Assembly Language
Step-by-Step

Assembly Language
Step-by-Step

Programming with Linux®

Third Edition

Jeff Duntemann

Wiley Publishing, Inc.

Assembly Language Step-by-Step

Published by
Wiley Publishing, Inc.
10475 Crosspoint Boulevard
Indianapolis, IN 46256
www.wiley.com

To the eternal memory of
Kathleen M. Duntemann, Godmother
1920– 1999
who gave me books when all I could do was put teeth marks on them.
There are no words for how much I owe you!

About the Author

Jeff Duntemann is a writer, editor, lecturer, and publishing industry analyst. In his thirty years in the technology industry he has been a computer programmer and systems analyst for Xerox Corporation, a technical journal editor for Ziff-Davis Publications, and Editorial Director for Coriolis Group Books and later Paraglyph Press. He is currently a technical publishing consultant and also owns Copperwood Press, a POD imprint hosted on lulu.com. Jeff lives with his wife Carol in Colorado Springs, Colorado.

Credits

Executive Editor
Carol Long

Project Editor
Brian Herrmann

Production Editor
Rebecca Anderson

Copy Editor
Luann Rouff

Editorial Director
Robyn B. Siesky

Editorial Manager
Mary Beth Wakefield

Production Manager
Tim Tate

**Vice President and Executive
Group Publisher**
Richard Swadley

**Vice President and Executive
Publisher**
Barry Pruett

Associate Publisher
Jim Minatel

Project Coordinator, Cover
Lynsey Stanford

Proofreader
Dr. Nate Pritts, Word One

Indexer
J&J Indexing

Cover Image
© Jupiter Images/Corbis/
Lawrence Manning

Acknowledgments

First of all, thanks are due to Carol Long and Brian Herrmann at Wiley, for allowing this book another shot, and then making sure it happened, on a much more aggressive schedule than last time.

As for all three previous editions, I owe Michael Abrash a debt of gratitude for constant sane advice on many things, especially the arcane differences between modern Intel microarchitectures.

Although they might not realize it, Randy Hyde, Frank Kotler, Beth, and all the rest of the gang on alt.lang.asm were very helpful in several ways, not least of which was hearing and answering requests from assembly language newcomers, thus helping me decide what must be covered in a book like this and what need not.

Finally, and as always, a toast to Carol for the support and sacramental friendship that has enlivened me now for 40 years, and enabled me to take on projects like this and see them through to the end.

Contents at a Glance

Introduction: "Why Would You Want to Do *That*?"   xxvii

Chapter 1   Another Pleasant Valley Saturday   1

Chapter 2   Alien Bases   15

Chapter 3   Lifting the Hood   45

Chapter 4   Location, Location, Location   77

Chapter 5   The Right to Assemble   109

Chapter 6   A Place to Stand, with Access to Tools   155

Chapter 7   Following Your Instructions   201

Chapter 8   Our Object All Sublime   237

Chapter 9   Bits, Flags, Branches, and Tables   279

Chapter 10 Dividing and Conquering   327

Chapter 11 Strings and Things   393

Chapter 12 Heading Out to C   439

Conclusion: Not the End, But Only the Beginning   503

Appendix A Partial x86 Instruction Set Reference   507

Appendix B Character Set Charts   583

Index   587

Contents

	Introduction: "Why Would You Want to Do *That*?"	**xxvii**
Chapter 1	**Another Pleasant Valley Saturday**	**1**
	It's All in the Plan	1
	Steps and Tests	2
	More Than Two Ways?	3
	Computers Think Like Us	4
	Had This Been the Real Thing . . .	4
	Do Not Pass Go	5
	The Game of Big Bux	6
	Playing Big Bux	8
	Assembly Language Programming As a Board Game	9
	Code and Data	10
	Addresses	11
	Metaphor Check!	12
Chapter 2	**Alien Bases**	**15**
	The Return of the New Math Monster	15
	Counting in Martian	16
	Dissecting a Martian Number	18
	The Essence of a Number Base	20
	Octal: How the Grinch Stole Eight and Nine	20
	Who Stole Eight and Nine?	21
	Hexadecimal: Solving the Digit Shortage	24
	From Hex to Decimal and from Decimal to Hex	28
	From Hex to Decimal	28
	From Decimal to Hex	29
	Practice. Practice! PRACTICE!	31

Arithmetic in Hex	32
Columns and Carries	35
Subtraction and Borrows	35
Borrows across Multiple Columns	37
What's the Point?	38
Binary	38
Values in Binary	40
Why Binary?	42
Hexadecimal As Shorthand for Binary	43
Prepare to Compute	44

Chapter 3   Lifting the Hood   **45**

RAXie, We Hardly Knew Ye . . .	45
Gus to the Rescue	46
Switches, Transistors, and Memory	47
One If by Land . . .	48
Transistor Switches	48
The Incredible Shrinking Bit	50
Random Access	52
Memory Access Time	53
Bytes, Words, Double Words, and Quad Words	54
Pretty Chips All in a Row	55
The Shop Foreman and the Assembly Line	57
Talking to Memory	58
Riding the Data Bus	59
The Foreman's Pockets	60
The Assembly Line	61
The Box That Follows a Plan	61
Fetch and Execute	63
The Foreman's Innards	64
Changing Course	65
What vs. How: Architecture and Microarchitecture	66
Evolving Architectures	67
The Secret Machinery in the Basement	68
Enter the Plant Manager	70
Operating Systems: The Corner Office	70
BIOS: Software, Just Not as Soft	71
Multitasking Magic	71
Promotion to Kernel	73
The Core Explosion	73
The Plan	74

Chapter 4	**Location, Location, Location**	**77**
	The Joy of Memory Models	77
	16 Bits'll Buy You 64K	79
	The Nature of a Megabyte	82
	Backward Compatibility and Virtual 86 Mode	83
	16-Bit Blinders	83
	The Nature of Segments	85
	A Horizon, Not a Place	88
	Making 20-Bit Addresses out of 16-Bit Registers	88
	16-Bit and 32-Bit Registers	90
	General-Purpose Registers	91
	Register Halves	93
	The Instruction Pointer	95
	The Flags Register	96
	The Three Major Assembly Programming Models	96
	Real Mode Flat Model	97
	Real Mode Segmented Model	99
	Protected Mode Flat Model	101
	What Protected Mode Won't Let Us Do Anymore	104
	Memory-Mapped Video	104
	Direct Access to Port Hardware	105
	Direct Calls into the BIOS	106
	Looking Ahead: 64-Bit "Long Mode"	106
	64-Bit Memory: What May Be Possible Someday vs. What We Can Do Now	107
Chapter 5	**The Right to Assemble**	**109**
	Files and What's Inside Them	110
	Binary Files vs. Text Files	111
	Looking at File Internals with the Bless Editor	112
	Interpreting Raw Data	116
	"Endianness"	117
	Text In, Code Out	121
	Assembly Language	121
	Comments	124
	Beware "Write-Only" Source Code!	124
	Object Code and Linkers	125
	Relocatability	128
	The Assembly Language Development Process	128
	The Discipline of Working Directories	129
	Editing the Source Code File	131

Assembling the Source Code File   131
Assembler Errors   132
Back to the Editor   133
Assembler Warnings   134
Linking the Object Code File   135
Linker Errors   136
Testing the .EXE File   136
Errors versus Bugs   137
Are We There Yet?   138
Debuggers and Debugging   138
Taking a Trip Down Assembly Lane   139
Installing the Software   139
Step 1: Edit the Program in an Editor   142
Step 2: Assemble the Program with NASM   143
Step 3: Link the Program with LD   146
Step 4: Test the Executable File   147
Step 5: Watch It Run in the Debugger   147
Ready to Get Serious?   153

Chapter 6   A Place to Stand, with Access to Tools   155
The Kate Editor   157
Installing Kate   157
Launching Kate   158
Configuration   160
Kate Sessions   162
Creating a New Session   162
Opening an Existing Session   163
Deleting or Renaming Sessions   163
Kate's File Management   164
Filesystem Browser Navigation   165
Adding a File to the Current Session   165
Dropping a File from the Current Session   166
Switching Between Session Files in the Editor   166
Creating a Brand-New File   166
Creating a Brand-New Folder on Disk   166
Deleting a File from Disk (Move File to Trash)   166
Reloading a File from Disk   167
Saving All Unsaved Changes in Session Files   167
Printing the File in the Editor Window   167
Exporting a File As HTML   167
Adding Items to the Toolbar   167
Kate's Editing Controls   168
Cursor Movement   169
Bookmarks   169
Selecting Text   170

Searching the Text	171
Using Search and Replace	172
Using Kate While Programming	172
Creating and Using Project Directories	173
Focus!	175
Linux and Terminals	176
The Linux Console	176
Character Encoding in Konsole	177
The Three Standard Unix Files	178
I/O Redirection	180
Simple Text Filters	182
Terminal Control with Escape Sequences	183
So Why Not GUI Apps?	185
Using Linux Make	186
Dependencies	187
When a File Is Up to Date	189
Chains of Dependencies	189
Invoking Make from Inside Kate	191
Using Touch to Force a Build	193
The Insight Debugger	194
Running Insight	195
Insight's Many Windows	195
A Quick Insight Run-Through	197
Pick Up Your Tools . . .	200
Chapter 7 **Following Your Instructions**	**201**
Build Yourself a Sandbox	201
A Minimal NASM Program	202
Instructions and Their Operands	204
Source and Destination Operands	204
Immediate Data	205
Register Data	207
Memory Data	209
Confusing Data and Its Address	210
The Size of Memory Data	211
The Bad Old Days	211
Rally Round the Flags, Boys!	212
Flag Etiquette	215
Adding and Subtracting One with INC and DEC	215
Watching Flags from Insight	216
How Flags Change Program Execution	218
Signed and Unsigned Values	221
Two's Complement and NEG	221
Sign Extension and MOVSX	224

Implicit Operands and MUL   225
    MUL and the Carry Flag   227
    Unsigned Division with DIV   228
    The x86 Slowpokes   229
Reading and Using an Assembly Language Reference   230
    Memory Joggers for Complex Memories   230
    An Assembly Language Reference for Beginners   231
    Flags   232
NEG: Negate (Two's Complement; i.e., Multiply by -1)   233
    Flags affected   233
    Legal forms   233
    Examples   233
    Notes   233
    Legal Forms   234
    Operand Symbols   234
    Examples   235
    Notes   235
    What's Not Here . . .   235

Chapter 8   Our Object All Sublime   **237**
The Bones of an Assembly Language Program   237
    The Initial Comment Block   239
    The .data Section   240
    The .bss Section   240
    The .text Section   241
    Labels   241
    Variables for Initialized Data   242
    String Variables   242
    Deriving String Length with EQU and $ 244
Last In, First Out via the Stack   246
    Five Hundred Plates per Hour   246
    Stacking Things Upside Down   248
    Push-y Instructions   249
    POP Goes the Opcode   251
    Storage for the Short Term   253
Using Linux Kernel Services Through INT80   254
    An Interrupt That Doesn't Interrupt Anything   254
    Getting Home Again   259
    Exiting a Program via INT 80h   260
    Software Interrupts versus Hardware Interrupts   261
    INT 80h and the Portability Fetish   262
Designing a Non-Trivial Program   264
    Defining the Problem   264
    Starting with Pseudo-code   265

Successive Refinement 266
Those Inevitable "Whoops!" Moments 270
Scanning a Buffer 271
"Off By One" Errors 273
Going Further 277

Chapter 9 Bits, Flags, Branches, and Tables 279

Bits Is Bits (and Bytes Is Bits) 279
Bit Numbering 280
"It's the Logical Thing to Do, Jim. . ." 280
The AND Instruction 281
Masking Out Bits 282
The OR Instruction 283
The XOR Instruction 284
The NOT Instruction 285
Segment Registers Don't Respond to Logic! 285
Shifting Bits 286
Shift By What? 286
How Bit Shifting Works 287
Bumping Bits into the Carry Flag 287
The Rotate Instructions 288
Setting a Known Value into the Carry Flag 289
Bit-Bashing in Action 289
Splitting a Byte into Two Nybbles 292
Shifting the High Nybble into the Low Nybble 293
Using a Lookup Table 293
Multiplying by Shifting and Adding 295
Flags, Tests, and Branches 298
Unconditional Jumps 298
Conditional Jumps 299
Jumping on the Absence of a Condition 300
Flags 301
Comparisons with CMP 301
A Jungle of Jump Instructions 302
"Greater Than" Versus "Above" 303
Looking for 1-Bits with TEST 304
Looking for 0 Bits with BT 306
Protected Mode Memory Addressing in Detail 307
Effective Address Calculations 308
Displacements 309
Base + Displacement Addressing 310
Base + Index Addressing 310
Index × Scale + Displacement Addressing 312
Other Addressing Schemes 313

LEA: The Top-Secret Math Machine   315
The Burden of 16-Bit Registers   317
Character Table Translation   318
Translation Tables   318
Translating with MOV or XLAT   320
Tables Instead of Calculations   325

Chapter 10   Dividing and Conquering   327
Boxes within Boxes   328
Procedures As Boxes for Code   329
Calling and Returning   336
Calls within Calls   338
The Dangers of Accidental Recursion   340
A Flag Etiquette Bug to Beware Of   341
Procedures and the Data They Need   342
Saving the Caller's Registers   343
Local Data   346
More Table Tricks   347
Placing Constant Data in Procedure Definitions   349
Local Labels and the Lengths of Jumps   350
"Forcing" Local Label Access   353
Short, Near, and Far Jumps   354
Building External Procedure Libraries   355
Global and External Declarations   356
The Mechanics of Globals and Externals   357
Linking Libraries into Your Programs   365
The Dangers of Too Many Procedures and Too Many
    Libraries   366
The Art of Crafting Procedures   367
Maintainability and Reuse   367
Deciding What Should Be a Procedure   368
Use Comment Headers!   370
Simple Cursor Control in the Linux Console   371
Console Control Cautions   377
Creating and Using Macros   378
The Mechanics of Macro Definition   379
Defining Macros with Parameters   385
The Mechanics of Invoking Macros   386
Local Labels Within Macros   387
Macro Libraries As Include Files   388
Macros versus Procedures: Pros and Cons   389

Chapter 11   Strings and Things   **393**

The Notion of an Assembly Language String   393
    Turning Your "String Sense" Inside-Out   394
    Source Strings and Destination Strings   395
    A Text Display Virtual Screen   395
REP STOSB, the Software Machine Gun   402
    Machine-Gunning the Virtual Display   403
    Executing the STOSB Instruction   404
    STOSB and the Direction Flag (DF)   405
    Defining Lines in the Display Buffer   406
    Sending the Buffer to the Linux Console   406
The Semiautomatic Weapon: STOSB without REP   407
    Who Decrements ECX?   407
    The LOOP Instructions   408
    Displaying a Ruler on the Screen   409
    MUL Is Not IMUL   410
    Adding ASCII Digits   411
    Adjusting AAA's Adjustments   413
    Ruler's Lessons   414
    16-bit and 32-bit Versions of STOS   414
MOVSB: Fast Block Copies   414
    DF and Overlapping Block Moves   416
    Single-Stepping REP String Instructions with Insight   418
Storing Data to Discontinuous Strings   419
    Displaying an ASCII Table   419
    Nested Instruction Loops   420
    Jumping When ECX Goes to 0   421
    Closing the Inner Loop   421
    Closing the Outer Loop   422
    Showchar Recap   423
Command-Line Arguments and Examining the Stack   424
    Virtual Memory in Two Chunks   424
    Anatomy of the Linux Stack   427
    Why Stack Addresses Aren't Predictable   429
    Setting Command-Line Arguments with Insight   429
    Examining the Stack with Insight's Memory View   430
String Searches with SCASB   432
    REPNE vs. REPE   435
    Pop the Stack or Address It?   436
    For Extra Credit . . .   438

Chapter 12   Heading Out to C   **439**

What's GNU?   440

The Swiss Army Compiler   441

Building Code the GNU Way   441

How to Use gcc in Assembly Work   443

Why Not gas?   444

Linking to the Standard C Library   445

C Calling Conventions   446

A Framework to Build On   447

Saving and Restoring Registers   447

Setting Up a Stack Frame   448

Destroying a Stack Frame   450

Characters Out via puts()   451

Formatted Text Output with printf()   452

Passing Parameters to printf()   454

Data In with fgets() and scanf()   456

Using scanf() for Entry of Numeric Values   458

Be a Time Lord   462

The C Library's Time Machine   462

Fetching time_t Values from the System Clock   464

Converting a time_t Value to a Formatted String   464

Generating Separate Local Time Values   465

Making a Copy of glibc's tm Struct with MOVSD   466

Understanding AT&T Instruction Mnemonics   470

AT&T Mnemonic Conventions   470

Examining gas Source Files Created by gcc   471

AT&T Memory Reference Syntax   474

Generating Random Numbers   475

Seeding the Generator with srand()   476

Generating Pseudorandom Numbers   477

Some Bits Are More Random Than Others   482

Calls to Addresses in Registers   483

How C Sees Command-Line Arguments   484

Simple File I/O   487

Converting Strings into Numbers with sscanf()   487

Creating and Opening Files   489

Reading Text from Files with fgets()   490

Writing Text to Files with fprintf()   493

Notes on Gathering Your Procedures into Libraries   494

Conclusion: Not the End, But Only the Beginning   **503**

Where to Now?   504

Stepping off Square One   506

Appenix A Partial x86 Instruction Set Reference **507**

Notes on the Instruction Set Reference 510

AAA: Adjust AL after BCD Addition 512

ADC: Arithmetic Addition with Carry 513

ADD: Arithmetic Addition 515

AND: Logical AND 517

BT: Bit Test 519

CALL: Call Procedure 521

CLC: Clear Carry Flag (CF) 523

CLD: Clear Direction Flag (DF) 524

CMP: Arithmetic Comparison 525

DEC: Decrement Operand 527

DIV: Unsigned Integer Division 528

INC: Increment Operand 529

INT: Software Interrupt 530

IRET: Return from Interrupt 531

J?: Jump on Condition 532

JCXZ: Jump If CX=0 534

JECXZ: Jump If ECX=0 535

JMP: Unconditional Jump 536

LEA: Load Effective Address 537

LOOP: Loop until CX/ECX=0 538

LOOPNZ/LOOPNE: Loop While CX/ECX > 0 and ZF=0 540

LOOPZ/LOOPE: Loop While CX/ECX > 0 and ZF=1 541

MOV: Move (Copy) Right Operand into Left Operand 542

MOVS: Move String 544

MOVSX: Move (Copy) with Sign Extension 546

MUL: Unsigned Integer Multiplication 547

NEG: Negate (Two's Complement; i.e., Multiply by -1) 549

NOP: No Operation 550

NOT: Logical NOT (One's Complement) 551

OR: Logical OR 552

POP: Pop Top of Stack into Operand 554

POPA/POPAD: Pop All GP Registers 555

POPF: Pop Top of Stack into 16-Bit Flags 556

POPFD: Pop Top of Stack into EFlags 557

PUSH: Push Operand onto Top of Stack 558

PUSHA: Push All 16-Bit GP Registers 559

PUSHAD: Push All 32-Bit GP Registers 560

PUSHF: Push 16-Bit Flags onto Stack 561

PUSHFD: Push 32-Bit EFlags onto Stack 562

RET: Return from Procedure 563

ROL: Rotate Left 564

ROR: Rotate Right   566

SBB: Arithmetic Subtraction with Borrow   568

SHL: Shift Left   570

SHR: Shift Right   572

STC: Set Carry Flag (CF)   574

STD: Set Direction Flag (DF)   575

STOS: Store String   576

SUB: Arithmetic Subtraction   577

XCHG: Exchange Operands   579

XLAT: Translate Byte via Table   580

XOR: Exclusive Or   581

Appendix B Character Set Charts   **583**

Index   **587**

Introduction: "Why Would You Want to Do *That*?"

It was 1985, and I was in a chartered bus in New York City, heading for a press reception with a bunch of other restless media egomaniacs. I was only beginning my media career (as Technical Editor for *PC Tech Journal*) and my first book was still months in the future. I happened to be sitting next to an established programming writer/guru, with whom I was impressed and to whom I was babbling about one thing or another. I won't name him, as he's done a lot for the field, and may do a fair bit more if he doesn't kill himself smoking first.

But I happened to let it slip that I was a Turbo Pascal fanatic, and what I really wanted to do was learn how to write Turbo Pascal programs that made use of the brand-new Microsoft Windows user interface. He wrinkled his nose and grimaced wryly, before speaking the Infamous Question:

"Why would you want to do *that*?"

I had never heard the question before (though I would hear it many times thereafter) and it took me aback. Why? Because, well, because ... I wanted to know how it *worked*.

"Heh. That's what C's for."

Further discussion got me nowhere in a Pascal direction. But some probing led me to understand that you *couldn't* write Windows apps in Turbo Pascal. It was impossible. Or ... the programming writer/guru didn't know how. Maybe both. I never learned the truth. But I did learn the meaning of the Infamous Question.

Note well: When somebody asks you, "Why would you want to do *that*?" what it really means is this: "You've asked me how to do something that is either impossible using tools that I favor or completely outside my experience, but I don't want to lose face by admitting it. So ... how 'bout those Black-hawks?''

I heard it again and again over the years:

Q: How can I set up a C string so that I can read its length without scanning it?

A: Why would you want to do *that?*

Q: How can I write an assembly language subroutine callable from Turbo Pascal?

A: Why would you want to do *that?*

Q: How can I write Windows apps in assembly language?

A: Why would you want to do *that?*

You get the idea. The answer to the Infamous Question is always the same, and if the weasels ever ask it of you, snap back as quickly as possible, *"Because I want to know how it works."*

That is a completely sufficient answer. It's the answer I've used every single time, except for one occasion a considerable number of years ago, when I put forth that I wanted to write a book that taught people how to program in assembly language as their *first* experience in programming.

Q: Good grief, why would you want to do *that?*

A: Because it's the best way there is to build the skills required to understand how *all the rest* of the programming universe works.

Being a programmer is one thing above all else: it is understanding how things work. Learning to be a programmer, furthermore, is almost entirely a process of leaning how things work. This can be done at various levels, depending on the tools you're using. If you're programming in Visual Basic, you have to understand how certain things work, but those things are by and large confined to Visual Basic itself. A great deal of machinery is hidden by the layer that Visual Basic places between the programmer and the computer. (The same is true of Delphi, Java, Python, and many other very high level programming environments.) If you're using a C compiler, you're a lot closer to the machine, and you see a lot more of that machinery—and must, therefore, understand how it works to be able to use it. However, quite a bit remains hidden, even from the hardened C programmer.

If, conversely, you're working in assembly language, you're as close to the machine as you can get. Assembly language hides *nothing,* and withholds no power. The flip side, of course, is that no magical layer between you and the machine will absolve any ignorance and "take care of" things for you. If you don't understand how something works, you're dead in the water—unless you know enough to be able to figure it out on your own.

That's a key point: My goal in creating this book is not entirely to teach you assembly language *per se*. If this book has a prime directive at all, it is to impart a certain disciplined curiosity about the machine, along with some basic context from which you can begin to explore the machine at its very lowest levels—that, and the confidence to give it your best shot. This is difficult stuff, but it's nothing you can't master given some concentration, patience, and the time it requires—which, I caution, may be considerable.

In truth, what I'm really teaching you here is how to learn.

What You'll Need

To program as I intend to teach, you're going to need an Intel x86-based computer running Linux. The text and examples assume at least a 386, but since Linux itself requires at least a 386, you're covered.

You need to be reasonably proficient with Linux at the user level. I can't teach you how to install and run Linux in this book, though I will provide hints where things get seriously non-obvious. If you're not already familiar with Linux, get a tutorial text and work through it. Many exist but my favorite is the formidable *Ubuntu 8.10 Linux Bible*, by William von Hagen. (*Linux for Dummies*, while well done, is not enough.)

Which Linux distribution/version you use is not extremely important, as long as it's based on at least the version 2.4 kernel, and preferably version 2.6. The distribution that I used to write the example programs was Ubuntu version 8.10. Which graphical user interface (GUI) you use doesn't matter, because all of the programs are written to run from the purely textual Linux console. The assembler itself, NASM, is also a purely textual creature.

Where a GUI is required is for the Kate editor, which I use as a model in the discussions of the logistics of programming. You can actually use any editor you want. There's nothing in the programs themselves that requires Kate, but if you're new to programming or have always used a highly language-specific editing environment, Kate is a good choice.

The debugger I cite in the text is the venerable Gdb, but mostly by way of Gdb's built-in GUI front end, Insight. Insight requires a functioning X Window subsystem but is not tied to a specific GUI system like GNOME or KDE.

You don't have to know how to install and configure these tools in advance, because I cover all necessary tool installation and configuration in the chapters, at appropriate times.

Note that other Unix implementations not based on the Linux kernel may not function precisely the same way under the hood. BSD Unix uses different conventions for making kernel calls, for example, and other Unix versions such as Solaris are outside my experience.

The Master Plan

This book starts at the beginning, and I mean the *beginning*. Maybe you're already there, or well past it. I respect that. I still think that it wouldn't hurt to start at the first chapter and read through all the chapters in order. Review is useful, and hey—you may realize that you didn't know *quite* as much as you thought you did. (Happens to me all the time!)

But if time is at a premium, here's the cheat sheet:

1. If you already understand the fundamental ideas of computer programming, skip Chapter 1.

2. If you already understand the ideas behind number bases other than decimal (especially hexadecimal and binary), skip Chapter 2.

3. If you already have a grip on the nature of computer internals (memory, CPU architectures, and so on) skip Chapter 3.

4. If you already understand x86 memory addressing, skip Chapter 4.

5. No. Stop. Scratch that. Even if you already understand x86 memory addressing, read Chapter 4.

Point 5 is there, and emphatic, for a reason: *Assembly language programming is about memory addressing*. If you don't understand memory addressing, nothing else you learn in assembly will help you one lick. So don't skip Chapter 4 no matter what else you know or think you know. Start from there, and see it through to the end. Load every example program, assemble each one, and run them all. Strive to understand every single line in every program. Take nothing on faith.

Furthermore, don't stop there. Change the example programs as things begin to make sense to you. Try different approaches. Try things that I don't mention. Be audacious. Nay, go nuts—bits don't have feelings, and the worst thing that can happen is that Linux throws a segmentation fault, which may hurt your program (and perhaps your self esteem) but does not hurt Linux. (They don't call it "protected mode" for nothing!) The only catch is that when you try something, understand why it *doesn't* work as clearly as you understand all the other things that do. *Take notes*.

That is, ultimately, what I'm after: to show you the way to understand what every however distant corner of your machine is doing, and how all its many pieces work together. This doesn't mean I explain every corner of it myself—no one will live long enough to do that. Computing isn't simple anymore, but if you develop the discipline of patient research and experimentation, you can probably work it out for yourself. Ultimately, that's the only way to learn it: by yourself. The guidance you find—in friends, on the Net, in books like this—is only guidance, and grease on the axles. You have to decide who is to be the master, you or the machine, and make it so. Assembly programmers are the only programmers who can truly claim to be the masters, and that's a truth worth meditating on.

A Note on Capitalization Conventions

Assembly language is peculiar among programming languages in that there is no universal standard for case sensitivity. In the C language, all identifiers are case sensitive, and I have seen assemblers that do not recognize differences in case at all. NASM, the assembler I present in this book, is case sensitive only for programmer-defined identifiers. The instruction mnemonics and the names of registers, however, are *not* case sensitive.

There are customs in the literature on assembly language, and one of those customs is to treat CPU instruction mnemonics and register names as uppercase in the text, and in lowercase in source code files and code snippets interspersed in the text. I'll be following that custom here. Within discussion text, I'll speak of MOV and registers EAX and EFLAGS. In example code, it will be mov and eax and eflags.

There are two reasons for this:

- In text discussions, the mnemonics and registers need to stand out. It's too easy to lose track of them amid a torrent of ordinary words.
- In order to read and learn from existing documents and source code outside of this one book, you need to be able to easily read assembly language whether it's in uppercase, lowercase, or mixed case. Getting comfortable with different ways of expressing the same thing is important.

This will grate on some people in the Unix community, for whom lowercase characters are something of a fetish. I apologize in advance for the irritation, while insisting to the end that it's still a fetish, and a fairly childish one at that.

Why Am I Here Again?

Wherever you choose to start the book, it's time to get under way. Just remember that whatever gets in your face, be it the weasels, the machine, or your own inexperience, the thing to keep in the forefront of your mind is this: *You're in it to figure out how it works.*

Let's go.

Jeff Duntemann
Colorado Springs, Colorado
June 5, 2009
www.duntemann.com/assembly.htm

Assembly Language
Step-by-Step

Another Pleasant Valley Saturday

Understanding What Computers Really Do

It's All in the Plan

"Quick, Mike, get your sister and brother up, it's past 7. Nicky's got Little League at 9:00 and Dione's got ballet at 10:00. Give Max his heartworm pill! (We're out of them, Ma, remember?) Your father picked a great weekend to go fishing. Here, let me give you 10 bucks and go get more pills at the vet's. My God, that's right, Hank needed gas money and left me broke. There's an ATM over by Kmart, and if I go there I can take that stupid toilet seat back and get the right one."

"I guess I'd better make a list. . . ."

It's another Pleasant Valley Saturday, and thirty-odd million suburban homemakers sit down with a pencil and pad at the kitchen table to try to make sense of a morning that would kill and pickle any lesser being. In her mind, she thinks of the dependencies and traces the route:

Drop Nicky at Rand Park, go back to Dempster and it's about 10 minutes to Golf Mill Mall. Do I have gas? I'd better check first—if not, stop at Del's Shell or I won't make it to Milwaukee Avenue. Milk the ATM at Golf Mill, then cross the parking lot to Kmart to return the toilet seat that Hank bought last weekend without checking what shape it was. Gotta remember to throw the toilet seat in the back of the van—write that at the top of the list.

By then it'll be half past, maybe later. Ballet is all the way down Greenwood in Park Ridge. No left turn from Milwaukee—but there's the sneak path around behind the mall. I have to remember not to turn right onto Milwaukee like I always do—jot that down. While I'm in Park Ridge I can check to see if Hank's new glasses are in—should call but they won't even be open until 9:30. Oh, and groceries—can do that while Dione dances. On the way back I can cut over to Oakton and get the dog's pills.

In about 90 seconds flat the list is complete:

- Throw toilet seat in van.
- Check gas—if empty, stop at Del's Shell.
- Drop Nicky at Rand Park.
- Stop at Golf Mill teller machine.
- Return toilet seat at Kmart.
- Drop Dione at ballet (remember the sneak path to Greenwood).
- See if Hank's glasses are at Pearle Vision—if they are, make sure they remembered the extra scratch coating.
- Get groceries at Jewel.
- Pick up Dione.
- Stop at vet's for heartworm pills.
- Drop off groceries at home.
- If it's time, pick up Nicky. If not, collapse for a few minutes, then pick up Nicky.
- Collapse!

In what we often call a "laundry list" (whether it involves laundry or not) is the perfect metaphor for a computer program. Without realizing it, our intrepid homemaker has written herself a computer program and then set out (acting as the computer) to execute it and be done before noon.

Computer programming is nothing more than this: you, the programmer, write a list of steps and tests. The computer then performs each step and test in sequence. When the list of steps has been executed, the computer stops.

A computer program is a list of steps and tests, nothing more.

Steps and Tests

Think for a moment about what I call a "test" in the preceding laundry list. A *test* is the sort of either/or decision we make dozens or hundreds of times on even the most placid of days, sometimes nearly without thinking about it.

Our homemaker performed a test when she jumped into the van to get started on her adventure. She looked at the gas gauge. The gas gauge would tell her one of two things: either she has enough gas or she doesn't. If she has enough gas, then she takes a right and heads for Rand Park. If she doesn't have enough gas, then she takes a left down to the corner and fills the tank at Del's Shell. Then, with a full tank, she continues the program by taking a U-turn and heading for Rand Park.

In the abstract, a test consists of those two parts:

- First, you take a look at something that can go one of two ways.
- Then you do one of two things, depending on what you saw when you took a look.

Toward the end of the program, our homemaker gets home, takes the groceries out of the van, and checks the clock. If it isn't time to get Nicky from Little League, then she has a moment to collapse on the couch in a nearly empty house. If it *is* time to get Nicky, then there's no rest for the ragged: she sprints for the van and heads back to Rand Park.

(Any guesses as to whether she really gets to collapse when the program finishes running?)

More Than Two Ways?

You might object, saying that many or most tests involve more than two alternatives. Ha-ha, sorry, you're dead wrong—*in every case*. Furthermore, you're wrong whether you think you are or not. Read this twice: *Except for totally impulsive or psychotic behavior, every human decision comes down to the choice between two alternatives.*

What you have to do is look a little more closely at what goes through your mind when you make decisions. The next time you buzz down to Yow Chow Now for fast Chinese, observe yourself while you're poring over the menu. The choice might seem, at first, to be of one item out of 26 Cantonese main courses. Not so. The choice, in fact, is between choosing one item and *not* choosing that one item. Your eyes rest on chicken with cashews. Naw, too bland. *That was a test*. You slide down to the next item. Chicken with black mushrooms. Hmm, no, had that last week. *That was another test*. Next item: Kung Pao chicken. Yeah, that's it! *That was a third test*.

The choice was not among chicken with cashews, chicken with black mushrooms, or Kung Pao chicken. Each dish had its moment, poised before the critical eye of your mind, and you turned thumbs up or thumbs down on it, individually. Eventually, one dish won, but it won in that same game of "to eat or not to eat."

Let me give you another example. Many of life's most complicated decisions come about due to the fact that 99.99867 percent of us are not nudists. You've been there: you're standing in the clothes closet in your underwear, flipping through your rack of pants. The tests come thick and fast. This one? No. This one? No. This one? No. This one? Yeah. You pick a pair of blue pants, say. (It's a Monday, after all, and blue would seem an appropriate color.) Then you stumble over to your sock drawer and take a look. Whoops, no blue socks. *That was a test.* So you stumble back to the clothes closet, hang your blue pants back on the pants rack, and start over. This one? No. This one? No. This one? Yeah. This time it's brown pants, and you toss them over your arm and head back to the sock drawer to take another look. Nertz, out of brown socks, too. So it's back to the clothes closet . . .

What you might consider a single decision, or perhaps two decisions inextricably tangled (such as picking pants and socks of the same color, given stock on hand), is actually a series of small decisions, always binary in nature: pick 'em or don't pick 'em. Find 'em or don't find 'em. The Monday morning episode in the clothes closet is a good analogy of a programming structure called a *loop*: you keep doing a series of things until you get it right, and then you stop (assuming you're not the kind of geek who wears blue socks with brown pants); but whether you get everything right always comes down to a sequence of simple either/or decisions.

Computers Think Like Us

I can almost hear the objection: "Sure, it's a computer book, and he's trying to get me to think like a computer." Not at all. Computers think like *us*. We designed them; how else could they think? No, what I'm trying to do is get you to take a long, hard look at how *you* think. We run on automatic for so much of our lives that we literally do most of our thinking without really thinking about it.

The very best model for the logic of a computer program is the very same logic we use to plan and manage our daily affairs. No matter what we do, it comes down to a matter of confronting two alternatives and picking one. What we might think of as a single large and complicated decision is nothing more than a messy tangle of many smaller decisions. The skill of looking at a complex decision and seeing all the little decisions in its tummy will serve you well in learning how to program. Observe yourself the next time you have to decide something. Count up the little decisions that make up the big one. You'll be surprised.

And, surprise! You'll be a programmer.

Had This Been the Real Thing . . .

Do not be alarmed. What you have just experienced was a metaphor. It was not the real thing. (The real thing comes later.) I use metaphors a lot in this book. A metaphor is a loose comparison drawn between something familiar (such as a Saturday morning laundry list) and something unfamiliar (such as a computer program). The idea is to anchor the unfamiliar in the terms of the familiar, so that when I begin tossing facts at you, you'll have someplace comfortable to lay them down.

The most important thing for you to do right now is keep an open mind. If you know a little bit about computers or programming, don't pick nits. Yes, there are important differences between a homemaker following a scribbled laundry list and a computer executing a program. I'll mention those differences all in good time.

For now, it's still Chapter 1. Take these initial metaphors on their own terms. Later on, they'll help a lot.

Do Not Pass Go

"There's a reason *bored* and *board* are homonyms," said my best friend, Art, one evening as we sat (two super-sophisticated twelve-year-olds) playing some game in his basement. (He may have been unhappy because he was losing.) Was it Mille Bornes? Or Stratego? Or Monopoly? Or something else entirely? I confess, I don't remember. I simply recall hopping some little piece of plastic shaped like a pregnant bowling pin up and down a series of colored squares that told me to do dumb things like go back two spaces or put $100 in the pot or nuke Outer Mongolia.

There are strong parallels to be drawn between that peculiar American pastime, the board game, and assembly-language programming. First of all, everything I said before still holds: board games, by and large, consist of a progression of steps and tests. In some games, such as Trivial Pursuit, *every* step on the board is a test: to see if you can answer, or not answer, a question on a card. In other board games, each little square along the path on the board contains some sort of instruction: Lose One Turn; Go Back Two Squares; Take a Card from Community Chest; and, of course, Go to Jail. Things happen in board games, and the path your little pregnant bowling pin takes as it works its way along the edge of the board will change along the way.

Many board games also have little storage locations marked on the board where you keep things: cards and play money and game tokens such as little plastic houses or hotels, or perhaps bombers and nuclear missiles. As the game progresses, you buy, sell, or launch your assets, and the contents of your storage locations change. Computer programs are like that too: there are places where you store things ("things" here being pure data, rather than physical tokens); and as the computer program executes, the data stored in those places will change.

Computer programs are not games, of course—at least, not in the sense that a board game is a game. Most of the time, a given program is running all by itself. There is only one "player" and not two or more. (This is not *always* true, but I don't want to get too far ahead right now. Remember, we're still in metaphor territory.) Still, the metaphor is useful enough that it's worth pursuing.

The Game of Big Bux

I've invented my own board game to continue down the road with this particular metaphor. In the sense that art mirrors life, the Game of Big Bux mirrors life in Silicon Valley, where money seems to be spontaneously created (generally in somebody else's pocket) and the three big Money Black Holes are fast cars, California real estate, and messy divorces. There is luck, there is work, and assets often change hands *very* quickly.

A portion of the Big Bux game board is shown in Figure 1-1. The line of rectangles on the left side of the page continues all the way around the board. In the middle of the board are cubbyholes to store your play money and game pieces; stacks of cards to be read occasionally; and short detours with names such as Messy Divorce and Start a Business, which are brief sequences of the same sort of action squares as those forming the path around the edge of the board. These are "side paths" that players take when instructed, either by a square on the board or a card pulled during the game. If you land on a square that tells you to Start a Business, you go through that detour. If you jump over the square, you don't take the detour, and just keep on trucking around the board.

Unlike many board games, you don't throw dice to determine how many steps around the board you take. Big Bux requires that you move *one* step forward on each turn, *unless* the square you land on instructs you to move forward or backward or go somewhere else, such as through a detour. This makes for a considerably less random game. In fact, Big Bux is a pretty linear experience, meaning that for the most part you go around the board until you're told that the game is over. At that point, you may be bankrupt; if not, you can total up your assets to see how well you've done.

There is some math involved. You start out with a condo, a cheap car, and $250,000 in cash. You can buy CDs at a given interest rate, payable each time you make it once around the board. You can invest in stocks and other securities whose value is determined by a changeable index in economic indicators, which fluctuates based on cards chosen from the stack called the Fickle Finger of Fate. You can sell cars on a secondary market, buy and sell houses, condos, and land; and wheel and deal with the other players. Each time you make it once around the board, you have to recalculate your net worth. All of this involves some addition, subtraction, multiplication, and division, but there's no math more complex than compound interest. Most of Big Bux involves nothing more than taking a step and following the instructions at each step.

Is this starting to sound familiar?

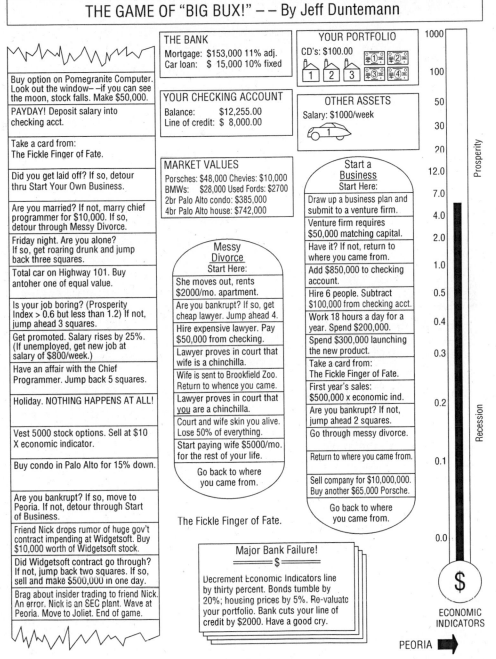

Figure 1-1: The Big Bux game board

Playing Big Bux

At one corner of the Big Bux board is the legend Move In, as that's how people start life in California—no one is actually *born* there. That's the entry point at which you begin the game. Once moved in, you begin working your way around the board, square by square, following the instructions in the squares.

Some of the squares simply tell you to do something, such as "Buy a Condo in Palo Alto for 15% down." Many of the squares involve a test of some kind. For example, one square reads: "Is your job boring? (Prosperity Index 0.3 but less than 4.0.) If not, jump ahead three squares." The test is actually to see if the Prosperity Index has a value between 0.3 and 4.0. Any value outside those bounds (that is, runaway prosperity or Four Horsemen–class recession) is defined as Interesting Times, and causes a jump ahead by three squares.

You always move one step forward at each turn, unless the square you land on directs you to do something else, such as jump forward three squares or jump back five squares, or take a detour.

The notion of taking a detour is an interesting one. Two detours are shown in the portion of the board I've provided. (The full game has others.) Taking a detour means leaving your main path around the edge of the game board and stepping through a series of squares somewhere else on the board. When you finish with the detour, you return to your original path right where you left it. The detours involve some specific process—for example, starting a business or getting divorced.

You can work through a detour, step by step, until you hit the bottom. At that point you simply pick up your journey around the board right where you left it. You may also find that one of the squares in the detour instructs you to go back to where you came from. Depending on the logic of the game (and your luck and finances), you may completely run through a detour or get thrown out of the detour somewhere in the middle. In either case, you return to the point from which you originally entered the detour.

Also note that you can take a detour from within a detour. If you detour through Start a Business and your business goes bankrupt, you leave Start a Business temporarily and detour through Messy Divorce. Once you leave Messy Divorce, you return to where you left Start a Business. Ultimately, you also leave Start a Business and return to wherever you were on the main path when you took the detour. The same detour (for example, Start a Business) can be taken from any of several different places along the game board.

Unlike most board games, the Game of Big Bux doesn't necessarily end. You can go round and round the board basically forever. There are three ways to end the game:

- *Retire*: To do this, you must have assets at a certain level and make the decision to retire.

- *Go bankrupt*: Once you have no assets, there's no point in continuing the game. Move to Peoria in disgrace.

- *Go to jail*: This is a consequence of an error of judgment, and is not a normal exit from the game board.

Computer programs are also like that. You can choose to end a program when you've accomplished what you planned, even though you could continue if you wanted. If the document or the spreadsheet is finished, save it and exit. Conversely, if the photo you're editing keeps looking worse and worse each time you select Sharpen, you stop the program without having accomplished anything. If you make a serious mistake, then the program may throw you out with an error message and corrupt your data in the bargain, leaving you with less than nothing to show for the experience.

Once more, *this is a metaphor*. Don't take the game board too literally. (Alas, Silicon Valley life was *way* too much like this in the go-go 1990s. It's calmer now, I've heard.)

Assembly Language Programming As a Board Game

Now that you're thinking in terms of board games, take a look at Figure 1-2. What I've drawn is actually a fair approximation of assembly language as it was used on some of our simpler computers about 25 or 30 years ago. The column marked "Program Instructions" is the main path around the edge of the board, of which only a portion can be shown here. This is the assembly language computer program, the actual series of steps and tests that, when executed, cause the computer to do something useful. Setting up this series of program instructions is what programming in assembly language actually *is*.

Everything else is odds and ends in the middle of the board that serve the game in progress. Most of these are storage locations that contain your data. You're probably noticing (perhaps with sagging spirits) that there are a *lot* of numbers involved. (They're weird numbers, too—what, for example, does "004B" mean? I deal with that issue in Chapter 2.) I'm sorry, but that's simply the way the game is played. Assembly language, at its innermost level, is nothing *but* numbers, and if you hate numbers the way most people hate anchovies, you're going to have a rough time of it. (I like anchovies, which is part of my legend. Learn to like numbers. They're not as salty.) Higher-level programming languages such as Pascal or Python disguise the numbers by treating them symbolically—but assembly language, well, it's you and the numbers.

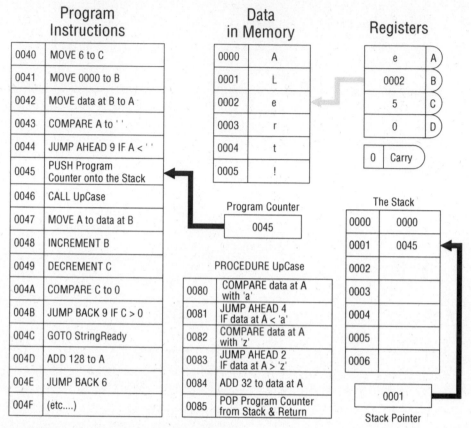

Figure 1-2: The Game of Assembly Language

I should caution you that the Game of Assembly Language represents no real computer processor like the Pentium. Also, I've made the names of instructions more clearly understandable than the names of the instructions in Intel assembly language. In the real world, instruction names are typically things like STOSB, DAA, INC, SBB, and other crypticisms that cannot be understood without considerable explanation. We're easing into this stuff sidewise, and in this chapter I have to sugarcoat certain things a little to draw the metaphors clearly.

Code and Data

Like most board games (including the Game of Big Bux), the assembly language board game consists of two broad categories of elements: game steps and places to store things. The "game steps" are the steps and tests I've been speaking of all along. The places to store things are just that: cubbyholes into which you can place numbers, with the confidence that those numbers will remain where you put them until you take them out or change them somehow.

In programming terms, the game steps are called *code*, and the numbers in their cubbyholes (as distinct from the cubbyholes themselves) are called *data*. The cubbyholes themselves are usually called *storage*. (The difference between the places you store information and the information you store in them is crucial. Don't confuse them.)

The Game of Big Bux works the same way. Look back to Figure 1-1 and note that in the Start a Business detour, there is an instruction reading "Add $850,000 to checking account." The checking account is one of several different kinds of storage in the Game of Big Bux, and money values are a type of data. It's no different conceptually from an instruction in the Game of Assembly Language reading ADD 5 to Register A. An ADD instruction in the code alters a data value stored in a cubbyhole named Register A.

Code and data are two very different kinds of critters, but they interact in ways that make the game interesting. The code includes steps that place data into storage (MOVE instructions) and steps that alter data that is already in storage (INCREMENT and DECREMENT instructions, and ADD instructions). Most of the time you'll think of code as being the master of data, in that the code writes data values into storage. Data does influence code as well, however. Among the tests that the code makes are tests that examine data in storage, the COMPARE instructions. If a given data value exists in storage, the code may do one thing; if that value does not exist in storage, the code will do something else, as in the Big Bux JUMP BACK and JUMP AHEAD instructions.

The short block of instructions marked PROCEDURE is a detour off the main stream of instructions. At any point in the program you can duck out into the procedure, perform its steps and tests, and then return to the very place from which you left. This allows a sequence of steps and tests that is generally useful and used frequently to exist in only one place, rather than as a separate copy everywhere it is needed.

Addresses

Another critical concept lies in the funny numbers at the left side of the program step locations and data locations. Each number is unique, in that a location tagged with that number appears only *once* inside the computer. This location is called an *address*. Data is stored and retrieved by specifying the data's address in the machine. Procedures are called by specifying the address at which they begin.

The little box (which is also a storage location) marked PROGRAM COUNTER keeps the address of the next instruction to be performed. The number inside the program counter is increased by one (we say, "incremented" each time an instruction is performed *unless the instructions tell the program counter to do something else*. For example: notice the JUMP BACK 9 instruction at address 004B. When this instruction is performed, the program counter will "back up" by nine locations. This is analogous to the "go back three spaces" concept in most board games.

Metaphor Check!

That's about as much explanation of the Game of Assembly Language as I'm going to offer for now. This is still Chapter 1, and we're still in metaphor territory. People who have had some exposure to computers will recognize and understand some of what Figure 1-2 is doing. (There's a real, traceable program going on in there—I dare you to figure out what it does—and how!) People with no exposure to computer innards at all shouldn't feel left behind for being utterly lost. I created the Game of Assembly Language solely to put across the following points:

- *The individual steps are very simple:* One single instruction rarely does more than move a single byte from one storage cubbyhole to another, perform very elementary arithmetic such as addition or subtraction, or compare the value contained in one storage cubbyhole to a value contained in another. This is good news, because it enables you to concentrate on the simple task accomplished by a single instruction without being overwhelmed by complexity. The bad news, however, is the following:

- *It takes a lot of steps to do anything useful:* You can often write a useful program in such languages as Pascal or BASIC in five or six lines. You can actually create useful programs in visual programming systems such as Visual Basic and Delphi *without writing any code at all.* (The code is still there ... but it is "canned" and all you're really doing is choosing which chunks of canned code in a collection of many such chunks will run.) A useful assembly language program cannot be implemented in fewer than about 50 lines, and anything challenging takes hundreds or thousands—or tens of thousands—of lines. The skill of assembly language programming lies in structuring these hundreds or thousands of instructions so that the program can still be read and understood.

- *The key to assembly language is understanding memory addresses:* In such languages as Pascal and BASIC, the compiler takes care of where something is located—you simply have to give that something a symbolic name, and call it by that name whenever you want to look at it or change it. In assembly language, you must always be cognizant of where things are in your computer's memory. Therefore, in working through this book, pay special attention to the concept of memory addressing, which is nothing more than the art of specifying where something is. The Game of Assembly Language is peppered with addresses and instructions that work with addresses (such as MOVE data at B to c, which means move the data stored at the address specified by register B to register C). Addressing is by far the trickiest part of assembly language, but master it and you've got the whole thing in your hip pocket.

Everything I've said so far has been orientation. I've tried to give you a taste of the big picture of assembly language and how its fundamental principles relate to the life you've been living all along. Life is a sequence of steps and tests, and so are board games—and so is assembly language. Keep those metaphors in mind as we proceed to get real by confronting the nature of computer numbers.

Alien Bases

Getting Your Arms around Binary and Hexadecimal

The Return of the New Math Monster

The year was 1966. Perhaps you were there. New Math burst upon the grade school curricula of the nation, and homework became a turmoil of number lines, sets, and alternate bases. Middle-class parents scratched their heads with their children over questions like, "What is 17 in Base Five?" and "Which sets does the null set belong to?" In very short order (I recall a period of about two months), the whole thing was tossed in the trash as quickly as it had been concocted by addle-brained educrats with too little to do.

This was a pity, actually. What nobody seemed to realize at the time was that, granted, we were learning New Math—except that *Old* Math had never been taught at the grade-school level either. We kept wondering of what possible use it was to know the intersection of the set of squirrels and the set of mammals. The truth, of course, was that it was no use at all. Mathematics in America has always been taught as *applied* mathematics—arithmetic—heavy on the word problems. If it won't help you balance your checkbook or proportion a recipe, it ain't real math, man. Little or nothing of the logic of mathematics has *ever* made it into the elementary classroom, in part because elementary school in America has historically been a sort of trade school for everyday life. Getting the little beasts fundamentally literate is difficult enough. Trying to get them to appreciate the beauty of alternate number systems simply went over the line for practical middle-class America.

I was one of the few who enjoyed fussing with math in the New-Age style back in 1966, but I gladly laid it aside when the whole thing blew over. I didn't have to pick it up again until 1976, when, after working like a maniac with a wire-wrap gun for several weeks, I fed power to my COSMAC ELF computer and was greeted by an LED display of a pair of numbers in *base 16!*

Mon dieu, New Math *redux* . . .

This chapter exists because at the assembly-language level, your computer does not understand numbers in our familiar base 10. Computers, in a slightly schizoid fashion, work in base 2 *and* base 16—all at the same time. If you're willing to confine yourself to higher-level languages such as C, Basic or Pascal, you can ignore these alien bases altogether, or perhaps treat them as an advanced topic once you get the rest of the language down pat. Not here. *Everything* in assembly language depends on your thorough understanding of these two number bases, so before we do anything else, we're going to learn how to count all over again—in Martian.

Counting in Martian

There is intelligent life on Mars.

That is, the Martians are intelligent enough to know from watching our TV programs these past 60 years that a thriving tourist industry would not be to their advantage. So they've remained in hiding, emerging only briefly to carve big rocks into the shape of Elvis's face to help the *National Enquirer* ensure that no one will ever take Mars seriously again. The Martians do occasionally communicate with science fiction writers like me, knowing full well that nobody has *ever* taken *us* seriously. Hence the information in this section, which involves the way Martians count.

Martians have three fingers on one hand, and only one finger on the other. Male Martians have their three fingers on the left hand, while females have their three fingers on the right hand. This makes waltzing and certain other things easier.

Like human beings and any other intelligent race, Martians started counting by using their fingers. Just as we used our 10 fingers to set things off in groups and powers of 10, the Martians used their four fingers to set things off in groups and powers of four. Over time, our civilization standardized on a set of 10 digits to serve our number system. The Martians, similarly, standardized on a set of four digits for their number system. The four digits follow, along with the names of the digits as the Martians pronounce them: Θ (xip), ∫ (foo), ∩ (bar), ≡ (bas).

Like our zero, xip is a placeholder representing no items, and while Martians sometimes count from xip, they usually start with foo, representing a single item. So they start counting: *Foo, bar, bas* . . .

Now what? What comes after bas? Table 2-1 demonstrates how the Martians count to what we would call 25.

Table 2-1: Counting in Martian, Base Fooby

MARTIAN NUMERALS	MARTIAN PRONUNCIATION	EARTH EQUIVALENT
Θ	Xip	0
ʃ	Foo	1
∩	Bar	2
≡	Bas	3
ʃΘ	Fooby	4
ʃʃ	Fooby-foo	5
ʃ∩	Fooby-bar	6
ʃ≡	Fooby-bas	7
∩Θ	Barby	8
∩ʃ	Barby-foo	9
∩∩	Barby-bar	10
∩≡	Barby-bas	11
≡Θ	Basby	12
≡ʃ	Basby-foo	13
≡∩	Basby-bar	14
≡≡	Basby-bas	15
ʃΘΘ	Foobity	16
ʃΘʃ	Foobity-foo	17
ʃΘ∩	Foobity-bar	18
ʃΘ≡	Foobity-bas	19
ʃʃΘ	Foobity-fooby	20
ʃʃʃ	Foobity-fooby-foo	21
ʃʃ∩	Foobity-fooby-bar	22
ʃʃ≡	Foobity-fooby-bas	23
ʃ∩Θ	Foobity-barby	24
ʃ∩ʃ	Foobity-barby-foo	25

With only four digits (including the one representing zero) the Martians can only count to bas without running out of digits. The number after bas has a new name, *fooby*. Fooby is the base of the Martian number system, and probably the most important number on Mars. Fooby is the number of fingers a Martian has. We would call it *four*.

The most significant thing about fooby is the way the Martians write it out in numerals: ⌈Θ. Instead of a single column, fooby is expressed in two columns. Just as with our decimal system, each column has a value that is a power of fooby. This means only that as you move from the rightmost column toward the left, each column represents a value fooby times the column to its right.

The rightmost column represents units, in counts of foo. The next column over represents fooby times foo, or (given that arithmetic works the same way on Mars as here, New Math notwithstanding) simply fooby. The next column to the left of fooby represents fooby times fooby, or foobity, and so on. This relationship should become clearer through Table 2-2.

Table 2-2: Powers of Fooby

⌈	Foo	x Fooby = ⌈Θ	(Fooby)
⌈Θ	Fooby	x Fooby = ⌈ΘΘ	(Foobity)
⌈ΘΘ	Foobity	x Fooby = ⌈ΘΘΘ	(Foobidity)
⌈ΘΘΘ	Foobidity	x Fooby = ⌈ΘΘΘΘ	(Foobididity)
⌈ΘΘΘΘ	Foobididity	x Fooby = ⌈ΘΘΘΘΘ	(Foobidididity)
⌈ΘΘΘΘΘ	Foobidididity	x Fooby = ⌈ΘΘΘΘΘΘ	and so on...

Dissecting a Martian Number

Any given column may contain a digit from xip to bas, indicating how many instances of that column's value are contained in the number as a whole. Let's work through an example. Look at Figure 2-1, which is a dissection of the Martian number ∩≡⌈Θ≡, pronounced "Barbididity-basbidity-foobity-bas." (A visiting and heavily disguised Martian precipitated the doo-wop craze while standing at a Philadelphia bus stop in 1954, counting his change.)

The rightmost column indicates how many units are contained in the number. The digit there is bas, indicating that the number contains bas units. The second column from the right carries a value of fooby times foo (fooby times one), or fooby. A xip in the fooby column indicates that there are no foobies in the number. The xip digit in ⌈Θ is a placeholder, just as zero is in our numbering system. Notice also that in the columnar sum shown to the right of the digit matrix, the foobies line is represented by a double xip. Not only is there a xip to indicate that there are no foobies, but also a xip holding

How is the following Martian number evaluated?

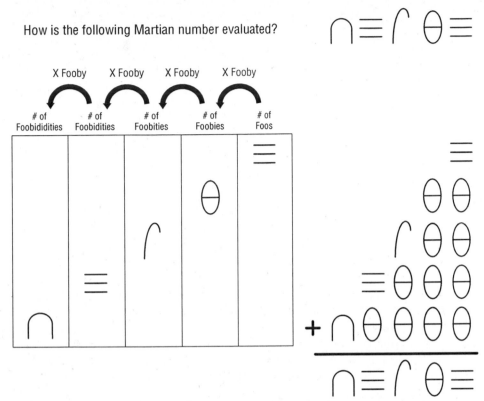

Figure 2-1: The anatomy of ∩≡⌠Θ≡

the foos place as well. This pattern continues in the columnar sum as we move toward the more significant columns to the left.

Fooby times fooby is foobity, and the ⌠ digit tells us that there is foo foobity (a single foobity) in the number. The next column, in keeping with the pattern, is foobity times fooby, or foobidity. In the columnar notation, foobidity is written as ⌠ΘΘΘ. The ≡ digit tells us that there are bas foobidities in the number. Bas foobidities is a number with its own name, basbidity, which may be written as ≡ΘΘΘ. Note the presence of basbidity in the columnar sum.

The next column to the left has a value of fooby times foobidity, or foobididity. The ∩ digit tells us that there are bar foobididities in the number. Bar foobididities (written ∩ΘΘΘΘ) is also a number with its own name, barbididity. Note also the presence of barbididity in the columnar sum, and the four xip digits that hold places for the empty columns.

The columnar sum expresses the sense of the way a number is assembled: the number contains barbididity, basbidity, foobity, and bas. Roll all that together by simple addition and you get ∩≡⌠Θ≡. The name is pronounced simply by hyphenating the component values: barbididity-basbidity-foobity-bas. Note that no part in the name represents the empty fooby column. In our own familiar base 10 we don't, for example, pronounce the number 401 as "four hundred, zero tens, one." We simply say, "four hundred one." In the same manner, rather than say "xip foobies," the Martians just leave it out.

As an exercise, given what I've told you so far about Martian numbers, figure out the Earthly value equivalent to ∩≡ ⌈Θ≡.

The Essence of a Number Base

Because tourist trips to Mars are unlikely to begin any time soon, of what Earthly use is knowing the Martian numbering system? Just this: it's an excellent way to see the sense in a number base without getting distracted by familiar digits and our universal base 10.

In a columnar system of numeric notation like both ours and the Martians', the *base* of the number system is the magnitude by which each column of a number exceeds the magnitude of the column to its right. In our base 10 system, each column represents a value *10* times the column to its right. In a base fooby system like the one used on Mars, each column represents a value fooby times that of the column to its right. (In case you haven't already caught on, the Martians are actually using base 4—but I wanted you to see it from the Martians' own perspective.) Each has a set of digit symbols, the number of which is equal to the base. In our base 10, we have 10 symbols, from 0 to 9. In base 4, there are four digits from 0 to 3. *In any given number base, the base itself can never be expressed in a single digit!*

Octal: How the Grinch Stole Eight and Nine

Farewell to Mars. Aside from lots of iron oxide and some terrific *a capella* groups, they haven't much to offer us 10-fingered folk. There are some similarly odd number bases in use here, and I'd like to take a quick detour through one that occupies a separate world right here on Earth: the world of Digital Equipment Corporation, better known as DEC.

Back in the Sixties, DEC invented the minicomputer as a challenger to the massive and expensive mainframes pioneered by IBM. (The age of minicomputers is long past, and DEC itself is history.) To ensure that no software could possibly be moved from an IBM mainframe to a DEC minicomputer, DEC designed its machines to understand only numbers expressed in base 8.

Let's think about that for a moment, given our experience with the Martians. In base 8, there must be eight digits. DEC was considerate enough not to invent its own digit symbols, so what it used were the traditional Earthly digits from 0 to 7. *There is no digit 8 in base 8!* That always takes a little getting used to, but it's part of the definition of a number base. DEC gave a name to its base 8 system: *octal*.

A columnar number in octal follows the rule we encountered in thinking about the Martian system: each column has a value *base* times that of the column to its right. (The rightmost column is units.) In the case of octal, each column has a value eight times that of the next column to the right.

Who Stole Eight and Nine?

This shows better than it tells. Counting in octal starts out in a very familiar fashion: 1, 2, 3, 4, 5, 6, 7 . . . *10*.

This is where the trouble starts. In octal, 10 comes after seven. What happened to eight and nine? Did the Grinch steal them? (Or the Martians?) Hardly. They're still there—but they have different names. In octal, when you say "10" you mean "8." Worse, when you say "11" you mean "9."

Unfortunately, what DEC did *not* do was invent clever names for the column values. The first column is, of course, the units column. The next column to the left of the units column is the tens column, just as it is in our own decimal system—but there's the rub, and the reason I dragged Mars into this: *Octal's "tens" column actually has a value of 8.*

A counting table will help. Table 2-3 counts up to 30 octal, which has a value of 24 decimal. I dislike the use of the terms *eleven*, *twelve*, and so on in bases other than 10, but the convention in octal has always been to pronounce the numbers as we would in decimal, only with the word *octal* after them. Don't forget to say *octal*—otherwise, people get *really* confused!

Remember, each column in a given number base has a value *base* times the column to its right, so the "tens" column in octal is actually the eights column. (They call it the tens column because it is written 10, and pronounced "ten.") Similarly, the column to the left of the tens column is the hundreds column (because it is written 100 and pronounced "hundreds"), but the hundreds column actually has a value of 8 times 8, or 64. The next column to the left has a value of 64 times 8, or 512, and the column left of that has a value of 512 times 8, or 4,096.

This is why when someone talks about a value of "ten octal," they mean 8; "one hundred octal," means 64; and so on. Table 2-4 summarizes the octal column values and their decimal equivalents.

A digit in the first column (the *units*, or *ones* column) indicates how many units are contained in the octal number. A digit in the next column to the left, the tens column, indicates how many eights are contained in the octal number. A digit in the third column, the hundreds column, indicates how many 64s are in the number, and so on. For example, 400 octal means that the number contains four 64s, which is 256 in decimal.

Table 2-3: Counting in Octal, Base 8

OCTAL NUMERALS	OCTAL PRONUNCIATION	DECIMAL EQUIVALENT
0	Zero	0
1	One	1
2	Two	2
3	Three	3
4	Four	4
5	Five	5
6	Six	6
7	Seven	7
10	Ten	8
11	Eleven	9
12	Twelve	10
13	Thirteen	11
14	Fourteen	12
15	Fifteen	13
16	Sixteen	14
17	Seventeen	15
20	Twenty	16
21	Twenty-one	17
22	Twenty-two	18
23	Twenty-three	19
24	Twenty-four	20
25	Twenty-five	21
26	Twenty-six	22
27	Twenty-seven	23
30	Thirty	24

Yes, it's confusing, in spades. The best way to make it all gel is to dissect a middling octal number, just as we did with a middling Martian number. This is what's happening in Figure 2-2: the octal number 76225 is pulled apart into columns and added up again.

Table 2-4: Octal Columns As Powers of Eight

OCTAL POWER OF 8		DECIMAL OCTAL
$1 = 8^0$	=	$1 \times 8 = 10$
$10 = 8^1$	=	$8 \times 8 = 100$
$100 = 8^2$	=	$64 \times 8 = 1000$
$1000 = 8^3$	=	$512 \times 8 = 10000$
$10000 = 8^4$	=	$4096 \times 8 = 100000$
$100000 = 8^5$	=	$32768 \times 8 = 1000000$
$1000000 = 8^6$	=	$262144 \times 8 = 10000000$

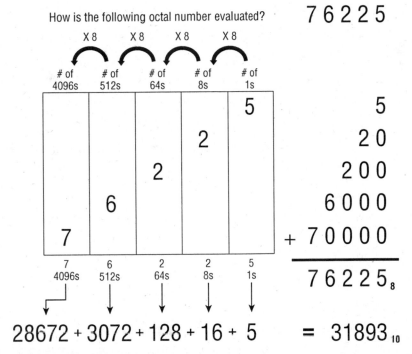

Figure 2-2: The anatomy of 76225 octal

It works here the same way it does in Martian, or in decimal, or in any other number base you could devise. In general (and somewhat formal) terms: each column has a value consisting of the number base raised to the power represented by the ordinal position of the column minus one. For example, the value of the first column is the number base raised to the 1 minus 1, or zero, power. Because any number raised to the zero power is one, the first column in *any* number base always has the value of one and is called the *units column*.

The second column has the value of the number base raised to the 2 minus 1, or first, power, which is the value of the number base itself. In octal this is 8; in decimal, 10; in Martian base fooby, fooby. The third column has a value consisting of the number base raised to the 3 minus 1, or second, power, and so on.

Within each column, the digit holding that column tells how many instances of that column's value is contained in the number as a whole. Here, the 6 in 76225 octal tells us that there are six instances of its column's value in the total value 76225 octal. The six occupies the fourth column, which has a value of $8^4 - 1$, which is 8^3, or 512. This tells us that there are six 512s in the number as a whole.

You can convert the value of a number in any base to decimal (our base 10) by determining the value of each column in the alien (non-decimal) base, multiplying the value of each column by the digit contained in that column (to create the decimal equivalent of each digit), and then finally taking the sum of the decimal equivalent of each column. This is done in Figure 2-2, and the octal number and its decimal equivalent are shown side by side. Note in Figure 2-2 the small subscript numerals on the right-hand side of the columnar sums. These subscripts are used in many technical publications to indicate a number base. The subscript in the value 76225_8, for example, indicates that the value 76225 is here denoting a quantity in octal, which is base 8. Unlike the obvious difference between Martian digits and our traditional decimal digits, there's really nothing about an octal number itself that sets it off as octal. (We encounter something of this same problem a little later when we confront hexadecimal.) The value 31893_{10}, by contrast, is shown by its subscript to be a base 10, or decimal, quantity. This is mostly done in scientific and research writing. In most computer publications (including this one) other indications are used, more on which later.

Now that we've looked at columnar notation from both a Martian and an octal perspective, make sure you understand how columnar notation works in any arbitrary base before continuing.

Hexadecimal: Solving the Digit Shortage

Octal is unlikely to be of use to you unless you do what a friend of mine did and restore an ancient DEC PDP8 computer that he had purchased as surplus from his university, by the pound. (He said it was considerably cheaper than potatoes, if not quite as easy to fry. Not quite.) As I mentioned earlier, the *real* numbering system to reckon with in the microcomputer world is base 16, which we call *hexadecimal*, or (more affectionately) simply ''hex.''

Hexadecimal shares the essential characteristics of any number base, including both Martian and octal: it is a columnar notation, in which each column has a value *16* times the value of the column to its right. It has 16 digits, running from 0 to . . . what?

We have a shortage of digits here. From zero through nine we're in fine shape. However, 10, 11, 12, 13, 14, and 15 need to be expressed with single symbols of some kind. Without any additional numeric digits, the people who developed hexadecimal notation in the early 1950s borrowed the first six letters of the alphabet to act as the needed digits.

Counting in hexadecimal, then, goes like this: 1, 2, 3, 4, 5, 6, 7, 8, 9, A, B, C, D, E, F, 10, 11, 12, 13, 14, 15, 16, 17, 18, 19, 1A, 1B, 1C, and so on. Table 2-5 restates this in a more organized fashion, with the decimal equivalents up to 32.

Table 2-5: Counting in Hexadecimal, Base 16

HEXADECIMAL NUMERALS	PRONUNCIATION (FOLLOW WITH "HEX")	DECIMAL EQUIVALENT
0	Zero	0
1	One	1
2	Two	2
3	Three	3
4	Four	4
5	Five	5
6	Six	6
7	Seven	7
8	Eight	8
9	Nine	9
A	A	10
B	B	11
C	C	12
D	D	13
E	E	14
F	F	15
10	Ten (or, One-oh)	16
11	One-one	17
12	One-two	18

Continued

Table 2-5 (continued)

HEXADECIMAL NUMERALS	PRONUNCIATION (FOLLOW WITH "HEX")	DECIMAL EQUIVALENT
13	One-three	19
14	One-four	20
15	One-five	21
16	One-six	22
17	One-seven	23
18	One-eight	24
19	One-nine	25
1A	One-A	26
1B	One-B	27
1C	One-C	28
1D	One-D	29
1E	One-E	30
1F	One-F	31
20	Twenty (or, Two-oh)	32

One of the conventions in hexadecimal that I favor is the dropping of words such as *eleven* and *twelve* that are a little too tightly bound to our decimal system and only promote gross confusion. Confronted by the number 11 in hexadecimal (usually written 11H to indicate what base we're speaking), we would say, "one-one hex." Don't forget to say "hex" after a hexadecimal number—again, to avoid gross confusion. This is unnecessary with the digits 0 through 9, which represent the exact same values in both decimal and hexadecimal.

Some people still say things like "twelve hex," which is valid, and means 18 decimal; but I don't care for it, and advise against it. This business of alien bases is confusing enough without giving the aliens Charlie Chaplin masks.

Each column in the hexadecimal system has a value 16 times that of the column to its right. (The rightmost column, as in *any* number base, is the units column and has a value of 1.) As you might guess, the values of the individual columns increase frighteningly fast as you move from right to left. Table 2-6 shows the values of the first seven columns in hexadecimal. For comparison's sake, note that the seventh column in decimal notation has a value of 1 million, whereas the seventh column in hexadecimal has a value of 16,777,216.

To help you understand how hexadecimal numbers are constructed, I've dissected a middling hex number in Figure 2-3, in the same fashion that

Table 2-6: Hexadecimal Columns As Powers of 16

HEXADECIMAL	POWER OF 16	DECIMAL	
1H	$= 16^0 =$	1 x 16 =	10H
10H	$= 16^1 =$	16 x 16 =	100H
100H	$= 16^2 =$	256 x 16 =	1000H
1000H	$= 16^3 =$	4096 x 16 =	10000H
10000H	$= 16^4 =$	65536 x 16 =	100000H
100000H	$= 16^5 =$	1048576 x 16 =	1000000H
1000000H	$= 16^6 =$	16777216 etc. . . .	

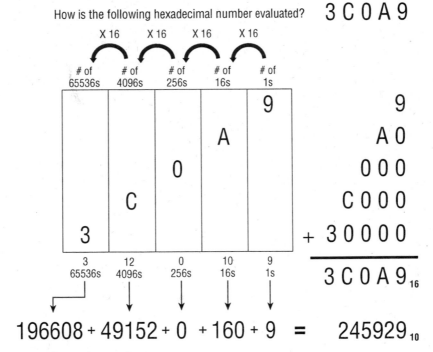

Figure 2-3: The anatomy of 3C0A9H

I dissected numbers earlier in both Martian base fooby, and in octal, base 8. Just as in octal, zero holds a place in a column without adding any value to the number as a whole. Note in Figure 2-3 that there are 0, that is, no, 256s present in the number 3C0A9H.

As in Figure 2-2, the decimal values of each column are shown beneath the column, and the sum of all columns is shown in both decimal and hex. (Note the subscripts!)

From Hex to Decimal and from Decimal to Hex

Most of the manipulation of hex numbers you'll be performing are simple conversions between hex and decimal, in both directions. The easiest way to perform such conversions is by way of a hex calculator, either a "real" calculator like the venerable TI Programmer (which I still have, wretched battery-eater that it is) or a software calculator with hexadecimal capabilities. The default Ubuntu Linux calculator will do math in decimal, hex, and binary if you select View → Scientific. The Windows calculator works exactly the same way: The default view is basic, and you have to select the Scientific view to get into any alien bases. The SpeedCrunch calculator installed by default with Kubuntu/KDE 4 works hex and binary from the get-go.

Using a calculator demands nothing of your gray matter, of course, and won't help you understand the hexadecimal number system any better. So while you're a relatively green student of alien bases, lay off anything that understands hex, be it hardware, software, or human associates.

In fact, the best tool while you're learning is a simple four-function memory calculator. The conversion methods I describe here all make use of such a calculator, as what I'm trying to teach you is number base conversion, not decimal addition or long division.

From Hex to Decimal

As you'll come to understand, converting hex numbers to decimal is a good deal easier than going the other way. The general method is to do what we've been doing all along in the number-dissection Figures 2-1, 2-2, and 2-3: derive the value represented by each individual column in the hex number, and then add all the column values in decimal.

Let's try an easy one. The hex number is 7A2. Start at the right column. This is the units column in any number system. You have 2 units, so enter 2 into your calculator. Now store that 2 into memory (or press the SUM button, if you have a SUM button).

So much for units. Keep in mind that what you're really doing is keeping a running tally of the values of the columns in the hex number. Move to the next column to the left. Remember that in hex, each column represents a value 16 times the value of the column to its right, so the second column from the right is the 16s column. (Refer to Table 2-6 if you lose track of the column values.) The 16s column has an A in it. A in hex is decimal 10. The total value of that column, therefore, is 16×10, or 160. Perform that multiplication on your calculator and add the product to the 2 that you stored in memory. (Again, the SUM button is a handy way to do this if your calculator has one.)

Remember what you're doing: evaluating each column in decimal and keeping a running total. Now move to the third column from the right. This one contains a 7. The value of the third column is 16×16, or 256. Multiply 256×7 on your calculator, and add the product to your running total.

You're done. Retrieve the running total from your calculator memory. The total should be 1,954, which is the decimal equivalent of 7A2H.

OK—let's try it again, more quickly, with a little less natter and a much larger number: C6F0DBH:

1. Evaluate the units column. $B \times 1 = 11 \times 1 = 11$. Start your running total with 11.

2. Evaluate the 16s column. $D \times 16 = 13 \times 16 = 208$. Add 208 to your running total.

3. Evaluate the 256s column. $0 \times 256 = 0$. Move on.

4. Evaluate the 4,096s column. $F \times 4,096 = 15 \times 4,096 = 61,440$. Add it to your running total.

5. Evaluate the 65,536s column. $6 \times 65,536 = 393,216$. Add it to the running total.

6. Evaluate the 1,048,576s column. $C \times ,048,576 = 12 \times 1,048,576 = 12,582,912$. Add it to your total.

The running total should be 13,037,787.

Finally, do it yourself without any help for the following number: 1A55BEH.

From Decimal to Hex

The lights should be coming on about now. This is good, because going in the other direction, from our familiar decimal base 10 to hex, is *much* harder and involves more math. What we have to do is find the hex column values "within" a decimal number—and that involves some considerable use of that fifth-grade bogeyman, long division.

But let's get to it, again starting with a fairly easy decimal number: 449. The calculator will be handy with a vengeance. Tap in the number 449 and store it in the calculator's memory.

What we need to do first is find the *largest* hex column value that is contained in 449 at least *once*. Remember grade-school *gazintas*? (12 *gazinta* 855 how many times?) Division is often introduced to students as a way of finding out how many times some number is present in—"goes into"—another. This is something like that. Looking back at Table 2-6, we can see that 256 is the largest power of 16, and hence the largest hex column value, that is present in 449 at least once. (The next largest power of 16—512—is obviously too large to be present in 449.)

Therefore, we start with 256, and determine how many times 256 "gazinta" 449: $449 / 256 = 1.7539$. At least once, but not quite twice, so 449 contains only one 256. Write down a 1 on paper. *Don't enter it into your calculator.* We're not keeping a running total here; if anything, you could say we're keeping a running remainder. The "1" is the leftmost hex digit of the hex value that is equivalent to decimal 449.

We know that only one 256 is contained in 449. What we must do now is *remove* that 256 from the original number, now that we've "counted" it by writing a 1 down on paper. Subtract 256 from 449. Store the difference, 193, into memory.

The 256 column has been removed from the number we're converting. Now we move to the next column to the right, the 16s. How many 16s are contained in 193? 193 / 16 = 12.0625. This means the 16s column in the hex equivalent of 449 contains a . . . 12? Hmm. Remember the digit shortage, and the fact that in hex, the value we call 12 is represented by the letter C. From a hex perspective, we have found that the original number contains C in the 16s column. Write a C down to the right of your 1: 1C. So far, so good.

We've got the 16s column, so just as with the 256s, we have to remove the 16s from what's left of the original number. The total value of the 16s column is C × 16 = 12 × 16 = 192. Bring the 193 value out of your calculator's memory, and subtract 192 from it. A lonely little 1 is all that's left.

So we're down to the units column. There is one unit in one, obviously. Write that 1 down to the right of the C in our hexadecimal number: 1C1. Decimal 449 is equivalent to hex 1C1.

Now perhaps you can appreciate why programmers like hexadecimal calculators so much.

Glance back at the big picture of the decimal-to-hex conversion. We're looking for the hexadecimal columns hidden in the decimal value. We find the largest column contained in the decimal number, find that column's value, and subtract that value from the decimal number. Then we look for the next smallest hex column, and the next smallest, and so on, removing the value of each column from the decimal number as we go. In a sense, we're dividing the number by consecutively smaller powers of 16 and keeping a running remainder by removing each column as we tally it.

Let's try it again. The secret number is 988,664:

1. Find the largest column contained in 988,664 from Table 2-6: 65,536. 988,664 / 65,536 = 15 and change. Ignore the change. 15 = F in hex. Write down the F.

2. Remove F × 65,536 from 988,664. Store the remainder: 5,624.

3. Move to the next smallest column. 5,624 / 4,096 = 1 and change. Write down the 1.

4. Remove 1 × 4,096 from the remainder: 5,624 − 4096 = 1528. Store the new remainder: 1,528.

5. Move to the next smallest column. 1,528 / 256 = 5 and change. Write down the 5.

6. Remove 5 × 256 from the stored remainder, 1,528. Store 248 as the new remainder.

7. Move to the next smallest column. 248 / 16 = 15 and change. 15 = F in hex. Write down the F.

8. Remove F × 16 from stored remainder, 248. The remainder, 8, is the number of units in the final column. Write down the 8.

There you have it: 988,664 decimal = F15F8H.

Note the presence of the *H* at the end of the hex number. From now on, every hex number in this book will have that H affixed to its hindparts. It's important because not *every* hex number contains letter digits to scream out the fact that the number is in base 16. There is a 157H as surely as a 157 decimal, and the two are *not* the same number. (Quick, now: by how much are they different?) Don't forget that H in writing your assembly programs, as I'll be reminding you later.

Practice. Practice! PRACTICE!

The best (actually, the only) way to get a gut feel for hex notation is to use it a lot. Convert *each* of the following hex numbers to decimal. Lay each number out on the dissection table and identify how many 1s, how many 16s, how many 256s, how many 4,096s, and so on, are present in the number, and then add them up in decimal:

CCH

157H

D8H

BB29H

7AH

8177H

A011H

99H

2B36H

FACEH

8DB3H

9H

That done, now turn it inside out, and convert each of the following decimal numbers to hex. Remember the general method: from Table 2-6, choose the largest power of 16 that is *less* than the decimal number to be converted. Find out how many times that power of 16 is present in the decimal number, and write it down as the leftmost hex digit of the converted number. Then subtract the total value represented by that hex digit from the decimal number. Repeat the process, using the next smallest power of 16, until you've subtracted the decimal number down to nothing.

39

413

22

67,349

6,992

41

1,117

44,919

12,331

124,217

91,198

307

112,374,777

(Extra credit for that last one.) If you need more practice, choose some decimal numbers and convert them to hex, and then convert them back. When you're done, check your work with whatever hex-capable calculator that you prefer.

Arithmetic in Hex

As you become more and more skilled in assembly language, you'll be doing more and more arithmetic in base 16. You may even (good grief) begin to do it in your head. Still, it takes some practice.

Addition and subtraction are basically the same as what we know in decimal, with a few extra digits tossed in for flavor. The trick is nothing more than knowing your addition tables up to 0FH. This is best done not by thinking to yourself, "Now, if C is 12 and F is 15, then C + F is 12 + 15, which is 27 decimal but 1BH." Instead, you should simply think, "C + F is 1BH."

Yes, that's asking a lot; but I ask you now, as I will ask you again on this journey, do you wanna hack assembly ... or do you just wanna fool around? It takes practice to learn the piano, and it takes practice to drive the core skills of assembly language programming down into your synapses where they belong.

So let me sound like an old schoolmarm and tell you to memorize the following. Make flash cards if you must:

```
   9        8        7        6        5
 + 1      + 2      + 3      + 4      + 5
 0AH      0AH      0AH      0AH      0AH

   A        9        8        7        6
 + 1      + 2      + 3      + 4      + 5
 0BH      0BH      0BH      0BH      0BH

   B        A        9        8        7        6
 + 1      + 2      + 3      + 4      + 5      + 6
 0CH      0CH      0CH      0CH      0CH      0CH

   C        B        A        9        8        7
 + 1      + 2      + 3      + 4      + 5      + 6
 0DH      0DH      0DH      0DH      0DH      0DH

   D        C        B        A        9        8        7
 + 1      + 2      + 3      + 4      + 5      + 6      + 7
 0EH      0EH      0EH      0EH      0EH      0EH      0EH

   E        D        C        B        A        9        8
 + 1      + 2      + 3      + 4      + 5      + 6      + 7
 0FH      0FH      0FH      0FH      0FH      0FH      0FH

   F        E        D        C        B        A        9        8
 + 1      + 2      + 3      + 4      + 5      + 6      + 7      + 8
 10H      10H      10H      10H      10H      10H      10H      10H

   F        E        D        C        B        A        9
 + 2      + 3      + 4      + 5      + 6      + 7      + 8
 11H      11H      11H      11H      11H      11H      11H

   F        E        D        C        B        A        9
 + 3      + 4      + 5      + 6      + 7      + 8      + 9
 12H      12H      12H      12H      12H      12H      12H

   F        E        D        C        B        A
 + 4      + 5      + 6      + 7      + 8      + 9
 13H      13H      13H      13H      13H      13H
```

F	E	D	C	B	A
+ 5	+ 6	+ 7	+ 8	+ 9	+ A
14H	14H	14H	14H	14H	14H

F	E	D	C	B
+ 6	+ 7	+ 8	+ 9	+ A
15H	15H	15H	15H	15H

F	E	D	C	B
+ 7	+ 8	+ 9	+ A	+ B
16H	16H	16H	16H	16H

F	E	D	C
+ 8	+ 9	+ A	+ B
17H	17H	17H	17H

F	E	D	C
+ 9	+ A	+ B	+ C
18H	18H	18H	18H

F	E	D
+ A	+ B	+ C
19H	19H	19H

F	E	D
+ B	+ C	+ D
1AH	1AH	1AH

F	E
+ C	+ D
1BH	1BH

F	E
+ D	+ E
1CH	1CH

F
+ E
1DH

F
+ F
1EH

If nothing else, this exercise should make you glad that computers don't work in base 64.

Columns and Carries

With all of these single-column additions committed (more or less) to memory, you can tackle multicolumn addition. It works pretty much the same way it does with decimal. Add each column starting from the right, and carry into the next column anytime a single column's sum exceeds 0FH.

For example:

```
  1       1
  2 F 3 1 A DH
+ 9 6 B A 0 7H
  C 5 E B B 4H
```

Carefully work this one through, column by column. The sum of the first column (that is, the rightmost) is 14H, which cannot fit in a single column, so we must carry the one into the next column to the left. Even with the additional 1, however, the sum of the second column is 0BH, which fits in a single column and no carry is required.

Keep adding toward the left. The second-to-last column will again overflow, and you need to carry the one into the last column. As long as you have your single-digit sums memorized, it's a snap.

Well, more or less.

Here's something you should take note of:

The most you can ever carry out of a single-column addition of two numbers is 1.

It doesn't matter what base you're in: 16, 10, fooby, or 2. You will either carry a 1 (in Martian, a foo) out of a column, or carry nothing at all. This fact surprises people for some reason, so ask yourself: what two single digits in old familiar base 10 can you add that will force you to carry a 2? The largest digit is 9, and $9 + 9 = 18$. Put down the 8 and carry the 1. Even if you have to add in a carry from a previous column, that will bring you up (at most) to 19. Again, you carry a 1 and no more. This is important when you add numbers on paper, or within the silicon of your CPU, as you'll learn in a few chapters.

Subtraction and Borrows

If you have your single-column sums memorized, you can usually grind your way through subtraction with a shift into a sort of mental reverse: "If E + 6 equals 14H, then 14H - E must equal 6." The alternative is memorizing an even larger number of tables, and since I haven't memorized them, I won't ask you to.

But over time, that's what tends to happen. In hex subtraction, you should be able to dope out any given single-column subtraction by turning a familiar hexadecimal sum inside-out; and just as with base 10, multicolumn subtractions are done column by column, one column at a time:

```
 F76CH
-A05BH
 5711H
```

During your inspection of each column, you should be asking yourself: "What number added to the bottom number yields the top number?" Here, you should know from your tables that B + 1 = C, so the difference between B and C is 1. The leftmost column is actually more challenging: What number added to A gives you F? Chin up; even I have to think about it on an off day.

The problems show up, of course, when the top number in a column is smaller than its corresponding bottom number. Then you have no recourse but to borrow.

Borrowing is one of those grade-school rote-learned processes that very few people really understand. (To understand it is tacit admittance that something of New Math actually stuck, horrors.) From a height, what happens in a borrow is that one count is taken from a column and applied to the column on its right. I say *applied* rather than *added to* because in moving from one column to the column on its right, that single count is multiplied by 10, where 10 represents the number base. (Remember that 10 in octal has a value of 8, while 10 in hexadecimal has a value of 16.)

It sounds worse than it is. Let's look at a borrow in action, and you'll get the idea:

```
 9 2H
-4 FH
```

Here, the subtraction in the rightmost column can't happen as-is because F is larger than 2, so we borrow from the next column to the left.

Nearly 50 years later, I can still hear old Sister Marie Bernard toughing it out on the blackboard, albeit in base 10: "Cross out the 9; make it an 8. Make the 2 a 12. And 12 minus F is what, class?" It's 3, Sister. And that's how a borrow works. (I hope the poor dear will forgive me for putting hex bytes in her mouth.)

Think about what happened there, functionally. *We subtracted 1 from the 9 and added 10H to the 2.* One obvious mistake is to subtract 1 from the 9 and add 1 to the 2, which (need I say it?) won't work. Think of it this way: we're moving part of one column's surplus value over to its right, where some extra value is needed. The *overall* value of the upper number doesn't change (which is why we call it a *borrow* and not a *steal*), but the recipient of the loan is increased by *10*, not *1*.

After the borrow, what we have looks something like this:

```
 8¹2H
- 4 FH
```

(On Sister Marie Bernard's blackboard, we crossed out the 9 and made it an 8. I just made it an 8. Silicon has advantages over chalk—except that the 8's earlier life as a 9 is not so obvious.)

Of course, once we're here, the columnar subtractions all work out, and we discover that the difference is 43H.

People sometimes ask if you ever have to borrow more than 1. The answer, plainly, is *no*. If you borrow 2, for example, you would add 20 to the recipient column, and *20 minus any single digit remains a two-digit number*. That is, the difference won't fit into a single column. Subtraction contains an important symmetry with addition:

> *The most you ever need to borrow in any single-column subtraction of two numbers is 1.*

Borrows across Multiple Columns

Understanding that much about borrows gets you most of the way there; but, as life is wont, you will *frequently* come across a subtraction similar to this:

```
  F 0 0 0H
- 3 B 6 CH
```

Column 1 needs to borrow, but neither column 2 nor column 3 has anything at all to lend. Back in grade school, Sister Marie Bernard would have rattled out with machine-gun efficiency: "Cross out the F, make it an E. Make the 0 a 10. Then cross it out, make it an F. Make the next 0 a 10; cross it out, make it an F. Then make the last 0 a 10. Got that?" (I got it. In Catholic school, the consequences of *not* getting it are too terrible to consider.)

What happens is that the middle two 0s act as loan brokers between the F and the rightmost 0, keeping their commission in the form of enough value to allow their own columns' subtractions to take place. Each column to the right of the last column borrows 10 from its neighbor to the left, and loans 1 to the neighbor on its right. After all the borrows trickle through the upper number, what we have looks like this (minus all of Sister's cross-outs):

```
  E F F¹0H
- 3 B 6 CH
```

At this point, each columnar subtraction can take place, and the difference is B494H.

In remembering your grade-school machinations, don't fall into the old decimal rut of thinking, "cross out the 10, make it a 9." In the world of hexadecimal, 10H - 1 = F. Cross out the 10, make it an *F*.

What's the Point?

. . . if you have a hex calculator, or a hex-capable screen calculator? The point is *practice*. Hexadecimal is the *lingua franca* of assemblers, to multiply mangle a metaphor. The more you burn a gut-level understanding of hex into your reflexes, the easier assembly language will be. Furthermore, understanding the internal structure of the machine itself will be *much* easier if you have that intuitive grasp of hex values. We're laying important groundwork here. Take it seriously now and you'll lose less hair later on.

Binary

Hexadecimal is excellent practice for taking on the strangest number base of all: *binary*. Binary is base 2. Given what you've learned about number bases so far, what can you surmise about base 2?

- Each column has a value two times the column to its right.
- There are only two digits (0 and 1) in the base.

Counting is a little strange in binary, as you might imagine. It goes like this: 0, 1, 10, 11, 100, 101, 110, 111, 1,000, and so on. Because it sounds absurd to say, "Zero, one, 10, 11, 100," and so on, it makes more sense to simply enunciate the individual digits, followed by the word *binary*. For example, most people say "one zero one one one zero one binary" instead of "one million, eleven thousand, one hundred one binary" when pronouncing the number 1011101—which sounds enormous until you consider that its value in decimal is only 93.

Odd as it may seem, binary follows all of the same rules we've discussed in this chapter regarding number bases. Converting between binary and decimal is done using the same methods described for hexadecimal earlier in this chapter.

Because counting in binary is as much a matter of counting columns as counting digits (as there are only two digits), it makes sense to take a long, close look at Table 2-7, which shows the values of the binary number columns out to 32 places.

One look at that imposing pyramid of zeroes implies that it's hopeless to think of pronouncing the larger columns as strings of digits: "One zero zero zero zero zero zero zero . . . " and so on. There's a crying need for a shorthand notation here, so I'll provide you with one in a little while—and its identity will surprise you.

Table 2-7: Binary Columns As Powers of 2

BINARY	POWER OF 2	DECIMAL
1	$=2^0=$	1
10	$=2^1=$	2
100	$=2^2=$	4
1000	$=2^3=$	8
10000	$=2^4=$	16
100000	$=2^5=$	32
1000000	$=2^6=$	64
10000000	$=2^7=$	128
100000000	$=2^8=$	256
1000000000	$=2^9=$	512
10000000000	$=2^{10}=$	1024
100000000000	$=2^{11}=$	2048
1000000000000	$=2^{12}=$	4096
10000000000000	$=2^{13}=$	8192
100000000000000	$=2^{14}=$	16384
1000000000000000	$=2^{15}=$	32768
10000000000000000	$=2^{16}=$	65536
100000000000000000	$=2^{17}=$	131072
1000000000000000000	$=2^{18}=$	262144
10000000000000000000	$=2^{19}=$	524288
100000000000000000000	$=2^{20}=$	1048576
1000000000000000000000	$=2^{21}=$	2097152
10000000000000000000000	$=2^{22}=$	4194304
100000000000000000000000	$=2^{23}=$	8388608
1000000000000000000000000	$=2^{24}=$	16777216
10000000000000000000000000	$=2^{25}=$	33554432
100000000000000000000000000	$=2^{26}=$	67108864
1000000000000000000000000000	$=2^{27}=$	134217720

Continued

Table 2-7 (*continued*)

BINARY	POWER OF 2	DECIMAL
10000000000000000000000000000	$=2^{28}=$	268435456
100000000000000000000000000000	$=2^{29}=$	536870912
1000000000000000000000000000000	$=2^{30}=$	1073741824
10000000000000000000000000000000	$=2^{31}=$	2147483648
100000000000000000000000000000000	$=2^{32}=$	4294967296

You might object that such large numbers as the bottommost in the table aren't likely to be encountered in ordinary programming. Sorry, but a 32-bit microprocessor such as the Pentium (and even its antiquated forbears like the 386 and 496) can swallow numbers like that in one electrical gulp, and eat billions of them for lunch. You *must* become accustomed to thinking in terms of such numbers as 2^{32}, which, after all, is only a trifling 4 billion in decimal. Think for a moment of the capacity of the hard drive on your own desktop computer. New midrange desktop PCs are routinely shipped with 500 gigabytes or more of hard disk storage. A gigabyte is a billion bytes, so that monster 32-bit number can't even count all the bytes on your hard drive! This little problem has actually bitten some vendors of old (no, sorry, the word is *legacy*) software. Twenty years ago, a 500-gigabyte hard drive seemed more like fantasy than science fiction. Now you can buy that fantasy for $99.95. More than one file utility from the DOS and early Windows eras threw up its hands in despair anytime it had to confront a disk drive with more than 2 gigabytes of free space.

Now, just as with octal and hexadecimal, there can be identity problems when using binary. The number 101 in binary is *not* the same as 101 in hex, or 101 in decimal. For this reason, always append the suffix "B" to your binary values to ensure that people reading your programs (including you, six weeks after the fact) know what number base you're working from.

Values in Binary

Converting a value in binary to one in decimal is done the same way it's done in hex—more simply, in fact, for the simple reason that you no longer have to count how many times a column's value is present in any given column. In hex, you have to see how many 16s are present in the 16s column, and so on. In binary, a column's value is either present (1 time) or not present (0 times).

Running through a simple example should make this clear. The binary number 11011010B is a relatively typical binary value in relatively simple computer work. (On the small side, actually—many common binary numbers are twice that size or more.) Converting 11011010B to decimal comes down to scanning it from right to left with the help of Table 2-7, and tallying any column's value where that column contains a 1, while ignoring any column containing a 0.

Clear your calculator and let's get started:

1. Column 0 contains a 0; skip it.

2. Column 1 contains a 1. That means its value, 2, is present in the value of the number. So we punch 2 into the calculator.

3. Column 2 is 0. Skip it.

4. Column 3 contains a 1. The column's value is 2^3, or 8; add 8 to the tally.

5. Column 4 also contains a 1; 2^4 is 16, which we add to our tally.

6. Column 5 is 0. Skip it.

7. Column 6 contains a 1; 2^6 is 64, so add 64 to the tally.

8. Column 7 also contains a 1. Column 7's value is 2^7, or 128. Add 128 to the tally, and what do we have? 218. That's the decimal value of 11011010B. It's as easy as that.

Converting from decimal to binary, while more difficult, is done *exactly* the same way as converting from decimal to hex. Go back and read that section again, searching for the *general method* used. In other words, see what was done and separate the essential principles from any references to a specific base such as hex.

I'll bet by now you can figure it out without much trouble.

As a brief aside, perhaps you noticed that I started counting columns from 0, rather than 1. A peculiarity of the computer field is that we always begin counting things from 0. Actually, to call it a peculiarity is unfair; the computer's method is the reasonable one, because 0 is a perfectly good number and should not be discriminated against. The rift occurred because in our real, physical world, counting things tells us *how many* things are there, whereas in the computer world counting things is more generally done to *name* them. That is, we need to deal with bit number 0, and then bit number 1, and so on, far more than we need to know how many bits there are.

This is not a quibble, by the way. The issue will come up again and again in connection with memory addresses, which, as I have said and will say again, are the key to understanding assembly language.

In programming circles, always begin counting from 0!

A practical example of the conflicts this principle can cause grows out of the following question: what year began our new millennium? Most people would intuitively say the year 2000—and back during the run-up to 2000 many people did—but technically the twentieth century continued its plodding pace until January 1, 2001. Why? *Because there was no year 0.* When historians count the years moving from BC to AD, they go right from 1 BC to 1 AD. Therefore, the first century began with year 1 and ended with year 100. The second century began with year 101 and ended with year 200. By extending the sequence, you can see that the twentieth century began in 1901 and ended in 2000. Conversely, if we had had the sense to begin counting years in the current era computer style, from year 0, the twentieth century would have ended at the end of 1999.

This is a good point to get some practice in converting numbers from binary to decimal and back. Sharpen your teeth on these:

```
110
10001
11111
11
101
1100010111010010
11000
1011
```

When that's done, convert these decimal values to binary:

```
77
42
106
255
18
6309
121
58
18,446
```

Why Binary?

If it takes eight whole digits (11011010) to represent an ordinary three-digit number such as 218, binary as a number base would seem to be a bad intellectual investment. Certainly for us it would be a waste of mental bandwidth, and even aliens with only two fingers would probably have come up with a better system.

The problem is, lights are either on or off.

This is just another way of saying (as I will discuss in detail in Chapter 3) that at the bottom of it, *computers are electrical devices*. In an electrical device, voltage is either present or it isn't; current either flows or it doesn't. Very early in the game, computer scientists decided that the presence of a voltage in a computer circuit would indicate a 1 digit, while lack of a voltage at that same point in the circuit would indicate a 0 digit. This isn't many digits, but it's enough for the binary number system. This is the only reason we use binary, but it's a rather compelling one, and we're stuck with it. However, you will not necessarily drown in ones and zeroes, because I've already taught you a form of shorthand.

Hexadecimal As Shorthand for Binary

The number 218 expressed in binary is 11011010B. Expressed in hex, however, the same value is quite compact: DAH. The two hex digits comprising DAH merit a closer look. AH (or 0AH as your assembler will require it, for reasons explained later) represents 10 decimal. Converting any number to binary simply involves detecting the powers of two within it. The largest power of 2 within 10 decimal is 8. Jot down a 1 digit and subtract 8 from 10. What's left is 2. Now, 4 is a power of 2, but there is no 4 hiding within 2, so we put a 0 to the right of the 1. The next smallest power of 2 is 2, and there is a 2 in 2. Jot down another 1 to the right of the 0. Two from 2 is 0, so there are no 1s left in the number. Jot down a final 0 to the right of the rest to represent the 1s column. What you have is this:

```
1 0 1 0
```

Look back at the binary equivalent of 218: 11011010. The last four digits are 1010—the binary equivalent of 0AH.

The same will work for the upper half of DAH. If you work out the binary equivalence for 0DH as we just did (and it would be good mental exercise), it is 1101. Look at the binary equivalent of 218 this way:

```
   218      decimal
1101 1010   binary
  D    A    hex
```

It should be dawning on you that you can convert long strings of binary ones and zeroes into more compact hex format by converting every four binary digits (starting from the right, *not* from the left!) into a single hex digit.

As an example, here is a 32-bit binary number that is not the least bit remarkable:

```
11110000000000001111101001101110
```

This is a pretty obnoxious collection of bits to remember or manipulate, so let's split it up into groups of four from the right:

```
1111 0000 0000 0000 1111 1010 0110 1110
```

Each of these groups of four binary digits can be represented by a single hexadecimal digit. Do the conversion now. You should get the following:

```
1111 0000 0000 0000 1111 1010 0110 1110
 F    0    0    0    F    A    6    E
```

In other words, the hex equivalent of that mouthful is

```
F000FA6E
```

In use, of course, you would append the H on the end, and also put a 0 at the beginning, so in any kind of assembly language work the number would actually be written 0F000FA6EH.

This is still a good-sized number, but unless you're doing things like counting hard drive space or other high-value things, such 32-bit numbers are the largest quantities you would typically encounter in journeyman-level assembly language programming.

Suddenly, this business starts looking a little more graspable.

Hexadecimal is the programmer's shorthand for the computer's binary numbers.

This is why I said earlier that computers use base 2 (binary) and base 16 (hexadecimal) both at the same time in a rather schizoid fashion. What I didn't say is that the computer isn't really the schizoid one; *you* are. At their very hearts (as I explain in Chapter 3) computers use *only* binary. Hex is a means by which you and I make dealing with the computer easier. Fortunately, every four binary digits may be represented by a hex digit, so the correspondence is clean and comprehensible.

Prepare to Compute

Everything up to this point has been necessary groundwork. I've explained conceptually what computers *do* and have given you the tools to understand the slightly alien numbers that they use; but I've said nothing so far about what computers actually *are*, and it's well past time. We will return to hexadecimal numbers repeatedly in this book; I've said nothing thus far about hex multiplication or bit-banging. The reason is plain: before you can bang a bit, you must know where the bits live. So, let's lift the hood and see if we can catch a few of them in action.

CHAPTER 3

Lifting the Hood

Discovering What Computers Actually Are

RAXie, We Hardly Knew Ye . . .

In January 1970 I was on the downwind leg of my senior year in high school, and the Chicago Public Schools had installed a computer somewhere. A truck full of these fancy IBM typewriter gadgets was delivered to Lane Tech, and a bewildered math teacher was drafted into teaching computer science (as they had the nerve to call it) to a high school full of rowdy males.

I figured it out fairly quickly. You pounded out a deck of these goofy computer cards on the card-punch machine, dropped them into the card hopper of one of the typewriter gadgets, and watched in awe as the typewriter danced its little golf ball over the green bar paper, printing out your inevitable list of error messages. It was fun. I got straight A's. I even kept the first program I ever wrote that did something useful: a little deck of cards that generated a table of parabolic correction factors for hand-figuring telescope mirrors, astronomy being my passion at the time. (I still have the card deck, though the gummy mess left behind by disintegrating rubber bands would not be healthy for a card reader, assuming that one still exists.)

The question that kept gnawing at me was exactly what sort of beast RAX (the computer's wonderfully appropriate name) actually was. What we had were ram-charged typewriters that RAX controlled over phone lines—that much I understood—but what was RAX itself?

I asked the instructor. In brief, the conversation went something like this:

Me: "Umm, sir, what exactly *is* RAX?"

He: "Eh? Um, a computer. An electronic computer."

Me: "That's what it says on the course notes; but I want to know what RAX is made of and how it works."

He: "Well, I'm sure RAX is all solid-state."

Me: "You mean, there's no levers and gears inside."

He: "Oh, there may be a few, but no vacuum tubes."

Me: "I wasn't worried about tubes. I suppose it has a calculator in it somewhere; but what makes it remember that A comes before B? How does it know what 'format' means? How does it tell time? What does it have to do to answer the phone?"

He: "Now, come on, that's why computers are so great! They put it all together so that we don't have to worry about that sort of thing! Who cares what RAX is? RAX knows FORTRAN and will execute any correct FORTRAN program. That's what matters, isn't it?"

He was starting to sweat. So was I. End of conversation.

That June I graduated with three inches of debugged and working FOR-TRAN punch cards in my book bag, and still had absolutely no clue as to what RAX was.

It has bothered me to this day.

Gus to the Rescue

I was thinking about RAX six years later, while on the Devon Avenue bus heading for work, with the latest copy of *Popular Electronics* in my lap. The lead story described a do-it-yourself project called the COSMAC ELF, which consisted of a piece of perfboard full of integrated circuit chips, all wired together, plus some toggle switches and a pair of LED numeric displays.

It was a computer. (Said so right on the label, heh.) The article described how to put it together, and that was about all. What did those chips do? What did the whole thing do? There was no fancy robotic typewriter anywhere in sight. It was driving me nuts.

As usual, my friend Gus Flassig got on the bus at Ashland Avenue and sat down beside me. I asked him what the COSMAC ELF did. He was the first human being to make the concept of a *physical* computer hang together for me:

These are memory chips. You load numbers into the memory chips by flipping these toggle switches in different binary code patterns, where "up" means a 1-bit, and "down" means a 0-bit. Each number in memory means something to the CPU chip. One number makes it add; another number makes it subtract; another makes it write different numbers into memory, and lots of other things. A program consists of a bunch of these instruction-numbers in a row in memory. The computer reads the first number, does what the number tells it to do, and then reads the second one, does what that number says to do, and so on until it runs out of numbers.

If you don't find that utterly clear, don't worry. I had the advantage of being an electronics hobbyist (so I knew what some of the chips did) and had already written some programs in RAX's FORTRAN. For me, my God, everything suddenly hit critical mass and exploded in my head until the steam started pouring out of my ears. I *got* it!

No matter what RAX was, I knew that it had to be something like the COSMAC ELF, only on a larger scale. I built an ELF. It was quite an education, and enabled me to understand the nature of computers at a very deep level. I don't recommend that anybody but total crazies wire-wrap their own computers out of loose chips anymore, although it was a common enough thing to do in the mid to late 1970s.

As a side note, someone has written a Windows-based simulation of the COSMAC ELF that looks just like the one I built, and it will actually accept and execute COSMAC programs. It's a lot of fun and might give you some perspective on what passed for hobby computing in early 1976. The URL is as follows:

```
http://incolor.inetnebr.com/bill_r/computer_simulators.htm
```

The site's author, Bill Richman, has also reprinted the *Popular Electronics* article from which I built the device. All fascinating reading—and a very good education in the deepest silicon concepts underlying computing as it was then and remains to this day.

In this chapter I will provide you with some of the insights that I obtained while assembling my own computer the hard way. (You wonder where the "hard" in "hardware" comes from? Not from the sound it makes when you bang it on the table, promise.)

Switches, Transistors, and Memory

Switches remember.

Think about it: you flip the wall switch by the door, and the light in the middle of the ceiling comes on. It stays on. When you leave the room, you flip the switch down again, and the light goes out. It stays out. Poltergeists notwithstanding, the switch will remain in the position you last left it until you or someone else comes back and flips it to its other position. Even if the bulb burns out, you can look at the position of the switch handle and know whether the light is on or off.

In a sense, the switch remembers what its last command was until you change it, and "overwrites" that command with a new one. In this sense, a light switch represents a sort of rudimentary memory element.

Light switches are more mechanical than electrical. This does not prevent them from acting as memory; indeed, the very first computer (Babbage's nineteenth-century Difference Engine) was entirely mechanical. In fact, the far larger version he designed but never finished was to have been *steam-powered*. Babbage's machine had a lot of little cams that could be flipped by other cams from one position to another. Numbers were encoded and remembered as patterns of cam positions.

One If by Land . . .

Whether a switch is mechanical, or electrical, or hydraulic, or something else is irrelevant. What counts is that a switch contains a pattern: on or off; up or down; flow or no flow. To that pattern can be assigned a meaning. Paul Revere told his buddy to set up a code in the Old North Church: "One if by land, two if by sea." Once lit, the lamps in the steeple remained lit (and thus remembered that very important code) long enough for Paul to call out the militia and whup the British.

In general, then, what we call *memory* is an aggregate of switches that retain a pattern long enough for that pattern to be read and understood by a person or a mechanism. For our purposes, those switches will be electrical, but keep in mind that both mechanical and hydraulic computers have been proposed and built with varying degrees of success.

Memory consists of containers for alterable patterns that retain an entered pattern until someone or something alters the pattern.

Transistor Switches

One problem with building a computer memory system of light switches is that light switches are pretty specialized: they require fingers to set them, and their output is a current path for electricity. Ideally, a computer memory switch should be operated by the same force it controls. This enables the patterns stored in memory to be passed on to other memory storage locations. In the gross electromechanical world, such a switch is called a *relay*.

A *relay* is a mechanical switch that is operated by electricity, for the purpose of controlling electricity. You "flip" a relay by feeding it a pulse of electricity, which powers a little hammer that whaps a lever to one side or another. This lever then opens or closes a set of electrical contacts, just as your garden-variety light switch does. Computers have been made out of relays, although as you might imagine, it was a long time ago, and (with a typical relay being about the size of an ice cube) they weren't especially powerful computers.

Fully electronic computers are made out of transistor switches. (*Very* early computers were also made with vacuum tube switches.) *Transistors* are tiny crystals of silicon that use the peculiar electrical properties of silicon to act as switches. I won't try to explain what those peculiar properties are, as that would take an entire book unto itself. Let's consider a transistor switch a sort of electrical black box, and describe it in terms of inputs and outputs.

Figure 3-1 shows a transistor switch. (It is a *field-effect* transistor, which in truth is only one type of transistor, but it is the type that our current computers are made of.) When an electrical voltage is applied to pin 1, current flows between pins 2 and 3. When the voltage is removed from pin 1, current ceases to flow between pins 2 and 3.

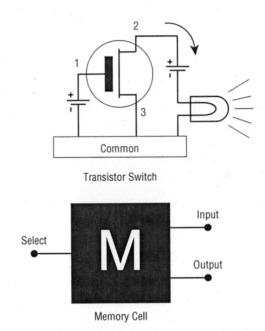

Figure 3-1: Transistor switches and memory cells

In real life, a tiny handful of other components (typically diodes and capacitors) are necessary to make things work smoothly in a computer memory context. These are not necessarily little gizmos connected by wires to the outside of the transistor (although in early transistorized computers they were), but are now cut from the same silicon crystal the transistor itself is cut from, and occupy almost no space at all. Taken together, the transistor switch and its support components are called a *memory cell*. I've hidden the electrical complexity of the memory cell within an appropriate black-box symbol in Figure 3-1.

A memory cell keeps the current flow through it to a minimum, because electrical current flow produces heat, and heat is the enemy of electrical components. The memory cell's circuit is arranged so that if you put a tiny voltage on its input pin and a similar voltage on its *select* pin, a voltage will appear *and remain* on its output pin. That output voltage remains in its set state until remove the voltage from the cell as a whole, or remove the voltage from the input pin while putting a voltage on the select pin.

The "on" voltage being applied to all of these pins is kept at a consistent level (except, of course, when it is removed entirely). In other words, you don't put 12 volts on the input pin and then change that to 6 volts or 17 volts. The computer designers pick a voltage and stick with it. The pattern is binary in nature: you either put a voltage on the input pin or you take the voltage away entirely. The output pin echoes that: it either holds a fixed voltage or no voltage at all.

We apply a code to that state of affairs: *The presence of voltage indicates a binary 1, and the lack of voltage indicates a binary 0.* This code is arbitrary. We could as well have said that the *lack* of voltage indicates a binary 1 and vice versa (and computers have been built this way for obscure reasons), but the choice is up to us. Having the *presence* of something indicate a binary 1 is more natural, and that is the way things have evolved in the computing mainstream.

A single computer memory cell, such as the transistor-based one we're speaking of here, holds one binary digit, either a 1 or a 0. This is called a bit. A *bit* is the indivisible atom of information. There is no half-a-bit, and no bit-and-a-half.

A bit is a single binary digit, either 1 or 0.

The Incredible Shrinking Bit

One bit doesn't tell us much. To be useful, we need to bring *a lot* of memory cells together. Transistors started out fairly small (the originals from the 1950s looked a lot like stovepipe hats for tin soldiers) and went down from there. The first transistors were created from little chips of germanium or silicon crystal about one-eighth of an inch square. The size of the crystal chip hasn't changed outrageously since then, but the transistors themselves have shrunk almost incredibly.

Whereas in the beginning one chip held one transistor, in time semiconductor designers crisscrossed the chip into four equal areas and made each area an independent transistor. From there it was an easy jump to add the other minuscule components needed to turn a transistor into a computer memory cell.

The chip of silicon was a tiny and fragile thing, and was encased in an oblong, molded-plastic housing, like a small stick of gum with metal legs for the electrical connections.

What we had now was a sort of electrical egg carton: four little cubbyholes, each of which could contain a single binary bit. Then the shrinking process began. First 8 bits, then 16, then multiples of 8 and 16, all on the same tiny silicon chip. By the late 1960s, 256 memory cells could occupy one chip of silicon, usually in an array of 8 cells by 32. In 1976, my COSMAC ELF computer contained two memory chips. On each chip was an array of memory cells 4 wide and 256 long. (Picture a *really* long egg carton.) Each chip could thus hold 1,024 bits.

This was a pretty typical memory chip capacity at that time. We called them "1K RAM chips" because they held roughly 1,000 bits of *random-access memory* (RAM). The *K* comes from *kilobit*—that is, one thousand bits. We'll get back to the notion of what *random access* means shortly.

Toward the mid-1970s, the great memory-shrinking act was kicking into high gear. One-kilobyte chips were crisscross divided into 4K chips containing 4,096 bits of memory. The 4K chips were almost immediately divided into 16K chips (16,384 bits of memory). These 16K chips were the standard when the IBM PC first appeared in 1981. By 1982, the chips had been divided once again, and 16K became 64K, with 65,536 bits inside that same little gum stick. Keep in mind that we're talking more than 65,000 transistors (plus other odd components) formed on a square of silicon about a quarter-inch on a side.

Come 1985 and the 64K chip had been pushed aside by its drawn-and-quartered child, the 256K chip (262,144 bits). Chips almost always increase in capacity by a factor of 4 simply because the current-generation chip is divided into 4 equal areas, onto each of which is then placed the same number of transistors that the previous generation of chip had held over the whole silicon chip.

By 1990, the 256K chip was history, and the 1-megabit chip was state of the art (*mega* is Greek for million). By 1992, the 4-megabit chip had taken over. The critter had a grand total of 4,194,304 bits inside it, still no larger than that stick of cinnamon gum. About that time, the chips themselves grew small and fragile enough so that four or eight of them were soldered to tiny printed circuit boards so that they would survive handling by clumsy human beings.

The game has continued apace, and currently you can purchase these little plug-in circuit board memory modules with as much as two *giga*bytes in them—which is over sixteen *billion* bits.

Will it stop here? Unlikely. More is better, and we're bringing some staggeringly powerful technology to bear on the creation of ever-denser memory systems. Some physicists warn that the laws of physics may soon call a time-out in the game, as the transistors are now so small that it gets hard pushing more than one electron at a time through them. At that point, some truly ugly limitations of life called quantum mechanics begin to get in the way. We'll find a way around these limitations (we always do), but in the process the whole nature of computer memory may change.

Random Access

Newcomers sometimes find "random" a perplexing and disturbing word with respect to memory, as *random* often connotes chaos or unpredictability. What the word really means here is "at random," indicating that you can reach into a random-access memory chip and pick out any of the bits it contains without disturbing any of the others, just as you might select one book at random from your public library's many shelves of thousands of books without sifting through them in order or disturbing the places of other books on the shelves.

Memory didn't always work this way. Before memory was placed on silicon chips, it was stored on electromagnetic machines of some kind, usually rotating magnetic drums or disks distantly related to the hard drives we use today. Rotating magnetic memory sends a circular collection of bits beneath a magnetic sensor. The bits pass beneath the sensor one at a time, and if you miss the one you want, like a Chicago bus in January, you simply have to wait for it to come by again. These are *serial-access devices*. They present their bits to you serially, in a fixed order, one at a time, and you have to wait for the one you want to come up in its order.

There's no need to remember that; we've long since abandoned serial-access devices for main computer memory. We still use such systems for *mass storage*, as I describe a bit later. Your hard drive is at its heart a serial-access device.

Random access works like this: inside the chip, each bit is stored in its own memory cell, identical to the memory cell diagrammed in Figure 3-1. Each of the however-many memory cells has a unique number. This number is a cell's (and hence a bit's) *address*. It's like the addresses on a street: the bit on the corner is number 0 Silicon Alley, and the bit next door is number 1, and so on. You don't have to knock on the door of bit 0 and ask which bit it is, and then go to the next door and ask there too, until you find the bit you want. If you have the address, you can zip right down the street and park square in front of the bit you intend to visit.

Each chip has a number of pins coming out of it. The bulk of these pins are called *address pins*. One pin is called a *data pin* (see Figure 3-2). The address pins are electrical leads that carry a binary address code. This address is a binary number, expressed in 1s and 0s only. You apply this address to the address pins by encoding a binary 1 as (let's say) 5 volts, and a binary 0 as 0 volts. Many other voltages have been used and are still used in computer hardware. What matters is that we all agree that a certain voltage on a pin represents a binary 1. Special circuits inside the RAM chip decode this address to one of the select inputs of the numerous memory cells inside the chip. For any given address applied to the address pins, only *one* select input will be raised to five volts, thereby selecting that memory cell.

Depending on whether you intend to read a bit or write a bit, the data pin is switched between the memory cells' inputs or outputs, as shown in Figure 3-2.

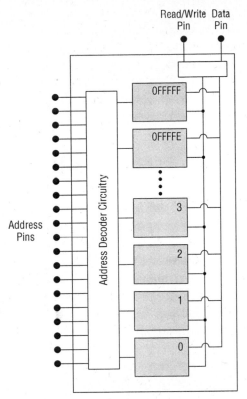

Figure 3-2: A RAM chip

That's all done internally to the chip. As far as you, on the outside, are concerned, once you've applied the address to the address pins, *voila!* The data pin will contain a voltage representing the value of the bit you requested. If that bit contained a binary 1, the data pin will contain a 5-volt signal; otherwise, the binary 0 bit will be represented by 0 volts.

Memory Access Time

Chips are graded by how long it takes for the data to appear on the data pin after you've applied the address to the address pins. Obviously, the faster the better, but some chips (for electrical reasons that again are difficult to explain) are faster than others.

The time values are so small as to seem almost insignificant: 30 nanoseconds is a typical memory chip access time. A nanosecond is a *billionth* of a second, so 30 nanoseconds is significantly less than one 10-millionth of a second. Great stuff—but to accomplish anything useful, a computer needs to access memory hundreds of thousands, millions, or (in most cases) *billions of times*. Those nanoseconds add up. If you become an expert assembly language programmer, you will jump through hoops to shave the number of memory accesses your program needs to perform, because memory access is the ultimate limiting factor in a computer's performance. Assembly language expert Michael Abrash, in fact, has published several books on doing exactly that, mostly in the realm of high-speed graphics programming. The gist of his advice can be (badly) summarized in just a few words: *Stay out of memory whenever you can!* (You'll soon discover just how difficult this is.)

Bytes, Words, Double Words, and Quad Words

The days are long gone (decades gone, in fact) when a serious computer could be made with only one memory chip. My poor 1976 COSMAC ELF needed at least two. Today's computers need many, irrespective of the fact that today's memory chips can hold a billion bits or more, rather than the ELF's meager 2,048 bits. Understanding how a computer gathers its memory chips together into a coherent memory *system* is critical when you wish to write efficient assembly language programs. Although there are infinite ways to hook memory chips together, the system I describe here is that of the Intel-based PC-compatible computer, which has ruled the world of desktop computing since 1982.

Our memory system must store our information. How we organize a memory system out of a hatful of memory chips will be dictated largely by how we organize our information.

The answer begins with this thing called a *byte*. The fact that the granddaddy of all computer magazines took this word for its title indicates its importance in the computer scheme of things. (Alas, *Byte* magazine ceased publishing late in 1998.) From a *functional* perspective, memory is measured in bytes. A byte is eight bits. Two bytes side by side are called a *word*, and two words side by side are called a *double word*. A *quad word*, as you might imagine, consists of two double words, for four words or eight bytes in all. Going in the other direction, some people refer to a group of four bits as a nybble—a *nybble* being somewhat smaller than a byte. (This term is now rare and becoming rarer.)

Here's the quick tour:

- A bit is a single binary digit, 0 or 1.
- A byte is 8 bits side by side.
- A word is 2 bytes side by side.
- A double word is 2 words side by side.
- A quad word is 2 double words side by side.

Computers were designed to store and manipulate human information. The basic elements of human discourse are built from a set of symbols consisting of letters of the alphabet (two of each, for uppercase and lowercase), numbers, and symbols, including commas, colons, periods, and exclamation marks. Add to these the various international variations on letters such as ä and ò plus the more arcane mathematical symbols, and you'll find that human information requires a symbol set of well over 200 symbols. (The symbol set used in all PC-style computers is provided in Appendix B.)

Bytes are central to the scheme because one symbol out of that symbol set can be neatly expressed in one byte. A byte is 8 bits, and 2^8 is 256. This means that a binary number 8 bits in size can be one of 256 different values, numbered from 0 to 255. Because we use these symbols so much, most of what we do in computer programs is done in byte-size chunks. In fact, except for the very odd and specialized kind of computers we are now building into intelligent food processors, *no* computer processes information in chunks smaller than 1 byte. Most computers today, in fact, process information one double word (four bytes, or 32 bits) at a time. Since 2003, PC-compatible computers have been available that process information one quad word (64 bits) at a time.

Pretty Chips All in a Row

One of the more perplexing things for beginners to understand is that a single RAM chip does not even contain *1* byte, though it might contain half a *billion* bits. The bulk of the individual RAM chips that we use today have no more than four data pins, and some only *one* data pin. Whole memory systems are created by combining individual memory chips in clever ways.

A simple example will help illustrate this. Consider Figure 3-3. I've drawn a memory system that distributes a single stored byte across eight separate RAM chips. Each of the black rectangles represents a RAM chip like the one shown in Figure 3-2. There is one bit from the byte stored within each of the eight chips, at the same address across all eight chips. The 20 address pins for all eight chips are connected together, "in parallel" as an electrician might say. When the computer applies a memory address to the 20 address lines, the address appears simultaneously on the address pins of all eight memory chips in the memory system. This way, a single address is applied simultaneously to the address pins of all eight chips, which deliver all eight bits simultaneously on the eight data lines, with one bit from each chip.

In the real world, such simple memory systems no longer exist, and there are many different ways of distributing chips (and their stored bits) across a memory system. Most memory chips today do in fact store more than one bit at each address. Chips storing 1, 2, 3, 4, or 8 bits per address are relatively common. How to design a fast and efficient computer memory system is an entire subdiscipline within electrical engineering, and as our memory chips are improved to contain more and more memory cells, the "best" way to design a physical memory system changes.

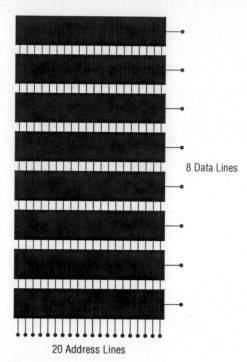

8 Data Lines

20 Address Lines

Figure 3-3: A 1-megabyte memory system

It's been a long time, after all, since we've had to plug individual memory chips into our computers. Today, memory chips are nearly always gathered together into plug-in Dual Inline Memory Modules (DIMMs) of various capacities. These modules are little green-colored circuit boards about 5 inches long and 1 inch high. In 2009, all desktop PC-compatible computers use such modules, generally in pairs. Each module typically stores 32 bits at each memory address (often, but not always, in eight individual memory chips, each chip storing four bits at each memory address) and a pair of modules acting together stores 64 bits at each memory address. The number of memory locations within each module varies, but the capacity is commonly 512 megabytes (MB), or 1 or 2 gigabytes (GB). (I will use the abbreviations MB and GB from now on.)

It's important to note that the way memory chips are combined into a memory system does *not* affect the way your programs operate. When a program that you've written accesses a byte of memory at a particular address, the computer takes care of fetching it from the appropriate place in that jungle of chips and circuit boards. One memory system arranged a certain way might bring the data back from memory *faster* than another memory system arranged a different way, but the addresses are the same, and the data is the same. From the point of view of your program, there is no functional difference.

To summarize: electrically, your computer's memory consists of one or more rows of memory chips, with each chip containing a *large* number of memory cells made out of transistors and other minuscule electrical components. Most of the time, to avoid confusion it's just as useful to forget about the transistors and even the rows of physical chips. (My high school computer science teacher was not *entirely* wrong but he was right for the wrong reasons.)

Over the years, memory systems have been accessed in different ways. Eight-bit computers (now ancient and almost extinct) accessed memory 8 bits (one byte) at a time. Sixteen-bit computers access memory 16 bits (one word) at a time. Today's mainstream 32-bit computers access memory 32 bits (one double word) at a time. Upscale computers based on newer 64-bit processors access memory 64 bits (one quad word) at a time. This can be confusing, so it's better in most cases to envision a very long row of byte-size containers, each with its own unique address. Don't assume that in computers which process information one word at a time that only *words* have addresses. It's a convention within the PC architecture that *every* byte has its own unique numeric address, irrespective of how many bytes are pulled from memory in one operation.

Every byte of memory in the computer has its own unique address, even in computers that process 2, 4, or 8 bytes of information at a time.

If this seems counterintuitive, yet another metaphor will help: when you go to the library to take out the three volumes of Tolkien's massive fantasy *The Lord of the Rings*, each of the three volumes has its own catalog number (essentially that volume's address in the library) but you take all three down at once and process them as a single entity. If you really want to, you can check only one of the books out of the library at a time, but doing so will require two more trips to the library later to get the other two volumes, which is a waste of your time and effort.

So it is with 32-bit or 64-bit computers. Every byte has its own address, but when a 32-bit computer accesses a byte, it actually reads 4 bytes starting at the address of the requested byte. You can use the remaining 3 bytes or ignore them if you don't need them—but if you later decide that you do need the other three bytes, you'll have to access memory again to get them. Best to save time and get it all at one swoop.

The Shop Foreman and the Assembly Line

All of this talk about reading things from memory and writing things to memory has thus far carefully skirted the question of *who* is doing the reading and writing. The who is almost always a single chip, and a remarkable chip it is, too: the *central processing unit*, or *CPU.* If you are the president and CEO of your personal computer, the CPU is your shop foreman, who sees that your orders are carried out down among the chips, where the work gets done.

Some would say that the CPU is what actually does the work, but while largely true, it's an oversimplification. Plenty of real work is done in the memory system, and in what are called *peripherals*, such as video display boards, USB and network ports, and so on. So, while the CPU does do a good deal of the work, it also parcels out quite a bit to other components within the computer, largely to enable itself to do a lot more quickly what it does best. Like any good manager, the foreman delegates to other computer subsystems whatever it can.

Most of the CPU chips used in the machines we lump together as a group and call PCs were designed by a company called Intel, which pretty much invented the single-chip CPU way back in the early 1970s. Intel CPUs have evolved briskly since then, as I'll describe a little later in this chapter. There have been many changes in the details over the years, but from a height, what any Intel or Intel-compatible CPU does is largely the same.

Talking to Memory

The CPU chip's most important job is to communicate with the computer's memory system. Like a memory chip, a CPU chip is a small square of silicon onto which a great many transistors—today, hundreds of *millions* of them!—have been placed. The fragile silicon chip is encased in a plastic or ceramic housing with a large number of electrical connection pins protruding from it. Like the pins of memory chips, the CPU's pins transfer information encoded as voltage levels, typically 3 to 5 volts. Five volts on a pin indicate a binary 1, and 0 volts on a pin indicate a binary 0.

Like memory chips, the CPU chip has a number of pins devoted to memory addresses, and these pins are connected to the computer's system of memory chips. I've drawn this in Figure 3-4, and the memory system to the left of the CPU chip is the same one that appears in Figure 3-3, just tipped on its side. When the CPU needs to read a byte (or a word, double word, or quad word) from memory, it places the memory address of the byte to be read on its address pins, encoded as a binary number. Some few nanoseconds later, the requested byte appears (also as a binary number) on the data pins of the memory chips. The CPU chip also has data pins, and it slurps up the byte presented by the memory chips through its own data pins.

The process, of course, also works in reverse: to write a byte into memory, the CPU first places the memory address where it wants to write onto its address pins. Some number of nanoseconds later (which varies from system to system depending on general system speed and how memory is arranged) the CPU places the byte it wants to write into memory on its data pins. The memory system obediently stores the byte inside itself at the requested address.

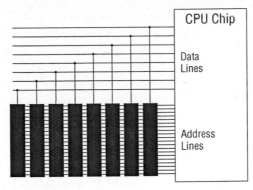

Figure 3-4: The CPU and memory

Figure 3-4 is, of course, purely conceptual. Modern memory systems are a great deal more complex than what is shown, but in essence they all work the same way: the CPU passes an address to the memory system, and the memory system either accepts data from the CPU for storage at that address or places the data found at that address on the computer's data bus for the CPU to process.

Riding the Data Bus

This give-and-take between the CPU and the memory system represents the bulk of what happens inside your computer. Information flows from memory into the CPU and back again. Information flows in other paths as well. Your computer contains additional devices called *peripherals* that are either sources or destinations (or both) for information.

Video display boards, disk drives, USB ports, and network ports are the most common peripherals in PC-type computers. Like the CPU and memory, they are all ultimately electrical devices. Most modern peripherals consist of one or two large chips and perhaps a couple of smaller chips that support the larger chips. Like both the CPU chip and memory chips, these peripheral devices have both address pins and data pins. Some peripherals, graphics boards in particular, have their own memory chips, and these days their own dedicated CPUs. (Your modern high-performance graphics board is a high-powered computer in its own right, albeit one with a very specific and limited mission.)

Peripherals "talk" to the CPU (that is, they pass the CPU data or take data from the CPU) and sometimes to one another. These conversations take place across the electrical connections linking the address pins and data pins that all devices in the computer have in common. These electrical lines are called a *data bus* and they form a sort of party line linking the CPU with all other parts of the computer. An elaborate system of electrical arbitration determines when and in what order the different devices can use this party line to talk with one another, but it happens in generally the same way: an address is placed on the bus, followed by some data. (How much data moves at once depends on the peripherals involved.) Special signals go out on the bus with the address to indicate whether the address represents a location in memory or one of the peripherals attached to the data bus. The address of a peripheral is called an *I/O address* to differentiate between it and a *memory address* such as those we've been discussing all along.

The data bus is the major element in the *expansion slots* present in most PC-type computers, and many peripherals (especially graphics adapters) are printed circuit boards that plug into these slots. The peripherals talk to the CPU and to memory through the data bus connections implemented as electrical pins in the expansion slots.

As convenient as expansion slots are, they introduce delays into a computer system. Increasingly, as time passes, peripherals are simply a couple of chips on one corner of the main circuit board (the *motherboard*) inside the computer.

The Foreman's Pockets

Every CPU contains a very few data storage cubbyholes called *registers*. These registers are at once the foreman's pockets and the foreman's workbench. When the CPU needs a place to tuck something away for a short while, an empty register is just the place. The CPU could always store the data out in memory, but that takes considerably more time than tucking the data in a register. Because the registers are actually inside the CPU, placing data in a register or reading it back again from a register is *fast*.

More important, registers are the foreman's workbench. When the CPU needs to add two numbers, the easiest and fastest way is to place the numbers in two registers and add the two registers together. The sum (in usual CPU practice) replaces one of the two original numbers that were added, but after that the sum could then be placed in yet another register, or added to still another number in another register, or stored out in memory, or take part in any of a multitude of other operations.

> *The CPU's immediate work-in-progress is held in temporary storage containers called* registers.

Work involving registers is always fast, because the registers are within the CPU and are specially connected to one another and to the CPU's internal machinery. Very little movement of data is necessary—and what data does move doesn't have to move very far.

Like memory cells and, indeed, like the entire CPU, registers are made out of transistors; but rather than having numeric addresses, registers have individual names such as EAX or EDI. To make matters even more complicated, while all CPU registers have certain common properties, some registers have unique special powers not shared by other registers. Understanding the behaviors and the limitations of CPU registers is something like following the Middle East peace process: There are partnerships, alliances, and always a bewildering array of secret agendas that each register follows. There's no general system describing such things; like irregular verbs in Spanish, you simply have to memorize them.

Most peripherals also have registers, and peripheral registers are even more limited in scope than CPU registers. Their agendas are quite explicit and in no wise secret. This does not prevent them from being confusing, as anyone who has tried programming a graphics board at the register level will attest. Fortunately, these days nearly all communication with peripheral devices is handled by the operating system, as I'll explain in the next chapter.

The Assembly Line

If the CPU is the shop foreman, then the peripherals are the assembly-line workers, and the data bus is the assembly line itself. (Unlike most assembly lines, however, the foreman works the line much harder than the rest of his crew!)

As an example: information enters the computer through a network port peripheral, which assembles bits received from a computer network cable into bytes of data representing characters and numbers. The network port then places the assembled byte onto the data bus, from which the CPU picks it up, tallies it or processes it in other ways, and then places it back on the data bus. The display board then retrieves the byte from the data bus and writes it into video memory so that you can see it on your screen.

This is a severely simplified description, but obviously a lot is going on inside the box. Continuous furious communication along the data bus between CPU, memory, and peripherals is what accomplishes the work that the computer does. The question then arises: who tells the foreman and crew what to do? *You* do. How do you do that? You write a program. Where is the program? It's in memory, along with all the rest of the data stored in memory. In fact, the program *is* data, and that is the heart of the whole idea of programming as we know it.

The Box That Follows a Plan

Finally, we come to the essence of computing: the nature of programs and how they direct the CPU to control the computer and get your work done.

We've seen how memory can be used to store bytes of information. These bytes are all binary codes, patterns of 1 and 0 bits stored as minute electrical voltage levels and collectively making up binary numbers. We've also spoken of symbols, and how certain binary codes may be interpreted as meaning something to us human beings, things such as letters, digits, punctuation, and so on.

Just as the alphabet and the numeric digits represent a set of codes and symbols that mean something to us humans, there is a set of codes that mean something to the CPU. These codes are called *machine instructions*, and their name is evocative of what they actually are: instructions to the CPU. When the CPU is executing a program, it picks a sequence of numbers off the data bus, one at a time. Each number tells the CPU to do something. The CPU knows how. When it completes executing one instruction, it picks the next one up and executes that. It continues doing so until something (a command in the program, or electrical signals such as a reset button) tells it to stop.

Let's take an example or two that are common to all modern IA-32 CPU chips from Intel. The 8-bit binary code 01000000 (40H) means something to the CPU. It is an order: *Add 1 to register AX and put the sum back in AX.* That's about as simple as they get. Most machine instructions occupy more than a single byte. Many are 2 bytes in length, and very many more are 4 bytes in length. The binary codes 11010110 01110011 (0B6H 073H) comprise another order: *Load the value 73H into register DH.* On the other end of the spectrum, the binary codes 11110011 10100100 (0F3H 0A4H) direct the CPU to do the following (take a deep breath): *Begin moving the number of bytes specified in register CX from the 32-bit address stored in registers DS and SI to the 32-bit address stored in registers ES and DI, updating the address in both SI and DI after moving each byte, and decreasing CX by one each time, and finally stopping when CX becomes zero.*

You don't have to remember all the details of those particular instructions right now; I'll come back to machine instructions in later chapters. The rest of the several hundred instructions understood by the Intel IA-32 CPUs fall somewhere in between these extremes in terms of complication and power. There are instructions that perform arithmetic operations (addition, subtraction, multiplication, and division) and logical operations (AND, OR, XOR, and so on), and instructions that move information around memory. Some instructions serve to "steer" the path that program execution takes within the logic of the program being executed. Some instructions have highly arcane functions and don't turn up very often outside of operating system internals. The important thing to remember right now is that *each instruction tells the CPU to perform one generally small and limited task.* Many instructions handed to the CPU in sequence direct the CPU to perform far more complicated tasks. Writing that sequence of instructions is what assembly language programming actually is.

Let's talk more about that.

Fetch and Execute

A computer program is nothing more than a table of these machine instructions stored in memory. There's nothing special about the table, nor about where it is positioned in memory. It could be almost anywhere, and the bytes in the table are nothing more than binary numbers.

The binary numbers comprising a computer program are special only in the way that the CPU treats them. When a modern 32-bit CPU begins running, it *fetches* a double word from an agreed-upon address in memory. (How this starting address is agreed upon doesn't matter right now.) This double word, consisting of 4 bytes in a row, is read from memory and loaded into the CPU. The CPU examines the pattern of binary bits contained in the double word, and then begins performing the task that the fetched machine instruction directs it to do.

Ancient 8088-based 8-bit machines such as the original IBM PC only fetched one byte at a time, rather than the four bytes that 32-bit Pentium-class machines fetch. Because most machine instructions are more than a single byte in size, the 8088 CPU had to return to memory to fetch a second (or a third or a fourth) byte to complete the machine instruction before it could actually begin to obey the instruction and begin performing the task it represented.

As soon as it finishes executing an instruction, the CPU goes out to memory and fetches the next machine instruction in sequence. Inside the CPU is a special register called the *instruction pointer* that quite literally contains the address of the next instruction to be fetched from memory and executed. Each time an instruction is completed, the instruction pointer is updated to point to the next instruction in memory. (There is some silicon magic afoot inside modern CPUs that "guesses" what's to be fetched next and keeps it on a side shelf so it will be there when fetched, only much more quickly—but the process as I've described it is true in terms of the outcome.)

All of this is done literally like clockwork. The computer has an electrical subsystem called a *system clock*, which is actually an oscillator that emits square-wave pulses at very precisely intervals. The immense number of microscopic transistor switches inside the CPU coordinate their actions according to the pulses generated by the system clock. In years past, it often took several clock cycles (basically, pulses from the clock) to execute a single instruction. As computers became faster, the majority of machine instructions executed in a single clock cycle. Modern CPUs can execute instructions in parallel, so multiple instructions can often execute in a single clock cycle.

So the process goes: fetch and execute; fetch and execute. The CPU works its way through memory, with the instruction pointer register leading the way. As it goes, it works: moving data around in memory, moving values around in registers, passing data to peripherals, crunching data in arithmetic or logical operations.

Computer programs are lists of binary machine instructions stored in memory. They are no different from any other list of data bytes stored in memory except in how they are interpreted when fetched by the CPU.

The Foreman's Innards

I made the point earlier that machine instructions are *binary* codes. This is something we often gloss over, yet to understand the true nature of the CPU, we have to step away from the persistent image of machine instructions as *numbers*. They are *not* numbers. They are binary *patterns* designed to throw electrical switches.

Inside the CPU are a *very* large number of transistors. (The Intel Core 2 Quad that I have on my desk contains 582 million transistors, and CPU chips with over a billion transistors are now in limited use.) Some small number of those transistors go into making up the foreman's pockets: machine registers for holding information. A significant number of transistors go into making up short-term storage called *cache* that I'll describe later. (For now, think of cache as a small set of storage shelves always right there at the foreman's elbow, making it unnecessary for the foreman to cross the room to get more materials.) The vast majority of those transistors, however, are switches connected to other switches, which are connected to still more switches in a mind-numbingly complex network.

The extremely simple machine instruction 01000000 (40H) directs the CPU to add 1 to the value stored in register AX, with the sum placed back in AX. When considering the true nature of computers, it's very instructive to think about the execution of machine instruction 01000000 in this way.

The CPU fetches a byte from memory. This byte contains the binary code 01000000. Once the byte is fully within the CPU, the CPU in essence lets the machine instruction byte push eight transistor switches. The lone 1 digit pushes its switch "up" electrically; the rest of the digits, all 0s, push their switches "down."

In a chain reaction, those eight switches flip the states of first dozens, then hundreds, then thousands, and in some cases tens of thousands of tiny transistor switches within the CPU. It isn't random—this furious nanomoment of electrical activity within the CPU operates utterly according to patterns etched into the silicon of the CPU by Intel's teams of engineers. Ultimately—perhaps after many thousands of individual switch throws—the value contained in register AX is suddenly one greater than it was before.

How this happens is difficult to explain, but you must remember that *any* number within the CPU can also be looked upon as a binary code, including values stored in registers. Also, most switches within the CPU contain more than one handle. These switches, called *gates*, work according to the rules of logic. Perhaps two, or three, or even more "up" switch throws have to arrive at a particular gate at the same time in order for one "down" switch throw to pass through that gate.

These gates are used to build complex internal machinery within the CPU. Collections of gates can add two numbers in a device called an *adder*, which again is nothing more than a crew of dozens of little switches working together first as gates and then as gates working together to form an adder.

As part of the cavalcade of switch throws kicked off by the binary code 01000000, the value in register AX was dumped trapdoor-style into an adder, while at the same time the number 1 was fed into the other end of the adder. Finally, rising on a wave of switch throws, the new sum emerges from the adder and ascends back into register AX—and the job is done.

The foreman of your computer, then, is made of switches—just like all the other parts of the computer. It contains a mind-boggling number of such switches, interconnected in even more mind-boggling ways. The important thing is that whether you are boggled or (like me on off-days) merely jaded by it all, the CPU, and ultimately the computer, *does exactly what we tell it to do.* We set up a list of machine instructions as a table in memory, and then, by golly, that mute silicon brick comes alive and starts earning its keep.

Changing Course

The first piece of genuine magic in the nature of computers is that a string of binary codes in memory tells the computer what to do, step by step. The second piece of that magic is really the jewel in the crown: *There are machine instructions that change the order in which machine instructions are fetched and executed.*

In other words, once the CPU has executed a machine instruction that does something useful, the next machine instruction may tell the CPU to go back and play it again—and again, and again, as many times as necessary. The CPU can keep count of the number of times that it has executed that particular instruction or list of instructions and keep repeating them until a prearranged count has been met. Alternately, it can arrange to skip certain sequences of machine instructions entirely if they don't need to be executed at all.

What this means is that the list of machine instructions in memory does not necessarily begin at the top and run without deviation to the bottom. The CPU can execute the first fifty or a hundred or a thousand instructions, then jump to the end of the program—or jump back to the start and begin again. It can skip and bounce up and down the list smoothly and at great speed. It can execute a few instructions up here, then zip down somewhere else and execute a few more instructions, then zip back and pick up where it left off, all without missing a beat or even wasting too much time.

How is this done? Recall that the CPU includes a special register that always contains the address of the next instruction to be executed. This register, the *instruction pointer*, is not essentially different from any of the other registers in the CPU. Just as a machine instruction can add one to register AX, another machine instruction can add/subtract some number to/from the address stored in the instruction pointer. Add 100 to the instruction pointer, and the CPU will *instantly* skip 100 bytes down the list of machine instructions before it continues. Subtract 100 from the address stored in the instruction pointer, and the CPU will *instantly* jump *back* 100 bytes up the machine instruction list.

Finally, the Third Whammy: *The CPU can change its course of execution based on the work it has been doing.* The CPU can decide whether to execute a given instruction or group of instructions, based on values stored in memory, or based on the individual state of several special one-bit CPU registers called *flags*. The CPU can count how many times it needs to do something, and then do that something that number of times. Or it can do something, and then do it again, and again, and again, checking each time (by looking at some data somewhere) to determine whether it's done yet, or whether it has to take another run through the task.

So, not only can you tell the CPU what to do, you can tell it where to go. Better, you can sometimes let the CPU, like a faithful bloodhound, sniff out the best course forward in the interest of getting the work done in the quickest possible way.

In Chapter 1, I described a computer program as a sequence of steps and tests. Most of the machine instructions understood by the CPU are steps, but others are tests. The tests are always two-way tests, and in fact the choice of what to do is always the same: jump or don't jump. *That's all.* You can test for any of numerous different conditions within the CPU, but the choice is *always* either jump to another place in the program or just keep truckin' along.

What vs. How: Architecture and Microarchitecture

This book is really about programming in assembly language for Intel's 32-bit x86 CPUs, and those 32-bit CPUs made by other companies to be compatible with Intel's. There are a *lot* of different Intel and Intel-compatible x86 CPU chips. A full list would include the 8086, 8088, 80286, 80386, 80486, the Pentium, Pentium Pro, Pentium MMX, Pentium II, Pentium D, Pentium III, Pentium 4, Pentium Xeon, Pentium II Xeon, Pentium Core, Celeron, and literally dozens of others, many of them special-purpose, obscure, and short-lived. (Quick, have you ever heard of the 80376?) Furthermore, those are only the CPU chips designed and sold by Intel. Other companies (primarily AMD) have designed their own Intel-compatible CPU chips, which adds dozens more to the full list; and within a single CPU type are often another three or four variants, with exotic names such as Coppermine, Katmai, Conroe, and so on. Still worse, there can be a Pentium III Coppermine and a Celeron Coppermine.

How does anybody keep track of all this?

Quick answer: Nobody really does. Why? For nearly all purposes, the great mass of details doesn't matter. The soul of a CPU is pretty cleanly divided into two parts: *what the CPU does* and *how the CPU does it*. We, as programmers, see it from the outside: what the CPU does. Electrical engineers and systems designers who create computer motherboards and other hardware systems incorporating Intel processors need to know some of the rest, but they are a small and hardy crew, and they know who they are.

Evolving Architectures

Our programmer's view from the outside includes the CPU registers, the set of machine instructions that the CPU understands, and special-purpose subsystems such as fast math processors, which may include instructions and registers of their own. All of these things are defined at length by Intel, and published online and in largish books so that programmers can study and understand them. Taken together, these definitions are called the CPU's *architecture*.

A CPU architecture evolves over time, as vendors add new instructions, registers, and other features to the product line. Ideally, this is done with an eye toward *backward compatibility*, which means that the new features do not generally replace, disable, or change the outward effects of older features. Intel has been very good about backward compatibility within its primary product line, which began in 1978 with the 8086 CPU and now goes by the catchall term "x86." Within certain limitations, even programs written for the ancient 8086 will run on a modern Pentium Core 2 Quad CPU. (Incompatibilities that arise are more often related to different operating systems than the details of the CPU itself.)

The reverse, of course, is not true. New machine instructions creep slowly into Intel's x86 product line over the years. A new machine instruction first introduced in 1996 will not be recognized by a CPU designed, say, in 1993; but a machine instruction first introduced in 1993 will almost always be present and operate identically in newer CPUs.

In addition to periodic additions to the instruction set, architectures occasionally make quantum leaps. Such quantum leaps typically involve a change in the "width" of the CPU. In 1986, Intel's 16-bit architecture expanded to 32 bits with the introduction of the 80386 CPU, which added numerous instructions and operational modes, and doubled the width of the CPU registers. In 2003, the x86 architecture expanded again, this time to 64 bits, again with new instructions, modes of operation, and expanded registers. However, CPUs that adhere to the expanded 64-bit architecture will still run software written for the older 32-bit architecture.

Intel's 32-bit architecture is called IA-32, and in this book that's what I'll be describing. The newer 64-bit architecture is called x86-64 for peculiar reasons, chief of which is that *Intel did not originate it*. Intel's major competitor, AMD, created a backward-compatible 64-bit x86 architecture in the early 2000s, and it was so well done that Intel had to swallow its pride and adopt it. (Intel's own 64-bit architecture, called IA-64 Itanium, was not backward compatible with IA-32 and was roundly rejected by the market.)

With only minor glitches, the newer 64-bit Intel architecture *includes* the IA-32 architecture, which in turn includes the still older 16-bit x86 architecture. It's useful to know which CPUs have added what instructions to the architecture, keeping in mind that when you use a "new" instruction, your code will not run on CPU chips made before that new instruction appeared. This is a solvable problem, however. There are ways for a program to ask a CPU how new it is, and limit itself to features present in that CPU. In the meantime, there are other things that it is *not* useful to know.

The Secret Machinery in the Basement

Because of the backward compatibility issue, CPU designers do not add new instructions or registers to an architecture without *very* good reason. There are other, better ways to improve a family of CPUs. The most important of these is increased processor throughput, which is *not* a mere increase in CPU clocking rates. The other is reduced power consumption. This is not even mostly a "green" issue. A certain amount of the power used by a CPU is wasted as heat; and waste heat, if not minimized, can cook a CPU chip and damage surrounding components. Designers are thus always looking for ways to reduce the power required to perform the same tasks.

Increasing processor throughput means increasing the number of instructions that the CPU executes over time. A lot of arcane tricks are associated with increasing throughput, with names like prefetching, L1 and L2 cache, branch prediction, hyper-pipelining, macro-ops fusion, along with plenty of others. Some of these techniques were created to reduce or eliminate bottlenecks within the CPU so that the CPU and the memory system can remain busy nearly all the time. Other techniques stretch the ability of the CPU to process multiple instructions at once.

Taken together, all of the electrical mechanisms by which the CPU does what its instructions tell it to do are called the CPU's *microarchitecture*. It's the machinery in the basement that you can't see. The metaphor of the shop foreman breaks down a little here. Let me offer you another one.

Suppose that you own a company that manufactures automatic transmission parts for Ford. You have two separate plants. One is 40 years old, and one has just been built. Both plants make *precisely* the same parts—they have to, because Ford puts them into its transmissions without knowing or caring which of your two plants manufactured them. A cam or a housing are thus identical within a ten-thousandth of an inch, whether they were made in your old plant or your new plant.

Your old plant has been around for a while, but your new plant was designed and built based on everything you've learned while operating the old plant for 40 years. It has a more logical layout, better lighting, and modern automated tooling that requires fewer people to operate and works longer without adjustment.

The upshot is that your new plant can manufacture those cams and housings much more quickly and efficiently, wasting less power and raw materials, and requiring fewer people to do it. The day will come when you'll build an even more efficient third plant based on what you've learned running the second plant, and you'll shut the first plant down.

Nonetheless, the cams and housings are the same, no matter where they were made. Precisely *how* they were made is no concern of Ford's or anyone else's. As long as the cams are built to the same measurements at the same tolerance, the "how" doesn't matter.

All of the tooling, the assembly line layouts, and the general structure of each plant may be considered that plant's microarchitecture. Each time you build a new plant, the new plant's microarchitecture is more efficient at doing what the older plants have been doing all along.

So it is with CPUs. Intel and AMD are constantly redesigning their CPU microarchitectures to make them more efficient. Driving these efforts are improved silicon fabrication techniques that enable more and more transistors to be placed on a single CPU die. More transistors mean more switches and more potential solutions to the same old problems of throughput and power efficiency.

The prime directive in improving microarchitectures, of course, is not to "break" existing programs by changing the way machine instructions or registers operate. That's why it's the secret machinery in the basement. CPU designers go to great lengths to maintain that line between what the CPU does and how those tasks are actually accomplished in the forest of those half-billion transistors.

All the exotic code names like Conroe, Katmai, or Yonah actually indicate tweaks in the microarchitecture. Major changes in the microarchitecture also have names: P6, NetBurst, Core, and so on. These are described in great detail online, but don't feel bad if you don't quite follow it all. Most of the time I'm hanging on by my fingernails too.

I say all this so that you, as a newly minted programmer, don't make more of Intel microarchitecture differences than you should. It is *extremely* rare (like, almost never) for a difference in microarchitecture detail to give you an exploitable advantage in how you code your programs. Microarchitecture is not a mystery (much about it is available online), but for the sake of your sanity you should probably treat it as one for the time being. We have many more important things to learn right now.

Enter the Plant Manager

What I've described so far is less "a computer" than "computation." A CPU executing a program does not a computer make. The COSMAC ELF device that I built in 1976 was an experiment, and at best a sort of educational toy.

It was a CPU with some memory, and just enough electrical support (through switches and LED digits) that I could enter machine code and see what was happening inside the memory chips. It was in no sense of the word *useful*.

My first useful computer came along a couple of years later. It had a keyboard, a CRT display (though not one capable of graphics) a pair of 8-inch floppy disk drives, and a printer. It was definitely useful, and I wrote numerous magazine articles and my first three books with it. I had a number of simple application programs for it, like the primordial WordStar word processor; but what made it useful was something else: an operating system.

Operating Systems: The Corner Office

An *operating system* is a program that manages the operation of a computer system. It's like any other program in that it consists of a sequence of machine instructions executed by the CPU. Operating systems are different in that they have special powers not generally given to word processors and spreadsheet programs. If we continue the metaphor of the CPU as the shop foreman, then the operating system is the plant manager. The entire physical plant is under its control. It oversees the bringing in of raw materials to the plant. It supervises the work that goes on inside the plant (including the work done by the shop foreman) and packages up the finished products for shipment to customers.

In truth, our early microcomputer operating systems weren't very powerful and didn't do much. They "spun the disks" and handled the storage of data to the disk drives, and brought data back from disks when requested. They picked up keystrokes from the keyboard, and sent characters to the video display. With some fiddling, they could send characters to a printer. That was about it.

The CP/M operating system was "state of the art" for desktop microcomputers in 1979. If you entered the name of a program at the keyboard, CP/M would go out to disk, load the program from a disk file into memory, and then literally hand over all power over the machine to the loaded program. When WordStar ran, it overwrote the operating system in memory, because memory was extremely expensive and there wasn't very much of it. Quite literally, only one program could run at a time. CP/M didn't come back until WordStar exited. Then CP/M would be reloaded from the floppy disk, and would simply wait for another command from the keyboard.

BIOS: Software, Just Not as Soft

So what brought CP/M back into memory, if it wasn't there when WordStar exited? Easy: *WordStar rebooted the computer*. In fact, every time a piece of software ran, CP/M went away. Every time that software exited, it rebooted the machine, and CP/M came back. There was so little to CP/M that rebooting it from a floppy disk took less than two seconds.

As our computer systems grew faster, and memory cheaper, our operating systems improved right along with our word processors and spreadsheets. When the IBM PC appeared, PC DOS quickly replaced CP/M. The PC had enough memory that DOS didn't go away when a program loaded, but rather remained in its place in memory while application software loaded above it. DOS could do a lot more than CP/M, and wasn't a great deal larger. This was possible because DOS had help.

IBM had taken the program code that handled the keyboard, the display, and the disk drives and burned it into a special kind of memory chip called *read-only memory (ROM)*. Ordinary random-access memory goes blank when power to it is turned off. ROM retains its data whether it has power or not. Thus, thousands of machine instructions did not have to be loaded from disk, because they were always there in a ROM chip soldered to the motherboard. The software on the ROM was called the Basic Input/Output System (BIOS) because it handled computer inputs (such as the keyboard) and computer outputs (such as the display and printer.)

Somewhere along the way, software like the BIOS, which existed on "non-volatile" ROM chips, was nicknamed *firmware*, because although it was still software, it was not quite as, well, *soft* as software stored in memory or on disk. All modern computers have a firmware BIOS, though the BIOS software does different things now than it did in 1981.

Multitasking Magic

DOS had a long reign. The first versions of Windows were not really whole new operating systems, but simply file managers and program launchers drawn on the screen in graphics mode. Down in the basement under the icons, DOS was still there, doing what it had always done.

It wasn't until 1995 that things changed radically. In that year, Microsoft released Windows 95, which had a brand-new graphical user interface, but something far more radical down in the basement. Windows 95 operated in 32-bit protected mode, and required at least an 80386 CPU to run. (I'll explain in detail what "protected mode" means in the next chapter.) For the moment, think of protected mode as allowing the operating system to definitely be The Boss, and no longer merely a peer of word processors and spreadsheets. Windows 95 did not make full use of protected mode, because it still had DOS and DOS applications to deal with, and such "legacy" software was written long before protected mode was an option. Windows 95 did, however, have something not seen previously in the PC world: *preemptive multitasking*.

Memory had gotten cheap enough by 1995 that it was possible to have not just one or two but several programs in memory at the same time. In an elaborate partnership with the CPU, Windows 95 created the convincing illusion that all of the programs in memory were running at once. This was done by giving each program loaded into memory a short *slice* of the CPU's time. A program would begin running on the CPU, and some number of its machine instructions would execute.

However, after a set period of time (usually a small fraction of a second) Windows 95 would "preempt" that first program, and give control of the CPU to the second program on the list. That program would execute instructions for a few milliseconds until it too was preempted. Windows 95 would go down the list, letting each program run for a little while. When it reached the bottom of the list, it would start again at the top and continue running through the list, round-robin fashion, letting each program run for a little while. The CPU was fast enough that the user sitting in front of the display would think that all the programs were running simultaneously.

Figure 3-5 may make this clearer. Imagine a rotary switch, in which a rotor turns continuously and touches each of several contacts in sequence, once per revolution. Each time it touches the contact for one of the programs, that program is allowed to run. When the rotor moves to the next contact, the previous program stops in its tracks, and the next program gets a little time to run.

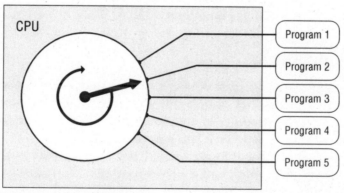

Figure 3-5: The idea of multitasking

The operating system can define a priority for each program on the list, so that some get more time to run than others. High-priority tasks get more clock cycles to execute, whereas low-priority tasks get fewer.

Promotion to Kernel

Much was made of Windows 95's ability to multitask, but in 1995 few people had heard of a Unix-like operating system called Linux, which a young Finn named Linus Torvalds had written almost as a lark, and released in 1991.

Linux did not have the elaborate graphical user interface that Windows 95 did, but it could handle multitasking, and had a much more powerful structure internally. The core of Linux was a block of code called the *kernel*, which took full advantage of IA-32 protected mode. The Linux kernel was entirely separate from the user interface, and it was protected from damage due to malfunctioning programs elsewhere in the system. System memory was tagged as either *kernel space* or *user space*, and nothing running in user space could write to (nor generally read from) anything stored in kernel space. Communication between kernel space and user space was handled through strictly controlled system calls (more on this later in the book).

Direct access to physical hardware, including memory, video, and peripherals, was limited to software running in kernel space. Programs wishing to make use of system peripherals could only get access through kernel-mode device drivers.

Microsoft released its own Unix-inspired operating system in 1993. Windows NT had an internal structure a great deal like Linux, with kernel and device drivers running in kernel space, and everything else running in user space. This basic design is still in use, for both Linux and Windows NT's successors, such as Windows 2000, Windows XP, Windows Vista, and Windows 7. The general design for true protected-mode operating systems is shown schematically in Figure 3-6.

The Core Explosion

In the early 2000s, desktop PCs began to be sold with two CPU sockets. Windows 2000/XP/Vista/7 and Linux all support the use of multiple CPU chips in a single system, through a mechanism called *symmetric multiprocessing* (SMP). Multiprocessing is "symmetric" when all processors are the same. In most cases, when two CPUs are available, the operating system runs its own code in one CPU, and user-mode applications are run in the other.

As technology improved, Intel and AMD were able to place two identical but entirely independent code execution units on a single chip. The result was the first dual-core CPUs, the AMD Athlon 64 X2 (2005) and the Intel Core 2 Duo (2006). Four-core CPUs became commonly available in 2007. (This book is being written on an Intel Core 2 Quad 6600.) CPUs with more than four cores are possible, of course, but there is still a lot of discussion as to how such an embarrassment of riches might be used, and as of now it's a seriously open question.

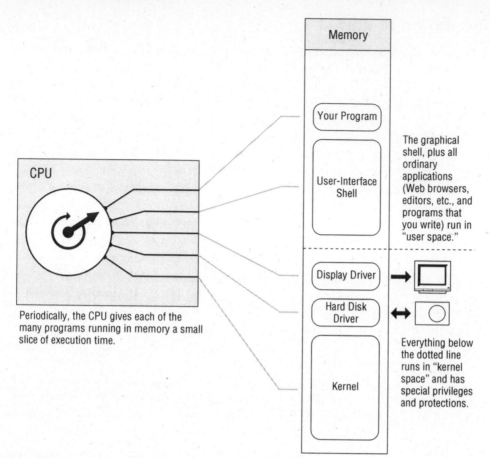

Memory

Your Program

User-Interface Shell

The graphical shell, plus all ordinary applications (Web browsers, editors, etc., and programs that you write) run in "user space."

Display Driver

Hard Disk Driver

Everything below the dotted line runs in "kernel space" and has special privileges and protections.

Kernel

CPU

Periodically, the CPU gives each of the many programs running in memory a small slice of execution time.

Figure 3-6: A mature, protected-mode operating system

The Plan

I can sum all of this up by borrowing one of the most potent metaphors for computing ever uttered: *The computer is a box that follows a plan.* These are the words of Ted Nelson, author of the uncanny book *Computer Lib/Dream Machines,* and one of those very rare people who have the infuriating habit of being right most of the time.

You write the plan. The computer follows it by passing the instructions, byte by byte, to the CPU. At the bottom of it, the process is a hellishly complicated electrical chain reaction involving hundreds of thousands of switches composed of many hundreds of thousands or even millions of transistors. That part of it, however, is hidden from you so that you don't have to worry about it. Once you tell all those heaps of transistors what to do, they know how to do it.

This plan, this list of machine instructions in memory, is your assembly language program. The whole point of this book is to teach you to correctly arrange machine instructions in memory for the use of the CPU.

With any luck at all, by now you have a reasonable conceptual understanding of both what computers do and what they are. It's time to start looking more closely at the nature of the operations that machine instructions direct the CPU to perform. For the most part, as with everything in computing, this is about memory, both the pedestrian memory out on the motherboard, and those kings of remembrance, the CPU registers.

Location, Location, Location

Registers, Memory Addressing, and Knowing Where Things Are

I wrote this book in large part because I could not find a beginning text on assembly language that I respected in the least. Nearly all books on assembly start by introducing the concept of an instruction set, and then begin describing machine instructions, one by one. This is moronic, and the authors of such books should be hung. *Even if you've learned every single instruction in an instruction set, you haven't learned assembly language.*

You haven't even come close.

The naive objection that a CPU exists to execute machine instructions can be disposed of pretty easily: it executes machine instructions once it has them in its electronic hands. The *real* job of a CPU, and the real challenge of assembly language, lies in locating the required instructions and data in memory. Any idiot can learn machine instructions. (Many do.) *The skill of assembly language consists of a deep comprehension of memory addressing.* Everything else is details—and easy details at that.

The Joy of Memory Models

Memory addressing is a difficult business, made much more difficult by the fact that there are a fair number of different ways to address memory in the x86 CPU family. Each of these ways is called a *memory model*. There are three major memory models that you can use with the more recent members of the x86

CPU family, and a number of minor variations on those three, especially the one in the middle.

In programming for 32-bit Linux, you're pretty much limited to one memory model, and once you understand memory addressing a little better, you'll be *very* glad of it. However, I'm going to describe all three in some detail here, even though the older two of the trio have become museum pieces. Don't skip over the discussion of those museum pieces. In the same way that studying fossils to learn how various living things evolved over time will give you a better understanding of livings things as they exist today, knowing a little about older Intel memory models will give you a more intuitive understanding of the one memory model that you're likely to *use*.

At the end of this chapter I'll briefly describe the 64-bit memory model that is only just now hitting the street in any numbers. That will be just a heads-up, however. In this book and for the next few years, 32-bit protected mode is where the action is.

The oldest and now ancient memory model is called the *real mode flat model*. It's thoroughly fossilized, but relatively straightforward. The elderly (and now retired) memory model is called the *real mode segmented model*. It may be the most hateful thing you ever learn in *any* kind of programming, assembly or otherwise. DOS programming at its peak used the real mode segmented model, and much Pepto Bismol was sold as a result. The newest memory model is called *protected mode flat model*, and it's the memory model behind modern operating systems such as Windows 2000/XP/Vista/7 and Linux. Note that protected mode flat model is available *only* on the 386 and newer CPUs that support the IA-32 architecture. The 8086, 8088, and 80286 do not support it. Windows 9x falls somewhere between models, and I doubt anybody except the people at Microsoft really understands all the kinks in the ways it addresses memory—maybe not even them. Windows 9x crashes all the time, and one main reason in my view is that it has a completely insane memory model. (Dynamic link libraries, or DLLs—a pox on *homo computationis*—are the other major reason.) Its gonzo memory model isn't the only reason you shouldn't consider writing Win 9x programs in assembly, but it's certainly the best one; and given that Windows 9x is now well on its way to being a fossil in its own right, you'll probably never have to.

I have a strategy in this book, and before we dive in, I'll lay it out: I will begin by explaining how memory addressing works under the real mode flat model, which was available under DOS. It's amazingly easy to learn. I discuss the real mode segmented model because you will keep stubbing your toe on it here and there and need to understand it, even if you never write a single line of code for it. Real work done today and for the near future lies in 32-bit protected mode flat model, for Windows, Linux, or any true 32-bit protected mode operating system. Key to the whole business is this: *Real mode flat model is very much like protected mode flat model in miniature.*

There is a big flat model and a little flat model. If you grasp real mode flat model, you will have no trouble with protected mode flat model. That monkey in the middle is just the dues you have to pay to consider yourself a real master of memory addressing.

So let's go see how this crazy stuff works.

16 Bits'll Buy You 64K

In 1974, the year I graduated from college, Intel introduced the 8080 CPU and basically invented microcomputing. (Yes, I'm an old guy, but I've been blessed with a sense of history—by virtue of having lived through quite a bit of it.) The 8080 was a white-hot little item at the time. I had one that ran at 1 MHz, and it was a pretty effective word processor, which is mostly what I did with it.

The 8080 was an 8-bit CPU, meaning it processed 8 bits of information at a time. However, it had 16 address lines coming out of it. The "bitness" of a CPU—how many bits wide its general-purpose registers are—is important, but to my view the far more important measure of a CPU's effectiveness is how many address lines it can muster in one operation. In 1974, 16 address lines was aggressive, because memory was *extremely* expensive, and most machines had 4K or 8K bytes (remember, that means 4,000 or 8,000) at most—and some had a lot less.

Sixteen address lines will address 64K bytes. If you count in binary (which computers always do) and limit yourself to 16 binary columns, you can count from 0 to 65,535. (The colloquial "64K" is shorthand for the number 66,536.) This means that every one of 65,536 separate memory locations can have its own unique address, from 0 up to 65,535.

The 8080 memory-addressing scheme was very simple: you put a 16-bit address out on the address lines, and you got back the 8-bit value that was stored at that address. Note well: there is *no* necessary relation between the number of address lines in a memory system and the size of the data stored at each location. The 8080 stored 8 bits at each location, but it could have stored 16 or even 32 bits at each location, and still have 16 memory address lines.

By far and away, the operating system most used with the 8080 was CP/M-80. CP/M-80 was a little unusual in that it existed at the *top* of installed memory—sometimes so that it could be contained in ROM, but mostly just to get it out of the way and allow a consistent memory starting point for *transient programs*, those that (unlike the operating system) were loaded into memory and run only when needed. When CP/M-80 read a program in from disk to run it, it would load the program into low memory, at address 0100H—that is, 256 bytes from the very bottom of memory. The first 256 bytes of memory were called the *program segment prefix (PSP)* and contained various odd bits of information as well as a general-purpose memory buffer for the program's disk input/output (I/O). The executable code itself did not begin until address 0100H.

I've drawn the 8080 and CP/M-80 memory model in Figure 4-1.

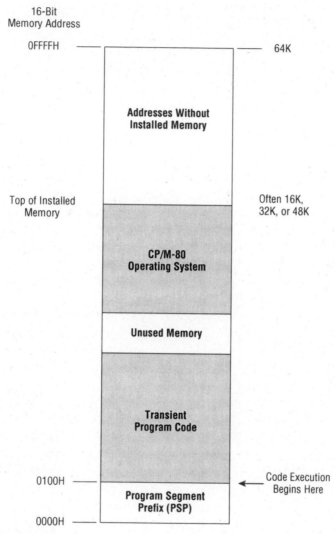

Figure 4-1: The 8080 memory model

The 8080's memory model as used with CP/M-80 was simple, and people used it a lot; so when Intel created its first 16-bit CPU, the 8086, it wanted to make it easy for people to translate older CP/M-80 software from the 8080 to the 8086—a process called *porting*. One way to do this was to make sure that a 16-bit addressing system such as that of the 8080 still worked. So, even though the 8086 could address 16 times as much memory as the 8080

(16 × 64K = 1MB), Intel set up the 8086 so that a program could take some 64K byte segment within that megabyte of memory and run entirely inside it, just as though it were the smaller 8080 memory system.

This was done by the use of *segment registers*, which are basically memory pointers located in CPU registers that point to a place in memory where things begin, be this data storage, code execution, or anything else. You'll learn a lot more about segment registers very shortly. For now, it's enough to think of them as pointers indicating where, within the 8086's megabyte of memory, a program ported from the 8080 world would begin (see Figure 4-2).

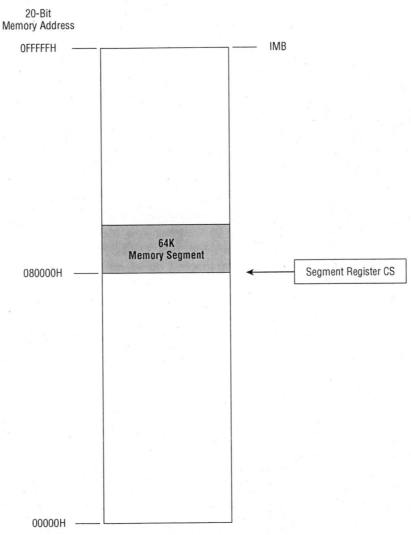

Figure 4-2: The 8080 memory model inside an 8086 memory system

When speaking of the 8086 and 8088, there are four segment registers to consider (again, we'll be dealing with them in detail very soon). For the purposes of Figure 4-2, consider the register called CS—which stands for *code segment*. Again, it's a pointer to a location within the 8086's megabyte of memory. This location acts as the starting point for a 64K region of memory, within which a quickly converted CP/M-80 program could run very happily.

This was very wise short-term thinking—and catastrophically bad long-term thinking. Any number of CP/M-80 programs were converted to the 8086 within a couple of years. The problems began big-time when programmers attempted to create new programs from scratch that had never seen the 8080 and had no need for the segmented memory model. Too bad—the segmented model dominated the architecture of the 8086. Programs that needed more than 64K of memory at a time had to use memory in 64K chunks, switching between chunks by switching values into and out of segment registers.

This was a nightmare. There is one good reason to learn it, however: understanding the way real-mode segmented memory addressing works will help you understand how the two x86 flat models work, and in the process you will come to understand the nature of the CPU a lot better.

The Nature of a Megabyte

When running in segmented real mode, the x86 CPUs can use up to one megabyte of directly addressable memory. This memory is also called *real mode memory*. As discussed briefly in Chapter 3, a megabyte of memory is actually not 1 million bytes of memory, but 1,048,576 bytes. As with the shorthand term "64K," a megabyte doesn't come out even in our base 10 because computers operate on base 2. Those 1,048,576 bytes expressed in base 2 are 10000000000000000000B bytes. That's 2^{20}, a fact that we'll return to shortly. The printed number 10000000000000000000B is so bulky that it's better to express it in the compatible (and much more compact) base 16, the hexadecimal system described in Chapter 2. The quantity 2^{20} is equivalent to 16^5, and may be written in hexadecimal as 100000H. (If the notion of number bases still confounds you, I recommend another trip through Chapter 2, if you haven't been through it already—or, perhaps, even if you have.)

Now, here's a tricky and absolutely critical question: In a bank of memory containing 100000H bytes, what's the address of the very last byte in the memory bank? The answer is *not* 100000H. The clue is the flip side to that question: What's the address of the *first* byte in memory? That answer, you might recall, is 0. *Computers always begin counting from 0.* (People generally begin counting from 1.) This disconnect occurs again and again in computer programming. From a computer programming perspective, the last in a row of four items is item number 3, because the first item in a row of four is item number 0. Count: 0, 1, 2, 3.

The address of a byte in a memory bank is just the number of that byte *starting from zero*. This means that the last, or highest, address in a memory bank containing one megabyte is 100000H minus one, or 0FFFFFH. (The initial zero, while not mathematically necessary, is there for the convenience of your assembler, and helps keep the assembler program from getting confused. Get in the habit of using an initial zero on any hex number beginning with the hex digits A through F.)

The addresses in a megabyte of memory, then, run from 00000H to 0FFFFFH. In binary notation, that is equivalent to the range of 00000000000000000000B to 11111111111111111111B. That's a lot of bits—20, to be exact. If you refer back to Figure 3-3 in Chapter 3, you'll see that a megabyte memory bank has 20 address lines. One of those 20 address bits is routed to each of those 20 address lines, so that any address expressed as 20 bits will identify one and only one of the 1,048,576 bytes contained in the memory bank.

That's what a megabyte of memory is: some arrangement of memory chips within the computer, connected by an address bus of 20 lines. A 20-bit address is fed to those 20 address lines to identify 1 byte out of the megabyte.

Backward Compatibility and Virtual 86 Mode

Modern x86 CPUs such as the Pentium can address much more memory than this, and I'll explain how and why shortly. With the 8086 and 8088 CPUs, the 20 address lines and one megabyte of memory was literally all they had. The 386 and later Intel CPUs could address 4 gigabytes of memory without carving it up into smaller segments. When a 32-bit CPU is operating in protected mode flat model, a segment *is* 4 gigabytes—so one segment is, for the most part, plenty.

However, a huge pile of DOS software written to make use of segments was still everywhere in use and had to be dealt with. So, to maintain *backward compatibility* with the ancient 8086 and 8088, newer CPUs were given the power to limit themselves to what the older chips could address and execute. When a Pentium-class CPU needs to run software written for the real mode segmented model, it pulls a neat trick that, temporarily, makes it *become* an 8086. This is called *virtual-86 mode*, and it provided excellent backward compatibility for DOS software.

When you launch an MS-DOS window or "DOS box" under Windows NT and later versions, you're using virtual-86 mode to create what amounts to a little real mode island inside the Windows protected mode memory system. It was the only good way to keep that backward compatibility, for reasons you will understand fairly soon.

16-Bit Blinders

In real mode segmented model, an x86 CPU can "see" a full megabyte of memory. That is, the CPU chips set themselves up so that they can use

20 of their 32 address pins and can pass a 20-bit address to the memory system. From that perspective, it seems pretty simple and straightforward. However, the bulk of the trouble you might have in understanding real mode segmented model stems from this fact: whereas those CPUs can see a full megabyte of memory, they are constrained to look at that megabyte through 16-bit blinders.

The blinders metaphor is closer to literal than you might think. Look at Figure 4-3. The long rectangle represents the megabyte of memory that the CPU can address in real mode segmented model. The CPU is off to the right. In the middle is a piece of metaphorical cardboard with a slot cut in it. The slot is 1 byte wide and 65,536 bytes long. The CPU can slide that piece of cardboard up and down the full length of its memory system. However, *at any one time*, it can access only 65,536 bytes.

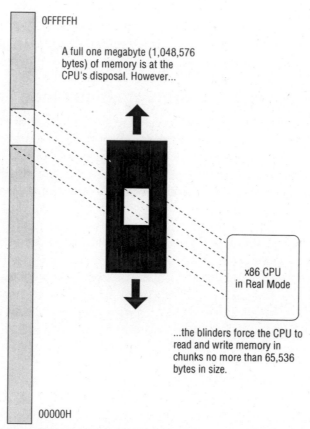

Figure 4-3: Seeing a megabyte through 64K blinders

The CPU's view of memory in real mode segmented model is peculiar. It is constrained to look at memory in chunks, where no chunk is larger than 65,536 bytes in length—again, what we call "64K." Making use of those chunks—that is, knowing which one is currently in use and how to move from one to another—is the real challenge of real mode segmented model programming. It's time to take a closer look at what segments are and how they work.

The Nature of Segments

We've spoken informally of segments so far as chunks of memory within the larger memory space that the CPU can see and use. In the context of real mode segmented model, a *segment* is a region of memory that begins on a paragraph boundary and extends for some number of bytes. In real mode segmented model, this number is less than or equal to 64K (65,536). You've seen the number 64K before, but *paragraphs*?

Time out for a lesson in old-time 86-family trivia. A *paragraph* is a measure of memory equal to 16 bytes. It is one of numerous technical terms used to describe various quantities of memory. We've looked at some of them before, and all of them are even multiples of 1 byte. Bytes are data atoms, remember; loose memory bits are more like subatomic particles, and they never exist in the absence of a byte (or more) of memory to contain them. Some of these terms are used more than others, but you should be aware of all of them, which are provided in Table 4-1.

Table 4-1: Collective Terms for Memory

NAME	VALUE IN DECIMAL	VALUE IN HEX
Byte	1	01H
Word	2	02H
Double word	4	04H
Quad word	8	08H
Ten byte	10	0AH
Paragraph	16	10H
Page	256	100H
Segment	65,536	10000H

Some of these terms, such as ten byte, occur very rarely, and others, such as page, occur almost never. The term *paragraph* was never common to begin with, and for the most part was used only in connection with the places in memory where segments may begin.

Any memory address evenly divisible by 16 is called a *paragraph boundary*. The first paragraph boundary is address 0. The second is address 10H; the third address 20H, and so on. (Remember that 10H is equal to decimal 16.) Any paragraph boundary may be considered the start of a segment.

This *doesn't* mean that a segment actually starts every 16 bytes up and down throughout that megabyte of memory. A segment is like a shelf in one of those modern adjustable bookcases. On the back face of the bookcase are a great many little slots spaced one-half inch apart. A shelf bracket can be inserted into any of the little slots. However, there aren't hundreds of shelves, but only four or five. Nearly all of the slots are empty and unused. They exist so that a much smaller number of shelves may be adjusted up and down the height of the bookcase as needed.

In a very similar manner, paragraph boundaries are little slots at which a segment may be begun. In real mode segmented model, a program may make use of only four or five segments, but each of those segments may begin at any of the 65,536 paragraph boundaries existing in the megabyte of memory available in the real mode segmented model.

There's that number again: 65,536—our beloved 64K. There are 64K different paragraph boundaries where a segment may begin. Each paragraph boundary has a number. As always, the numbers begin from 0, and go to 64K minus one; in decimal 65,535, or in hex 0FFFFH. Because a segment may begin at any paragraph boundary, the number of the paragraph boundary at which a segment begins is called the *segment address* of that particular segment.

We rarely, in fact, speak of paragraphs or paragraph boundaries at all. When you see the term *segment address* in connection with real mode segmented model, keep in mind that each segment address is 16 bytes (one paragraph) farther along in memory than the segment address before it. In Figure 4-4, each shaded bar is a segment address, and segments begin every sixteen bytes. The highest segment address is 0FFFFH, which is 16 bytes from the very top of real mode's 1 megabyte of memory.

In summary: segments may begin at any segment address. There are 65,536 segment addresses evenly distributed across real mode's full megabyte of memory, sixteen bytes apart. A segment address is more a permission than a compulsion; for all the 64K possible segment addresses, only five or six are ever actually used to begin segments at any one time. Think of segment addresses as slots where segments may be placed.

So much for segment addresses; now, what of segments themselves? The most important thing to understand about a segment is that it may be up to 64K bytes in size, but it doesn't *have* to be. A segment may be only one byte long, or 256 bytes long, or 21,378 bytes long, or any length at all short of 64K bytes.

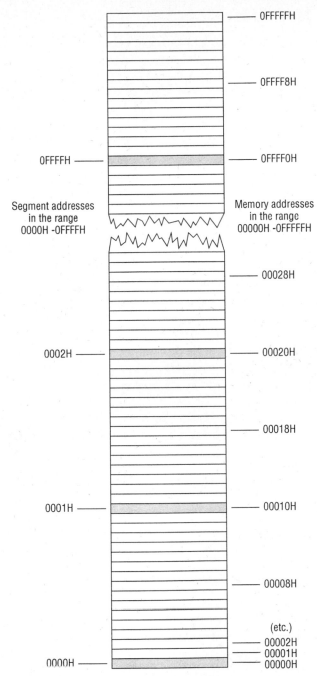

Figure 4-4: Memory addresses versus segment addresses

A Horizon, Not a Place

You define a segment primarily by stating where it begins. What, then, defines how *long* a segment is? Nothing, really—and we get into some really tricky semantics here. A segment is more a *horizon* than a *place*. Once you define where a segment begins, that segment can encompass any location in memory between that starting place and the horizon—which is 65,536 bytes down the line.

Nothing dictates, of course, that a segment must use all of that memory. In most cases, when a segment is defined at some segment address, a program considers only the next few hundred or perhaps few thousand bytes as part of that segment, unless it's a really world-class program. Most beginners reading about segments think of them as some kind of memory allocation, a protected region of memory with walls on both sides, reserved for some specific use.

This is about as far from true as you can get. In real mode nothing is protected within a segment, and segments are not reserved for any specific register or access method. Segments can overlap. (People often don't think about or realize this.) In a very real sense, segments don't really exist, *except* as horizons beyond which a certain type of memory reference cannot go. It comes back to that set of 64K blinders that the CPU wears, as I drew in Figure 4-3. I think of it this way: *A segment is the location in memory at which the CPU's 64K blinders are positioned.* In looking at memory through the blinders, you can see bytes starting at the segment address and going on until the blinders cut you off, 64K bytes down the way.

The key to understanding this admittedly metaphysical definition of a segment is knowing how segments are used—and understanding that finally requires a detailed discussion of registers.

Making 20-Bit Addresses out of 16-Bit Registers

A *register*, as I've mentioned informally in earlier chapters, is a memory location *inside* the CPU chip, rather than outside the CPU in a memory bank somewhere. The 8088, 8086, and 80286 are often called 16-bit CPUs because their internal registers are almost all 16 bits in size. The 80386 and its twenty years' worth of successors are called 32-bit CPUs because most of their internal registers are 32 bits in size. Since the mid-2000s, many of the new x86 CPUs are 64 bits in design, with registers that are 64 bits wide. (More about this at the end of the chapter.) The x86 CPUs have a fair number of registers, and they are an interesting crew indeed.

Registers do many jobs, but perhaps their most important single job is holding addresses of important locations in memory. If you recall, the 8086 and 8088 have 20 address pins, and their megabyte of memory (which is the real mode segmented memory we're talking about) requires addresses 20 bits in size.

How do you put a 20-bit memory address in a 16-bit register? You don't. You put a 20-bit address in *two* 16-bit registers.

What happens is this: all memory locations in real mode's megabyte of memory have not one address but *two*. Every byte in memory is assumed to reside in a segment. A byte's complete address, then, consists of the address of its segment, along with the distance of the byte from the start of that segment. Recall that the address of the segment is the byte's *segment address*. The byte's distance from the start of the segment is the byte's *offset address*. Both addresses must be specified to completely describe any single byte's location within the full megabyte of real mode memory. When written out, the segment address comes first, followed by the offset address. The two are separated with a colon. Segment:offset addresses are always written in hexadecimal.

I've drawn Figure 4-5 to help make this a little clearer. A byte of data we'll call "MyByte" exists in memory at the location marked. Its address is given as 0001:0019. This means that MyByte falls within segment 0001H and is located 0019H bytes from the start of that segment. It's a convention in x86 programming that when two numbers are used to specify an address with a colon between them, you do *not* end each of the two numbers with an *H* for hexadecimal. Addresses written in segment:offset form are assumed to be in hexadecimal.

The universe is perverse, however, and clever eyes will perceive that MyByte can have two other perfectly legal addresses: 0:0029 and 0002:0009. How so? Keep in mind that a segment may start every 16 bytes throughout the full megabyte of real memory. A segment, once begun, embraces all bytes from its origin to 65,535 bytes further up in memory. There's nothing wrong with segments overlapping, and in Figure 4-5 we have three overlapping segments. MyByte is 2DH bytes into the first segment, which begins at segment address 0000H. MyByte is 1DH bytes into the second segment, which begins at segment address 0001H. It's not that MyByte is in two or three places at once. It's in only one place, but that one place may be described in any of three ways.

It's a little like Chicago's street-numbering system. Howard Street is 76 blocks north of Chicago's "origin," Madison Street. Howard Street is also four blocks north of Touhy Avenue. You can describe Howard Street's location relative to either Madison Street or Touhy Avenue, depending on what you want to do.

An arbitrary byte somewhere in the middle of real mode's megabyte of memory may fall within literally thousands of different segments. Which segment the byte is *actually* in is strictly a matter of convention.

In summary: to express a 20-bit address in two 16-bit registers is to put the segment address into one 16-bit register, and the offset address into another 16-bit register. The two registers taken together identify one byte among all 1,048,576 bytes in real mode's megabyte of memory.

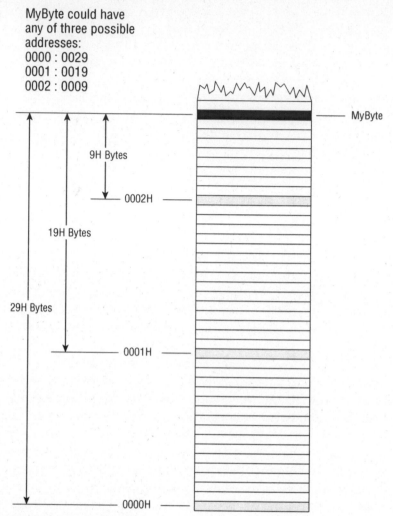

MyByte could have
any of three possible
addresses:
0000 : 0029
0001 : 0019
0002 : 0009

MyByte

9H Bytes

0002H

19H Bytes

29H Bytes

0001H

0000H

Figure 4-5: Segments and offsets

Is this awkward? You bet, but it was the best we could do for a good many years.

16-Bit and 32-Bit Registers

Think of the segment address as the starting position of real mode's 64K blinders. Typically, you would move the blinders to encompass the location where you wish to work, and then leave the blinders in one place while moving around within their 64K limits.

This is exactly how registers tend to be used in real mode segmented model assembly language. The 8088, 8086, and 80286 have exactly four segment registers specifically designated as holders of segment addresses. The 386 and later CPUs have two more that can also be used in real mode. (You need to be aware of the CPU model you're running on if you intend to use the two additional segment registers, because the older CPUs don't have them at all.) Each segment register is a 16-bit memory location existing within the CPU chip itself. No matter what the CPU is doing, if it's addressing some location in memory, then the segment address of that location is present in one of the six segment registers.

The segment registers have names that reflect their general functions: CS, DS, SS, ES, FS, and GS. FS and GS exist only in the 386 and later Intel x86 CPUs—but are still 16 bits in size. *All segment registers are 16 bits in size, irrespective of the CPU*. This is true even of the 32-bit CPUs.

- *CS stands for code segment.* Machine instructions exist at some offset into a code segment. The segment address of the code segment of the currently executing instruction is contained in CS.

- *DS stands for data segment.* Variables and other data exist at some offset into a data segment. There may be many data segments, but the CPU may only use one at a time, by placing the segment address of that segment in register DS.

- *SS stands for stack segment.* The *stack* is a very important component of the CPU used for temporary storage of data and addresses. I explain how the stack works a little later; for now simply understand that, like everything else within real mode's megabyte of memory, the stack has a segment address, which is contained in SS.

- *ES stands for extra segment.* The extra segment is exactly that: a spare segment that may be used for specifying a location in memory.

- *FS and GS are clones of ES.* They are both additional segments with no specific job or specialty. Their names come from the fact that they were created after ES (think, E, F, G). Don't forget that they exist *only* in the 386 and later x86 CPUs!

General-Purpose Registers

The segment registers exist only to hold segment addresses. They can be forced to do a very few other things in real mode, but by and large, segment registers should be considered specialists in holding segment addresses. The x86 CPUs have a crew of generalist registers to do the rest of the work of assembly language computing. Among many other things, these *general-purpose registers* are used to hold the offset addresses that must be paired with segment addresses to pin down a single location in memory. They also hold values for arithmetic manipulation, for bit-shifting (more on this later) and many other things. They are truly the craftsman's pockets inside the CPU.

But we come here to one of the biggest and most obvious differences between the older 16-bit x86 CPUs (the 8086, 8088, and 80286) and the newer 32-bit x86 CPUs starting with the 386: the *size* of the general-purpose registers. When I wrote the very first edition of this book in 1989, the 8088 still ruled the PC computing world, and I limited myself to discussing what the 8088 had within it.

Those days are long gone. The fully 32-bit 386 is considered an antique, and the original 1993 Pentium is seen as ever more quaint as the years go by. It's a 32-bit world now, and the time will come when it's a 64-bit world. The "bitness" of the world is almost entirely defined by the width of the x86 CPU registers.

Like the segment registers, the general-purpose registers are memory locations existing inside the CPU chip itself; and like the segment registers, they all have names rather than numeric addresses. The general-purpose registers really are generalists in that all of them share a large suite of capabilities. However, some of the general-purpose registers also have what I call a "hidden agenda": a task or set of tasks that only it can perform. I explain all these hidden agendas as I go—keeping in mind that some of the hidden agendas are actually limitations of the older 16-bit CPUs. The newer general-purpose registers are much more, well, *general*.

In our current 32-bit world, the general-purpose registers fall into three general classes: the 16-bit general-purpose registers, the 32-bit extended general-purpose registers, and the 8-bit register halves. These three classes do not represent three entirely distinct sets of registers at all. The 16-bit and 8-bit registers are actually names of regions *inside* the 32-bit registers. Register growth in the x86 CPU family has come about by *extending* registers existing in older CPUs. Adding a room to your house doesn't make it two houses—just one bigger house. And so it has been with the x86 registers.

There are eight 16-bit general-purpose registers: AX, BX, CX, DX, BP, SI, DI, and SP. (SP is a little less general than the others, but we'll get to that.) These all existed in the 8086, 8088, and 80286 CPUs. They are all 16 bits in size, and you can place any value in them that may be expressed in 16 bits or fewer. When Intel expanded the x86 architecture to 32 bits in 1986, it doubled the size of all eight registers and gave them new names by prefixing an *E* in front of each register name, resulting in EAX, EBX, ECX, EDX, EBP, ESI, EDI, and ESP.

So, were these just bigger registers, or new registers?

Both.

As with a lot of things in assembly language, this becomes a lot clearer by drawing a diagram. Figure 4-6 shows how SI, DI, BP, and SP doubled in size and got new names—without entirely losing their old ones.

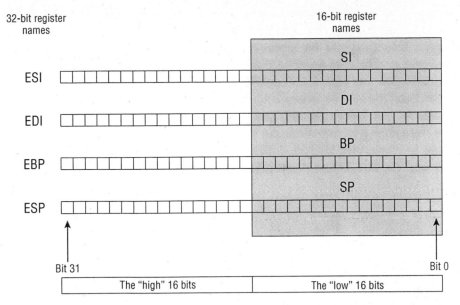

Figure 4-6: Extending 16-bit general-purpose registers

Each of the four registers shown in Figure 4-6 is fully 32 bits in size. However, in each register, the lower 16 bits have a name of their own. The lower 16 bits of ESI, for example, may be referenced as SI. The lower 16 bits of EDI may be referenced as DI. If you're writing programs to run in real mode on an 8088 machine such as the ancient IBM PC, you can *only* reference the DI part—the high 16 bits don't exist on that CPU!

Unfortunately, the *high* 16 bits of the 32-bit general-purpose registers do not have their own names. You can access the low 16 bits of ESI as SI, but to get at the high 16 bits, you must refer to ESI and get the whole 32-bit shebang.

Register Halves

The same is true for the other four general-purpose registers, EAX, EBX, ECX, and EDX, but there's an additional twist: the low 16 bits are themselves divided into two 8-bit halves, so what we have are register names on not two but *three* levels. The 16-bit registers AX, BX, CX, and DX are present as the lower 16-bit portions of EAX, EBX, ECX, and EDX; but AX, BX, CX, and DX are themselves divided into 8-bit halves, and assemblers recognize special names for the two halves. The A, B, C, and D are retained, but instead of the X, a half is specified with an *H* (for high half) or an *L* (for low half). Each register half is one byte (8 bits) in size. Thus, making up 16-bit register AX, you have byte-sized register halves AH and AL; within BX there is BH and BL, and so on.

Again, this can best be understood in a diagram (see Figure 4-7). As I mentioned earlier, one quirk of this otherwise very useful system is that there is no name for the *high* 16-bit portion of the 32-bit registers. In other words, you can read the low 16 bits of EAX by specifying AX in an assembly language instruction, but there's no way to specify the high 16 bits by themselves. This keeps the naming conventions for the registers a little simpler (would you like to have to remember EAXH, EBXH, ECXH, and EDXH on top of everything else?), and the lack is not felt as often as you might think.

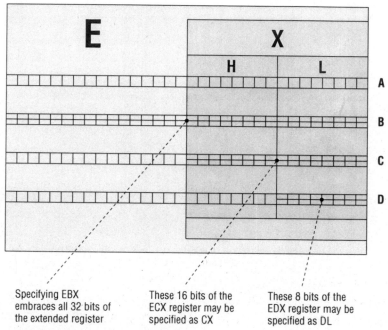

Specifying EBX embraces all 32 bits of the extended register

These 16 bits of the ECX register may be specified as CX

These 8 bits of the EDX register may be specified as DL

Figure 4-7: 8-bit, 16-bit, and 32-bit registers

One nice thing about the 8-bit register halves is that you can read and change one half of a 16-bit number without disturbing the other half. This means that if you place the word-sized hexadecimal value 76E9H into register AX, you can read the byte-sized value 76H from register AH, and 0E9H from register AL. Better still, if you then store the value 0AH into register AL and then read back register AX, you'll find that the original value of 76E9H has been changed to 760AH.

Being able to treat the AX, BX, CX, and DX registers as 8-bit halves can be extremely handy in situations where you're manipulating a lot of 8-bit quantities. Each register half can be considered a separate register, providing you with twice the number of places to put things while your program works.

As you'll see later, finding a place to stick a value in a pinch is one of the great challenges facing assembly language programmers.

Keep in mind that this dual nature involves *only* the 16-bit general-purpose registers AX, BX, CX, and DX. The other 16-bit general-purpose registers, SP, BP, SI, and DI, are not similarly equipped. There are no SIH and SIL 8-bit registers, for example, as convenient as that would sometimes be.

The Instruction Pointer

Yet another type of register lives inside the x86 CPUs. The *instruction pointer* (usually called IP or, in 32-bit protected mode, EIP) is in a class by itself. In radical contrast to the gang of eight general-purpose registers, IP is a specialist *par excellence*—more of a specialist than even the segment registers. It can do only one thing: it contains the offset address of the next machine instruction to be executed in the current code segment.

A *code segment* is an area of memory where machine instructions are stored. The steps and tests of which a program is made are contained in code segments. Depending on the programming model you're using (more on this shortly) there may be many code segments in a program, or only one. The *current code segment* is that code segment whose segment address is currently stored in code segment register CS. At any given time, the machine instruction currently being executed exists within the current code segment. In real mode segmented model, the value in CS can change frequently. In the two flat models, the value in CS (almost) never changes—and certainly never changes at the bidding of an application program. (As you'll see later, in protected mode all the segment registers "belong" to the operating system and are not changeable by ordinary programs.)

While executing a program, the CPU uses IP to keep track of where it is in the current code segment. Each time an instruction is executed, IP is *incremented* by some number of bytes. The number of bytes is the size of the instruction just executed. The net result is to bump IP further into memory, so that it points to the start of the *next* instruction to be executed. Instructions come in different sizes, ranging typically from 1 to 6 bytes. (Some of the more arcane forms of the more arcane instructions may be even larger.) The CPU is careful to increment IP by just the right number of bytes, so that it does in fact end up pointing to the start of the next instruction, and not merely into the middle of the last instruction or some other instruction.

If IP contains the offset address of the next machine instruction, then where is the segment address? The segment address is kept in the code segment register CS. Together, CS and IP contain the full address of the next machine instruction to be executed.

The nature of this address depends on what CPU you're using, and the programming model for which you're using it. In the 8088, 8086, and 80286,

IP is 16 bits in size. In the 386 and later CPUs, IP (like all the other registers except the segment registers) graduates to 32 bits in size and becomes EIP.

In real mode segmented model, CS and IP working together give you a 20-bit address pointing to one of the 1,048,576 bytes in real-mode memory. In both of the two flat models (more on which shortly), CS is set by the operating system and held constant. IP does all the instruction pointing that you, the programmer, have to deal with. In the 16-bit flat model (real mode flat model), this means IP can follow instruction execution all across a full 64K segment of memory. The 32-bit flat model does far more than double that; 32 bits can represent 4,294,967,290 different memory addresses. Therefore, in 32-bit flat model (that is, protected mode flat model), IP can follow instruction execution across over 4 gigabytes of memory—which used to be an unimaginable amount of memory, and now is commonplace.

IP is notable in being the *only* register that can be neither read from nor written to directly. There are tricks that may be used to obtain the current value in IP, but having IP's value is not as useful as you might think, and you won't often have to do it.

The Flags Register

There is one additional type of register inside the CPU: what is generically called the *flags register*. It is 16 bits in size in the 8086, 8088, and 80286, and its formal name is FLAGS. It is 32 bits in size in the 386 and later CPUs, and its formal name in the 32-bit CPUs is EFLAGS. Most of the bits in the flags register are used as single-bit registers called *flags*. Each of these individual flags has a name, such as CF, DF, OF, and so on, and each has a very specific meaning within the CPU.

When your program performs a test, what it tests are one or another of the single-bit flags in the flags register. Because a single bit may contain one of only two values, 1 or 0, a test in assembly language is truly a two-way affair: either a flag is set to 1 or it isn't. If the flag is set to 1, the program takes one action; if the flag is set to 0, the program takes a different action.

The flags register is almost never dealt with as a unit. What happens is that many different machine instructions test the various flags to decide which way to go on some either-or decision. We're concentrating on memory addressing at the moment, so for now I'll simply promise to go into flag lore in more detail at more appropriate moments later in the book, when we discuss machine instructions that test the various flags in the flags register.

The Three Major Assembly Programming Models

I mentioned earlier in this chapter that three major programming models are available for use on the x86 CPUs, though two of them are now considered archaic. The differences between them lie (mostly) in the use of registers to address memory. (The other differences, especially on the high end, are for the most part hidden from you by the operating system.) This section describes the three models, all of which we'll touch on throughout the course of the rest of this book.

Real Mode Flat Model

In real mode, if you recall, the CPU can see only one megabyte (1,048,576) of memory. You can access every last one of those million-odd bytes by using the segment:offset register trick shown earlier to form a 20-bit address out of two 16-bit addresses contained in two registers. Or, you can be content with 64K of memory, and not fool with segments at all.

In the real mode flat model, your program and all the data it works on must exist within a single 64K block of memory. Sixty-four kilobytes! Pfeh! What could you possibly accomplish in only 64K bytes? Well, the first version of WordStar for the IBM PC fit in 64K. So did the first three major releases of Turbo Pascal—in fact, the Turbo Pascal program itself occupied a lot less than 64K because it compiled its programs into memory. The whole Turbo Pascal package—compiler, text editor, and some odd tools—came to just over 39K. Thirty-nine kilobytes! You can't even write a letter to your mother (using Microsoft Word) in that little space these days!

True, true. But that's mostly because we don't have to. Memory has become *very* cheap, and our machines now contain what by historical standards is a staggering amount of it. We've gotten lazy and hoggish and wasteful, simply because we can get away with it.

Spectacular things once happened in 64K, and while you may never be called upon to limit yourself to real mode flat model, the discipline that all those now gray-haired programmers developed for it is very useful. More to the point, real mode flat model is the "little brother" of protected mode flat model, which is the code model you will use when programming under Linux. If you learn the ways of real mode flat model, protected mode flat model will be a snap. (Any trouble you'll have won't be with assembly code or memory models, but with the byzantine requirements of Linux and its canonical code libraries.)

Real mode flat model is shown diagrammatically in Figure 4-8. There's not much to it. The segment registers are all set to point to the beginning of the 64K block of memory you can work with. (The operating system sets them when it loads and runs your program.) They all point to that same place and never change as long as your program is running. That being the case, you can simply forget about them. Poof! No segment registers, no fooling with segments, and none of the ugly complication that comes with them.

Because a 16-bit register such as BX can hold any value from 0 to 65,535, it can pinpoint any single byte within the full 64K your program has to work with. Addressing memory can thus be done without the explicit use of the segment registers. The segment registers are still functioning, of course, from the CPU's point of view. They don't disappear and are still there, but the operating system sets them to values of its own choosing when it launches your program, and those values will be good as long as your program runs. You don't have to access the segment registers in any way to write your program.

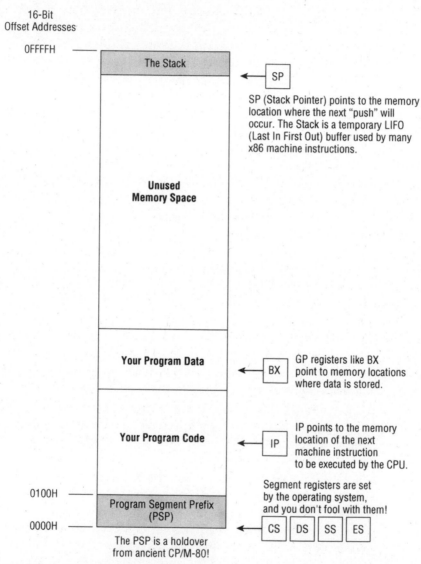

Figure 4-8: Real mode flat model

Most of the general-purpose registers may contain addresses of locations in memory. You use them in conjunction with machine instructions to bring data in from memory and write it back out again.

At the top of the single segment that your program exists within, you'll see a small region called the *stack*. The stack is a LIFO (last in, first out) storage location with some very special uses. I will explain what the stack is and how it works in considerable detail later.

Real Mode Segmented Model

The first two editions of this book focused entirely on real mode segmented model, which was the mainstream programming model throughout the MS-DOS era, and still comes into play when you launch an MS-DOS window to run a piece of "legacy" software. It's a complicated, ugly system that requires you to remember a lot of little rules and gotchas, but it's useful to understand because it illustrates the nature and function of segments very clearly. Note that under both flat models you can squint a little and pretend that segments and segment registers don't really exist, but they are both still there and operating, and once you get into some of the more exotic styles of programming, you will need to be aware of them and grasp how they work.

In real mode segmented model, your program can see the full 1MB of memory available to the CPU in real mode. It does this by combining a 16-bit segment address with a 16-bit offset address. It doesn't just glom them together into a 32-bit address, however. You need to think back to the discussion of segments earlier in this chapter. A segment address is not really a memory address. A segment address specifies one of the 65,535 slots at which a segment may begin. One of these slots exists every 16 bytes from the bottom of memory to the top. Segment address 0000H specifies the first such slot, at the very first location in memory. Segment address 0001H specifies the next slot, which lies 16 bytes higher in memory. Jumping up-memory another 16 bytes gets you to segment address 0002H, and so on. You can translate a segment address to an actual 20-bit memory address by multiplying it by 16. Segment address 0002H is thus equivalent to memory address 0020H, which is the 32nd byte in memory.

But such multiplication isn't something you have to do. The CPU handles the combination of segments and offsets into a full 20-bit address internally. *Your* job is to tell the CPU where the two different components of that 20-bit address are. The customary notation is to separate the segment register and the offset register by a colon, as shown in the following example:

```
SS:SP
SS:BP
ES:DI
DS:SI
CS:BX
```

Each of these five register combinations specifies a full 20-bit address. ES:DI, for example, specifies the address as the distance in DI from the start of the segment called out in ES.

I've drawn a diagram outlining real mode segmented model in Figure 4-9. In contrast to real mode flat model (shown in Figure 4-8), the diagram here shows *all* of memory, not just the one little 64K chunk that your real mode flat model program is allocated when it runs. A program written for real mode segmented model can see all of real mode memory.

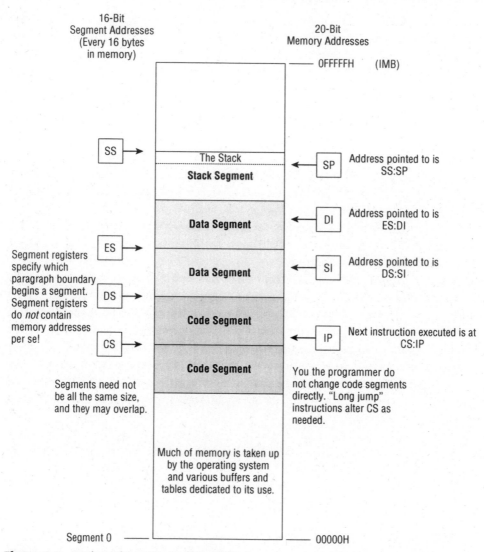

Figure 4-9: Real mode segmented model

The diagram shows two code segments and two data segments. In practice you can have any reasonable number of code and data segments, not just two of each. You can access two data segments at the same time, because you have two segment registers available to do the job: DS and ES. (In the 386 and later processors, you have two additional segment registers, FS and GS.) Each can specify a data segment, and you can move data from one segment to another using any of several machine instructions. However, you only have *one* code segment register, CS. CS always points to the current code segment, and the next instruction to be executed is pointed to by the IP register. You don't load values directly into CS to change from one code segment to another. Machine instructions called *jumps* change to another code segment as necessary. Your program can span several code segments, and when a jump instruction (of which there are several kinds) needs to take execution into a different code segment, it changes the value in CS for you.

There is only one stack segment for any single program, specified by the stack segment register SS. The stack pointer register SP points to the memory address (relative to SS, albeit in an upside-down direction) where the next stack operation will take place. The stack requires some considerable explaining, which I take up in several places later in this book.

You need to keep in mind that in real mode, there will be pieces of the operating system (and if you're using an 8086 or 8088, that will be the *whole* operating system) in memory with your program, along with important system data tables. You can destroy portions of the operating system by careless use of segment registers, which will cause the operating system to crash and take your program with it. This is the danger that prompted Intel to build new features into its 80386 and later CPUs to support a "protected" mode. In protected mode, application programs (that is, the programs that you write, as opposed to the operating system or device drivers) cannot destroy the operating system or other application programs that happen to be running elsewhere in memory via multitasking. That's what the *protected* means.

Finally, although it's true that there was a sort of rudimentary protected mode present in the 80286, no operating system ever really used it, and it's not much worth discussing today.

Protected Mode Flat Model

Intel's CPUs have implemented a very good protected mode architecture since the 386 appeared in 1986. However, application programs cannot make use of protected mode all by themselves. The operating system must set up and manage a protected mode before application programs can run within it. MS-DOS couldn't do this, and Microsoft Windows couldn't really do it either until Windows NT first appeared in 1994. Linux, having no real-mode "legacy" issues to deal with, has operated in protected mode since its first appearance in 1992.

Protected mode assembly language programs may be written for both Linux and Windows releases from NT forward. (I exclude Windows 9x for technical reasons. Its memory model is an odd proprietary hybrid of real mode and protected mode, and very difficult to completely understand—and now almost entirely irrelevant.) Note well that programs written for Windows need not be graphical in nature. The easiest way to program in protected mode under Windows is to create *console applications*, which are text-mode programs that run in a text-mode window called a *console*. The console is controlled through a command line almost identical to the one in MS-DOS. Console applications use protected mode flat model and are fairly straightforward compared to writing Windows GUI applications. The default mode for Linux is a text console, so it's even easier to create assembly programs for Linux, and a lot more people appear to be doing it. The memory model is very much the same.

I've drawn the protected mode flat model in Figure 4-10. Your program sees a single block of memory addresses running from zero to a little over 4 gigabytes. Each address is a 32-bit quantity. All of the general-purpose registers are 32 bits in size, so one GP register can point to any location in the full 4GB address space. The instruction pointer is 32 bits in size as well, so EIP can indicate any machine instruction anywhere in the 4GB of memory.

The segment registers still exist, but they work in a radically different way. Not only don't you have to fool with them; you *can't*. The segment registers are now considered part of the operating system, and in almost all cases you can neither read nor change them directly. Their new job is to define where your 4GB memory space exists in physical or virtual memory. Physical memory may be much larger than 4GB, and currently 4GB of memory is not especially expensive. However, a 32-bit register can only express 4,294,967,296 different locations. If you have more than 4GB of memory in your computer, the operating system must arrange a 4GB region within memory, and your programs are limited to operating in this region. Defining where in your larger memory system this 4GB region falls is the job of the segment registers, and the operating system keeps them very close to its vest.

I won't say a great deal about virtual memory in this book. It's a system whereby a much larger memory space can be "mapped" onto disk storage, so that even with only 4GB of physical memory in your machine, the CPU can address a "virtual" memory space millions of bytes larger. Again, this is handled by the operating system, and handled in a way that is almost completely transparent to the software that you write.

It's enough to understand that when your program runs, it receives a 4GB address space in which to play, and any 32-bit register can potentially address any of those 4 billion memory locations, all by itself. This is an oversimplification, especially for ordinary Intel-based desktop PCs. Not all of the 4GB is at your program's disposal, and there are certain parts of the memory space that you can't use or even look at. Unfortunately, the rules are specific to the operating system you're running under, and I can't generalize too far without specifying Linux or Windows NT or some other protected-mode OS.

But it's worth taking a look back at Figure 4-8 and comparing real mode flat model to protected mode flat model. The main difference is that in real mode flat model, your program owns the full 64K of memory that the operating system hands it. In protected mode flat model, you are given a portion of 4GB of memory as your own, while other portions still belong to the operating system. Apart from that, the similarities are striking: a general-purpose (GP) register can *by itself* specify any memory location in the full memory address space, and the segment registers are really the tools of the operating system—not you, the programmer. (Again, in protected mode flat model, a GP register can *hold* the address of any location in its 4GB space, but attempting to actually read from or write to certain locations will be forbidden by the OS and trigger a runtime error.)

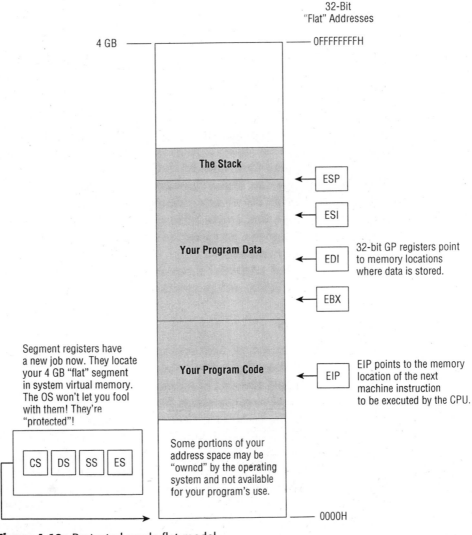

Figure 4-10: Protected mode flat model

Note that we haven't really talked about machine instructions in detail yet, and we've been able to pretty crisply define the universe in which machine instructions exist and work. Memory addressing and registers are key in this business. If you know them, the instructions will be a snap. If you don't know them, the instructions won't do you any good!

What difficulty exists in programming for protected mode flat model lies in understanding the operating system, its requirements, and its restrictions. This can be a substantial amount of learning: Windows NT and Linux are major operating systems that can take years of study to understand well. I'm going to introduce you to protected mode assembly programming in flat model in this book, but you're going to have to learn the operating system on your own. This book is only the beginning—there's a long road out there to be walked, and you're barely off the curb.

What Protected Mode Won't Let Us Do Anymore

People coming to this book with some knowledge of DOS may recall that in the DOS environment, the entire machine was "wide open" to access from DOS programs. DOS, of course, was a 16-bit operating system, and could only access the lowest 1MB of memory address space. However, a lot of interesting things resided in that address space, and they were no farther away than loading an address into DS:AX and having fun. Those days are long gone, and we're all better off for it, but there was an intoxicating simplicity in performing a lot of useful functions that I confess that I miss. That simplicity made explaining basic assembly language techniques a lot easier, as people who have read the earlier editions of this book may remember.

It's useful to understand what protected mode no longer allows us to do, especially if (like me) you were active as a programmer in the DOS era.

Memory-Mapped Video

The original IBM PC used a very simple and extremely clever mechanism for displaying text and low-resolution (by today's standards) graphics. A video adapter board contained a certain amount of memory, and this memory was "mapped in" to the PC's physical memory space. In other words, there was no "magic" involved in accessing the video board's memory. Simply writing data to a segment:offset memory address somewhere within the range of memory contained on the video adapter board displayed something on the monitor.

This technique allowed programs to display full screens of text that just "popped" into view, without any sense of the text gradually appearing from the top to the bottom, even on early machines with bogglingly slow CPU chips. The organization of the memory buffer was simple: starting at address 0B00:0 (or 0B800:0 for color displays) was an array of two-byte words. The first byte in each word was an ASCII character code. For example, the number 41H encoded the capital letter 'A'. The second byte was a text attribute: the color of the glyph, the color of the background portion of the character cell, or special presentations like underlining.

This arrangement made it very easy and very fast to display text using relatively simple assembly language libraries. Unfortunately, direct access like this to system peripherals is a violation of protected mode's protections. The "why" is simple: Protected mode makes it possible for multiple programs to execute at the same time, and if more than one executing program attempted to change display memory at the same time, video chaos would result. Good ol' DOS was strictly a single-tasking operating system, so only one program was ever running at a time anyway.

To have multitasking in a way that makes sense, an operating system has to "manage" access to video, through elaborate video-display code libraries that in turn access the display hardware through driver software running alongside the kernel in kernel space. Drivers enable the operating system to confine a single program's video output to a window on the screen, so that any reasonable number of running programs can display their output simultaneously without bumping into output from all the other programs.

Now, with all that said, there *is* a way to set up a buffer in user memory and then tell Linux to use it for video display. This involves some fusswork around the Linux framebuffer device dev/fb0 and the mmap and ioctl functions, but it is nowhere near as simple, and nowhere near as fast. The mechanism is useful for porting ancient DOS programs to Linux, but for new programs, it's far more trouble than it's worth. Later in this book I'll demonstrate the favored Linux method for handling text screen output, using a console window and VT100 control sequences.

Direct Access to Port Hardware

Back in the DOS era, PCs had serial and parallel ports controlled by separate controller chips on the motherboard. Like everything else in the machine, these controller chips could be directly accessed by any software running under DOS. By writing bit-mapped control values to the chips and creating custom interrupt service routines, one could create custom "fine-tuned" serial interface software, which enabled the plodding 300-character-per-second dial-up modems of that time to work as fast as they were capable. That was routine, but with some cleverness, you could make standard computer hardware do things it was not really intended to do. By studying the hardware controllers for the machine's parallel port, for example, I was able to write a two-way communications system in assembly that moved data very quickly from one computer to another through their parallel ports. (This was actually pre-PC, using CP/M for the Z80 CPU.)

Again, as with video, the requirements of multitasking demand that the operating system manage access to ports, which it does through drivers and code libraries; but unlike video, using drivers for interface to ports is actually *much* simpler than completely controlling the ports yourself, and I do not mourn those "bad old days."

Direct Calls into the BIOS

The third DOS-era technique we've had to surrender to the rigors of protected mode is direct calls to PC BIOS routines. As I explained in Chapter 3, IBM placed a code library in read-only memory for basic management of video and peripherals like ports. In the DOS era it was possible for software to call into these BIOS routines directly and without limitation. In earlier editions of this book, I explained how this was done in connection with management of text video.

Protected mode reserves BIOS calls to the operating system, but in truth, even protected-mode operating systems do little with direct BIOS calls these days. Almost all low-level access to hardware is done through installable drivers. Operating systems mostly make BIOS calls to determine hardware configuration information for things like power management.

As a sort of consolation prize, Linux provides a list of low-level functions that may be called through a mechanism very similar to BIOS calls, using software interrupt 80H. I'll explain what software interrupts are and how they're used later in this book.

Looking Ahead: 64-Bit "Long Mode"

The future is already with us, and you can buy it at Fry's. All but the least expensive desktop PCs these days contain AMD or Intel CPUs that are technically 64 bits "wide." In order to use these 64-bit features, you need an operating system that was explicitly compiled for them and knows how to manage them. Both Windows and Linux are available in versions compiled for 64-bit "long mode." Windows Vista and Windows XP have both been available in 64-bit versions for some time. Windows 7 will be (as best we know) available in both 32-bit and 64-bit versions. For both Windows and Ubuntu Linux, you have to choose which version you want. One size does not "fit all." In this book I'm focusing on the 32-bit version of Linux, with the reassurance that everything will run on 64-bit Linux in 32-bit compatibility mode. However, it's useful to get a sense of what long mode offers, so that you can explore it on your own as your programming skills mature.

The 64-bit x86 architecture has a peculiar history: in 2000, Intel's competitor AMD announced a 64-bit superset of the IA-32 architecture. AMD did not release CPUs implementing this new architecture until 2003, but it was a pre-emptive strike in the CPU wars. Intel already had a 64-bit architecture called IA-64 Itanium, but Itanium was a clean break with IA-32, and IA-32 software would not run on Itanium CPUs without recompilation, and, in some cases, recoding. The industry wanted backward compatibility, and the response to AMD's new architecture was so enthusiastic that Intel was forced to play catch-up and implement an AMD-compatible architecture, which it named Intel 64. Intel's first AMD-compatible 64-bit CPUs were released in late 2004. The vendor-neutral term "x86-64" is now being applied to features implemented identically by both companies.

The x86-64 architecture defines three general modes: real mode, protected mode, and long mode. Real mode is a compatibility mode that enables the CPU to run older real-mode operating systems and software like DOS and Windows 3.1. In real mode the CPU works just like an 8086 or other x86 CPU does in real mode, and supports real mode flat model and real mode segmented model. Protected mode is also a compatibility mode, and makes the CPU "look like" an IA-32 CPU to software, so that x86-64 CPUs can run Windows 2000/XP/Vista/7 and other 32-bit operating systems like Linux, plus their 32-bit drivers and applications.

Long mode is a true 64-bit mode; and when the CPU is in long mode, all registers are 64 bits wide, and all machine instructions that act on 64-bit operands are available.

All of the registers available in IA-32 are there, and have been extended to 64 bits in width. The 64-bit versions of the registers are renamed beginning with an R: EAX becomes RAX, EBX becomes RBX, and so on. Over and above the familiar general-purpose registers present in IA-32, there are eight brand-new 64-bit general-purpose registers with no 32-bit counterparts. These brand-new registers are named R8 through R15. I haven't said much about the x86 architecture's fast math features, and won't in this book, but x86-64 adds eight 128-bit SSE registers to IA-32's eight, for a total of 16.

All of these new registers are like manna from heaven to assembly programmers seeking increases in execution speed. The fastest place to store data is in registers, and programmers who suffered under the register scarcity of the early x86 CPUs will look at that pile of internal wealth and gasp.

64-Bit Memory: What May Be Possible Someday vs. What We Can Do Now

As I've described earlier, 32 bits can address only 4 gigabytes of memory. Various tricks have been used to make more memory available to programs running on IA-32 CPUs. In 64-bit long mode we have something like the opposite problem: 64 bits can address such a boggling immensity of memory that memory systems *requiring* 64 bits' worth of address space will not be created for a good many years yet. (I hedge a little here by reminding myself and all of you that we've said things like that before, only to get our noses rubbed in it.)

64 bits can address 16 exabytes. An exabyte is 2^{60} bytes, which may be described more comprehensibly as a billion gigabytes, which is a little over one quintillion bytes. Our computer hardware will get there someday, but we're not there yet. The kicker for the here and now is this: managing all the bits in those 64-bit addresses takes transistors within the CPU's microarchitecture. So rather than waste transistors on the chip managing memory address lines that will not be used within the expected lifetime of the CPU chip (or even the x86-64 architecture itself), chipmakers have limited the number of address lines that are actually functional within current chip implementations.

The x86-64 CPU chips that you can buy today implement 48 address bits for virtual memory, and only 40 bits for physical memory. That's still far more physical memory than you can stuff into any physical computer at present: 2^{40} represents one terabyte; basically a little over a thousand gigabytes, or one trillion bytes. I know of higher-end machines that can accept 64GB. A terabyte is a few years off yet.

I say all this to emphasize that you're not cheating yourself out of anything by programming for the IA-32 architecture now and for the next few years. The NASM assembler that I'll be describing in the next chapter can generate code for 64-bit long mode, and if you have a 64-bit version of Linux installed, you can write code for it right now. There are some differences in the way that 64-bit Linux handles function calls, but 64-bit long mode is still a flat model, and it is far more similar to 32-bit flat model than 32-bit flat model is to the benighted real mode segmented model that we suffered under for the first 15 or 20 years of the PC era.

That's enough for the time being about the platform on which our code will run. It's time to start talking about the process of writing assembly language programs, and the tools with which we'll be doing it.

CHAPTER 5

The Right to Assemble

The Process of Creating Assembly Language Programs

Rudyard Kipling's poem "In the Neolithic Age" (1895) gives us a tidy little scold on tribal certainty. Having laid about himself successfully with his trusty diorite tomahawk, the poem's Neolithic narrator eats his former enemies while congratulating himself for following the One True Tribal Path. Alas, his totem pole has other thoughts, and in a midnight vision puts our cocky narrator in his place:

"There are nine and sixty ways of constructing tribal lays,
And *every single one of them is right!*"

The moral of the poem: Trust your totem pole. What's true of tribal lays is also true of programming methodologies. There are at *least* nine and sixty ways of making programs, and I've tried most of them over the years. They're all different, but they all work, in that they all produce programs that can be loaded and run—once the programmer figures out how to follow a particular method and use the tools that go with it.

Still, although all these programming techniques work, they are not interchangeable, and what works for one programming language or tool set will not apply to another programming language or tool set. In 1977 I learned to program in a language called APL (A Programming Language; how profound) by typing in lines of code and watching what each one did. That was the way that APL worked: Each line was mostly an independent entity, which performed a calculation or some sort of array manipulation, and once you

109

pressed Enter the line would crunch up a result and print it for you. (I learned it on a Selectric printer/terminal.) You could string lines together, of course, and I did, but it was an intoxicating way to produce a program from an initial state of total ignorance, testing everything one single microstep at a time.

Later I learned BASIC almost the same way that I learned APL, and later still Perl, but there were other languages that demanded other techniques. Pascal and C both required significant study beforehand, because you can't just hammer in one line and execute it independently. Much later still, when Windows went mainstream, Visual Basic and especially Delphi changed the rules radically. Programming became a sort of stimulus-response mechanism, in which the operating system sent up stimuli called *events* (keystrokes, mouse clicks, and so on) and simple programs consisted mostly of responses to those events.

Assembly language is not constructed the same way that C, Java, or Pascal is constructed. Very pointedly, you *cannot* write assembly language programs by trial and error, nor can you do it by letting other people do your thinking for you. It is a complicated and tricky process compared to BASIC or Perl or such visual environments as Delphi, Lazarus, or Gambas. You have to pay attention. You have to read the sheet music. And most of all, you have to practice.

In this chapter I'm going to teach you assembly language's tribal lays as I've learned them.

Files and What's Inside Them

All programming is about processing files. Some programming methods hide some of those files, and all methods to some extent strive to make it easier for human beings to understand what's inside those files; but the bottom line is you'll be creating files, processing files, reading files, and executing files.

Most people understand that a file is a collection of data stored on a medium of some kind: a hard disk drive, a thumb drive or Flash card, an optical disk, or an occasional exotic device of some sort. The collection of data is given a name and manipulated as a unit. Your operating system governs the management of files on storage media. Ultimately, it brings up data from within a file for you to see, and writes the changes that you make back to the file or to a new file that you create with the operating system's help.

Assembly language is notable in that it hides almost nothing from you; and to be good at it, you have to be willing to go inside any file that you deal with and understand it down to the byte and often the bit level. This takes longer, but it pays a huge dividend in knowledge: you will know how everything works. APL and BASIC, by contrast, were mysteries. I typed in a line, and the computer spat back a response. What happened in between was hidden very well. In assembly language, you see it *all*. The trick is to understand what you're looking at.

Binary Files vs. Text Files

The looking isn't always easy. If you've worked with Windows or Linux (and before that, DOS) for any length of time, you may have a sense of the differences between files in terms of how you "look at" them. A simple text file is opened and examined in a simple text editor. A word processor file is opened in the species of word processor that created it. A PowerPoint presentation file is opened from inside the PowerPoint application. If you try to load it into Word or Excel, the application will display garbage, or (more likely) politely refuse to obey the open command. Trying to open an executable program file in a word processor or other text editor will generally get you either nowhere or screen garbage.

Text files are files that can be opened and examined meaningfully in a text editor, such as Notepad in Windows, or any of the many text editors available for Linux. *Binary files* are files containing values that do not display meaningfully as text. Most higher-end word processors confuse the issue by manipulating text and then mixing the text with formatting information that does not translate into text, but instead dictates things such as paragraph spacing, line height, and so on. Open a Word or OpenOffice document in a simple text editor and you'll see what I mean.

Text files contain uppercase and lowercase letters and numeric digits, plus odd symbols like punctuation. There are 94 such visible characters. Text files also contain a group of characters called *whitespace*. Whitespace characters give text files their structure by dividing them into lines and providing space within lines. These include the familiar space character, the tab character, the newline character that indicates a line end, and sometimes a couple of others. There are also fossil characters such as the BEL character, which was used decades ago to ring the little mechanical brass bell in teletype machines, and while BEL is technically considered whitespace, most text editors simply ignore it.

Text files in the PC world are a little more complicated, because there are another 127 characters containing glyphs for mathematical symbols, characters with accent marks and other modifiers, Greek letters, and "box draw" characters that were widely used in ancient times for drawing screen forms, before graphical user interfaces such as Windows and Gnome. How well these additional characters display in a text editor or terminal window depends entirely on the text editor or terminal window and how it is configured.

Text files become even more complex when you introduce non-Western alphabets through the Unicode standard. Explaining Unicode in detail is beyond the scope of this book, but good introductions are available on Wikipedia and elsewhere.

Text files are easy to display, edit, and understand. Alas, there's a *lot* more to the programming world than text files. In previous chapters, I defined what a computer program is, from the computer's perspective. A program is, metaphorically, a long journey in very small steps. These steps are a list of binary values representing machine instructions that direct the CPU to do what it must to accomplish the job at hand. These machine instructions, even in their hexadecimal shorthand form, are gobbledygook to human beings. Here's a short sequence of binary values expressed in hexadecimal:

```
FE FF A2 37 4C 0A 29 00 91 CB 60 61 E8 E3 20 00 A8 00 B8 29 1F FF 69 55
```

Is this part of a real program or isn't it? You'd probably have to ask the CPU to find out, unless you were a machine-code maniac of the kind that hasn't been seen since 1978. (It isn't.)

But the CPU has no trouble with programs presented in this form. In fact, the CPU can't handle programs any other way. The CPU itself simply isn't equipped to understand and obey a string of characters such as

```
LET X = 42
```

or even something that we out here would call assembly language:

```
mov eax,42
```

To the CPU, it's binary only. The CPU just *might* interpret a sequence of text characters as binary machine instructions, but if this happened it would be pure coincidence, and the coincidence would not go on longer than three or four characters' worth. Nor would the sequence of instructions be likely to do anything useful.

From a height, the process of assembly language programming (or programming in many other languages) consists of taking human-readable text files and translating them somehow into files containing sequences of binary machine instructions that the CPU can understand. You, as a programmer, need to understand which files are which (a lot more on this later) and how each is processed. Also, you need to be able to "open" an executable binary file and examine the binary values that it contains.

Looking at File Internals with the Bless Editor

Very fortunately, there are utilities that can open, display, and enable you to change characters or binary bytes inside *any* kind of file. These are called *binary editors* or *hexadecimal editors*, and the best of them in my experience (at least for the Linux world) is the Bless Hex Editor. It was designed to operate under graphical user interfaces such as Gnome, and it is very easy to figure out by exploring the menus.

Bless is not installed by default under Ubuntu. You can download it free of charge from its home page:

```
http://home.gna.org/bless/
```

However, you can very easily install it from the Ubuntu Applications menu. Select Add/Remove and leave the view set to All (the default). Type **Bless** in the Search field, and the Bless Hex Editor should be the only item to appear. (Give it a few seconds to search; the item won't appear instantaneously.) Check its check box to select it for installation, and then click Apply. Once installed, the Bless Hex Editor will be available in Applications → Programming, or you can create a desktop launcher for it if you prefer.

Demonstrating Bless will also demonstrate why it's necessary for programmers to understand even text files at the byte level. In the listings archive for this book (see the Introduction for the URL) are two files, samwindows.txt and samlinux.txt. Extract them both. Launch Bless, and using the File → Open command, open samlinux.txt. When that file has been opened, use File → Open again to open samwindows.txt. What you'll see should look like Figure 5-1.

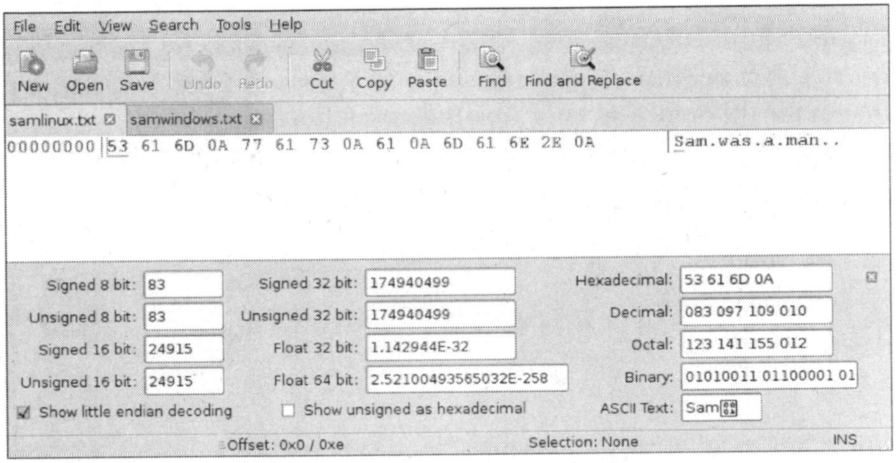

Figure 5-1: Displaying a Linux text file with the Bless Hex Editor

I've shortened the display pane vertically just to save space here on the printed page; after all, the file itself is only about 15 bytes long. Each opened file has a tab in the display pane, and you can switch instantly between files by clicking on the tabs.

The display pane is divided into three parts. The left column is the offset column. It contains the offset from the beginning of the file for the first byte displayed on that line in the center column. The offset is given in hexadecimal. If you're at the beginning of the file, the offset column will be 00000000. The center column is the hex display column. It displays a line of data bytes from the file in hexadecimal format. How many bytes are shown depends on how you size the Bless window and what screen resolution you're using. The minimum number of bytes displayed is (somewhat oddly) seventeen. In the center column the display is always in hexadecimal, with each byte separated from adjacent bytes by a space. The right column is the same line of data with any "visible" text characters displayed as text. Nondisplayable binary values are represented by period characters.

If you click on the samwindows.txt tab, you'll see the same display for the other file, which was created using the Windows Notepad text editor. The samwindows.txt file is a little longer, and you have a second line of data bytes in the center column. The offset for the second line is 00000012. This is the offset in hex of the first (and in this case, the only) byte in the second line.

Why are the two files different? Bring up a terminal window and use the `cat` command to display both files. The display in either case will be identical:

```
Sam
was
a
man.
```

Figure 5-2 shows the Bless editor displaying samwindows.txt. Look carefully at the two files as Bless displays them (or at Figures 5-1 and 5-2) and try to figure out the difference on your own before continuing.

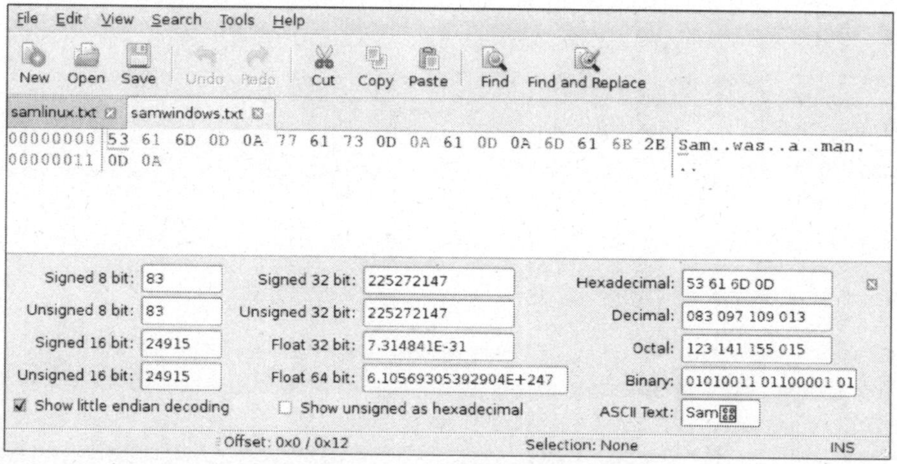

Figure 5-2: Displaying a Windows text file with the Bless editor

At the end of each line of text in both files is a 0AH byte. The Windows version of the file has a little something extra: a 0DH byte preceding each 0AH byte. The Linux file lacks the 0DH bytes. As standardized as "plain" text files are, there can be minor differences depending on the operating system under which the files were created. As a convention, Windows text files (and DOS text files in older times) mark the end of each line with two characters: 0DH followed by 0AH. Linux (and nearly all Unix-descendent operating systems) mark the end of each line with a 0AH byte only.

As you've seen in using `cat` on the two files, Linux displays both versions identically and accurately. However, if you were to take the Linux version of the file and load it into the Windows Notepad text editor, you'd see something a little different, as shown in Figure 5-3.

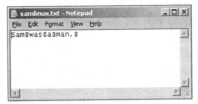

Figure 5-3: A Linux text file displayed under Windows

Notepad expects to see both the 0DH and the 0AH at the end of each text line, and doesn't understand a lonely 0AH value as an end-of-line (EOL) marker. Instead, it inserts a thin rectangle everywhere it sees a 0AH, as it would for any single character that it didn't know how to display or interpret. Not all Windows software is that fussy. Many or most other Windows utilities understand that 0AH is a perfectly good EOL marker.

The 0DH bytes at the end of each line are another example of a "fossil" character. Decades ago, in the Teletype era, there were two separate electrical commands built into Teletype machines to handle the end of a text line when printing a document. One command indexed the paper upward to the next line, and the other returned the print head to the left margin. These were called *line feed* and *carriage return*, respectively. Carriage return was encoded as 0DH and line feed as 0AH. Most computer systems and software now ignore the carriage return code, though a few (like Notepad) still require it for proper display of text files.

This small difference in text file standards won't be a big issue for you, and if you're importing files from Windows into Linux, you can easily remove the extra carriage return characters manually, or—what a notion!—write a small program in assembly to do it for you. What's important for now is that you understand how to load a file into the Bless Hex Editor (or whatever hex editor you prefer; there are many) and inspect the file at the individual byte level.

You can do more with Bless than just look. Editing of a loaded file can be done in either the center (binary) column or the right (text) column. You can bounce the edit cursor between the two columns by pressing the Tab key. Within either column, the cursor can be moved from byte to byte by using the standalone arrow keys. Bless respects the state of the Insert key, and you can either type over or insert bytes as appropriate.

I shouldn't have to say that once you've made changes to a file, save it back to disk by clicking the Save button.

Interpreting Raw Data

Seeing a text file as a line of hexadecimal values is a very good lesson in a fundamental principle of computing: *Everything is made of bits, and bit patterns mean what we agree that they mean.* The capital letter "S" that begins both of the two text files displayed in Bless is the hexadecimal number 53H. It is also the decimal number 83. At the very bottom, it is a pattern of eight bits: 01010011. Within this file, we agree among ourselves that the bit pattern 01010011 represents a capital "S." In an executable binary file, the bit pattern 01010011 might mean something entirely different, depending on where in the file it happened to be, and what other bit patterns existed nearby in the file.

This is why the lower pane of the Bless Hex Editor exists. It takes the sequence of bytes that begins at the cursor and shows you all the various ways that those bytes may be interpreted. Remember that you won't always be looking at text files in a hex editor like Bless. You may be examining a data file generated by a program you're writing, and that data file may represent a sequence of 32-bit signed integers; or a sequence of unsigned 16-bit integers; or a sequence of 64-bit floating-point numbers; or a mixture of any or all of the above. All you'll see in the center pane is a series of hexadecimal values. What those values represent depends on what program wrote those values to the file and what those values stand for in the "real" world. Are they dollar amounts? Measurements? Data points generated by some sort of instrument? That's up to you—and to the software that you use. The file, as with all files, is simply a sequence of binary patterns stored somewhere that we display (using Bless) as hexadecimal values to make them easier to understand and manipulate.

Bounce the cursor around the list of hex values in the center column and watch how the interpretations in the bottom pane change. Note that some of the interpretations look at only one byte (8 bits), others two bytes (16 bits), or four bytes (32 bits), or eight bytes (64 bits). In every case the sequence of bytes being interpreted begins at the cursor and goes toward the right. For example, with the cursor at the first position in the file:

- 53H may be interpreted as decimal value 83.
- 53 61H may be interpreted as decimal 21345.
- 53 61 6D 0AH may be interpreted as decimal 1398893834.
- 53 61 6D 0A 77 61 73 0AH may be interpreted as the floating-point number 4.54365038640977[93].

(The differences between a signed value and an unsigned value will have to wait until later in this book.) The important thing to understand is that in all cases it's the very same sequence of bytes at the very same location within the file. All that changes is how many bytes we look at, and what kind of value we want that sequence of bytes to represent.

This may become clearer later when we begin writing programs that work on numbers. And, speaking of numbers . . .

"Endianness"

In the lower-left corner of the bottom pane of the Bless editor is a check box marked "Show little endian decoding." By default the box is not checked, but in almost all cases it should be. The box tells Bless whether to interpret sequences of bytes as numeric values in "big endian" order or in "little endian" order. If you click and unclick the check box, the values displayed in the lower pane will change radically, even if you don't move the cursor. When you change the state of that check box, you are changing the way that the Bless editor interprets a sequence of bytes in a file as some sort of number.

If you recall from Chapter 4, a single byte can represent numbers from 0 to 255. If you want to represent a number larger than 255, you must use more than one byte to do it. A sequence of two bytes in a row can represent any number from 0 to 65,535. However, once you have more than one byte representing a numeric value, *the order of the bytes becomes crucial.*

Let's go back to the first two bytes in either of the two files we loaded earlier into Bless. They're nominally the letters "S" and "a," but that is simply another interpretation. The hexadecimal sequence 53 61H may also be interpreted as a number. The 53H appears first in the file. The 61H appears after it (see Figures 5-1 and 5-2). So, taken together as a single 16-bit value, the two bytes become the hex number 53 61H.

Or do they? Perhaps a little weirdly, it's not that simple. See Figure 5-4. The left part of the figure is a little excerpt of the information shown in the Bless hex display pane for our example text file. It shows only the first two bytes and their offsets from the beginning of the file. The right portion of the figure is the very same information, but reversed left-for-right, as though seen in a mirror. It's the same bytes in the same order, but we see them differently. What we assumed at first was the 16-bit hex number 53 61H now appears to be 61 53H.

Did the number change? Not from the computer's perspective. All that changed was the way we printed it on the page of this book. By custom, people reading English start at the left and read toward the right. The layout of the Bless hex editor display reflects that. But many other languages in the world, including Hebrew and Arabic, start at the right margin and read toward the left. An Arabic programmer's first impulse might be to see the two bytes as 61 53H, especially if he or she is using software designed for the Arabic language conventions, displaying file contents from right to left.

It's actually more confusing than that. Western languages (including English) are a little schizoid, in that they read *text* from left to right, but

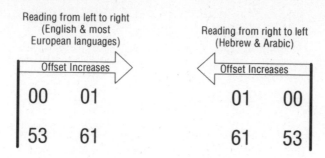

So is it "53 61H" or "61 53H" ?

Figure 5-4: Differences in display order vs. differences in evaluation order

evaluate numeric columns from right to left. The number 426 consists of four hundreds, two tens, and six ones, not four ones, two tens, and six hundreds. By convention here in the West, the least significant column is at the right, and the values of the columns increase from right to left. The most significant column is the leftmost.

Confusion is a bad idea in computing. So whether or not a sequence of bytes is displayed from left to right or from right to left, we all have to agree on which of those bytes represents the least significant figure in a multibyte number, and which the most significant figure. In a computer, we have two options:

- We can agree that the least significant byte of a multibyte value is at the lowest offset, and the most significant byte is at the highest offset.

- We can agree that the most significant byte of a multibyte is at the lowest offset, and the least significant byte is at the highest offset.

These two choices are mutually exclusive. A computer must operate using one choice or the other; they cannot both be used at the same time at the whim of a program. Furthermore, this choice is not limited to the operating system, or to a particular program. The choice is baked right into the silicon of the CPU and its instruction set. A computer architecture that stores the least significant byte of a multibyte value at the lowest offset is called *little endian*. A computer architecture that stores the most significant byte of a multibyte value at the lowest offset is called *big endian*.

Figure 5-5 should make this clearer. In big endian systems, a multibyte value begins with its *most* significant byte. In little endian systems, a multibyte value begins with its *least* significant byte. Think: big endian, big end first; little endian, little end first.

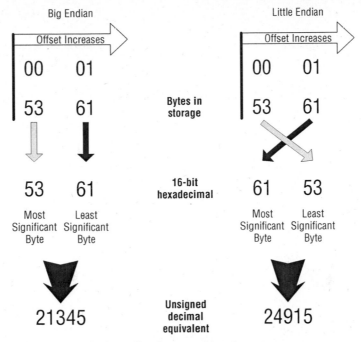

Figure 5-5: Big endian vs. little endian for a 16-bit value

There are *big* differences at stake here! The two bytes that begin our example text file represent the decimal number 21,345 in a big endian system, but 24,915 in a little endian system.

It's possible to do quite a bit of programming without being aware of a system's "endianness." If you program in higher-level languages like Visual Basic, Delphi, or C, most of the consequences of endianness are hidden by the language and the language compiler—at least until something goes wrong at a low level. Once you start reading files at a byte level, you have to know how to read them; and if you're programming in assembly language, you had better be comfortable with endianness going in.

Reading hex displays of numeric data in big endian systems is easy, because the digits appear in the order that Western people expect, with the most significant digits on the left. In little endian systems, everything is reversed; and the more bytes used to represent a number, the more confusing it can become. Figure 5-6 shows the endian differences between evaluations of a 32-bit value. Little endian programmers have to read hex displays of multibyte values as though they were reading Hebrew or Arabic, from right to left.

Remember that endianness differences apply not only to bytes stored in files but also to bytes stored in memory. When (as I'll explain later) you inspect numeric values stored in memory with a debugger, all the same rules apply.

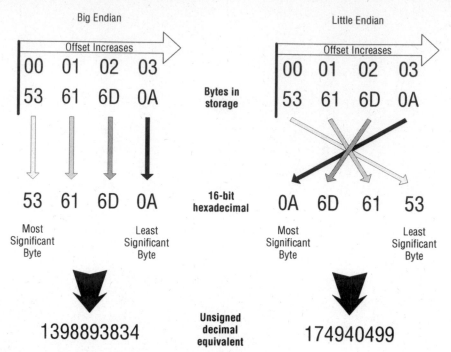

Figure 5-6: Big endian vs. little endian for a 32-bit value

So, which "endianness" do Linux systems use? Both! (Though not at the same time . . .) Again, it's not about operating systems. The entire x86 hardware architecture, from the lowly 8086 up to the latest Core 2 Quad, is little endian. Other hardware architectures, such as Motorola's 68000 and the original PowerPC, and most IBM mainframe architectures like System/370, are big endian. More recent hardware architectures have been designed as *bi-endian*, meaning they can be configured (with some difficulty) to interpret numeric values one way or the other at the hardware level. Alpha, MIPS, and Intel's Itanium architecture are bi-endian.

If (as mostly likely) you're running Linux on an ordinary x86 CPU, you'll be little endian, and you should check the box on the Bless editor labeled "Show little endian decoding." Other programming tools may offer you the option of selecting big endian display or little endian display. Make sure that whatever tools you use, you have the correct option selected.

Linux, of course, can be made to run on *any* hardware architecture, so using Linux doesn't guarantee that you will be facing a big endian or little endian system, and that's one reason I've gone on at some length about endianness here. You have to know from studying the system what endianness is currently in force, though you can learn it by inspection: store a 32-bit integer to memory and then look at it with a debugger or a hex editor like Bless. If you know your hex (and you had *better*!) the system's endianness will jump right out at you.

Text In, Code Out

From a height, all programming is a matter of processing files. The goal is to take one or more human-readable text files and then process them to create an executable program file that you can load and run under whatever operating system you're using. For this book, that would be Linux, but the general process that I describe in this section applies to almost any kind of programming under almost any operating system.

Programming as a process varies wildly by language and by the set of tools that support the language. In modern graphical interactive development environments such as Visual Basic and Delphi, much of file processing is done "behind the scenes" while you, the programmer, are staring at one or more files on display and pondering your next move. In assembly language that's not the case. Most assembly language programmers use a much simpler tool set, and explicitly process the files as sequences of discrete steps entered from a command line or a script file.

However it's done, the general process of converting text files to binary files is one of translation, and the programs that do it are as a class called translators. A *translator* is a program that accepts human-readable source files and generates some kind of binary file. The output binary file could be an executable program file that the CPU can understand, or it could be a font file, or a compressed binary data file, or any of a hundred other types of binary file.

Program translators are translators that generate machine instructions that the CPU can understand. A program translator reads a source code file line by line, and writes a binary file of machine instructions that accomplishes the computer actions described by the source code file. This binary file is called an *object code file*.

A *compiler* is a program translator that reads in source code files written in higher-level languages such as C or Pascal and writes out object code files.

An *assembler* is a special type of compiler. It, too, is a program translator that reads source code files and outputs object code files for execution by the CPU. However, an assembler is a translator designed specifically to translate what we call *assembly language* into object code. In the same sense that a language compiler for Pascal or C++ compiles a source code file to an object code file, we say that an assembler *assembles* an assembly language source code file to an object code file. The process, one of translation, is similar in both cases. Assembly language, however, has an overwhelmingly important characteristic that sets it apart from compilers: *total control over the object code*.

Assembly Language

Some people define assembly language as a language in which one line of source code generates one machine instruction. This has never been literally true, as some lines in an assembly language source code file are instructions to the translator program (rather than to the CPU) and do not generate machine instructions at all.

Here's a better definition:

Assembly language is a translator language that allows total control over every individual machine instruction generated by the translator program. Such a translator program is called an assembler.

Pascal or C++ compilers, conversely, make a multitude of invisible and inalterable decisions about how a given language statement will be translated into a sequence of machine instructions. For example, the following single Pascal statement assigns a value of 42 to a numeric variable called I:

```
I := 42;
```

When a Pascal compiler reads this line, it outputs a series of four or five machine instructions that take the literal numeric value 42 and store it in memory at a location encoded by the name I. Normally, you—the Pascal programmer—have *no idea* what these four or five instructions actually are, and you have utterly no way of changing them, even if you know a sequence of machine instructions that is faster and more efficient than the sequence used by the compiler. The Pascal compiler has its own way of generating machine instructions, and you have no choice but to accept what it writes to its object code file to accomplish the work of the Pascal statements you wrote in the source code file.

To be fair, modern high-level language compilers generally implement something called *in-line assembly*, which allows a programmer to "take back" control from the compiler and "drop in" a sequence of machine instructions of his or her own design. A great deal of modern assembly language work is done this way, but it's actually considered an advanced technique, because you first have to understand how the compiler generates its own code before you can "do better" using in-line assembly. (And don't assume, as many do, that you can do better than the compiler without a *great* deal of study and practice!)

An assembler sees *at least* one line in the source code file for every machine instruction that it generates. It typically sees more lines than that, and the additional lines deal with various other things, but *every* machine instruction in the final object code file is controlled by a corresponding line in the source code file.

Each of the CPU's many machine instructions has a corresponding *mnemonic* in assembly language. As the word suggests, these mnemonics began as devices to help programmers remember a particular binary machine instruction. For example, the mnemonic for binary machine instruction 9CH, which pushes the flags register onto the stack, is PUSHF—which is a country mile easier to remember than 9CH.

When you write your source code file in assembly language, you arrange series of mnemonics, typically one mnemonic per line in the source code text file. A portion of a source code file might look like this:

```
mov eax,4               ; 04H specifies the sys_write kernel call
mov ebx,1               ; 01H specifies stdout
mov ecx,Message         ; Load starting address of display string into ECX
mov edx,MessageLength   ; Load the number of chars to display into EDX
int 80H;                ; Make the kernel call
```

Here, the words MOV and MOV at the left margin are the mnemonics. The numbers and textual items to the immediate right of each mnemonic are that mnemonic's *operands*. There are various kinds of operands for various machine instructions, and some instructions (such as PUSHF mentioned previously) use no operands at all.

Taken together, a mnemonic and its operands are called an *instruction*. (Words to the right of the semicolons are comments, and are not part of the instructions.) This is the word I'll be using most of the time in this book to indicate the human-readable proxy of one of the CPU's pure binary machine code instructions. To talk about the binary code specifically, I'll always refer to a *machine instruction*.

The assembler's most important job is to read lines from the source code file and write machine instructions to an object code file (see Figure 5-7).

Mnemonic Operands   Comment

mov ebp,esp   ; Save the stack pointer in ebp

The assembler reads a line like this from the source code file, and writes the equivalent machine instruction to an object code file:

8BH ECH

Figure 5-7: What the assembler does

Comments

To the right of each instruction is text starting with a semicolon. This text is called a *comment*, and its purpose should be obvious: to cast some light on what the associated assembly language instruction is *for*. The instruction MOV EBX, ESP places the current value of the stack pointer into register ebx—but *why*? What is the instruction accomplishing in the context of the assembly language program that you're writing? Comments provide the why.

Structurally, a comment begins with the first semicolon on a line, and continues toward the right to the EOL marker at the end of that line. A comment does not need to be on the same line with an instruction. Much useful description in assembly language programs exists in *comment blocks*, which are sequences of lines consisting solely of comment text. Each line in a comment block begins with a semicolon at the left margin.

Far more than in any other programming language, comments are critical to the success of your assembly language programs. My own recommendation is that *every* instruction in your source code files should have a comment to its right. Furthermore, every group of instructions that act together in some way should be preceded by a comment block that explains that group of instructions "from a height" and how they work together.

Comments are one area where understanding how a text file is structured is very important—because in assembly language, comments end at the ends of lines. In most other languages such as Pascal and C, comments are placed *between* pairs of comment delimiters like (* and *), and EOL markers at line ends are ignored.

In short: *Comments begin at semicolons and end at EOL.*

Beware "Write-Only" Source Code!

This is as good a time as any to point out a serious problem with assembly language. The instructions themselves are almost vanishingly terse, and doing anything useful takes a *lot* of them. In addition, whereas each instruction states what it does, there is *nothing* to indicate a context within which that instruction operates. You can build that context into your Pascal or Basic code with some skill and discipline (along with identifiers that point to their purpose), but in assembly language you can add context only through comments.

Without context, assembly language starts to turn into what is called "write-only" code. It can happen like this: on November 1, in the heat of creation, you crank out about 300 instructions in a short utility program that does something important. You go back on January 1 to add a feature to the program—and discover that *you no longer remember how it works*. The individual instructions are all correct, and the program assembles and runs as it should, but knowledge of how it all came together and how it works from a height have vanished under the weight of Christmas memories and eight weeks of doing other things. In other words, you *wrote* it, but you can no longer *read* it, or change it. Voila! Write-only code.

Although it's true that comments do take up room in your source code disk files, they are *not* copied into your object code files, and a program with loads of comments in its source code runs *exactly* as fast as the same program with no comments at all.

You will be making a considerable investment in time and energy when you write assembly language programs—far more than in "halfway to heaven" languages such as C and C++, and unthinkably more than in "we do it all for you" IDEs such as Delphi, Lazarus, and Gambas. It's more difficult than just about any other way of writing programs; and if you don't comment, you may end up having to simply toss out hundreds of lines of inexplicable code and write it again, *from scratch*.

Work smart. Comment till you drop.

Object Code and Linkers

Assemblers read your source code files and generate an object code file containing the machine instructions that the CPU understands, plus any data you've defined in the source code.

There's no reason at all why an assembler could not read a source code file and write out a finished, executable program as its object code file, but this is almost never done. The assembler I'm teaching in this book, NASM, can do that for DOS programs, and can write out .COM executable files for the real mode flat model. More modern operating systems such as Linux and Windows are too complex for that, and in truth, there's no real payoff in such one-step assembly except when you're first learning to write assembly language.

So the object code files produced by modern assemblers are a sort of intermediate step between source code and executable program. This intermediate step is a type of binary file called an *object module*, or simply an object code file.

Object code files cannot themselves be run as programs. An additional step, called *linking*, is necessary to turn object code files into executable program files.

The reason for object code files as intermediate steps is that a single large source code file may be divided up into numerous smaller source code files to keep the files manageable in size and complexity. The assembler assembles the various fragments separately, and the several resulting object code files are then woven together into a single executable program file. This process is shown in Figure 5-8.

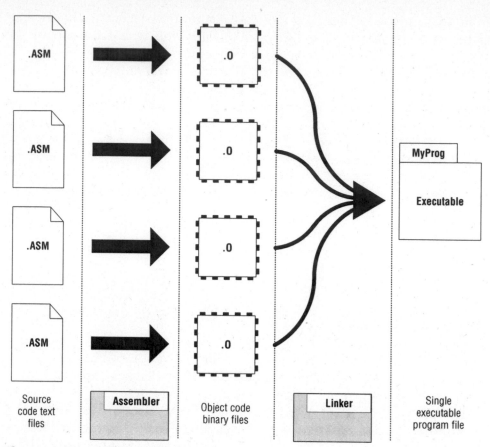

Figure 5-8: The assembler and linker

When you're first learning assembly programming, it's unlikely that you'll be writing programs spread out across several source code files. This may make the linker seem extraneous, as there's only one piece to your program and nothing to link together. Not so: the linker does more than just stitch lumps of object code together into a single piece. It ensures that function calls out of one object module arrive at the target object module, and that all the many memory references actually reference what they're supposed to reference. The assembler's job is obvious; the linker's job is subtle. Both are necessary to produce a finished, working executable file.

Besides, you'll very quickly get to the point where you begin extracting frequently used portions of your programs into your own personal code libraries. There are two reasons for doing this:

1. You can move tested, proven routines into separate libraries and link them into any program you write that might need them. This way, you

can reuse code and not build the same old wheels every time you begin a new programming project in assembly language.

2. Once portions of a program are tested and found to be correct, there's no need to waste time assembling them over and over again along with newer, untested portions of a program. Once a major program grows to tens of thousands of lines of code (and you'll get there sooner than you might think!) you can save a significant amount of time by assembling only the portion of a program that you are currently working on, linking the finished portions into the final program without re-assembling *every* single part of the whole thing every time you assemble *any* part of it.

The linker's job is complex and not easily described. Each object module may contain the following:

- Program code, including named procedures
- References to named procedures lying outside the module
- Named data objects such as numbers and strings with predefined values
- Named data objects that are just empty space "set aside" for the program's use later
- References to data objects lying outside the module
- Debugging information
- Other, less common odds and ends that help the linker create the executable file

To process several object modules into a single executable module, the linker must first build an index called a *symbol table*, with an entry for every named item in every object module it links, with information about what name (called a *symbol*) refers to what location within the module. Once the symbol table is complete, the linker builds an image of how the executable program will be arranged in memory when the operating system loads it. This image is then written to disk as the executable file.

The most important thing about the image that the linker builds relates to addresses. Object modules are allowed to refer to symbols in other object modules. During assembly, these *external references* are left as holes to be filled later—naturally enough, because the module in which these external symbols exist may not have been assembled or even written yet. As the linker builds an image of the eventual executable program file, it learns where all of the symbols are located within the image, and thus can drop real addresses into all of the external reference holes.

Debugging information is, in a sense, a step backward: portions of the source code, which was all stripped out early in the assembly process, are put back in the object module by the assembler. These portions of the source code are mostly the names of data items and procedures, and they're embedded in the object file to make it easier for the programmer (you!) to see the names of data items when you debug the program. (I'll go into this more deeply later.) Debugging information is optional; that is, the linker does not need it to build a proper executable file. You choose to embed debugging information in the object file while you're still working on the program. Once the program is finished and debugged to the best of your ability, you run the assembler and linker one more time, without requesting debugging information. This is important, because debugging information can make your executable files *hugely* larger than they otherwise would be, and generally a little slower.

Relocatability

Very early computer systems like 8080 systems running CP/M-80 had a very simple memory architecture. Programs were written to be loaded and run at a specific physical memory address. For CP/M, this was 100H. The programmer could assume that any program would start at 100H and go up from there. Memory addresses of data items and procedures were actual physical addresses, and every time the program ran, its data items were loaded and referenced at *precisely* the same place in memory.

This all changed with the arrival of the 8086 and 8086-specific operating systems such as CP/M-86 and PC DOS. Improvements in the Intel architecture introduced with the 8086 made it unnecessary for the program to be assembled for running at a specific physical address. All references within an executable program were specified as relative to the beginning of the program. A variable, for example, would no longer be reliably located at the physical address 02C7H in memory. Instead, it was reliably located at an offset from the beginning of the file. This offset was always the same; and because all references were relative to the beginning of the executable program file, it didn't matter where the program was placed in physical memory when it ran.

This feature is called *relocatability*, and it is a necessary part of any modern computer system, especially when multiple programs may be running at once. Handling relocatability is perhaps the largest single part of the linker's job. Fortunately, it does this by itself and requires no input from you. Once the job is done and the smoke clears, the file translation job is complete, and you have your executable program file.

The Assembly Language Development Process

As you can see, there are a lot of different file types and a fair number of programs involved in the process of writing, assembling, and testing an assembly language program. The process itself sounds more complex than it is. I've drawn you a map to help you keep your bearings during the discussions in the rest of this chapter. Figure 5-9 shows the most common form that the assembly language development process takes, in a "view from a height." At first glance it may look like a map of the Los Angeles freeway system, but in reality the flow is fairly straightforward, and you'll do it enough that it will become second nature in just a couple of evenings spent flailing at a program or two.

In a nutshell, the process cooks down to this:

1. Create your assembly language source code file in a text editor.

2. Use your assembler to create an object module from your source code file.

3. Use your linker to convert the object module (and any previously assembled object modules that are part of the project) into a single executable program file.

4. Test the program file by running it, using a debugger if necessary.

5. Go back to the text editor in step 1, fix any mistakes you may have made earlier, and write new code as necessary.

6. Repeat steps 1–5 until done.

The Discipline of Working Directories

Programmers generally count from 0, and if we're counting steps in the assembly language development process, step 0 consists of setting up a system of directories on your Linux PC to manage the files you'll be creating and processing as you go.

There's a rule here that you need to understand and adopt right up front: *Store only one project in a directory.* That is, when you want to write a Linux program called TextCaser, create a directory called TextCaser, and keep nothing in that directory but files directly related to the TextCaser project. If you have another project in the works called TabExploder, give that project its own separate directory. This is good management practice, first of all, and it prevents your makefiles from getting confused. (More on this later when I take up make and makefiles.)

I recommend that you establish a directory scheme for your assembly development projects, and my experience suggests something like this: Create a directory under your Linux Home directory called "asmwork" (or make up some other suitably descriptive name) and create your individual project directories as subdirectories under that overall assembly language directory.

By the way, it's OK to make the name of a directory the same as the name of the main .ASM file for the project; that is, textcaser.asm is perfectly happy living in a directory called textcaser.

At this point, if you haven't already downloaded and unpacked the listings archive for this book, I suggest you do that—you're going to need one of the

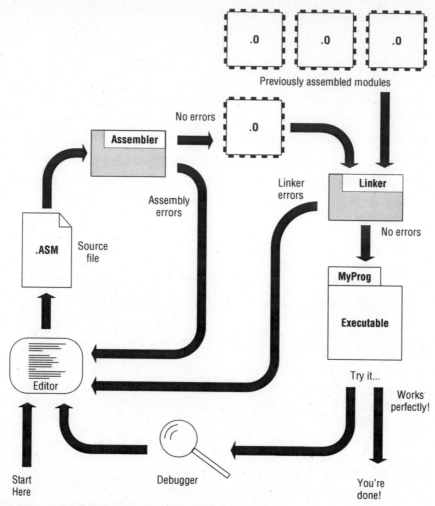

Figure 5-9: The assembly language development process

files in the archive for the demonstration in this section. The archive file is called asmsbs3e.zip, and it can be found at

    www.copperwood.com/pub

or, alternatively, at

    www.junkbox.com/pub

(I have these two domains on two different Internet hosting services so that at least one of them will always be up and available. The file is identical, whichever site you download it from.)

When unpacked, the listings archive will create individual project directories under whatever parent directory you choose. I recommend unpacking it under your asmwork directory, or whatever you end up naming it.

Editing the Source Code File

You begin the actual development process by typing your program code into a text editor. *Which* text editor doesn't matter very much, and there are dozens from which to choose. (I'll recommend a very good one in the next chapter.) The only important thing to keep in mind is that word processors such as Microsoft Word and OpenOffice Writer embed a lot of extra binary data in their document files, above and beyond the text that you type. This binary data controls things such as line spacing, fonts and font size, page headers and footers, and many other things that your assembler has no need for and no clue about. Assemblers are not always good at ignoring such data, which may cause errors at assembly time.

Ubuntu Linux's preinstalled text editor, gedit (which may be found in the Applications → Accessories menu), is perfectly good, especially when you're just starting out and aren't processing thousands of lines of code for a single program.

As for how you come up with what you type in, well, that's a separate question, and one that I address in a good portion of Chapter 8. You will certainly have a pile of notes, probably some pseudo-code, some diagrams, and perhaps a formal flowchart. These can all be done on your screen with software utilities, or with a pencil on a paper quadrille pad. (Maybe I'm just old, but I still use the pad and pencil.)

Assembly language source code files are almost always saved to disk with an .ASM file extension. In other words, for a program named MyProg, the assembly language source code file would be named MyProg.asm.

Assembling the Source Code File

As you can see from the flow in Figure 5-9, the text editor produces a source code text file with an .ASM extension. This file is then passed to the assembler program itself, for translation to an object module file. Under Linux and with the NASM assembler that I'm focusing on in this book, the file extension will be .O.

When you invoke the assembler from the command line, you provide it with the name of the source code file that you want it to process. Linux will load the assembler from disk and run it, and the assembler will open the source code file that you named on the command line. Almost immediately afterward (especially for the small learning programs that you'll be poking at in this book) it will create an object file with the same name as the source file, but with an .O file extension.

As the assembler reads lines from the source code file, it will examine them, build a symbol table summarizing any named items in the source code file, construct the binary machine instructions that the source code lines represent, and then write those machine instructions and symbol information to the object module file. When the assembler finishes and closes the object module file, its job is done and it terminates. On modern PCs and with programs representing fewer than 500 lines of code, this happens in a second or less.

Assembler Errors

Note well: the previous paragraphs describe what happens if the .ASM file is *correct*. By correct, I mean that the file is completely comprehensible to the assembler, and can be translated into machine instructions without the assembler getting confused. If the assembler encounters something it doesn't understand when it reads a line from the source code file, the misunderstood text is called an *error*, and the assembler displays an *error message*.

For example, the following line of assembly language will confuse the assembler and prompt an error message:

```
mov eax,evx
```

The reason is simple: there's no such thing as EVX. What came out as EVX was actually intended to be "EBX," which is the name of a CPU register. (The *V* key is right next to the *B* key and can be struck by mistake without your fingers necessarily knowing that they erred. Done that!)

Typos like this are by far the easiest kind of error to spot. Others that take some study to find involve transgressions of the assembler's many rules—which in most cases are the CPU's rules. For example:

```
mov ax,ebx
```

This looks like it should be correct, as AX and EBX are both real registers. However, on second thought, you may notice that AX is a 16-bit register, whereas EBX is a 32-bit register. You are not allowed to copy a 32-bit register into a 16-bit register.

You don't have to remember the instruction operand details here; we'll go into the rules later when we look at the individual instructions themselves. For now, simply understand that some things that may look reasonable to you (especially as a beginner) are simply against the rules for technical reasons and are considered errors.

And these are easy ones. There are much, *much* more difficult errors that involve inconsistencies between two otherwise legitimate lines of source code. I won't offer any examples here, but I want to point out that errors can be truly ugly, hidden things that can take a lot of study and torn hair to find. Toto, we are definitely *not* in BASIC anymore . . .

The error messages vary from assembler to assembler, and they may not always be as helpful as you might hope. The error NASM displays upon encountering the "EVX" typo follows:

```
testerr.asm:20: symbol 'evx' undefined
```

This is pretty plain, assuming that you know what a "symbol" is. And it tells you where to look: The 20 is the line number where it noticed the error. The error message NASM offers when you try to load a 32-bit register into a 16-bit register is far less helpful:

```
testerr.asm:22: invalid combination of opcode and operands
```

This lets you know you're guilty of performing illegal acts with an opcode and its operands, but that's it. *You* have to know what's legal and what's illegal to really understand what you did wrong. As in running a stop sign, ignorance of the law is no excuse, and unlike the local police department, the assembler will catch you *every* time.

Assembler error messages do not absolve you from understanding the CPU's or the assembler's rules.

This will become very clear the first time you sit down to write your own assembly code. I hope I don't frighten you too terribly by warning you that for more abstruse errors, the error messages may be almost no help at all.

You may make (or *will* make—let's get real) more than one error in writing your source code files. The assembler will display more than one error message in such cases, but it may not necessarily display an error for *every* error present in the source code file. At some point, multiple errors confuse the assembler so thoroughly that it cannot necessarily tell right from wrong anymore. While it's true that the assembler reads and translates source code files line by line, a cumulative picture of the final assembly language program is built up over the course of the whole assembly process. If this picture is shot too full of errors, then in time the whole picture collapses.

The assembler will terminate, having printed numerous error messages. *Start at the first one*, make sure you understand it (take notes!) and keep going. If the errors following the first one don't make sense, fix the first one or two and assemble again.

Back to the Editor

The way to fix errors is to load the offending source code file back into your text editor and start hunting up errors. This loopback is shown in Figure 5-9. It may well be the highway you see the most of on this particular map.

The assembler error message almost always contains a line number. Move the cursor to that line number and start looking for the false and the fanciful. If you find the error immediately, fix it and start looking for the next. Assuming that you're using Ubuntu's GNOME graphical desktop, it's useful to keep the terminal window open at the same time as your editor window, so that you don't have to scribble down a list of line numbers on paper, or redirect the compiler's output to a text file. With a 19″ monitor or better, there's plenty of room for multiple windows at once.

(There is a way to make NASM write its error messages to a text file during the assembly process, which you'll see in the next chapter.)

Assembler Warnings

As taciturn a creature as an assembler may appear to be, it will sometimes display *warning messages* during the assembly process. These warning messages are a monumental puzzle to beginning assembly language programmers: are they errors or aren't they? Can I ignore them or should I fool with the source code until they go away?

Alas, there's no crisp answer. Sorry about that.

Assembly-time warnings are the assembler acting as experienced consultant, and hinting that something in your source code is a little dicey. This something may not be serious enough to cause the assembler to stop assembling the file, but it may be serious enough for you to take note and investigate. For example, NASM will flag a warning if you define a named label but put no instruction after it. That may not be an error, but it's probably an omission on your part, and you should take a close look at that line and try to remember what you were thinking when you wrote it. (This may not always be easy, when it's three ayem or three weeks after you originally wrote the line in question.)

If you're a beginner doing ordinary, 100-percent-by-the-book sorts of things, you should crack your assembler reference manual and figure out why the assembler is tut-tutting you. Ignoring a warning *may* cause peculiar bugs to occur later during program testing. Or, ignoring a warning message may have no undesirable consequences at all. I feel, however, that it's always better to know what's going on. Follow this rule:

Ignore an assembler warning message only if you know exactly what it means.

In other words, until you understand why you're getting a warning message, treat it as though it were an error message. Only when you fully understand why it's there and what it means should you try to make the decision whether to ignore it or not.

In summary: the first part of the assembly language development process (as shown in Figure 5-9) is a loop. You must edit your source code file, assemble it, and return to the editor to fix errors until the assembler spots no further errors. *You cannot continue until the assembler gives your source code file a clean bill of health.* I also recommend studying any warnings offered by the assembler until you understand them clearly. Fixing the condition that triggered the warning is always a good idea, especially when you're first starting out.

When no further errors are found, the assembler will write an .O file to disk, and you will be ready to go on to the next step.

Linking the Object Code File

As I explained a little earlier in this chapter, the linking step is non-obvious and a little mysterious to newcomers, especially when you have only one object code module in play. It is nonetheless crucial, and whereas it was possible in ancient times to assemble a simple DOS assembly language program directly to an executable file without a linking step, the nature of modern operating systems such as Linux and Windows makes this impossible.

The linking step is shown on the right half of Figure 5-9. In the upper-right corner is a row of .O files. These .O files were assembled earlier from correct .ASM files, yielding object module files containing machine instructions and data objects. When the linker links the .O file produced from your in-progress .ASM file, it adds in the previously assembled .O files. The single executable file that the linker writes to disk contains the machine instructions and data items from all of the .O files that were handed to the linker when the linker was invoked.

Once the in-progress .ASM file is completed and made correct, its .O file can be put up on the rack with the others and added to the *next* in-progress .ASM source code file that you work on. Little by little you construct your application program out of the modules you build and test one at a time.

A very important bonus is that some of the procedures in an .O module may be used in a future assembly language program that hasn't even been begun yet. Creating such libraries of "toolkit" procedures can be an extraordinarily effective way to save time by reusing code, without even passing it through the assembler again!

There are numerous assemblers in the world (though only a few really good ones) and plenty of linkers as well. Linux comes with its own linker, called ld. (The name is actually short for "load," and "loader" was what linkers were originally called, in the First Age of Unix, back in the 1970s.) We'll use ld for very simple programs in this book, but in Chapter 12 we're going to take up a Linux peculiarity and use a C compiler for a linker ... sort of.

As I said, we're not doing BASIC anymore.

As with the assembler, invoking the linker is done from the Linux terminal command line. Linking multiple files involves naming each file on the command line, along with the desired name of the output executable file. You may also need to enter one or more command-line switches, which give the linker additional instructions and guidance. Few of these will be of interest while you're a beginner, and I'll discuss the ones you need along the way.

Linker Errors

As with the assembler, the linker may discover problems as it weaves multiple .O files together into a single executable program file. Linker errors are subtler than assembler errors, and they are usually harder to find. Fortunately, they are less common and not as easy to make.

As with assembler errors, linker errors are "fatal"; that is, they make it impossible to generate the executable file; and when the linker encounters one, it will terminate immediately. When you're presented with a linker error, you have to return to the editor and figure out the problem. Once you've identified the problem (or *think* you have) and changed something in the source code file to fix it, you must reassemble and then relink the program to see if the linker error went away. Until it does, you have to loop back to the editor, try something else, and assemble/link once more.

If possible, avoid doing this by trial and error. Read your assembler and linker documentation. Understand what you're doing. The more you understand about what's going on within the assembler and the linker, the easier it will be to determine what's giving the linker fits.

(Hint: It's almost always *you*!)

Testing the .EXE File

If you receive no linker errors, the linker will create a single executable file that contains all the machine instructions and data items present in all of the .O files named on the linker command line. The executable file is your program. You can run it to see what it does by simply naming it on the terminal command line and pressing Enter.

The Linux path comes into play here, though if you have any significant experience with Linux at all, you already know this. The terminal window is a purely textual way of looking at your working directory, and all of the familiar command-line utilities will operate on whatever is in your working directory. However, remember that your working directory is *not* in your path unless you explicitly put it there, and although people argue about this and always have, there are good reasons for not putting your working directory into your path.

When you execute a program from the terminal window command line, you must tell Linux where the program is by prefixing the name of the program with the ./ specifier, which simply means "in the working directory." This is unlike DOS, in which whatever directory is current is also on the search path for executable programs. A command-line invocation of your program under Linux might look like this:

```
./myprogram
```

This is when the fun *really* starts.

Errors versus Bugs

When you launch your program in this way, one of two things will happen: The program will work as you intended it to or you'll be confronted with the effects of one or more program bugs. A *bug* is anything in a program that doesn't work the way you want it to. This makes a bug somewhat more subjective than an error. One person might think red characters displayed on a blue background is a bug, while another might consider it a clever New Age feature and be quite pleased. Settling bug-versus-feature conflicts like this is up to you. You should have a clear idea of what the program is supposed to do and how it works, backed up by a written spec or other documentation of some kind, and this is the standard by which you judge a bug.

Characters in odd colors are the least of it. When working in assembly language, it is *extremely* common for a bug to abort the execution of a program with little or no clue on the display as to what happened. If you're lucky, the operating system will spank your executable and display an error message. This is one you will see far too often:

```
Segmentation Fault
```

Such an error is called a *runtime error* to differentiate it from assembler errors and linker errors. Often, your program will not annoy the operating system. It just won't do what you expect it to do, and it may not say much in the course of its failure.

Very fortunately, Linux is a rugged operating system designed to take buggy programs into account, and it is *extremely* unlikely that one of your programs will "blow the machine away," as happened so often in the DOS era.

All that being said, and in the interest of keeping the Babel effect at bay, I think it's important here to carefully draw the distinction between errors and bugs. An *error* is something wrong with your source code file that either the assembler or the linker kicks out as unacceptable. An error prevents the assembly or link process from going to completion and will thus prevent a final .EXE file from being produced.

A *bug*, by contrast, is a problem discovered during *execution* of a program. Bugs are not detected by either the assembler or the linker. Bugs can be benign, such as a misspelled word in a screen message or a line positioned on the wrong screen row; or a bug can force your program to abort prematurely. If your program attempts to do certain forbidden things, Linux will terminate it and present you with a message. These are called *runtime errors*, but they are actually caused by bugs.

Both errors and bugs require that you go back to the text editor and change something in your source code file. The difference here is that most errors are reported with a line number indicating where you should look in your source code file to fix the problem. Bugs, conversely, are left as an exercise for the student. You have to hunt them down, and neither the assembler nor the linker will give you much in the line of clues.

Are We There Yet?

Figure 5-9 announces the exit of the assembly language development process as happening when your program works perfectly. A very serious question is this: How do you know when it works perfectly? Simple programs assembled while learning the language may be easy enough to test in a minute or two; but any program that accomplishes anything useful at all will take *hours* of testing at *minimum*. A serious and ambitious application could take weeks—or months—to test thoroughly. A program that takes various kinds of input values and produces various kinds of output should be tested with as many different combinations of input values as possible, and you should examine every possible output every time.

Even so, finding every last bug in a nontrivial program is considered by some to be an impossible ideal. Perhaps—but you should strive to come as close as possible, in as efficient a fashion as you can manage. I'll have more to say about bugs and debugging throughout the rest of this book.

Debuggers and Debugging

The final—and almost certainly the most painful—part of the assembly language development process is debugging. *Debugging* is simply the systematic process by which bugs are located and corrected. A *debugger* is a utility program designed specifically to help you locate and identify bugs.

Debuggers are among the most mysterious and difficult to understand of all classes of software. Debuggers are part X-ray machine and part magnifying glass. A debugger loads into memory *with* your program and remains in memory, side by side with your program. The debugger then puts tendrils down into your program and enables some truly peculiar things to be done.

One of the problems with debugging computer programs is that they operate so quickly. Tens or hundreds of thousands of machine instructions can be executed in a single second, and if one of those instructions isn't quite right, it's long gone before you can identify which one it was by staring at the screen. A debugger enables you to execute the machine instructions in a program *one at a time*, which enables you to pause indefinitely between each instruction to examine the effects of the last instruction that executed. The debugger also enables you to look at the contents of any location in the block of memory allowed to your program, as well as the values stored in any CPU register, during that pause between instructions.

Debuggers can do all of this mysterious stuff because they are necessary, and the CPU has special features baked into its silicon to make debuggers possible. How they work internally is outside the scope of this book, but it's a fascinating business, and once you're comfortable with x86 CPU internals I encourage you to research it further.

Some debuggers have the ability to display the source code with the machine instructions, so that you can see which lines of source code text correspond to which binary opcodes. Others enable you to locate a program variable by name, rather than simply by memory address.

Many operating systems are shipped with a debugger. DOS and early versions of Windows were shipped with DEBUG, and in earlier editions of this book I explained DEBUG in detail. Linux has a very powerful debugger called *gdb*, which I introduce in the next chapter, along with a separate graphical utility used to manage it. Many other debuggers are available, and I encourage you to try them as your skills develop.

Taking a Trip Down Assembly Lane

You can stop asking, "Are we there yet?" where "there" means "ready to build an actual working program." We are indeed there, and for the rest of this chapter we're going to take a simple program and run it through the process shown graphically in Figure 5-9.

You don't have to write the program yourself. I've explained the process, but I haven't gone into any of the machine instructions or the CPU registers in detail. I'll provide you with a very simple program, and give you enough explanation of its workings that it's not a total mystery. In subsequent chapters, we'll look at machine instructions and their operation in great detail. In the meantime, you must understand the assembly language development process, or knowing how the instructions work won't help you in the slightest.

Installing the Software

One of the fantastic things about Linux is the boggling array of software available for it, nearly all of which is completely free of charge. If you've used Linux for any length of time you've probably encountered products such as OpenOffice, Kompozer, Gnumeric, and Evolution. Some of these are preinstalled when you install the operating system. The rest are obtained through the use of a *package manager*. A package manager is a catalog program that lives on your PC and maintains a list of all the free software packages available for Linux. You choose the ones you want, and the package manager will go online, download them from their online homes (called *repositories*), and then install them for you.

Actually, two package managers are installed with Ubuntu Linux. One is the Gnome Application Installer, and this is the one that you see in the Applications menu, as the item Add/Remove. This package manager is there for its simplicity, but it doesn't list every free software package that you might want. Tucked away in the System → Administration menu is the Synaptic Package Manager, which can (at least in theory) access any free software product that has been committed to a known public repository. We're going to use the Synaptic Package Manager to obtain the rest of the software we need for the examples in this book.

Needless to say, you need an active Internet connection to use Ubuntu's package managers. Broadband is helpful, but the two packages we need to download are not very large and will transfer through a dial-up Internet connection if you're reasonably patient.

If you're coming from the Windows world, it's good to understand that under Linux you don't have to worry about where software is being installed. Almost all software is installed in the /usr directory hierarchy, in a place on your file search path. You can open a terminal window and navigate to any directory as your working directory, and then launch an installed application by naming it on the command line.

In this chapter, we need a number of things in order to take a quick tour through the assembly language development process: an editor, an assembler, a linker, and a debugger:

- The gedit editor is preinstalled with Ubuntu Linux.
- The NASM assembler will have to be installed.
- The Linux linker ld is preinstalled.
- The debugger situation is a little more complex. The canonical Linux debugger, Gdb, is preinstalled. However, Gdb is more of a debugger "engine" than a complete debugger. To make it truly useful (especially to beginners), you have to download something to make its controls easier to handle and its output easier to understand. This is a program called *KDbg*, which is a "front end" to Gdb. I explain how this works in the next chapter. For now, just take it on faith.

The Synaptic Package Manager enables you to select multiple packages to install in one operation. Bring up Synaptic. It will refresh its index for a few seconds, and then present you with the window shown in Figure 5-10.

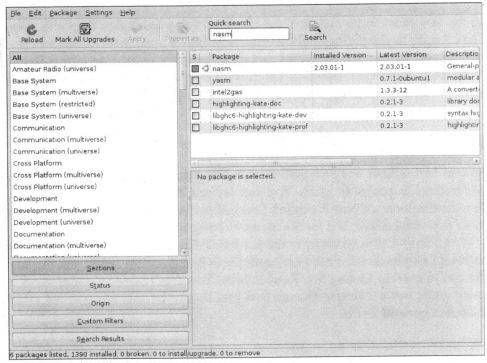

Figure 5-10: The Synaptic Package Manager

Click in the Quick Search field to give it the focus, and then type **NASM**. You don't need to click Search; Synaptic will search incrementally as you type, and display any packages that it thinks match your entered search text. NASM should be the first item shown. At the left edge of the results pane will be a column of check boxes. Click on the check box for NASM. You will get a confirming dialog, and from it select Mark for Installation. Now, depending on the version of NASM, you may next be presented with a dialog asking you, "Mark additional required changes?" These are additional things (typically code libraries) required to install the product, so click the Mark button. Once you confirm the additional changes, the NASM line will change to green, indicating that NASM is queued for installation. Whatever files NASM depends on will also "turn green."

Do the same thing for KDbg. Type **Kdbg** in Quick Search, and enable its check box when it appears. It also requires additional libraries for installation, so click Mark when that dialog appears.

When all required installation line items are "green," click the Apply button at the top of the window. A confirming Summary dialog will appear, listing all the line items to be installed and the hard drive space that they will take. Click Apply in the dialog, and Synaptic will take it from there. Downloading smallish products such as NASM and KDbg won't take long on a broadband connection. After both products are present on your PC, Synaptic will install everything, and when the Changes Applied dialog appears, you're done!

Step 1: Edit the Program in an Editor

Several text editors are preinstalled with Ubuntu, and the easiest of them to understand is probably gedit. You can launch it from the Applications → Accessories menu, where it's called Text Editor. Later I'll present Kate, a much more powerful editor, but for the moment bring up gedit.

With File → Open, navigate to the eatsyscall directory from the book listings archive. Double-click the eatsyscall.asm file in that directory. gedit will display the file, shown in Listing 5-1. Read it over. You don't have to understand it completely, but it's simple enough that you should be able to dope out what it does in general terms.

Listing 5-1: eatsyscall.asm

```
;   Executable name  : EATSYSCALL
;   Version          : 1.0
;   Created date     : 1/7/2009
;   Last update      : 1/7/2009
;   Author           : Jeff Duntemann
;   Description      : A simple assembly app for Linux, using NASM 2.05,
;                      demonstrating the use of Linux INT 80H syscalls
;                      to display text.
;
;   Build using these commands:
;     nasm -f elf -g -F stabs eatsyscall.asm
;     ld -o eatsyscall eatsyscall.o
;

SECTION .data           ; Section containing initialized data

EatMsg: db "Eat at Joe's!",10
EatLen: equ $-EatMsg
```

Listing 5-1: eatsyscall.asm (*continued*)

```
SECTION .bss            ; Section containing uninitialized data
SECTION .text           ; Section containing code

global _start           ; Linker needs this to find the entry point!

_start:
    nop                 ; This no-op keeps gdb happy (see text)
    mov eax,4           ; Specify sys_write syscall
    mov ebx,1           ; Specify File Descriptor 1: Standard Output
    mov ecx,EatMsg      ; Pass offset of the message
    mov edx,EatLen      ; Pass the length of the message
    int 80H             ; Make syscall to output the text to stdout

    mov eax,1           ; Specify Exit syscall
    mov ebx,0           ; Return a code of zero
    int 80H             ; Make syscall to terminate the program
```

At this point you could modify the source code file if you wanted to, but for the moment just read it over. It belongs to a species of demo programs called "Hello world!" and simply displays a single line of text in a terminal window. (You have to start somewhere!)

Step 2: Assemble the Program with NASM

The NASM assembler does not have a user interface as nontechnical people understand "user interface" today. It doesn't put up a window, and there's no place for you to enter filenames or select options in check boxes. NASM works via text only, and you communicate with it through a terminal and a Linux console session. It's like those old DOS days when everything had to be entered on the command line. (How soon we forget!)

Open a terminal window. Many different terminal utilities are available for Ubuntu Linux. The one I use most of the time is called Konsole, but they will all work here. Terminal windows generally open with your home directory as the working directory. Once you have the command prompt, navigate to the "eatsyscall" project directory using the cd command:

```
myname@mymachine:~$ cd asmwork/eatsyscall
```

If you're new to Linux, make sure you're in the right directory by checking the directory contents with the ls command. The file eatsyscall.asm should at least be there, either extracted from the listings archive for this book, or entered by you in a text editor.

Assuming that the file eatsyscall.asm is present, assemble it by (carefully) entering the following command and pressing Enter:

```
nasm -f elf -g -F stabs eatsyscall.asm
```

When NASM finds nothing wrong, it will say nothing, and you will simply get the command prompt back. That means the assembly worked! If you entered the eatsyscall.asm file yourself and typed something incorrectly, you may get an error. Make sure the file matches Listing 5-1.

Now, what did all that stuff that you typed into the terminal mean? I've dissected the command line you just entered in Figure 5-11. A NASM invocation begins with the name of the program itself. Everything after that are parameters that govern the assembly process. The ones shown here are nearly all of the ones you're likely to need while first learning the assembly language development process. There are others with more arcane purposes, and all of them are summarized in the NASM documentation. Let's go through the ones used here, in order:

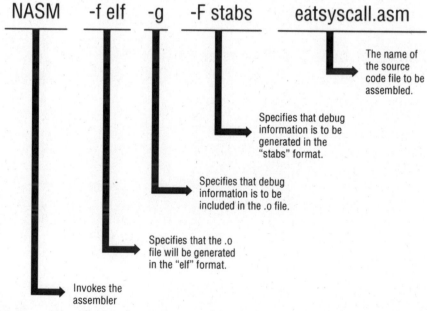

Figure 5-11: The anatomy of a NASM command line

-f elf: There are a fair number of useful object file formats, and each one is generated differently. The NASM assembler is capable of generating most of them, including other formats, such as bin, aout, coff, and ELF64, that you probably won't need, at least for awhile. The -f command tells NASM which format to use for the object code file it's about to generate. In 32-bit IA-32 Linux work, the format is ELF32, which can be specified on the command line as simply elf.

-g: While you're still working on a program, you want to have debugging information embedded in the object code file so that you can use a debugger to spot problems. (More on how this is done shortly.) The -g command tells NASM to include debugging information in the output file.

-F stabs: As with the output file, there are different formats in which NASM can generate debug information. Again, as with the output file format, if you're working in IA-32 Linux, you'll probably be using the STABS format for debug information, at least while you're starting out. There is a more powerful debug format called DWARF that can also be used with ELF (get it?), and NASM will generate DWARF data instead of STABS data if you replace "stabs" with "dwarf" in this command. Remember too that Linux commands are case sensitive. The -f command and the -F command are distinct, so watch that Shift key!

eatsyscall.asm: The last item on the NASM command line is always the name of file to be assembled. Again, as with everything in Linux, the filename is case sensitive. EATSYSCALL.ASM and EatSysCall.asm (as well as all other case variations) are considered entirely different files.

Unless you give NASM other orders, it will generate an object code file and name it using the name of the source code file and the file extension .O. The "other orders" are given through the -o option. If you include a -o command in a NASM command line, it must be followed by a filename, which is the name you wish NASM to give to the generated object code file. For example:

```
nasm -f elf -g -F stabs eatsyscall.asm -o eatdemo.o
```

Here, NASM will assemble the source file eatsyscall.asm to the object code file eatdemo.o.

Now, before moving on to the link step, verify that the object code file has been created by using the ls command to list your working directory contents. The file eatsyscall.o should be there.

Step 3: Link the Program with LD

So far so good. Now you have to create an executable program file by using the Linux linker utility, ld. After ensuring that the object code file eatsyscall.o is present in your working directory, type the following linker command into the terminal:

```
ld -o eatsyscall eatsyscall.o
```

If the original program assembled without errors or warnings, the object file should link without any errors as well. As with NASM, when ld encounters nothing worth mentioning, it says nothing at all. No news is good news in the assembly language world.

The command line for linking is simpler than the one for assembling, as shown in Figure 5-12. The "ld" runs the linker program itself. The -o command specifies an output filename, which here is eatsyscall. In the DOS and Windows world, executable files almost always use the .exe file extension. In the Linux world, executables generally have no file extension at all.

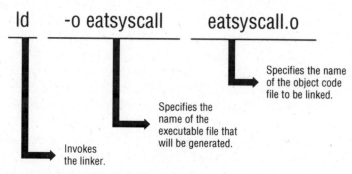

Figure 5-12: The anatomy of an ld command line

Note that if you do *not* specify an executable filename with the -o command, ld will create a file with the default name a.out. If you ever see a mysterious file named a.out in one of your project directories, it probably means you ran the linker without the -o command.

The last things you enter on the ld command line are the names of the object files to be linked. In this case there is only one, but once you begin using code libraries (whether your own or those written by others) you'll have to enter the names of any libraries you're using on the command line. The order in which you enter them doesn't matter. Just make sure that they're all there.

Step 4: Test the Executable File

Once the linker completes an error-free pass, your finished executable file will be waiting for you in your working directory. It's error-free if the assembler and linker digested it without displaying any error messages. However, error-free does not imply bug-free. To make sure it works, just name it on the terminal command line:

```
./eatsyscall
```

Linux newcomers need to remember that *your working directory is not automatically on your search path*, and if you simply type the name of the executable on the command line (without the "working directory" prefix "./"), Linux will not find it. But when named with the prefix, your executable will load and run, and print out its 13-character advertisement:

```
Eat at Joe's!
```

Victory! But don't put that terminal window away just yet . . .

Step 5: Watch It Run in the Debugger

Assuming that you entered Listing 5-1 correctly (or unpacked it from the listings archive), there are no bugs in eatsyscall.asm. That's an uncommon circumstance for programmers, especially those just starting out. Most of the time you'll need to start bug-hunting almost immediately. The easiest way to do this is to load your executable file into a debugger so that you can single-step it, pausing after the execution of each machine instruction in order to see what effect each instruction has on the registers and any variables defined in memory.

Two programs work together to provide you with an enjoyable (well, tolerable) debugging experience: gdb and KDbg. The gdb utility does the way-down-deep CPU magic that debuggers do, and KDbg arranges it all nicely on your display and allows you to control it. To kick off a debugging session, invoke KDbg from the terminal window command line, followed by the name of your executable file:

```
kdbg eatsyscall
```

KDbg is not so nearly mute as NASM and ld. It's a KDE app, and puts up a nice graphical window that should look very much like what's shown in

Figure 5-13. The eatsyscall program source code should be displayed in the center pane. If the top pane doesn't say "Register" in its upper-left corner, select View → Registers and make sure the Registers item has an X beside it.

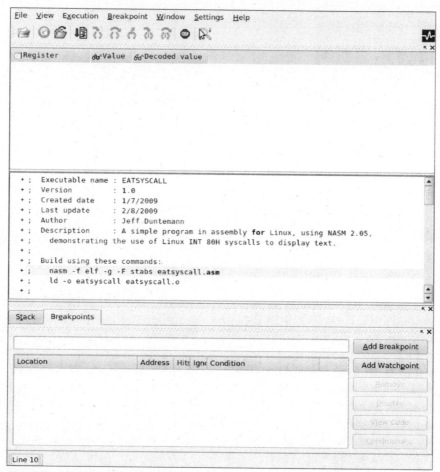

Figure 5-13: KDbg's startup window

To make a little more room to see your source code, close KDbg's bottom pane. Click the small X in the upper-right corner of the pane. KDbg is capable of displaying a lot of different things in a lot of different windows; but for this quick run-through, having the source code pane and the registers display pane will be enough. Having other windows open will simply confuse you.

If you recall from the overview earlier in this chapter, debuggers need to be told where to stop initially, before you can tell them to begin single-stepping a program—otherwise, they will scoot through execution of the whole program too quickly for you to follow. You have to set an initial breakpoint. The way to do this is to scroll the source code display down until you can see the code that follows the label _start: at the left edge of the program text. Move down two lines and left-click in the empty space at the left edge of the source code pane, between the window's frame and the plus symbol. A red dot should appear where you clicked. This red dot indicates that you have now set a breakpoint on that line of code, which in this case is the instruction MOV EAX, 4. (Make sure you insert a breakpoint at this instruction, and not at the NOP instruction immediately above it in the program!)

Once you have the initial breakpoint set, click the Run button in the top toolbar. The button looks like a page with a downward-pointing arrow to its left. (Hover the mouse pointer over the button and it should say Run.) Two things will happen, essentially instantaneously (see Figure 5-14):

- The red dot indicating the breakpoint will be overlain by a green triangle pointing to the right. The triangle indicates the place in the program where execution has paused, and it points at the next instruction that will execute. Note well that the instruction where execution pauses for a breakpoint *has not been executed yet*.

- The top pane, which was blank previously, is now filled with a listing of the CPU registers. It's a longish list because it includes all the CPU flags and floating-point processor registers, but you only need to see the top group for this demo.

At this point, the general-purpose registers will all be shown containing zeroes. Your program has begun running, but the only instruction that has run yet is the NOP instruction, which does ... nothing. (It's a placeholder, and why it's here in this program will have to wait until the next chapter.)

This will soon change. To do the first single-step, click the Step Into By Instruction button. Hover the mouse pointer over the buttons until you find it. (The button has the focus in Figure 5-14.) As the name of the button suggests, clicking the button triggers the execution of one machine instruction. The green triangle moves one line downward.

Up in the Registers window, things are not the same. Two lines have turned red. The red color indicates that the values shown have changed during the execution of the single step that we just took. The EIP register is the instruction pointer, and it keeps track of which instruction will be executed next. More interesting right now is the state of the EAX register. What had been 0x0 is now 0x4. If you look at the source code, the instruction we just executed was this:

```
mov eax,4
```

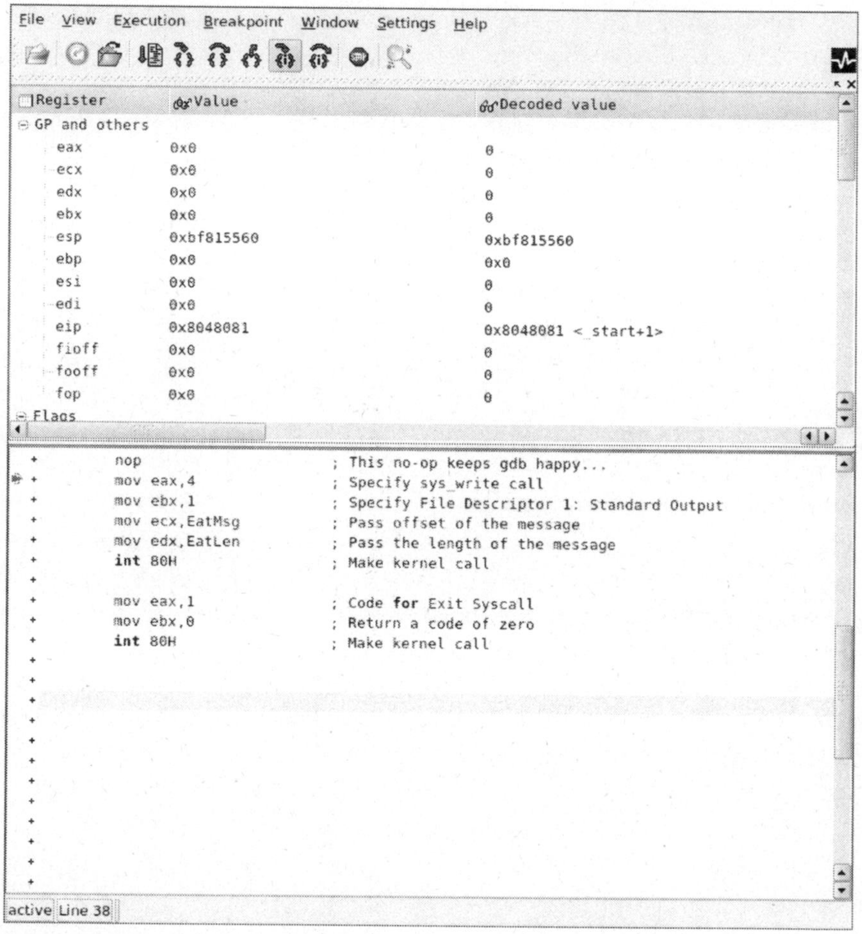

Figure 5-14: KDbg, ready to single-step

The "MOV" mnemonic tells us that data is being moved. The left operand is the destination (where data is going) and the right operand is the source (where data is coming from.) What happened is that the instruction put the value 4 in register EAX.

Click the Step Into By Instruction button again. The pointer will again move down a line. And again, the red lines in the Registers window indicate what was changed by executing the instruction. The instruction pointer changed again; that shouldn't be a surprise. Every time we execute an instruction, EIP will be red. This time, EAX has turned black again and EBX has turned red. The value in EBX has changed from 0 to 1. (The notation "0x1" is just another way of telling us that the value is given in hexadecimal.) Clearly, we've moved the value 1 into register EBX; and that's the instruction we just executed:

```
mov ebx,1
```

Click the button again. This time, register ECX will change radically (see Figure 5-15). The precise number you see on your PC for ECX will differ from the precise number I saw when I took the screen shot. The value depends on the individual Linux system, how much memory you have, and what the Linux OS is doing elsewhere in memory. What matters is that a 32-bit hexadecimal value has been moved into ECX. This instruction did the work:

```
mov ecx,EatMsg
```

So what did we actually move? If you scroll up into the earlier part of the source code temporarily, you'll see that EatMsg is a quoted string of ordinary characters reading "Eat at Joe's!" and not a 32-bit number; but note the comment to the right of the instruction: "Pass offset of the message." What we actually loaded into ECX was not the message itself but the message's address in memory. Technically, in IA-32 protected mode, a data item like EatMsg has both a segment address and an offset address. The segment address, however, is the property of the operating system, and we can safely ignore it when doing this kind of simple user-space programming. Back in the DOS era, when we had to use the real mode segmented memory model, we had to keep track of the segment registers too; doing it the protected mode way means one less headache. (Don't worry; there are plenty more!)

Click Step Into By Instruction again, and register EDX will be given the value 0xe, or (in decimal) 14. This is the length of the character string EatMsg.

At this point all the setup work has been done with respect to moving various values where they need to go. Click the button and execute the next instruction:

```
int 80H
```

It looks like nothing has happened—nothing in the Registers window changed—but hold on. Go into KDbg's menus and select View → Output. A simple terminal window will appear—and there's EatMsg, telling the world where to go for lunch (see Figure 5-16).

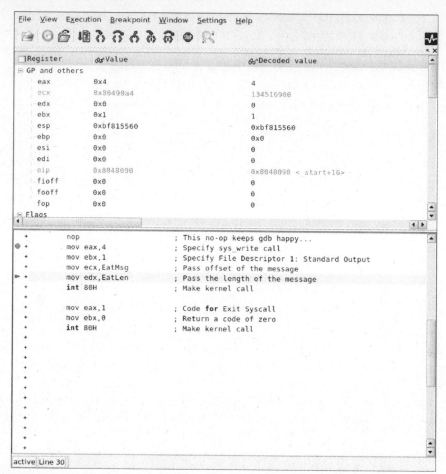

Figure 5-15: Moving a memory address into a register

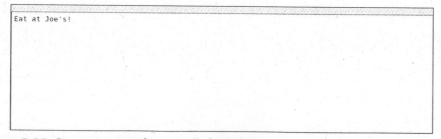

Figure 5-16: Program output in a terminal window

The INT 80H instruction is a special one. It generates a Linux system call (affectionately referred to as a *syscall*) named sys_write, which sends data to the currently active terminal window.

Sending EatMsg to the output window is all that the eatsyscall program was designed to do. Its work is done, and the last three instructions in the program basically tidy up and leave. Click the button and step through them, watching to see that EAX and EBX receive new values before the final INT 80H, which signals Linux that this program is finished. You'll get a confirmation of that in the bottom line of KDbg's window, which will say "Program exited normally" along with the source code line where this exit happened.

One question that may have occurred to you is this: Why is the stepper button called "Step *Into* By Instruction"? We just bounced down to the next line; we did not step our way *into* anything. A full answer will have to wait for a couple of chapters, until we get into procedures, but the gist of it is this: KDbg gives you the option to trace execution step by step into an assembly language procedure, or to let the computer run full speed while executing the procedure. The button Step Into By Instruction specifies to go through a procedure step by step. The button Step Over By Instruction (the next button to the right) allows the procedure to execute at full speed, and pick up single-stepping on the other side of the procedure call.

Why step over a procedure call? Mainly this: procedures are often library procedures, which you or someone else may have written months or years ago. If they are already debugged and working, stepping through them is probably a waste of time. (You can, however, learn a great deal about how the procedure works by watching it run one instruction at a time.)

Conversely, if the procedures are new to the program at hand, you may need to step through them just as carefully as you step through the main part of the program. KDbg gives you the option. This simple program has no procedures, so the Step Into and Step Over buttons do precisely the same thing: execute the next instruction in sequence.

The three single-stepping buttons to the left of Step Into By Instruction are for use when debugging code in higher-level languages such as C. They enable stepping by one high-level *statement* at a time, not simply one machine instruction at a time. These buttons don't apply to assembly language programming and I won't be discussing them further.

Ready to Get Serious?

I've taken this chapter slowly; and if you're impatient, you may be groaning by now. Bear with me. I want to make sure that you *very* clearly understand the component steps of the assembly language programming process. Everything in this book up until now has been conceptual groundwork, but at this point the necessary groundwork has been laid. It's time to pull out some serious tools, investigate the programmer's view of the Linux operating system, and begin writing some programs.

A Place to Stand, with Access to Tools

The Linux Operating System and the Tools That Shape the Way You Work

Archimedes, the primordial engineer, had a favorite saying: "Give me a lever long enough, and a place to stand, and I will move the Earth." The old guy was not much given to metaphor, and was speaking literally about the mechanical advantage of *really* long levers, but behind his words there is a larger truth about work in general: to get something done, you need a place to work, with access to tools. My radio bench down in the basement is set up that way: a large, flat space to lay ailing transmitters down on, and a shelf above where my oscilloscope, VTVM, frequency counter, signal generator, signal tracer, and dip meter are within easy reach. On the opposite wall, just two steps away, is a long line of shelves where I keep parts (including my legendary collection of tubes), raw materials such as sheet metal, circuit board stock, and scrap plastic, and equipment I don't need very often.

In some respects, an operating system is your place to stand while getting your computational work done. All the tools you need should be right there within easy reach, and there should be a standard, comprehensible way to access them. Storage for your data should be "close by" and easy to browse and search. The Linux operating system meets this need like almost nothing else in the desktop computing world today.

Ancient operating systems like DOS gave us our "place to stand" in a limited way. DOS provided access to disk storage, and a standard way to load and run software, and not much more. The tool set was small, but it was a good start, and about all that we could manage on 6 MHz 8088 machines.

In some ways, the most interesting thing about DOS is that it was created as a "dumbed down" version of a much more powerful operating system, Unix, which had been developed by AT&T's research labs in the 1960s and 1970s. At the time that the IBM PC appeared, Unix ran only on large and expensive mainframe computers. The PC didn't have the raw compute power to run Unix itself, but DOS was created with a hierarchical file system very much like the Unix file system, and its command line provided access to a subset of tools that worked very much like Unix tools.

The x86 PC grew up over the years, and by 1990 or so Intel's CPUs were powerful enough to run an operating system modeled on Unix. The PC grew up, and Unix "grew down" until the two met in the middle. In 1991 the young Finnish programmer Linus Torvalds wrote a Unix "lookalike" that would run on an inexpensive 386-based PC. It was based on an implementation of Unix called Minix, which was written in the Netherlands in the late 1980s as a Unix lookalike capable of running on small computers. Torvalds' Linux operating system eventually came to dominate the Unix world. Other desktop variations of Unix appeared, the most important of which was BSD (Berkeley Software Distribution) Unix, which spawned several small-system implementations and eventually became the core of Apple's OS/X operating system for the Mac.

That's our place to stand, and it's a good one; but in terms of access to tools, it also helps to have a sort of software workbench designed specifically for the type of work we're doing at the moment. The NASM assembler is powerful but taciturn, and inescapably tied to the command line, as are most of the venerable Unix tools you'll find in Linux. In the previous chapter, we ran through a simple development project the old hard way, by typing commands at the command line. You need to know how that works, but it's by no means the best we can do.

The legendary success of Turbo Pascal for DOS in the 1980s was largely due to the fact that it integrated an editor and a compiler together, and presented a menu that enabled easy and fast movement between the editor, to write code; to the compiler, to compile code into executable files; and to DOS, where those files could be run and tested. Programming in Turbo Pascal was easier to grasp and much faster than traditional methods, which involved constantly issuing commands from the command line.

Turbo Pascal was the first really successful commercial product to provide an interactive development environment (IDE) for programmers. Others had appeared earlier (particularly the primordial UCSD p-System) but Turbo Pascal put the idea on the map.

The Kate Editor

A little remarkably, there is no true equivalent to Turbo Pascal in the Linux assembly language field. The reason for this may seem peculiar to you, the beginner: seasoned assembly language programmers either create their own development environments (they are, after all, the programming elite) or simply work from the naked operating system command prompt. The appeal of a Turbo Pascal–type IDE is not so strong to them as it may be to you. However, there is a movement to IDEs for programming among the higher-level languages such as C, C++, and Python. I think that assembly language programmers will come along eventually. (Two general-purpose IDEs to watch are Eclipse and KDevelop, though neither is much used for assembly language work at this time.)

In the meantime, I'm going to present a simple IDE for you to use while you're learning assembly language. It has the virtue of simplicity, and for the sorts of small programs you'll be writing while you get up to speed, I've not found anything else like it. It's called Kate, and it's been around since 2002. As a text editor, Kate is unusual for a number of reasons:

- It is "aware" of assembly language source code formatting conventions, and will highlight different elements of assembly source code in different colors.

- It includes features for managing your text files, as well as editing them, through a side pane.

- It integrates a terminal window within its larger MDI (multiple document interface) display, where you can launch programs to test them, and a debugger to single-step them and examine memory.

- It has project support in the form of *sessions*, where a session is the "state" of Kate while you're working on a particular project.

- It is available as a software component; and by the use of KDE's KParts technology, it can be built into programs that you write for yourself.

Kate is in fact the editing component used in the "big" IDE KDevelop and the Access-like database manager Kexi. Although Kate originated in the KDE world and depends upon the Qt code libraries, it will install and run without any difficulty in the GNOME-based Ubuntu Linux distribution.

Installing Kate

If you're using Ubuntu Linux, Kate is most easily installed from the Applications → Add/Remove menu item. Type "**kate**" in the Search field and it will come right up. Check the box for installation, confirm the dependency installs that it requires, and the package manager will do the rest. After you select Kate, go back and search for KWrite, and check that for install as well. KWrite is a simple editor based on the same editor engine as Kate; and while it can be useful in its own right, you should install it for the sake of the Kate plugins that it installs. Peculiarly, Kate itself does not install its own plugins, and double peculiarly, KWrite cannot use the plugins that it installs for Kate. (Nobody ever said this business always makes sense!)

Launching Kate

After installation, Kate can be launched from Ubuntu's Applications menu, in the Accessories group. If you're used to keeping icons in the desktop's top panel, you can place Kate's icon there. Do it this way: pull down the Applications → Accessories → Kate menu item, but before left-clicking on Kate's item to open it, right-click on the item instead. A context menu will appear, the top item of which is "Add this launcher to panel." Right-click this menu item, and Kate's icon will be placed in the top panel. See Figure 6-1, where I've already placed the icon in the panel so you can see where it appears: just to the right of the Help button.

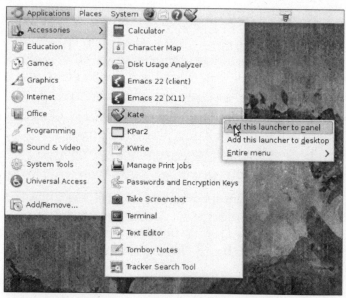

Figure 6-1: Placing Kate's icon in the panel

If you prefer a desktop icon to a panel icon, the same context menu also presents an item enabling you to place Kate's launcher icon on the desktop. Where you place it is up to you.

One thing I do *not* recommend is launching Kate from a terminal command line. This will work, but the terminal will then display debugging information on the Kate program itself while Kate runs. Whether this is a bug or a feature depends on who you are, but all the activity in the terminal window is distracting, and irrelevant to the projects that *you're* working on.

The first time you start Kate, before you see the editor screen itself, you'll see an empty Session Chooser dialog (see Figure 6-2). You haven't created any sessions yet, so none are listed there. You can create a new one once you've digested what sessions are and how they work (more on this shortly), but for the moment, click Default Session to highlight it, and then click Open Session. The main Kate window will appear, overlain by the Tip of the Day window. Some people find "splash tips" dialogs like this annoying, but when you're first learning Kate they can be useful. If you don't want to see them, uncheck the Show Tips on Startup check box.

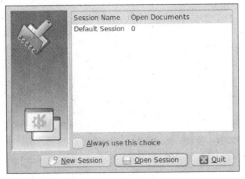

Figure 6-2: The Session Chooser dialog

The default Kate screen layout (see Figure 6-3) is very simple. The editor pane is on the right, and the manager sidebar is on the left. Note that if you *don't* see the button for Filesystem Browser on the left margin of the manager sidebar, and for the Terminal in the bottom margin, it generally means that you haven't installed the KWrite editor, which installs several plug-ins for Kate's use. These include the Terminal plugin, which is essential for building and running the examples presented in this book. Make sure that KWrite is installed or your Kate install won't be complete!

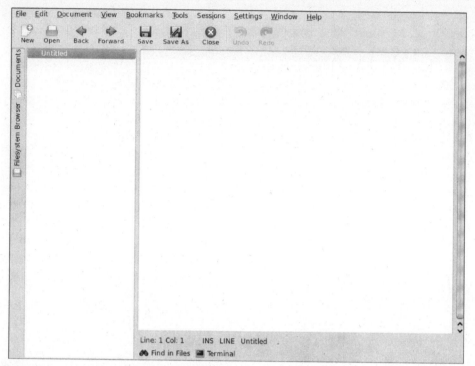

Figure 6-3: The default Kate screen layout

Configuration

The Kate editor supports a blizzard of configurable options. Some of these are more useful than others, and in truth most do not really apply to assembly language programming. Those that do apply will make your programming life a great deal easier. Here are the options you should set up after installing Kate:

- **Editor Mode:** Select Tools → Mode → Assembler → Intel x86 (**NASM**). This helps Kate recognize NASM syntax.

- **Syntax Highlighting:** Select Tools → Highlighting → Assembler → Intel x86 (**NASM**). This enables Kate to highlight source code mnemonics and symbols in the editor window.

- **Enable line number display:** Pull down the View menu and click on the check box marked Show Line Numbers. Line number display can also be toggled on and off with the F11 function key. I refer to individual lines within programs by line number, and having line numbers displayed will make it easier for you to zero in on the line under discussion.

- **Enable the icon border display:** Select View → Show Icon Border. This is where bookmarks are indicated (with a star); and if you intend to use bookmarks in your files, the icon border must be visible. Note that you can toggle the icon border on and off at any time by pressing F6.

- **Enable external tools:** Select Settings → Configure Kate and click on the Plugins line in the options tree view. This will bring up Kate's Plugin Manager dialog (see Figure 6-4). Three plugins should have been enabled simply by installing KWrite: the Terminal tool view, the Find in Files tool view, and the File system browser. Find and check the check box for External Tools.

- **Enable Terminal synchronization:** In the Plugins dialog, select Terminal. There's only one check box, and when checked, Kate will change the working directory (as shown in the Terminal pane) to the directory where the currently opened file resides. In essence, this means that whenever you open a session, the working directory will change to the directory where the session's files live. This is important, and I will assume that this option is checked when describing Kate's operation elsewhere in this book.

- **Enable Kate File Templates:** As with the previous item, this is found in the Plugins dialog. Find the Kate File templates item and check the box.

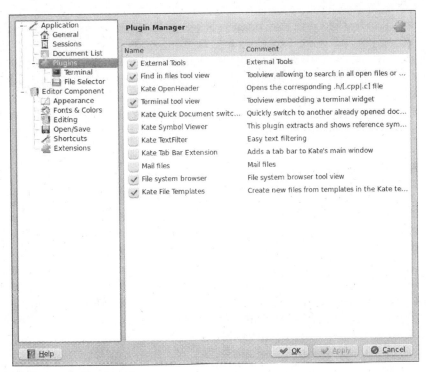

Figure 6-4: Kate's Plugins Manager

Most of the other options are either tweaks to the display or things pertinent to higher-level languages such as C and C++. As you explore Kate you may find a few things you want to customize, but initially this is all you need to change.

Kate Sessions

If you're like most programmers, you don't usually work on only one project at a time. I always have five or six in play, and I tinker with one or another as time allows and inspiration directs. Each project lives in its own directory, and each project has several files—for the ambitious ones, sometimes ten or twenty. When I decide I've had enough tangling with one project and want to move to another, I don't want to have to close Kate, change the working directory to that of another project, run Kate again, and then load the pertinent files into Kate. This is how we used to work years ago, and it's a lot more bother than it needs to be, especially when your editor has a feature like Kate's sessions.

A *session* is basically the current state of a project and all its various files and settings, saved on disk. When you want to begin working on a project, you load its session file from disk. Bang! All the files associated with the project are there in the sidebar, and the terminal pane has moved to the project's directory. The last file you had open will be open again, with the cursor at the place where you left it the last time you worked on it.

When you close a session, change sessions, or shut Kate down, Kate saves the current state of the session to disk before bringing in a new session or shutting itself down. You can move from one project to another in only seconds.

Handling sessions is easy. The following sections describe all the common tasks of session management.

Creating a New Session

When you launch Kate, it first presents you with the Session Chooser dialog (refer to Figure 6-1). The dialog will list all the sessions that exist, and provide a button for creating a new session. If you're starting a new project, click New Session. Kate will open with a brand-new, blank session.

You can also create a new session from within Kate at any time, by selecting Sessions → New from the menu. These new sessions do not have names, and are not saved as sessions until you load a file. I suggest giving a new session a name immediately. This is done by selecting Sessions → Save As from the menu. A small dialog will appear in which you can enter a session name. Enter the name of the new session, and click OK.

The name of a session can be anything. It does not have to be the name of the main .ASM file, nor does it have to be of a limited length, nor conform to

Linux file-naming conventions. Note that the name of a new session will *not* appear in the window title until you load a file into the editor.

Once you have a named session, you can begin opening files and working with them. You can resize Kate's window, and the size of the window will be retained as an aspect of the session, so if your source code files are of a different width for some reason, you can resize Kate to display the full width of the source, and Kate will remember the window dimensions when you switch sessions.

Opening an Existing Session

As with creating a new session, opening an existing session can be done when you launch Kate. The Session Chooser dialog will show you all existing Kate sessions. Highlight the session you want and click Open Session.

Sessions can also be opened from Kate's Sessions menu. Two items on the Sessions menu allow this:

- Sessions → Open brings up a dialog in which you can highlight a session and then click its Open button.
- Sessions → Quick Open brings up a submenu listing all Kate sessions. Select one and left-click to open the session.

There is no Close Session option. You can close a session only by loading a different session or creating a new session, or by closing down Kate entirely. If you want a blank session, you must create a new one, remembering that unless and until saved under a particular name, a new session is not retained by Kate.

Deleting or Renaming Sessions

Deleting or renaming sessions is done using the Manage Sessions dialog, which you can invoke by selecting Sessions → Manage from the Kate menus. The dialog displays all existing sessions. Once you click to select a particular session, you can either click the Rename button to rename it or click the Delete button to delete it entirely.

Note that *deleting a session has no effect whatsoever on the files or the directory associated with the session.* All that is deleted is Kate's record of the session. Your files are not affected.

Another way to rename a session is to select Sessions → Save As and save the current session under a new name. After that, delete the original session from the Manage Sessions dialog.

Kate's File Management

Kate makes it easy to load existing files into the editor window, browse your session working directory, create new files, rename files, and move unneeded files to the Trash.

The primary mechanism for file management is the sidebar on the left side of the Kate window. Absent other plugins that use it, the management sidebar serves two functions:

- When in the Document view, the sidebar displays the documents associated with the current session. You can click on one of the document listing lines to load a document into the editor window. When a file in the Document view contains unsaved changes, that file's entry will display a floppy disk icon.

- When in the Filesystem Browser view, the sidebar shows you what files are present in the session working directory.

Vertically oriented icon buttons in the left margin of the sidebar enable you to choose which of the two views to display. Figure 6-5 shows the management sidebar in the Filesystem Browser view. The difference between the two views is slightly subtle but worth remembering: the Document view shows you what files are part of the current Kate session. The Filesystem Browser view shows you what files are present *on disk*, in the working directory for the project described by the current session. Removing a file from the Document view removes the document from the session. Removing a file from the Filesystem Browser view deletes the file from disk. Don't get the two mixed up!

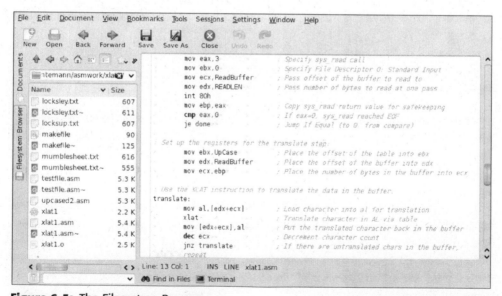

Figure 6-5: The Filesystem Browser

If you have enough horizontal space on your display, you can display file details in the Filesystem Browser. By default, Kate displays only the filename in the browser. To display file details, right-click anywhere in the Filesystem Browser. From the context menu that appears, select View → Detailed View. The Detailed view provides the size of the file, its type, and the date and time that the file was last modified. This typically triples the width of the management sidebar, but it can be handy if you have a lot of files in your working directory.

The following sections briefly describe the most important file management tasks that you can perform from within Kate.

Filesystem Browser Navigation

At the top of the Filesystem Browser is a horizontal row of eight small buttons. These buttons are used to navigate your folder. Here's what the buttons do, starting from the button on the left and working right:

- The blue, upward-pointing arrow moves the browser to the parent folder of the current folder. When you reach root, the arrow is grayed out.
- The blue arrow pointing to the left moves the browser back to the folder where it was before the last move. This works the same way that the Back button does in Web browsers and standalone file managers.
- The blue arrow pointing to the right moves you forward into a folder that you have already visited. This works the same way that the Forward button does in Web browsers and standalone file managers.
- The house icon moves you to your home folder.
- The next two icons govern the detail level in the Filesystem Browser view. The one to the left selects the Short view. The one to the right selects the Detailed view.
- The gold star icon brings up a submenu that enables you to manage folder bookmarks.
- The blue, two-headed arrow brings you back to the folder where the file currently in the editor is stored.

Adding a File to the Current Session

From the Filesystem Browser view: click on any file and it will be loaded into the editor and added to the session. If you click on a binary file, rather than a text file, Kate will pop up a dialog warning you that binary files cannot be edited, and if saved out to disk from Kate can be corrupted. (Kate is a text editor, and unlike hex editors such as Bless, it cannot edit binary files.) Until you explicitly close the file added to the session, it will remain part of the session.

Dropping a File from the Current Session

From the Document view: right-click on the file that you wish to drop from the session and select Close from the context menu. The file will be dropped, but remember that *it will not be deleted*—simply dropped from the list of files associated with the current session.

Switching Between Session Files in the Editor

From the Document view: click on the file that you want to load into the editor and it will become the file under edit. Changes made to the file formerly in the edit window will *not* be written to disk simply by switching the file currently in the window! When you click on filenames in the Document view, you're simply switching which file is on display in the window. All of the files in the session can be under edit; you're simply bouncing quickly between views. You can also switch between session files using the blue Back and Forward arrows in the main toolbar.

Creating a Brand-New File

Click the New button on the main toolbar, or select File → New from the main menu. A new file with the temporary name Untitled will appear in the Document view, and will become the file on display in the editor window. You can begin entering text immediately, but the file will not be saved to disk until you select or click Save As and give the new file a name. Shortcut: Ctrl+N.

Creating a Brand-New Folder on Disk

From the Filesystem Browser view: right-click on "blank space" anywhere outside the list of files (i.e., don't right-click on a file's entry) and select New Folder from the context menu. A dialog will appear in which you can enter a name for the new folder, which by default is created beneath the current directory.

Deleting a File from Disk (Move File to Trash)

From the Filesystem Browser view: highlight the file to be deleted and right-click on it. From the context menu select Move to Trash. Kate will present a confirmation dialog to ensure you intended to trash the file. Click the Trash button and the file will be moved to the Trash folder. Shortcut: Del.

Reloading a File from Disk

Select File → Reload from the main menu. This command can be handy if you make changes to a file that you didn't intend to, and want to return to the state of the file the last time it was saved to disk. The command will load the file from disk back into the editor window, and any unsaved changes to the file will be lost. Shortcut: F5.

Saving All Unsaved Changes in Session Files

Select File → Save All from the main menu. If you have any newly created files that have not yet been saved to disk, Kate will present a Save As dialog for the new file, enabling you to name and save it. Note that whereas Kate saves all unsaved changes to disk when you exit the program, if power fails while you're working, some or all of your unsaved changes may be lost. This is why I added a Save All button to the main toolbar, and why I click it every so often during long sessions. (I'll explain how to add the button to the toolbar a little later.) Shortcut: Ctrl+L.

Printing the File in the Editor Window

Select File → Print from the main menu. The Print dialog will appear, allowing you to select which printer to print to, and otherwise configure the print job. Shortcut: Ctrl+P.

Exporting a File As HTML

Select File → Export as HTML from the main menu. This is useful if you have the need to post one of your source code files on the Web. The command pops up a Save As dialog, and will create a new HTML file under the name you enter, containing the current file in the editor window, with source code formatting added. The idea is that the exported HTML file will appear in a Web browser precisely as it appears in the Kate editor window, syntax highlighting and all.

Adding Items to the Toolbar

Kate's default toolbar already contains buttons for the commands you use most often. The toolbar is configurable, however, and there is at least one button that I think should be up there: the Save All button. With one click, the Save All command saves all unsaved changes to disk, for all files open as part of the current session. It's a good idea to hit Save All every few minutes, on the outside chance that the power goes out before you exit Kate or manually save changes on the individual files.

Here's how it's done: Select Settings → Configure Toolbars. The Toolbar dialog will appear (see Figure 6-6). Scroll down the list of available actions on the left side of the dialog until the Save All command comes into view. Click it to highlight it. Then click the right-pointing arrow. The Save All command will move into the list on the right side of the dialog, which represents those buttons present on the main toolbar.

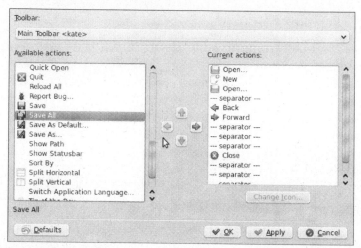

Figure 6-6: The Toolbar dialog

By default, Save All will be added to the list of toolbar buttons at the bottom. If you want the Save All button to be up with the Save and Save As buttons, click the Save All button item to highlight it, and then click the upward-pointing arrow to move the Save All button upward through the button items.

There's a peculiarity in the version of Kate I was using while writing this book: the Save and Save As buttons do not "show" in the button list on the right side of the dialog. To get Save All to join its salvational brothers, move it up until it is just below the separator line located right under the two blue arrows. Then click OK, and you'll see Save All in your toolbar, right where it should be. Click it early and often!

Kate's Editing Controls

Kate's most important purpose, of course, is to edit your source code files. Most of the time you'll spend inside Kate will be spent working on your source code, so it's useful to commit its editing controls to memory as quickly as you can. Of course, nothing does that like practice, but to get started, the following sections explain how to move around in Kate and perform the basic editing tasks.

Cursor Movement

Basic cursor movement follows conventional practice on PC-type systems:

- The left and right arrow keys move the cursor one position left or right. If the cursor is at either extreme of a line, cursor movement wraps to adjacent lines as expected.

- Ctrl+left arrow moves the cursor left by one word. Ctrl+right arrow moves the cursor right by one word. Both wrap at line ends.

- The up and down arrow keys move the cursor one line up or down.

- Ctrl+up arrow and Ctrl+down arrow scroll the *view* up or down without moving the cursor. Let go of the Ctrl key, and the next arrow press returns the view to the current cursor position. (This enables you to look up or down the file for a moment without losing your place, i.e., where you're currently working on the text.)

- Home moves the cursor to the left end of the current line. However, if the text is indented, the cursor will move only to the leftmost visible character.

- Ctrl+Home moves to the beginning of the document.

- End moves the cursor to the right end of the current line.

- Ctrl+End moves to the end of the document.

- Pg Up and Pg Dn move the cursor up or down, respectively, by the number of lines displayed in the window at its current size (e.g., if the screen is sized to show 30 lines, Pg Up and Pg Dn will move the cursor by 30 lines).

- You can move to a particular line in the file by pressing Ctrl+G. A page number field will appear at the bottom of the editor window. Enter the number of the destination line in the field and press Enter to move to that line.

Bookmarks

Kate enables you to set bookmarks in your files. These are a handy way to provide quick navigation to important points in the file, especially when your files begin to run to hundreds or even thousands of lines. For example, I generally set bookmarks on the starting lines of the .DATA, .BSS, and .TEXT sections (more on this in later chapters) so that if I have to add or edit a predefined data item I can "teleport" back to the .DATA section instantly without scrolling and hunting for it visually.

The easiest way to set a bookmark is by clicking in the icon border immediately to the left of the line you wish to bookmark. This requires that the icon border be visible; if it isn't, press F6 to display it. When a bookmark is set, the icon border at the bookmarked line will show a small yellow star icon.

You can also set a bookmark by placing the cursor on the line to be bookmarked and right-clicking the line. Select Bookmarks → Set Bookmark from the context menu. Any line with a bookmark set on it will be highlighted via background color.

Bookmarks are toggles: Clicking in the icon border (or pressing the shortcut Ctrl+B) will set a bookmark; clicking on the bookmark's gold star icon or pressing Ctrl+B again will clear that bookmark.

All bookmarks in a single file may be cleared at once by selecting Bookmarks → Clear All Bookmarks.

To move to a bookmark, bring down the Sessions menu and do one of two things:

- Find the bookmark that you want in the list at the bottom of the menu and click on it. The bookmark is tagged with the line number and the source code text where the bookmark was placed.

- Select either Previous or Next to move to the next bookmark up or down from the current cursor position.

Selecting Text

As in any text editor, text may be selected in Kate for deletion, for moving via click-and-drag, or for placing onto the clipboard. Selecting text can be done in several ways:

- Place the mouse cursor over a word and double-click the word to select it.

- Place the mouse cursor anywhere in a line and triple-click to select the entire line.

- Place the mouse cursor where you want to begin a selection, and then press the left mouse button and drag the mouse to the opposite end of the desired selection. Interestingly, selecting text this way automatically copies the selection into the clipboard, but with a twist: text selected this way is stored in a separate clipboard, and can be pasted into the document *only* by clicking the middle mouse button, if you have one. Ctrl+V or selecting Edit → Paste won't do it. Text selected earlier with Ctrl+C or Edit → Copy will still be on the conventional clipboard. Note that on most modern mice, the mouse wheel acts as a middle button and may be clicked just like the left and right buttons. Text selected by click-and-drag may be manipulated by the conventional edit commands such as Ctrl+C, Ctrl+X, and Ctrl+V.

- By selecting Edit → Block Selection Mode (shortcut: Ctrl+Shift+B) you can select rectangular areas of text without respecting line lengths. When Block Selection Mode is in force, dragging the mouse with the left button pressed will select an area with the starting point at one corner and the ending point (where you release the left mouse button) at the opposite corner.

- From the keyboard, text may be selected by holding down the Shift key while navigating with the various navigation keys. The cursor will move as normally, and all text between the original cursor position and the new cursor position will be selected.

Selected text may be dragged to a new position in the file in the usual way: by pressing and holding the left mouse button while moving the mouse pointer.

Searching the Text

Kate's text search feature operates out of a built-in dialog called the *search bar* that appears when needed at the bottom of the editor window. There are two forms of the search bar: one for simple incremental searches, and another for managing search and replace operations.

Select Edit → Find or press Ctrl+F to bring up the incremental search bar. By default, the search bar that appears manages a simple, incremental search mechanism. Enter text in the Find field, and while you're entering the text, Kate will search for the first incremental match of the text that you're typing (see Figure 6-7).

In Figure 6-7, I typed **DoneMsg** and Kate found and highlighted the first instance of that text in the file while I was still typing. The highlighted text is selected, and may be moved by dragging, or cut or copied using the conventional edit commands. The Next and Previous buttons search for the same text after the current cursor position or before it, respectively.

The Options menu at the right end of the search bar allows some refinements to the search process. If you select Options → Highlight All, Kate will select the next instance of the search text as expected, but will also highlight *all* instances of the search text anywhere in the file, in a different color. If you select Options → Match case, the search will be case sensitive; otherwise, case differences in the text are ignored.

The incremental search bar may be hidden by clicking the red close button at the upper-left corner of the bar.

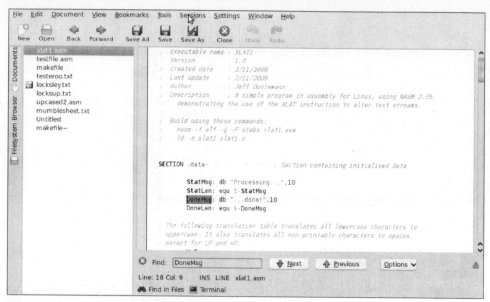

Figure 6-7: The incremental search bar

Using Search and Replace

Search and replace is handled by a second search bar, which may be invoked by selecting Edit → Replace or pressing Ctrl+R (see Figure 6-8). You enter text in the Find field; and as with simple search, Kate performs an incremental search to find and select the first instance in the file. If you type in replacement text in the Replace field, Kate will replace the text in the Find field with the text in the Replace field when you click the Replace button. Or, if you click the Replace All button, Kate will perform the search and replace operation on the entire file, replacing all instances of the text in the Find field with the text in the Replace field.

The several options governing the search are displayed as buttons (on the right) and not drop-down menu items. The options work as they do for the incremental search bar. There is one additional option: if you check Selection Only, the search and replace operation will occur only within whatever text is selected.

The search and replace bar may be hidden by clicking the red close button in the bar's upper-left corner.

Using Kate While Programming

At least for the programs I present in this book, Kate is going to be the "workbench" where we edit, assemble, link, test, and debug our code. In other words, you run Kate from the Applications menu or from a desktop or panel launcher, and then everything else you do you do from inside Kate.

"Inside" here has an interesting wrinkle: Kate has its own built-in Linux terminal window, and this terminal window enables us to launch other tools from inside Kate: specifically, the Make utility (more on this in the next section) and whatever debugger you decide to use. Anything you can do from the Linux console you can do in Kate's terminal window, which by default connects to the Linux console.

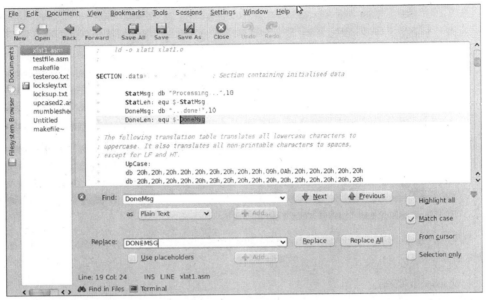

Figure 6-8: The search and replace bar

Although you can launch Kate itself from inside a terminal window, I don't recommend this. When launched from a terminal, Kate posts status information relating to its own internal machinery to the window pretty much continuously. This is for the sake of the programmers who are working on Kate, but it's of little or no value to Kate's users, and yet another distraction on your screen. It's much better to create a desktop or panel launcher icon and launch Kate from the icon.

Creating and Using Project Directories

As explained earlier in this section, an assembly language project maps neatly onto Kate's idea of a session. A project should reside in its own directory under your assembly language work directory, which in turn should reside under your Ubuntu Home directory. All files associated with the project (except for library files shared among projects) should remain in that project's directory. In this book, I'll refer to your overall assembly language work directory as "asmwork."

The example code archive I've created for this book is a ZIP archive, and when you extract the archive to your hard drive in your asmwork directory, it will create a project directory for each of the example programs. To open these "readymade" project directories from Kate for the first time, do this:

1. Launch Kate.
2. When the Session Chooser dialog appears, click New Session.
3. Click the Open button on the main toolbar, or select File → Open. Use the Open File dialog that appears to navigate to the project directory that you want, starting from your Home directory.
4. When the files in the project directory are displayed, open the source code files and makefile. You can do this in one operation by holding Ctrl down while clicking on all the files you wish to open. All selected files will be highlighted. Then click the dialog's Open button to open them all.
5. Once all the opened files are displayed in the Documents view in the Kate sidebar, save the new session with a descriptive name. This is done by selecting Sessions → Save As and typing the name for the new session in the Session Name dialog that appears. Click OK, and you have a new Kate session for that project directory.

When you want to create a brand-new project for which no directory exists yet, do this:

1. Launch Kate.
2. When the Session Chooser dialog appears, click New Session.
3. Click the Filesystem Browser button to display the Filesystem Browser view.
4. Navigate to your assembly language working directory ("asmwork," for example) using the Filesystem Browser.
5. Right-click anywhere in the Filesystem Browser view, and from the context menu select New Folder. Type a name for the new directory and click OK.
6. Save the new session under a new name, as described in step 5.

At this point you can begin entering source code text for your new project. Don't forget to save it periodically, by clicking Save All.

Kate's terminal window is not displayed by default. You can display it by clicking the Terminal icon at the bottom edge of Kate's window. Note that the terminal will not display a brand-new project directory that you just created until you save at least one document from Kate into that directory. Kate synchronizes the terminal to the location of the document shown in the editor window, and until there's a document in the editor window that's been saved to a specific location in your directory tree, there's nowhere for the terminal window to "go."

Once you have a project directory and have begun saving files into that directory from Kate, your workflow will go something like this:

1. Enter and make changes to your source code files and make-file in Kate's editor window. Save all changes to disk.

2. Build your project by clicking in the terminal window to give it the focus, and then enter the **make** command at the terminal command line. Assuming you've created a makefile for the project, the Make utility will launch NASM and the linker, and will show any errors that occur during the build. (More on Make later in this chapter.)

3. Test the executable built by Make by ensuring that the terminal window has the focus, and then enter *./myprog*, where *"myprog"* is the name of the executable file that you want to test.

4. If you want to observe your program running in a debugger, make sure the terminal window has the focus, and then enter the name of the debugger, followed by the name of the executable—for example, **insight myprog**. The debugger will appear with your program loaded and read to observe. When you're done debugging, exit the debugger to return to Kate.

5. Return to the editor by clicking on the editor window to give it the focus, and continue working on your source files.

Focus!

The issue of where the focus is may trip you up when you're first getting used to working with Kate. In any modern windowing environment like GNOME or KDE, the focus is basically the screen component that receives keystrokes you type. Most of the time, you'll be typing into Kate's editor window, because the editor window has the focus while you're editing. If you don't explicitly move the focus to the terminal, you'll end up typing **make** or other Linux commands into your source code files—and if you don't notice that you're doing this (and it's very easy to forget in the heat of software creation), you may find the text pointed up by NASM in an error message the next time you try to assemble the project.

It's easy to tell if the terminal window has the focus or not: if the terminal's block cursor is a hollow box, the focus is elsewhere. If the terminal's block cursor is a filled box, the terminal has the focus.

Linux and Terminals

Unix people hated to admit it at the time, but when it was created, Unix really was a mainframe operating system like IBM's, and it supported multiple simultaneous users via timesharing. Each user communicated with the central computer through separate, standalone terminals, especially those from the Digital Equipment Corporation's VT series.

These terminals did *not* display the graphical desktops that have been mainstream since 1995 so. They were text-only devices, typically presenting 25 lines of 80 characters each, without icons or windows. Some applications used the full screen, presenting numbered menus and fill-in fields for data entry. The bulk of the Unix software tools, especially those used by programmers, were controlled from the command line, and sent back scroll-up-from-the-bottom output.

Linux works the same way. Put most simply, Linux *is* Unix. Linux does not use external "dumb terminals" like the 1970s DEC VT100, but the DEC-style terminal-oriented software machinery is still there inside Linux and still functioning, in the form of terminal emulation.

The Linux Console

There are any number of terminal emulator programs for Linux and other Unix implementations like BSD. Ubuntu comes with one called the *GNOME Terminal*, and you can download and install many others from the Applications → Add/Remove menu item. The one that I use for the discussions in this book and recommend generally is called Konsole. Do install it if you haven't already.

When you open a terminal emulator program under Linux, you get a text command line with a flashing cursor, much like the old DOS command line or the Command Prompt utility in Windows. The terminal program does its best to act like one of those old DEC CRT serial terminals from the First Age of Unix. By default, a terminal emulator program uses the PC keyboard and display for its input and output. What it connects to is a special Linux device called *dev/console*, which is a predefined device that provides communication with the Linux system itself.

It's useful to remember that a terminal program is just a program, and you can have several different varieties of terminal program installed on your Linux machine, and multiple instances of each running, all at the same time. However, there is only *one* Linux console, by which I mean the device named dev/console that channels commands to the Linux system and returns the system's responses. By default, a terminal emulator program connects to dev/console when it launches. If you want, you can use a Linux terminal emulator to connect to other things through a network, though how that works and how to do it are outside the scope of this book.

The simplest way of communicating with a Linux program is through a terminal emulator like the Konsole program, the one I'll refer to in this book. The alternative to a terminal emulator is to write your programs for a windowing system of some kind. Describing Linux desktop managers and the X Window system that operates beneath them would itself take an entire book (or several), and involves layers of complexity that really have nothing to do with assembly language. Therefore, in this book the example programs operate strictly from the terminal emulator command line.

Character Encoding in Konsole

There's not much to configure in a terminal emulator program, at least while taking your first steps in assembly language. One thing that does matter for the example programs in this book is *character encoding*. A terminal emulator has to put characters into its window, and one of the configurable options is related to what glyphs correspond to which 8-bit character code.

Note well that this has nothing directly to do with fonts. A glyph is a specific recognizable symbol, like the letter "A" or the @ sign. How that symbol is rendered graphically depends on what font you use. Rendered in different fonts, a particular glyph might be fatter or thinner or have little feet or flourishes of various kinds. You can display an "A" in any number of fonts, but assuming that the font is not excessively decorative (and such fonts exist), you can still tell that a particular glyph is an "A."

Character encoding maps a numeric value to a particular glyph. In our familiar Western ASCII standard, the number 65 is associated with the glyph we recognize as an uppercase "A." In a different character encoding, one created to render an entirely different, non-Roman alphabet (such as Hebrew, Arabic, or Thai) the number 65 might be associated with an entirely different glyph.

This book was written in a Roman alphabet for a Western and mostly English-speaking audience, so our terminal emulator's default glyphs for the alphabet will do just fine. However, the ASCII character set really only goes from character 0 up to character 127. Eight bits can express values up to 256, so there are another 128 "high" characters beyond the top end of the ASCII standard. There's no strong standard for which glyphs appear when those 128 high characters are displayed, certainly nothing as strong as the ASCII standard for the lower 128 characters. Different character encoding schemes for the high 128 include many different glyphs, most of them Roman characters with modifiers (umlaut, circumflex, tilde, accents, and so on), the major Greek letters, and symbols from mathematics and logic.

When IBM released its original PC in 1981, it included glyphs that it had created for its mainframe terminals years earlier, to enable boxes to be rendered on terminal screens that were text-only and could not display pixel graphics. These glyphs turned out to be very useful for delimiting fill-in forms and other things. The PC's ROM-based character set eventually came to be called *Code Page 437 (CP437)*, which includes a lot of other symbols, such as the four card suits.

A similar character encoding scheme was later used in IBM's Unix implementation, AIX, and was called IBM-850. IBM-850 includes a subset of the box-draw characters in CP437, plus a lot of Roman alphabet characters with modifiers, to enable the correct rendering of text in Western languages other than English.

Linux terminal emulators do not encode either the CP437 encoding scheme or the IBM-850 scheme (and thus its box-border characters) by default. The IBM-850 encoding scheme is available, but you have to select it from the menus. Later in the book we'll need those box-draw characters, and this is as good a place as any to describe how to select them. (By the way, at this writing I have not seen a Linux terminal emulator capable of displaying IBM's original CP437 character set, but if you know of one do pass it along.)

Launch Konsole and pull down the Settings → Manage Profiles item. Konsole comes with one profile, named Shell. In the Manage Profiles dialog that appears, select New Profile, and give it a name like "Shell Box." In the Edit Profile dialog, select the Advanced tab, and look for the Encoding drop-down at the bottom of the pane. Click Select, and from the list presented, hover over Western European until the list of encodings appears. Select IBM850, and then click OK (see Figure 6-9).

When the Shell Box profile is in force, the IBM box-border characters will be available for use in your programs.

The Three Standard Unix Files

Computers have been described as machines that move data around, and that's not a bad way to see it. That said, the best way to get a grip on program input and output via terminal emulators is to understand one of Unix's fundamental design principles: *Everything is a file*. A file can be a collection of data on disk, as I explained in some detail in Chapter 5; but in more general terms, a file is an endpoint on a path taken by data. When you write to a file, you're sending data along a path to an endpoint. When you read from a file, you are accepting data from an endpoint. The path that the data takes between files may be entirely within a single computer, or it may be between computers along a network of some kind. Data may be processed and changed along the path, or it may simply move from one endpoint to another without modification. No matter. Everything is a file, and all files are treated more or less identically by Unix's internal file machinery.

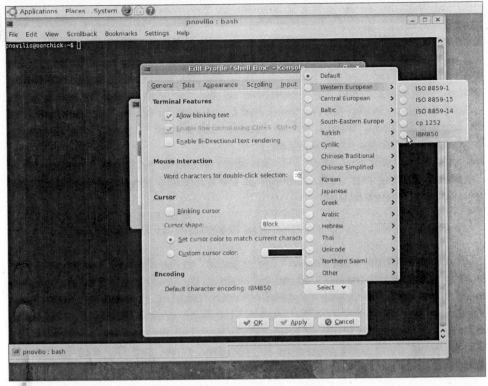

Figure 6-9: Changing Konsole's character encoding to IBM-850

The "everything is a file" dictum applies to more than collections of data on disk. Your keyboard is a file: it's an endpoint that generates data and sends it somewhere. Your display is a file: it's an endpoint that receives data from somewhere and puts it where you can see it. Unix files do not have to be text files. Binary files (like the executables created by NASM and the linker) are handled the same way.

Table 6-1 lists the three standard files defined by Unix. These files are always open to your programs while the programs are running.

Table 6-1: The Three Standard Unix Files

FILE	C IDENTIFIER	FILE DESCRIPTOR	DEFAULTS TO
Standard Input	stdin	0	Keyboard
Standard Output	stdout	1	Display
Standard Error	stderr	2	Display

At the bottom of it, a file is known to the operating system by its file descriptor, which is just a number. The first three such numbers belong to the three standard files. When you open an existing file or create a new file from within a program, Linux will return a file descriptor value specific to the file you've opened or created. To manipulate the file, you call into the operating system and pass it the file descriptor of the file you want to work with. Table 6-1 also provides the conventional identifiers by which the standard files are known in the C world. When people talk about "stdout," for example, they're talking about file descriptor 1.

If you refer back to Listing 5-1, the short example program I presented in Chapter 5 during our walk-through of the assembly language development process, you'll see this line:

```
mov ebx,1              ; Specify File Descriptor 1: Standard Output
```

When we sent the little slogan "Eat at Joe's!" to the display, we were in fact writing it to file descriptor 1, standard output. By changing the value to 2, we could have sent the slogan to standard error instead. It wouldn't have been displayed any differently on the screen. Standard error is identical in all ways to standard output in terms of how data is handled. By custom, programs like NASM send their error messages to standard error, but the text written to standard error isn't marked as an "error message" or displayed in a different color or character set. Standard error and standard output exist so that we can keep our program's output separate from our program's errors and other messages related to how and what the program is doing.

This will make a lot more sense once you understand one of the most useful basic mechanisms of all Unix-descended systems: I/O redirection.

I/O Redirection

By default, standard output goes to the display (generally a terminal emulator window), but that's just the default. You can change the endpoint for a data stream coming from standard output. The data from standard output can be sent to a file on disk instead. A file is a file; data traffic between files is handled the same way by Linux, so switching endpoints is no big trick. Data from standard output can be sent to an existing file or it can be sent to a new file created when your program is run.

By default, input to your programs comes from the keyboard, but all the keyboard sends is text. This text could also come from another text file. Switching the source of data sent to your programs is no more difficult than switching the destination of its output. The mechanism for doing so is called *I/O redirection*, and we're going to use it for a lot of the example programs in this book.

You've probably already used I/O redirection in your Linux work, even if you didn't know it by name. All of Linux's basic shell commands send their output to standard output. The `ls` command, for example, sends a listing of the contents of the working directory to standard output. You can capture that listing by redirecting the text emitted by `ls` into a Linux disk file. To do so, enter this command at the command line:

```
ls > dircontents.txt
```

The file dircontents.txt is created if it doesn't already exist, and the text emitted by `ls` is stored in dircontents.txt. You can then print the file or load it into a text editor.

The ">" symbol is one of two redirection operators. The "<" symbol works the other way, and redirects standard input away from the keyboard and to another file, typically a text file stored on disk. This is less useful for handing keyboard commands to a program than it is for providing the raw material on which the program is going to work.

Let's say you want to write a program to force all the lowercase text in a file to uppercase characters. (This is a wonderfully contrarian thing to do, as uppercase characters make some Unix people half-nuts.) You can write the program to obtain its text from standard input and send its text to standard output. This is very easy to do from a programming standpoint—and in fact we'll be doing it a little further along in the book.

You can test your program by typing a line of text at the keyboard:

```
i want live things in their pride to remain.
```

Your program would process the preceding line of text and send the processed text to standard output, where it would be posted to the terminal emulator display:

```
I WANT LIVE THINGS IN THEIR PRIDE TO REMAIN.
```

Well, the test was a success: it looks like things worked inside the program. The next step is to test uppercaser on some real files. You don't have to change the uppercaser program at all. Just enter this at the shell prompt:

```
uppercaser < santafetrail.txt > vachelshouting.txt
```

By the magic of I/O redirection, your program will read all the text from a disk file called santafetrail.txt, force any lowercase characters to uppercase, and then write the uppercase text to the disk file vachelshouting.txt.

The redirection operators can be thought of as arrows pointing in the direction that data is moving. Data is being taken from the file santafetrail.txt and sent to the uppercaser program; thus the symbol < points from the input file to the program where it's going. The uppercaser program is sending data to the output file vachelshouting.txt, and thus the redirection operator points away from the name of the program and toward the name of the output file.

From a height, what's going on looks like what I've drawn in Figure 6-10. I/O redirection acts as a sort of data switch, steering streams of data away from the standard files to named source and destination files of your own choosing.

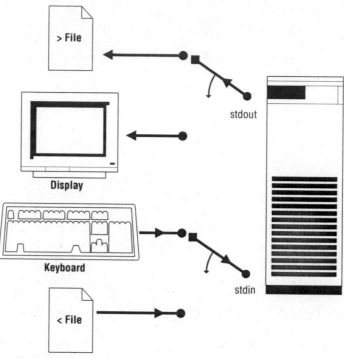

Figure 6-10: I/O redirection

Simple Text Filters

We're actually going to create a little program called uppercaser later, and that's exactly what it's going to do: read text from a text file, process the text, and write the processed text to an output file. Inside the program, we'll be reading from standard input and writing to standard output. This makes it unnecessary for the program to prompt the user for input and output filenames, create the output file, and so on. Linux will do all that for us, which makes for a much easier programming task.

Programs that work this way represent a standard mechanism in the greater Unix world, called a *filter*. You've already met a couple of them. The NASM assembler itself is a filter: it takes text files full of assembly language source code, processes them, and writes out a binary file full of object code and symbol information. The Linux linker reads in one or more files full of object code and symbol information, and writes out an executable program file. NASM and the linker operate on more than simple text, but that's OK. A file is a file is a file, and the machinery that Linux uses to operate on files doesn't distinguish between text and binary files.

Filter programs don't always use I/O redirection to locate their inputs and outputs. NASM and most linkers pick their source and destination filenames off the command line, which is a useful trick discussed later in the book. Still, I/O redirection makes programming simple text filter programs *much* easier.

Once you grasp how filter programs work, you'll begin to understand why the standard error file exists and what it does. A filter program processes input data into output data. Along the way, it may need to post an error message, or simply confirm to us that it's still plugging along and hasn't fallen into an endless loop. For that, we need a communication channel independent of the program's inputs and outputs. Standard error provides such a communication channel. Your program can post textual status and error messages to the terminal emulator display by writing those messages to the standard error file, all during the time that it's working and the standard output file is busy writing program output to disk.

Standard error can be redirected just as standard output is. For example, if you wanted to capture your program's status and/or error messages to a disk file named joblog.txt, you would launch the program from the terminal command line this way:

```
uppercaser < santafetrail.txt > vachelshouting.txt 2> joblog.txt
```

Here, the 2> operator specifies that file descriptor 2 (which, if you recall, is standard error) is being redirected to joblog.txt.

If you redirect output (from whatever source) to an existing disk file, redirection will replace whatever may already be in the file with new data, and the old data will be overwritten and lost. If you want to append redirected data to the end of an existing file that already contains data, you must use the >> append operator instead.

Terminal Control with Escape Sequences

By default, output to a terminal emulator window enters at the left end of the bottom line, and previously displayed lines scroll up with the addition of each new line at the bottom. This is perfectly useful, but it's not pretty and certainly doesn't qualify as a "user interface" in any honest sense. There were plenty of "full screen" applications written for the Unix operating system in ancient times, and they wrote their data entry fields and prompts all over the screen. When color display terminals became available, text could be displayed in different colors, on fields with backgrounds set to white or to some other color to contrast with the text.

How was this done? The old DEC VT terminals like the VT100 could be controlled by way of special sequences of characters embedded in the stream of data sent to the terminal from standard output or standard error. These sequences of characters were called *escape sequences*, because they were an "escape" (albeit a temporary one) from the ordinary stream of data being sent up to be displayed.

The VT terminals watched the data streams that they were displaying, and picked out the characters in the escape sequences for separate interpretation. One escape sequence would be interpreted as a command to clear the display; another escape sequence would be interpreted as a command to display the next characters on the screen starting five lines from the top of the screen and thirty characters from the left margin. There were dozens of such recognized escape sequences, and they enabled the relatively crude text terminals of the day to present neatly formatted text to the user one full screen at a time.

A Linux terminal emulator like Konsole is a program written to "look like" one of those old DEC terminals, at least in terms of how it displays data on our 21st century LCD computer monitors. Send the character sequence "Eat at Joe's!" to Konsole, and Konsole puts it up obediently in its window, just like the old VT100s did. You've already seen that, with Listing 5-1. Konsole, however, watches the stream of characters that we send to it, and it knows those escape sequences as well. The key to Konsole's vigilance lies in a special character that is normally invisible: ESC, the numeric equivalent of which is 27, or 01Bh. When Konsole sees an ESC character come in on the stream of text that it is displaying, it looks very carefully at the next several characters. If the first three characters after the ESC character are [2J, then Konsole recognizes that as the escape sequence that commands it to clear its display. If, however, the four characters after the ESC are [11H, then Konsole sees an escape sequence commanding it to move the cursor to the home position in the upper-left corner of the display.

There are literally dozens of different escape sequences, all of them representing commands to do things such as move the cursor around; change the foreground and background colors of characters; switch fonts or character encodings; erase lines, portions of lines, or portions of the entire screen; and so on. Programs running in a terminal window can take complete control over the display by sending carefully crafted escape sequences to standard output. (We'll do some of this a little later; just keep in mind that there are caveats, and the whole business is not as simple as it sounds.) Prior to the era of graphical user interface (GUI) applications, sending escape sequences to terminals (or terminal emulators) was precisely how display programming under Unix was done.

So Why Not GUI Apps?

This brings us to an interesting question. This book has been in print now for over 20 years, and I get a lot of mail about it. The #1 question (after the inevitable "Will you do my CS102 project for me?") is this: how can I write GUI apps? Most of my correspondents mean Windows apps, but here and there people ask about writing assembly apps for GNOME, KDE, or MOTIF as well. I learned my lesson years ago, and never respond by saying, "Why would you want to do *that?*" but instead respond with the honest truth: it's a project that represents a huge amount of research and effort, for relatively little payoff.

Conversely, if you *do* learn to write GUI apps for Windows or Linux, you will understand how those operating systems' UI mechanisms work, and that can certainly be valuable if you have the time and energy to devote to it.

The problem is that there is an *enormous* barrier to entry. Before you can write your first GUI app in assembly, you have to know how it *all* works, and for this particular challenge, there is a lot of "all." GUI apps require managing *signals* (in Windows, *events*) sent up by the operating system, indicating that keys have been pressed or mouse buttons clicked. GUI apps have to manage a large and complex "widget set" of buttons and menus and fill-out fields, and a mind-boggling number of Application Programming Interface (API) calls. There is memory to manage and redrawing to do when part of an app's screen display area gets "dirty" (overwritten by something else or updated by the app) or when the user resizes the app's window or windows.

The internals of Windows GUI programming is one of the ugliest things I've ever seen. (Linux is just as complex, though not as ugly.) Fortunately, it's a very standardized sort of ugliness, and easily encapsulated within code libraries that don't change much from one application to another. This is why graphical IDEs and very high-level programming language products are so popular: they hide most of the ugliness of interfacing to the operating system's GUI machinery behind a set of standard class libraries working within an application framework. You can write very good apps in Delphi or Visual Basic (for Windows) or Lazarus or Gambas for Linux, with only a sketchy understanding of what's going on way down deep. If you want to work in assembly, you basically have to know it all before you even start.

This means that you have to start somewhere else. If you genuinely want to write assembly language GUI apps for one of the Linux desktop managers, approach it this way:

1. Study Linux programming in a capable native-code high-level language such as Pascal, C, or C++. Intermediate language systems such as Python, Basic, or Perl won't help you much here.

2. Get good at that language. Study the code that it generates by loading it into a debugger, or compile to assembly language source and study the generated assembly source code files.

3. Learn how to write and link assembly language functions to programs written in your chosen high-level language.

4. Study the underlying windowing mechanism. For Linux, this would be the X Window technology, on which several good books have been written. My favorite: *The Joy of X* by Niall Mansfield (Addison-Wesley, 1994).

5. Study the details of a particular desktop environment and widget set, be it GNOME, KDE, xfce, or some other. (There are many, and some, such as xfce and WindowLab, were designed to be "lightweight" and relatively simple.) The best way to do this is to write apps for it in your chosen high-level language, and study the assembly language code that the compiler emits.

6. Finally, try creating your own assembly code by imitating what the compiler generates.

Don't expect to find a lot of help online. Unix (and thus Linux) are heavily invested in the culture of portability, which requires that the bulk of the operating system and all apps written for it be movable to a new hardware platform by a simple recompile. Assembly language is the hated orphan child in the Unix world (almost as hated as my own favorite high-level language, Pascal), and many cultural tribalists will try to talk you out of doing anything ambitious in assembly. Resist—but remember that you will be very much on your own.

If you're simply looking for a more advanced challenge in assembly language, look into writing network apps using Unix sockets. This involves *way* less research, and the apps you produce may well be useful for administering servers or other "in the background" software packages that do not require graphical user interfaces. Several books exist on sockets programming, most of them by W. Richard Stevens. Read up; it's a fascinating business.

Using Linux Make

If you've done any programming in C at all, you're almost certainly familiar with the idea of the Make utility. The Make mechanism grew up in the C world, and although it's been adopted by many other programming languages and environments, it's never been adopted quite as thoroughly as in the C world.

What the Make mechanism does is build executable program files from their component parts. The Make utility is a puppet master that executes other programs according to a master plan, which is a simple text file called a *makefile*. The makefile (which by default is named "makefile") is a little like a computer program in that it specifies how something is to be done; but unlike a computer program, it doesn't specify the precise sequence of operations to be taken. What it does is specify what pieces of a program are required to build other pieces of the program, and in doing so ultimately defines what it takes to build the final executable file. It does this by specifying certain rules called *dependencies*.

Dependencies

Throughout the rest of this book we'll be looking at teeny little programs with 250 lines of code or less. In the real world, useful programs can take thousands, tens of thousands, or even millions of lines of source code. Managing such an immense quantity of source code is *the* central problem in software engineering. Writing programs in a modular fashion is the oldest and most frequently used method of dealing with program complexity. Cutting up a large program into smaller chunks and working on the chunks separately helps a great deal.

In ambitious programs, some of the chunks are further cut into even smaller chunks, and sometimes the various chunks are written in more than one programming language. Of course, that creates the additional challenge of knowing how the chunks are created and how they all fit together. For that you really need a blueprint.

A makefile is such a blueprint.

In a modular program, each chunk of code is created somehow, generally by using a compiler or an assembler and a linker. Compilers, assemblers, and linkers take one or more files and create new files from them. An assembler, as you've learned, takes a .ASM file full of assembly language source code and uses it to create a linkable object code file. You can't create the object code file without having and working with the source code file. The object code file *depends* on the source code file for its very existence.

Similarly, a linker connects multiple object code files together into a single executable file. The executable file depends on the existence of the object code files for its existence. The contents of a makefile specify which files are necessary to create which other files, and what steps are necessary to accomplish that creation. The Make utility looks at the rules (dependencies) in the makefile and invokes whatever compilers, assemblers, and other utilities it deems necessary to build the final executable or library file.

There are numerous flavors of Make utilities, and not all makefiles are comprehensible to all Make utilities everywhere. The Unix Make utility is pretty standard, however, and the one that comes with Linux is the one we'll be discussing here.

Let's take an example that actually makes a simple Linux assembly program. Typically, in creating a makefile, you begin by determining which file or files are necessary to create the executable program file. The executable file is created in the link step, so the first dependency you have to define is which files the linker requires to create the executable file. The dependency itself can be pretty simply stated:

```
eatsyscall: eatsyscall.o
```

This merely says that in order to generate the executable file eatsyscall (presented in Chapter 5 as Listing 5-1), we first need to have the file eatsyscall.o. The preceding line is actually a dependency line written as it should be for inclusion in a make file. In any but the smallest programs (such as this one), the linker will have to link more than one .O file. So this is probably the simplest possible sort of dependency: one executable file depends on one object code file. If additional files must be linked to generate the executable file, these are placed in a list, separated by spaces:

```
linkbase: linkbase.o linkparse.o linkfile.o
```

This line tells us that the executable file "linkbase" depends on *three* object code files, and all three of these files must exist before we can generate the executable file that we want.

Lines like these tell us what files are required, but not what must be done with them. That's an essential part of the blueprint, and it's handled in a line that follows the dependency line. The two lines work together. Here's both lines for our simple example:

```
eatsyscall: eatsyscall.o
        ld -o eatsyscall.o eatsyscall
```

At least for the Linux version of Make, *the second line must be indented by a single tab character at the beginning of the line.* I emphasize this because Make will hand you an error if the tab character is missing at the beginning of the second line. *Using space characters to indent will not work.* A typical "missing tab" error message (which beginners see a lot) looks like this:

```
Makefile:2: *** missing separator. Stop.
```

Here, a tab was missing at the beginning of line 2.

The two lines of the makefile taken together should be pretty easy to understand: the first line tells us what file or files are required to do the job. The second line tells us how the job is to be done—in this case, by using the Ld linker to link eatsyscall.o into the executable file eatsyscall.

Nice and neat: we specify which files are necessary and what has to be done with them. The Make mechanism, however, has one more very important aspect: knowing whether the job as a whole actually has to be done at all.

When a File Is Up to Date

It may seem idiotic to say so, but once a file has been compiled or linked, it's been done, and it doesn't have to be done again ... *until you modify one of the required source or object code files*. The Make utility knows this. It can tell whether a compile or a link task needs to be done at all; and if the job doesn't have to be done, Make will refuse to do it.

How does Make know whether the job needs doing? Consider this dependency:

```
eatsyscall: eatsyscall.o
```

Make looks at this and understands that the executable file eatsyscall depends on the object code file eatsyscall.o, and that you can't generate eatsyscall without having eatsyscall.o. It also knows when both files were last changed, so if the executable file eatsyscall is *newer* than eatsyscall.o, then it deduces that any changes made to eatsyscall.o are already reflected in eatsyscall. (It can be absolutely sure of this because the only way to generate eatsyscall is by processing eatsyscall.o.)

The Make utility pays close attention to Linux timestamps. Whenever you edit a source code file, or generate an object code file or an executable file, Linux updates that file's timestamp to the moment that the changes were finally completed; and even though you may have created the original file six months ago, by convention a file is *newer* than another if the time value in its timestamp is more recent than that of another file, even one that was created only 10 minutes ago.

(In case you're unfamiliar with the notion of a *timestamp*, it's simply a value that an operating system keeps in a file system directory for every file in the directory. A file's timestamp is updated to the current clock time whenever the file is changed.)

When a file is newer than all of the files that it depends upon (according to the dependencies called out in the make file), that file is said to be *up to date*. Nothing will be accomplished by generating it again, because all the information contained in the component files is reflected in the dependent file.

Chains of Dependencies

So far, this may seem like a lot of fuss to no great purpose; but the real value in the Make mechanism begins to appear when a single make file contains *chains* of dependencies. Even in the simplest makefiles, there will be dependencies that depend on other dependencies. Our completely trivial example program requires two dependency statements in its make file.

Consider that the following dependency statement specifies how to generate an executable file from an object code (.O) file:

```
eatsyscall: eatsyscall.o
    ld -o eatsyscall.o eatsyscall
```

The gist here is that to build the eatsyscall file, you start with eatsyscall.o and process it according to the recipe in the second line. OK . . . so where does eatsyscall.o come from? That requires a second dependency statement:

```
eatsyscall.o: eatsyscall.asm
    nasm –f elf -g -F stabs eatsyscall.asm
```

Here we explain that to generate eatsyscall.o, we need eatsyscall.asm, and to generate it we follow the recipe in the second line. The full makefile would contain nothing more than these two dependencies:

```
eatsyscall: eatsyscall.o
    ld -o eatsyscall.o eatsyscall
eatsyscall.o: eatsyscall.asm
    nasm –f elf -g -F stabs eatsyscall.asm
```

These two dependency statements define the two steps that we must take to generate an executable program file from our very simple assembly language source code file eatlinux.asm. However, it's not obvious from the two dependencies shown here that all the fuss is worthwhile. Assembling eatlinux.asm pretty much requires that we link eatlinux.o to create eatlinux. The two steps go together in virtually all cases.

But consider a real-world programming project, in which there are hundreds of separate source code files. Only some of those files might be "on the rack" in an editor and undergoing change on any given day. However, to build and test the final program, *all* of the files are required. Does that mean all the compilation steps and assembly steps are required? Not at all.

An executable program is knit together by the linker from one or more—often *many* more—object code files. If all but (let's say) two of the object code files are up to date, there's no reason to compile the other 147 source code files. You just compile the two source code files that have been changed, and then link all 149 object code files into the executable.

The challenge, of course, is correctly remembering *which* two files have changed—and ensuring that *all* changes that have been recently made to *any* of the 149 source code files are reflected in the final executable file. That's a lot of remembering, or referring to notes, and it gets worse when more than one person is working on the project, as is typically the case in nearly all commercial software development shops. The Make utility makes remembering any of this unnecessary. Make figures it out and does only what must be done—no more, no less.

The Make utility looks at the makefile, and at the timestamps of all the source code and object code files called out in the makefile. If the executable file is newer than all of the object code files, nothing needs to be done; but if *any* of the object code files are newer than the executable file, then the executable file must be relinked. And if one or more of the source code files are newer than either the executable file or their respective object code files, some compiling or assembling must be done before any linking is done.

What Make does is start with the executable file and look for chains of dependency moving away from that. The executable file depends on one or more object files, which depend on one or more source code files, and Make walks the path up the various chains, taking note of what's newer than what and what must be done to put it all right. Make then executes the compiler, assembler, and linker selectively to ensure that the executable file is ultimately newer than all of the files on which it depends. Make ensures that all work that needs to be done gets done.

Furthermore, Make avoids spending unnecessary time compiling and assembling files that are already up to date and therefore do not need to be compiled or assembled. Given that a full build (by which I mean the recompilation/reassembly and relinking of every single file in the project) can take hours on an ambitious program, Make saves an enormous amount of idle time when all you need to do is test changes made to one small part of the program.

There is actually a lot more to the Unix Make facility than this, but what I've described are the fundamental principles. You have the power to make compiling conditional, inclusion of files conditional, and much more. You won't need to fuss with such things on your first forays into assembly language (or C programming, for that matter), but it's good to know that the power is there as your programming skills improve and you take on more ambitious projects.

Invoking Make from Inside Kate

Running Make is about as easy as anything you'll ever do in programming: you type make on the command line and press Enter. Make will handle the rest. There is only one command-line option of interest to beginners, and that is -k. The -k option instructs Make to stop building any file in which an error occurs and leave the previous copy of the target file undisturbed. (It continues building any other files that need building.) Absent the -k option, Make may overwrite your existing object code and executable files with incomplete copies, which isn't the end of the world but is sometimes a nuisance, and confusing. If this doesn't make total sense to you right now, don't worry—it's a good idea to use -k until you're *really* sure you don't need it. That said, for simple projects in which there is one project per directory, and a makefile named "makefile," invoking Make is no more than this:

```
make -k
```

Anytime you make *any* change to one of your source code files, no matter how minor, you will have to run Make to test the consequences of that change. As a beginner you will probably be learning by the "tweak and try" method, which means that you might change only one instruction on one line of your source code file, and then "see what that does."

If you do tend to learn this way (and there's nothing wrong with it!), then you're going to be running Make *a lot*. The famous EMACS text editor includes a key binding that enables you to run Make with a single keystroke. We can do the same thing with Kate, so that as soon as you save changes to a file, you can press a single key to turn Make loose on your project.

To give yourself a Make key, you have to add a key binding, not to Kate but to the Konsole terminal emulator program. Konsole is "embedded" in Kate, and when you open the terminal window under the source code window, what you're opening is in fact a copy of Konsole. Defining the key binding for Konsole adds it to all copies of Konsole, including the one embedded in Kate.

The option is buried deep in Konsole's menu tree, so read carefully:

1. Launch Konsole from the desktop, *not* from within Kate.

2. Select Settings → Manage profiles from Konsole's main menu.

3. Create a new profile is you haven't already. Earlier in this chapter I described how to create a new profile for Konsole to provide the IBM-850 character encoding (for the sake of the old box-border character set); if you created a new profile back then, select it and open it.

4. When the Edit Profile dialog appears, click the Input tag.

5. When the Key Bindings dialog appears, make sure that xFree 4 is selected. This is the default using Konsole under Ubuntu 8.10. Click Edit.

6. When the Edit Key Binding List dialog appears, scroll down the list of bindings until you see ScrollLock in the Key Combination column. We're going to hijack the ScrollLock key, which I consider the most expendable key in the standard PC keyboard. If you use ScrollLock for something, you may have to choose a different key.

7. Double-click in the Output column to the right of ScrollLock. This enables you to enter a string that will be emitted to standard output by Konsole anytime the ScrollLock key is pressed when Konsole has the focus. Type the following string: **make -k/r** (see Figure 6-11).

8. Click OK in the Edit Key Bindings List dialog, and click OK in the Key Bindings dialog. Then click Close in the Manage Profiles dialog. You're done!

Test the new key binding by bringing up Konsole and pressing the ScrollLock key. Konsole should type `make -k` on the command line, followed by Enter. (That's what the `/r` means in the key binding string.) Make will be invoked and, depending on whether Konsole was open to a project directory with a make file in it, build your project.

Now you can launch Kate, open its terminal window, and do the same thing. Press ScrollLock, and Make will be invoked in the terminal window. Each press of the ScrollLock key will invoke Make again.

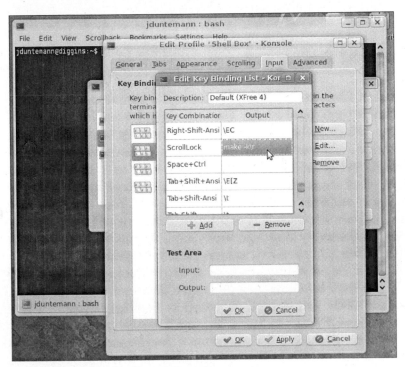

Figure 6-11: Adding a key binding to Konsole

Using Touch to Force a Build

As I said earlier, if your executable file is newer than all of the files that it depends on, Make will refuse to perform a build—after all, in its understanding of the process, when your executable file is newer than everything it depends on, there's no work to do.

However, there is the occasional circumstance when you want Make to perform a build even when the executable is up to date. The one you'll most likely encounter as a beginner is when you're tinkering with the makefile itself. If you've changed your makefile and want to test it, but your executable is up-to-date, you need to engage in a little persuasion. Linux has a command called touch that has one job only: to update the timestamp in a file to the current time. If you invoke touch on your source code file, it will magically become "newer" than the executable file, and Make will obediently build it.

Invoke `touch` in a terminal window, followed by the name of the file to be touched:

```
touch eatsyscall.asm
```

Then invoke Make again, and the build will happen—assuming that your makefile is present and correct!

The Insight Debugger

At the end of Chapter 5, I took you through a simple development cycle of edit/assemble/link/test/debug. The debugger I used for that run-through was KDbg, which I chose because of its simplicity and ease of use. KDbg has a problem, however: it doesn't completely understand assembly language executables, and doesn't display data in memory as it does for executables written in other languages such as C and C++. So although KDbg is useful for peeking at registers while you bounce through your code one instruction at a time, it is not the end-all of debuggers, and you will very quickly bump up against its assembly language limitations. (At this writing, the online help system for KDbg is broken and its help file is inaccessible.)

There are a lot of debuggers, and a lot of debugger "front ends" like KDbg. KDbg itself is not really a debugger. It's a software control panel for the standard GNU debugger, Gdb, which is installed automatically with all versions of Linux. When you use KDbg you're really using Gdb, and Gdb is a foundational component of Linux software development. The Gdb debugger has no user interface. It works strictly in a terminal window, using text only, and is one of the most miserably difficult pieces of software I have ever used. It veritably begs for some sort of graphical user interface, which is why Gdb front ends such as KDbg and DDD (Data Display Debugger) exist.

Gdb has been around almost as long as the GNU project, which dates back to 1985. About fifteen years ago, several people decided that GUI platforms were the future, and that the Gdb debugger needed a GUI of its own. The Insight interface was originally a collaboration between the Red Hat Linux organization and Cygnus Solutions, a GNU support company. The two firms merged in 1999, and Red Hat has continued work on Insight ever since then.

Insight is different from KDbg, DDD, and the other Gdb front-end products. Insight is actually a *part* of Gdb, and provides a second "view" of Gdb's operation, a windowed view for use on graphical desktops such as GNOME, KDE, xfce, and all the rest. This view is comprehensive, and if the whole thing is open on your desktop at one time it's probably a little intimidating. The good news is that Insight is modular, with different windows displaying different views of the project on the workbench. You can turn off the views that you don't need or don't yet understand, and the debugger will then come across as a little less overwhelming.

For the rest of this chapter I'm going to explain Insight's various views and how you can load your programs into it and observe them. For the rest of this book, when I speak of "the debugger," Gdb/Insight is the one I mean.

Running Insight

Insight is installed with Linux itself, and there is nothing more to go looking for. You can launch it from any terminal emulator, such as Konsole, simply by naming it on the command line. In practice, you generally load the program under test at the same time you run Insight, by naming the program on the command line after "insight". For example, to use the program from Listing 5-1, you'd navigate to the eatsyscall project directory, open a Konsole window, and run Insight this way:

```
insight eatsyscall
```

If you're going to debug the program with I/O redirection, the redirection has to be entered along with the name of the executable on the command line when you invoke Insight:

```
insight eatsyscall > eattalk.txt
```

It doesn't matter what terminal window you launch Insight from. I recommend launching it from Kate's terminal window, after you open the Kate session corresponding to the project that you want to debug. When Kate opens a session, it navigates to the directory where the session files reside, so you don't have to worry about Insight being able to find your executable or source files when you launch it.

Insight's Many Windows

The first time you run Insight, you may see as many as ten different windows pop up all over your screen. (Different versions of Insight may launch different numbers of windows by default.) Each of the ten windows is a different view into the project that you're debugging. The primary Insight window is called the *source code window*. The other nine windows may be "turned off" if you want; and while you're a beginner, only three of them will be truly useful on assembly language projects.

All of Insight's windows may be opened from the Views menu. Each window may be closed separately by clicking on the close button in the upper-right corner of the window. Table 6-2 summarizes the nine views. For the purposes of following along with the examples in this book, you only need the source code window plus the Registers view and the Memory view.

Table 6-2: Insight's Views

WINDOW	SHORTCUT	PURPOSE
Stack	Ctrl+S	Summarizes and navigates existing stack frames
Registers	Ctrl+R	Summarizes CPU registers
Memory	Ctrl+M	Dumps memory from a given address
Watch Expressions	Ctrl+T	Displays and edits watched values
Local Variables	Ctrl+L	Displays local variables in the stack frame
Breakpoints	Ctrl+B	Summarizes all existing breakpoints
Console	Ctrl+N	Opens a command-line interface to Gdb
Function Browser	Ctrl+F	Finds functions and allows breakpoints to be set
Thread List	Ctrl+H	Summarizes threads belonging to the executable

Several of Insight's windows are pretty C-specific, and won't be of much help to you. Seeing and setting watches on local variables depends on having debug information in your executable that assembly programs just don't provide. Other windows are outside the scope of a beginners' book: the Thread List view only applies to multithreaded programs, which is an advanced topic that I can't cover in this book. For short programs, you don't need the Breakpoints view because you can see the breakpoints in the source code window. The Console view enables you to control Gdb through its traditional command-line interface, which although difficult to master may be of use to you later.

The Stack view comes into its own once you begin defining callable procedures, and especially when you begin calling functions out of the standard C library, as I'll explain toward the end of the book. For the next few chapters, you're mainly going to be looking at your source code, the CPU registers, and memory.

If you have a smallish display, arranging Kate and Insight on the same screen so that both may be seen in their entirety can be a bit of a trick. (Don't even try it on anything smaller than a 22″ diagonal.) It's not a problem, however, as you can be either editing your program or debugging it—you can't do both at once. So after you've done your edits and have invoked Make to build your project, launch Insight from Kate's terminal window. Once you've seen enough of your project's misbehavior, close Insight and return to Kate for another stint at the editor. Insight's window state is persistent, and the next time you run Insight, only the windows you had open the last time will appear, and in the same places on your display, too.

The only significant configuration option you should change for Insight is to select the "Windows-style" toolbar icon set. Select Preferences → Global, and in the Global Preferences dialog that appears, pull down the Icons menu and select Windows-Style Icon Set. Click OK. The Windows-style icons are more detailed and will help you remember what the buttons mean while you're still learning your way around.

A Quick Insight Run-Through

I explained how debuggers single-step your programs in Chapter 5, and Insight works the same way. Let's load Listing 5-1 into Insight and see what it can do, especially with respect to looking at memory data. Open Kate and its session for the eatsyscall project. Make sure that the project has been built and that an executable is present in the project directory. Then launch Insight:

```
insight eatsyscall
```

The only views you want this time are the main window (the source code view) plus the Registers view and the Memory view. Close any others that may have opened. What you see should look something like Figure 6-12.

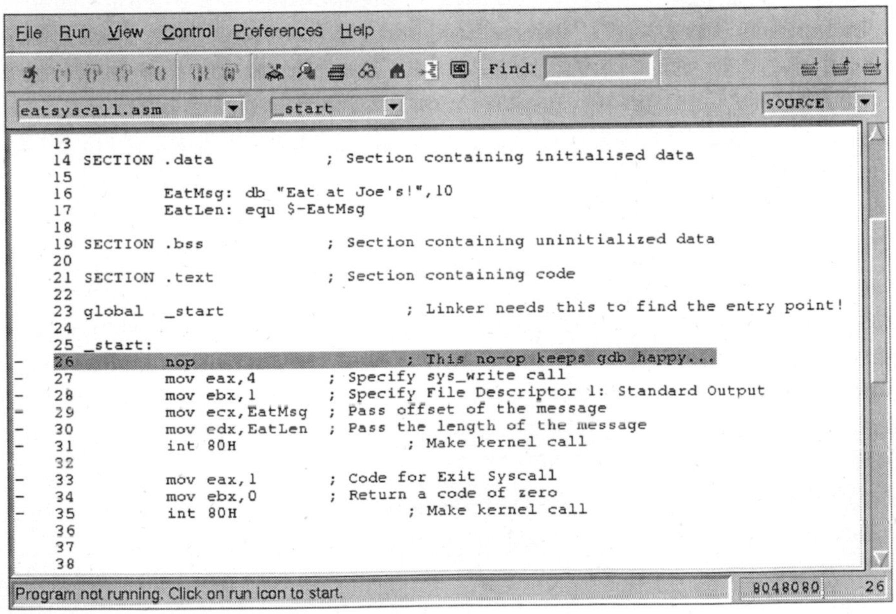

Figure 6-12: Insight's source code window

Insight's windows are not as nicely drawn as those of KDbg, but on the upside, all of its controls have "hover help." When you hover the mouse pointer over one of the controls, a label pops up that tells you what the control is. Insight's defaults are fairly good, and you generally don't have to do any setup before single-stepping a program.

When it loads an executable for debugging, Insight highlights the first executable instruction. This looks like execution is paused at a breakpoint, but not so: There are no breakpoints set by default, and the program is not running. The highlight simply tells you where execution will begin when you run the program.

As with KDbg, an initial breakpoint must be set. You set a breakpoint by clicking on the dash character in the leftmost column of the source-code display. A dash is present on each line that contains an instruction and therefore can accept a breakpoint. (You can't set a breakpoint on data definitions, or anything but an instruction.) Breakpoints are toggles: click the dash, and the breakpoint is shown by the presence of a red square; click the red square, and the breakpoint is removed, with the display returning to the dash.

Click on the dash next to the MOV EAX, 4 instruction. You'll get your breakpoint, and now you can run the program. Insight's navigation controls are the leftmost two groups of buttons in the toolbar. You start the program by clicking the Run icon (which shows a running man) or pressing R. Execution will begin, and pause at your breakpoint. Two other things will happen:

- Insight will place what looks like a breakpoint at the program's first instruction (here, a NOP instruction) but *it will not stop there*. The highlight will move to your initial breakpoint. The reason for this involves the internals of C programs, which I won't explain in detail here.

- The Registers view and the Memory view, which had been empty, will now "light up" and show real data.

Like KDbg, Insight was really designed for C programming, and some of the controls apply more to C than to assembly. To single-step simple programs, click the Step Asm Instruction button. The highlighted instruction will execute, and the highlight will move to the next instruction in sequence. The two buttons for instruction stepping differ when you begin writing code with subroutine calls (as I'll demonstrate in a later chapter) but for programs as simple as eatsyscall, the two buttons do exactly the same thing.

The Registers view shows the current state of CPU registers, and any register that changed during the last instruction executed is highlighted in green. Step down the program until the highlight rests on the first INT 80H instruction. Four registers have been loaded in preparation for the syscall, as you'll see in the Registers view, shown in Figure 6-13.

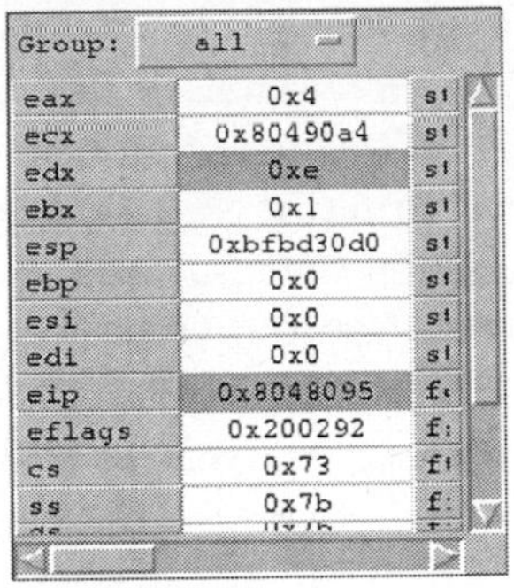

Figure 6-13: Insight's Registers view during program execution

The EDX register is the one highlighted in green because it was loaded in the last instruction that Insight executed. The EIP register (the instruction pointer) will be green virtually all the time, because it changes whenever an instruction is executed—that is, at every step.

The Registers view window (refer to Figure 6-13) is scaled back significantly. The CPU has a lot of registers, and the Registers view will obediently display all of them. You can get a sense for the full list of registers by maximizing the Registers view window. With the window maximized, Insight will show you the segment registers (which belong to the operating system and are not available for your use) and the math processor registers, which you won't be using during your first steps in assembly. It's possible to select only the general-purpose registers for display, and this is done by clicking the Group button at the top of the Registers view and selecting General from the menu that appears. You can get the same effect by sizing the window, and which you choose is up to you.

When you begin running your program, the Memory view window loads data starting at the first named data item in your .data section. In Listing 5-1, there's only one data item, the `EatMsg` string. You'll see the "Eat at Joe's" message at the beginning of the displayed data (see Figure 6-14).

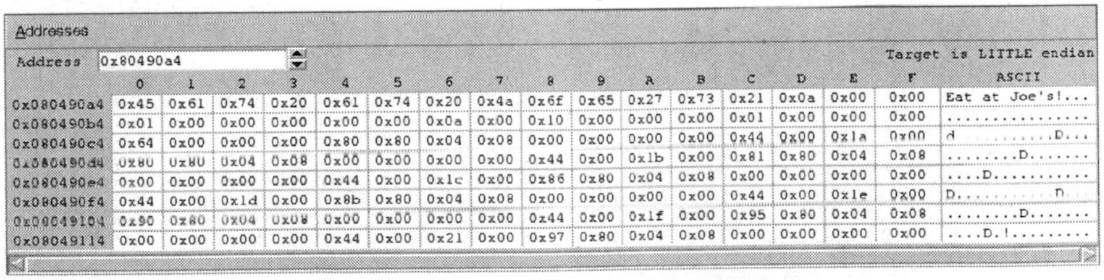

Figure 6-14: Insight's Memory view during program execution

Like the Registers view, the Memory view is updated after every instruction. In more powerful programs that manipulate data in memory, you can watch the contents of memory change as you step through the program's machinery. Insight's Memory view is much like the Bless Hex Editor introduced in Chapter 5. Memory is displayed in two forms: on the left, as rows of 16 individual hexadecimal numeric values, and on the right, as rows of 16 ASCII characters. Data values that fall outside the range of displayable ASCII characters are displayed as period characters.

The memory view has another very useful trick: You can change data in memory at any time. Changes can be made in either the hexadecimal values section of the view, or in the ASCII section of the view. Give it a try: click on the ASCII view so that the cursor appears just after the "e" in "Joe's." Backspace three characters, type **Sam**, and press Enter. You've changed "Joe" to "Sam" in memory. (Your files on disk are not affected.)

To verify the change, click the Continue button, which (in contrast to stepping) continues execution without pause until the next breakpoint, or until the end of the program, whichever comes first. (Continue is the fifth button from the left on the main toolbar.) Your program will run to completion, and if you look at the program's output in Kate's terminal window, you'll see that you've hijacked Joe's advertising slogan and given it to Sam.

Pick Up Your Tools . . .

At this point, you have the background you need and the tools you need. It's time (finally!) to sit down and begin looking at the x86 instruction set in detail, and then begin writing programs in earnest.

Following Your Instructions

Meeting Machine Instructions Up Close and Personal

As comedian Bill Cosby once said: I told you *that* story so I could tell you *this* one. . . .   We're over a third of the way through this book, and I haven't even begun describing in detail the principal element in PC assembly language: the x86 instruction set. Most books on assembly language, even those targeted at beginners, assume that the instruction set is as good a place as any to start their story, without considering the mass of groundwork without which most beginning programmers get totally lost and give up.

Orientation is crucial. That's why I began at the *real* beginning, and took 200 pages to get to where the other guys start.

Keep in mind that this book was created to supply that essential groundwork and orientation for your first steps in the language itself. It is *not* a complete course in PC assembly language. Once you run off the end of this book, you'll have one leg up on any of the numerous other books on assembly language from this and other publishers.

And it's high time that we got to the heart of things, way down where the software meets the silicon.

Build Yourself a Sandbox

The best way to get acquainted with the x86 machine instructions is to build yourself a sandbox and just have fun. An assembly language program doesn't need to run correctly from Linux. It doesn't even need to be complete, as programs go. All it has to be is comprehensible to NASM and the linker, and that in itself doesn't take a lot of doing.

In my personal techie jargon, a *sandbox* is a program intended to be run *only* in a debugger. If you want to see what effects an instruction has on memory or one of the registers, single-stepping it in Insight will show you vividly. The program doesn't need to return visible results on the command line. It simply has to contain correctly formed instructions.

In practice, my sandbox idea works this way: you create a makefile that assembles and links a program called sandbox.asm. You create a minimal NASM program in source code and save it to disk as newsandbox.asm. Anytime you want to play around with machine instructions, you open newsandbox.asm and save it out again as sandbox.asm, overwriting any earlier version of sandbox.asm that may exist. You can add instructions for observation, and use the Linux make utility to generate an executable. Then you load the executable into Insight and execute the instructions one at a time, carefully watching what each one does in the various Insight views.

It's possible that your experiments will yield a useful combination of machine instructions that's worth saving. In that case, save the sandbox file out as experiment1.asm (or whatever descriptive name you want to give it) and you can build that sequence into a "real" program whenever you're ready.

A Minimal NASM Program

So what does a program require to be assembled by NASM? In truth, not much. Listing 7-1 is the source code for what I use as a starter sandbox. It presents more, in fact, than NASM technically requires, but nothing more than it needs to be useful as a sandbox.

Listing 7-1: newsandbox.asm

```
section .data
section .text

        global _start

_start:
        nop
; Put your experiments between the two nops...


; Put your experiments between the two nops...
        nop

section .bss
```

NASM will in fact assemble a source code file that contains no instruction mnemonics at all—though in fairness, the instructionless executable will not be run by Linux. What we *do* need is a starting point that is marked as global—here, the label _start. We also need to define a data section and a text section as shown. The data section holds named data items that are to be given initial values when the program runs. The old "Eat at Joe's" ad message from Listing 5-1 was a named data item in the data section. The text section holds program code. Both of these sections are needed to create an executable.

The section marked .bss isn't strictly essential, but it's good to have if you're going to be experimenting. The .bss section holds uninitialized data—that is, space for data items that are given no initial values when the program begins running. These are empty buffers, basically, for data that will be generated or read from somewhere while the program is running. By custom, the .bss section is located after the .text section. (I'll have a lot more to say about the .bss section and uninitialized data in upcoming chapters.)

To use newsandbox.asm, create a session in Kate called sandbox, and load the newsandbox.asm file into that session. Save it out immediately as sandbox.asm, so that you don't modify newsandbox.asm. Create a makefile containing these lines:

```
sandbox: sandbox.o
        ld -o sandbox sandbox.o
sandbox.o: sandbox.asm
        nasm -f elf -g -F stabs sandbox.asm -l sandbox.lst
```

(This file and Listing 7-1. are already in the sandbox directory that will be created when you unpack the listings archive for this book.)

There are two NOP instructions in sandbox.asm, and they are there to make it easier to watch the program in the debugger. To play around with machine instructions, place them between the two comments. Build the executable with Make, and load the executable into Insight:

```
insight sandbox
```

Set a breakpoint at the first instruction you place between the comments, and click Run. Execution will begin, and stop at your breakpoint. To observe the effects of that instruction, click the Step Asm button. Here's why the second NOP instruction is there: when you single-step an instruction, there has to be an instruction *after* that instruction for execution to pause on. If the first instruction in your sandbox is the last instruction, execution will "run off the edge" on your first single step and your program will terminate. When that happens, Insight's Registers and Memory views will go blank, and you won't be able to see the effects of that one instruction!

The notion of running off the edge of the program is an interesting one. If you click the Continue button you'll see what happens when you don't properly end the program: Linux will hand up a segmentation fault, which can have a number of causes. However, what happened in this case is that your program attempted to execute a location *past* the end of the text section. Linux knows how long your program is, and it won't allow you to execute any instructions that were not present in your program when it was loaded.

There's no lasting harm in that, of course. Linux is *very* good at dealing with misbehaving and malformed programs, and nothing you're likely to do by accident will have any effect on Linux itself. You can avoid generating the segmentation fault by selecting Run → Kill from the Insight main menu. The Kill command does just that: it stops the program being debugged, even if it's paused at a breakpoint or during single-stepping.

Instructions and Their Operands

The single most common activity in assembly language work is getting data from here to there. There are several specialized ways to do this, but only one truly general way: the MOV instruction. MOV can move a byte, word (16 bits), or double word (32 bits) of data from one register to another, from a register into memory, or from memory into a register. What MOV *cannot* do is move data directly from one address in memory to a different address in memory. (To do that, you need two separate MOV instructions—one from memory to a register, and another from that register back out to memory.)

The name MOV is a bit of a misnomer, since what actually happens is that data is *copied* from a source to a destination. Once copied to the destination, however, the data does not vanish from the source, but continues to exist in both places. This conflicts a little with our intuitive notion of moving something, which usually means that something disappears from a source and reappears at a destination.

Source and Destination Operands

Most machine instructions, MOV included, have one or more *operands*. (Some instructions have no operands, or operate on registers or memory implicitly. When this is the case, I'll make a point of mentioning it in the text.) Consider this machine instruction:

```
mov eax,1
```

There are two operands in the preceding instruction. The first is EAX, and the second is the digit 1. By convention in assembly language, the first (leftmost) operand belonging to a machine instruction is the *destination operand*. The second operand from the left is the *source operand*.

With the MOV instruction, the sense of the two operands is pretty literal: the source operand is copied to the destination operand. In the preceding instruction, the source operand (the literal value 1) is copied into the destination operand EAX. The sense of source and destination is not nearly so literal in other instructions, but a rule of thumb is this: whenever a machine instruction causes a new value to be generated, that new value is placed in the destination operand.

Three different flavors of data may be used as operands: *memory data, register data*, and *immediate data*. I've laid out some example MOV instructions on the dissection pad in Table 7-1 to give you a flavor for how the different types of data are specified as operands to the MOV instruction.

Table 7-1: MOV and Its Operands

MACHINE INSTRUCTION	DESTINATION OPERAND	SOURCE OPERAND	OPERAND NOTES
MOV	EAX,	42h	Source is immediate data
MOV	EBX,	EDI	Both are 32-bit register data
MOV	BX,	CX	Both are 16-bit register data
MOV	DL,	BH	Both are 8-bit register data
MOV	[EBP],	EDI	Destination is 32-bit memory data at the address stored in ebp
MOV	EDX,	[ESI]	Source is 32-bit memory data at the address stored in ESI

Immediate Data

The MOV EAX, 42h instruction in Table 7-2 is a good example of using what is called immediate data, accessed through an addressing mode called *immediate addressing*. Immediate addressing gets its name from the fact that the item being addressed is data built right into the machine instruction itself. The CPU does not have to go anywhere to find immediate data. It's not in a register, nor is it stored in a data item somewhere out there in memory. Immediate data is always right inside the instruction being fetched and executed.

Immediate data must be of an appropriate size for the operand. For example, you can't move a 16-bit immediate value into an 8-bit register section such as AH or DL. NASM will not allow you to assemble an instruction like this:

```
mov cl,067EFh
```

CL is an 8-bit register, and 067EFh is a 16-bit quantity. Won't go!

Because it's built right into a machine instruction, you might think that immediate data would be quick to access. This is true only to a point: fetching *anything* from memory takes more time than fetching anything from a register, and instructions are, after all, stored in memory. So, while addressing immediate data is somewhat quicker than addressing ordinary data stored in memory, neither is anywhere near as quick as simply pulling a value from a CPU register.

Also keep in mind that *only* the source operand may be immediate data. The destination operand is the place where data *goes*, not where it comes from. Because immediate data consists of literal constants (numbers such as 1, 0, 42, or 07F2Bh), trying to copy something *into* immediate data, rather than *from* immediate data, simply has no meaning and is always an error.

NASM allows some interesting forms of immediate data. For example, the following is perfectly legal, if not necessarily as useful as it looks at first glance:

```
mov eax,'WXYZ'
```

This is a good instruction to load into your sandbox and execute in the debugger. Look at the contents of register EAX in the registers view:

```
0x5a595857
```

This may seem weird, but look close: the numeric equivalents of the uppercase ASCII characters W, X, Y, and Z have been loaded nose-to-tail into EAX. If you're not up on your ASCII, take a look at the chart in Appendix B. W is 57h, X is 58h, Y is 59h, and Z is 5Ah. Each character equivalent is 8 bits in size, so four of them fit snugly into 32-bit register EAX. However ... they're backwards!

Well, no. Recall the concept of "endianness" introduced early in Chapter 5 (and if you don't recall, do go back and read that section again). The x86 architecture is "little endian," meaning that the least significant byte in a multibyte sequence is stored at the lowest address. This applies to registers as well, and makes sense once you understand how to refer to units of storage within a register.

The confusion results from our schizoid habit of reading text from left to right, while reading numbers from right to left. Take a look at Figure 7-1. Treated as a sequence of text characters, the "W" in "WXYZ" is considered the least significant element. EAX, however, is a container for numbers, where the least significant column is always (for Western languages) on the right. The least significant byte in EAX we call AL, and that's where the "W" goes. The second-to-least significant byte in EAX we call AH, and that's where the "X" goes. The two most significant bytes in EAX do not have separate names and may not be addressed individually, but they are still 8-bit bytes and may contain 8-bit values like ASCII characters. The most significant character in the sequence "WXYZ" is the "Z," and it's stored in the most significant byte of EAX.

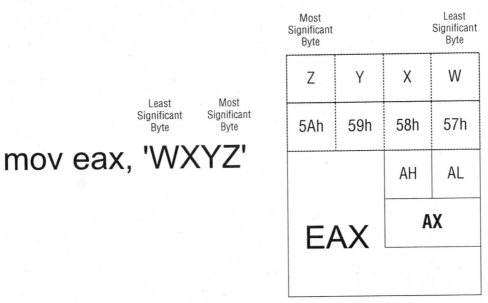

Figure 7-1: Character strings as immediate data

Register Data

Data stored inside a CPU register is known as *register data*, and accessing register data directly is an addressing mode called *register addressing*. Register addressing is done by simply naming the register you want to work with. Here are some entirely legal examples of register data and register addressing:

```
mov ebp,esi      ; 32-bit
mov bl,ch        ; 8-bit
add di,ax        ; 16-bit
add ecx,edx      ; 32-bit
```

The last two examples point up the fact that we're not speaking *only* of the MOV instruction here. The ADD instruction does just what you might expect, adding the source and destination operands. The sum replaces whatever was in the destination operand. Irrespective of the instruction, register addressing happens any time data in a register is acted on directly.

The assembler keeps track of certain things that don't make sense, and one such situation is having a 16-bit register half and a full 32-bit register within the same instruction. Such operations are not legal—after all, what would it mean to move a 4-byte source into a 2-byte destination? And while moving a 2-byte source into a 4-byte destination might seem possible and even reasonable, the CPU does not support it and it cannot be done directly.

Watching register data in the debugger is a good way to get a gut sense for how this works, especially when you're just starting out. Let's practice a little. Enter the following instructions into your sandbox, build the executable, and load the sandbox executable into the debugger:

```
mov ax,067FEh
mov bx,ax
mov cl,bh
mov ch,bl
```

Set a breakpoint on the first of the four instructions, and then click Run. Single-step through the four instructions, watching carefully what happens to the AX, BX, and CX register sections. (Remember that Insight's Registers view does not show the 8-bit or 16-bit register sections individually. AX is part of EAX, and CL is part of ECX, and so on.) Once you're done, select Run → Kill to terminate the program. Keep in mind that if you select Continue or try to step past the end of the program, Linux will hand you a segmentation fault for not terminating the program properly. Nothing will be harmed by the fault; remember that the sandbox is not expected to be a complete and proper Linux program. It's good practice to "kill" the program rather than generate the fault, however.

Here's a summary of what happened: the first instruction is an example of immediate addressing using 16-bit registers. The 16-bit hexadecimal value 067FEH was moved into the AX register. The second instruction used register addressing to copy register data from AX into BX.

The third instruction and fourth instruction both move data between 8-bit register segments, rather than 16-bit register segments. These two instructions accomplish something interesting. Look at the last register display, and compare the value of BX and CX. By moving the value from BX into CX one byte at a time, it was possible to reverse the order of the two bytes making up BX. The high half of BX (sometimes called the *most significant byte*, or MSB, of BX) was moved into the low half of CX. Then the low half of BX (sometimes called the *least significant byte*, or LSB, of BX) was moved into the high half of CX. This is just a sample of the sorts of tricks you can play with the general-purpose registers.

Just to disabuse you of the notion that the MOV instruction should be used to exchange the two halves of a 16-bit register, let me suggest that you do the following. Go back to Kate and add the following instruction to the end of your sandbox:

```
xchg cl,ch
```

Rebuild the sandbox and head back into the debugger to see what happens. The XCHG instruction exchanges the values contained in its two operands. What was interchanged before is interchanged again, and the value in CX will match the values already in AX and BX. A good idea while writing your first assembly language programs is to double-check the instruction set periodically to see that what you have cobbled together with four or five instructions is not possible using a single instruction. The x86 instruction set is very good at fooling you in that regard.

Note one caution here: Sometimes a "special case" is faster in terms of machine execution time than a more general case. Dividing by a power of 2 can be done using the DIV instruction, but it can also be done by using the SHR (Shift Right) instruction. DIV is more general (you can use it to divide by any unsigned integer, not simply powers of 2), but it is a great deal slower—on some species of x86 processor, as much as ten times slower! (I'll have more to say about DIV later in this chapter.)

Memory Data

Immediate data is built right into its own machine instruction. Register data is stored in one of the CPU's collections of internal registers. In contrast, *memory data* is stored somewhere in the sliver of system memory "owned" by a program, at a 32-bit memory address.

With one or two important exceptions (the string instructions, which I cover to a degree—but not exhaustively—later), only *one* of an instruction's two operands may specify a memory location. In other words, you can move an immediate value to memory, or a memory value to a register, or some other similar combination, but you *can't* move a memory value directly to another memory value. This is just an inherent limitation of the current generation of x86 CPUs, and we have to live with it, inconvenient as it is at times.

To specify that you want the data at the memory location contained in a register, rather than the data in the register itself, you use square brackets around the name of the register. In other words, to move the word in memory at the address contained in EBX into register EAX, you would use the following instruction:

```
mov eax, [ebx]
```

The square brackets may contain more than the name of a single 32-bit register, as you'll learn in detail later. For example, you can add a literal constant to a register within the brackets, and NASM will do the math:

```
mov eax, [ebx+16]
```

Ditto adding two general-purpose registers, like so:

```
mov eax, [ebx+ecx]
```

And, as if that weren't enough, you can add two registers plus a literal constant:

```
mov eax,[ebx+ecx+11]
```

Not everything goes, of course. Whatever is inside the brackets is called the *effective address* of a data item in memory, and there are rules dictating what can be a valid effective address and what cannot. At the current evolution of the x86 hardware, two registers may be added together to form the effective address, but not three or more. In other words, the following are *not* legal effective address forms:

```
mov eax,[ebx+ecx+edx]
mov eax,[ebx+ecx+esi+edi]
```

The more complicated forms of effective addresses are easier to demonstrate than explain, but we have to cover a few other things first. They're especially useful when you're dealing with lookup tables, which I'll go into later. For now, the most important thing to do is *not* confuse a data item with where it exists!

Confusing Data and Its Address

This sounds banal, but trust me, it's an easy enough thing to do. Back in Listing 5-1, we had this data definition, and this instruction:

```
EatMsg: db "Eat at Joe's!"
  .    .    .    .
mov ecx,EatMsg
```

If you've had any exposure to high-level languages like Pascal, your first instinct might be to assume that whatever data is stored in EatMsg will be copied into ECX. Assembly doesn't work that way. That MOV instruction actually copies the *address* of EatMsg, not what's stored *in* (actually, at) EatMsg. In assembly language, variable names represent addresses, *not* data!

So how do you actually "get at" the data represented by a variable like EatMsg? Again, it's done with square brackets:

```
mov edx,[EatMsg]
```

What this instruction does is go out to the location in memory specified by the address represented by EatMsg, pull the first 32 bits' worth of data from that address, and load that data into EDX starting with the least significant byte in EDX. Given the contents we've defined for EatMsg, that would be the four characters "E,", "a," "t," and " ".

The Size of Memory Data

What if you only want to work with a single character, and not the first four? What if you don't want all 32 bits? Basically, if you want to use one byte of data, you need to load it into a byte-size container. The register EAX is 32 bits in size. However, you can address the least significant byte of EAX as AL. AL is one byte in size, and by using AL you can bring back the first byte of EatMsg this way:

```
mov al,[EatMsg]
```

AL, of course, is contained within EAX—it's not a separate register. (Refer to Figure 7-1 if this isn't immediately clear to you.) But the name "AL" allows you to fetch only one byte at a time from memory.

You can perform a similar trick using the name AX to refer to the lower 2 bytes (16 bits) of EAX:

```
mov ax,[EatMsg]
```

This time, the characters "E" and "a" are read from memory and placed in the two least significant bytes of EAX.

Where the size issue gets tricky is when you write data in a register out to memory. NASM does not "remember" the size of variables, as higher-level languages do. It knows where EatMsg *starts* in memory, and that's it. You have to tell NASM how many bytes of data to move. This is done by a *size specifier*. For example:

```
mov [EatMsg],byte 'G'
```

Here, you tell NASM that you only want to move a single byte out to memory by using the BYTE size specifier. Other size specifiers include WORD (16 bits) and DWORD (32 bits).

The Bad Old Days

Be glad you're learning x86 assembly now, as it was a *lot* more complicated in years past. In real mode under DOS, there were several restrictions on the components of an effective address that just don't exist today, in 32-bit protected mode. In real mode, only certain of the x86 general-purpose registers could hold a memory address: BX, BP, SI, and DI. The others, AX, CX, and DX, could not.

Worse, an address had two parts, as you learned in Chapter 4. You had to be mindful of which segment an address was in, and you had to make sure you specified the segment where it was not obvious, using constructs like [DS:BX] or [ES:BP]. You had to fool with diabolical things called ASSUMEs, about which the less said, the better. (If you are for some reason forced to program in real mode segmented model for the x86, try to find a copy of the 2000 edition of this book, in which I take on the whole mess in gruesome detail.)

In so many ways, life is just better now.

Rally Round the Flags, Boys!

Although I mentioned it in the overview of the x86 architecture, we haven't yet studied the EFlags register in detail. EFlags is a veritable junk drawer of disjointed little bits of information, and it's tough (and perhaps misleading) to just sit down and describe all of them in detail at once. Instead, I will describe the CPU flags briefly here, and then in more detail as we encounter them while discussing the various instructions that use them in this and future chapters.

A *flag* is a single bit of information whose meaning is independent of any other bit. A bit can be *set* to 1 or *cleared* to 0 by the CPU as its needs require. The idea is to tell you, the programmer, the state of certain conditions inside the CPU, so that your program can test for and act on the states of those conditions. Much more rarely, you, the programmer, set a flag as a way of signaling something to the CPU.

Consider a row of country mailboxes, each with its own little red flag on the side. Each flag can be up or down; and if the Smiths' flag is up, it tells the mailman that the Smiths have placed mail in their box to be picked up. The mailman looks to see whether the Smiths' flag is raised (a test) and, if so, opens the Smiths' mailbox and picks up the waiting mail.

EFlags as a whole is a single 32-bit register buried inside the CPU. It's the 32-bit extended descendent of the 16-bit Flags register present in the 8086/8088 CPUs. Each of those 32 bits is a flag, though only a few are commonplace, and fewer still are useful when you're just learning your way around. Many, furthermore, are still undefined by Intel and not (yet) used.

It's a bit of a mess, but took a look at Figure 7-2, which summarizes all flags currently defined in the x86 architecture. The flags I've put against a gray background are the arcane ones that you can safely ignore for the moment.

Each of the EFlags register's flags has a two- or three-letter symbol by which most programmers know them. I use those symbols in this book, and you should become familiar with them. The most common flags, their symbols, and brief descriptions of what they stand for follows:

- **OF:** The **Overflow flag** is set when the result of an arithmetic operation on a signed integer quantity becomes too large to fit in the operand it originally occupied. OF is generally used as the "carry flag" in signed arithmetic.

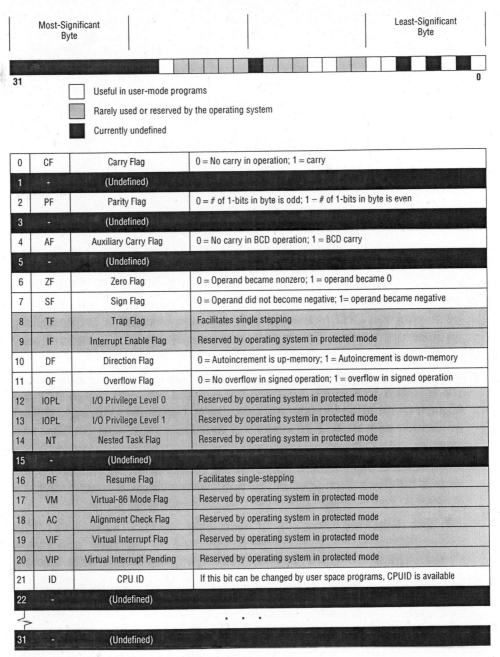

Most-Significant Byte			Least-Significant Byte

31   0

☐ Useful in user-mode programs

▨ Rarely used or reserved by the operating system

■ Currently undefined

0	CF	Carry Flag	0 = No carry in operation; 1 = carry
1	-	(Undefined)	
2	PF	Parity Flag	0 = # of 1-bits in byte is odd; 1 − # of 1-bits in byte is even
3	-	(Undefined)	
4	AF	Auxiliary Carry Flag	0 = No carry in BCD operation; 1 = BCD carry
5	-	(Undefined)	
6	ZF	Zero Flag	0 = Operand became nonzero; 1 = operand became 0
7	SF	Sign Flag	0 = Operand did not become negative; 1= operand became negative
8	TF	Trap Flag	Facilitates single stepping
9	IF	Interrupt Enable Flag	Reserved by operating system in protected mode
10	DF	Direction Flag	0 = Autoincrement is up-memory; 1 = Autoincrement is down-memory
11	OF	Overflow Flag	0 = No overflow in signed operation; 1 = overflow in signed operation
12	IOPL	I/O Privilege Level 0	Reserved by operating system in protected mode
13	IOPL	I/O Privilege Level 1	Reserved by operating system in protected mode
14	NT	Nested Task Flag	Reserved by operating system in protected mode
15	-	(Undefined)	
16	RF	Resume Flag	Facilitates single-stepping
17	VM	Virtual-86 Mode Flag	Reserved by operating system in protected mode
18	AC	Alignment Check Flag	Reserved by operating system in protected mode
19	VIF	Virtual Interrupt Flag	Reserved by operating system in protected mode
20	VIP	Virtual Interrupt Pending	Reserved by operating system in protected mode
21	ID	CPU ID	If this bit can be changed by user space programs, CPUID is available
22	-	(Undefined)	
· · ·			
31	-	(Undefined)	

Figure 7-2: The x86 EFlags register

- **DF:** The **Direction flag** is an oddball among the flags in that it tells the CPU something that you want it to know, rather than the other way around. It dictates the direction that activity moves (up-memory or down-memory) during the execution of string instructions. When DF is set, string instructions proceed from high memory toward low memory. When DF is cleared, string instructions proceed from low memory toward high memory.

- **IF:** The **Interrupt enable flag** is a two-way flag. The CPU sets it under certain conditions, and you can set it yourself using the STI and CLI instructions. When IF is set, interrupts are enabled and may occur when requested. When IF is cleared, interrupts are ignored by the CPU. Ordinary programs could set and clear this flag with impunity in real mode, back in the DOS era. Under Linux, IF is for the use of the operating system and sometimes its drivers. If you try to use the STI and CLI instructions within one of your programs, Linux will hand you a general protection fault and your program will be terminated. Consider IF off limits.

- **TF:** When set, the **Trap flag** allows debuggers to manage single-stepping, by forcing the CPU to execute only a single instruction before calling an interrupt routine. This is not an especially useful flag for ordinary programming and I won't have anything more to say about it.

- **SF:** The **Sign flag** becomes set when the result of an operation forces the operand to become negative. By *negative*, we only mean that the highest-order bit in the operand (the *sign bit*) becomes 1 during a signed arithmetic operation. Any operation that leaves the sign positive will clear SF.

- **ZF:** The **Zero flag** becomes set when the results of an operation become zero. If the destination operand instead becomes some nonzero value, ZF is cleared. You'll be using this one a lot for conditional jumps.

- **AF:** The **Auxiliary carry flag** is used only for BCD arithmetic. BCD arithmetic treats each operand byte as a pair of 4-bit "nybbles" and allows something approximating decimal (base 10) arithmetic to be done directly in the CPU hardware by using one of the BCD arithmetic instructions. These instructions are not much used anymore; I discuss BCD arithmetic only briefly in this book.

- **PF:** The **Parity flag** will seem instantly familiar to anyone who understands serial data communications, and utterly bizarre to anyone who doesn't. PF indicates whether the number of set (1) bits in the low-order byte of a result is even or odd. For example, if the result is 0F2H, then PF will be cleared because 0F2H (11110010) contains an odd number of 1 bits. Similarly, if the result is 3AH (00111100), then PF will be set because there is an even number (four) of 1 bits in the result. This flag is a carryover from the days when all computer communications were done through a serial port, for which a system of error detection called *parity checking* depends on knowing whether a count of set bits in a character byte is even or odd. PF is used only rarely and I won't be describing it further.

- **CF:** The **Carry flag** is used in unsigned arithmetic operations. If the result of an arithmetic or shift operation "carries out" a bit from the operand, CF becomes set. Otherwise, if nothing is carried out, CF is cleared.

Flag Etiquette

What I call "flag etiquette" is the way a given instruction affects the flags in the EFlags register. You *must* remember that the descriptions of the flags just described are generalizations *only* and are subject to specific restrictions and special cases imposed by individual instructions. Flag etiquette for individual flags varies widely from instruction to instruction, even though the *sense* of the flag's use may be the same in every case.

For example, some instructions that cause a zero to appear in an operand set ZF, while others do not. Sadly, there's no system to it and no easy way to keep it straight in your head. When you intend to use the flags in testing by way of conditional jump instructions, you have to check each individual instruction to see how the various flags are affected.

Flag etiquette is a highly individual matter. Check an instruction reference for each instruction to see if it affects the flags. Assume nothing!

A simple lesson in flag etiquette involves the two instructions INC and DEC.

Adding and Subtracting One with INC and DEC

Several x86 machine instructions come in pairs. Simplest among those are INC and DEC, which increment and decrement an operand by one, respectively.

Adding one to something or subtracting one from something are actions that happen *a lot* in computer programming. If you're counting the number of times that a program is executing a loop, or counting bytes in a table, or doing something that advances or retreats one count at a time, INC or DEC can be very quick ways to make the actual addition or subtraction happen.

Both INC and DEC take only one operand. An error will be flagged by the assembler if you try to use either INC or DEC with two operands, or without any operands.

Try both by adding the following instructions to your sandbox. Build the sandbox as usual, load the executable into Insight, and step through it:

```
mov eax,0FFFFFFFFh
mov ebx,02Dh
```

```
dec ebx
inc eax
```

Watch what happens to the EAX and EBX registers. Decrementing EBX predictably turns the value 2DH into value 2CH. Incrementing 0FFFFFFFFH, on the other hand, rolls over the EAX register to 0, because 0FFFFFFFFH is the largest unsigned value that can be expressed in a 32-bit register. Adding 1 to it rolls it over to zero, just as adding 1 to 99 rolls the rightmost two digits of the sum to zero in creating the number 100. The difference with INC is that *there is no carry*. The Carry flag is not affected by INC, so don't try to use it to perform multidigit arithmetic.

Watching Flags from Insight

The EFlags register is a register, just as EAX is, and its value is updated in Insight's Registers view. Unfortunately, you don't see the individual flags in the view. Instead, the overall hexadecimal value of EFlags is given, as if each of the flag bits were a bit in a hexadecimal number. This isn't especially useful if what you're doing is watching what an instruction does to a particular flag. Executing the DEC EBX instruction above changes the value in EFlags from 0292h to 0202h. Something changed in our rack of flags, but what?

This is one place where the Insight debugger interface really falls short, especially for people exploring the x86 instruction set for the first time. There is no simple view for EFlags that presents the values of the individual flags. To see which flags changed individually, you have to open the Console view and execute Gdb commands on its console command line.

Select View → Console from the Insight main menu. The Console view is very plain: just a blank terminal with the prompt (gdb) in the upper-right corner. Step the sandbox down to the DEC EBX instruction, but before executing the instruction, type this command in the Console view:

```
info reg
```

What you see should look like Figure 7-3. Gdb's info command displays the current status of something, and the reg parameter tells Gdb that we want to look at the current state of the registers. You get more than EFlags, of course. By default, all of the general-purpose registers and the segment registers are displayed. The math processor registers will not be, and that's good for our purposes.

Look at the line in Figure 7-3 showing the value of EFlags. The hex value of the register as a whole is shown, but after that value is a list of register names within square brackets. Flags that are set are shown; flags that are cleared are not shown. Prior to executing the DEC EBX instruction, the AF, SF, and IF flags are set. Now execute the DEC EBX instruction. Then enter the info reg command into the Console view again. The line showing the value of EFlags has changed to this:

```
eflags          0x202    [IF]
```

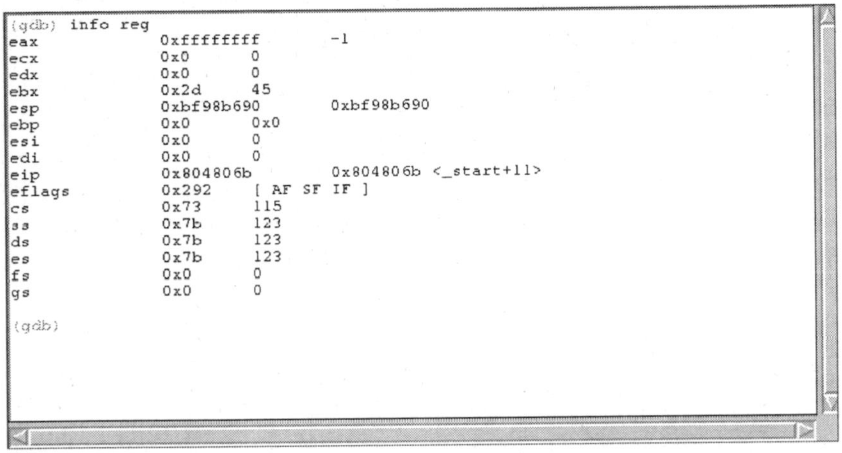

```
(gdb) info reg
eax             0xffffffff          -1
ecx             0x0       0
edx             0x0       0
ebx             0x2d      45
esp             0xbf98b690          0xbf98b690
ebp             0x0       0x0
esi             0x0       0
edi             0x0       0
eip             0x804806b           0x804806b <_start+11>
eflags          0x292     [ AF SF IF ]
cs              0x73      115
ss              0x7b      123
ds              0x7b      123
es              0x7b      123
fs              0x0       0
gs              0x0       0

(gdb)
```

Figure 7-3: Displaying the registers from the Insight Console view

So what happened? A look at the page for the DEC instruction in Appendix A will give you some hints: DEC affects the OF, SF, ZF, AF, and PF flags. The DEC EBX instruction cleared all of them. Here's why:

- The Overflow flag (OF) was cleared because the operand, interpreted as a signed integer, did not become too large to fit in EBX. This may not help you if you don't know what makes a number "signed," so let's leave it at that for the moment.

- The Sign flag (SF) was cleared because the high bit of EBX did not become 1 as a result of the operation. Had the high bit of EBX become 1, the value in EBX, interpreted as a signed integer value, would have become negative, and SF is set when a value becomes negative. As with OF, SF is not very useful unless you're doing signed arithmetic.

- The Zero flag (ZF) was cleared because the destination operand did not become zero. Had it become zero, ZF would have been set to 1.

- The Auxiliary carry flag (AF) was cleared because there was no BCD carry out of the lower four bits of EBX into the next higher four bits.

- The Parity flag (PF) was cleared because the number of 1 bits in the operand after the decrement happened was three, and PF is cleared when the number of bits in the destination operand is odd. Check it yourself: the value in EBX after the DEC instruction is 02Ch. In binary, this is 00101100. There are three 1 bits in the value, and thus PF is cleared.

The DEC instruction does not affect the IF flag, which remained set. In fact, almost nothing changes the IF flag, and user-mode applications like the sandbox (and everything else you're likely to write while learning assembly) are forbidden to change IF.

Now, execute the INC EAX instruction, and re-display the registers in the Console view. Boom! Lots of action this time:

- The Parity flag (PF) was set because the number of 1-bits in EAX is now zero, and PF is set when the number of 1-bits in the operand becomes even. 0 is considered an even number.

- The Auxiliary carry flag (AF) was set because the lower four bits in EAX went from FFFF to 0000. This implies a carry out of the lower four bits to the upper four bits, and AF is set when a carry out of the lower four bits of the operand happens.

- The Zero flag (ZF) was set because EAX became zero.

- As before, the IF flag doesn't change, and remains set at all times.

How Flags Change Program Execution

Watching the flags change value after instructions execute is a good way to learn flag etiquette, but once you have a handle on how various instructions change the flags, you can close the Console view. The real value of the flags doesn't lie in their values per se, but in how they affect the flow of machine instructions in your programs.

There is a whole category of machine instructions that "jump" to a different location in your program based on the current value in one of the flags. These instructions are called *conditional jump* instructions, and most of the flags in EFlags have one or more associated conditional jump instructions. They're listed in Appendix A on page 534.

Think back to the notion of "steps and tests" introduced in Chapter 1. Most machine instructions are steps taken in a list that runs generally from top to bottom. The conditional jump instructions are the tests. They test the condition of one of the flags, and either keep on going or jump to a different part of your program.

The simplest example of a conditional jump instruction, and the one you're likely to use the most, is JNZ, Jump If Not Zero. The JNZ instruction tests the value of the Zero flag. If ZF is set (that is, equal to 1), then nothing happens and the CPU executes the next instruction in sequence. However, if ZF is *not* set (that is, equal to 0), then execution travels to a new destination in your program.

This sounds worse than it is. You don't have to worry about adding or subtracting anything. In nearly all cases, the destination is provided as a *label*.

Labels are descriptive names given to locations in your programs. In NASM, a label is a character string followed by a colon, generally placed on a line containing an instruction.

Like so many things in assembly language, this will become clearer with a simple example. Load up a fresh sandbox, and type in the following instructions:

```
        mov eax,5
DoMore: dec eax
        jnz DoMore
```

Build the sandbox and load it into Insight. Watch the value of EAX in the Registers view as you step into it. In particular, watch what happens in the source code window when you execute the JNZ instruction. JNZ jumps to the label named as its operand if ZF is 0. If ZF = 1, it "falls through" to the next instruction.

The DEC instruction decrements the value in EAX. As long as the value in EAX does not change to 0, the Zero flag remains cleared. And as long as the Zero flag is cleared, JNZ jumps back to the label DoMore. So for five passes, DEC takes EAX down a notch, and JNZ jumps back to DoMore. But as soon as DEC takes EAX down to 0, the Zero flag becomes set, and JNZ "falls through" to the NOP instruction at the end of the sandbox.

Constructs like this are called *loops*, and are very common in all programming, not just assembly language. The preceding loop isn't useful but it demonstrates how you can repeat an instruction as many times as you need to, by loading an initial value in a register and decrementing that value once for each pass through the loop. The JNZ instruction tests ZF each time through, and knows to stop the loop when the counter goes to 0.

We can make the loop a little more useful without adding a lot of complication. What we do need to add is a data item for the loop to work on. Load Listing 7-2 into Kate, build it, and then load it into Insight.

Listing 7-2: kangaroo.asm

```
section .data

        Snippet db "KANGAROO"

section .text
global  _start
_start:
        nop
; Put your experiments between the two nops...

        mov ebx,Snippet
```

(continued)

Listing 7-2: kangaroo.asm (*continued*)

```
        mov eax,8
DoMore: add byte [ebx],32
        inc ebx
        dec eax
        jnz DoMore

; Put your experiments between the two nops...
        nop
```

The only difference from the generic sandbox program is the variable Snippet and the six instructions between the NOPS. Step through the program, making sure that you have Insight's Memory view open.

After eight passes through the loop, "KANGAROO" has become "kangaroo". How? Look at the ADD instruction located at the label DoMore. Earlier in the program, we copied the memory address of Snippet into register EBX. The ADD instruction adds the literal value 32 to whatever number is at the address stored in BX. If you look at Appendix B, you'll notice that the difference between the value of ASCII uppercase letters and ASCII lowercase letters is 32. A capital "K" has the value 4Bh, and a lowercase "k" has the value 6Bh. 6Bh − 4Bh is 20h, which in decimal is 32, so if we treat ASCII letters as numbers, we can add 32 to an uppercase letter and transform it into a lowercase letter.

The loop makes eight passes, one for each letter in "KANGAROO." After each ADD, the program increments the address in EBX, which puts the next character of "KANGAROO" in the crosshairs. It also decrements EAX, which had been loaded with the number of characters in the variable Snippet before the loop began. So within the same loop, the program is counting up along the length of Snippet in EBX, while counting down in EAX. When EAX goes to zero, it means that we've gone through all of the characters in Snippet, and we're done.

The operands of the ADD instruction are worth a closer look. Putting EBX inside square brackets references the contents of Snippet, rather than its address. But more important, the BYTE size specifier tells NASM that we're only writing a single byte to the memory address in EBX. NASM has no way to know otherwise. It's possible to write one byte, two bytes, or four bytes to memory at once, depending on what you need to do. However, you have to tell NASM what you want.

Don't forget that kangaroo.asm is still a sandbox program, suitable only for single-stepping in a debugger. If you just "let it run," it will generate a segmentation fault when execution moves past the final NOP instruction. Once you single-step to that final NOP, kill the program and either begin execution again or exit the debugger.

Signed and Unsigned Values

In assembly language we can work with both signed and unsigned numeric values. Signed values, of course, are values that can become negative. An unsigned value is always positive. There are instructions for the four basic arithmetic operations in the x86 instruction set, and these instructions can operate on both signed and unsigned values. (With multiplication and division, there are separate instructions for signed and unsigned calculations, as I'll explain shortly.)

The key to understanding the difference between signed and unsigned numeric values is knowing where the CPU puts the sign. It's not a dash character, but actually a bit in the binary pattern that represents the number. The highest bit in the most significant byte of a signed value is the *sign bit*. If the sign bit is a 1-bit, the number is negative. If the sign bit is a 0 bit, the number is positive.

Keep in mind through all of this that whether a given binary pattern represents a signed or an unsigned value depends on how you choose to use it. If you intend to perform signed arithmetic, the high bit of a register value or memory location is considered the sign bit. If you do not intend to perform signed arithmetic, then the high bits of the very same values in the very same places will simply be the most significant bits of unsigned values. The signed nature of a value lies in how you treat the value, and not in the nature of the underlying bit pattern that represents the value.

For example, does the binary number 10101111 represent a signed value or an unsigned value? The question is meaningless without context: if you need to treat the value as a signed value, you treat the high-order bit as the sign bit, and the value is -81. If you need to treat the value as an unsigned value, you treat the high bit as just another digit in a binary number, and the value is 175.

Two's Complement and NEG

One mistake beginners sometimes commit is assuming that you can make a value negative by setting the sign bit to 1. Not so! You can't simply take the value 42 and make it -42 by setting the sign bit. The value you get will certainly be negative, but it will *not* be -42.

One way to get a sense for the way negative numbers are expressed in assembly language is to decrement a positive number down into negative territory. Bring up a clean sandbox and enter these instructions:

```
        mov eax,5
DoMore: dec eax
        Jmp DoMore
```

Build the sandbox as usual and load the executable into Insight. Note that we've added a new instruction here, and a hazard: the JMP instruction does *not* look at the flags. When executed, it *always* jumps to its operand, hence the mnemonic. So execution will bounce back to the label DoMore each and every time that JMP executes. If you're sharp you'll notice that there's no way out of this particular sequence of instructions, and, yes, this is the legendary "endless loop" that you'll fall into now and then.

Therefore, make sure you set a breakpoint on the initial MOV instruction, and don't just let the program rip. Or ... go ahead! (Nothing will be harmed.) Without breakpoints, what you'll see is that Insight's "running man" icon becomes a stop sign. When you see the stop sign icon, you'll know that the program is not paused for stepping, but is running freely. If you click on the stop sign, Insight will stop the program. Under DOS, you would have been stuck and had to reboot. Linux and Gdb make for a much more robust programming environment, one that doesn't go down in flames on your least mistake.

Start single-stepping the sandbox and watch EAX in the Registers view. The starting value of 5 will count down to 4, and 3, and 2, and 1, and 0, and then ... 0FFFFFFFFh! That's the 32-bit expression of the simple value -1. If you keep on decrementing EAX, you'll get a sense for what happens:

```
0FFFFFFFFh (-1)
0FFFFFFFEh (-2)
0FFFFFFFDh (-3)
0FFFFFFFCh (-4)
0FFFFFFFBh (-5)
0FFFFFFFAh (-6)
0FFFFFFF9h (-7)
```

...and so on. When negative numbers are handled in this fashion, it is called *two's complement*. In x86 assembly language, negative numbers are stored as the two's complement form of their absolute value, which if you remember from eighth-grade math is the distance of a number from 0, in either the positive or the negative direction.

The mathematics behind two's complement is surprisingly subtle, and I direct you to Wikipedia for a fuller treatment than I can afford in this book:

http://en.wikipedia.org/wiki/Two's_complement

The magic of expressing negative numbers in two's complement form is that the CPU doesn't really need to subtract at the level of its transistor logic. It simply generates the two's complement of the subtrahend and adds it to the minuend. This is relatively easy for the CPU, and it all happens transparently to your programs, where subtraction is done about the way you'd expect.

The good news is that you almost never have to calculate a two's complement value manually. There is a machine instruction that will do it for you: NEG. The NEG instruction will take a positive value as its operand, and negate that value—that is, make it negative. It does so by generating the two's complement form of the positive value. Load the following instructions into a clean sandbox and single-step them in Insight. Watch EAX in the Registers view:

```
mov eax,42
neg eax
add eax,42
```

In one swoop, 42 becomes 0FFFFFFD6h, the two's complement hexadecimal expression of -42. Add 42 to this value, and watch EAX go to 0.

At this point, the question may arise: What are the largest positive and negative numbers that can be expressed in one, two, or four bytes? Those two values, plus all the values in between, constitute the *range* of a value expressed in a given number of bits. I've laid this out in Table 7-2.

Table 7-2: Ranges of Signed Values

VALUE SIZE	GREATEST NEGATIVE VALUE		GREATEST POSITIVE VALUE	
	DECIMAL	HEX	DECIMAL	HEX
Eight Bits	−128	80h	127	7Fh
Sixteen Bits	−32768	8000h	32767	7FFFh
Thirty-Two Bits	−2147483648	80000000h	2147483647	7FFFFFFFh

If you're sharp and know how to count in hex, you may notice something here from the table: the greatest positive value and the greatest negative value for a given value size are *one count apart*. That is, if you're working in 8 bits and add one to the greatest positive value, 7Fh, you get 80h, the greatest negative value.

You can watch this happen by executing the following two instructions in a sandbox:

```
mov eax,07FFFFFFh
inc eax
```

This example will only be meaningful in conjunction with a trick I haven't shown you yet: Insight's Registers view allows you to display a register's value in three different formats. By default, Insight displays all register values in hex. However, you can right-click on any given register in the Registers view window, and select between Hex, Decimal, and Unsigned. The three formats work this way:

- Hexadecimal format presents the value in hex.
- Decimal format presents the value as a signed value, treating the high bit as the sign bit.
- Unsigned format presents the value as an unsigned value, treating the high bit as just another binary bit in the number as a whole.

So before you execute the two instructions given above, right-click on EAX in the Registers view and select Decimal. After the MOV instruction executes, EAX will show the decimal value 2147483647. That's the highest signed value possible in 32 bits. Increment the value with the INC instruction, and instantly the value in EAX becomes -2147483648.

Sign Extension and MOVSX

There's a subtle gotcha to be avoided when you're working with signed values in different sizes. The sign bit is the high bit in a signed byte, word, or double word. But what happens when you have to move a signed value into a larger register or memory location? What happens, for example, if you need to move a signed 16-bit value into a 32-bit register? If you use the MOV instruction, nothing good. Try this:

```
mov ax,-42
mov ebx,eax
```

The hexadecimal form of -42 is 0FFD6h. If you have that value in a 16-bit register like AX, and use MOV to move the value into a 32-bit register like EBX, *the sign bit will no longer be the sign bit*. In other words, once -42 travels from a 16-bit container into a 32-bit container, it changes from -42 to 65494. The sign bit is still there. It hasn't been cleared to zero. However, in a 32-bit register, the old sign bit is now just another bit in a binary value, with no special meaning.

This example is a little misleading. First of all, we can't literally move a value from AX into EBX. The MOV instruction will only handle operands of the same size. However, remember that AX is simply the lower two bytes of EAX. We can move AX into EBX by moving EAX into EBX, and that's what we did in the preceding example.

And, alas, Insight is not capable of showing us signed 8-bit or 16-bit values. Insight can only display EAX, and we can see AL, AH, or AX only by seeing them inside EAX. That's why, in the preceding example, Insight shows the value we thought was -42 as 65494. Insight's Registers view has no concept of a sign bit except in the highest bit of a 32-bit value. This is a shortcoming of the Insight program itself, and I hope that someone will eventually enhance the Registers view to allow signed 8-bit and 16-bit values to be displayed as such.

The x86 CPU provides us with a way out of this trap, in the form of the MOVSX instruction. MOVSX means "Move with Sign Extension," and it is one of many instructions that were not present in the original 8086/8088 CPUs. MOVSX was introduced with the 386 family of CPUs, and because Linux will not run on anything older than a 386, you can assume that any Linux PC supports the MOVSX instruction.

Load this into a sandbox and try it:

```
mov ax,-42
movsx ebx,ax
```

Remember that Insight cannot display AX individually, and so will show EAX as containing 65494. However, when you move AX into EBX with MOVSX, the value of EBX will then be shown as -42. What happened is that the MOVSX instruction performed *sign extension* on its operands, taking the sign bit from the 16-bit quantity in AX and making it the sign bit of the 32-bit quantity in EBX.

MOVSX is different from MOV in that its operands may be of different sizes. MOVSX has three possible variations, which I've summarized in Table 7-3.

Table 7-3: The MOVSX Instruction

MACHINE INSTRUCTION	DESTINATION OPERAND	SOURCE OPERAND	OPERAND NOTES
MOVSX	r16	r/m8	8-bit signed to 16-bit signed
MOVSX	r32	r/m8	8-bit signed to 32-bit signed
MOVSX	r32	r/m16	16-bit signed to 32-bit signed

Note that the destination operand can *only* be a register. The notation here is one you'll see in many assembly language references in describing instruction operands. The notation "r16" is an abbreviation for "any 16-bit register." Similarly, "r/m" means "register or memory" and is followed by the bit size. For example, "r/m16" means "any 16-bit register or memory location."

With all that said, you may find after solving some problems in assembly language that signed arithmetic is used less often than you think. It's good to know how it works, but don't be surprised if you go years without ever needing it.

Implicit Operands and MUL

Most of the time, you hand values to machine instructions through one or two operands placed right there on the line beside the mnemonic. This is good, because when you say MOV EAX, EBX you know *precisely* what's moving, where it comes from, and where it's going. Alas, that isn't always the case. Some instructions act on registers or even memory locations that are not stated in a list of operands. These instructions do in fact have operands, but they represent assumptions made by the instruction. Such operands are called *implicit operands*, and they do not change and cannot be changed. To add to the confusion, most instructions that have implicit operands have explicit operands as well.

The best examples of implicit operands in the x86 instruction set are the multiplication and division instructions. Excluding the instructions in the dedicated math processors (x87, MMX, and SSE, which I won't be covering in this book) the x86 instruction set has two sets of multiply and divide instructions. One set, MUL and DIV, handle unsigned calculations. The other, IMUL and IDIV, handle signed calculations. Because MUL and DIV are used much more frequently than their signed-math alternates, they are what I discuss in this section.

The MUL instruction does what you'd expect: it multiplies two values and returns a product. Among the basic math operations, however, multiplication has a special problem: it generates output values that are often *hugely* larger than the input values. This makes it impossible to follow the conventional pattern in x86 instruction operands, whereby the value generated by an instruction goes into the destination operand.

Consider a 32-bit multiply operation. The largest unsigned value that will fit in a 32-bit register is 4,294,967,295. Multiply that even by two and you've got a 33-bit product, which will no longer fit in any 32-bit register. This problem has plagued the x86 architecture (all computer architectures, in fact) since the beginning. When the x86 was a 16-bit architecture, the problem was where to put the product of two 16-bit values, which can easily overflow a 16-bit register.

Intel's designers solved the problem the only way they could: by using *two* registers to hold the product. It's not immediately obvious to non-mathematicians, but it's true (try it on a calculator!) that the largest product of two binary numbers can be expressed in no more than twice the number of bits required by the larger factor. Simply put, any product of two 16-bit values will fit in 32 bits, and any product of two 32-bit values will fit in 64 bits. Therefore, while two registers may be needed to hold the product, no *more* than two registers will ever be needed.

Which brings us to the MUL instruction. MUL is an odd bird from an operand standpoint: it takes only one operand, which contains one of the factors to be multiplied. The other factor is implicit, as is the pair of registers that receives the product of the calculation. MUL thus looks deceptively simple:

```
mul ebx
```

More is involved here than just EBX. The implicit operands depend on the size of the explicit one. This gives us three variations, which I've summarized in Table 7-4.

Table 7-4: The MUL Instruction

MACHINE INSTRUCTION	EXPLICIT OPERAND (FACTOR 1)	IMPLICIT OPERAND (FACTOR 2)	IMPLICIT OPERAND (PRODUCT)
mul	r/m8	AL	AX
mul	r/m16	AX	DX and AX
mul	r/m32	EAX	EDX and EAX

The first factor is given in the single explicit operand, which can be a value either in a register or in a memory location. The second factor is implicit, and always in the "A" general-purpose register appropriate to the size of the first factor. If the first factor is an 8-bit value, the second factor is always in the 8-bit register AL. If the first factor is a 16-bit value, the second factor is always in the 16-bit register AX, and so on.

Once the product requires more than 16 bits, the "D" register is drafted to hold the high-order portion of the product. By "high-order" here I mean the portion of the product that won't fit in the "A" register. For example, if you multiply two 16-bit values and the product is 02A456Fh, then register AX will contain 0456Fh, and the DX register will contain 02Ah.

Note well that even when a product is small enough to fit in the first of the two registers holding the product, the high-order register (whether AH, DX, or EDX) is zeroed out. Registers often become scarce in assembly work, but even if you're *sure* that your multiplications always involve small products, you can't use the high-order register for anything else while a MUL instruction is executed.

Also, take note that immediate values cannot be used as operands for MUL; that is, you can't do the following, as useful as it would often be to state the first factor as an immediate value:

```
mul 42
```

MUL and the Carry Flag

Not all multiplications generate large enough products to require two registers. Most of the time you'll find that 32 bits is more than enough. So how can you tell whether or not there are significant figures in the high-order register? MUL very helpfully sets the Carry flag (CF) when the value of the product overflows the low-order register. If, after a MUL, you find CF set to 0, you can ignore the high-order register, secure in the knowledge that the entire product is in the lower order of the two registers.

This is worth a quick sandbox demonstration. First try a "small" multiplication for which the product will easily fit in a single 32-bit register:

```
mov eax,447
mov ebx,1739
mul ebx
```

Remember that we're multiplying EAX by EBX here. Step through the three instructions, and after the MUL instruction has executed, look at the Registers view to see the product in EDX and EAX. EAX contains 777333, and EDX contains 0. Now type info reg in the Console view and look at the current state of the various flags. No sign of CF, meaning that CF has been cleared to 0.

Next, add the following instructions to your sandbox, after the three shown in the preceding example:

```
mov eax,0FFFFFFFFh
mov ebx,03B72h
mul ebx
```

Step through them as usual, watching the contents of EAX, EDX, and EBX in the Registers view. After the MUL instruction, type info reg in the Console view once more. The Carry flag (CF) has been set to 1. (So have the Overflow flag, OF, Sign flag, SF, and Parity flag, PF, but those are not generally useful in unsigned arithmetic.) What CF basically tells you here is that there are significant figures in the high-order portion of the product, and these are stored in EDX for 32-bit multiplies.

Unsigned Division with DIV

I recall stating flatly in class as a third grader that division is multiplication done backwards, and I was closer to the truth than poor Sister Agnes Eileen was willing to admit at the time. It's certainly true enough for there to be a strong resemblance between the x86 unsigned multiply instruction MUL and the unsigned division instruction DIV. DIV does what you'd expect from your third-grade training: it divides one value by another and gives you a quotient and a remainder. Remember, we're doing integer, not decimal, arithmetic here, so there is no way to express a decimal quotient like 17.76 or 3.14159. These require the "floating point" machinery on the math processor side of the x86 architecture, which is a vast and subtle subject that I won't be covering in this book.

In division, you don't have the problem that multiplication has, of generating large output values for some input values. If you divide a 16-bit value by another 16-bit value, you will never get a quotient that will not fit in a 16-bit register. Nonetheless, it would be useful to be able to divide very large numbers, so Intel's engineers created something very like a mirror image of MUL: you place a dividend value in EDX and EAX, which means that it may be up to 64 bits in size. 64 bits can hold a *whomping* big number: 18,446,744,073,709,551,615. The divisor is stored in DIV's only explicit operand, which may be a register or in memory. (As with MUL, you cannot use an immediate value as the operand.) The quotient is returned in EAX, and the remainder in EDX.

That's the situation for a full, 32-bit division. As with MUL, DIV's implicit operands depend on the size of the explicit operand, here acting as the divisor. There are three "sizes" of DIV operations, as summarized in Table 7-5.

Table 7-5: The DIV Instruction

MACHINE INSTRUCTION	EXPLICIT OPERAND (DIVISOR)	IMPLICIT OPERAND (QUOTIENT)	IMPLICIT OPERAND (REMAINDER)
DIV	r/m8	AL	AH
DIV	r/m16	AX	DX
DIV	r/m32	EAX	EDX

The DIV instruction does not affect any of the flags. However, division does have a special problem: *Using a value of 0 in either the dividend or the divisor is undefined*, and will generate a Linux arithmetic exception that terminates your program. This makes it important to test the value in both the divisor and the dividend before executing DIV, to ensure you haven't let any zeroes into the mix.

You may object that ordinary grade-school math allows you to divide zero by a nonzero value, with a result that is always zero. That's true mathematically, but it's not an especially useful operation, and in the x86 architecture dividing zero by *anything* is *always* an error.

I'll demonstrate a useful application of the DIV instruction later in this book, when we build a routine to convert pure binary values to ASCII strings that can be displayed on the PC screen.

The x86 Slowpokes

A common beginner's question about MUL and DIV concerns the two "smaller" versions of both instructions (see Tables and 7-5). If a 32-bit multiply or divide can handle anything the IA32 implementation of the x86 architecture can stuff in registers, why are the smaller versions even necessary? Is it all a matter of backward compatibility with older 16-bit CPUs?

Not entirely. In many cases, it's a matter of speed. The DIV and MUL instructions are close to the slowest instructions in the entire x86 instruction set. They're certainly not as slow as they used to be, but compared to other instructions like MOV or ADD, they're goop. Furthermore, the 32-bit version of both instructions is slower than the 16-bit version, and the 8-bit version is the fastest of all.

Now, speed optimization is a very slippery business in the x86 world. Having instructions in the CPU cache versus having to pull them from memory is a speed difference that swamps most speed differences among the instructions themselves. Other factors come into play in the most recent Pentium-class CPUs that make generalizations about instruction speed almost impossible, and certainly impossible to state with any precision.

If you're only doing a few isolated multiplies or divides, don't let any of this bother you. Instruction speed becomes important inside loops, where you're doing a lot of calculations constantly, as in graphics rendering and video work (and if you're doing anything like that, you should probably be using the math processor portion of the x86 architecture instead of MUL and DIV). My own personal heuristic is to use the smallest version of MUL and DIV that the input values allow—tempered by the even stronger heuristic that most of the time, *instruction speed doesn't matter*. When you become experienced enough at assembly to make performance decisions at the instruction level, you will know it. Until then, concentrate on making your programs bug-free and leave speed to the CPU.

Reading and Using an Assembly Language Reference

Assembly language programming is about details. Good grief, is it about details. There are broad similarities among instructions, but it's the differences that get you when you start feeding programs to the unforgiving eye of the assembler.

Remembering a host of tiny, tangled details involving several dozen different instructions is brutal and unnecessary. Even the Big Guys don't try to keep it all between their ears at all times. Most keep some other sort of reference document handy to jog their memory about machine instruction details.

Memory Joggers for Complex Memories

This problem has existed for a long time. Thirty-five years ago, when I first encountered microcomputers, a complete and useful instruction set memory-jogger document could fit on two sides of a trifold card that could fit in your shirt pocket. Such cards were common and you could get them for almost any microprocessor. For reasons unclear, they were called *blue cards*, though most were printed on ordinary white cardboard.

By the early 1980s, what was once a card had now become an 89-page booklet, sized to fit in your pocket. The Intel *Programmer's Reference Pocket Guide* for the 8086 family of CPUs was shipped with Microsoft's Macro Assembler, and everybody I knew had one. (I still have mine.) It really did fit in a shirt pocket, as long as nothing else tried to share the space.

The power and complexity of the x86 architecture exploded in the mid-80s, and a full summary of all instructions in all their forms, plus all the necessary explanations, became book material; and as the years passed, it required not one but several books to cover it completely. Intel provides PDF versions of its processor documentation as free downloads, and you can get them here:

```
www.intel.com/products/processor/manuals/
```

They're worth having—but forget cramming them in your pocket. The instruction set reference alone represents *1,600 pages* in two fat books, and there are four or five other essential books to round out the set.

Perhaps the best compromise I've seen is the *Turbo Assembler Quick Reference Guide* from Borland. It's a 5″ × 8″ spiral-bound lay-flat booklet of only 140 pages, published as part of the documentation set of the Turbo Assembler product in 1990. The material on the assembler directives does not apply to NASM, but the instruction reference covers the 32-bit forms of all instructions through the 486, which is nearly everything a beginning assembly student is likely to use.

Copies of the *Turbo Assembler Quick Reference Guide* can often be found in the $5 to $10 price range on the online used book sites like Alibris (www.alibris.com) and ABE Books (www.abebooks.com).

An Assembly Language Reference for Beginners

The problem with assembly language references is that to be complete, they cannot be small. However, a great deal of the complexity of the x86 in the modern day rests with instructions and memory addressing machinery that are of use only to operating systems and drivers. For smallish applications running in user mode they simply do not apply.

So in deference to people just starting out in assembly language, I have put together a beginner's reference to the most common x86 instructions, in Appendix A. It contains at least a page on every instruction I cover in this book, plus a few additional instructions that everyone ought to know. It does *not* include descriptions on *every* instruction, but only the most common and most useful. Once you are skillful enough to use the more arcane instructions, you should be able to read Intel's x86 documentation and run with it.

On page 233 is a sample entry from Appendix A. Refer to it during the following discussion.

The instruction's mnemonic is at the top of the page, highlighted in a shaded box to make it easy to spot while flipping quickly through the appendix. To the mnemonic's right is the name of the instruction, which is a little more descriptive than the naked mnemonic.

Flags

Immediately beneath the mnemonic is a minichart of CPU flags in the EFlags register. As mentioned earlier, the EFlags register is a collection of 1-bit values that retain certain essential information about the state of the machine for short periods of time. Many (but by no means all) x86 instructions change the values of one or more flags. The flags may then be individually tested by one of the Jump On Condition instructions, which change the course of the program depending on the states of the flags.

Each of the flags has a name, and each flag has a symbol in the flags minichart. Over time, you'll eventually know the flags by their two-character symbols, but until then the full names of the flags are shown to the right of the minichart. The majority of the flags are not used frequently in beginning assembly language work. Most of what you'll be paying attention to, flagswise, are the Zero flag (ZF) and the Carry flag (CF).

There will be an asterisk (*) beneath the symbol of any flag affected by the instruction. *How* the flag is affected depends on what the instruction does. You'll have to divine that from the Notes section. When an instruction affects no flags at all, the word <none> appears in the flags minichart.

In the example page here, the minichart indicates that the NEG instruction affects the Overflow flag, the Sign flag, the Zero flag, the Auxiliary carry flag, the Parity flag, and the Carry flag. How the flags are affected depends on the results of the negation operation on the operand specified. These possibilities are summarized in the second paragraph of the Notes section.

NEG: Negate (Two's Complement; i.e., Multiply by -1)

Flags Affected

```
O D I T S Z A P C    OF: Overflow flag   TF: Trap flag AF: Aux carry
F F F F F F F F F     DF: Direction flag  SF: Sign flag PF: Parity flag
*       * * * *       IF: Interrupt flag  ZF: Zero flag CF: Carry flag
```

Legal Forms

```
NEG r8
NEG m8
NEG r16
NEG m16
NEG r32        386+
NEG m32        386+
```

Examples

```
NEG AL
NEG DX
NEG ECX
NEG BYTE [BX]    ; Negates BYTE quantity at [BX]
NEG WORD [DI]    ; Negates WORD quantity at [BX]
NEG DWORD [EAX]  ; Negates DWORD quantity at [EAX]
```

Notes

This is the assembly language equivalent of multiplying a value by -1. Keep in mind that negation is *not* the same as simply inverting each bit in the operand. (Another instruction, NOT, does that.) The process is also known as generating the *two's complement* of a value. The two's complement of a value added to that value yields zero. -1 = $FF; -2 = $FE; -3 = $FD; and so on.

If the operand is 0, then CF is cleared and ZF is set; otherwise, CF is set and ZF is cleared. If the operand contains the maximum negative value (−128 for 8-bit or −32,768 for 16-bit), then the operand does not change, but OF and CF are set. SF is set if the result is negative, or else SF is cleared. PF is set if the low-order 8 bits of the result contain an even number of set (1) bits; otherwise, PF is cleared.

Note that you *must* use a size specifier (BYTE, WORD, DWORD) with memory data!

```
r8 = AL AH BL BH CL CH DL DH      r16 = AX BX CX DX BP SP SI DI
sr = CS DS SS ES FS GS            r32 = EAX EBX ECX EDX EBP ESP ESI EDI
m8 = 8-bit memory data            m16 = 16-bit memory data
m32 = 32-bit memory data          i8 = 8-bit immediate data
i16 = 16-bit immediate data       i32 = 32-bit immediate data
d8 = 8-bit signed displacement    d16 = 16-bit signed displacement
d32 = 32-bit unsigned displacement
```

Legal Forms

A given mnemonic represents a single x86 instruction, but each instruction may include more than one legal form. The form of an instruction varies by the type and order of the operands passed to it.

What the individual forms actually represent are different binary number opcodes. For example, beneath the surface, the POP AX instruction is the binary number 058h, whereas the POP SI instruction is the binary number 05Eh. Most opcodes are not single 8-bit values, and most are at least two bytes long, and often four or more.

Sometimes there will be special cases of an instruction and its operands that are shorter than the more general cases. For example, the XCHG instruction, which exchanges the contents of the two operands, has a special case when one of the operands is register AX. Any XCHG instruction with AX as one of the operands is represented by a single-byte opcode. The general forms of XCHG (for example, XCHG r16,r16) are always two bytes long instead. This implies that there are actually two different opcodes that will do the job for a given combination of operands (for example, XCHG AX,DX). True enough—and some assemblers are smart enough to choose the shortest form possible in any given situation. If you are hand-assembling a sequence of raw opcode bytes, say, for use in a higher-level language inline assembly statement, you need to be aware of the special cases, and all special cases are marked as such in the Legal Forms section.

When you want to use an instruction with a certain set of operands, be sure to check the Legal Forms section of the reference guide for that instruction to ensure that the combination is legal. More forms are legal now than they were in the bad old DOS days, and many of the remaining restrictions involve segment registers, which you will not be able to use when writing ordinary 32-bit protected mode user applications. The MOV instruction, for example, cannot move data from memory to memory, and in real mode there are restrictions regarding how data may be placed in segment registers.

In the example reference page on the NEG instruction, you can see that a segment register cannot be an operand to NEG. (If it could, there would be a NEG sr (discussed in the next section) item in the Legal forms list.)

Operand Symbols

The symbols used to indicate the nature of the operands in the Legal Forms section are summarized at the bottom of every instruction's page in Appendix A. They're close to self-explanatory, but I'll take a moment to expand upon them slightly here:

▪ **r8:** An 8-bit register half, one of AH, AL, BH, BL, CH, CL, DH, or DL

- **r16:** A 16-bit general-purpose register, one of AX, BX, CX, DX, BP, SP, SI, or DI

- **r32:** A 32-bit general-purpose register, one of EAX, EBX, ECX, EDX, EBP, ESP, ESI, or EDI

- **sr:** One of the segment registers, CS, DS, SS, ES, FS, or GS

- **m8:** An 8-bit byte of memory data

- **m16:** A 16-bit word of memory data

- **m32:** A 32-bit word of memory data

- **i8:** An 8-bit byte of immediate data

- **i16:** A 16-bit word of immediate data

- **i32:** A 32-bit word of immediate data

- **d8:** An 8-bit signed displacement. We haven't covered these yet, but a *displacement* is the distance between the current location in the code and another place in the code to which you want to jump. It's *signed* (that is, either negative or positive) because a positive displacement jumps you higher (forward) in memory, whereas a negative displacement jumps you lower (back) in memory. We examine this notion in detail later.

- **d16:** A 16-bit signed displacement. Again, for use with jump and call instructions.

- **d32:** A 32-bit signed displacement

Examples

Whereas the Legal Forms section shows what combinations of operands is legal for a given instruction, the Examples section shows examples of the instruction in actual use, just as it would be coded in an assembly language program. I've tried to provide a good sampling of examples for each instruction, demonstrating the range of different possibilities with the instruction.

Notes

The Notes section of the reference page describes the instruction's action briefly and provides information about how it affects the flags, how it may be limited in use, and any other detail that needs to be remembered, especially things that beginners would overlook or misconstrue.

What's Not Here . . .

Appendix A differs from most detailed assembly language references in that it does not include the binary opcode encoding information, nor indications of how many machine cycles are used by each form of the instruction.

The binary encoding of an instruction is the actual sequence of binary bytes that the CPU digests and recognizes as the machine instruction. What we would call POP AX, the machine sees as the binary number 58h. What we call ADD SI,07733h, the machine sees as the 4-byte sequence 81h 0C6h 33h 77h. Machine instructions are encoded into anywhere from one to four (sometimes more) binary bytes depending on what instruction they are and what their operands are. Laying out the system for determining what the encoding will be for any given instruction is extremely complicated, in that its component bytes must be set up bit by bit from several large tables. I've decided that this book is not the place for that particular discussion and have left encoding information out of the reference appendix. (This issue is one thing that makes the Intel instruction reference books as big as they are.)

Finally, I've included nothing anywhere in this book that indicates how many machine cycles are expended by any given machine instruction. A *machine cycle* is one pulse of the master clock that makes the PC perform its magic. Each instruction uses some number of those cycles to do its work, and the number varies all over the map depending on criteria that I won't be explaining in this book. Worse, the number of machine cycles used by a given instruction varies from one model of Intel processor to another. An instruction may use fewer cycles on the Pentium than on the 486, or perhaps more. (In general, x86 instructions have evolved to use fewer clock cycles over the years, but this is not true of every single instruction.)

Furthermore, as Michael Abrash explains in his immense book *Michael Abrash's Graphics Programming Black Book* (Coriolis Group Books, 1997), knowing the cycle requirements for individual instructions is rarely sufficient to allow even an expert assembly language programmer to calculate how much time a given series of instructions will take to execute. The CPU cache, prefetching, branch prediction, hyperthreading, and any number of other factors combine and interact to make such calculations almost impossible except in broad terms. He and I both agree that it is no fit subject for beginners, and if you'd like to know more at some point, I suggest hunting down his book and seeing for yourself.

CHAPTER 8

Our Object All Sublime

Creating Programs That Work

They don't call it "assembly" for nothing. Facing the task of writing an assembly language program brings to mind images of Christmas morning: you've spilled 1,567 small metal parts out of a large box marked *Land Shark HyperBike* (some assembly required) and now you have to somehow put them all together with nothing left over. (In the meantime, the kids seem more than happy playing in the box.)

I've actually explained just about all you absolutely *must* understand to create your first assembly language program. Still, there is a nontrivial leap from here to there; you are faced with many small parts with sharp edges that can fit together in an infinity of different ways, most wrong, some workable, but only a few that are ideal.

So here's the plan: in this chapter I'll present you with the completed and operable Land Shark HyperBike—which I will then tear apart before your eyes. This is the best way to learn to assemble: by pulling apart programs written by those who know what they're doing. Over the course of this chapter we'll pull a few more programs apart, in the hope that by the time it's over you'll be able to move in the other direction all by yourself.

The Bones of an Assembly Language Program

Back in Listing 5-1 in Chapter 5, I presented perhaps the simplest correct program for Linux that will do anything visible and still be comprehensible and expandable. Since then we've been looking at instructions in a sandbox through the Insight debugger. That's a good way to become familiar with individual instructions, but very quickly a sandbox just isn't enough. Now that you have a grip on the most common x86 instructions (and know how to set up a sandbox to experiment with and get to know the others), we need to move on to complete programs.

As you saw when you ran it, the program eatsyscall displays one (short) line of text on your display screen:

```
Eat at Joe's!
```

And for that, you had to feed 35 lines of text to the assembler! Many of those 35 lines are comments and unnecessary in the strictest sense, but they serve as internal documentation, enabling you to understand what the program is doing (or, more important, *how* it's doing it) six months or a year from now.

The program presented here is the very same one you saw in Listing 5-1, but I repeat it here so that you don't have to flip back and forth during the discussion on the following pages:

```
;   Executable name : EATSYSCALL
;   Version         : 1.0
;   Created date    : 1/7/2009
;   Last update     : 1/7/2009
;   Author          : Jeff Duntemann
;   Description     : A simple assembly app for Linux, using NASM 2.05,
;                     demonstrating the use of Linux INT 80H syscalls
;                     to display text.
;
;   Build using these commands:
;       nasm -f elf -g -F stabs eatsyscall.asm
;       ld -o eatsyscall eatsyscall.o
;

SECTION .data          ; Section containing initialized data

EatMsg:  db "Eat at Joe's!",10
EatLen:  equ $-EatMsg

SECTION .bss           ; Section containing uninitialized data

SECTION .text          ; Section containing code

global _start          ; Linker needs this to find the entry point!

_start:
        nop                    ; This no-op keeps gdb happy (see text)
        mov eax,4              ; Specify sys_write syscall
        mov ebx,1              ; Specify File Descriptor 1: Standard Output
```

```
mov ecx,EatMsg    ; Pass offset of the message
mov edx,EatLen    ; Pass the length of the message
int 80H           ; Make syscall to output the text to stdout

mov eax,1         ; Specify Exit syscall
mov ebx,0         ; Return a code of zero
int 80H           ; Make syscall to terminate the program
```

The Initial Comment Block

One of the aims of assembly language coding is to use as few instructions as possible to get the job done. This does *not* mean creating as short a source code file as possible. The size of the source file has *nothing* to do with the size of the executable file assembled from it! The more comments you put in your file, the better you'll remember how things work inside the program the next time you pick it up. I think you'll find it amazing how quickly the logic of a complicated assembly language program goes cold in your head. After no more than 48 hours of working on other projects, I've come back to assembly projects and had to struggle to get back to flank speed on development.

Comments are neither time nor space wasted. IBM used to recommend *one line of comments per line of code*. That's good—and should be considered a *minimum* for assembly language work. A better course (that I will in fact follow in the more complicated examples later) is to use one short line of commentary to the right of each line of code, along with a comment block at the start of each sequence of instructions, that work together to accomplish some discrete task.

At the top of every program should be a sort of standardized comment block, containing some important information:

- The name of the source code file
- The name of the executable file
- The date you created the file
- The date you last modified the file
- The name of the person who wrote it
- The name and version of the assembler used to create it
- An "overview" description of what the program or library does. Take as much room as you need. It doesn't affect the size or speed of the executable program
- A copy of the commands used to build the file, taken from the makefile if you use a makefile (You should.)

The challenge with an initial comment block lies in updating it to reflect the current state of your project. None of your tools are going to do that automatically. It's up to you.

The .data Section

Ordinary user-space programs written in NASM for Linux are divided into three sections. The order in which these sections fall in your program really isn't important, but by convention the .data section comes first, followed by the .bss section, and then the .text section.

The .data section contains data definitions of initialized data items. Initialized data is data that has a value before the program begins running. These values are part of the executable file. They are loaded into memory when the executable file is loaded into memory for execution. You don't have to load them with their values, and no machine cycles are used in their creation beyond what it takes to load the program as a whole into memory.

The important thing to remember about the .data section is that the more initialized data items you define, the larger the executable file will be, and the longer it will take to load it from disk into memory when you run it.

You'll examine in detail how initialized data items are defined shortly.

The .bss Section

Not all data items need to have values before the program begins running. When you're reading data from a disk file, for example, you need to have a place for the data to go after it comes in from disk. Data buffers like that are defined in the .bss section of your program. You set aside some number of bytes for a buffer and give the buffer a name, but you don't say what values are to be present in the buffer.

There's a crucial difference between data items defined in the .data section and data items defined in the .bss section: data items in the .data section add to the size of your executable file. Data items in the .bss section do not. A buffer that takes up 16,000 bytes (or more, sometimes *much* more) can be defined in .bss and add almost nothing (about 50 bytes for the description) to the executable file size.

This is possible because of the way the Linux loader brings the program into memory. When you build your executable file, the Linux linker adds information to the file describing all the symbols you've defined, including symbols naming data items. The loader knows which data items do not have initial values, and it allocates space in memory for them when it brings the executable in from disk. Data items with initial values are read in with their values.

The very simple program eatsyscall.asm does not need any buffers or other uninitialized data items, and technically does not require that a .bss section be defined. I added one simply to show you how one is defined. Having an empty .bss section does not increase the size of your executable file, and deleting an empty .bss section does not make your executable file any smaller.

The .text Section

The actual machine instructions that make up your program go into the .text section. Ordinarily, no data items are defined in .text. The .text section contains symbols called *labels* that identify locations in the program code for jumps and calls, but beyond your instruction mnemonics, that's about it.

All global labels must be declared in the .text section, or the labels cannot be "seen" outside your program by the Linux linker or the Linux loader. Let's look at the labels issue a little more closely.

Labels

A label is a sort of bookmark, describing a place in the program code and giving it a name that's easier to remember than a naked memory address. Labels are used to indicate the places where jump instructions should jump to, and they give names to callable assembly language procedures. I'll explain how that's all done in later chapters.

Here are the most important things to know about labels:

- *Labels must begin with a letter, or else with an underscore, period, or question mark.* These last three have special meanings to the assembler, so don't use them until you know how NASM interprets them.

- *Labels must be followed by a colon when they are defined.* This is basically what tells NASM that the identifier being defined is a label. NASM will punt if no colon is there and will not flag an error, but the colon nails it, and prevents a mistyped instruction mnemonic from being mistaken for a label. Use the colon!

- *Labels are case sensitive.* So `yikes:`, `Yikes:`, and `YIKES:` are three completely different labels. This differs from practice in a lot of other languages (Pascal particularly), so keep it in mind.

Later, you'll see such labels used as the targets of jump and call instructions. For example, the following machine instruction transfers the flow of instruction execution to the location marked by the label `GoHome`:

```
jmp GoHome
```

Notice that the colon is *not* used here. The colon is only placed where the label is *defined*, not where it is *referenced*. Think of it this way: use the colon when you are *marking* a location, not when you are *going* there.

There is only one label in eatsyscall.asm, and it's a little bit special. The _start label indicates where the program begins. Every Linux assembly language program has to be marked this way, and with the precise label _start. (It's case sensitive, so don't try using _START or _Start.) Furthermore, this label must be marked as global at the top of the .text section, as shown.

This is a requirement of the Linux operating system. Every executable program for Linux has to have a label _start in it somewhere, irrespective of the language it's written in: C, Pascal, assembly, no matter. If the Linux loader can't find the label, it can't load the program correctly. The global specifier tells the linker to make the _start label visible from outside the program's borders.

Variables for Initialized Data

The identifier EatMsg in the .data section defines a *variable*. Specifically, EatMsg is a string variable (more on which follows), but as with all variables, it's one of a class of items called *initialized data:* something that comes with a value, and not just a box into which we can place a value at some future time. A variable is defined by associating an identifier with a *data definition directive*. Data definition directives look like this:

```
MyByte      db 07h          ; 8 bits in size
MyWord      dw 0FFFFh       ; 16 bits in size
MyDouble    dd 0B8000000h   ; 32 bits in size
```

Think of the DB directive as "Define Byte." DB sets aside one byte of memory for data storage. Think of the DW directive as "Define Word." DW sets aside one word (16 bits, or 2 bytes) of memory for data storage. Think of the DD directive as "Define Double." DD sets aside a double word in memory for storage, typically for full 32-bit memory addresses.

String Variables

String variables are an interesting special case. A *string* is just that: a sequence, or string, of characters, all in a row in memory. One string variable is defined in eatsyscall.asm:

```
EatMsg: db "Eat at Joe's!",10
```

Strings are a slight exception to the rule that a data definition directive sets aside a particular quantity of memory. The DB directive ordinarily sets aside one byte only, but a string may be any length you like. Because there is no data directive that sets aside 17 bytes, or 42, strings are defined simply by associating a label with the place where the string *starts*. The EatMsg label and its DB directive specify one byte in memory as the string's starting point. The number of characters in the string is what tells the assembler how many bytes of storage to set aside for that string.

Either single quote (') or double quote (") characters may be used to delineate a string, and the choice is up to you *unless* you're defining a string value that itself contains one or more quote characters. Notice in eatsyscall.asm that the string variable EatMsg contains a single-quote character used as an apostrophe. Because the string contains a single-quote character, you *must* delineate it with double quotes. The reverse is also true: if you define a string that contains one or more double-quote characters, you must delineate it with single-quote characters:

```
Yukkh: db 'He said, "How disgusting!" and threw up.',10
```

You may combine several separate substrings into a single string variable by separating the substrings with commas. This is a perfectly legal (and sometimes useful) way to define a string variable:

```
TwoLineMsg: db "Eat at Joe's...",10,"...Ten million flies can't ALL be
wrong!",10
```

What's with the numeric literal 10 tucked into the previous example strings? In Linux text work, the end-of-line (EOL) character has the numeric value of 10. It indicates to the operating system where a line submitted for display to the Linux console ends. Any subsequent text displayed to the console will be shown on the next line down, at the left margin. In the variable TwoLineMsg, the EOL character in between the two substrings will direct Linux to display the first substring on one line of the console, and the second substring on the next line of the console below it:

```
Eat at Joe's!
Ten million flies can't ALL be wrong!
```

You can concatenate such individual numbers within a string, but you must remember that, as with EOL, *they will not appear as numbers*. A string is a string of *characters*. A number appended to a string will be interpreted by most operating system routines as an ASCII character. The correspondence between numbers and ASCII characters is shown in Appendix B. To show numbers in a string, you must represent them as ASCII characters, either as character literals, like "7," or as the numeric equivalents to ASCII characters, like 37h.

In ordinary assembly work, nearly all string variables are defined using the DB directive, and may be considered strings of bytes. (An ASCII character is one byte in size.) You can define string variables using DW or DD, but they're handled a little differently than those defined using DB. Consider these variables:

```
WordString: dw 'CQ'
DoubleString: dd 'Stop'
```

The DW directive defines a word-length variable, and a word (16 bits) may hold two 8-bit characters. Similarly, the DD directive defines a double word (32-bit) variable, which may hold four 8-bit characters. The different handling comes in when you load these named strings into registers. Consider these two instructions:

```
mov ax,wordstring
mov edx,DoubleString
```

In the first MOV instruction, the characters "CQ" are placed into register AX, with the "C" in AL and the "Q" in AH. In the second MOV instruction, the four characters "Stop" are loaded into EDX in little-endian order, with the "S" in the lowest-order byte of EDX, the "t" in the second-lowest byte, and so on. This sort of thing is a lot less common (and less useful) than using DB to define character strings, and you won't find yourself doing it very often.

Because eatsyscall.asm does not incorporate any uninitialized data, I'll hold off discussing such definitions until we look at the next example program.

Deriving String Length with EQU and $

Beneath the definition of EatMsg in the eatsyscall.asm file is an interesting construct:

```
EatLen: equ $-EatMsg
```

This is an example of a larger class of things called *assembly-time calculations*. What we're doing here is calculating the length of the string variable EatMsg, and making that length value accessible through the label EatLen. At any point in your program, if you need to use the length of EatMsg, you can use the label EatLen.

A statement containing the directive EQU is called an *equate*. An equate is a way of associating a value with a label. Such a label is then treated very much like a named constant in Pascal. Any time the assembler encounters an equate during an assembly, it will swap in the equate's value for its name. For example:

```
FieldWidth equ 10
```

The preceding tells the assembler that the label `FieldWidth` stands for the numeric value 10. Once that equate is defined, the following two machine instructions are *exactly* the same:

```
mov eax,10
mov eax,FieldWidth
```

There are two advantages to this:

- An equate makes the instruction easier to understand by using a descriptive name for a value. We know what the value 10 is for here; it's the width of a field.
- An equate makes programs easier to change down the road. If the field width changes from 10 to 12 at some point, we need only change the source code file at one line, rather than everywhere we access the field width.

Don't underestimate the value of this second advantage. Once your programs become larger and more sophisticated, you may find yourself using a particular value dozens or hundreds of times within a single program. You can either make that value an equate and change one line to alter a value used 267 times, or you can go through your code and change all 267 uses of the value individually—except for the five or six that you miss, causing havoc when you next assemble and run your program.

Combining assembly language calculation with equates allows some wonderful things to be done very simply. As I'll explain shortly, to display a string in Linux, you need to pass both the address of the string and its length to the operating system. You can make the length of the string an equate this way:

```
EatMsg db "Eat at Joe's!",10
EatLen equ 14
```

This works, because the `EatMsg` string is in fact 14 characters long, including the EOL character; but suppose Joe sells his diner to Ralph, and you swap in "Ralph" for "Joe." You have to change not only the ad message, but also its length:

```
EatMsg db "Eat at Ralph's!",10
EatLen equ 16
```

What are the chances that you're going to forget to update the `EatLen` equate with the new message length? Do that sort of thing often enough, and you *will*. With an assembly-time calculation, you simply change the definition of the string variable, and its length is automatically calculated by NASM at assembly time.

How? This way:

```
EatLen: equ $-EatMsg
```

It all depends on the magical "here" token, expressed by the humble dollar sign. As explained earlier, at assembly time NASM chews through your source code files and builds an intermediate file with a .o extension. The $ token marks the spot where NASM is in the intermediate file (*not* the source code file!). The label EatMsg marks the beginning of the advertising slogan string. Immediately after the last character of EatMsg is the label EatLen. Labels, remember, are not data, but *locations*—and, in the case of assembly language, addresses. When NASM reaches the label EatLen, the value of $ is the location immediately after the last character in EatMsg. The assembly-time calculation is to take the location represented by the $ token (which, when the calculation is done, contains the location just past the end of the EatMsg string) and subtract from it location of the beginning of the EatMsg string. End − Beginning = Length.

This calculation is performed every time you assemble the file, so anytime you change the contents of EatMsg, the value EatLen will be recalculated automatically. You can change the text within the string any way you like, and never have to worry about changing a length value anywhere in the program.

Assembly-time calculation has other uses, but this is the most common one, and the only one you're likely to use as a beginner.

Last In, First Out via the Stack

The little program eatsyscall.asm doesn't do much: it displays a short text string in the Linux console. Explaining how it does that one simple thing, however, will take a little doing, and before I can even begin, I have to explain one of the key concepts of not only the x86 architecture but in fact all computing: the *stack*.

The stack is a storage mechanism built right into the x86 hardware. Intel didn't invent it; the stack has been an integral part of computer hardware since the 1950s. The name is appropriate, and for a usable metaphor I can go back to my high school days, when I was a dishwasher for Resurrection Hospital on Chicago's northwest side.

Five Hundred Plates per Hour

There were many different jobs in the hospital dish room back then, but what I did most of the time was pull clean plates off a moving conveyor belt that emerged endlessly from the steaming dragon's mouth of a 180° dishwashing machine. This was hot work, but it was a lot less slimy than stuffing the dirty plates into the other end of the machine.

When you pull 500 plates per hour out of a dishwashing machine, you had better have some place efficient to stash them. Obviously, you could simply stack them on a table, but stacked ceramic plates in any place habituated by rowdy teenage boys is asking for tableware mayhem. What the hospital had instead was an army of little wheeled stainless-steel cabinets equipped with one or more spring-loaded circular plungers accessed from the top. When you had a handful of plates, you pushed them down into the plunger. The plunger's spring was adjusted such that the weight of the added plates pushed the whole stack of plates down just enough to make the new top plate flush with the top of the cabinet.

Each plunger held about 50 plates. We rolled one up next to the dragon's mouth, filled it with plates, and then rolled it back into the kitchen where the clean plates were used at the next meal shift to set patients' trays.

It's instructive to follow the path of the first plate out of the dishwashing machine on a given shift. That plate got into the plunger first and was subsequently shoved down into the bottom of the plunger by the remaining 49 plates that the cabinet could hold. After the cabinet was rolled into the kitchen, the kitchen staff pulled plates out of the cabinet one by one as they set trays. The *first* plate out of the cabinet was the *last* plate in. The *last* plate out of the cabinet had been the *first* plate to go in.

The x86 stack (and most other stacks in other computer architectures) is like that. It's called a last in, first out, or *LIFO*, stack. Instead of plates, we push chunks of data onto the top of the stack, and they remain on the stack until we pull them off in reverse order.

The stack doesn't exist in some separate alcove of the CPU. It exists in ordinary memory, and in fact what we call "the stack" is really a way of managing data in memory. The stack is a place where we can tuck away one or two (or however many) 32-bit double words for the time being, and come back to them a little later. Its primary virtue is that it does not require that we give the stored data a name. We put that data on the stack, and we retrieve it later not by its memory address but by its position.

The jargon involving use of the stack reflects my dishwasher's metaphor: When we place something on the stack, we say that we *push* it; when we retrieve something from the stack, we say that we *pop* it. The stack grows or shrinks as data is pushed onto it or popped off of it. The most recently pushed item on the stack is said to be at the "top of the stack." When we pop an item from the stack, what we get is the item at the top of the stack. I've drawn this out conceptually in Figure 8-1.

In the x86 architecture, the top of the stack is marked by a register called the *stack pointer*, with the formal name ESP. It's a 32-bit register, and it holds the memory address of the last item pushed onto the stack.

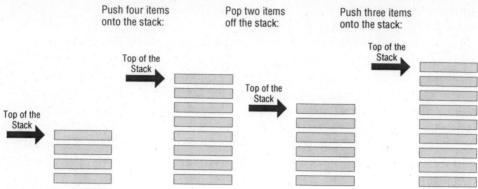

Figure 8-1: The stack

Stacking Things Upside Down

Making things a little trickier to visualize is the fact that the x86 stack is basically upside-down. If you picture a region of memory with the lowest address at the bottom and the highest address at the top, the stack begins up at the ceiling, and as items are pushed onto the stack, the stack grows downward, toward low memory.

Figure 8-2 shows in broad terms how Linux organizes the memory that it gives to your program when it runs. At the bottom of memory are the three sections that you define in your program: .text at the lowest addresses, followed by .data, followed by .bss. The stack is located all the way at the opposite end of your program's memory block. In between the end of the .bss section and the top of the stack is basically empty memory.

C programs routinely use this free memory space to allocate variables "on the fly" in a region called the *heap*. Assembly programs can do that as well, though it's not as easy as it sounds and I can't cover it in this book. The important thing to remember is that the stack and your program proper (code and named data) play in opposite corners of the sandbox. The stack grows toward the rest of your program, but unless you're doing *really* extraordinary—or stupid—things, there's little or no chance that the stack will grow so large as to collide with your program's named data items or machine instructions. If that happens, Linux will calmly issue a segmentation fault and your program will terminate.

The only caution I should offer regarding Figure 8-2 is that the relative sizes of the program sections versus the stack shouldn't be seen as literal. You may have thousands of bytes of program code and tens of thousands of bytes of data in a middling assembly program, but for that the stack is still quite small: a few hundred bytes at most, and generally less than that.

Note that when your program begins running, the stack is not completely empty. Some useful things are there waiting for you, as I'll explain a little later.

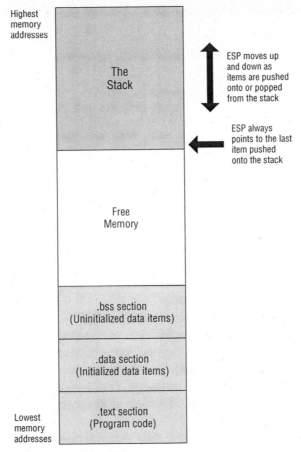

Figure 8-2: The stack in program memory

Push-y Instructions

You can place data onto the stack in several ways, but the most straightforward way involves a group of five related machine instructions: PUSH, PUSHF, PUSHFD, PUSHA, and PUSHAD. All work similarly, and differ mostly in what they push onto the stack:

- PUSH pushes a 16-bit or 32-bit register or memory value that is specified by you in your source code.
- PUSHF pushes the 16-bit Flags register onto the stack.
- PUSHFD pushes the full 32-bit EFlags register onto the stack.
- PUSHA pushes all eight of the 16-bit general-purpose registers onto the stack.

- PUSHAD pushes all eight of the 32-bit general-purpose registers onto the stack.

Here are some examples of the PUSH family of instructions in use:

```
pushf        ; Push the Flags register
pusha        ; Push AX, CX, DX, BX, SP, BP, SI, and DI, in that order, all at
             ; once
pushad       ; Push EAX, ECX, EDX, EBX, ESP, ESP, EBP, ESI, and EDI, all at
             ; once
push ax      ; Push the AX register
push eax     ; Push the EAX register
push [bx]    ; Push the word stored in memory at BX
push [edx]   ; Push the doubleword in memory at EDX
push edi     ; Push the EDI register
```

Note that PUSHF and PUSHFD take no operands. You'll generate an assembler error if you try to hand them operands; the two instructions push the flags and that's all they're capable of doing.

PUSH works as follows for 32-bit operands: First ESP is decremented by 32 bits (4 bytes) so that it points to an empty area of the stack segment that is four bytes long. Then whatever is to be pushed onto the stack is written to memory at the address in ESP. Voila! The data is safe on the stack, and ESP has crawled two bytes closer to the bottom of memory. PUSH can also push 16-bit values onto the stack; and when it does, the only difference is that ESP moves by 2 bytes instead of 4.

PUSHF works the same way, except that what it writes is the 16-bit Flags register.

PUSHA also works the same way, except that it pushes all eight 16-bit general-purpose registers at once, thus using 16 bytes of stack space at one swoop. PUSHA was added to the instruction set with the 286, and is not present in the 8086/8088 CPUs.

PUSHFD and PUSHAD were added to the x86 instruction set with the 386 CPU. They work the same way that their 16-bit alternates do, except that they push 32-bit registers rather than 16-bit registers. PUSHFD pushes the 32-bit EFlags register onto the stack. PUSHAD pushes all eight 32-bit general-purpose registers onto the stack in one blow.

Because Linux requires at least a 386 to function, you can assume that any Linux installation supports PUSHA, PUSHFD, and PUSHAD.

All memory between SP's initial position and its current position (the top of the stack) contains real data that was explicitly pushed on the stack and will presumably be popped from the stack later. Some of that data was pushed onto the stack by the operating system before running your program, and we'll talk about that a little later in the book.

What can and cannot be pushed onto the stack is complicated and depends on what CPU you're using. Any of the 16-bit and 32-bit general-purpose registers may be pushed individually onto the stack. None of the x86 CPUs can push 8-bit registers onto the stack. In other words, you can't push AL or BH or any other of the 8-bit registers. Immediate data can be pushed onto the stack, but only if you have a 286 or later CPU. (This will always be true under Linux.) User-mode Linux programs cannot push the segment registers onto the stack under any circumstances.

Keeping track of all this used to be a problem in the DOS era, but you're very unlikely to be running code on CPUs earlier than the 386 these days, and never under Linux.

POP Goes the Opcode

In general, what is pushed must be popped, or you can end up in any of several different kinds of trouble. Getting an item of data *off* the stack is done with another quintet of instructions: POP, POPF, POPFD, POPA, and POPAD. As you might expect, POP is the general-purpose one-at-a-time popper, while POPF and POPFD are dedicated to popping the flags off of the stack. POPA pops 16 bytes off the stack into the eight general-purpose 16-bit registers. POPAD is the flip side of PUSHAD and pops the top 32 bytes off the stack into the eight general-purpose 32-bit registers. Here are some examples:

```
popf       ; Pop the top 2 bytes from the stack into Flags
popa       ; Pop the top 16 bytes from the stack into AX, CX, DX, BX,
           ; BP, SI, and DI...but NOT SP!
popad      ; Pop the top 32 bytes from the stack into EAX, ECX, EDX, EBX,
           ; EBP, ESI and EDI...but NOT ESP!!!
pop cx     ; Pop the top 2 bytes from the stack into CX
pop esi    ; Pop the top 4 bytes from the stack into ESI
pop [ebx]  ; Pop the top 4 bytes from the stack into memory at EBX
```

As with PUSH, POP only operates on 16-bit or 32-bit operands. Don't try to pop data from the stack into an 8-bit register such as AH or CL.

POP works pretty much the way PUSH does, but in reverse. As with PUSH, how much comes off the stack depends on the size of the operand. Popping the stack into a 16-bit register takes the top two bytes off the stack. Popping the stack into a 32-bit register takes the top four bytes off the stack. Note well that nothing in the CPU or in Linux remembers the size of the data items that you place on the stack. *It's up to you to know the size of the last item pushed onto the stack.* If the last item you pushed was a 16-bit register, popping the stack into a 32-bit register will take two more bytes off the stack than you pushed. There may be (rare) circumstances when you may want to do this, but you certainly don't want to do it by accident!

When a POP instruction is executed, things work in this order: first, the data at the address currently stored in ESP (whether 16 bits or 32 bits' worth, depending on the operand) is copied from the stack and placed in POP's operand, whatever you specified that to be. After that, ESP is incremented (rather than decremented) by the size of the operand, so that in effect ESP moves either two or four bytes up the stack, away from low memory.

It's significant that ESP is decremented *before* placing a word on the stack at push time, but incremented *after* removing a word from the stack at pop time. Certain other CPUs outside the x86 universe work in the opposite manner, which is fine—just don't get them confused. For x86, the following is always true: *Unless the stack is completely empty, SP points to real data, not empty space.*

Ordinarily, you don't have to remember that fact, as PUSH and POP handle it all for you and you don't have to manually keep track of what ESP is pointing to. If you decide to manipulate the stack pointer directly, it helps to know the sequence of events behind PUSH and POP—an advanced topic not covered in this book.

One important note about POPA and POPAD: The value stored in the stack pointer is *not* affected! In other words, PUSHA and PUSHAD will push the current stack pointer value onto the stack. However, POPA and POPAD discard the stack pointer value that they find on the stack and do not change the value in SP/ESP. That makes sense: changing the stack pointer value while the CPU is busily working on the stack would invite chaos.

Figure 8-3 shows the stack's operation in a little more detail. The values of the four 16-bit "X" general-purpose registers at some hypothetical point in a program's execution are shown at the top of the figure. AX is pushed first on the stack. Its least significant byte is at ESP, and its most significant byte is at ESP+1. (Remember that both bytes are pushed onto the stack at once, as a unit!)

Each time one of the 16-bit registers is pushed onto the stack, ESP is decremented two bytes down toward low memory. The first three columns show AX, BX, and CX being pushed onto the stack, respectively; but note what happens in the fourth column, when the instruction POP DX is executed. The stack pointer is incremented by two bytes and moves away from low memory. DX now contains a copy of the contents of CX. In effect, CX was pushed onto the stack, and then immediately popped off into DX.

That's a mighty roundabout way to copy the value of CX into DX. MOV DX,CX is a lot faster and more straightforward. However, moving register values via the stack is sometimes necessary. Remember that the MOV instruction will *not* operate on the Flags or EFlags registers. If you want to load a copy of Flags or EFlags into a register, you must first push Flags or EFlags onto the stack with PUSHF or PUSHFD, and then pop the flags' values off the stack into the register of your choice with POP. Getting Flags into BX is thus done like this:

```
PUSHF  ; Push the Flags register onto the stack..
POP DX ; ..and pop it immediately into BX
```

Not all bits of EFlags may be changed with POPFD. Bits VM and RF are not affected by popping a value off the stack into EFlags.

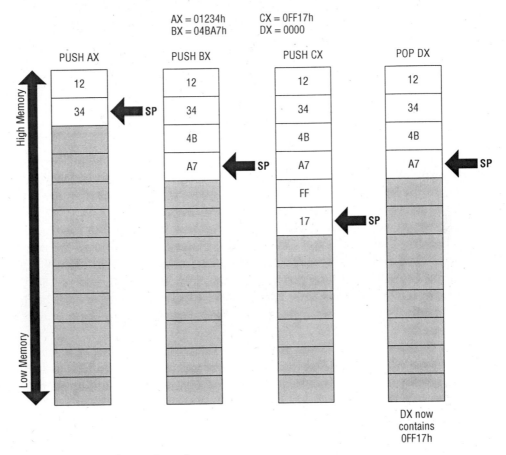

Figure 8-3: How the stack works

Storage for the Short Term

The stack should be considered a place to stash things for the short term. Items stored on the stack have no names, and in general must be taken off the stack in the reverse order in which they were put on. Last in, first out, remember. LIFO!

One excellent use of the stack allows the all-too-few registers to do multiple duty. If you need a register to temporarily hold some value to be operated on by the CPU and all the registers are in use, push one of the busy registers onto the stack. Its value will remain safe on the stack while you use the register for other things. When you're finished using the register, pop its old value off the stack—and you've gained the advantages of an additional register without really having one. (The cost, of course, is the time you spend moving that register's value onto and off of the stack. It's not something you want to do in the middle of a frequently repeated loop!)

Short-term storage during your program's execution is the simplest and most obvious use of the stack, but its most important use is probably calling procedures and Linux kernel services. And now that you understand the stack, you can take on the mysterious INT instruction.

Using Linux Kernel Services Through INT80

Everything else in eatsyscall.asm is leading to the single instruction that performs the program's only real work: displaying a line of text in the Linux console. At the heart of the program is a call into the Linux operating system, performed using the INT instruction, with a parameter of 80h.

As explained in Chapter 6, an operating system is something like a god and something like a troll, and Linux is no different. It controls all the most important elements of the machine in godlike fashion: the disk drives, the printer, the keyboard, various ports (Ethernet, USB, Bluetooth, and so forth), and the display. At the same time, Linux is like a troll living under a bridge to all those parts of your machine: you tell the troll what you want done, and the troll will go do it for you.

One of the services that Linux provides is simple (far too simple, actually) access to your PC's display. For the purposes of eatsyscall.asm (which is just a lesson in getting your first assembly language program written and operating), simple services are enough.

So—how do we use Linux's services? We have to request those services through the Linux kernel. The way there is as easy to use as it is tricky to understand: through software interrupts.

An Interrupt That Doesn't Interrupt Anything

As one new to the x86 family of processors back in 1981, the notion of a *software interrupt* drove me nuts. I kept looking and looking for the interrupter and interruptee. Nothing was being interrupted.

The name is unfortunate, though I admit that there is some reason for calling software interrupts as such. They are in fact courteous interrupts—if you can still call an interrupt an interrupt when it is so courteous that it does no interrupting at all.

The nature of software interrupts and Linux services is best explained by a real example illustrated twice in eatsyscall.asm. As I hinted previously, Linux keeps library routines—sequences of machine instructions focused on a single task—tucked away within itself. Each sequence does something useful—read something from a file, send something to a file, fetch the current time, access the network port, and so on. Linux uses these to do its own work, and it also makes them available (with its troll hat on) to you, the programmer, to access from your own programs.

Well, here is the critical question: how do you find something tucked away inside of Linux? All sequences of machine instructions, of course, have addresses, so why not just publish a list of the addresses of all these useful routines?

There are two problems here: first, allowing user space programs intimate access to operating system internals is dangerous. Malware authors could modify key components of the OS to spy on user activities, capture keystrokes and forward them elsewhere, and so on. Second, the address of any given sequence of instructions changes from one installation to another—nay, from one day to another, as software is installed and configured and removed from the PC. Linux is evolving and being improved and repaired on an ongoing basis. Ubuntu Linux releases two major updates every year in the spring and in the fall, and minor automatic updates are brought down to your PC regularly through the Update Manager. Repairing and improving code involves adding, changing, and removing machine instructions, which changes the size of those hidden code sequences—and, as a consequence, their location.

The solution is ingenious. There is a way to call service routines inside Linux that doesn't depend on knowing the addresses of anything. Most people refer to it as the *kernel services call gate*, and it represents a heavily guarded gateway between user space, where your programs run, and kernel space, where god/troll Linux does its work. The call gate is implemented via an x86 software interrupt.

At the very start of x86 memory, down at segment 0, offset 0, is a special lookup table with 256 entries. Each entry is a complete memory address including segment and offset portions, for a total of 4 bytes per entry. The first 1,024 bytes of memory in *any* x86 machine are reserved for this table, and no other code or data may be placed there.

Each of the addresses in the table is called an *interrupt vector*. The table as a whole is called the *interrupt vector table*. Each vector has a number, from 0 to 255. The vector occupying bytes 0 through 3 in the table is vector 0. The vector occupying bytes 4 through 7 is vector 1, and so on, as shown in Figure 8-4.

None of the addresses is burned into permanent memory the way the PC BIOS routines are. When your machine starts up, Linux and BIOS fill many of the slots in the interrupt vector table with addresses of certain service routines within themselves. Each version of Linux knows the location of its innermost parts, and when you upgrade to a new version of Linux, that new version will fill the appropriate slots in the interrupt vector table with upgraded and accurate addresses.

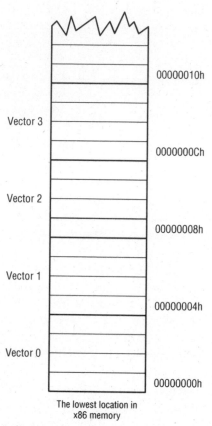

Figure 8-4: The interrupt vector table

What *doesn't* change from Linux version to Linux version is the *number* of the interrupt that holds a particular address. In other words, since the very first Linux release, interrupt number 80h has pointed the way into darkest Linux to the *services dispatcher*, a sort of multiple-railway switch with spurs heading out to the many (almost 200) individual Linux kernel service routines. The address of the dispatcher is different with most Linux distributions and versions, but regardless of which Linux distro or which version of a distro that you have, programs can access the dispatcher by way of slot 80h in the interrupt vector table.

Furthermore, programs don't have to go snooping the table for the address themselves. In fact, that's forbidden under the restrictions of protected mode. The table belongs to the operating system, and you can't even go down there and look at it. However, you don't have to access addresses in the table directly. The x86 CPUs include a machine instruction that has special powers to make use of the interrupt vector table. The INT (INTerrupt) instruction is used by eatsyscall.asm to request the services of Linux in displaying its ad slogan string on the screen. At two places, eatsyscall.asm has an INT 80h instruction. When an INT 80h instruction is executed, the CPU goes down to the interrupt vector table, fetches the address from slot 80h, and then jumps execution to that address. The transition from user space to kernel space is clean and completely controlled. On the other side of the address stored in table slot 80h, the dispatcher picks up execution and performs the service that your program requests.

The process is shown in Figure 8-5. When Linux loads at boot time, one of the many things it does to prepare the machine for use is put correct addresses in several of the vectors in the interrupt vector table. One of these addresses is the address of the kernel services dispatcher, which goes into slot 80h.

Later, when you type the name of your program eatsyscall on the Linux console command line, Linux loads the eatsyscall executable into user space memory and allows it to execute. To gain access to kernel services, eatsyscall executes INT 80h instructions as needed. Nothing in your program needs to know anything more about the Linux kernel services dispatcher than its number in the interrupt vector table. Given that single number, eatsyscall is content to remain ignorant and simply let the INT 80h instruction and interrupt vector 80h take it where it needs to go.

On the northwest side of Chicago, where I grew up, there was a bus that ran along Milwaukee Avenue. All Chicago bus routes have numbers, and the Milwaukee Avenue route is number 56. It started somewhere in the tangled streets just north of downtown, and ended up in a forest preserve just inside the city limits. The Forest Preserve District ran a swimming pool called Whelan Pool in that forest preserve. Kids all along Milwaukee Avenue could not necessarily have told you the address of Whelan Pool, but they could tell you in a second how to get there: Just hop on bus number 56 and take it to the end of the line. It's like that with software interrupts. Find the number of the vector that reliably points to your destination and ride that vector to the end of the line, without worrying about the winding route or the precise address of your destination.

Behind the scenes, the INT 80h instruction does something else: it pushes the address of the *next* instruction (that is, the instruction immediately following the INT 80h instruction) onto the stack, before it follows vector 80h into the Linux kernel. Like Hansel and Gretel, the INT 80h instruction was pushing some breadcrumbs to the stack as a way of helping the CPU find its way back to the eatsyscall program after the excursion down into Linux—but more on that later.

Now, the Linux kernel services dispatcher controls access to 200 individual service routines. How does it know which one to execute? You have to tell the dispatcher which service you need, which you do by placing the service's number in register EAX. The dispatcher may require other information as well, and will expect you to provide that information in the correct place—almost always in various registers—before it begins its job.

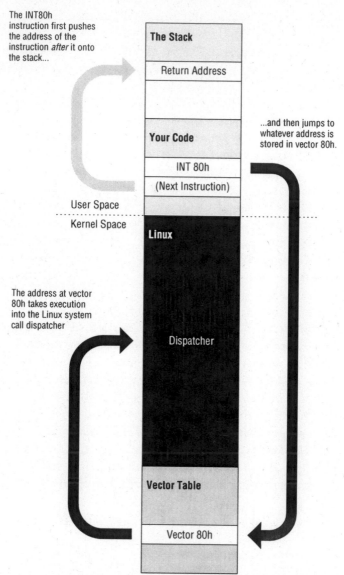

Figure 8-5: Riding an interrupt vector into Linux

Look at the following lines of code from eatsyscall.asm:

```
mov eax,4        ; Specify sys_write syscall
mov ebx,1        ; Specify File Descriptor 1: Standard Output
```

```
mov  ecx,EatMsg    ; Pass offset of the message
mov  edx,EatLen    ; Pass the length of the message
int  80H           ; Make syscall to output the text to stdout
```

This sequence of instructions requests that Linux display a text string on the console. The first line sets up a vital piece of information: the number of the service that we're requesting. In this case, it's to sys_write, service number 4, which writes data to a Linux file. Remember that in Linux, just about everything is a file, and that includes the console. The second line tells Linux *which* file to write to: standard output. Every file must have a numeric file descriptor, and the first three (0, 1, and 2) are standard and never change. The file descriptor for standard output is 1.

The third line places the address of the string to be displayed in ECX. That's how Linux knows what it is that you want to display. The dispatcher expects the address to be in ECX, but the address is simply where the string begins. Linux also needs to know the string's length, and we place that value in register EDX.

With the kernel service number, the address of the string, and the string's length tucked into their appropriate registers, we take a trip to the dispatcher by executing INT 80h. The INT instruction is all it takes. *Boom!*—execution crosses the bridge into kernel space, where Linux the troll reads the string at ECX and sends it to the console through mechanisms it keeps more or less to itself. Most of the time, that's a good thing: there can be too much information in descriptions of programming machinery, just as in descriptions of your personal life.

Getting Home Again

So much for getting into Linux. How does execution get back home again? The address in vector 80h took execution into the kernel services dispatcher, but how does Linux know where to go to pass execution back into eatsyscall? Half of the cleverness of software interrupts is knowing how to get there, and the other half—just as clever—is knowing how to get back.

To continue execution where it left off prior to the INT 80h instruction, Linux has to look in a completely reliable place for the return address, and that completely reliable place is none other than the top of the stack.

I mentioned earlier (without much emphasis) that the INT 80h instruction pushes an address to the top of the stack before it launches off into the unknown. This address is the address of the *next* instruction in line for execution: the instruction immediately following the INT 80h instruction. This location is completely reliable because, just as there is only one interrupt vector table in the machine, there is only one stack in operation at any one time. This means that there is only one top of the stack—that is, at the address pointed to by ESP—and Linux can always send execution back to the program that called it by popping the address off the top of the stack and jumping to that address.

The process is shown in Figure 8-6, which is the continuation of Figure 8-5. Just as the INT instruction pushes a return address onto the stack and then jumps to the address stored in a particular vector, there is a "combination" instruction that pops the return address off the stack and then jumps to the address. The instruction is IRET (for Interrupt RETurn), and it completes this complex but reliable system of jumping to an address when you don't know the address. The trick, once again, is knowing where the address can reliably be found, and in this case that's the stack.

There's actually a little more to what the software interrupt mechanism pushes onto and pops from the stack, but it happens transparently enough that I don't want to complicate the explanation at this point—and you're unlikely to be writing your own software interrupt routines for a while. That's programming in kernel territory, which I encourage you to pursue; but when you're just starting out, it's still a ways down the road.

Exiting a Program via INT 80h

There is a second INT 80h instruction in eatsyscall.asm, and it has a humble but crucial job: shutting down the program and returning control to Linux. This sounds simpler than it is, and once you understand Linux internals a little more, you'll begin to appreciate the work that must be done both to launch a process and to shut one down.

From your own program's standpoint, it's fairly simple: You place the number of the sys_exit service in EAX, place a return code in EBX, and then execute INT 80h:

```
mov eax,1        ; Specify Exit syscall
mov ebx,0        ; Return a code of zero
int 80H          ; Make the syscall to terminate the program
```

The return code is a numeric value that you can define however you want. Technically, there are no restrictions on what it is (aside from having to fit in a 32-bit register), but by convention a return value of 0 means "everything worked OK; shutting down normally." Return values other than 0 typically indicate an error of some sort. Keep in mind that in larger programs, you have to watch out for things that don't work as expected: a disk file cannot be found, a disk drive is full, and so on. If a program can't do its job and must terminate prematurely, it should have some way of telling you (or, in some cases, another program) what went wrong. The return code is a good way to do this.

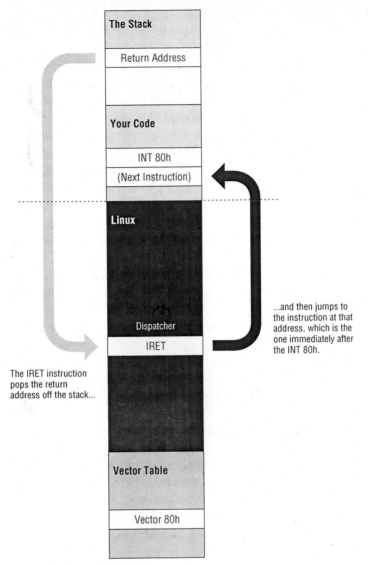

Figure 8-6: Returning home from an interrupt

Exiting this way is not just a nicety. *Every* program you write *must* exit by making a call to sys_exit through the kernel services dispatcher. If a program just "runs off the edge" it will in fact end, but Linux will hand up a segmentation fault and you'll be none the wiser as to what happened.

Software Interrupts versus Hardware Interrupts

You're probably still wondering why a mechanism like this is called an "interrupt," and it's a reasonable question with historical roots. Software interrupts evolved from an older mechanism that *did* involve some genuine interrupting: hardware interrupts. A *hardware interrupt* is your CPU's mechanism for paying attention to the world outside itself.

A fairly complex electrical system built into your PC enables circuit boards to send signals to the CPU. An actual metal pin on the CPU chip is moved from one voltage level to another by a circuit board device such as a disk drive controller or a serial port board. Through this pin, the CPU is tapped on the shoulder by the external device. The CPU recognizes this tap as a hardware interrupt. Like software interrupts, hardware interrupts are numbered, and for each interrupt number there is a slot reserved in the interrupt vector table. In this slot is the address of an interrupt service routine (ISR) that performs some action relevant to the device that tapped the CPU on the shoulder. For example, if the interrupt signal came from a serial port board, the CPU would then allow the serial port board to transfer a character byte from itself into the CPU.

The only real difference between hardware and software interrupts lies in the event that triggers the trip through the interrupt vector table. With a software interrupt, the triggering event is part of the software—that is, an INT instruction. With a hardware interrupt, the triggering event is an electrical signal applied to the CPU chip itself without any INT instruction taking a hand in the process. The CPU itself pushes the return address onto the stack when it recognizes the electrical pulse that triggers the interrupt; however, when the ISR is done, an IRET instruction sends execution home, just as it does for a software interrupt.

The mechanism explained here for returning "home" after a software interrupt call is in fact more universal than it sounds. Later in this book we'll begin dividing our own programs into procedures, which are accessed through a pair of instructions: CALL and RET. CALL pushes the address of the next instruction on the stack and then jumps into a procedure; a RET instruction at the end of the procedure pops the address off the top of the stack and allows execution to pick up just after the CALL instruction.

INT 80h and the Portability Fetish

Ten years ago, while I was preparing the two Linux-related chapters included in the second edition of this book, I watched a debate on the advisability of incorporating direct INT 80h access to Linux kernel calls in user space programs. A couple of people all but soiled themselves screaming that INT 80h calls are to be made *only* by the standard C library, and that assembly language calls for kernel services should always be made indirectly, by calling routines in the C library that then make the necessary INT 80h kernel calls.

The violence of the debate indicated that we were no longer discussing something on its technical merits, and had crossed over into fetish territory.

I bring it up here because people like this are still around, and if you hang out in Linux programming circles long enough you will eventually run into them. My advice is to avoid this debate if you can. There's no point in arguing it, and, mercifully, the explosion of new ways to write Linux programs since 2000 has mostly put the portability fetish into eclipse.

But it cooks down to this: The Unix world has long held the ideal that a program should be able to be recompiled *without changes* and run correctly on a different Unix version or even Unix running on an entirely different CPU architecture. This is only barely possible, and then only for relatively simple programs written in a single language (C), which make use of a "least common denominator" subset of what a computer system is able to provide. Get into elaborate GUI applications and modern peripherals, and you will be confronted with multiple incompatible software libraries with hugely complex Application Programming Interfaces (APIs), plus device driver quirks that aren't supposed to exist—but discourteously do.

Add to this the ongoing evolution of all these APIs and new, higher-level programming languages like Python, where code you wrote last year may not even compile on the *same* platform this year, and you're faced with a conclusion I came to many years ago: *Drop-in portability is a myth.* Our platforms are now so complex that *every* application is platform-specific. Cross-platform coding can be done, but source code has to change, and usually compromises have to be made by using *conditional compilation*—basically, a set of IF statements inside your programs that change the program source based on a set of parameters passed to the compiler: if you're compiling for Linux on x86, compile these statements; if you're compiling for BSD Unix under x86, compile these other statements, and so on. Conditional compilation is simply a mask over the cruel underlying reality: *Computers are different.* Computer systems evolve. It's not 1970 anymore.

Making calls to Linux kernel services as I've explained in this section is indeed specific to the Linux implementation of Unix. Other Unix implementations handle kernel calls in different ways. In the BSD family of Unix operating systems, the kernel services dispatcher is also called via INT 80h, but parameters are passed to the kernel on the stack, rather than in registers. We can argue on technical merits whether this is better or worse, but it's *different*, and your Linux assembly programs will *not* run under BSD Unix. If that's an issue for you, assembly language may not be the way to go. (For more or less "portable" coding I suggest learning Python, which is a wonderful and very high-level language, and present on nearly all Unix implementations.)

However, among Linux distributions and even across years' worth of Linux updates, the list of kernel services itself has changed only a little, and then primarily on the more arcane services added to the kernel in recent years. If assembly code written under one x86 distribution of Linux will not run identically under another x86 distribution, it's *not* because of the way you called kernel services.

Assembly language is not and cannot be portable. That's not what it's for. Don't let anybody try to persuade you otherwise.

Designing a Non-Trivial Program

At this point, you know just about everything you need to know to design and write small utilities that perform significant work—work that may even be useful. In this section we'll approach the challenge of writing a utility program from the engineering standpoint of solving a problem. This involves more than just writing code. It involves stating the problem, breaking it down into the problem's component parts, and then devising a solution to the problem as a series of steps and tests that may be implemented as an assembly language program.

There's a certain "chicken and egg" issue with this section: it's difficult to write a non-trivial assembly program without conditional jumps, and difficult to explain conditional jumps without demonstrating them in a non-trivial program. I've touched on jumps a little in previous chapters, and take them up in detail in Chapter 9. The jumps I'm using in the demo program in this section are pretty straightforward; if you're a little fuzzy on the details, read Chapter 9 and then return to this section to work through the examples.

Defining the Problem

Years ago, I was on a team that was writing a system that gathered and validated data from field offices around the world and sent that data to a large central computing facility, where it would be tabulated, analyzed, and used to generate status reports. This sounds easy enough, and in fact gathering the data itself from the field offices was not difficult. What made the project difficult was that it involved several separate and very different types of computers that saw data in entirely different and often incompatible ways. The problem was related to the issue of data encoding that I touched on briefly in Chapter 6. We had to deal with three different encoding systems for data characters. A character that was interpreted one way on one system would not be considered the same character on one of the other systems.

To move data from one system to one of the others, we had to create software that translated data encoding from one scheme to another. One of the schemes used a database manager that did not digest lowercase characters well, for reasons that seemed peculiar even then and are probably inconceivable today. We had to translate any lowercase characters into uppercase before we could feed data files into that system. There were other encoding issues as well, but that was an important one, and because it's a simple problem to describe and then solve, it's a good first exercise in genuine assembly language program design.

At the very highest level, the problem to be solved here can be stated this way: *Convert any lowercase characters in a data file to uppercase.*

With that in mind, it's a good idea to take notes on the problem. In particular, take notes on the limitations of any proposed solution. We used to call these notes the "bounds" of the solution, and they need to be kept in mind while thinking about the program that will solve the problem:

- We'll be working under Linux.
- The data exists in disk files.
- We do not know ahead of time how large any of the files will be.
- There is no maximum or minimum size for the files.
- We will use I/O redirection to pass filenames to the program.
- All the input files are in the same encoding scheme. The program can assume that an "a" character in one file is encoded the same way as an "a" in another file. (In our case, this is ASCII.)
- We must preserve the original file in its original form, rather than read data from the original file and then write it back to the original file. (That's because if the process crashes, we've destroyed the original file without completely generating an output file.)

In a real-world project there might be pages and pages of these notes, but just a few facts here will serve to shape our simple solution to the character-case problem. Note that these notes expand on what must be done, and to some extent put limits on the nature of the eventual solution, but do not attempt to say *how* it must be done. That's what we do in the next step.

Starting with Pseudo-code

Once you understand the nature of the problem as thoroughly as possible, you can begin crafting a solution. At the outset, this very much resembles the process described in Chapter 1, where someone makes a "to do" list of tasks for running the day's errands. You state a solution in a very broad form and in as few statements as possible. Then, little by little, you refine the stated solution by breaking down the larger steps into the smaller steps that the larger steps contain.

In our case, the solution is fairly easy to state in broad terms. To get started, here's one form that the statement might take:

```
Read a character from the input file.
Convert the character to uppercase (if necessary)
```

```
Write the character to the output file.
Repeat until done.
```

This really is a solution, if perhaps an extreme "view from a height." It's short on *details,* but not short on function. If we execute the steps listed, we'll have a program that does what we need it to do. Note well that the preceding statements are not statements written in any programming language. They're certainly not assembly language instructions. They're descriptions of several actions, independent of any particular system for accomplishing those actions. Lists of statements like this, because they are deliberately *not* written as code for a particular programming environment, are called *pseudo-code.*

Successive Refinement

From our first complete but detail-challenged statement of the solution, we move toward a more detailed statement of the solution. We do this by refining the pseudo-code statements so that each is more specific about how the action being described is to be done. We repeat this process, adding more details every time, until what we have can be readily translated into actual assembly language instructions. This process, called *successive refinement*, is not specific to assembly language. It's used with all programming languages to one degree or another, but it works especially well with assembly.

Let's stare at the pseudo-code given above and create a new version with additional details. We know we're going to be using Linux for the program—it's part of the spec, and one of the bounds of any solution—so we can begin adding details specific to the Linux way of doing such things. The next refinement might look like this:

```
Read a character from standard input (stdin)
Test the character to see if it's lowercase.
If the character is lowercase, convert it to uppercase by subtracting 20h.
Write the character to standard output (stdout).
Repeat until done.
Exit the program by calling sys_exit.
```

At each refinement pass, look long and hard at each action statement to see what details it may hide, and expand those details in the next refinement. Sometimes this will be easy; sometimes, well, not so easy. In the preceding version, the statement "Repeat until done" sounds pretty plain and obvious at first, until you think about what "done" means here: running out of data in the input file. How do we know when the input file is out of characters? This may require some research, but in most operating systems (including Linux) the routine that you call to read data from a file returns a value. This value can indicate a successful read, a read error, or special-case results like "end of file" (EOF). The precise details can be added later; what matters here is that we have to test for EOF when we read characters from the file. An expanded (and slightly rearranged) version of the solution pseudo-code might look like this:

```
Read a character from standard input (stdin)
Test if we have reached End Of File (EOF)
If we have reached EOF, we're done, so jump to exit
Test the character to see if it's lowercase.
If the character is lowercase, convert it to uppercase by subtracting 20h.
Write the character to standard output (stdout).
Go back and read another character.
Exit the program by calling sys_exit.
```

And so we go, adding detail each time. Notice that this is starting to look a little more like program code now. So be it: as the number of statements increases, it helps to add labels to those statements that represent jump targets, so that we don't get the jump targets mixed up, even in pseudo-code. It also helps to break the pseudo-code up into blocks, with related statements grouped together. Sooner or later we'll get to something like the following:

```
Read:   Set up registers for the sys_read kernel call.
        Call sys_read to read from stdin.
        Test for EOF.
        If we're at EOF, jump to Exit.

        Test the character to see if it's lowercase.
        If it's not a lowercase character, jump to Write.
        Convert the character to uppercase by subtracting 20h.

Write:  Set up registers for the Write kernel call.
        Call sys_write to write to stdout.
        Jump back to Read and get another character.

Exit:   Set up registers for terminating the program via sys_exit.
        Call sys_exit.
```

This is a good example of "bending" the pseudo-code statement in the direction of the operating system and programming language that you're going to use. All programming languages have their quirks, their limitations, and a general "shape," and if you keep this shape in mind while you craft your pseudo-code, making the final transition to real code will be easier.

At some point your pseudo-code will have all the details it can contain and still remain pseudo-code. To go further, you will have to begin turning your pseudo-code into real assembly code. This means you have to take each statement and ask yourself: Do I know how to convert this pseudo-code statement into one or more assembly language statements? It's especially true while you're a beginner, but even after you've earned your chops as an assembly language programmer, you may not know everything that there is to be known. In most programming languages (including assembly) there are often several or sometimes many different ways to implement a particular action. Some may be faster than others; some may be slower but easier to read and modify. Some solutions may be limited to a subset of the full line of x86 CPUs. Does your program need to run on creaky old 386 or 486 CPUs? Or can you assume that everyone will have at least a Pentium? (Your original sheets of notes should include such bounding conditions for any usable solution to the original problem.)

The jump from pseudo-code to instructions may seem like a big one, but the good news is that once you've converted your pseudo-code to instructions, you can make the text an assembly language source code file and turn NASM loose on it to spot your syntactic boo-boos. Expect to spend some time fixing assembly errors and then program bugs, but if you've gone through the refinement process with a clear head and reasonable patience, you may be surprised at how good a program you have on your first attempt.

A competent translation of the preceding pseudo-code to real assembly is shown in Listing 8-1. Read through it and see if you can follow the translation from the pseudo-code, knowing what you already know about assembly language. The code shown will work, but it is not "finished" in any real sense. It's a "first cut" for real code in the successive refinement process. It needs better comments, first of all—but more than anything else, it needs some hard thinking about how good and how complete a solution it is to the original problem. *A working program is not necessarily a finished program.*

Listing 8-1: uppercaser1.asm

```
section .bss
        Buff resb 1

section .data

section .text
        global _start

_start:
        nop                 ; This no-op keeps the debugger happy

Read:   mov eax,3           ; Specify sys_read call
        mov ebx,0           ; Specify File Descriptor 0: Standard Input
        mov ecx,Buff        ; Pass address of the buffer to read to
        mov edx,1           ; Tell sys_read to read one char from stdin
        int 80h             ; Call sys_read

        cmp eax,0           ; Look at sys_read's return value in EAX
```

Listing 8-1: uppercaser1.asm (*continued*)

```
        je Exit           ; Jump If Equal to 0 (0 means EOF) to Exit
                          ; or fall through to test for lowercase
        cmp byte [Buff],61h  ; Test input char against lowercase 'a'
        jb Write          ; If below 'a' in ASCII chart, not lowercase
        cmp byte [Buff],7Ah  ; Test input char against lowercase 'z'
        ja Write          ; If above 'z' in ASCII chart, not lowercase
                          ; At this point, we have a lowercase character
        sub byte [Buff],20h  ; Subtract 20h from lowercase to give uppercase...

                          ; ...and then write out the char to stdout
Write:  mov eax,4         ; Specify sys_write call
        mov ebx,1         ; Specify File Descriptor 1: Standard output
        mov ecx,Buff      ; Pass address of the character to write
        mov edx,1         ; Pass number of chars to write
        int 80h           ; Call sys_write...
        jmp Read          ; ...then go to the beginning to get another character

Exit:   mov eax,1         ; Code for Exit Syscall
        mov ebx,0         ; Return a code of zero to Linux
        int 80H           ; Make kernel call to exit program
```

This looks scary, but it consists almost entirely of instructions and concepts we've already discussed. A few notes on things you might not completely understand at this point:

- Buff is an uninitialized variable, and therefore located in the .bss section of the program. Buff has no initial value, and contains nothing until we read a character from stdin and store it there.

- When a call to sys_read returns a 0, sys_read has reached the end of the file it's reading from. If it returns a positive value, this value is the number of characters it has read from the file. In this case, since we only requested one character, sys_read returns either a count of 1, or a 0 indicting that we're out of characters.

- The CMP instruction compares its two operands and sets the flags accordingly. The conditional jump instruction that follows each CMP instruction takes action based on the state of the flags. (More on this in the next chapter.)

- The JB (Jump If Below) instruction jumps if the preceding CMP's left operand is lower in value than its right operand.

- The JA (Jump If Above) instruction jumps if the preceding CMP's left operand is higher in value than its right operand.

- Because a memory address (like Buff) simply points to a location in memory of no particular size, you must place the qualifier BYTE between

CMP and its memory operand to tell NASM that you want to compare two 8-bit values. In this case, the two 8-bit values are an ASCII character like "w" and a hex value like 7Ah.

Running the executable program is done by using I/O redirection. The command line for uppercaser1 looks like this:

```
./uppercaser1 > outputfile < inputfile
```

Both "inputfile" and "outputfile" can be any text file. Here's one thing to try:

```
./uppercaser1 > allupper.txt < uppercaser1.asm
```

The file allupper.txt will be created when you run the program, and it will be filled with the source code for the program, with all characters forced to uppercase.

Those Inevitable "Whoops!" Moments

Especially while you're a beginner, you may discover as you attempt this last step going from pseudo-code to machine instructions that you've misunderstood something or forgotten something, and that your pseudo-code isn't complete or correct. (Or both!) You may also realize that there are better ways to do something in assembly statements than what a literal translation of the pseudo-code might give you. Learning is a messy business, and no matter how good you think you are, you will always be learning.

A good example, and one that may actually have occurred to you in reading over the preceding assembly code, is this: *The program has no error detection*. It assumes that whatever input filename the user enters for I/O redirection is an existing and not corrupt file with data in it, that there will be room on the current drive for the output file, and so on. That's a dangerous way to operate, though heaven knows it's been done. File-related Linux system calls return error values, and any program that uses them should examine those error values and take action accordingly.

In short, there will be times when you have to seriously rearrange your pseudo-code partway through the process, or even scrap it entirely and begin again. These insights have an annoying habit of occurring when you're in that final stage of converting pseudo-code to machine instructions. Be ready.

There's another issue that may have occurred to you if you know anything at all about low-level file I/O: the Linux sys_read kernel call isn't limited to returning a single character at one go. You pass the address of a buffer to sys_read, and sys_read will attempt to fill that buffer with as many characters from the input file as you tell it to. If you set up a buffer 500 bytes in size, you can ask `sys_read` to bring in 500 characters from stdin and put them in that buffer. A single call to `sys_read` can thus give you 500 characters (or 1,000, or 16,000) to work on, all at once. This reduces the amount of time that Linux spends chasing back and forth between its file system and your program, but it also changes the shape of the program in significant ways. You fill the buffer, and then you have to step through the buffer one character at a time, converting whatever is there in lowercase to uppercase.

Yes, you should have known that upfront, while refining a pseudo-code solution to your problem—and after you've been at it for awhile, you will. There is a daunting number of such details that you need at your mental fingertips, and you won't commit them all to indelible memory in an afternoon. Now and then, such a revelation may force you to "back up" an iteration or two and recast some of your pseudo-code.

Scanning a Buffer

That's the case with the current example. The program needs error handling, which in this case mostly involves testing the return values from `sys_read` and `sys_write` and displaying meaningful messages on the Linux console. There's no technical difference between displaying error messages and displaying slogans for greasy-spoon diners, so you can add error handling yourself as an exercise.

The more interesting challenge, however, involves buffered file I/O. The Unix read and write kernel calls are buffer-oriented and not character-oriented, so we have to recast our pseudo-code to fill buffers with characters, and then process the buffers.

Let's go back to pseudo-code and give it a try:

```
Read:    Set up registers for the sys_read kernel call.
         Call sys_read to read a buffer full of characters from stdin.
         Test for EOF.
         If we're at EOF, jump to Exit.


         Set up registers as a pointer to scan the buffer.
Scan:    Test the character at buffer pointer to see if it's lowercase.
         If it's not a lowercase character, skip conversion.
         Convert the character to uppercase by subtracting 20h.
         Decrement buffer pointer.
       . If we still have characters in the buffer, jump to Scan.

Write:   Set up registers for the Write kernel call.
         Call sys_write to write the processed buffer to stdout.
         Jump back to Read and get another buffer full of characters.

Exit:    Set up registers for terminating the program via sys_exit.
         Call sys_exit.
```

This adds everything you need to read a buffer from disk, scan and convert the characters in the buffer, and then write the buffer back out to disk. (Of course, the buffer has to be enlarged from one character to some useful size, like 1024 characters.) The gist of the buffer trick is to set up a pointer into the buffer, and then examine and (if necessary) convert the character at the address expressed by the pointer. Then you move the pointer to the next character in the buffer and do the same thing, repeating the process until you've dealt with all the characters in the buffer.

Scanning a buffer is a very good example of an assembly language loop. At each pass through the loop we have to test something to determine whether we're finished and should exit the loop. The "something" in this case is the pointer. We can set the pointer to the beginning of the buffer and test to see when it reaches the end, or we could set the pointer to the end of the buffer and work our way forward, testing to see when we reach the beginning of the buffer.

Both approaches will work, but starting at the end and working our way forward toward the beginning of the buffer can be done a little more quickly and with fewer instructions. (I'll explain why shortly.) Our next refinement should start talking specifics: which registers do what, and so on:

```
Read:    Set up registers for the sys_read kernel call.
         Call sys_read to read a buffer full of characters from stdin.
         Store the number of characters read in esi
         Test for EOF (eax = 0).
         If we're at EOF, jump to Exit.

         Put the address of the buffer in ebp.
         Put the number of characters read into the buffer in ecx.
Scan:    Compare the byte at [ebp+ecx] against 'a'.
         If the byte is below 'a' in the ASCII sequence, jump to Next.
         Compare the byte at [ebp+ecx] against 'z'.
         If the byte is above 'z' in the ASCII sequence, jump to Next.
         Subtract 20h from the byte at [ebp+ecx].
Next:    Decrement ecx by one.
         Jump if not zero to Scan.

Write:   Set up registers for the Write kernel call.
         Call sys_write to write the processed buffer to stdout.
         Jump back to Read and get another buffer full of characters.

Exit:    Set up registers for terminating the program via sys_exit.
         Call sys_exit.
```

This refinement recognizes that there is not one test to be made, but two. Lowercase characters represent a range in the ASCII sequence, and ranges have beginnings and ends. We have to determine if the character under examination falls within the range. Doing that requires testing the character to see if it's either below the lowest character in the lowercase range ("a") or above the highest character in the lowercase range ("z"). If the character in question is not lowercase, no processing is required, and we jump to the code that bumps the pointer to the next character.

Navigating within the buffer involves two registers. The address of the beginning of the buffer is placed in EBP. The number of characters in the buffer is placed in the ECX register. If you add the two registers, you'll get the address of the last character in the buffer. If you decrement the character counter in ECX, the sum of EBP and ECX will point to the second-to-last character in the buffer. Each time you decrement ECX, you'll have the address to a character one closer to the start of the buffer. When ECX is decremented to zero, you'll be at the beginning of the buffer, and all the characters will have been processed.

"Off By One" Errors

But wait ... that's not entirely true. There's a bug in the pseudo-code, and it's one of the commonest beginner bugs in all assembly language: the legendary "off by one" error. The sum of EBP and ECX will point one address *past* the end of the buffer. And when the count in ECX goes to zero, one character—the one at the very beginning of the buffer—will remain unexamined and (if it's lowercase) untouched. The easiest way to explain where this bug comes from is to draw it out, as I've done in Figure 8-7.

There's a very short text file in the listings archive for this book called gazabo.txt. It contains only the single nonsense word "gazabo" and the EOL marker, for a total of seven characters. Figure 8-7 shows the gazabo.txt file as it would look after Linux loads it into a buffer in memory. The address of the buffer has been loaded into register EBP, and the number of characters (here, 7) into ECX. If you add EBP and ECX, the resulting address goes past the end of the buffer into unused (you hope!) memory.

This kind of problem can occur any time you begin mixing address offsets and counts of things. Counts begin at 1, and offsets begin at 0. Character #1 is actually at offset 0 from the beginning of the buffer, character #2 is at offset 1, and so on. We're trying to use a value in ECX as *both* a count and an offset, and if the offsets into the buffer are assumed to begin with 0, an off-by-one error is inevitable.

The solution is simple: decrement the address of the buffer (which is stored in EBP) by 1 before beginning the scan. EBP now points to the memory location immediately *before* the first character in the buffer. With EBP set up this way, we can use the count value in ECX as both a count *and* an offset. By the time the value in ECX is decremented to 0, we've processed the "g" character, and we exit the loop.

Before DEC EBP:

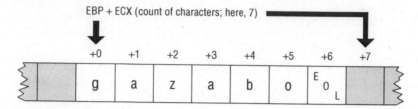

After DEC EBP:

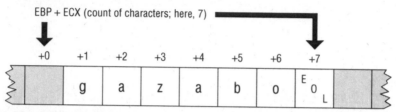

Figure 8-7: The "off by one" error

At this point I'm going to take that scary jump to actual machine instructions, but for the sake of brevity, will show only the loop itself:

```
; Set up the registers for the convert buffer step:
        mov ecx,esi          ; Place the number of bytes read into ecx
        mov ebp,Buff         ; Place address of the buffer into ebp
        dec ebp              ; Adjust address of buffer by 1

; Go through the buffer and convert lowercase to uppercase characters:
Scan:
        cmp byte [ebp+ecx],61h  ; Test input char against lowercase 'a'
        jb Next                 ; If below 'a' in ASCII, not lowercase
        cmp byte [ebp+ecx],7Ah  ; Test input char against lowercase 'z'
        ja Next                 ; If above 'z' in ASCII, not lowercase
                                ; At this point, we have a lowercase char
        sub byte [ebp+ecx],20h  ; Subtract 20h to give uppercase...
Next:   dec ecx
        jnz Scan
```

The state of the buffer and the pointer registers before beginning the scan is shown in the second part of Figure 8-7. The first time through, the value in ECX is the count of characters in the buffer. The sum EBP + ECX points at the EOL character at the buffer's end. The next time through, ECX is decremented to 6, and EBP + ECX points at the "o" in "gazabo." Each time we decrement ECX, we look at the Zero flag by using the JNZ instruction, which jumps back to the Scan label when the Zero flag is *not* set. On the last pass through the loop, ECX contains 1, and EBP + ECX points to the "g" in the very first location in the buffer. Only when ECX is decremented to zero does JNZ "fall through" and the loop end.

Purists may think that decrementing the address in EBP before the loop begins is a dicey hack. They're half-right: after being decremented, EBP points to a location in memory outside the bounds of the buffer. If the program tried to write to that location, another variable might be corrupted, or a segmentation fault might result. The logic of the loop doesn't require writing to that particular address, but it could easily be done by mistake.

The "proper" way to handle the off-by-one error is to leave EBP pointing at the true start of the buffer, and decrement ECX at the beginning of the loop, rather than the end. Testing ECX against 0 must still be done, but at the end of the loop, with a separate CMP instruction. This works fine, and the pointer always points to memory locations within Buff:

```
; Set up the registers for the convert buffer step:
        mov ecx,esi             ; Place the number of bytes read into ecx
        mov ebp,Buff            ; Place address of buffer into ebp

; Go through the buffer and convert lowercase to uppercase characters:
Scan:
        dec ecx                 ; Decrement the char counter
        cmp byte [ebp+ecx],61h  ; Test input char against lowercase 'a'
        jb Next                 ; If below 'a' in ASCII, not lowercase
        cmp byte [ebp+ecx],7Ah  ; Test input char against lowercase 'z'
        ja Next                 ; If above 'z' in ASCII, not lowercase
                                ; At this point, we have a lowercase char
        sub byte [ebp+ecx],20h  ; Subtract 20h to give uppercase...
Next:   cmp ecx,0               ; See if the char counter is at 0
        jnz Scan                ; If not, jump back and loop again
```

However, this comes at a cost: there is one more instruction inside the loop than there used to be. It doesn't matter much when you're only going to go through the loop a small number of times. But it's good practice to keep your loops as tight as possible, by not using any more instructions inside a loop than absolutely necessary. Even tiny slices of time add up, and if the loop will need to run thousands, tens of thousands, or millions of times, execution could slow down noticeably.

The completed program, with all pseudo-code converted to assembly code, is shown in Listing 8-2.

Listing 8-2: uppercaser2.asm

```
;   Executable name : uppercaser2
;   Version         : 1.0
;   Created date    : 3/25/2009
;   Last update     : 3/25/2009
```

(continued)

Listing 8-2: uppercaser2.asm (*continued*)

```
;  Author        : Jeff Duntemann
;  Description   : A simple program in assembly for Linux,using NASM 2.05,
;    demonstrating simple text file I/O (through redirection) for reading an
;    input file to a buffer in blocks, forcing lowercase characters to
;    uppercase, and writing the modified buffer to an output file.
;
;  Run it this way:
;    uppercaser2 > (output file) < (input file)
;
;  Build using these commands:
;    nasm -f elf -g -F stabs uppercaser2.asm
;    ld -o uppercaser2 uppercaser2.o
;
SECTION .bss                    ; Section containing uninitialized data

        BUFFLEN equ 1024        ; Length of buffer
        Buff:   resb BUFFLEN    ; Text buffer itself

SECTION .data                 ; Section containing initialised data

SECTION .text                 ; Section containing code

global  _start                ; Linker needs this to find the entry point!

_start:
        nop                   ; This no-op keeps gdb happy...

; Read a buffer full of text from stdin:
read:
        mov eax,3             ; Specify sys_read call
        mov ebx,0             ; Specify File Descriptor 0: Standard Input
        mov ecx,Buff          ; Pass offset of the buffer to read to
        mov edx,BUFFLEN       ; Pass number of bytes to read at one pass
        int 80h               ; Call sys_read to fill the buffer
        mov esi,eax           ; Copy sys_read return value for safekeeping
        cmp eax,0             ; If eax=0, sys_read reached EOF on stdin
        je Done               ; Jump If Equal (to 0, from compare)

; Set up the registers for the process buffer step:
        mov ecx,esi           ; Place the number of bytes read into ecx
        mov ebp,Buff          ; Place address of buffer into ebp
        dec ebp               ; Adjust count to offset

; Go through the buffer and convert lowercase to uppercase characters:
Scan:
```

Listing 8-2: uppercaser2.asm (*continued*)

```
        cmp byte [ebp+ecx],61h  ; Test input char against lowercase 'a'
        jb Next             ; If below 'a' in ASCII, not lowercase
        cmp byte [ebp+ecx],7Ah  ; Test input char against lowercase 'z'
        ja Next             ; If above 'z' in ASCII, not lowercase
                            ; At this point, we have a lowercase char
        sub byte [ebp+ecx],20h  ; Subtract 20h to give uppercase...
Next:   dec ecx             ; Decrement counter
        jnz Scan            ; If characters remain, loop back

; Write the buffer full of processed text to stdout:
Write:
        mov eax,4           ; Specify sys_write call
        mov ebx,1           ; Specify File Descriptor 1: Standard output
        mov ecx,Buff        ; Pass offset of the buffer
        mov edx,esi         ; Pass the # of bytes of data in the buffer
        int 80h             ; Make sys_write kernel call
        jmp read            ; Loop back and load another buffer full

; All done! Let's end this party:
Done:
        mov eax,1           ; Code for Exit Syscall
        mov ebx,0           ; Return a code of zero
        int 80H             ; Make sys_exit kernel call
```

Going Further

This general process will serve you well no matter what language you program in. Here are some notes as you proceed, on this project and all your future projects:

- Keep in mind that nothing says you have to convert everything from pseudo-code to machine instructions at one pass. Successive refinement is, well, *successive*. A perfectly reasonable statement for the problem could include a mixture of instructions and pseudo-code. Over time you'll evolve a technique that works for you, and as you become more confident as a programmer, you'll make fewer refinement passes, and better ones.

- Don't be afraid to draw pictures. Pencil sketches of pointers, buffers, and so on, scribbled on a quadrille pad, can be enormously helpful when trying to get a handle on a complicated loop or any process with a lot of moving parts.

▪ *Save your notes*, no matter how ugly. Memories of the programming process get stale. If you write a utility and use it for six months, you may need a refresher on how its innards operate before attempting to enhance it. Toss everything in a file folder, including paper printouts of pseudo-code written to disk files.

The program we developed in this chapter is a simple example of a Unix *text filter*. Filters are very common in Unix work, and I'll be returning to the concept in later chapters. In the meantime, go back and add error checking to the uppercaser program, on both read and write. You may have to locate a Linux system call reference, but that's good practice too. Research may be the single toughest part of programming, and that's not going to get any easier; trust me.

Bits, Flags, Branches, and Tables

Easing into Mainstream Assembly Coding

As you've seen by now, my general method for explaining things starts with the "view from a height" and then moves down toward the details. That's how I do things because that's how people learn: by plugging individual facts into a larger framework that makes it clear how those facts relate to one another. It's possible (barely) to move from details to the big picture, but across 56 years of beating my head against various subjects in the pursuit of knowledge, it's become very clear that having the overall framework in place first makes it *a lot* easier to establish all those connections between facts. It's like carefully placing stones into a neat pile before shoveling them into a box. If the goal is to get the stones into a box, it's much better to have the box in place before starting to pick up the stones.

And so it is here. The big picture is mostly in place. From now on in this book, we'll be looking at the details of assembly code, and seeing how they fit into that larger view.

Bits Is Bits (and Bytes Is Bits)

Assembly language is big on bits.

Bits, after all, are what bytes are made of, and one essential assembly language skill is building bytes and taking them apart again. A technique called *bit mapping* is widely used in assembly language. Bit mapping assigns special meanings to individual bits within a byte to save space and squeeze the last little bit of utility out of a given amount of memory.

There is a family of instructions in the x86 instruction set that enables you to manipulate the bits within the bytes by applying Boolean logical operations between bytes on a bit-by-bit basis. These are the *bitwise logical instructions*: AND, OR, XOR, and NOT. Another family of instructions enables you to slide bits back and forth within a single byte or word. These are the most frequently used shift/rotate instructions: ROL, ROR, RCL, RCR, SHL, and SHR. (There are a few others that I will not be discussing in this book.)

Bit Numbering

Dealing with bits requires that we have a way of specifying which bits we're dealing with. By convention, bits in assembly language are numbered, starting from 0, at the *least-significant bit* in the byte, word, or other item we're using as a bitmap. The least-significant bit is the one with the least value in the binary number system. It's also the bit on the far right if you write the value down as a binary number in the conventional manner.

I've shown this in Figure 9-1, for a 16-bit word. Bit numbering works exactly the same way no matter how many bits you're dealing with: bytes, words, double words, or more. Bit 0 is always on the right-hand end, and the bit numbers increase toward the left

Most significant bit   Least significant bit

Figure 9-1: Bit numbering

When you count bits, start with the bit on the right, and number them from 0.

"It's the Logical Thing to Do, Jim. . ."

Boolean logic sounds arcane and forbidding, but remarkably, it reflects the realities of ordinary thought and action. The Boolean operator AND, for instance, pops up in many of the decisions you make every day of your life. For example, to write a check that doesn't bounce, you must have money in your checking account AND checks in your checkbook. Neither alone will do the job. You can't write a check that you don't have, and a check without money behind it will bounce. People who live out of their checkbooks (and they always seem to end up ahead of me in the checkout line at Safeway) must use the AND operator frequently.

When mathematicians speak of Boolean logic, they manipulate abstract values called True and False. The AND operator works like this. Condition1

AND Condition2 will be considered True if *both* Condition1 and Condition2 are True. If either condition is False, the result will be False.

There are in fact four different combinations of the two input values, so logical operations between two values are usually summarized in a form called a *truth table*. The truth table for the logical operator AND (not the AND instruction yet; we'll get to that shortly) is shown in Table 9-1.

Table 9-1: The AND Truth Table for Formal Logic

CONDITION1	OPERATOR	CONDITION2	RESULT
False	AND	False	False
False	AND	True	False
True	AND	False	False
True	AND	True	True

There's nothing mysterious about the truth table. It's just a summary of all possibilities of the AND operator as applied to two input conditions. The important thing to remember about AND is that *only* when both input values are True is the result also True.

That's the way mathematicians see AND. In assembly language terms, the AND instruction looks at two bits and yields a third bit based on the values of the first two bits. By convention, we consider a 1 bit to be True and a 0 bit to be False. The *logic* is identical; we're just using different symbols to represent True and False. Keeping that in mind, we can rewrite AND's truth table to make it more meaningful for assembly language work (see Table 9-2).

Table 9-2: The AND Truth Table for Assembly Language

BIT 1	OPERATOR	BIT 2	RESULT BIT
0	AND	0	0
0	AND	1	0
1	AND	0	0
1	AND	1	1

The AND Instruction

The AND instruction embodies this concept in the x86 instruction set. The AND instruction performs the AND logical operation on two like-size operands and replaces the destination operand with the result of the operation as a whole. (Remember that the destination operand, as always, is the operand closest to the mnemonic.) In other words, consider this instruction:

```
and al,bl
```

What will happen here is that the CPU will perform a gang of eight bitwise AND operations on the eight bits in AL and BL. Bit 0 of AL is ANDed with bit 0 of BL, bit 1 of AL is ANDed with bit 1 of BL, and so on. Each AND operation generates a result bit, and that bit is placed in the destination operand (here, AL) *after* all eight AND operations occur. This is a common thread among machine instructions that perform some operation on two operands and produce a result: The result replaces the first operand (the destination operand) and not the second!

Masking Out Bits

A major use of the AND instruction is to isolate one or more bits out of a byte value or a word value. *Isolate* here simply means to set all *unwanted* bits to a reliable 0 value. As an example, suppose we are interested in testing bits 4 and 5 of a value to see what those bits are. To do that, we have to be able to ignore the other bits (bits 0 through 3 and 6 through 7), and the only way to safely ignore bits is to set them to 0.

AND is the way to go. We set up a *bit mask* in which the bit numbers that we want to inspect and test are set to 1, and the bits we wish to ignore are set to 0. To mask out all bits but bits 4 and 5, we must set up a mask in which bits 4 and 5 are set to 1, with all other bits at 0. This mask in binary is 00110000B, or 30H. (To verify it, count the bits from the right-hand end of the binary number, starting with 0.) This bit mask is then ANDed against the value in question. Figure 9-2 shows this operation in action, with the 30H bit mask just described and an initial value of 9DH.

The three binary values involved are shown laid out vertically, with the least-significant bit (that is, the right-hand end) of each value at the top. You should be able to trace each AND operation and verify it by looking at Table 9-2.

The end result is that all bits except bits 4 and 5 are *guaranteed* to be 0 and can thus be safely ignored. Bits 4 and 5 could be either 0 or 1. (That's why we need to test them; we don't *know* what they are.) With the initial value of 9DH, bit 4 turns out to be a 1, and bit 5 turns out to be a 0. If the initial value were something else, bits 4 and 5 could both be 0, both be 1, or some combination of the two.

Don't forget: the result of the AND instruction replaces the destination operand after the operation is complete.

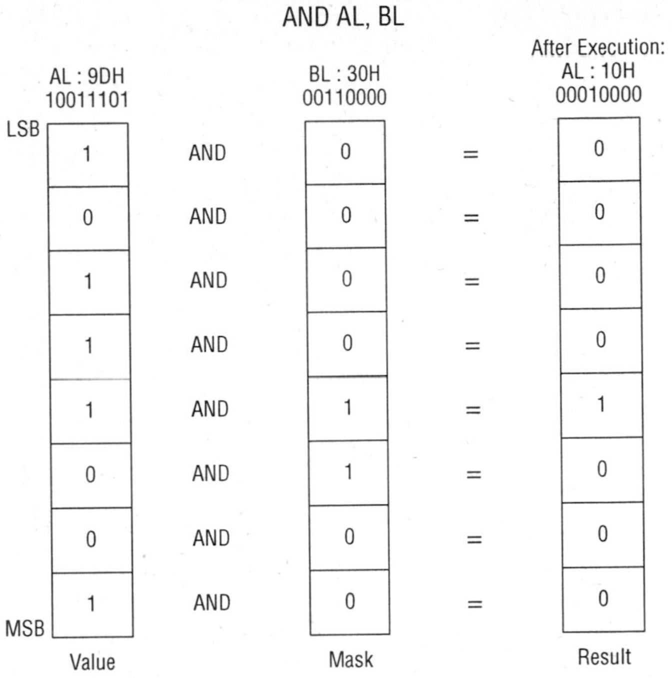

AND AL, BL

Figure 9-2: The anatomy of an AND instruction

The OR Instruction

Closely related to the AND logical operation is OR, which, like the AND logical operation, has an embodiment with the same name in the x86 instruction set. Structurally, the OR instruction works identically to AND. Only its truth table is different: While AND requires that both its operands be 1 for the result to be 1, OR is satisfied that at least *one* operand has a 1 value. The truth table for OR is shown in Table 9-3.

Table 9-3: The OR Truth Table for Assembly Language

BIT 1	OPERATOR	BIT 2	RESULT BIT
0	OR	0	0
0	OR	1	1
1	OR	0	1
1	OR	1	1

Because it's unsuitable for isolating bits, OR is used much more rarely than AND.

The XOR Instruction

In a class by itself is the exclusive OR operation, embodied in the XOR instruction. XOR, again, does in broad terms what AND and OR do: it performs a logical operation on its two operands, and the result replaces the destination operand. The logical operation, however, is *exclusive or*, meaning that the result is 1 only if the two operands are *different* (that is, 1 and 0 or 0 and 1). The truth table for XOR, shown in Table 9-4, should make this slightly slippery notion a little clearer.

Table 9-4: The XOR Truth Table for Assembly Language

BIT 1	OPERATOR	BIT 2	RESULT BIT
0	XOR	0	0
0	XOR	1	1
1	XOR	0	1
1	XOR	1	0

Look over Table 9-4 carefully! In the first and last cases, where the two operands are the *same*, the result is 0. In the middle two cases, where the two operands are *different*, the result is 1.

Some interesting things can be done with XOR, but most of them are a little arcane for a beginners' book. One non-obvious use of XOR is this: XORing any value against *itself* yields 0. In other words, if you execute the XOR instruction with both operands as the same register, that register will be cleared to 0:

```
xor eax,eax    ; Zero out the eax register
```

In the old days, this was faster than loading a 0 into a register from immediate data using MOV. Although that's no longer the case, it's an interesting trick to know. How it works should be obvious from reading the truth table, but to drive it home I've laid it out in Figure 9-3.

Follow each of the individual XOR operations across the figure to its result value. Because each bit in AL is XORed against itself, in every case the XOR operations happen between two operands that are identical. Sometimes both are 1, sometimes both are 0, but in every case the two are the same. With the XOR operation, when the two operands are the same, the result is always 0. Voila! Zero in a register.

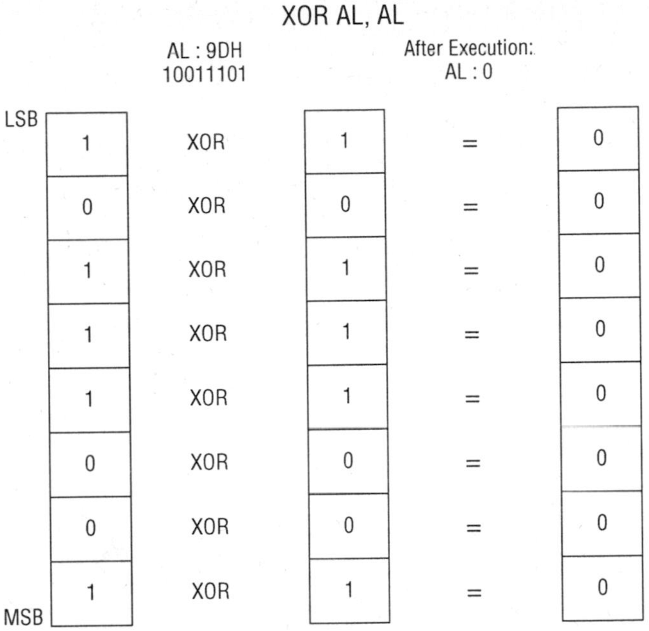

XOR AL, AL

AL : 9DH
10011101

After Execution:
AL : 0

LSB

1	XOR	1	=	0
0	XOR	0	=	0
1	XOR	1	=	0
1	XOR	1	=	0
1	XOR	1	=	0
0	XOR	0	=	0
0	XOR	0	=	0
1	XOR	1	=	0

MSB

Figure 9-3: Using XOR to zero a register

The NOT Instruction

Easiest to understand of all the bitwise logical instructions is NOT. The truth table for NOT is simpler than the others we've looked at because NOT only takes one operand. And what it does is simple as well: NOT takes the state of each bit in its single operand and changes that bit to its opposite state. What was 1 becomes 0, and what was 0 becomes 1, as shown in Table 9-5.

Table 9-5: The NOT Truth Table for Assembly Language

BIT	OPERATOR	RESULT BIT
0	NOT	1
1	NOT	0

Segment Registers Don't Respond to Logic!

You won't be directly accessing the x86 segment registers until you get into the depths of operating system programming. The segment registers belong to the OS, and user-space programs cannot change them in any way.

But even when you begin working at the operating-system level, the segment registers have significant limitations. One such limitation is that they cannot be used with any of the bitwise logic instructions. If you try, the assembler will hand you an "Illegal use of segment register" error. If you need to perform a logical operation on a segment register, you must first copy the segment register's value into one of the registers EAX, EBX, ECX, EDX, EBP, ESI, or EDI; perform the logical operation on the GP register; and then copy the result in the GP register back into the segment register.

The general-purpose registers are called "general purpose" for a reason, and the segment registers are not in any way general-purpose. They are specialists in memory addressing, and if you have to modify segment values, the general approach is to do the work in a general-purpose register and then move the modified value into the segment register in question.

Shifting Bits

The other way of manipulating bits within a byte is a little more straightforward: you *shift* them to one side or the other. There are a few wrinkles to the process, but the simplest shift instructions are pretty obvious: SHL SHifts its operand Left, whereas SHR SHifts its operand Right.

All of the shift instructions (including the slightly more complex ones I'll describe a little later) have the same general form, illustrated here by the SHL instruction:

```
shl <register/memory>,<count>
```

The first operand is the target of the shift operation—that is, the value that you're going to be shifting. It can be register data or memory data, but not immediate data. The second operand specifies the number of bits by which to shift.

Shift By What?

This <count> operand has a peculiar history. On the ancient 8086 and 8088, it could be one of two things: the immediate digit 1 or the register CL. (*Not* CX!) If you specified the count as 1, then the shift would be by one bit. If you wished to shift by more than one bit at a time, you had to load the shift count into register CL. In the days before the x86 general-purpose registers became truly general-purpose, counting things used to be CX's (and hence CL's) "hidden agenda." It would count shifts, passes through loops, string elements, and a few other things. That's why it's sometimes called the *count register* and can be remembered by the C in *count*.

Although you can shift by a number as large as 255, it really only makes sense to use shift count values up to 32. If you shift any bit in a double word by 32, you shift it completely out of the 32-bit double word—not to mention out of any byte or word!

Starting with the 286 and for all more recent x86 CPUs, the `<count>` operand may be any immediate value from 1 to 255. As Linux requires at least a 386 to run, the ancient restrictions on where the shift count value had to be no longer apply when you're programming under Linux.

How Bit Shifting Works

Understanding the shift instructions requires that you think of the numbers being shifted as *binary* numbers, and not hexadecimal or decimal numbers. (If you're fuzzy on binary notation, take another focused pass through Chapter 2.) A simple example would start with register AX containing a value of 0B76FH. Expressed as a binary number (and hence as a bit pattern), 0B76FH is as follows:

```
1011011101101111
```

Keep in mind that each digit in a binary number is one bit. If you execute an SHL AX, 1 instruction, what you'd find in AX after the shift is the following:

```
0110111011011110
```

A 0 has been inserted at the right-hand end of the number, and the whole shebang has been bumped toward the left by one digit. Notice that a 1 bit has been bumped off the left end of the number into cosmic nothingness.

Bumping Bits into the Carry Flag

Well, not *exactly* cosmic nothingness. The last bit shifted out of the left end of the binary number is bumped into a temporary bucket for bits called the *Carry flag*, generally abbreviated as CF. The Carry flag is one of those informational bits gathered together as the EFlags register, which I described in Chapter 7. You can test the state of the Carry flag with a branching instruction, as I'll explain a little later in this chapter.

However, keep in mind when using shift instructions that *a lot* of different instructions use the Carry flag—not only the shift instructions. If you bump a bit into the Carry flag with the intent of testing that bit later to see what it is, test it *before* you execute another instruction that affects the Carry flag. This includes all the arithmetic instructions, all the bitwise logical instructions, a few other miscellaneous instructions—and, of course, all the other shift instructions.

If you shift a bit into the Carry flag and then immediately execute another shift instruction, that first bit *will* be bumped off the end of the world and into cosmic nothingness.

The Rotate Instructions

That said, if a bit's destiny is *not* to be lost in cosmic nothingness, you need to use the rotate instructions RCL, RCR, ROL, and ROR instead. The rotate instructions are almost identical to the shift instructions, but with a crucial difference: a bit bumped off one end of the operand reappears at the opposite end of the operand. As you rotate an operand by more than one bit, the bits march steadily in one direction, falling off the end and immediately reappearing at the opposite end. The bits thus "rotate" through the operand as the rotate instruction is executed.

Like so many things, this shows better than it tells. Take a look at Figure 9-4. The example shown here is the ROL (Rotate Left) instruction, but the ROR instruction works the very same way, with the bits moving in the opposite direction. An initial binary value of 10110010 (0B2h) is placed in AL. When an ROL AL,1 instruction is executed, all the bits in AL march toward the left by one position. The 1-bit in bit 7 exits AL stage left, but runs around and reappears immediately from stage right.

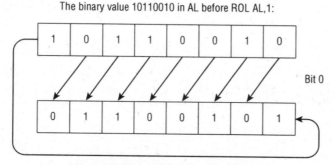

The binary value 10110010 in AL before ROL AL,1:

ROL shifts all bits left and moves bit 7 to bit 0.
What was 10110010 is now 01100101.

Figure 9-4: How the rotate instructions work

Again, ROR works exactly the same way, but the movement of bits is from left to right instead of (as with ROL) right to left. The number of bits by which an operand is rotated can be either an immediate value or a value in CL.

There is a second pair of rotate instructions in the x86 instruction set: RCR (Rotate Carry Right) and RCL (Rotate Carry Left). These operate as ROL and ROR do, but with a twist: The bits that are shifted out the end of an operand and reenter the operand at the beginning travel by way of the Carry flag. The path that any single bit takes in a rotate through CF is thus one bit longer than it would be in ROL and ROR. I've shown this graphically in Figure 9-5.

As with the shift instructions, there's no advantage to rotating a value by more than 31 bits. (If you rotate a value by 32 bits, you end up with the same

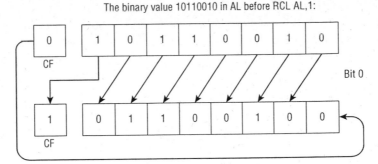

The binary value 10110010 in AL before RCL AL,1:

RCL shifts all bits left and moves bit 7 to the Carry flag.
The 0-bit previously in the Carry flag is moved into bit 0.

Figure 9-5: How the rotate through carry instructions work

value in the operand that you started with.) The rotate instructions bump bits off one end of the operand and then feed them back into the opposite end of the operand, to begin the trip again. If you mentally follow a single bit through the rotation process, you'll realize that after 32 rotations, any given bit is where it was when you started rotating the value. What's true of one bit is true of them all, so 31 rotations is as much as will be useful on a 32-bit value. This is why, in protected mode programming (and on the old 286 as well), the shift-by count is truncated to 5 bits before the instruction executes. After all, the largest value expressible in 5 bits is . . . 32!

Setting a Known Value into the Carry Flag

It's also useful to remember that previous instructions can leave values in CF, and those values will be rotated into an operand during an RCL or RCR instruction. Some people have the mistaken understanding that CF is forced to 0 before a shift or rotate instruction, which is not true. If another instruction leaves a 1-bit in CF immediately before an RCR or RCL instruction, that 1-bit will obediently enter the destination operand, whether you want it to or not.

If starting out a rotate with a known value in CF is important, there is a pair of x86 instructions that will do the job for you: CLC and STC. CLC clears the Carry flag to 0. STC sets the Carry flag to one. Neither instruction takes an operand, and neither has any other effects beyond changing the value in the Carry flag.

Bit-Bashing in Action

As you saw in earlier chapters, Linux has a fairly convenient method for displaying text to your screen. The problem is that it only displays *text*—if you want to display a numeric value from a register as a pair of hex digits, Linux won't help. You first have to convert the numeric value into its string representation, and then display the string representation by calling the sys_write kernel service via INT 80h.

Converting hexadecimal numbers to hexadecimal digits isn't difficult, and the code that does the job demonstrates several of the new concepts we're exploring in this chapter. The code in Listing 9-1 is the bare-bones core of a hex dump utility, rather like a read-only version of the Bless Hex Editor. When you redirect its input from a file of any kind, it will read that file 16 bytes at a time, and display those 16 bytes in a line, as 16 hexadecimal values separated by spaces.

Listing 9-1: hexdump1.asm

```
;   Executable name  : hexdump1
;   Version          : 1.0
;   Created date      : 4/4/2009
;   Last update       : 4/4/2009
;   Author            : Jeff Duntemann
;   Description       : A simple program in assembly for Linux, using NASM 2.05,
;       demonstrating the conversion of binary values to hexadecimal strings.
;       It acts as a very simple hex dump utility for files, though without the
;       ASCII equivalent column.
;
;   Run it this way:
;       hexdump1 < (input file)
;
;   Build using these commands:
;       nasm -f elf -g -F stabs hexdump1.asm
;       ld -o hexdump1 hexdump1.o
;
SECTION .bss                        ; Section containing uninitialized data

        BUFFLEN equ 16        ; We read the file 16 bytes at a time
        Buff:   resb BUFFLEN  ; Text buffer itself

SECTION .data               ; Section containing initialized data

        HexStr: db " 00 00 00 00 00 00 00 00 00 00 00 00 00 00 00 00",10
        HEXLEN  equ $-HexStr

        Digits: db "0123456789ABCDEF"

SECTION .text               ; Section containing code

global _start               ; Linker needs this to find the entry point!
```

Listing 9-1: hexdump1.asm (*continued*)

```
_start:
        nop             ; This no-op keeps gdb happy...

; Read a buffer full of text from stdin:
Read:
        mov eax,3       ; Specify sys_read call
        mov ebx,0       ; Specify File Descriptor 0: Standard Input
        mov ecx,Buff    ; Pass offset of the buffer to read to
        mov edx,BUFFLEN ; Pass number of bytes to read at one pass
        int 80h         ; Call sys_read to fill the buffer
        mov ebp,eax     ; Save # of bytes read from file for later
        cmp eax,0       ; If eax=0, sys_read reached EOF on stdin
        je Done         ; Jump If Equal (to 0, from compare)

; Set up the registers for the process buffer step:
        mov esi,Buff    ; Place address of file buffer into esi
        mov edi,HexStr  ; Place address of line string into edi
        xor ecx,ecx     ; Clear line string pointer to 0

; Go through the buffer and convert binary values to hex digits:
Scan:
        xor eax,eax     ; Clear eax to 0

; Here we calculate the offset into HexStr, which is the value in ecx X 3
        mov edx,ecx     ; Copy the character counter into edx
        shl edx,1       ; Multiply pointer by 2 using left shift
        add edx,ecx     ; Complete the multiplication X3

; Get a character from the buffer and put it in both eax and ebx:
        mov al,byte [esi+ecx] ; Put a byte from the input buffer into al
        mov ebx,eax     ; Duplicate the byte in bl for second nybble

; Look up low nybble character and insert it into the string:
        and al,0Fh      ; Mask out all but the low nybble
        mov al,byte [Digits+eax]   ; Look up the char equivalent of nybble
        mov byte [HexStr+edx+2],al ; Write LSB char digit to line string

; Look up high nybble character and insert it into the string:
        shr bl,4        ; Shift high 4 bits of char into low 4 bits
        mov bl,byte [Digits+ebx] ; Look up char equivalent of nybble
        mov byte [HexStr+edx+1],bl ; Write MSB char digit to line string

; Bump the buffer pointer to the next character and see if we're done:
        inc ecx         ; Increment line string pointer
        cmp ecx,ebp     ; Compare to the number of chars in the buffer
        jna Scan        ; Loop back if ecx is <= number of chars in buffer

; Write the line of hexadecimal values to stdout:
```

(continued)

Listing 9-1: hexdump1.asm (*continued*)

```
        mov eax,4       ; Specify sys_write call
        mov ebx,1       ; Specify File Descriptor 1: Standard output
        mov ecx,HexStr  ; Pass offset of line string
        mov edx,HEXLEN  ; Pass size of the line string
        int 80h         ; Make kernel call to display line string
        jmp Read        ; Loop back and load file buffer again

; All done! Let's end this party:
Done:
        mov eax,1       ; Code for Exit Syscall
        mov ebx,0       ; Return a code of zero
        int 80H         ; Make kernel call
```

The hexdump1 program is at its heart a filter program, and has the same general filter machinery used in the uppercaser2 program from Chapter 8. The important parts of the program for this discussion are the parts that read 16 bytes from the input buffer and convert them to a string of characters for display to the Linux console. This is the code between the label Scan and the INT 80h exit call. I'll be referring to that block of code in the discussion that follows.

Splitting a Byte into Two Nybbles

Remember that the values read by Linux from a file are read into memory as binary values. Hexadecimal is a way of displaying binary values, and in order to display binary values as displayable ASCII hexadecimal digits, you have to do some converting.

Displaying a single 8-bit binary value requires two hexadecimal digits. The bottom four bits in a byte are represented by one digit (the least-significant, or rightmost, digit) and the top four bits in a byte are represented by another digit (the most significant, or leftmost, digit). The binary value 11100110, for example, is the equivalent of E6 in hex. (I covered all this in detail in Chapter 2.) Converting an 8-bit value into two 4-bit digits must be done one digit at a time, which means that we have to separate the single byte into two 4-bit quantities, which are often called *nybbles*.

In the hexdump1 program, a byte is read from Buff and is placed in two registers, EAX and EBX. This is done because separating the high from the low nybble in a byte is destructive, in that we basically zero out the nybble that we don't want.

To isolate the low nybble in a byte, we need to *mask out* the unwanted nybble. This is done with an AND instruction:

```
and al,0Fh
```

The immediate constant 0Fh expressed in binary is 00001111. If you follow the operation through the AND truth table (Table 9-2) you'll see that any bit ANDed against 0 is 0. We AND the high nybble of register AL with 0000, which zeros out anything that might be there. ANDing the low nybble against 1111 leaves whatever was in the low nibble precisely as it was.

When we're done, we have the low nybble of the byte read from Buff in AL.

Shifting the High Nybble into the Low Nybble

Masking out the high nybble from the input byte in AL destroys it. We need the high nybble, but we have a second copy of the input byte in EBX, and that's the copy from which we'll extract the high nybble. As with the low nybble, we'll actually work with the least significant eight bits of EBX, as BL. Remember that BL is just a different way of referring to the low eight bits of EBX. It's not a different register. If a value is loaded into EBX, its least significant eight bits are in BL.

We could mask out the low nybble in BL with an AND instruction, leaving behind the high nybble, but there's a catch: masking out the low four bits of a byte does not make the high four bits a nybble. We have to somehow move the high four bits of the input byte into the low four bits.

The fastest way to do this is simply to shift BL to the right by four bits. This is what the SHR BL,4 instruction does. The low nybble is simply shifted off the edge of BL, into the Carry flag, and then out into cosmic nothingness. After the shift, what was the high nybble in BL is now the low nybble.

At this point, we have the low nybble of the input byte in AL, and the high nybble of the input byte in BL. The next challenge is converting the four-bit number in a nybble (like 1110) into its displayable ASCII hex digit—in this case, the character E.

Using a Lookup Table

In the .data section of the program is the definition of a very simple *lookup table*. The Digits table has this definition:

```
Digits db '0123456789ABCDEF'
```

The important thing to note about the Digits table is that each digit occupies a position in the string whose offset from the start of the string is the value it represents. In other words, the ASCII character "0" is at the very start of the string, zero bytes offset from the string's beginning. The character "7" lies seven bytes from the start of the string, and so on.

We "look up" a character in the Digits table using a memory reference:

```
mov al,byte [Digits+eax]
```

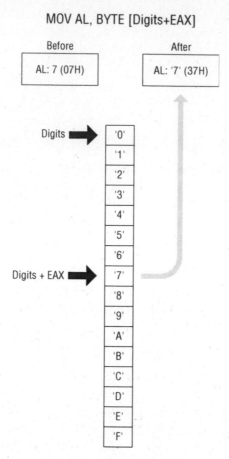

MOV AL, BYTE [Digits+EAX]

Figure 9-6: Using a lookup table

As with most of assembly language, everything here depends on memory addressing. The first hex digit character in the lookup table is at the address in Digits. To get at the desired digit, we must *index* into the lookup table. We do this by adding an offset into the table to the address inside the brackets. This offset is the nybble in AL.

Adding the offset in AL to the address of Digits (using EAX) takes us right to the character that is the ASCII equivalent of the value in AL. I've drawn this out graphically in Figure 9-6.

There are two possibly confusing things about the MOV instruction that fetches a digit from Digits and places it in AL:

- We must use EAX in the memory reference rather than AL, because AL cannot take part in effective address calculations. Don't forget that AL is "inside" EAX! (More on effective address calculations a little later in this chapter.)

- We are replacing the nybble in AL with its character equivalent. The instruction first fetches the character equivalent of the nybble from the table, and then stores the character equivalent back into AL. The nybble that was in AL is now gone.

So far, we've read a character from the lookup table into AL. The conversion of that nybble is done. The next task sounds simple but is actually surprisingly tricky: writing the ASCII hex digit character now in AL into the display string at HexStr.

Multiplying by Shifting and Adding

The hexdump1 program reads bytes from a file and displays them in lines, with 16 bytes represented in hex in each line. A portion of the output from the program is shown here:

```
3B 20 20 45 78 65 63 75 74 61 62 6C 65 20 6E 61
6D 65 20 3A 20 45 40 54 53 59 53 43 40 4C 4C 0D
0A 3B 20 20 56 65 72 73 69 6F 6E 20 20 20 20 20
20 20 20 20 3A 20 30 2E 30 0D 0A 3B 20 20 43 72
65 60 74 65 64 20 64 60 74 65 20 20 20 20 3A 20
30 2F 37 2F 32 30 30 39 0D 0A 3B 20 20 4C 60 73
74 20 75 70 64 60 74 65 20 20 20 20 20 3A 20 32
2F 30 38 2F 32 30 30 39 0D 0A 3B 20 20 40 75 74
68 6F 72 20 20 20 20 20 20 20 20 20 20 3A 20 4A
```

Each of these lines is a display of the same item: HexStr, a string of 48 characters with an EOL on the end. Each time hexdump1 reads a block of 16 bytes from the input file, it formats them as ASCII hex digits and inserts them into HexStr. In a sense, this is another type of table manipulation, except that instead of looking up something in a table, we're writing values into a table, based on an index.

One way to think about HexStr is as a table of 16 entries, each entry three characters long (see Figure 9-7). In each entry, the first character is a space, and the second and third characters are the hex digits themselves. The space characters are already there, as part of the original definition of HexStr in the .data section. The original "empty" HexStr has 0 characters in all hex digit positions. To "fill" HexStr with "real" data for each line's display, we have to scan through HexStr in an assembly language loop, writing the low nybble character and the high nybble character separately.

The tricky business here is that for each pass through the loop, we have to "bump" the index into HexStr by three instead of just by one. The offset of one of those three-byte entries in HexStr is the index of the entry multiplied

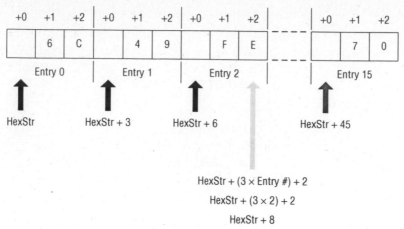

Figure 9-7: A table of 16 three-byte entries

by three. I've already described the MUL instruction, which handles arbitrary unsigned multiplication in the x86 instruction set. MUL, however, is very slow as instructions go. It has other limitations as well, especially the ways in which it requires specific registers for its implicit operands.

Fortunately, there are other, faster ways to multiply in assembly, with just a little cleverness. These ways are based on the fact that it's very easy and very fast to multiply by powers of two, using the SHL (Shift Left) instruction. It may not be immediately obvious to you, but each time you shift a quantity one bit to the left, you're multiplying that quantity by two. Shift a quantity two bits to the left, and you're multiplying it by four. Shift it three bits to the left, and you're multiplying by eight, and so on.

You can take my word for it, or you can actually watch it happen in a sandbox. Set up a fresh sandbox in Kate and enter the following instructions:

```
mov al,3
shl al,1
shl al,1
shl al,2
```

Build the sandbox and load the executable into Insight. Set the EAX display field in the Registers view to Decimal. (This must be done *after* the sandbox program is running, by right-clicking on the EAX field and selecting Decimal from the context menu.) Then step through the instructions, watching the value of EAX change in the Registers view for each step.

The first instruction loads the value 3 into AL. The next instruction shifts AL to the left by one bit. The value in AL becomes 6. The second SHL instruction shifts AL left by one bit again, and the 6 becomes 12. The third SHL instruction shifts AL by two bits, and the 12 becomes 48. I've shown this graphically in Figure 9-8.

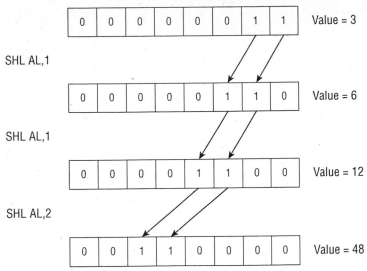

Figure 9-8: Multiplying by shifting

What if you want to multiply by 3? Easy: you multiply by 2 and then add one more copy of the multiplicand to the product. In the hexdump1 program, it's done this way:

```
mov edx,ecx    ; Copy the character counter into edx
shl edx,1      ; Multiply pointer by 2 using left shift
add edx,ecx    ; Complete the multiplication X3
```

Here, the multiplicand is loaded from the loop counter ECX into EDX. EDX is then shifted left by one bit to multiply it by 2. Finally, ECX is added once to the product EDX to make it multiplication by 3.

Multiplication by other numbers that are not powers of two may be done by combining a SHL and one or more ADDS. To multiply a value in ECX by 7, you would do this:

```
mov edx,ecx    ; Keep a copy of the multiplicand in ecx
shl edx,2      ; Multiply edx by 4
add edx,ecx    ; Makes it X 5
add edx,ecx    ; Makes it X 6
add edx,ecx    ; Makes it X 7
```

This may look clumsy, but remarkably enough, it's still faster than using MUL! (There's an even faster way to multiply by 3 that I'll show you a little later in this chapter.)

Once you understand how the string table HexStr is set up, writing the hex digits into it is straightforward. The least-significant hex digit is in AL, and the most significant hex digit is in BL. Writing both hex digits into `HexString` is done with a three-part memory address:

```
mov byte [HexStr+edx+2],al ; Write the LSB char digit to line string
mov byte [HexStr+edx+1],bl ; Write the MSB char digit to line string
```

Refer back to Figure 9-7 to work this out for yourself: you begin with the address of `HexStr` as a whole. EDX contains the offset of the first character in a given entry. To obtain the address of the entry in question, you add `HexStr` and EDX. However, that address is of the first character in the entry, which in `HexStr` is always a space character. The position of the LSB digit in an entry is the entry's offset +2, and the position of the MSB digit in an entry is the entry's offset +1. The address of the LSB digit is therefore `HexStr` + the offset of the entry, + 2. The address of the MSB digit is therefore `HexStr` + the offset of the entry, + 1.

Flags, Tests, and Branches

From a height, the idea of conditional jump instructions is simple, and without it, you won't get much done in assembly. I've been using conditional jumps informally in the last few example programs without saying much about them, because the sense of the jumps was pretty obvious from context, and they were necessary to demonstrate other things. But underneath the simplicity of the idea of assembly language jumps lies a great deal of complexity. It's time to get down and cover that in detail.

Unconditional Jumps

A *jump* is just that: an abrupt change in the flow of instruction execution. Ordinarily, instructions are executed one after the other, in order, moving from low memory toward high memory. *Jump instructions* alter the address of the next instruction to be executed. Execute a jump instruction, and *zap!* All of a sudden you're somewhere else. A jump instruction can move execution forward in memory or backward. It can bend execution back into a loop. (It can also tie your program logic in knots.)

There are two kinds of jumps: conditional and unconditional. An *unconditional* jump is a jump that *always* happens. It takes this form:

```
jmp <label>
```

When this instruction executes, the sequence of execution moves to the instruction located at the label specified by `<label>`. It's just that simple.

Conditional Jumps

A *conditional* jump instruction is one of those fabled tests I introduced in Chapter 1. When executed, a conditional jump tests something—usually one, occasionally two, or, much more rarely, three of the flags in the EFlags register. If the flag or flags being tested happen to be in a particular state, execution will jump to a label somewhere else in the code segment; otherwise, it simply falls through to the next instruction in sequence.

This two-way nature is important. A conditional jump instruction either jumps or it falls through. Jump or no jump. It can't jump to one of two places, or three. Whether it jumps or not depends on the current value of a very small set of bits within the CPU.

As I mentioned earlier in this book while discussing the EFlags register as a whole, there is a flag that is set to 1 by certain instructions when the result of that instruction is zero: the Zero flag (ZF). The DEC (DECrement) instruction is a good example. DEC subtracts one from its operand. If by that subtraction the operand becomes zero, ZF is set to 1. One of the conditional jump instructions, JZ (Jump if Zero), tests ZF. If ZF is found set to 1, then a jump occurs, and execution transfers to the label after the ZF mnemonic. If ZF is found to be 0, then execution falls through to the next instruction in sequence. This may be the commonest conditional jump in the entire x86 instruction set. It's often used when you're counting a register down to zero while executing a loop, and when the count register goes to zero by virtue of the DEC instruction, the loop ends, and execution picks up again right after the loop.

Here's a simple (if slightly bizarre) example, using instructions you should already understand:

```
          mov word [RunningSum],0 ; Clear the running total
          mov ecx,17              ; We're going to do this 17 times
WorkLoop:
          add word [RunningSum],3 ; Add three to the running total
          dec ecx                 ; Subtract 1 from the loop counter
          jz  SomewhereElse       ; If the counter is zero, we're done!
          jmp WorkLoop
```

Before the loop begins, we set up a value in ECX, which acts as the count register and contains the number of times we're going to run through the loop. The body of the loop is where something gets done on each pass through the loop. In this example it's a single ADD instruction, but it could be dozens or hundreds of instructions long.

After the work of the loop is accomplished, the count register is decremented by 1 with a DEC instruction. Immediately afterward, the JZ instruction tests the Zero flag. Decrementing ECX from 17 to 16, or from 4 to 3, does not set ZF, and the JZ instruction simply falls through. The instruction after JZ is an unconditional jump instruction, which obediently and consistently takes execution back to the WorkLoop label every time.

Now, decrementing ECX from 1 to 0 *does* set ZF, and that's when the loop ends. JZ finally takes us out of the loop by jumping to SomewhereElse (a label in the larger program not shown here), and execution leaves the loop.

If you're sharp enough, you may realize that this is a lousy way to set up a loop. (That doesn't mean it's never been done, or that you yourself may not do it in a late-night moment of impatience.) What we're really looking for each time through the loop is when a condition—the Zero flag—*isn't* set, and there's an instruction for that too.

Jumping on the Absence of a Condition

There are quite a few conditional jump instructions, of which I'll discuss several but not all in this book. Their number is increased by the fact that almost every conditional jump instruction has an alter ego: a jump when the specified condition is *not* set to 1.

The JZ instruction provides a good example of jumping on a condition. JZ jumps to a new location in the code segment if the Zero flag (ZF) is set to 1. JZ's alter ego is JNZ (Jump if Not Zero). JNZ jumps to a label if ZF is 0, and falls through if ZF is 1.

This may be confusing at first, because JNZ jumps when ZF is equal to 0. Keep in mind that the name of the instruction applies to the *condition* being tested and not necessarily the binary bit value of the flag. In the previous code example, JZ jumped when the DEC instruction decremented a counter to zero. The condition being tested is something connected with an earlier instruction, *not* simply the state of ZF.

Think of it this way: a condition raises a flag. "Raising a flag" means setting the flag to 1. When one of numerous instructions forces an operand to a value of zero (which is the condition), the Zero flag is raised. The logic of the instruction refers to the condition, *not* to the flag.

As an example, let's improve the little loop shown earlier by changing the loop logic to use JNZ:

```
          mov word [RunningSum],0 ; Clear the running total
          mov ecx,17              ; We're going to do this 17 times
WorkLoop:
          add word [RunningSum],3 ; Add three to the running total
          dec ecx                 ; Subtract 1 from the loop counter
          jnz  WorkLoop           ; If the counter is zero, we're done!
```

The JZ instruction has been replaced with a JNZ instruction. That makes much more sense, since to close the loop we have to jump, and we only close the loop while the counter is greater than 0. The jump back to label WorkLoop will happen only while the counter is greater than 0.

Once the counter decrements to 0, the loop is considered finished. JNZ falls through, and the code that follows the loop (not shown here) executes. The point is that if you can position the program's next task immediately after the JNZ instruction, you don't need to use the JMP instruction *at all*. Instruction execution will just flow naturally into the next task that needs performing. The program will have a more natural and less convoluted top-to-bottom flow and will be easier to read and understand.

Flags

Back in Chapter 7, I explained the EFlags register and briefly described the purposes of all the flags it contains. Most flags are not terribly useful, especially when you're first starting out as a programmer. The Carry flag (CF) and the Zero flag (ZF) will be 90 percent of your involvement in flags as a beginner, with the Direction flag (DF), Sign flag (SF), and Overflow flag (OF) together making up an additional 99.98 percent. It might be a good idea to reread that part of Chapter 7 now, just in case your grasp of flag etiquette has gotten a little rusty.

As explained earlier, JZ jumps when ZF is 1, whereas JNZ jumps when ZF is 0. Most instructions that perform some operation on an operand (such as AND, OR, XOR, INC, DEC, and all arithmetic instructions) set ZF according to the results of the operation. On the other hand, instructions that simply move data around (such as MOV, XCHG, PUSH, and POP) do not affect ZF or any of the other flags. (Obviously, POPF affects the flags by popping the top-of-stack value into them.) One irritating exception is the NOT instruction, which performs a logical operation on its operand but does *not* set any flags—even when it causes its operand to become 0. Before you write code that depends on flags, *check your instruction reference* to ensure that you have the flag etiquette down correctly for that instruction. The x86 instruction set is nothing if not quirky.

Comparisons with CMP

One major use of flags is in controlling loops. Another is in comparisons between two values. Your programs will often need to know whether a value in a register or memory is equal to some other value. Further, you may want to know if a value is greater than a value or less than a value if it is not equal to that value. There is a jump instruction to satisfy every need, but something has to set the flags for the benefit of the jump instruction. The CMP (CoMPare) instruction is what sets the flags for comparison tasks.

CMP's use is straightforward and intuitive. The second operand is compared with the first, and several flags are set accordingly:

```
cmp <op1>,<op2>     ; Sets OF, SF, ZF, AF, PF, and CF
```

The sense of the comparison can be remembered if you simply recast the comparison in arithmetic terms:

```
Result = <op1> - <op2>
```

CMP is very much a subtraction operation whereby the result of the subtraction is thrown away, and only the flags are affected. The second operand is subtracted from the first. Based on the results of the subtraction, the other flags are set to appropriate values.

After a CMP instruction, you can jump based on several arithmetic conditions. People who have a reasonable grounding in math, and FORTRAN or Pascal programmers, will recognize the conditions: *Equal, Not equal, Greater than, Less than, Greater than or equal to,* and *Less than or equal to.* The sense of these operators follows from their names and is exactly like the sense of the equivalent operators in most high-level languages.

A Jungle of Jump Instructions

There is a bewildering array of jump instruction mnemonics, but those dealing with arithmetic relationships sort out well into just six categories, one category for each of the six preceding conditions. Complication arises from the fact that there are *two* mnemonics for each machine instruction—for example, JLE (Jump if Less than or Equal) and JNG (Jump if Not Greater than). These two mnemonics are *synonyms* in that the assembler generates the identical binary opcode when it encounters either mnemonic. The synonyms are a convenience to you, the programmer, in that they provide two alternate ways to think about a given jump instruction. In the preceding example, *Jump if Less Than or Equal to* is logically identical to *Jump if Not Greater Than.* (Think about it!) If the importance of the preceding compare were to see whether one value is less than or equal to another, you'd use the JLE mnemonic. Conversely, if you were testing to be sure that one quantity was not greater than another, you'd use JNG. The choice is yours.

Another complication is that there is a separate set of instructions for signed and unsigned arithmetic comparisons. I haven't spoken much about assembly language math in this book, and thus haven't said much about the difference between signed and unsigned quantities. A *signed* quantity is one in which the high bit of the quantity is considered a built-in flag indicating whether the quantity is negative. If that bit is 1, then the quantity is considered negative. If that bit is 0, then the quantity is considered positive.

Signed arithmetic in assembly language is complex and subtle, and not as useful as you might immediately think. I won't be covering it in detail in this book, though nearly all assembly language books treat it to some extent. All you need know to get a high-level understanding of signed arithmetic is that in signed arithmetic, negative quantities are legal and the most significant bit of a value is treated as the sign bit. (If the sign bit is set to 1, then the value is considered negative.)

Unsigned arithmetic, on the other hand, does not recognize negative numbers, and the most significant bit is just one more bit in the binary number expressed by the quantity.

"Greater Than" Versus "Above"

To tell the signed jumps apart from the unsigned jumps, the mnemonics use two different expressions for the relationship between two values:

- *Signed values* are thought of as being *greater than* or *less than*. For example, to test whether one signed operand is greater than another, you would use the JG (Jump if Greater) mnemonic after a CMP instruction.

- *Unsigned values* are thought of as being *above* or *below*. For example, to tell whether one unsigned operand is greater than (above) another, you would use the JA (Jump if Above) mnemonic after a CMP instruction.

Table 9-6 summarizes the arithmetic jump mnemonics and their synonyms. Any mnemonics containing the words *above* or *below* are for unsigned values, whereas any mnemonics containing the words *greater* or *less* are for signed values. Compare the mnemonics with their synonyms and note how the two represent opposite viewpoints from which to look at identical instructions.

Table 9-6 simply serves to expand the mnemonics into a more comprehensible form and associate a mnemonic with its synonym. Table 9-7, on the other hand, sorts the mnemonics by logical condition and according to their use with signed and unsigned values. Also listed in Table 9-7 are the flags whose values are tested by each jump instruction. Notice that some of the jump instructions require one of two possible flag values in order to take the jump, while others require *both* of two flag values.

Several of the signed jumps compare two of the flags against one another. JG, for example, will jump when either ZF is 0, or when the Sign flag (SF) is equal to the Overflow flag (OF). I won't spend any more time explaining the nature of the Sign flag or the Overflow flag. As long as you have the sense of each instruction under your belt, understanding exactly how the instructions test the flags can wait until you've gained some programming experience.

Some people have trouble understanding how the JE and JZ mnemonics are synonyms, as are JNE and JNZ. Think again of the way a comparison is done within the CPU: the second operand is subtracted from the first, and if the result is 0 (indicating that the two operands were in fact equal), then the Zero flag is set to 1. That's why JE and JZ are synonyms: both are simply testing the state of the Zero flag.

Table 9-6: Jump Instruction Mnemonics and Their Synonyms

MNEMONICS		SYNONYMS	
JA	Jump if Above	JNBE	Jump if Not Below or Equal
JAE	Jump if Above or Equal	JNB	Jump if Not Below
JB	Jump if Below	JNAE	Jump if Not Above or Equal
JBE	Jump if Below or Equal	JNA	Jump if Not Above
JE	Jump if Equal	JZ	Jump if result is Zero
JNE	Jump if Not Equal	JNZ	Jump if result is Not Zero
JG	Jump if Greater	JNLE	Jump if Not Less than or Equal
JGE	Jump if Greater or Equal	JNL	Jump if Not Less
JL	Jump if Less	JNGE	Jump if Not Greater or Equal
JLE	Jump if Less or Equal	JNG	Jump if Not Greater

Looking for 1-Bits with TEST

The x86 instruction set recognizes that bit testing is done a lot in assembly language, and it provides what amounts to a CMP instruction for bits: TEST. TEST performs an AND logical operation between two operands, and then sets the flags as the AND instruction would, *without* altering the destination operation, as AND also would. Here's the TEST instruction syntax:

```
test <operand>,<bit mask>
```

The bit mask operand should contain a 1 bit in each position where a 1 bit is to be sought in the operand, and 0 bits in all the other bits.

What TEST does is perform the AND logical operation between the instruction's destination operand and the bit mask, and then set the flags as the AND instruction would do. The result of the AND operation is discarded, and the destination operand doesn't change. For example, if you want to determine whether bit 3 of AX is set to 1, you would use this instruction:

```
test ax,08h        ; Bit 3 in binary is 00001000B, or 08h
```

Bit 3, of course, does not have the numeric value 3—you have to look at the bit pattern of the mask and express it as a binary or hexadecimal value. (Bit 3 represents the value 8 in binary.) Using binary for literal constants is perfectly legal in NASM, and often the clearest expression of what you're doing when you're working with bit masks:

```
test ax,00001000B    ; Bit 3 in binary is 00001000B, or 08h
```

Table 9-7: Arithmetic Tests Useful After a CMP Instruction

CONDITION	PASCAL OPERATOR	UNSIGNED VALUES	JUMPS WHEN	SIGNED VALUES	JUMPS WHEN
Equal	=	JE	ZF=1	JE	ZF=1
Not Equal	<>	JNE	ZF=0	JNE	ZF=0
Greater than	>	JA	CF=0 and ZF=0	JG	ZF=0 or SF=OF
Not Less than or equal to		JNBE	CF=0 and ZF=0	JNLE	ZF=0 or SF=OF
Less than	<	JB	CF=1	JL	SF<>OF
Not Greater than or equal to		JNAE	CF=1	JNGE	SF<>OF
Greater than or equal to	>=	JAE	CF=0	JGE	SF=OF
Not Less than		JNB	CF=0	JNL	SF=OF
Less than or equal to	<=	JBE	CF=1 or ZF=1	JLE	ZF=1 or SF<>OF
Not Greater than		JNA	CF=1 or ZF=1	JNG	ZF=1 or SF<>OF

Destination operand AX doesn't change as a result of the operation, but the AND truth table is asserted between AX and the binary pattern 00001000. If bit 3 in AX is a 1 bit, then the Zero flag is cleared to 0. If bit 3 in AX is a 0 bit, then the Zero flag is set to 1. Why? If you AND 1 (in the bit mask) with 0 (in AX), you get 0. (Look it up in the AND truth table, shown previously in Table 9-2.) And if all eight bitwise AND operations come up 0, the result is 0, and the Zero flag is raised to 1, indicating that the result is 0.

Key to understanding TEST is thinking of TEST as a sort of "Phantom of the Opcode," where the opcode is AND. TEST puts on a mask (as it were) and *pretends* to be AND, but then doesn't follow through with the results of the operation. It simply sets the flags *as though* an AND operation had occurred.

The CMP instruction is another Phantom of the Opcode and bears the same relation to SUB as TEST bears to AND. CMP subtracts its second operand from its first, but doesn't follow through and store the result in the first operand. It just sets the flags *as though* a subtraction had occurred. As you've already seen, this can be mighty useful when combined with conditional jump instructions.

Here's something important to keep in mind: TEST *is only useful for finding 1 bits*. If you need to identify 0 bits, you must first flip each bit to its opposite state with the NOT instruction. NOT changes all 1 bits to 0 bits, and all 0 bits to 1 bits. Once all 0 bits are flipped to 1 bits, you can test for a 1 bit where you need to find a 0 bit. (Sometimes it helps to map it out on paper to keep it all straight in your head.)

Finally, TEST will *not* reliably test for two or more 1 bits in the operand *at one time*. TEST doesn't check for the presence of a bit pattern; *it checks for the presence of a single 1 bit*. In other words, if you need to confirm that *both* bits 4 and 5 are set to 1, TEST won't hack it.

Looking for 0 Bits with BT

As I explained earlier, TEST has its limits: it's not cut out for determining when a bit is set to 0. TEST has been with us since the very earliest X86 CPUs, but the 386 and newer processors have an instruction that enables you to test for either 0 bits or 1 bits. BT (Bit Test) performs a very simple task: it copies the specified bit from the first operand into the Carry flag (CF). In other words, if the selected bit was a 1 bit, the Carry flag becomes set. If the selected bit was a 0 bit, the Carry flag is cleared. You can then use any of the conditional jump instructions that examine and act on the state of CF.

BT is easy to use. It takes two operands: the destination operand is the value containing the bit in question; the source operand is the ordinal number of the bit that you want to test, counting from 0:

```
bt <value containing bit>,<bit number>
```

Once you execute a BT instruction, you should immediately test the value in the Carry flag and branch based on its value. Here's an example:

```
bt eax,4    ; Test bit 4 of AX
jnc quit    ; We're all done if bit 4 = 0
```

Note something to be careful of, especially if you're used to using TEST: *You are not creating a bit mask*. With BT's source operand you are specifying the ordinal number of a bit. The literal constant 4 shown above is the bit's *number* (counting from 0), not the bit's *value*, and that's a crucial difference.

Also note that we're branching if CF is *not* set; that's what JNC (Jump if Not Carry) does.

I hate to discuss code efficiency too much in a beginners' book, but there is a caution here: the BT instruction is pretty slow as instructions go—and bit-banging is often something you do a great many times inside tight loops, where instruction speed can be significant. Using it here and there is fine, but if you're inside a loop that executes thousands or millions of times, consider whether there might be a better way to test bits. Creaky old TEST is much faster, but TEST only tests for 1 bits. Depending on your application, you may be able to test for 0 bits more quickly another way, perhaps shifting a value into the Carry flag with SHL or SHR, using NOT to invert a value. There are no hard-and-fast rules, and everything depends on the dynamics of what you're doing. (That's why I'm not teaching optimization systematically in this book!)

Protected Mode Memory Addressing in Detail

In so many ways, life is *better* now. And I'm not just talking about modern dentistry, plug-and-play networking, and four-core CPUs. I used to program in assembly for the real-mode 8088 CPUs in the original IBM PC—and I remember real-mode memory addressing.

Like dentistry in the 1950s, 8088-based real-mode memory addressing was just ... painful. It was a hideous ratbag of restrictions and gotchas and limits and Band-Aids, all of which veritably screamed out that the CPU was *desperately* hungry for more transistors on the die. Addressing memory, for example, was limited to EBX and EBP in most instructions, which meant a lot of fancy footwork when several separate items had to be addressed in memory all at the same time. And thinking about segment management still makes me shudder.

Well, in the past 20 years our x86 CPUs got pretty much all the transistors they wanted, and the bulk of those infuriating real-mode memory addressing limitations have simply gone away. You can address memory with *any* of the general-purpose registers. You can even address memory directly with the stack pointer ESP, something that its 16-bit predecessor SP could not do. (You shouldn't *change* the value in ESP without considerable care, but ESP can now take part in addressing modes from which the stack pointer was excluded in 16-bit real-mode land.)

Protected mode on the 386 CPU introduced a general-purpose memory-addressing scheme in which all the GP registers can participate equally. I've sketched it out in Figure 9-9, which may well be the single most important figure in this entire book. Print it out and tape it to the wall next to your machine. Refer to it often. *Memory addressing is the key skill in assembly language work.* If you don't understand that, nothing else matters at *all.*

When I first studied and understood this scheme, wounds still bleeding from 16-bit 8088 real-mode segmented memory addressing, it looked too good to be true. But true it is! Here are the rules:

■ The base and index registers may be any of the 32-bit general-purpose registers, including ESP.

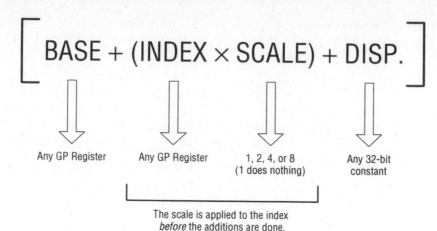

The scale is applied to the index
before the additions are done.

Figure 9-9: Protected mode memory addressing

- The displacement may be any 32-bit constant. Obviously, 0, while legal, isn't useful.

- The scale must be one of the values 1, 2, 4, or 8. That's it! The value 1 is legal but doesn't do anything useful, so it's never used.

- The index register is multiplied by the scale before the additions are done. In other words, it's not (base + index) × scale. Only the index register is multiplied by the scale.

- All of the elements are optional and may be used in almost any combination.

- 16-bit and 8-bit registers may *not* be used in memory addressing.

This last point is worth enlarging upon. There are several different ways you can address memory, by gathering the components in the figure in different combinations. Examples are shown in Table 9-8.

Effective Address Calculations

Each of the rows in Table 9-8 summarizes a method of expressing a memory address in 32-bit protected mode. All but the first two involve a little arithmetic among two or more terms within the brackets that signify an address. This arithmetic is called *effective address calculation*, and the result of the calculation is the *effective address*. The term is "effective address" in that it means that address that will ultimately be used to read or write memory, irrespective of how it is expressed. Effective address calculation is done by the instruction, when the instruction is executed.

The effective address in the Base scheme is simply the 32-bit quantity stored in the GP register between the brackets. No calculation is involved, but what you see in the source code is not a literal or symbolic address. So although the

Table 9-8: Protected Mode Memory-Addressing Schemes

SCHEME	EXAMPLE	DESCRIPTION
[BASE]	[edx]	Base only
[DISPLACEMENT]	[0F3h] or [<variable>]	Displacement, either literal constant or symbolic address
[BASE + DISPLACEMENT]	[ecx + 033h]	Base plus displacement
[BASE + INDEX]	[eax + ecx]	Base plus index
[INDEX × SCALE]	[ebx * 4]	Index times scale
[INDEX × SCALE + DISPLACEMENT]	[eax * 8 + 65]	Index times scale plus displacement
[BASE + INDEX × SCALE]	[esp + edi * 2]	Base plus index times scale
[BASE + INDEX × SCALE + DISPLACEMENT]	[esi + ebp * 4 + 9]	Base plus index times scale plus displacement

instruction is coded with a register name between the brackets, the address that will be sent out to the memory system when the code executes is stored inside the register.

The only case in which the effective address is right there on the line with the instruction mnemonic would be a literal address within the brackets. This is almost never done, because it's extremely unlikely that you will know a precise 32-bit numeric address at assembly time.

Most of the time there's some arithmetic going on. In the Base + Index scheme, for example, the contents of the two GP registers between the brackets are added when the instruction is executed to form the effective address.

Displacements

Among the several components of a legal address, the displacement term is actually one of the most slippery to understand. As I indicated in the previous paragraph, the displacement term can be a literal address, but in all my years of protected-mode assembly programming I've never done it, nor seen anyone else do it. When the displacement term stands alone, it is virtually always a symbolic address. By that I mean a named data item that you've defined in your .data or .bss sections, like the HexStr variable from the hexdump1 program in Listing 9-1:

```
mov eax,[HexStr]
```

What is placed in EAX here is the address given to the variable HexStr when the program is loaded into memory. Like all addresses, it's just a number, but it's determined at runtime rather than at assembly time, as a literal constant numeric address would be.

A lot of beginners get confused when they see what looks like two displacement terms between the brackets in a single address. The confusion stems from the fact that if NASM sees two (or more) constant values in a memory reference, it will combine them at assembly time into a single displacement value. That's what's done here:

```
mov eax,[HexStr+3]
```

The address referred to symbolically by the variable named HexStr is simply added to the literal constant 3 to form a single displacement value. The key characteristic of a displacement term is that *it is not in a register*.

Base + Displacement Addressing

A simple and common addressing scheme is Base + Displacement, and I demonstrated it in the hexdump1 program in Listing 9-1. The instruction that inserts an ASCII character into the output line looks like this:

```
mov byte [HexStr+edx+2]
```

This is a perfect example of a case where there are two displacement terms that NASM combines into one. The variable name HexStr resolves to a number (the 32-bit address of HexStr) and it is easily added to the literal constant 2, so there is actually only one base term (EDX) and one displacement term.

Base + Index Addressing

Perhaps the most common single addressing scheme is Base + Index, in which the effective address is calculated by adding the contents of two GP registers within the brackets. I demonstrated this addressing scheme in Chapter 8, in the uppercaser2 program in Listing 8-2. Converting a character in the input buffer from lowercase to uppercase is done by subtracting 20h from it:

```
sub byte [ebp+ecx],20h
```

The address of the buffer was earlier placed in EBP, and the number in ECX is the offset from the buffer start of the character being processed during any given pass through the loop. Adding the address of the buffer with an offset into the buffer yields the effective address of the character acted upon by the SUB instruction.

But wait ... why not use Base + Displacement addressing? This instruction would be legal:

```
sub byte [Buff+ecx],20h
```

However, if you remember from the program (and it would be worth looking at it again, and reading the associated text), we had to decrement the address of Buff by one before beginning the loop. But wait some more ... could we have NASM do that little tweak by adding a second displacement term of -1? Indeed we could, and it would work. The central loop of the uppercaser2 program would then look like this:

```
; Set up the registers for the process buffer step:
        mov ecx,esi   ; Place the number of bytes read into ecx
        mov ebp,Buff  ; Place address of buffer into ebp
;       dec ebp  ** We don't need this instruction anymore! **

; Go through the buffer and convert lowercase to uppercase characters:
Scan:
        cmp byte [Buff-1+ecx],61h  ; Test input char against lowercase 'a'
        jb Next        ; If below 'a' in ASCII, not lowercase
        cmp byte [Buff-1+ecx],7Ah  ; Test input char against lowercase 'z'
        ja Next        ; If above 'z' in ASCII, not lowercase
                       ; At this point, we have a lowercase char
        sub byte [Buff-1+ecx],20h  ; Subtract 20h to give uppercase...
Next:   dec ecx        ; Decrement counter
        jnz Scan       ; If characters remain, loop back
```

The initial DEC EBP instruction is no longer necessary. NASM does the math, and the address of Buff is decremented by one within the effective address expression when the program loads. This is actually the correct way to code this particular loop, and I thought long and hard about whether to show it in Chapter 8 or wait until I could explain memory addressing schemes in detail.

Some people find the name "Base + Displacement" confusing, because in most cases the Displacement term contains an address, and the Base term is a register containing an offset into a data item at that address. The word "displacement" resembles the word "offset" in most people's experience, hence the confusion. This is one reason I don't emphasize the names of the various memory addressing schemes in this book, and certainly don't recommend memorizing the names. *Understand how effective address calculation works*, and ignore the names of the schemes.

Index × Scale + Displacement Addressing

Base + Index addressing is what you'll typically use to scan through a buffer in memory byte by byte, but what if you need to access a data item in a buffer or table where each data item is not a single byte, but a word or a double word? This requires slightly more powerful memory addressing machinery.

As a side note here, the word *array* is the general term for what I've been calling a buffer or a table. Other writers may call a table an array, especially when the context of the discussion is a high-level language, but all three terms cook down to the same definition: a sequence of data items in memory, all of the same size and same internal definition. In the programs shown so far, we've looked at only very simple tables and buffers consisting of a sequence of one-byte values all in a row. The Digits table in the hexdump1 program in Listing 9-1 is such a table:

```
Digits: db "0123456789ABCDEF"
```

It's 16 single-byte ASCII characters in a row in memory. You can access the "C" character within Digits this way, using Base + Displacement addressing:

```
mov ecx,12
mov edx,[Digits+ecx]
```

What if you have a table containing 32-bit values? Such a table is easy enough to define:

```
Sums: dd "15,12,6,0,21,14,4,0,0,19"
```

The DD qualifier tells NASM that each item in the table Sums is a 32-bit double word quantity. The literal constants plug a numeric value into each element of the table. The address of the first element (here, 15) in Sums is just the address of the table as a whole, contained in the variable Sums.

What is the address of the second element, 12? And how do you access it from assembly code? Keep in mind that memory is addressed byte by byte, and not double word by double word. The second entry in the table is at an offset of four bytes into the table. If you tried to reference the second entry in the table using an address [Sums + 1], you would get one of the bytes inside the first table element's double word, which would not be useful.

This is where the concept of *scaling* comes in. An address may include a scale term, which is a multiplier and may be any of the literal constants 2, 4, or 8. (The literal constant 1 is technically legal, but because the scale is a multiplier, 1 is not a useful scale value.) The product of the index and the scale terms is added to the displacement to give the effective address. This is known as the Index × Scale + Displacement addressing scheme.

Typically, the scale term is the size of the individual elements in the table. If your table consists of 2-byte word values, the scale would be 2. If your table consists of 4-byte double word values, the scale would be 4. If your table consists of 8-byte quad word values, the scale would be 8.

The best way to explain this is with a diagram. In Figure 9-10, we're confronted with the address [DDTable + ECX*4]. DDTable is a table of double word (32-bit) values. DDTable's address is the displacement. The ECX register is the index, and for this example it contains 2, which is the number of the table element that you want to access. Because it's a table of 4-byte double words, the scale value is 4.

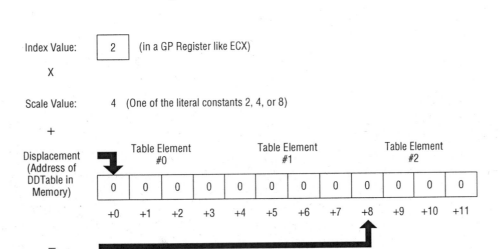

Figure 9-10: How address scaling works

Because each table element is four bytes in size, the offset of element #2 from the start of the table is 8. The effective address of the element is calculated by first multiplying the index by the scale, and then adding the product to the address of DDTable. There it is!

Other Addressing Schemes

Any addressing scheme that includes scaling works just this way. The differences lie in what other terms are figured into the effective address. The Base + Index × Scale scheme adds a scaled index to a base value in a register rather than displacement:

```
mov ecx,2              ; Index is in ecx
```

```
mov ebp,DDTable        ; Table address is in ebp
mov edx,[ebp+ecx*4]    ; Put the selected element into edx
```

You won't always be working with the address of a predefined variable like DDTable. Sometimes the address of the table will come from somewhere else, most often a two-dimensional table consisting of a number of subtables in memory, each subtable containing some number of elements. Such tables are accessed in two steps: first you derive the address of the inner table in the outer table, and then you derive the address of the desired element within the inner table.

The most familiar example of this sort of two-dimensional table is something I presented in earlier editions of this book, for DOS. The 25-line × 80-character text video memory buffer under DOS was a two-dimensional table. Each of the 25 lines was a table of 80 characters, and each character was represented by a 2-byte word. (One byte was the ASCII value, and the other byte specified attributes like color, underlining, and so on.) Therefore, the buffer as a whole was an overall table of 25 smaller tables, each containing 80 2-byte word values.

That sort of video access system died with DOS; Linux does not allow you direct access to PC video memory. It was done a lot in the DOS era, however, and is a good example of a two-dimensional table.

Scaling will serve you well for tables with 2-byte, 4-byte, or 8-byte elements. What if your table consists of 3-byte elements? Or 5-byte elements? Or 17-byte elements? Alas, in such cases you have to do some additional calculations in order to zero in on one particular element. Effective address calculation won't do the whole job itself. I've already given you an example of such a table in Listing 9-1. The line display string is a table of 3-byte elements. Each element contains a space character followed by the two hex digit characters. Because the elements are each three characters long, scaling cannot be done within the instruction, and must be handled separately.

It's not difficult. Scaling for the 3-byte elements in the HexStr table in the hexdump1 program is done like this:

```
mov edx,ecx     ; Copy the character counter into edx
shl edx,1       ; Multiply counter by 2 using left shift
add edx,ecx     ; Complete the multiplication X3
```

The calculation to multiply a value in EDX by 3 is done with a combination of an SHL instruction to multiply by 2, followed by an ADD instruction that adds a third copy of the index value to the shifted index value, effectively multiplying the original count value by 3.

Scaling for other index values can be done the same way. Scaling by 5 would be done by shifting the index value left by 2 bits, thus multiplying it by 4, followed by adding another copy of the index value to complete the multiplication by 5. In general terms, to scale an index value by X:

1. Find the largest power of 2 less than X.

2. Shift the index value left by that power of 2.

3. Add a copy of the original index value to the shifted copy as many times as it takes to complete the multiplication by X.

For example, if X is 11, the scale calculation would be done this way:

```
mov edx,ecx      ; Copy the index into edx
shl edx,3        ; Multiply index by 8 by shifting counter left 3 times
add edx,ecx      ; Add first of three additional copies of index
add edx,ecx      ; Add second of three additional copies of index
add edx,ecx      ; Add third of three additional copies of index
```

This works best for relatively small-scale values; once you get past 20 there will be a lot of ADD instructions. At that point, the solution is not to calculate the scale, but to look up the scale in a table specially defined for a given scale value. For example, suppose your table elements are each 25 bytes long. You could define a table with multiples of 25:

```
ScaleValues: dd 0,25,50,75,100,125,150,175,200,225,250,275,300
```

To scale an index value of 6 for an entry size of 25, you would look up the product of 6 × 25 in the table this way:

```
mov ecx,6
mov eax,[ScaleValues+ecx*4]
```

The value in EAX now contains the effective address of the first byte of element 6, counting elements (as usual) from 0.

LEA: The Top-Secret Math Machine

But wait (as they say on late-night TV), there's more. One of the oddest instructions, and in some respects the most wonderful instruction, in the x86 architecture is LEA, Load Effective Address. On the surface, what it does is simple: It calculates an effective address given between the brackets of its source operand, and loads that address into any 32-bit general-purpose register given as its destination operand. Refer back to the previous paragraph and the MOV instruction that looks up the element with index 6 in the table ScaleValues. In order to look up the item at index 6, it has to first calculate the effective address of the item at index 6. This address is then used to access memory.

What if you'd like to save that address in a register to use it later? That's what LEA does. Here's LEA in action:

```
lea ebx,[ScaleValues+ecx*4]
```

What happens here is that the CPU calculates the effective address given inside the brackets, and loads that address into the EBX register. Keep in mind that the individual entries in a table do not have labels and thus cannot be referenced directly. LEA enables you to calculate the effective address of any element in a table (or any calculable address at all!) and drop that address in a register.

In itself this is very useful, but LEA also has an "off-label" purpose: doing fast math without shifts, adds, or pokey MUL. If you remember, there is a calculation in the hexdump1 program that multiplies by three using a shift and an add:

```
mov edx,ecx      ; Copy the character counter into edx
shl edx,1        ; Multiply pointer by 2 using left shift
add edx,ecx      ; Complete the multiplication X3
```

The preceding works, but look at what we can use that does exactly the same thing:

```
mov edx,ecx           ; Copy the character counter into edx
lea edx,[edx*2+edx]   ; Multiply edx X 3
```

Not only is this virtually always faster than shifts combined with adds, it's also clearer from your source code what sort of calculation is actually being done. The fact that what ends up in EDX may not in fact be the legal address of anything is unimportant. *LEA does not try to reference the address it calculates.* It does the math on the stuff inside the brackets and drops it into the destination operand. Job over. Memory is not touched, and the flags are not affected.

Of course, you're limited to what calculations can be done on effective addresses; but right off the top, you can multiply any GP register by 2, 3, 4, 5, 8, and 9, while tossing in a constant too! It's not arbitrary math, but multiplying by 2, 3, 4, 5, 8, and 9 comes up regularly in assembly work, and you can combine LEA with shifts and adds to do more complex math and "fill in the holes." You can also use multiple LEA instructions in a row. Two consecutive LEA instructions can multiple a value by 10, which is useful indeed:

```
lea ebx,[ebx*2]        ; Multiply ebx X 2
lea ebx,[ebx*4+ebx]    ; Multiply ebx X 5 for a total of X 10
```

Some people consider this use of LEA a scurvy trick, but in all the years I've worked in x86 assembly I've never seen a downside. Before throwing five or six instructions into the pot to cook up a particular multiplication, see if two or three LEAs can do it instead. LEA does its work in one machine cycle, and x86 math doesn't get any faster than that!

The Burden of 16-Bit Registers

There's a slightly dark flip side to protected mode's graduation to 32-bit registers: Using the 16-bit general-purpose registers AX, BX, CX, DX, SP, BP, SI, and DI will slow you down. Now that 32-bit registers rule, making use of the 16-bit registers is considered a special case that adds to the size of the opcodes that the assembler generates, slowing your program code down. Now, note well that by "use" I mean explicitly reference in your source code. The AX register, for example, is still there inside the silicon of the CPU (as part of the larger EAX register), and simply placing data there won't slow you down. You just can't place data in AX by using "AX" as an operand in an opcode and not slow down. This syntax generates a slow opcode:

```
mov ax,542
```

You can do the same thing as follows, and the opcode that NASM generates will execute much more quickly:

```
mov eax,542
```

I haven't mentioned this until now because I consider it an advanced topic: You have to walk before you run, and trying to optimize your code before you fully understand what makes code fast and what makes code slow is a proven recipe for confusion and disappointment. A scattering of references to the 16-bit registers in a program will not make the program significantly slower. What you want to avoid is using 16-bit register references inside a tight loop, where the loop will be executed thousands or tens of thousands of times. (Or more!)

In some circumstances, both the 8-bit and 16-bit registers are absolutely necessary—for example, when writing 8-bit or 16-bit values to memory. NASM will not let you do this:

```
mov byte [ebx],eax
```

The BYTE qualifier makes the first operand an 8-bit operand, and NASM will complain that there is a "mismatch in operand size." If you need to write an isolated 8-bit value (like an ASCII character) into memory, you need to put the character in one of the 8-bit registers, like this:

```
mov byte [ebx],al
```

That generates a (moderately) slower opcode, but there's no getting around it. Keep in mind, with modern CPUs especially, that code performance of individual opcodes is swamped by other CPU machinery like cache, hyper-threading, prefetch, and so on. In general, statistical terms, using 32-bit registers makes it more likely that your code will run faster, but a scattering of 16-bit or 8-bit register references will not make a huge difference except in certain cases (like within tight loops) and even then, the performance hit is difficult to predict and almost impossible to quantify.

Put simply: use 32-bit registers wherever you can, but don't agonize over it.

Character Table Translation

There is a type of table lookup that is (or perhaps was) so common that Intel's engineers baked a separate instruction into the x86 architecture for it. The type of table lookup is what I was alluding to toward the end of Chapter 8: *character conversion*. In the early 1980s I needed to convert character sets in various ways, the simplest of which was forcing all lowercase characters to uppercase. And in Chapter 8 we built a simple program that went through a file one buffer at a time, bringing in characters, converting all lowercase characters to uppercase, and then writing them all back out again to a new file.

The conversion itself was simple: by relying on the ASCII chart for the relationship between all uppercase characters and their associated lowercase characters, we could convert a lowercase character to uppercase by simply subtracting 20h (32) from the character. That's reliable, but in a sense a sort of special case. It just so happens that ASCII lowercase characters are always 32 higher on the chart than uppercase characters. What do you do if you need to convert all "vertical bar" (ASCII 124) characters to exclamation points? (I had to do this once because one of the knucklehead mainframes couldn't digest vertical bars.) You can write special code for each individual case that you have to deal with . . .

. . . or you can use a translation table.

Translation Tables

A translation table is a special type of table, and it works the following way: you set up a table of values, with one entry for every possible value that must be translated. A number (or a character, treated as a number) is used as an index into the table. At the index position in the table is a value that is used to replace the original value that was used as the index. In short, the original value indexes into the table and finds a new value that replaces the original value, thus translating the old value to a new one.

We've done this once before, in the hexdump1.asm program in Listing 9-1. Recall the Digits table:

```
Digits: db "0123456789ABCDEF"
```

This is a translation table, though I didn't call it that at the time. The idea, if you recall, was to separate the two 4-bit halves of an 8-bit byte, and convert those 4-bit values into ASCII characters representing hexadecimal digits. The focus at the time was separating the bytes into two nybbles via bitwise logical operations, but translation was going on there as well.

The translation was accomplished by these three instructions:

```
mov al,byte [esi+ecx]      ; Put a byte from the input buffer into al
and al,0Fh                 ; Mask out all but the low nybble
mov al,byte [Digits+eax]   ; Look up the char equivalent of nybble
```

The first instruction loads a byte from the input buffer into the 8-bit AL register. The second instruction masks out all but the low nybble of AL. The third instruction does a memory fetch: It uses the value in AL to index into the Digits table, and brings back whatever value was in the ALth entry in the table. (This has to be done using EAX between the brackets, because AL cannot take part in effective address calculations. Just remember that AL is the lowest-order byte in the EAX register.) If AL held 0, then the effective address calculation added 0 to the address of Digits, bringing back the 0th table entry, which is the ASCII character for 0. If AL held 5, then effective address calculation added 5 to the address of Digits, bringing back the fifth table entry, which is the ASCII character for 5. And so it would go, for all 16 possible values that may be expressed in a 4-bit nibble. Basically, the code is used to translate a number to its corresponding ASCII character.

There are only 16 possible hexadecimal digits, so the conversion table in hexdump1 only needs to be 16 bytes long. A byte contains enough bits to represent 256 different values, so if we're going to translate byte-size values, we need a table with 256 entries. Technically, the ASCII character set only uses the first 128 values, but as I described earlier in this book, the "high" 128 values have often been assigned to special characters such as non-English letters, "box-draw" characters, mathematical symbols, and so on. One common use of character translation is to convert any characters with values higher than 128 to something lower than 128, to avoid havoc in older systems that can't deal with extended ASCII values.

Such a table is easy enough to define in an assembly language program:

```
UpCase:
        db 20h,20h,20h,20h,20h,20h,20h,20h,20h,09h,0Ah,20h,20h,20h,20h,20h
        db 20h,20h,20h,20h,20h,20h,20h,20h,20h,20h,20h,20h,20h,20h,20h,20h
        db 20h,21h,22h,23h,24h,25h,26h,27h,28h,29h,2Ah,2Bh,2Ch,2Dh,2Eh,2Fh
        db 30h,31h,32h,33h,34h,35h,36h,37h,38h,39h,3Ah,3Bh,3Ch,3Dh,3Eh,3Fh
        db 40h,41h,42h,43h,44h,45h,46h,47h,48h,49h,4Ah,4Bh,4Ch,4Dh,4Eh,4Fh
        db 50h,51h,52h,53h,54h,55h,56h,57h,58h,59h,5Ah,5Bh,5Ch,5Dh,5Eh,5Fh
        db 60h,41h,42h,43h,44h,45h,46h,47h,48h,49h,4Ah,4Bh,4Ch,4Dh,4Eh,4Fh
        db 50h,51h,52h,53h,54h,55h,56h,57h,58h,59h,5Ah,7Bh,7Ch,7Dh,7Eh,20h
```

```
db 20h,20h,20h,20h,20h,20h,20h,20h,20h,20h,20h,20h,20h,20h,20h,20h
db 20h,20h,20h,20h,20h,20h,20h,20h,20h,20h,20h,20h,20h,20h,20h,20h
db 20h,20h,20h,20h,20h,20h,20h,20h,20h,20h,20h,20h,20h,20h,20h,20h
db 20h,20h,20h,20h,20h,20h,20h,20h,20h,20h,20h,20h,20h,20h,20h,20h
db 20h,20h,20h,20h,20h,20h,20h,20h,20h,20h,20h,20h,20h,20h,20h,20h
db 20h,20h,20h,20h,20h,20h,20h,20h,20h,20h,20h,20h,20h,20h,20h,20h
db 20h,20h,20h,20h,20h,20h,20h,20h,20h,20h,20h,20h,20h,20h,20h,20h
db 20h,20h,20h,20h,20h,20h,20h,20h,20h,20h,20h,20h,20h,20h,20h,20h
```

The UpCase table is defined in 16 lines of 16 separate hexadecimal values. The fact that it's split across 16 lines is purely for readability on the screen or printed page and does not affect the binary table that NASM generates in the output .o file. Once it's in binary, it's 256 8-bit values in a row.

A quick syntactic note here: When defining tables (or any data structure containing multiple predefined values), commas are used to separate values within a single definition. There is no need for commas at the end of the lines of the DB definitions in the table. Each DB definition is separate and independent, but because they are adjacent in memory, we can treat the 16 DB definitions as a single table.

Any translation table can be thought of as expressing one or more "rules" governing what happens during the translation process. The UpCase table shown above expresses these translation rules:

- All lowercase ASCII characters are translated to uppercase.

- All printable ASCII characters less than 127 that are *not* lowercase are translated to themselves. (They're not precisely "left alone," but translated to the same characters.)

- All "high" character values from 127 through 255 are translated to the ASCII space character (32, or 20h.)

- All non-printable ASCII characters (basically, values 0–31, plus 127) are translated to spaces *except* for values 9 and 10.

- Character values 9 and 10 (tab and EOL) are translated as themselves.

Not bad for a single data item, eh? (Just imagine how much work it would be to do all that fussing purely with machine instructions!)

Translating with MOV or XLAT

So how do you use the UpCase table? Very simply:

1. Load the character to be translated into AL.

2. Create a memory reference using AL as the base term and UpCase as the displacement term, and MOV the byte at the memory reference into AL, replacing the original value used as the base term.

The MOV instruction would look like this:

```
mov al,byte [UpCase+al]
```

There's only one problem: *NASM won't let you do this.* The AL register can't take part in effective address calculations, nor can any of the other 8-bit registers. Enter XLAT.

The XLAT instruction is hard-coded to use certain registers in certain ways. Its two operands are implicit:

- The address of the translation table must be in EBX.

- The character to be translated must be in AL.

- The translated character will be returned in AL, replacing the character originally placed in AL.

With the registers set up in that way, the XLAT instruction is used all by its lonesome:

```
xlat
```

I'll be honest here: XLAT is less of a win than it used to be. In 32-bit protected mode, the same thing can be done with the following instruction:

```
mov al,byte [UpCase+eax]
```

There's only one catch: you must clear out any "leftover" values in the high 24 bits of EAX, or you could accidentally index far beyond the bounds of the translation table. The XLAT instruction uses only AL for the index, ignoring whatever else might be in the rest of EAX. Clearing EAX before loading the value to be translated into AL is done with a simple XOR EAX, EAX or MOV EAX, 0.

In truth, given XLAT's requirement that it use AL and EBX, it's a wash, but the larger topic of character translation via tables is really what I'm trying to present here. Listing 9-2 puts it all into action. The program as shown does exactly what the uppercaser2 program in Listing 8-2 does: it forces all lowercase characters in an input file to uppercase and writes them to an output file. I didn't call it "uppercaser3" because it is a general-purpose character translator. In this particular example, it translates lowercase characters to uppercase, but that's simply one of the rules that the UpCase table expresses. Change the table, and you change the rules. You can translate any or all of the 256 different values in a byte to any 256 value or values.

I've added a second table to the program for you to experiment with. The Custom table expresses these rules:

- All printable ASCII characters less than 127 are translated to themselves. (Again, they're not precisely "left alone" but translated to the same characters.)

- All "high" character values from 127 through 255 are translated to the ASCII space character (32, or 20h).

- All non-printable ASCII characters (basically, values 0–31, plus 127) are translated to spaces *except* for values 9 and 10.

- Character values 9 and 10 (tab and EOL) are translated as themselves.

Basically, it leaves all printable characters (plus tab and EOL) alone, and converts all other character values to 20h, the space character. You can substitute the label Custom for UpCase in the program, make changes to the Custom table, and try it out. Convert that pesky vertical bar to an exclamation point. Change all "Z" characters to "Q." Changing the rules is done by changing the table. The code does not change at all!

Listing 9-2: xlat1.asm

```
;   Executable name  : XLAT1
;   Version          : 1.0
;   Created date     : 2/11/2009
;   Last update      : 4/5/2009
;   Author           : Jeff Duntemann
;   Description      : A simple program in assembly for Linux, using NASM 2.05,
;     demonstrating the use of the XLAT instruction to alter text streams.
;
;   Build using these commands:
;     nasm -f elf -g -F stabs xlat1.asm
;     ld -o xlat1 xlat1.o
;

SECTION .data              ; Section containing initialized data

        StatMsg: db "Processing...",10
        StatLen: equ $-StatMsg
        DoneMsg: db "...done!",10
        DoneLen: equ $-DoneMsg

; The following translation table translates all lowercase characters to
; uppercase. It also translates all non-printable characters to spaces,
; except for LF and HT.
        UpCase:
        db 20h,20h,20h,20h,20h,20h,20h,20h,20h,09h,0Ah,20h,20h,20h,20h,20h
        db 20h,20h,20h,20h,20h,20h,20h,20h,20h,20h,20h,20h,20h,20h,20h,20h
        db 20h,21h,22h,23h,24h,25h,26h,27h,28h,29h,2Ah,2Bh,2Ch,2Dh,2Eh,2Fh
        db 30h,31h,32h,33h,34h,35h,36h,37h,38h,39h,3Ah,3Bh,3Ch,3Dh,3Eh,3Fh
        db 40h,41h,42h,43h,44h,45h,46h,47h,48h,49h,4Ah,4Bh,4Ch,4Dh,4Eh,4Fh
        db 50h,51h,52h,53h,54h,55h,56h,57h,58h,59h,5Ah,5Bh,5Ch,5Dh,5Eh,5Fh
        db 60h,41h,42h,43h,44h,45h,46h,47h,48h,49h,4Ah,4Bh,4Ch,4Dh,4Eh,4Fh
        db 50h,51h,52h,53h,54h,55h,56h,57h,58h,59h,5Ah,7Bh,7Ch,7Dh,7Eh,20h
```

Listing 9-2: xlat1.asm (*continued*)

```
        db 20h,20h,20h,20h,20h,20h,20h,20h,20h,20h,20h,20h,20h,20h,20h,20h
        db 20h,20h,20h,20h,20h,20h,20h,20h,20h,20h,20h,20h,20h,20h,20h,20h
        db 20h,20h,20h,20h,20h,20h,20h,20h,20h,20h,20h,20h,20h,20h,20h,20h
        db 20h,20h,20h,20h,20h,20h,20h,20h,20h,20h,20h,20h,20h,20h,20h,20h
        db 20h,20h,20h,20h,20h,20h,20h,20h,20h,20h,20h,20h,20h,20h,20h,20h
        db 20h,20h,20h,20h,20h,20h,20h,20h,20h,20h,20h,20h,20h,20h,20h,20h
        db 20h,20h,20h,20h,20h,20h,20h,20h,20h,20h,20h,20h,20h,20h,20h,20h
        db 20h,20h,20h,20h,20h,20h,20h,20h,20h,20h,20h,20h,20h,20h,20h,20h

; The following translation table is "stock" in that it translates all
; printable characters as themselves, and converts all non-printable
; characters to spaces except for LF and HT. You can modify this to
; translate anything you want to any character you want.
        Custom:
        db 20h,20h,20h,20h,20h,20h,20h,20h,20h,09h,0Ah,20h,20h,20h,20h,20h
        db 20h,20h,20h,20h,20h,20h,20h,20h,20h,20h,20h,20h,20h,20h,20h,20h
        db 20h,21h,22h,23h,24h,25h,26h,27h,28h,29h,2Ah,2Bh,2Ch,2Dh,2Eh,2Fh
        db 30h,31h,32h,33h,34h,35h,36h,37h,38h,39h,3Ah,3Bh,3Ch,3Dh,3Eh,3Fh
        db 40h,41h,42h,43h,44h,45h,46h,47h,48h,49h,4Ah,4Bh,4Ch,4Dh,4Eh,4Fh
        db 50h,51h,52h,53h,54h,55h,56h,57h,58h,59h,5Ah,5Bh,5Ch,5Dh,5Eh,5Fh
        db 60h,61h,62h,63h,64h,65h,66h,67h,68h,69h,6Ah,6Bh,6Ch,6Dh,6Eh,6Fh
        db 70h,71h,72h,73h,74h,75h,76h,77h,78h,79h,7Ah,7Bh,7Ch,7Dh,7Eh,20h
        db 20h,20h,20h,20h,20h,20h,20h,20h,20h,20h,20h,20h,20h,20h,20h,20h
        db 20h,20h,20h,20h,20h,20h,20h,20h,20h,20h,20h,20h,20h,20h,20h,20h
        db 20h,20h,20h,20h,20h,20h,20h,20h,20h,20h,20h,20h,20h,20h,20h,20h
        db 20h,20h,20h,20h,20h,20h,20h,20h,20h,20h,20h,20h,20h,20h,20h,20h
        db 20h,20h,20h,20h,20h,20h,20h,20h,20h,20h,20h,20h,20h,20h,20h,20h
        db 20h,20h,20h,20h,20h,20h,20h,20h,20h,20h,20h,20h,20h,20h,20h,20h
        db 20h,20h,20h,20h,20h,20h,20h,20h,20h,20h,20h,20h,20h,20h,20h,20h
        db 20h,20h,20h,20h,20h,20h,20h,20h,20h,20h,20h,20h,20h,20h,20h,20h


SECTION .bss                  ; Section containing uninitialized data


        READLEN      equ 1024      ; Length of buffer
        ReadBuffer: resb READLEN   ; Text buffer itself


SECTION .text                 ; Section containing code


global _start                 ; Linker needs this to find the entry point!


_start:
        nop                   ; This no-op keeps gdb happy...


; Display the "I'm working..." message via stderr:
        mov eax,4        ; Specify sys_write call
        mov ebx,2        ; Specify File Descriptor 2: Standard error
        mov ecx,StatMsg  ; Pass offset of the message
        mov edx,StatLen  ; Pass the length of the message
```

(continued)

Listing 9-2: xlat1.asm (*continued*)

```
        int 80h          ; Make kernel call

; Read a buffer full of text from stdin:
read:
        mov eax,3        ; Specify sys_read call
        mov ebx,0        ; Specify File Descriptor 0: Standard Input
        mov ecx,ReadBuffer  ; Pass offset of the buffer to read to
        mov edx,READLEN     ; Pass number of bytes to read at one pass
        int 80h
        mov ebp,eax      ; Copy sys_read return value for safekeeping
        cmp eax,0        ; If eax=0, sys_read reached EOF
        je done          ; Jump If Equal (to 0, from compare)

; Set up the registers for the translate step:
        mov ebx,UpCase   ; Place the offset of the table into ebx
        mov edx,ReadBuffer  ; Place the offset of the buffer into edx
        mov ecx,ebp      ; Place the number of bytes in the buffer into ecx

; Use the xlat instruction to translate the data in the buffer:
; (Note: the commented out instructions do the same work as XLAT;
; un-comment them and then comment out XLAT to try it!
translate:
;       xor eax,eax               ; Clear high 24 bits of eax
        mov al,byte [edx+ecx]     ; Load character into AL for translation
;       mov al,byte [UpCase+eax]  ; Translate character in AL via table
        xlat                      ; Translate character in AL via table
        mov byte [edx+ecx],al     ; Put the translated char back in the buffer
        dec ecx          ; Decrement character count
        jnz translate    ; If there are more chars in the buffer, repeat

; Write the buffer full of translated text to stdout:
write:
        mov eax,4               ; Specify sys_write call
        mov ebx,1               ; Specify File Descriptor 1: Standard output
        mov ecx,ReadBuffer      ; Pass offset of the buffer
        mov edx,ebp             ; Pass the # of bytes of data in the buffer
        int 80h                 ; Make kernel call
        jmp read                ; Loop back and load another buffer full

; Display the "I'm done" message via stderr:
done:
        mov eax,4               ; Specify sys_write call
        mov ebx,2               ; Specify File Descriptor 2: Standard error
        mov ecx,DoneMsg         ; Pass offset of the message
        mov edx,DoneLen         ; Pass the length of the message
        int 80h                 ; Make kernel call

; All done! Let's end this party:
```

Listing 9-2: xlat1.asm *(continued)*

```
        mov eax,1           ; Code for Exit Syscall
        mov ebx,0           ; Return a code of zero
        int 80H             ; Make kernel call
```

Tables Instead of Calculations

Standardization among computer systems has made character translation a lot less common than it used to be, but translation tables can be extremely useful in other areas. One of them is to perform faster math. Consider the following table:

```
Squares: db 0,1,4,9,16,25,36,49,64,81,100,121,144,169,196,225
```

No mystery here: Squares is a table of the squares of the numbers from 0–15. If you needed the square of 14 in a calculation, you could use MUL, which is very slow as instructions go, and requires two GP registers; or you could simply fetch down the result from the Squares table:

```
mov ecx,14
mov al,byte [Squares+ecx]
```

Voila! EAX now contains the square of 14. You can do the same trick with XLAT, though it requires that you use certain registers. Also remember that XLAT is limited to 8-bit quantities. The Squares table shown above is as large a squares value table as XLAT can use, because the next square value (of 16) is 256, which cannot be expressed in 8 bits.

Making the entries of a squares value lookup table 16 bits in size will enable you to include the squares of all integers up to 255. And if you give each entry in the table 32 bits, you can include the squares of integers up to 65,535—but that would be a *very* substantial table!

I don't have the space in this book to go very deeply into floating-point math, but using tables to look up values for things like square roots was once done very frequently. In recent years, the inclusion of math processors right on the CPU makes such techniques a lot less compelling. Still, when confronted with an integer math challenge, you should always keep the possibility of using table lookups somewhere in the corner of your mind.

CHAPTER 10

Dividing and Conquering

Using Procedures and Macros to Battle Program Complexity

Complexity kills—programs, at least. This was one of the first lessons I ever learned as a programmer, and it has stuck with me all these intervening 30-odd years.

So listen well: there is a programming language called APL (an acronym for *A Programming Language*, how clever) that has more than a little Martian in it. APL was the first computer language I ever learned (on a major IBM mainframe), and when I learned it, I learned a little more than just APL.

APL uses a very compact notation, including its very own character set, which bears little resemblance to our familiar ASCII. The character set has dozens of odd little symbols, each of which is capable of some astonishing power such as matrix inversion. You can do more in one line of APL than you can in one line of anything else I have ever learned since. The combination of the strange symbol set and the vanishingly compact notation makes it very hard to read and remember what a line of code in APL actually *does*.

So it was in 1977. Having mastered (or so I thought) the whole library of symbols, I set out to write a text formatter program. The program would justify right and left, center headers, and do a few other things of a sort that we take for granted today but which were still very exotic in the seventies.

The program grew over a period of a week to about 600 lines of squirmy little APL symbols. I got it to work, and it worked fine—as long as I didn't try to format a column that was more than 64 characters wide. Then everything came out scrambled.

Whoops. I printed the whole thing out and sat down to do some serious debugging. Then I realized with a feeling of sinking horror that, having finished the last part of the program, *I had no idea how the first part worked anymore.*

The special APL symbol set was only part of the problem. I soon came to realize that the most important mistake I had made was writing the whole thing as one 600-line monolithic block of code lines. There were no functional divisions, nothing to indicate what any 10-line portion of the code was trying to accomplish.

The Martians had won. I did the only thing possible: I scrapped it, and settled for ragged margins in my text. Like I said, complexity kills. This is as true of assembly language as it is true of APL, Java, C, Pascal, or any other programming language that has ever existed. Now that you can write reasonably complex programs in assembly, you had better learn how to manage that complexity, or you will find yourself abandoning a great deal of code simply because you can no longer remember (or figure out) how it works.

Boxes within Boxes

Managing complexity is the great challenge in programming. Key to the skill is something that sounds like Eastern mysticism, but which is really just an observation from life: *Within any action is a host of smaller actions.* Look inside your common activities. When you brush your teeth you do the following:

- Pick up your toothpaste tube.
- Unscrew the cap.
- Place the cap on the sink counter.
- Pick up your toothbrush.
- Squeeze toothpaste onto the brush from the middle of the tube.
- Put your toothbrush into your mouth.
- Work it back and forth vigorously.

And so on. When you brush your teeth, you perform every one of those actions. However, when you think about the sequence, you don't run through the whole list. You bring to mind the simple concept called "brushing teeth."

Furthermore, when you think about what's behind the action we call "getting up in the morning," you might assemble a list of activities like this:

- Shut off the clock radio.
- Climb out of bed.
- Put on your robe.

- Let the dogs out.
- Make breakfast.
- Eat breakfast.
- Brush your teeth.
- Shave.
- Shower.
- Get dressed.

Brushing your teeth is certainly on the list, but within the activity you call "brushing your teeth" is a whole list of smaller actions, as described earlier. The same can be said for most of the activities shown in the preceding list. How many individual actions, for example, does it take to put a reasonable breakfast together? And yet in one small, if sweeping, phrase, "getting up in the morning," you embrace that whole host of small and still smaller actions without having to laboriously trace through each one.

What I'm describing is the "Chinese boxes" method of fighting complexity. Getting up in the morning involves hundreds of little actions, so we divide the mass up into coherent chunks and set the chunks into little conceptual boxes. "Making breakfast" is in one box, "brushing teeth" is in another, "getting dressed" in still another, and so on. Closer inspection of any single box shows that its contents can be divided further into numerous boxes, and those smaller boxes into even smaller boxes.

This process doesn't (and can't) go on forever, but it should go on as long as it needs to in order to satisfy this criterion: *The contents of any one box should be understandable with only a little scrutiny.* No single box should contain anything so subtle or large and involved that it takes hours of staring and hair-pulling to figure it out.

Procedures As Boxes for Code

The mistake I made in writing my APL text formatter is that I threw the whole collection of 600 lines of APL code into one huge box marked "text formatter."

While I was writing it, I should have been keeping my eyes open for sequences of code statements that worked together at some identifiable task. When I spotted such sequences, I should have set them off as *procedures* and given each a descriptive name. Each sequence would then have a memory tag (its name) for the sequence's function. If it took 10 statements to justify a line of text, those 10 statements should have been named JustifyLine, and so on.

Xerox's legendary APL programmer Jim Dunn later told me that I shouldn't ever write an APL procedure that wouldn't fit on a single 25-line terminal screen. "More than 25 lines and you're doing too much in one procedure. Split it up,'' he said. Whenever I worked in APL after that, I adhered to that sage rule of thumb. The Martians still struck from time to time, but when they did, it was no longer a total loss.

All computer languages in common use today implement procedures in one form or another, and assembly language is no exception. Your assembly language program may have numerous procedures. In fact, there's no limit to the *number* of procedures you can include in a program, as long as the total number of bytes of code contained by all the procedures together, plus whatever data they use, does not exceed the two-and-change gigabytes that Linux will allocate to a single user-space program

Needless to say, that's a *lot* of code. Even the largest commercial applications like OpenOffice aren't that big. Whatever complexity you can generate in assembly language can be managed with procedures.

Let's start in early with an example of procedures in action. Read Listing 10-1 closely and let's look at what makes it work, and (more to the point) what helps it remain comprehensible.

Listing 10-1: hexdump2.asm

```
;   Executable name  : hexdump2
;   Version          : 1.0
;   Created date     : 4/15/2009
;   Last update      : 4/20/2009
;   Author           : Jeff Duntemann
;   Description      : A simple hex dump utility demonstrating the use of
;                      assembly language procedures
;
;   Build using these commands:
;     nasm -f elf -g -F stabs hexdump2.asm
;     ld -o hexdump2 hexdump2.o
;

SECTION .bss                      ; Section containing uninitialized data

   BUFFLEN EQU 10
   Buff resb BUFFLEN

SECTION .data                     ; Section containing initialized data

; Here we have two parts of a single useful data structure, implementing
; the text line of a hex dump utility. The first part displays 16 bytes in
; hex separated by spaces. Immediately following is a 16-character line
; delimited by vertical bar characters. Because they are adjacent, the two
; parts can be referenced separately or as a single contiguous unit.
; Remember that if DumpLin is to be used separately, you must append an
; EOL before sending it to the Linux console.
```

Listing 10-1: hexdump2.asm (*continued*)

```
DumpLin: db " 00 00 00 00 00 00 00 00 00 00 00 00 00 00 00 00 "
DUMPLEN  EQU $-DumpLin
ASCLin:  db "|................|",10
ASCLEN   EQU $-ASCLin
FULLLEN  EQU $-DumpLin

; The HexDigits table is used to convert numeric values to their hex
; equivalents. Index by nybble without a scale: [HexDigits+eax]
HexDigits: db "0123456789ABCDEF"

; This table is used for ASCII character translation, into the ASCII
; portion of the hex dump line, via XLAT or ordinary memory lookup.
; All printable characters "play through" as themselves. The high 128
; characters are translated to ASCII period (2Eh). The non-printable
; characters in the low 128 are also translated to ASCII period, as is
; char 127.
DotXlat:
        db 2Eh,2Eh,2Eh,2Eh,2Eh,2Eh,2Eh,2Eh,2Eh,2Eh,2Eh,2Eh,2Eh,2Eh,2Eh,2Eh
        db 2Eh,2Eh,2Eh,2Eh,2Eh,2Eh,2Eh,2Eh,2Eh,2Eh,2Eh,2Eh,2Eh,2Eh,2Eh,2Eh
        db 20h,21h,22h,23h,24h,25h,26h,27h,28h,29h,2Ah,2Bh,2Ch,2Dh,2Eh,2Fh
        db 30h,31h,32h,33h,34h,35h,36h,37h,38h,39h,3Ah,3Bh,3Ch,3Dh,3Eh,3Fh
        db 40h,41h,42h,43h,44h,45h,46h,47h,48h,49h,4Ah,4Bh,4Ch,4Dh,4Eh,4Fh
        db 50h,51h,52h,53h,54h,55h,56h,57h,58h,59h,5Ah,5Bh,5Ch,5Dh,5Eh,5Fh
        db 60h,61h,62h,63h,64h,65h,66h,67h,68h,69h,6Ah,6Bh,6Ch,6Dh,6Eh,6Fh
        db 70h,71h,72h,73h,74h,75h,76h,77h,78h,79h,7Ah,7Bh,7Ch,7Dh,7Eh,2Eh
        db 2Eh,2Eh,2Eh,2Eh,2Eh,2Eh,2Eh,2Eh,2Eh,2Eh,2Eh,2Eh,2Eh,2Eh,2Eh,2Eh
        db 2Eh,2Eh,2Eh,2Eh,2Eh,2Eh,2Eh,2Eh,2Eh,2Eh,2Eh,2Eh,2Eh,2Eh,2Eh,2Eh
        db 2Eh,2Eh,2Eh,2Eh,2Eh,2Eh,2Eh,2Eh,2Eh,2Eh,2Eh,2Eh,2Eh,2Eh,2Eh,2Eh
        db 2Eh,2Eh,2Eh,2Eh,2Eh,2Eh,2Eh,2Eh,2Eh,2Eh,2Eh,2Eh,2Eh,2Eh,2Eh,2Eh
        db 2Eh,2Eh,2Eh,2Eh,2Eh,2Eh,2Eh,2Eh,2Eh,2Eh,2Eh,2Eh,2Eh,2Eh,2Eh,2Eh
        db 2Eh,2Eh,2Eh,2Eh,2Eh,2Eh,2Eh,2Eh,2Eh,2Eh,2Eh,2Eh,2Eh,2Eh,2Eh,2Eh
        db 2Eh,2Eh,2Eh,2Eh,2Eh,2Eh,2Eh,2Eh,2Eh,2Eh,2Eh,2Eh,2Eh,2Eh,2Eh,2Eh
        db 2Eh,2Eh,2Eh,2Eh,2Eh,2Eh,2Eh,2Eh,2Eh,2Eh,2Eh,2Eh,2Eh,2Eh,2Eh,2Eh


SECTION .text            ; Section containing code


;-----------------------------------------------------------------------
; ClearLine: Clear a hex dump line string to 16 0 values
; UPDATED:  4/15/2009
; IN:       Nothing
; RETURNS:  Nothing
; MODIFIES: Nothing
; CALLS:    DumpChar
; DESCRIPTION: The hex dump line string is cleared to binary 0 by
;              calling DumpChar 16 times, passing it 0 each time.

ClearLine:
```

(*continued*)

Listing 10-1: hexdump2.asm (*continued*)

```
        Pushad          ; Save all caller's GP registers
        mov edx,15      ; We're going to go 16 pokes, counting from 0
.poke:  mov eax,0       ; Tell DumpChar to poke a '0'
        call DumpChar   ; Insert the '0' into the hex dump string
        sub edx,1       ; DEC doesn't affect CF!
        jae .poke       ; Loop back if EDX >= 0
        popad           ; Restore all caller's GP registers
        ret             ; Go home


;-------------------------------------------------------------------------------
; DumpChar:     "Poke" a value into the hex dump line string.
; UPDATED:      4/15/2009
; IN:           Pass the 8-bit value to be poked in EAX.
;               Pass the value's position in the line (0-15) in EDX
; RETURNS:      Nothing
; MODIFIES:     EAX, ASCLin, DumpLin
; CALLS:        Nothing
; DESCRIPTION:  The value passed in EAX will be put in both the hex dump
;               portion and in the ASCII portion, at the position passed
;               in EDX, represented by a space where it is not a
;               printable character.

DumpChar:
        push ebx        ; Save caller's EBX
        push edi        ; Save caller's EDI
; First we insert the input char into the ASCII portion of the dump line
        mov bl,byte [DotXlat+eax]   ; Translate nonprintables to '.'
        mov byte [ASCLin+edx+1],bl  ; Write to ASCII portion
; Next we insert the hex equivalent of the input char in the hex portion
; of the hex dump line:
        mov ebx,eax                 ; Save a second copy of the input char
        lea edi,[edx*2+edx]         ; Calc offset into line string (EDX X 3)
; Look up low nybble character and insert it into the string:
        and eax,0000000Fh           ; Mask out all but the low nybble
        mov al,byte [HexDigits+eax] ; Look up the char equiv. of nybble
        mov byte [DumpLin+edi+2],al ; Write the char equiv. to line string
; Look up high nybble character and insert it into the string:
        and ebx,000000F0h           ; Mask out all the but second-lowest nybble
        shr ebx,4                   ; Shift high 4 bits of byte into low 4 bits
        mov bl,byte [HexDigits+ebx] ; Look up char equiv. of nybble
        mov byte [DumpLin+edi+1],bl ; Write the char equiv. to line string
;Done! Let's go home:
        pop edi                     ; Restore caller's EDI
        pop ebx                     ; Restore caller's EBX
        ret                         ; Return to caller
```

Listing 10-1: hexdump2.asm (*continued*)

```
;-------------------------------------------------------------------
; PrintLine:   Displays DumpLin to stdout
; UPDATED:     4/15/2009
; IN:          Nothing
; RETURNS:     Nothing
; MODIFIES:    Nothing
; CALLS:       Kernel sys_write
; DESCRIPTION: The hex dump line string DumpLin is displayed to stdout
;              using INT 80h sys_write. All GP registers are preserved.

PrintLine:
        pushad              ; Save all caller's GP registers
        mov eax,4           ; Specify sys_write call
        mov ebx,1           ; Specify File Descriptor 1: Standard output
        mov ecx,DumpLin     ; Pass offset of line string
        mov edx,FULLLEN     ; Pass size of the line string
        int 80h             ; Make kernel call to display line string
        popad               ; Restore all caller's GP registers
        ret                 ; Return to caller


;-------------------------------------------------------------------
; LoadBuff:    Fills a buffer with data from stdin via INT 80h sys_read
; UPDATED:     4/15/2009
; IN:          Nothing
; RETURNS:     # of bytes read in EBP
; MODIFIES:    ECX, EBP, Buff
; CALLS:       Kernel sys_write
; DESCRIPTION: Loads a buffer full of data (BUFFLEN bytes) from stdin
;              using INT 80h sys_read and places it in Buff. Buffer
;              offset counter ECX is zeroed, because we're starting in
;              on a new buffer full of data. Caller must test value in
;              EBP: If EBP contains zero on return, we hit EOF on stdin.
;              Less than 0 in EBP on return indicates some kind of error.

LoadBuff:
        push eax            ; Save caller's EAX
        push ebx            ; Save caller's EBX
        push edx            ; Save caller's EDX
        mov eax,3           ; Specify sys_read call
        mov ebx,0           ; Specify File Descriptor 0: Standard Input
        mov ecx,Buff        ; Pass offset of the buffer to read to
        mov edx,BUFFLEN     ; Pass number of bytes to read at one pass
        int 80h             ; Call sys_read to fill the buffer
        mov ebp,eax         ; Save # of bytes read from file for later
        xor ecx,ecx         ; Clear buffer pointer ECX to 0
        pop edx             ; Restore caller's EDX
        pop ebx             ; Restore caller's EBX
```

(continued)

Listing 10-1: hexdump2.asm (*continued*)

```
        pop eax         ; Restore caller's EAX
        ret             ; And return to caller


GLOBAL _start

; --------------------------------------------------------------------
; MAIN PROGRAM BEGINS HERE
;---------------------------------------------------------------------
_start:
        nop             ; No-ops for GDB
        nop

; Whatever initialization needs doing before the loop scan starts is here:
        xor esi,esi     ; Clear total byte counter to 0
        call LoadBuff   ; Read first buffer of data from stdin
        cmp ebp,0       ; If ebp=0, sys_read reached EOF on stdin
        jbe Exit

; Go through the buffer and convert binary byte values to hex digits:
Scan:
        xor eax,eax         ; Clear EAX to 0
        mov al,byte[Buff+ecx] ; Get a byte from the buffer into AL
        mov edx,esi         ; Copy total counter into EDX
        and edx,0000000Fh   ; Mask out lowest 4 bits of char counter
        call DumpChar       ; Call the char poke procedure

; Bump the buffer pointer to the next character and see if buffer's done:
        inc esi         ; Increment total chars processed counter
        inc ecx         ; Increment buffer pointer
        cmp ecx,ebp     ; Compare with # of chars in buffer
        jb .modTest     ; If we've processed all chars in buffer...
        call LoadBuff   ; ...go fill the buffer again
        cmp ebp,0       ; If ebp=0, sys_read reached EOF on stdin
        jbe Done        ; If we got EOF, we're done

; See if we're at the end of a block of 16 and need to display a line:
.modTest:
        test esi,0000000Fh  ; Test 4 lowest bits in counter for 0
        jnz Scan            ; If counter is *not* modulo 16, loop back
        call PrintLine      ; ...otherwise print the line
        call ClearLine      ; Clear hex dump line to 0's
        jmp Scan            ; Continue scanning the buffer

; All done! Let's end this party:
Done:
        call PrintLine  ; Print the "leftovers" line
Exit:   mov eax,1       ; Code for Exit Syscall
        mov ebx,0       ; Return a code of zero
        int 80H         ; Make kernel call
```

I admit, that looks a little scary. It's more than 200 lines of code, and by a significant fraction the largest program in this book so far. What it does, however, is fairly simple. It's a straightforward extension of the hexdump1 program from Listing 9-1. If you recall, a hex dump program takes a file of any kind (text, executable, binary data, whatever) and displays it on the screen (here, on the Linux console) such that each byte in the program is given in hexadecimal. Listing 9-1 did that much. What hexdump2 adds is a second display column in which any printable ASCII characters (letters, numbers, symbols) are shown in their "true" form, with nonprintable characters represented by a space-holder character. This space-holder character is typically an ASCII period character, but that's merely a convention; it could be anything at all.

You can display a hex dump of any Linux file using hexdump2, invoking it this way:

```
$./hexdump2 < (filename)
```

The I/O redirection operator < takes whatever data exists in the file you name to its right and pipes that data into standard input. The hexdump2 program takes data from standard input and prints it out in hex dump format, 16 bytes to a line, for as many lines as it takes to show the entire file.

For example, a hex dump of the hexdump2 program's own makefile is shown here:

```
68 65 78 64 75 6D 70 32 3A 20 68 65 78 64 75 6D |hexdump2: hexdum|
70 32 2E 6F 0A 09 6C 64 20 2D 6F 20 68 65 78 64 |p2.o..ld -o hexd|
75 6D 70 32 20 68 65 78 64 75 6D 70 32 2E 6F 0A |ump2 hexdump2.o.|
68 65 78 64 75 6D 70 32 2E 6F 3A 20 68 65 78 64 |hexdump2.o: hexd|
75 6D 70 32 2E 61 73 6D 0A 09 6E 61 73 6D 20 2D |ump2.asm..nasm -|
66 20 65 6C 66 20 2D 67 20 2D 46 20 73 74 61 62 |f elf -g -F stab|
73 20 68 65 78 64 75 6D 70 32 2E 61 73 6D 0A 00 |s hexdump2.asm..|
```

Makefiles are pure text, so there aren't a lot of nonprintable characters in the dump. Notice, however, that tab and EOL, the two nonprintable characters generally present in Linux text files, are clearly visible, both in hex form in the left column and as periods in the right column. This is useful, because when the file is shown as pure text on the console, tab characters and EOL characters are invisible. (They have visible *effects*, but you can't see the characters themselves.) Having a hex dump of a file shows you precisely where any tab and EOL characters fall in the file, and how many of them exist in any particular place.

Given the complexity of hexdump2, it may be useful to show you how the program works through pseudo-code before we get too deeply into the mechanics of how a procedure mechanism operates internally. Here is how the program works, from a (high) height:

```
As long as there is data available from stdin, do the following:
    Read data from stdin
```

```
        Convert data bytes to a suitable hexadecimal/ASCII display form
  Insert formatted data bytes into a 16-byte hex dump line
        Every 16 bytes, display the hex dump line
```

This is a good example of an early pseudo-code iteration, when you know roughly what you want the program to do but are still a little fuzzy on exactly how to do it. It should give you a head-start understanding of the much more detailed (and *how*-oriented) pseudo-code that follows:

```
Zero out the byte count total (ESI) and offset counter (ECX)
Call LoadBuff to fill a buffer with first batch of data from stdin
        Test number of bytes fetched into the buffer from stdin
              If the number of bytes was 0, the file was empty; jump to Exit
Scan:  Get a byte from the buffer and put it in AL
        Derive the byte's position in the hex dump line string
        Call DumpChar to poke the byte into the line string
        Increment the total counter and the buffer offset counter
        Test and see if we've processed the last byte in the buffer:
              If so, call LoadBuff to fill the buffer with data from stdin
                Test number of bytes fetched into the buffer from stdin
                   If the number of bytes was 0, we hit EOF; jump to Exit
        Test and see if we've poked 16 bytes into the hex dump line
        If so, call PrintLine to display the hex dump line
Loop back to Scan
Exit:  Shut down the program gracefully per Linux requirements
```

Unlike the examples of pseudo-code presented in Chapter 8, there are explicit references to procedures here. I think that they may be almost self-explanatory from context, which is the sign of a good procedure. For example, "Call LoadBuff" means "execute a procedure that loads the buffer." That's what LoadBuff does, and that's *all* LoadBuff does. You don't have to confront all the details of how LoadBuff does its work. This makes it easier to grasp the larger flow of logic expressed by the program as a whole.

Look again through the Listing 10-1 code proper and see if you can understand how the preceding pseudo-code relates to the actual machine instructions. Once you have a grip on that, we can begin talking about procedures in more depth.

Calling and Returning

Right near the beginning of the main program block in hexdump2 is a machine instruction I haven't used before in this book:

```
call LoadBuff
```

The label `LoadBuff` refers to a procedure. As you might have gathered (especially if you've programmed in an older language such as BASIC or FORTRAN), `CALL LoadBuff` simply tells the CPU to go off and execute a procedure named `LoadBuff`, and then come back when `LoadBuff` finishes running. `LoadBuff` is defined earlier in Listing 10-1, but for clarity in the following discussion I reproduce it below.

`LoadBuff` is a good first example of a procedure because it's fairly straight-line in terms of its logic, and it uses instructions and concepts already discussed. Like assembly language programs generally, a procedure like `LoadBuff` starts executing at the top, runs sequentially through the instructions in its body, and at some point ends. The end does not necessarily have to be at the very bottom of the sequence of instructions, but the "end" of a procedure is always the place where the procedure goes back to the part of the program that called it. This place is wherever you see `CALL`'s alter ego, `RET` (for "return").

```
LoadBuff:
        push eax            ; Save caller's EAX
        push ebx            ; Save caller's EBX
        push edx            ; Save caller's EDX
        mov eax,3           ; Specify sys_read call
        mov ebx,0           ; Specify File Descriptor 0: Standard Input
        mov ecx,Buff        ; Pass offset of the buffer to read to
        mov edx,BUFFLEN     ; Pass number of bytes to read at one pass
        int 80h             ; Call sys_read to fill the buffer
        mov ebp,eax         ; Save # of bytes read from file for later
        xor ecx,ecx         ; Clear buffer pointer ECX to 0
        pop edx             ; Restore caller's EDX
        pop ebx             ; Restore caller's EBX
        pop eax             ; Restore caller's EAX
        ret                 ; And return to caller
```

In a very simple example like `LoadBuff`, `RET` is at the very end of the sequence of instructions in the procedure. However, `RET` may be anywhere in the procedure, and in some situations you may find it simplest to have more than one `RET` in a procedure. Which `RET` actually takes execution back to the caller depends on what the procedure does and what circumstances it encounters, but that's immaterial. Each `RET` is an "exit point" back to the code that called the procedure, and (more important) all `RET` instructions within a procedure take execution back to the very same location: the instruction immediately after the `CALL` instruction that invoked the procedure.

The important points of procedure structure are these:

- A procedure must begin with a label, which is (as you should recall) an identifier followed by a colon.

- Somewhere within the procedure, there must be at least one RET instruction.

- There may be more than one RET instruction. Execution has to come back from a procedure by way of a RET instruction, but there can be more than one exit door from a procedure. Which exit is taken depends on the procedure's flow of execution, but with conditional jump instructions you can have exits anywhere it satisfies the requirements of the procedure's logic.

- A procedure may use CALL to call another procedure. (More on this shortly.)

The means by which CALL and RET operate may sound familiar: CALL first pushes the address of the *next* instruction after itself onto the stack. Then CALL transfers execution to the address represented by the label that names the procedure—in this case, LoadBuff. The instructions contained in the procedure execute. Finally, the procedure is terminated by the instruction RET. The RET instruction pops the address off the top of the stack and transfers execution to that address. Because the address pushed was the address of the first instruction *after* the CALL instruction, execution continues as though CALL had not changed the flow of instruction execution at all (see Figure 10-1).

This should remind you strongly of how software interrupts work, as I explained in connection with the INT instruction in Chapter 8. The main difference is that the caller *does* know the exact address of the code it wishes to call. Apart from that, it's very close to being the same process. Note, however, that RET and IRET are *not* interchangeable. CALL works with RET just as INT works with IRET. Don't get those return instructions confused!

Calls within Calls

Within a procedure you can do anything that you can do within the main program itself. This includes calling other procedures from within a procedure, and making INT 80h calls to Linux kernel services.

There's a simple example in hexdump2: The ClearLine procedure calls the DumpChar procedure to "clear" the hex dump line variable DumpLin:

```
ClearLine:
        pushad              ; Save all caller's GP registers
        mov edx,15          ; We're going to go 16 pokes, counting from 0
.poke:  mov eax,0           ; Tell DumpChar to poke a '0'
        call DumpChar       ; Insert the '0' into the hex dump string
        sub edx,1           ; DEC doesn't affect CF!
        jae .poke           ; Loop back if EDX >= 0
        popad               ; Restore all caller's GP registers
        ret                 ; Go home
```

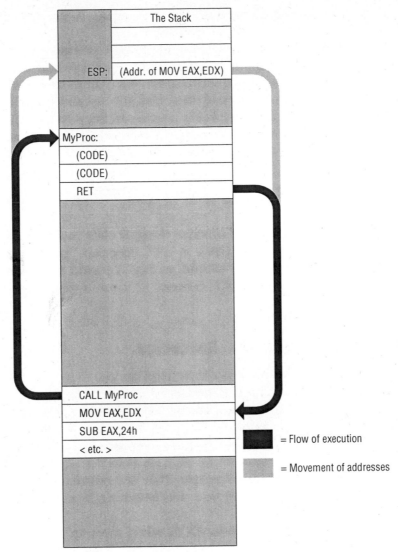

Figure 10-1: Calling a procedure and returning

Basically, what ClearLine does is make a special-case use of the DumpChar procedure, which I'll explain in detail shortly. When filled with data and displayed to the console, the DumpLin variable looks like this:

```
75 6D 70 32 2E 61 73 6D 0A 09 6E 61 73 6D 20 2D |ump2.asm..nasm -|
```

Each two-character hex value, and each ASCII character in the ASCII column on the right, was inserted by a single call to DumpChar. It takes 16 calls to DumpChar to "fill" the DumpLin variable. At that point it can be displayed. After DumpLin is displayed to the console, hexdump2 continues its loop and begins filling DumpLin again. Every 16 calls to DumpChar, hexdump2 displays DumpLin to the console . . . except for the *last* time.

A file being dumped to the console might not be a precise multiple of 16 bytes long, so the final display of DumpLin could be of a partial line of two, three, nine, eleven, or however many characters less than sixteen, which I call the "leftovers." When a partial line is displayed, the last several bytes in the line dump may be "old" data sent to the console on the previous display of DumpLin. To avoid this, DumpLin is cleared to zero values immediately after each display. This is what ClearLine does. After a call to ClearLine, DumpLin looks like this:

```
00 00 00 00 00 00 00 00 00 00 00 00 00 00 00 00 |................|
```

ClearLine does the simple and obvious thing: It calls DumpChar 16 times, each time passing DumpChar the value 0 in EAX. DumpChar "pokes" an ASCII equivalent of both the hex value 00 and an ASCII period to represent the 0 value in all positions in the ASCII column. (0 is not a displayable ASCII character.)

The Dangers of Accidental Recursion

Calling procedures from within procedures requires you to pay at least a little attention to one thing: stack space. Remember that each procedure call pushes a 32-bit return address onto the stack. This return address is not removed from the stack until the RET instruction for that procedure executes. If you execute another CALL instruction before returning from a procedure, then the second CALL instruction pushes another return address onto the stack. If you keep calling procedures from within procedures, then one return address will pile up on the stack for each CALL until you start returning from all those *nested* procedures.

This used to be a real issue under DOS, when memory was scarce and programs might allocate only a few hundred bytes of memory to the stack, sometimes less. Each address pushed onto the stack makes the stack grow down toward the .data and .text sections of the program. Calling too "deep" could make the stack collide with data or code, causing a program crash that typically took DOS with it. Under Linux you have a *great* deal more memory, and you would have to nest procedures literally millions deep to get into trouble, and that would be an ambitious program indeed.

However, you can still get in trouble by misusing an advanced programming technique called *recursion*. In recursion, a procedure calls *itself* to get its work done. This often seems peculiar to beginners, but it's a respected and legitimate way to express a certain kind of program logic. The trick with recursion, of course, is knowing when to stop. For every CALL to itself, a recursive procedure must eventually execute a RET. Even if the recursive procedure calls itself dozens or hundreds of times, as long as the CALL instructions balance the RET instructions, nothing bad will happen.

Problems begin when you write a recursive procedure badly, and the logic that determines when to use that all-important RET instruction is miscoded. When to return is generally governed by a conditional jump instruction. Get the sense or the flag etiquette of that instruction wrong, and the procedure never returns, but continues calling itself again, and again, and again. On a modern PC, an assembly language procedure can call itself a million times in a second or less. At that point the stack collides with the code, and Linux hands you a segmentation fault.

I'm not going to be explaining recursion in this book, and I only mention it because it's possible to use recursion *accidentally*. In keeping with our current example, suppose you were coding ClearLine late at night, and at the point where ClearLine calls DumpChar, you muddleheadedly write CALL ClearLine where you intended to write CALL DumpChar. Don't shake your head: I've done it more than once, and sooner or later you'll do it too. Clearline was not designed to be recursive, so it will go into a not-quite-endless loop, calling itself until it runs out of stack space and triggers a segmentation fault.

Add "accidental recursion" to the list of bugs you look for when Linux hands you a segmentation fault. It belongs to the class of bugs I call "uncommon, but inevitable."

A Flag Etiquette Bug to Beware Of

And while we're talking bugs, the ClearLine procedure is pretty simple, and does a simple job. It also provides a useful teaching moment about a flags-related bug that trips up beginners regularly. Take a look at the following alternate way of coding ClearLine:

```
ClearLine:
        pushad          ; Save all caller's GP registers
        mov edx,15      ; We're going to go 16 pokes
.Poke:  mov eax,0       ; Tell DumpChar to poke a '0'
        call DumpChar   ; Insert the '0' into the hex dump string
        dec edx         ; THIS WON'T WORK!!!!!
        jae .Poke       ; Loop back if EDX >= 0
        popad           ; Restore all caller's GP registers
        ret             ; Go home
```

Would this work? If you think so, think again. Yes, we're counting down from 15 to 0, making 16 passes through a simple loop. Yes, the DEC instruction is used a lot in loops, when we're counting down to zero. But this loop is a little different, as we need to do some work when the counter value in EDX is 0, and then decrement one more time. The conditional jump shown is JAE, Jump Above or Equal. It must jump back to Poke when the value in EDX goes below zero. DEC will count a counter down to zero and then below zero just fine, so why won't JAE jump after DEC? The sense is right.

The flag etiquette, however, is wrong. If you check the instruction reference on page 534 for JAE, you'll see that it jumps when CF=0. The CPU doesn't understand the "sense" in JAE. It's not a mind; it's just a very small pile of very clean sand. All it understands is that the JAE instruction jumps when CF=0. If you look up the DEC instruction on page 528 and scrutinize the flags list, you'll see that DEC *doesn't affect CF at all*, and CF is what JAE examines before it decides whether to jump or not jump.

This is why we use the SUB instruction to decrement the counter register in this case, because SUB *does* affect CF, and allows the JAE instruction to work correctly. There are no speed issues; SUB is precisely as fast as DEC. The lesson here is that you need to understand how the conditional jump instructions interpret the various flags. The sense of a jump can be deceiving. It's the flag etiquette that matters.

Procedures and the Data They Need

Programs get their work done by acting on data: data in buffers, data in named variables, and data in registers. Procedures are often created to do a single type of manipulation on a particular type of data. Programs that call such procedures treat them as data meat-grinders: data of one sort goes in, and transformed data of another sort comes out.

In addition, data is often handed to a procedure in order to control or direct the work that it does. A procedure may need a count value to know how many times to execute an operation, for example, or it may need a bit mask to apply to some data values for some reason, and it may not be precisely the same bit mask every time.

When you write procedures, you need to decide what data the procedure needs to do its work, and how that data will be made available to the procedure. There are two general classes of data in assembly work (and in most programming in non-exotic languages,) differentiated by method of access: *global* and *local*.

Global data is very common in pure assembly work, especially for smallish programs like the ones presented in this book. Global data is accessible to any code anywhere in the program. A global data item is defined in the .data or .bss sections of the program. CPU registers are also containers for global data, because the registers are part of the CPU and may be accessed from anywhere in a program.

The notion of global data gets more complex when you separate a program into a main program and multiple groups of procedures called *libraries*, as I'll explain a little later in this chapter.

For simple programs, the obvious way to pass data to a procedure is often the best: Place the data in one or more registers and then call the procedure. We've seen this mechanism at work already, in making calls to Linux kernel services through INT 80h. You place the service number in EAX, the file descriptor in EBX, the address of a string in ECX, and the length of the string in EDX. Then you make the call with INT 80h.

It's no different for ordinary procedures. You write a procedure under the assumption that when the procedure begins running, the values that it needs will be in particular registers. You have to make sure that the code calling the procedure places the right values in the right registers before calling the procedure, but it's really no more complex than that.

Tables, buffers, and other named data items are accessed from procedures just as they are from any other part of the program, via memory addressing expressions "between the brackets."

Saving the Caller's Registers

Once you start writing significant programs in assembly, you'll realize that you can never have enough registers, and (unlike higher-level languages like C and Pascal) you can't just create more when you need them. Registers have to be used carefully, and you'll find that within any significant program, all registers are generally in use all of the time.

Ducking out into a procedure from inside your main program (or from inside another procedure) carries a specific and subtle problem. You can call a procedure from anywhere—which means that *you won't always know what registers are already in use when the procedure is called*. As explained in the previous section, registers are the primary way that callers pass values into procedures, and the primary way that procedures return values to callers. A procedure needs registers to work, and so do other procedures and the main program. No procedure can assume that EAX or EBP or any other register will always be "free" any time that it's called.

This is why well-written procedures always save the values of any registers that they modify before they begin loading new values into registers, or making other changes to data in registers. If a procedure only examines a register value (but doesn't change it), then this saving doesn't need to be done. For example, a procedure may assume that a certain register contains a counter value that it needs to index into a table, and it can use that register freely as long as no changes to its value are made. However, whenever a register is changed by a procedure (unless the caller explicitly expects a return value into a register), it should be saved, and then restored before the procedure executes RET to go back to the caller.

Saving the caller's register values is done with PUSH:

```
push ebx
push esi
push edi
```

Each PUSH instruction pushes a 32-bit register value onto the stack. Those values will remain safely on the stack until they are popped back into the same registers just prior to returning to the caller:

```
pop edi
pop esi
pop ebx
ret
```

There's an absolutely crucial detail here, one that causes a multitude of very peculiar program bugs: *The caller's values must be popped from the stack in the reverse order from how they were pushed.* In other words, if you push EBX, followed by ESI, followed by EDI, you must pop them from the stack as EDI, followed by ESI, followed by EBX. The CPU will obediently pop them into any registers in any order you specify, but if you get the order wrong, you will essentially be *changing* the caller's registers instead of saving them. What had been in EBX may now be in EDI, and the caller's program logic may simply go berserk.

I showed how this happens when I originally explained the stack in Chapter 8, but it may not have sunk in at the time. Take a quick flip back to Figure 8-3 on page 253 and see what happens in the rightmost column. The value of CX was pushed onto the stack, but the next instruction was POP DX. What had been in CX was now in DX. If that's what you want, fine—and sometimes it may be the best way to solve a particular problem; but if you're pushing register values to preserve them, the order of the pushes and pops is absolutely critical.

In some cases a procedure uses most or all of the general-purpose registers, and there is a pair of instructions that will push and pop all GP registers at one go. Look back to the ClearLine procedure shown earlier. The very first instruction in the procedure is PUSHAD, and the very last before the RET is POPAD. PUSHAD pushes all GP registers onto the stack, including the stack pointer ESP. POPAD pops all those pushed register values back into their correct registers, in the correct order. (The value of ESP is a special case, and even though its value was pushed onto the stack, PUSHAD discards the copy of ESP popped from the stack when it executes.)

I used PUSHAD and POPAD in ClearLine for a particular reason: ClearLine returns no values to the caller. It does a simple job, and all of its actions are focused on the DumpLin variable. Because it doesn't need the registers to send anything back to the caller, I chose to preserve everything, even registers unaffected by ClearLine.

Isn't this wasteful? Not necessarily. Yes, it takes time to push a register on the stack, but remember: in *every* case where you weigh whether one instruction takes more time to execute than another, you must consider how many times that instruction is executed. If an instruction is within a tight loop that executes sequentially tens of thousands or millions of times, instruction speed is important. On the other hand, if an instruction is executed only a few times over the course of a program's run, its speed is at best a minor consideration. ClearLine executes only once for every 16 bytes that hexdump2 processes; and even using PUSHAD and POPAD, its execution time is a fraction of the time taken by the INT 80h call to Linux kernel services that precedes it, in the PrintLine procedure.

PrintLine is the same way: the time it takes to execute is "swamped" by the time required by the INT 80h call to sys_write that it makes, so using PUSHAD and POPAD in no way affects the perceived speed of the program as a whole.

Of course, if the caller expects a procedure to pass a value back in a register, the procedure cannot use PUSHAD and POPAD. In such cases, you simply have to discern which registers must be preserved for the caller, and which registers have to carry some results back on return. For a good example, consider the LoadBuff procedure shown on page 337. LoadBuff preserves three of the caller's registers: EAX, EBX, and EDX. However, it makes changes to two of the other registers, ECX and EBP, without preserving them.

Why? The ECX register contains a "global" value: the position of the next character to be processed in the file buffer variable Buff. LoadBuff is called when one buffer full of data has been completely processed, and a new load of data must be brought in from stdin. When the buffer is refilled, the buffer counter has to be reset to 0 so that the processing can begin again and work through the new data from its beginning. LoadBuff does this, and the reset ECX is passed back to the caller.

EBP has a mission, too: it carries back the number of bytes loaded into Buff by the INT 80h call to sys_read. The call to sys_read requests the number of bytes specified by the BUFFLEN equate near the beginning of the program. However, because few files will be exact multiples of BUFFLEN long, the number of bytes in the last batch of data brought from stdin will be less than BUFFLEN. This value is also considered global, and is used by the main program to determine when the current buffer has been completely processed.

Note that the caller can preserve its own registers, and this is done sometimes. For example, consider this sequence of instructions:

```
push ebx
push edx
```

```
call CalcSpace
pop edx
pop ebx
```

This is really no different, functionally, from preserving the registers inside the procedure. However, there may be more than one call to CalcSpace within the program. There may be dozens of calls, or hundreds, and each such call requires five instructions instead of only one. If preserving registers is done within the procedure, the preservation requires only five instructions, period, irrespective of how many places in the code call the procedure.

There are no hard-and-fast rules about knowing which registers to preserve. You need to know how the registers are being used at any given point in the program, and code accordingly. (Taking good notes on register use as you design the program is important.) The only advice I would offer is conservative, and errs on the side of avoiding bugs: preserve any registers that you know are neither being used globally, nor being used to pass values back to the caller. The time taken by register preservation is minor compared to the aggravation of bugs caused by register conflicts.

Local Data

Local data, in contrast to global data, is data that is accessible (also called "visible") only to a particular procedure or in some cases a library. (Again, let's postpone discussion of code libraries for the time being.) When procedures have local data, it's almost always data that is placed on the stack when a procedure is called.

The PUSH instructions place data on the stack. When a part of your code calls a procedure with the CALL instruction, it can pass data down to that procedure by using PUSH one or more times before the CALL instruction. The procedure can then access these PUSHed data items on the stack. However, a word of warning: The procedure can't just pop those data items off the stack into registers, because *the return address is in the way*.

Remember that the first thing CALL does is push the address of the next machine instruction onto the stack. When your procedure gets control, that return address is at the top of the stack (TOS, as we say), ready for the inevitable RET instruction to use to go home. Anything pushed onto the stack by the caller before the CALL instruction is *above* the return address. These items can still be accessed using ordinary memory addressing and the stack pointer ESP. You cannot, however, use POP to get at them without popping and repushing the return address.

This works and I've done it a time or two, but it's slow, and unnecessary once you understand the nature of a *stack frame* and how to address memory within one. I'll take up the notion of stack frames later in this book, as it is absolutely crucial once you begin calling library procedures written in C or other higher-level languages. For now, simply understand that global data is defined in the .data and .bss sections of your program, whereas local data is placed on the stack for the "local" use of a particular call to a particular procedure. Local data takes some care and discipline to use safely, for reasons explained later.

More Table Tricks

The hexdump2 program works very much like the hexdump1 program from Listing 9-1, but it has a few more tricks in its black bag. One worth noting lies in the definition of the hex dump line variable DumpLin:

```
DumpLin:    db " 00 00 00 00 00 00 00 00 00 00 00 00 00 00 00 00 "
DUMPLEN     EQU $-DumpLin
ASCLin:     db "|................|",10
ASCLEN      EQU $-ASCLin
FULLLEN     EQU $-DumpLin
```

What we have here is a variable declared in two parts. Each part may be used separately, or (as is usually done) the two parts may be used together. The first section of DumpLin is the string containing 16 hex digits. Its length is defined by the DUMPLEN equate. (Note that my personal convention is to place the names of equates in uppercase. Equates are not the same species of animal as variables, and I find it makes programs more readable to set equates off so that they can be distinguished from variables at a glance. This is not a NASM requirement; you can name equates in lower or mixed case as you choose.)

The second section of DumpLin is the ASCII column, and it has its own label, ASCLin. A program that only needed the ASCII column could use the ASCLin variable all by itself, along with its associated length equate, ASCLEN. Now, because the two sections of DumpLin are adjacent in memory, referencing DumpLin allows you to reference both sections as a unit—for example, when you want to send a line to stdout via INT 80h. In this case, the equate that calculates the length of the whole line is FULLLEN.

It's useful to have separate names for the two sections because data is not written to or read from the two sections in anything like the same ways. Take a look at the following DumpChar procedure:

```
DumpChar:
        push ebx                  ; Save caller's EBX
        push edi                  ; Save caller's EDI
; First we insert the input char into the ASCII portion of the dump line
        mov bl,byte [DotXlat+eax]   ; Translate nonprintables to '.'
        mov byte [ASCLin+edx+1],bl ; Write to ASCII portion
```

```
; Next we insert the hex equivalent of the input char in the hex portion
; of the hex dump line:
        mov ebx,eax              ; Save a second copy of the input char
        lea edi,[edx*2+edx]      ; Calc offset into line string (ECX X 3)
; Look up low nybble character and insert it into the string:
        and eax,0000000Fh        ; Mask out all but the low nybble
        mov al,byte [HexDigits+eax]  ; Look up the char equiv. of nybble
        mov byte [DumpLin+edi+2],al  ; Write the char equiv. to line string
; Look up high nybble character and insert it into the string:
        and ebx,000000F0h        ; Mask out all the but second-lowest nybble
        shr ebx,4                ; Shift high 4 bits of byte into low 4 bits
        mov bl,byte [HexDigits+ebx] ; Look up char equiv. of nybble
        mov byte [DumpLin+edi+1],bl ; Write the char equiv. to line string
;Done! Let's go home:
        pop edi                  ; Restore caller's EDI
        pop ebx                  ; Restore caller's EBX
        ret                      ; Return to caller
```

Writing to the ASCII column is very simple, because each character in the ASCII column is a single byte in memory, and the effective address of any one position in ASCLin is easy to calculate:

```
mov byte [ASCLin+edx+1],bl   ; Write to ASCII portion
```

Each position in the hex dump portion of the line, however, consists of three characters: a space followed by two hex digits. Considered as a table, addressing a specific entry in DumpLin requires a scale of 3 in the effective address calculation:

```
lea edi,[edx*2+edx]     ; Calc offset into line string (EDX X 3)
```

The two parts of the hex dump line are dealt with very differently from a data manipulation standpoint, and only act together when they are sent to stdout. It's useful, then, to give each of the two sections its own label. Structs in C and records in Pascal are handled very much the same way "under the skin."

The DotXlat table is another example of character translation, and as with all such translation tables, expresses the rules needed to display all 256 different ASCII values consistently in a text line:

- All printable characters translate as themselves.

- All nonprintable characters (which includes all control characters and all characters from 127 and up) translate as ASCII periods. ("dots," hence the name of the table.)

Placing Constant Data in Procedure Definitions

By now you're used to thinking of code as living in the .text section, and data as living in the .data or .bss sections. In almost all cases this is a good way to organize things, but there's no absolute requirement that you separate code and data in this way. It's possible to define data within a procedure using NASM's pseudo-instructions, including DB, DW, and DD. I've created a useful procedure that shows how this is done, and it's a good example of when to do it.

The `Newlines` procedure enables you to issue some number of newline characters to stdout, specified by a value passed to the subroutine in EDX:

```
;----------------------------------------------------------------------
; Newlines:    Sends between 1-15 newlines to the Linux console
; UPDATED:     4/19/2009
; IN:          EDX: # of newlines to send, from 1 to 15
; RETURNS:     Nothing
; MODIFIES:    Nothing. All caller registers preserved.
; CALLS:       Kernel sys_write
; DESCRIPTION: The number of newline chareacters (0Ah) specified in EDX
;              is sent to stdout using using INT 80h sys_write. This
;              procedure demonstrates placing constant data in the
;              procedure definition itself, rather than in the .data or
;              .bss sections.

Newlines:
        Pushad              ; Save all caller's registers
        cmp edx,15          ; Make sure caller didn't ask for more than 15
        ja .exit            ; If so, exit without doing anything
        mov ecx,EOLs        ; Put address of EOLs table into ECX
        mov eax,4           ; Specify sys_write
        mov ebx,1           ; Specify stdout
        int 80h             ; Make the kernel call
.exit   popad               ; Restore all caller's registers
        ret                 ; Go home!
EOLs    db 10,10,10,10,10,10,10,10,10,10,10,10,10,10,10
```

The table `EOLs` contains 15 EOL characters. If you recall, when the EOL character is sent to stdout, the console interprets it as a newline, in which the cursor position of the console is bumped down one line. The caller passes the desired number of newlines in EDX. The `Newlines` procedure first checks to ensure that the caller hasn't requested more newlines than there are EOL characters in the table, and then plugs the address of the `EOLs` table and the requested number into a conventional call to `sys_write` using INT 80h. Basically, `sys_write` displays the first ECX characters of the `EOLs` table to the console, which interprets the data as ECX newlines.

Having the data right in the procedure means that it's easy to cut and paste the procedure definition from one program into another without leaving the essential table of EOL characters behind. Because the only code that ever uses the EOLs table is the Newlines procedure itself, there's no benefit to placing the EOLs table in the more centrally visible .data section. And although the EOLs table is not local in the technical sense (it is not placed on the stack by a caller to Newlines) it "looks" local, and keeps your .data and .bss sections from becoming a little more cluttered with data that is referenced from only a single procedure.

Local Labels and the Lengths of Jumps

Sooner or later, as your programs get longer and more complex, you're going to accidentally reuse a label. I won't be presenting any particularly long or complex programs in this book, so having problems with code labels conflicting with one another won't be a practical issue; but as you begin to write more serious programs you'll eventually be writing hundreds or even (with some practice and persistence) thousands of lines of assembly code in a single source code file. You will soon find that duplicate code labels will be a problem. How will you always remember that you already used the label Scan on line 187 of a 2,732-line program?

You won't; and sooner or later (especially if you're crunching buffers and tables a lot) you'll try to use the label Scan again. NASM will call you on it with an error.

This is a common enough problem (especially with obviously useful labels such as Scan) that NASM's authors created a feature to deal with it: *local labels*. Local labels are based on the fact that nearly all labels in assembly work (outside of names of subroutines and major sections) are "local" in nature, by which I mean that they are only referenced by jump instructions that are *very* close to them—perhaps only two or three instructions away. Such labels are usually parts of tight loops and are not referenced from far away in the code, and are often referenced from only one place.

Here's an example, from the main body of hexdump2.asm:

```
Scan:
        xor eax,eax            ; Clear EAX to 0
        mov al,byte[Buff+ecx]  ; Get a byte from the buffer into AL
        mov edx,esi            ; Copy total counter into EDX
        and edx,0000000Fh      ; Mask out lowest 4 bits of char counter
        call DumpChar          ; Call the char poke procedure

; Bump the buffer pointer to the next character and see if buffer's done:
        inc esi                ; Increment total chars processed counter
```

```
        inc ecx              ; Increment buffer pointer
        cmp ecx,ebp          ; Compare with # of chars in buffer
        jb .modTest          ; If we've processed all chars in buffer...
        call LoadBuff        ; ...go fill the buffer again
        cmp ebp,0            ; If ebp=0, sys_read reached EOF on stdin
        jbe Done             ; If we got EOF, we're done

; See if we're at the end of a block of 16 and need to display a line:
.modTest:
        test esi,0000000Fh   ; Test 4 lowest bits in counter for 0
        jnz Scan             ; If counter is *not* modulo 16, loop back
        call PrintLine       ; ...otherwise print the line
        call ClearLine       ; Clear hex dump line to 0's
        jmp Scan             ; Continue scanning the buffer
```

Note that the label .modTest has a period in front of it. This period marks it as a local label. Local labels are local to the first *nonlocal* label (that is, the first label not prefixed by a period; we call these *global*) that precedes them in the code. In this particular case, the global label to which .modTest belongs is Scan. The block shown above is the portion of the main body of the program that scans the input file buffer, formats the input data into lines of 16 bytes, and displays those lines to the console.

In what way does a global label "own" a local label? It's a question of visibility within the source code: a local label cannot be referenced *higher* in the source code file than the global label that owns it, which, again, is the first global label above it in the file.

In this case, the local label .modTest cannot be referenced above the global label Scan. This means that there could conceivably be a second local label .modTest in the program, on the "other side" of Scan. As long as a global label exists between two local labels with the same name, NASM has no trouble distinguishing them.

Local labels may also exist within procedures. In another example from hexdump2.asm, there is a local label .poke in the ClearLine procedure. It belongs to the ClearLine label, and thus cannot be referenced from any other procedure elsewhere in the program or library. (Don't forget that procedure names are global labels.) This isolation within a single procedure isn't immediately obvious, but it's true, and stems from the fact that "below" a procedure in a program or library there is always either another procedure or the _start label at the beginning of the main program. It's obvious once you see it drawn out, as I've done in Figure 10-2.

Some notes on local labels:

■ Local labels within procedures are *at least* local to the procedures in which they are defined. (This is the point of Figure 10-2.) You may, of course, have global labels within procedures, which limits the visibility of local labels even further.

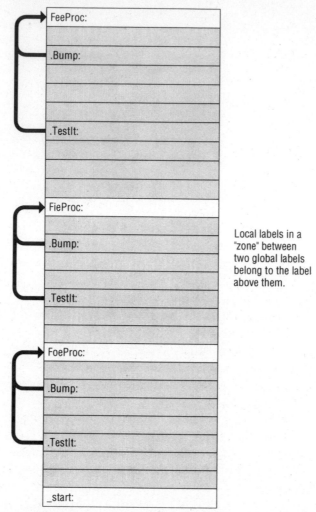

Figure 10-2: Local labels and the globals that own them

- It's perfectly legal and often helpful to define global labels that are never referenced, simply to provide ownership of local labels. If you're writing a utility program that executes in straightforward fashion without a lot of jumping or long-distance looping back, you may go a long way without needing to insert a global label. I like to use global labels to set off major functional parts of a program, whether those labels are ever referenced or not. This enables me to use local labels freely within those major functional modules.

- Local labels, unfortunately, are not accessible as breakpoints from the command-line interface of the Gdb debugger. I'm not entirely sure why this is so, but Gdb refuses to set a breakpoint on a local label from the command line. Of course, you can set a breakpoint on any line containing a machine instruction from the source code window of Insight, irrespective of labels. In general, use the command-line interface of Gdb only when you have to; it has peculiar limitations.

- If you're writing dense code with a lot of intermixed global and local labels, be careful that you don't try to JMP to a local label on the other side of a global label. This is one reason *not* to have 15 local labels called .scan or .loopback within one part of a program—you can easily get them confused, and in trying to jump to one five instructions up, you may unknowingly be jumping to one seven instructions down. NASM won't warn you if there is a local label with the same name on your side of a global label and you try to jump to a local label on the other side of the global label. Bugs like this can be insanely difficult to find sometimes. Like any tool, local labels have to be used carefully to be of greatest benefit.

- Here's a rule of thumb that I use: local labels and all jumps to them should occur within a single screen of code. In other words, you should be able to see both a local label and everything that refers to it without scrolling your program editor. This is just a guide to help you keep track of the sense in your programs, but I've found it very useful in my own work.

- I also use a code style convention that makes the first character after the dot in a local label a lowercase character, and the first character of all global labels an uppercase character. Nothing in NASM requires this, but I find it helpful to distinguish global labels from local labels at a glance. Thus, .poke is easily identifiable as local (periods are tiny!) and Scan is easily identified as global.

"Forcing" Local Label Access

Every so (not very) often, you may find the need to access a local label from the "other side" of its global label owner. NASM offers a way to do this, though I'll admit that I've never had the need. The key to forcing access to a local label outside of its scope (the area of your program from which it is normally visible) is understanding how NASM treats local labels "under the skin."

A local label has an implicit definition that includes the global label to which it belongs. The local label .modTest that I discussed earlier in this section belongs to the global label Scan. Internally, NASM knows .modtest as Scan.modTest. If there were another .modtest local label elsewhere in the program (belonging, let's say, to a global label Calc), then you could force a jump to it by including the name of its owner in the jump instruction:

```
jne Calc.modTest
```

In a sense, a local label is just the "tail" of a global label; and if you need to, you can access a local label by prepending the label of its global owner, thereby converting it to a global label.

Again, I've never had to do this and I don't consider it good practice, but it's good to know that the capability is there if the need ever arises.

Short, Near, and Far Jumps

One of the oddest assembler errors you may ever encounter can appear in a completely correct program; and if you work with NASM long enough and create programs large enough, you *will* encounter it. Here it is:

```
error: short jump is out of range
```

This error occurs when a conditional jump instruction is too far from the label that it references, where "too far" means too many locations away in memory. This only applies to conditional jumps; the unconditional jump instruction JMP is not subject to this error.

The problem arises because of the different ways that NASM can generate a binary opcode for a particular conditional jump instruction. There are two different kinds of conditional jumps, based on how far away the jump target label is. A jump target that lies within 127 bytes of the conditional jump instruction is called a *short jump*. A jump target that is farther away than 127 bytes but still within the current code segment is called a *near jump*. (A near jump can be as far as 2GB away from the instruction, which may stretch your conception of the word "near.")

There is a third kind of jump called a *far jump*, which involves leaving the current code segment entirely for whatever reason. In the old DOS real-mode world, this meant specifying both a segment address and an offset address for the jump target, and they were not used very often, though I used them a time or two. In the 32-bit protected mode world, far jumps are *extremely* rare and involve all sorts of operating system complexity that I won't go into in this book.

The problem really lies with the difference between short jumps and near jumps. A short conditional jump instruction generates a short—and hence compact—binary opcode. Short jump opcodes are always two bytes in size, no more. Near jump opcodes are either 4 or 6 bytes in size, depending on various factors. Compact code means fast code, and taking a short jump is (slightly) faster in most cases than taking a near jump. Furthermore, if you use short jumps most of the time, your executable files will be smaller.

Given that 90% or more of the conditional jump instructions you'll write target program locations only a few instructions away, it makes sense for NASM to generate opcodes for short jumps by default. In fact, *NASM generates opcodes for short jumps unless you explicitly tell it to use near jumps.* A near jump is specified using the NEAR qualifier:

```
jne Scan        ; Short jump, to within 127 bytes in either direction
jne near Scan   ; Near jump, anywhere in the current code segment
```

Beginners tend to run into the "short jump out of range" error this way: You begin a program, and put a label like Exit: at the end, expecting to jump to the Exit label from several different parts of the program. When the program is new and still fairly small, it may work fine. However, eventually code added to the middle of the program forces conditional jumps near the beginning of the program more than 127 bytes away from the Exit label at the end. Bang! NASM hands you the "short jump out of range" error.

The fix is easy: For any jump that NASM calls "out of range," insert the NEAR qualifier between the mnemonic and the target label. Leave the others alone.

Building External Procedure Libraries

You'll notice that the hexdump2 program shown in Listing 10-1 has most of its bulk separated out into procedures. This is as it should be, for the sake of keeping the program comprehensible and maintainable. However, the procedures declared within hexdump2.asm are only usable by the hexdump2 program itself. If you were to write a more powerful program that for whatever reason needed to display a hex/ASCII dump of some data, those procedures could be used again—but not while they're inside hexdump2.

The answer is to move hexdump2's procedures out of hexdump2 completely, and place them in an entirely separate source code file. This file can then be assembled separately to a .o file, which in turn can be linked by the Linux linker into other programs that you may write in the future. A source code file like this is a procedure *library*. It may be full of procedures but it has no main program portion, and no _start: label to indicate where execution begins. All it contains are procedures, and it cannot be translated by the linker into its own executable program.

I describe the separate assembly process in Chapter 5, and show it pictorially in Figures 5-8 and 5-9 on pages 126 and 130, respectively. A single (and fairly simple) program might consist of three or four separate .asm files, each of which is assembled separately to a separate .o file. To produce the final executable file, the Linux linker, Ld, weaves all of the .o files together, resolving all of the references from one to the other, finally creating the executable file.

From the standpoint of the assembly process, each separate .asm file is considered a *module*, whether it contains a _start: label, and thus a program, or simply contains procedures. Each module contains code and possibly some data definitions. When all the declarations are done correctly, all of the modules may freely "talk" to one another via procedure calls, and any procedure may refer to any data definition anywhere among the files that the linker combines. Each executable file may contain only one _start: label, so among the several modules linked into an executable file, only one may contain a _start: label and thus be a program proper.

This sounds harder than it is. The trick is simply to get all the declarations right . . .

Global and External Declarations

. . . and that is *much* less of a trick than it used to be. Back in the bad old DOS days, you had to define code segments and data segments for the use of your separately assembled libraries, and ensure that those segments were marked as PUBLIC, and on and on and on. For protected-mode user-space programs under Linux, there is only *one* segment, containing code, data, and stack—literally everything that a program has. Most of the manual "connecting" that we used to have to do is now done automatically by NASM, the linker, and the Linux loader. Creating libraries is now a snap, no more complex than creating programs, and in some ways even easier.

The very heart of programming in modules is delaying resolution of addresses until link time. You may already have experienced the problem of address resolution if you've begun writing your own programs in assembly. It can happen by accident: If you intend to write a procedure in a program but in your manic enthusiasm write the code that references that (as yet unwritten) procedure's label first, NASM will gleefully give you an error message:

```
error: symbol 'MyProc' undefined
```

In modular programming, you're frequently going to be calling procedures that don't exist anywhere in the source code file that you're actually working on. How do you get past the assembler's watchdogs?

The answer is to declare a procedure *external*. This works very much like it sounds: The assembler is told that a given label will have to be found outside the program somewhere, in another module, later. Once told that, NASM is happy to give you a pass on an undefined label. You've promised NASM that you'll provide it later, and NASM accepts your promise. It will flag the reference as external and keep going without calling foul on the undefined label.

The promise that you make to NASM looks like this:

```
EXTERN MyProc
```

Here, you've told the assembler that the label MyProc represents a procedure and that it will be found somewhere external to the current module. That's all the assembler needs to know to withhold its error message; and having done that, the assembler's part in the bargain is finished. It leaves in place an empty socket in your program where the address of the external procedure may be plugged in later. I sometimes think of it as an eyelet into which the external procedure will later hook.

Over in the other module where procedure MyProc actually exists, it isn't enough just to define the procedure. An eyelet needs a hook. You have to warn the assembler that MyProc will be referenced from outside the module. The assembler needs to forge the hook that will hook into the eyelet. You forge the hook by declaring the procedure *global*, meaning that other modules anywhere else in the program may freely reference the procedure. Declaring a procedure global is no more complex than declaring it external:

```
GLOBAL MyProc
```

In short: a procedure declared GLOBAL where it is defined may be referenced from anywhere its label is declared EXTERNAL.

With both the hook and the eyelet in place, who actually connects them? The linker does that during the link operation. At link time, the linker takes the two .o files generated by the assembler, one from your program and the other from the module containing MyProc, and combines them into a single executable file. (The number of .o files isn't limited to two; you can have almost any number of separately assembled external modules in a single program.) When the executable file created by the linker is loaded and run, the program can call MyProc as cleanly and quickly as though both had been declared in the same source code file.

This process is summarized graphically in Figure 10-3.

What works for procedures works for data as well, and it can work in either direction. Your program can declare any named variable as GLOBAL, and that variable may then be used by any module in which the same variable name is declared as external with the EXTERN directive. Finally, procedure libraries themselves may share data and procedures among themselves in any combination, as long as all of the global and external declarations are handled correctly.

A program or module containing procedures or variables declared as global is often said to *export* those items. Similarly, a program or module that uses procedures or variables that are external to it is said to *import* those items.

The Mechanics of Globals and Externals

The hexdump2 program in Listing 10-1 contains several procedures. Let's pull those procedures out of the main program module and create a separately assembled library module from them, so that we can see how it all works.

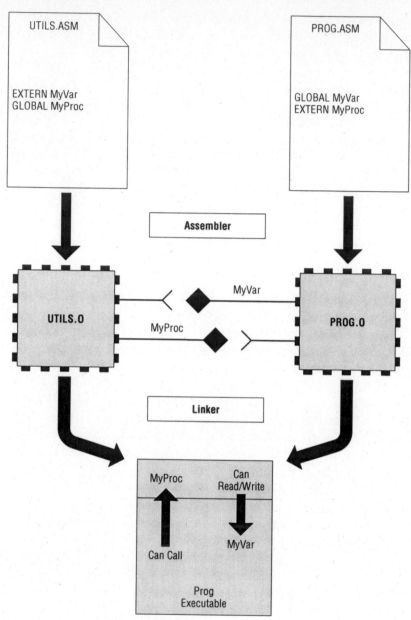

Figure 10-3: Connecting globals and externals

I've described the source code requirements of assembly language programs in detail in the last few chapters. Separately assembled library modules are similar to programs and may have all three of the sections (.text, .data, and .bss) that program modules may have. There are two major differences, however, related to things that library modules lack:

- *External modules do not contain a main program and hence have no start address.* That is, no label `_start:` exists in a library to indicate to the linker that this is the point at which code execution is to begin. Library modules are not intended to be run by themselves, so a `_start:` label in a library module is both unnecessary and grounds for a fatal linker error if `_start:` already exists in the main program module.

- *External modules do not return to Linux.* If only the main program module contains a `_start:` label, then only the main program module should contain the code to make the required `sys_exit` `INT 80h` call shutting down the program and giving control back to Linux. As a general rule of thumb, *never make a call to* `sys_exit` *from within a procedure*, whether it's a procedure located in the same module as the main program, or a procedure located in an external library module.

First, take a look at Listing 10-2, which contains a program called hexdump3. It does precisely the same things as hexdump2. It's a lot shorter than hexdump2 from a source code standpoint, because most of its machinery has been outsourced. Outsourced where? You don't know yet—and you don't have to. NASM will put off resolving the addresses of the missing procedures as long as you list all the missing procedures using the EXTERN directive.

Listing 10-2: hexdump3.asm

```
;   Executable name : hexdump3
;   Version         : 1.0
;   Created date    : 4/15/2009
;   Last update     : 4/20/2009
;   Author          : Jeff Duntemann
;   Description     : A simple hex dump utility demonstrating the use of
;                     separately assembled code libraries via EXTERN
;
;
;   Build using these commands:
;     nasm -f elf -g -F stabs hexdump3.asm
;     ld -o hexdump3 hexdump3.o <path>/textlib.o
;
SECTION .bss                       ; Section containing uninitialized data
        BUFFLEN EQU 10
        Buff resb BUFFLEN


SECTION .data                      ; Section containing initialised data


SECTION .text                      ; Section containing code


EXTERN ClearLine, DumpChar, PrintLine
```

(continued)

Listing 10-2: hexdump3.asm (*continued*)

```
GLOBAL _start

_start:
        nop                      ; This no-op keeps gdb happy...
        nop
        xor esi,esi              ; Clear total chars counter to 0

; Read a buffer full of text from stdin:
Read:
        mov eax,3                ; Specify sys_read call
        mov ebx,0                ; Specify File Descriptor 0: Standard Input
        mov ecx,Buff             ; Pass offset of the buffer to read to
        mov edx,BUFFLEN          ; Pass number of bytes to read at one pass
        int 80h                  ; Call sys_read to fill the buffer
        mov ebp,eax              ; Save # of bytes read from file for later
        cmp eax,0                ; If eax=0, sys_read reached EOF on stdin
        je Done                  ; Jump If Equal (to 0, from compare)

; Set up the registers for the process buffer step:
        xor ecx,ecx              ; Clear buffer pointer to 0

; Go through the buffer and convert binary values to hex digits:
Scan:
        xor eax,eax              ; Clear EAX to 0
        mov al,byte[Buff+ecx]    ; Get a char from the buffer into AL
        mov edx,esi              ; Copy total counter into EDX
        and edx,0000000Fh        ; Mask out lowest 4 bits of char counter
        call DumpChar            ; Call the char poke procedure

; Bump the buffer pointer to the next character and see if buffer's done:
        inc ecx                  ; Increment buffer pointer
        inc esi                  ; Increment total chars processed counter
        cmp ecx,ebp              ; Compare with # of chars in buffer
        jae Read                 ; If we've done the buffer, go get more

; See if we're at the end of a block of 16 and need to display a line:
        test esi,0000000Fh       ; Test 4 lowest bits in counter for 0
        jnz Scan                 ; If counter is *not* modulo 16, loop back
        call PrintLine           ; ...otherwise print the line
        call ClearLine           ; Clear hex dump line to 0's
        jmp Scan                 ; Continue scanning the buffer

; All done! Let's end this party:
Done:
        call PrintLine           ; Print the "leftovers" line
        mov eax,1                ; Code for Exit Syscall
        mov ebx,0                ; Return a code of zero
        int 80H                  ; Make kernel call
```

External declarations of multiple items may be put on a single line, separated by commas, as in hexdump3:

```
EXTERN ClearLine, DumpChar, PrintLine
```

There does not have to be a single EXTERN directive. Several may exist in a module; each external identifier, in fact, may have its own EXTERN directive. It's up to you. When you have a longish list of external identifiers, however, don't make this mistake, which is an error:

```
EXTERN InitBlock, ReadBlock, ValidateBlock, WriteBlock, CleanUp,
       ShowStats, PrintSummary    ; ERROR!
```

EXTERN declarations do *not* span line boundaries. (In fact, almost nothing in assembly language spans line boundaries, especially with NASM. Pascal and C programmers run up against this peculiarity fairly often.) If you have too many external declarations to fit on a single line with a single EXTERN, place additional EXTERN directives on subsequent lines. There is no limit to the number of EXTERN directives in a single module.

To make hexdump3 link into a functioning executable program, we have to create an external library module for all of its procedures. All that's needed are the procedures and their data in the proper sections, and the necessary GLOBAL declarations, as shown in Listing 10-3.

Listing 10-3: textlib.asm

```
;   Library name   : textlib
;   Version        : 1.0
;   Created date   : 4/10/2009
;   Last update    : 4/20/2009
;   Author         : Jeff Duntemann
;   Description    : A linkable library of text-oriented procedures and tables
;
;   Build using these commands:
;     nasm -f elf -g -F stabs textlib.asm
;
SECTION .bss                        ; Section containing uninitialized data
        BUFFLEN EQU 10
        Buff    resb BUFFLEN

SECTION .data                       ; Section containing initialised data

; Here we have two parts of a single useful data structure, implementing the
; text line of a hex dump utility. The first part displays 16 bytes in hex
; separated by spaces. Immediately following is a 16-character line delimited
```

(continued)

Listing 10-3: textlib.asm (*continued*)

```
; by vertical bar characters. Because they are adjacent, they can be
; referenced separately or as a single contiguous unit. Remember that if
; DumpLin is to be used separately, you must append an EOL before sending it
; to the Linux console.
DumpLin:        db " 00 00 00 00 00 00 00 00 00 00 00 00 00 00 00 00 "
DUMPLEN         EQU $-DumpLin
ASCLin:         db "|...............|",10
ASCLEN          EQU $-ASCLin
FULLLEN         EQU $-DumpLin


; The HexDigits table is used to convert numeric values to their hex
; equivalents. Index by nybble without a scale: [HexDigits+eax]
HexDigits:      db "0123456789ABCDEF"


; This table allows us to generate text equivalents for binary numbers.
; Index into the table by the nybble using a scale of 4:
; [BinDigits + ecx*4]
BinDigits: db "0000","0001","0010","0011"
           db "0100","0101","0110","0111"
           db "1000","1001","1010","1011"
           db "1100","1101","1110","1111"


; This table is used for ASCII character translation, into the ASCII
; portion of the hex dump line, via XLAT or ordinary memory lookup.
; All printable characters "play through" as themselves. The high 128
; characters are translated to ASCII period (2Eh). The non-printable
; characters in the low 128 are also translated to ASCII period, as is
; char 127.
DotXlat:
      db 2Eh,2Eh,2Eh,2Eh,2Eh,2Eh,2Eh,2Eh,2Eh,2Eh,2Eh,2Eh,2Eh,2Eh,2Eh,2Eh
      db 2Eh,2Eh,2Eh,2Eh,2Eh,2Eh,2Eh,2Eh,2Eh,2Eh,2Eh,2Eh,2Eh,2Eh,2Eh,2Eh
      db 20h,21h,22h,23h,24h,25h,26h,27h,28h,29h,2Ah,2Bh,2Ch,2Dh,2Eh,2Fh
      db 30h,31h,32h,33h,34h,35h,36h,37h,38h,39h,3Ah,3Bh,3Ch,3Dh,3Eh,3Fh
      db 40h,41h,42h,43h,44h,45h,46h,47h,48h,49h,4Ah,4Bh,4Ch,4Dh,4Eh,4Fh
      db 50h,51h,52h,53h,54h,55h,56h,57h,58h,59h,5Ah,5Bh,5Ch,5Dh,5Eh,5Fh
      db 60h,61h,62h,63h,64h,65h,66h,67h,68h,69h,6Ah,6Bh,6Ch,6Dh,6Eh,6Fh
      db 70h,71h,72h,73h,74h,75h,76h,77h,78h,79h,7Ah,7Bh,7Ch,7Dh,7Eh,2Eh
      db 2Eh,2Eh,2Eh,2Eh,2Eh,2Eh,2Eh,2Eh,2Eh,2Eh,2Eh,2Eh,2Eh,2Eh,2Eh,2Eh
      db 2Eh,2Eh,2Eh,2Eh,2Eh,2Eh,2Eh,2Eh,2Eh,2Eh,2Eh,2Eh,2Eh,2Eh,2Eh,2Eh
      db 2Eh,2Eh,2Eh,2Eh,2Eh,2Eh,2Eh,2Eh,2Eh,2Eh,2Eh,2Eh,2Eh,2Eh,2Eh,2Eh
      db 2Eh,2Eh,2Eh,2Eh,2Eh,2Eh,2Eh,2Eh,2Eh,2Eh,2Eh,2Eh,2Eh,2Eh,2Eh,2Eh
      db 2Eh,2Eh,2Eh,2Eh,2Eh,2Eh,2Eh,2Eh,2Eh,2Eh,2Eh,2Eh,2Eh,2Eh,2Eh,2Eh
      db 2Eh,2Eh,2Eh,2Eh,2Eh,2Eh,2Eh,2Eh,2Eh,2Eh,2Eh,2Eh,2Eh,2Eh,2Eh,2Eh
      db 2Eh,2Eh,2Eh,2Eh,2Eh,2Eh,2Eh,2Eh,2Eh,2Eh,2Eh,2Eh,2Eh,2Eh,2Eh,2Eh
      db 2Eh,2Eh,2Eh,2Eh,2Eh,2Eh,2Eh,2Eh,2Eh,2Eh,2Eh,2Eh,2Eh,2Eh,2Eh,2Eh


SECTION .text                    ; Section containing code
```

Listing 10-3: textlib.asm (*continued*)

```
GLOBAL ClearLine, DumpChar, Newlines, PrintLine      ; Procedures
GLOBAL DumpLin, HexDigits, BinDigits                 ; Data items

;-------------------------------------------------------------------
; ClearLine:   Clear a hex dump line string to 16 0 values
; UPDATED:     4/13/2009
; IN:          Nothing
; RETURNS:     Nothing
; MODIFIES:    Nothing
; CALLS:       DumpChar
; DESCRIPTION: The hex dump line string is cleared to binary 0.

ClearLine:
        push edx           ; Save caller's EDX
        mov edx,15         ; We're going to go 16 pokes, counting from 0
.Poke:  mov eax,0          ; Tell DumpChar to poke a '0'
        call DumpChar      ; Insert the '0' into the hex dump string
        sub edx,1          ; DEC doesn't affect CF!
        jae .Poke          ; Loop back if EDX >= 0
        pop edx            ; Restore caller's EDX
        ret                ; Go home

;-------------------------------------------------------------------
; DumpChar:    "Poke" a value into the hex dump line string.
; UPDATED:     4/13/2009
; IN:          Pass the 8-bit value to be poked in EAX.
;              Pass the value's position in the line (0-15) in EDX
; RETURNS:     Nothing
; MODIFIES:    EAX
; CALLS:       Nothing
; DESCRIPTION: The value passed in EAX will be placed in both the hex dump
;              portion and in the ASCII portion, at the position passed
;              in ECX, represented by a space where it is not a printable
;              character.

DumpChar:
        push ebx                   ; Save EBX on the stack so we don't trash
        push edi
; First we insert the input char into the ASCII portion of the dump line
        mov bl,byte [DotXlat+eax]    ; Translate nonprintables to '.'
        mov byte [ASCLin+edx+1],bl   ; Write to ASCII portion
; Next we insert the hex equivalent of the input char in the hex portion
; of the hex dump line:
        mov ebx,eax                ; Save a second copy of the input char
        lea edi,[edx*2+edx]        ; Calc offset into line string (ECX X 3)
; Look up low nybble character and insert it into the string:
        and eax,0000000Fh          ; Mask out all but the low nybble
        mov al,byte [HexDigits+eax] ; Look up the char equivalent of nybble
```

(continued)

Listing 10-3: textlib.asm (*continued*)

```
        mov byte [DumpLin+edi+2],al ; Write char equivalent to line string
; Look up high nybble character and insert it into the string:
        and ebx,000000F0h        ; Mask out all the but second-lowest nybble
        shr ebx,4                ; Shift high 4 bits of char into low 4 bits
        mov bl,byte [HexDigits+ebx] ; Look up char equivalent of nybble
        mov byte [DumpLin+edi+1],bl ; Write the char equiv. to line string
;Done! Let's go home:
        pop ebx                  ; Restore caller's EBX register value
        pop edi                  ; Restore caller's EDI register value
        ret                      ; Return to caller


;-------------------------------------------------------------------------
; Newlines:     Sends between 1 and 15 newlines to the Linux console
; UPDATED:      4/13/2009
; IN:           # of newlines to send, from 1 to 15
; RETURNS:      Nothing
; MODIFIES:     Nothing
; CALLS:        Kernel sys_write
; DESCRIPTION:  The number of newline chareacters (0Ah) specified in EDX
;               is sent to stdout using using INT 80h sys_write. This
;               procedure demonstrates placing constant data in the
;               procedure definition itself, rather than in the .data or
;               .bss sections.

Newlines:
        pushad              ; Save all caller's registers
        cmp edx,15          ; Make sure caller didn't ask for more than 15
        ja .exit            ; If so, exit without doing anything
        mov ecx,EOLs        ; Put address of EOLs table into ECX
        mov eax,4           ; Specify sys_write
        mov ebx,1           ; Specify stdout
        int 80h             ; Make the kernel call
.exit   popad               ; Restore all caller's registers
        ret                 ; Go home!
EOLs:   db 10,10,10,10,10,10,10,10,10,10,10,10,10,10,10


;-------------------------------------------------------------------------
; PrintLine:    Displays the hex dump line string via INT 80h sys_write
; UPDATED:      4/13/2009
; IN:           Nothing
; RETURNS:      Nothing
; MODIFIES:     Nothing
; CALLS:        Kernel sys_write
; DESCRIPTION:  The hex dump line string is displayed to stdout using
;               INT 80h sys_write.

PrintLine:
        pushad                      ; Push all GP registers
```

Listing 10-3: textlib.asm (*continued*)

```
        mov eax,4              ; Specify sys_write call
        mov ebx,1              ; Specify File Descriptor 1: Standard output
        mov ecx,DumpLin        ; Pass offset of line string
        mov edx,FULLLEN        ; Pass size of the line string
        int 80h                ; Make kernel call to display line string
        popad                  ; Pop all GP registers
        ret                    ; Go home!
```

There are two lines of global identifier declarations, each line with its own GLOBAL directive. As a convention in my own work, I separate declarations of procedures and named data items, and give each their own line:

```
GLOBAL ClearLine, DumpChar, Newlines, PrintLine  ; Procedures
GLOBAL DumpLin, HexDigits, BinDigits             ; Data items
```

Any procedure or data item that is to be exported (that is, made available outside the module) must be declared on a line after a GLOBAL directive. You don't have to declare everything in a module global. In fact, one way to manage complexity and prevent certain kinds of bugs is to think hard about and strictly limit what other modules can "see" in their fellow modules. A module can have "private" procedures and named data items that can only be referenced from inside the module. Making these items private is in fact the default: Just don't declare them global.

Note well that all items declared global must be declared global *before* they are defined in the source code. In practice, this means that you need to declare global procedures at the top of the .text section, before any of the procedures are actually defined. Similarly, all global named data items must be declared in the .data section before the data items are defined.

Equates can be exported from modules, though this is an innovation of the NASM assembler and not necessarily true of all assemblers. Just place the label associated with an equate in a list of EXTERN definitions, and other modules will be able to see and use the equate, though equates are necessarily considered read-only values, like Pascal constants.

Linking Libraries into Your Programs

For all the previous example programs presented in this book, the make files are fairly simple. Here, for example, is the makefile for the hexdump2 program:

```
hexdump2: hexdump2.o
        ld -o hexdump2 hexdump2.o
hexdump2.o: hexdump2.asm
        nasm -f elf -g -F stabs hexdump2.asm
```

The linker invocation converts hexdump2.o into the executable file hexdump2, and that's all it has to do. Adding a library file complicates the picture slightly. The linker now must do some actual linking of multiple files. Additional library files in the .o format are added to the linker invocation after the name of the main program's linkable file. There can be any (reasonable) number of .o files in a link step. To build hexdump3, we only need two. Here is the makefile for hexdump3:

```
hexdump3: hexdump3.o
        ld -o hexdump3 hexdump3.o ../textlib/textlib.o
hexdump3.o: hexdump3.asm
        nasm -f elf -g -F stabs hexdump3.asm
```

The textlib.o file is simply placed on the linker invocation line after the .o file for the program itself. There is one wrinkle in the preceding makefile: the library file is on a path relative to the directory containing the hexdump3 project. Placing "../textlib/" in front of the textlib.o filename allows the linker to reach "up, across, and down" through the Linux file system into the project directory for the library itself. Otherwise, you'd have to place textlib.o in the same directory as hexdump3, or else copy it to a directory under usr/lib, which is on the default search path.

A directory under usr/lib would actually be a very good place for it, *once it's finished*. While you're still actively working on a library, it's best to keep it in a project directory in the same tree as all your other project directories so you can fix bugs and add features that don't occur to you until you've used it for a while building other programs.

The Dangers of Too Many Procedures and Too Many Libraries

You can have too much of a good thing. I've seen code libraries that consist of literally hundreds of files, each file containing a single procedure. These are not procedures that stand alone, either. They call one another right and left, in a thick web of execution that is very difficult to trace at the source-code level, especially if you've inherited such a library from someone else and must get a grip (often very quickly) on how the mechanisms implemented by the library actually work. Absent very detailed text documentation, there's no "view from a height" to help you grasp what calls what from where. If the library came from somewhere else and is used like a "block box," that may not be a catastrophe, but I still like to know how any libraries I use work.

There is, alas, a valid reason for creating libraries this way: when you link a library to a program, *the whole library is added to the executable file*, even those procedures and data definitions that are never referenced from the main program. If every procedure is assembled separately into its own cozy little

.o file, the linker will add *only* those procedures to your program that will actually be called by (and thus executed by) the program.

Much depends on where your code ends up. If your goal is the smallest possible executable file, this is significant; and there are some continents in the assembly language world (especially those relating to embedded systems) where every byte counts and *dead code* that never runs adds needless cost to the low-end hardware on which the code must run.

Assembly language code size won't be an issue on ordinary Linux PCs with 3GB of memory and 250GB of disk. If that's where your code will run, you may be better off having fewer libraries and more comprehensible source code, even if you end up with a few thousand bytes of code in your executable files that never actually meet the CPU face-to-face.

The Art of Crafting Procedures

There's a little more to creating procedures than simply slicing out a section of code from one of your programs and making a CALL and RET sandwich out of it. The primary purpose of procedures is to make your code more maintainable, by gathering together instructions that serve a common purpose into named entities. Don't forget about the Martians, and how they abducted my hapless APL text formatter in 1977. Maintainability is probably the single toughest nut to crack in software design, and maintainability depends utterly on comprehensibility. The whole idea in crafting libraries of procedures is to make your code comprehensible—primarily to you, but very possibly to other people who may inherit or will attempt to use your code.

Therefore, in this section I'm going to talk a little bit about how to think about procedures and the process of their creation, with code maintainability in mind.

Maintainability and Reuse

The single most important purpose of procedures is to manage complexity in your programs by replacing a sequence of machine instructions with a descriptive name. The close runner-up is code reuse. There's no point in writing the same common mechanisms from scratch every time you begin a new project. Write 'em once, write 'em well, and use 'em forever.

The two purposes interact. Code reuse aids code maintainability in several ways:

- Reuse means that there is less code in total to maintain across the breadth of all your projects.

- Reuse maintains your time and effort investment in debugging.

- Reuse forces you to maintain certain coding conventions across your projects over time (because your libraries require it), which gives your projects a "family resemblance" to one another that makes them easier to grasp after you've been away from them for a while.

- Reuse means you will have fewer code sequences that do pretty much the same thing but in slightly different ways.

This last point is subtle but very important. When you're debugging, what you're constantly referring to in the back of your head is an understanding of how each section of your program works. You'd like this understanding to be unique to every program that you write, but it doesn't work that way. Memory is imprecise, and memories of separate but very similar things tend to blur together. (Quick: Is that a 1972 Impala or a 1973 Impala?) In programming, details matter crucially, and in assembly language programming, there are *a lot* of details. If you scratch-wrote a `RefreshText` procedure three times for three different programs that differ in only minor ways, you may be relying on an understanding of one `RefreshText` implementation when staring at another. The farther back in time these similar-but-not-identical procedures go, the more likely you are to confuse them, and waste time sorting out the little quirks of how each one operates.

If there's only one `RefreshText` procedure, however, then there's only one understanding of `RefreshText` to be recalled. All of the reuse advantage points above cook down to this: managing complexity by simply reducing the amount of complexity that must be managed.

Deciding What Should Be a Procedure

So when should a block of instructions be pulled out and made a procedure? There are no hard-and-fast rules, but there are some useful heuristics that are worth discussing:

- Look for actions that happen a lot within a program.

- Look for actions that may not happen a lot within any single program, but which tend to happen in the same ways in many or most programs.

- When programs get large (and by "large" I mean well beyond the tutorial book demo class; let's say 1,000 lines or so), look for functional blocks that can be made into procedures so that the overall flow of execution in the main program becomes easier to understand. (More on this in a moment.)

- Look for actions within a program that may change over time in response to forces outside your control (data specifications, third-party libraries, and so on), and isolate those actions in procedures.

In short: think big, and think long-term. You aren't going to be a beginner forever. Try to anticipate your programming efforts "down the road" and create procedures of general usefulness. "General" here means not only useful within the single program you happen to be working on right now, but also useful in programs that you will be writing in the future.

There's no "minimum size" for procedures if they're called frequently enough. Extremely simple procedures—even ones with as few as four or five instructions—don't themselves hide a great deal of complexity. They *do* give certain frequently used actions descriptive names, which is valuable in itself. They can also provide standard basic building blocks for the creation of larger and more powerful procedures. That said, a short code sequence (5 to 10 instructions) that is only called once or perhaps twice within a middling program of several hundred machine instructions is a poor candidate for a procedure, *unless* it is a candidate for reuse in future programs. Then it belongs in a code library, and code can't be in a library unless it's in a procedure.

Nor is there any "maximum size" for procedures, and in some circumstances very large procedures make sense—if they serve some well-defined purpose. Remember that procedures don't always need to be in libraries. You may find it useful to define large procedures that are called only once when your program becomes big enough to require breaking it down into functional chunks for comprehensibility's sake. A thousand-line assembly language program might split well into a sequence of seven or eight largish procedures. Each procedure is meant to be called only once from the main program, but this allows your main program to be short, easily grasped, and clearly indicative of what the program is doing:

```
Start: call Initialize  ; Open spec files, create buffers
       call OpenFile     ; Open the target data file
Input: call GetRec       ; Fetch a record from the open file
       cmp eax,0          ; Test for EOF on file read
       je Done            ; If we've hit EOF, time to shut 'er down
       call ProcessRec   ; Crunch the rec
       call VerifyRec    ; Validate the modified data against the spec
       call WriteRec     ; Write the modified record out to the file
       jmp Input          ; Go back and do it all again
Done:  call CloseFile    ; Close the opened file
       call CleanUp      ; Delete the temp files
       mov eax,1          ; Specify exit syscall
       mov ebx,[StatusCode]   ; Pass status code back to OS
       int 80h            ; Return to Linux
```

This clean and readable and provides a necessary view from a height when you begin to approach a thousand-line assembly language program. Remember that the Martians are always hiding somewhere close by, anxious to turn your programs into unreadable hieroglyphics.

There's no weapon against them with half the power of procedures.

Use Comment Headers!

As time goes on, you'll find yourself creating dozens or even hundreds of procedures in the cause of managing complexity. The libraries of "canned" procedures that most high-level language vendors supply with their compilers just don't exist with NASM. By and large, when you need some function or another, you'll have to write it yourself.

Keeping such a list of routines straight is no easy task when you've written them all yourself. You *must* document the essential facts about each individual procedure or you'll forget them, or remember them incorrectly and act on bad information. (The resultant bugs are often devilishly hard to find because you're *sure* you remember everything there is to know about that proc. After all, *you* wrote it!)

I powerfully recommend adding a comment header to every procedure you write, no matter how simple. Such a header should at least contain the following information:

- The name of the procedure
- The date it was last modified
- The name of each entry point, if the procedure has multiple entry points
- What the procedure does
- What data items the caller must pass to it to make it work correctly
- What data (if any) is returned by the procedure, and where that data is returned (for example, in register ECX)
- What registers or data items the procedure modifies
- What other procedures, if any, are called by the procedure
- Any "gotchas" that need to be kept in mind while writing code that uses the procedure

In addition to that, other information is sometimes helpful in comment headers:

- The version of the procedure, if you use versioning
- The date it was created
- The name of the person who wrote the procedure, if you're dealing with code shared within a team

A typical workable procedure header might look something like this:

```
;-----------------------------------------------------------------------
; LoadBuff:     Fills a buffer with data from stdin via INT 80h sys_read
; UPDATED:      4/15/2009
```

```
; IN:          Nothing
; RETURNS:     # of bytes read in EBP
; MODIFIES:    ECX, EBP, Buff
; CALLS:       Kernel sys_read
; DESCRIPTION: Loads a buffer full of data (BUFFLEN bytes) from stdin
;              using INT 80h sys_read and places it in Buff. Buffer
;              offset counter ECX is zeroed, because we're starting in
;              on a new buffer full of data. Caller must test value in
;              EBP: If EBP contains zero on return, we hit EOF on stdin.
;              Less than 0 in EBP on return indicates some kind of error.
```

A comment header does *not* relieve you of the responsibility of commenting the individual lines of code within the procedure! As I've said many times, it's a good idea to put a short comment to the right of every line that contains a machine instruction mnemonic, and (in longer procedures) a comment block describing every major functional block within the procedure.

Simple Cursor Control in the Linux Console

As a segue from assembly language procedures into assembly language macros, I'd like to spend a little time on the details of controlling the Linux console display from within your programs. Let's return to our little greasy-spoon advertising display for Joe's diner. Let's goose it up a little, first clearing the Linux console and then centering the ad text on the cleared display. I'm going to present the same program twice, first with several portions expressed as procedures, and later with the same portions expressed as macros.

Procedures first, as shown in Listing 10-4.

Listing 10-4: eatterm.asm

```
;  Executable name : eatterm
;  Version         : 1.0
;  Created date    : 4/21/2009
;  Last update     : 4/23/2009
;  Author          : Jeff Duntemann
;  Description     : A simple program in assembly for Linux, using
;                    NASM 2.05, demonstrating the use of escape
;                    sequences to do simple "full-screen" text output
;
;  Build using these commands:
;    nasm -f elf -g -F stabs eatterm.asm
;    ld -o eatterm eatterm.o
;
;
section .data                    ; Section containing initialised data
```

(continued)

Listing 10-4: eatterm.asm (*continued*)

```
SCRWIDTH:   equ 80              ; By default we assume 80 chars wide
PosTerm:    db 27,"[01;01H"     ; <ESC>[<Y>;<X>H
POSLEN:     equ $-PosTerm       ; Length of term position string
ClearTerm:  db 27,"[2J"         ; <ESC>[2J
CLEARLEN    equ $-ClearTerm     ; Length of term clear string
AdMsg:      db "Eat At Joe's!"  ; Ad message
ADLEN:      equ $-AdMsg         ; Length of ad message
Prompt:     db "Press Enter: "  ; User prompt
PROMPTLEN:  equ $-Prompt        ; Length of user prompt

; This table gives us pairs of ASCII digits from 0-80. Rather than
; calculate ASCII digits to insert in the terminal control string,
; we look them up in the table and read back two digits at once to
; a 16-bit register like DX, which we then poke into the terminal
; control string PosTerm at the appropriate place. See GotoXY.
; If you intend to work on a larger console than 80 X 80, you must
; add additional ASCII digit encoding to the end of Digits. Keep in
; mind that the code shown here will only work up to 99 X 99.
Digits: db "000102030405060708091011121314151617181 9"
        db "202122232425262728293031323334353637383 9"
        db "404142434445464748495051525354555657585 9"
        db "606162636465666768697071727374757677787980"


SECTION .bss              ; Section containing uninitialized data


SECTION .text             ; Section containing code


;------------------------------------------------------------------------
; ClrScr:      Clear the Linux console
; UPDATED:     4/21/2009
; IN:          Nothing
; RETURNS:     Nothing
; MODIFIES:    Nothing
; CALLS:       Kernel sys_write
; DESCRIPTION: Sends the predefined control string <ESC>[2J to the
;              console, which clears the full display

ClrScr:
        push eax          ; Save pertinent registers
        push ebx
        push ecx
        push edx
        mov ecx,ClearTerm ; Pass offset of terminal control string
        mov edx,CLEARLEN  ; Pass the length of terminal control string
        call WriteStr     ; Send control string to console
        pop edx           ; Restore pertinent registers
```

Listing 10-4: eatterm.asm (*continued*)

```
        pop ecx
        pop ebx
        pop eax
        ret                 ; Go home


;-------------------------------------------------------------------
; GotoXY:     Position the Linux Console cursor to an X,Y position
; UPDATED:    4/21/2009
; IN:         X in AH, Y in AL
; RETURNS:    Nothing
; MODIFIES:   PosTerm terminal control sequence string
; CALLS:      Kernel sys_write
; DESCRIPTION: Prepares a terminal control string for the X,Y coordinates
;             passed in AL and AH and calls sys_write to position the
;             console cursor to that X,Y position. Writing text to the
;             console after calling GotoXY will begin display of text
;             at that X,Y position.

GotoXY:
        pushad              ; Save caller's registers
        xor ebx,ebx         ; Zero EBX
        xor ecx,ecx         ; Ditto ECX
; Poke the Y digits:
        mov bl,al                     ; Put Y value into scale term EBX
        mov cx,word [Digits+ebx*2] ; Fetch decimal digits to CX
        mov word [PosTerm+2],cx     ; Poke digits into control string
; Poke the X digits:
        mov bl,ah                     ; Put X value into scale term EBX
        mov cx,word [Digits+ebx*2] ; Fetch decimal digits to CX
        mov word [PosTerm+5],cx     ; Poke digits into control string
; Send control sequence to stdout:
        mov ecx,PosTerm     ; Pass address of the control string
        mov edx,POSLEN      ; Pass the length of the control string
        call WriteStr       ; Send control string to the console
; Wrap up and go home:
        popad               ; Restore caller's registers
        ret                 ; Go home


;-------------------------------------------------------------------
; WriteCtr:   Send a string centered to an 80-char wide Linux console
; UPDATED:    4/21/2009
; IN:         Y value in AL, String address in ECX, string length in EDX
; RETURNS:    Nothing
; MODIFIES:   PosTerm terminal control sequence string
; CALLS:      GotoXY, WriteStr
; DESCRIPTION: Displays a string to the Linux console centered in an
;             80-column display. Calculates the X for the passed-in
```

(continued)

Listing 10-4: eatterm.asm (*continued*)

```
;                 string length, then calls GotoXY and WriteStr to send
;                 the string to the console

WriteCtr:
        push ebx        ; Save caller's EBX
        xor ebx,ebx     ; Zero EBX
        mov bl,SCRWIDTH ; Load the screen width value to BL
        sub bl,dl       ; Take diff. of screen width and string length
        shr bl,1        ; Divide difference by two for X value
        mov ah,bl       ; GotoXY requires X value in AH
        call GotoXY     ; Position the cursor for display
        call WriteStr   ; Write the string to the console
        pop ebx         ; Restore caller's EBX
        ret             ; Go home


;-----------------------------------------------------------------------
; WriteStr:    Send a string to the Linux console
; UPDATED:     4/21/2009
; IN:          String address in ECX, string length in EDX
; RETURNS:     Nothing
; MODIFIES:    Nothing
; CALLS:       Kernel sys_write
; DESCRIPTION: Displays a string to the Linux console through a
;              sys_write kernel call

WriteStr:
        push eax        ; Save pertinent registers
        push ebx
        mov eax,4       ; Specify sys_write call
        mov ebx,1       ; Specify File Descriptor 1: Stdout
        int 80H         ; Make the kernel call
        pop ebx         ; Restore pertinent registers
        pop eax
        ret             ; Go home


global _start           ; Linker needs this to find the entry point!

_start:
        nop             ; This no-op keeps gdb happy...

; First we clear the terminal display...
        call ClrScr

; Then we post the ad message centered on the 80-wide console:
        mov al,12       ; Specy line 12
        mov ecx,AdMsg   ; Pass address of message
```

Listing 10-4: eatterm.asm (*continued*)

```
        mov edx,ADLEN    ; Pass length of message
        call WriteCtr    ; Display it to the console

; Position the cursor for the "Press Enter" prompt:
        mov ax,0117h     ; X,Y = 1,23 as a single hex value in AX
        call GotoXY      ; Position the cursor

; Display the "Press Enter" prompt:
        mov ecx,Prompt       ; Pass offset of the prompt
        mov edx,PROMPTLEN    ; Pass the length of the prompt
        call WriteStr        ; Send the prompt to the console

; Wait for the user to press Enter:
        mov eax,3        ; Code for sys_read
        mov ebx,0        ; Specify File Descriptor 0: Stdin
        int 80H          ; Make kernel call

; ...and we're done!
Exit:   mov eax,1        ; Code for Exit Syscall
        mov ebx,0        ; Return a code of zero
        int 80H          ; Make kernel call
```

There's some new machinery here. All the programs I've presented so far in this book simply send lines of text sequentially to standard output, and the console displays them sequentially, each on the next line down, scrolling at the bottom.

This can be very useful, but it isn't the best we can do. Back on page 183 in Chapter 6, I briefly described the way that the Linux console can be controlled by sending it *escape sequences* embedded in the stream of text traveling from your program to stdout. It would be useful to reread that section if you don't recall it, as I won't recap deeply here.

The simplest example of an escape sequence for controlling the console clears the entire console display to blanks (basically, space characters). In the eatterm program, this sequence is a string variable called ClearTerm:

```
ClearTerm: db 27,"[2J"    ; <ESC>[2J
```

The escape sequence is four characters long. It begins with ESC, a nonprintable character that we usually describe by its decimal value in the ASCII table, 27. (Or hex, which is 1Bh.) Immediately following the ESC character are the three printable characters [2J. They're printable, but they're not printed because they follow ESC. The console watches for ESC characters, and interprets any characters following ESC specially, according to a large and very complicated scheme. Particular sequences represent particular commands to the console, like this one, which clears the display.

There is no marker at the end of an escape sequence to indicate that the sequence is finished. The console knows each and every escape sequence to the letter, including how long each is, and there are no ambiguities. In the case of the ClearTerm sequence, the console knows that when it sees the J character, the sequence is complete. It then clears its display and resumes displaying characters that your program sends to stdout.

Nothing special has to be done in terms of sending an escape sequence to the console. The escape sequence goes to stdout by way of an INT 80h call, just as all other text does. You can embed escape sequences in the middle of printable text by careful arrangement of DB directives in the .text sections of your programs. Remember that even though escape sequences are not shown on the console display, they must still be counted when you pass the length of a text sequence to sys_write via INT 80h.

The escape sequence to clear the display is easy to understand because it's always the same and always does exactly the same thing. The sequence that positions the cursor is a lot trickier, because it takes parameters that specify the X,Y position to which the cursor is to be moved. Each of these parameters is a two-digit textual number in ASCII that must be embedded in the sequence by your program before the sequence is sent to stdout. All of the trickiness in moving the cursor around the Linux console involves embedding those X and Y parameters in the escape sequence.

The default sequence as defined in eatterm is called PosTerm:

```
PosTerm: db 27,"[01;01H" ; <ESC>[<Y>;<X>H
```

As with ClearTerm it begins with an ESC character. Sandwiched between the [character and the H character are the two parameters. The Y value comes first, and is separated from the X value by a semicolon. Note well that these are *not* binary numbers, but two ASCII characters representing numeric digits—in this case, ASCII 48 (0) and ASCII 49 (1). You can't just poke the binary value "1" into the escape sequence. The console doesn't understand the binary value 1 as ASCII 49. Binary values for the X and Y positions must first be converted to their ASCII equivalents and then inserted into the escape sequence.

This is what the GotoXY procedure does. Binary values are converted to their ASCII equivalents by looking up the ASCII characters in a table. The Digits table presents two-digit ASCII representations of numeric values from 0 through 80. Values under 10 have leading 0s, as in 01, 02, 03, and so on. Here's where the magic happens inside GotoXY:

```
; Poke the Y digits:
        mov bl,al                    ; Put Y value into scale term EBX
        mov cx,word [Digits+ebx*2]   ; Fetch decimal digits to CX
        mov word [PosTerm+2],cx      ; Poke digits into control string
; Poke the X digits:
```

```
        mov bl,ah                    ; Put X value into scale term EBX
        mov cx,word [Digits+ebx*2]   ; Fetch decimal digits to CX
        mov word [PosTerm+5],cx      ; Poke digits into control string
```

The x,y values are passed in the two 8-bit registers AL and AH. Each is placed in a cleared EBX that becomes a term in an effective address starting at Digits. Because each element of the Digits table is two characters in size, we have to scale the offset by two.

The trick (if there is one) is bringing down both ASCII digits with one memory reference, and placing them in the 16-bit register CX. With the two ASCII digits in CX, we then poke them both simultaneously into their proper position in the escape sequence string. The y value begins at offset 2 into the string, and the x value begins at offset 5.

Once the PosTerm string has been modified for a particular X,Y coordinate pair, the string is sent to stdout, and interpreted by the console as an escape sequence that controls the cursor position. The next character sent to the console will appear at the new cursor position, and subsequent characters will follow at subsequent positions until and unless another cursor control sequence is sent to the console.

When you run programs that issue cursor control codes, make sure that your console window is larger than the maximum x and y values that your cursor will take on; otherwise, the lines will fold and nothing will show up quite where you intend it to. The eatterm program has a Digits table good up to 80 × 80. If you want to work across a larger display, you have to expand the Digits table with ASCII equivalents of two-digit values up to 99. Because of the way the table is set up and referenced, you can only fetch two-digit values, and thus with the code shown here you're limited to a 99 × 99 character console.

Console Control Cautions

This all sounds great—but it isn't quite as great as it sounds. The very fundamental control sequences like clearing the display and moving the cursor are probably universal, and will likely work identically on any Linux console you might find. Certainly they work on GNOME Terminal and Konsole, the two most popular console terminal utilities for Debian-based Linux distros.

Unfortunately, the history of Unix terminals and terminal control is a very spotted story; and for the more advanced console control functions, the sequences may not be supported, or may be different from one console implementation to another. To ensure that everything works, your programs would have to probe the console to find out what terminal spec it supports, and then issue escape sequences accordingly.

This is a shame. In Konsole, the following escape sequence turns the console background green:

```
GreenBack: db 27,"[42m"
```

This is true in Konsole. How universal this sequence and others like it are, I just don't know. Ditto the multitude of other console control commands, through which you can turn the PC keyboard LEDs on and off, alter foreground colors, display with underlining, and so on. More on this (in the terse Unix style) can be found in the Linux man pages under the keyword "console_codes." I encourage you to experiment, keeping in mind that different consoles (especially those on non-Linux Unix implementations) may react in different ways to different sequences.

Still, controlling console output isn't the worst of it. The holy grail of console programming is to create full-screen text applications that "paint" a form on the console, complete with data entry fields, and then allow the user to tab from one field to another, entering data in each field. This is made diabolically difficult in Linux by the need to access individual keystrokes at the console keyboard, through something called *raw mode*. Just explaining how raw mode works would take most of a chapter and involve a lot of fairly advanced Linux topics, for which I don't have space in this book.

The standard Unix way to deal with the console is a C library called ncurses, and while ncurses may be called from assembly, it's a fat and ugly thing indeed. A better choice for assembly programmers is a much newer library written specifically for NASM assembly language, called LinuxAsmTools. It was written by Jeff Owens, and it does nearly all of what ncurses does without C's brute-force calling conventions and boatloads of C cruft. LinuxAsmTools is free and may be found here: http://linuxasmtools.net/.

Creating and Using Macros

There is more than one way to split an assembly language program into more manageable chunks. Procedures are the most obvious way, and certainly the easiest to understand. The mechanism for calling and returning from procedures is built right into the CPU and is independent of any given assembler product.

Today's major assemblers provide another complexity-management tool: *macros*. Macros are a different breed of cat entirely. Whereas procedures are implemented by using CALL and RET instructions built right into the instruction set, macros are a trick of the assembler and do not depend on any particular instruction or group of instructions.

Simply put, a macro is a label that stands for some sequence of text lines. This sequence of text lines can be (but is not necessarily) a sequence of instructions.

When the assembler encounters the macro label in a source code file, it replaces the macro label with the text lines that the macro label represents. This is called *expanding* the macro, because the name of the macro (occupying one text line) is replaced by several lines of text, which are then assembled just as though they had appeared in the source code file all along. (Of course, a macro doesn't have to be several lines of text. It can be only one—but then there's a lot less advantage to using it!)

Macros bear some resemblance to include files in high-level languages such as Pascal. In Borland Pascal and newer Pascals like FreePascal, an include command might look like this:

```
{$I ENGINE.DEF}
```

When this include command is encountered, the compiler goes out to disk and finds the file named ENGINE.DEF. It then opens the file and starts feeding the text contained in that file into the source code file at the point where the include command was placed. The compiler then processes those lines as though they had always been right there in the source code file.

You might think of a macro as an include file that's built into the source code file. It's a sequence of text lines that is defined once, given a descriptive name, and then dropped into the source code repeatedly as needed by simply using the name.

This process is shown in Figure 10-4. The source code as stored on disk has a definition of the macro, bracketed between the %MACRO and %ENDMACRO directives. Later in the file, the name of the macro appears several times. When the assembler processes this file, it copies the macro definition into a buffer somewhere in memory. As it assembles the text read from disk, the assembler drops the statements contained in the macro into the text wherever the macro name appears. The disk file is not affected; the expansion of the macros occurs *only* in memory.

The Mechanics of Macro Definition

A macro definition looks a little like a procedure definition, framed between a pair of special NASM directives: %MACRO and %ENDMACRO. Note that the %ENDMACRO directive is on the line *after* the last line of the macro. Don't make the mistake of treating %ENDMACRO like a label that marks the macro's last line.

One minor shortcoming of macros vis-à-vis procedures is that macros can have only *one* entry point. A macro, after all, is a sequence of code lines that are inserted into your program in the midst of the flow of execution. You don't call a macro, and you don't return from it. The CPU runs through it just as the CPU runs through any sequence of instructions.

Many or most procedures may be expressed as macros with a little care. In Listing 10-5, I've taken the program from Listing 10-4 and converted all the procedures to macros so that you can see the differences between the two approaches.

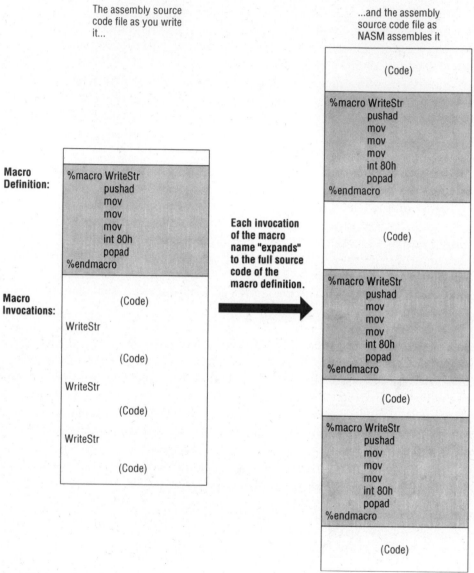

Figure 10-4: How macros work

Listing 10-5: eatmacro.asm

```
;   Executable name : eatmacro
;   Version          : 1.0
;   Created date     : 4/21/2009
;   Last update      : 4/23/2009
```

Listing 10-5: eatmacro.asm *(continued)*

```
;  Author        : Jeff Duntemann
;  Description   : A simple program in assembly for Linux, using
;                  NASM 2.05, demonstrating the use of escape
;                  sequences to do simple "full-screen" text output
;                  through macros rather than procedures
;
;  Build using these commands:
;    nasm -f elf -g -F stabs eatmacro.asm
;    ld -o eatmacro eatmacro.o
;
;
section .data            ; Section containing initialised data

SCRWIDTH:  equ 80                ; By default we assume 80 chars wide
PosTerm:   db 27,"[01;01H"       ; <ESC>[<Y>;<X>H
POSLEN:    equ $-PosTerm         ; Length of term position string
ClearTerm: db 27,"[2J"           ; <ESC>[2J; clears display
CLEARLEN   equ $-ClearTerm       ; Length of term clear string
AdMsg:     db "Eat At Joe's!"    ; Ad message
ADLEN:     equ $-AdMsg           ; Length of ad message
Prompt:    db "Press Enter: "    ; User prompt
PROMPTLEN: equ $-Prompt          ; Length of user prompt

; This table gives us pairs of ASCII digits from 0-80. Rather than
; calculate ASCII digits to insert in the terminal control string,
; we look them up in the table and read back two digits at once to
; a 16-bit register like DX, which we then poke into the terminal
; control string PosTerm at the appropriate place. See GotoXY.
; If you intend to work on a larger console than 80 X 80, you must
; add additional ASCII digit encoding to the end of Digits. Keep in
; mind that the code shown here will only work up to 99 X 99.
Digits: db "00010203040506070809101112131415161718191920"
        db "20212223242526272829303132333435363738392939"
        db "40414243444546474849505152535455565758592959"
        db "60616263646566676869707172737475767778792980"


SECTION .bss             ; Section containing uninitialized data


SECTION .text            ; Section containing code


;-----------------------------------------------------------------
; ExitProg:    Terminate program and return to Linux
; UPDATED:     4/23/2009
; IN:          Nothing
; RETURNS:     Nothing
; MODIFIES:    Nothing
; CALLS:       Kernel sys_exit
; DESCRIPTION: Calls sys_edit to terminate the program and return
```

(continued)

Listing 10-5: eatmacro.asm (*continued*)

```
;                     control to Linux

%macro ExitProg 0
        mov eax,1       ; Code for Exit Syscall
        mov ebx,0       ; Return a code of zero
        int 80H         ; Make kernel call
%endmacro


;-----------------------------------------------------------------------
; WaitEnter:   Wait for the user to press Enter at the console
; UPDATED:     4/23/2009
; IN:          Nothing
; RETURNS:     Nothing
; MODIFIES:    Nothing
; CALLS:       Kernel sys_read
; DESCRIPTION: Calls sys_read to wait for the user to type a newline at
;              the console

%macro WaitEnter 0
        mov eax,3       ; Code for sys_read
        mov ebx,0       ; Specify File Descriptor 0: Stdin
        int 80H         ; Make kernel call
%endmacro


;-----------------------------------------------------------------------
; WriteStr:    Send a string to the Linux console
; UPDATED:     4/21/2009
; IN:          String address in %1, string length in %2
; RETURNS:     Nothing
; MODIFIES:    Nothing
; CALLS:       Kernel sys_write
; DESCRIPTION: Displays a string to the Linux console through a
;              sys_write kernel call

%macro WriteStr 2       ; %1 = String address; %2 = string length
        push eax        ; Save pertinent registers
        push ebx
        mov ecx,%1      ; Put string address into ECX
        mov edx,%2      ; Put string length into EDX
        mov eax,4       ; Specify sys_write call
        mov ebx,1       ; Specify File Descriptor 1: Stdout
        int 80H         ; Make the kernel call
        pop ebx         ; Restore pertinent registers
        pop eax
%endmacro
```

Listing 10-5: eatmacro.asm (*continued*)

```
;-------------------------------------------------------------------
; ClrScr:      Clear the Linux console
; UPDATED:     4/23/2009
; IN:          Nothing
; RETURNS:     Nothing
; MODIFIES:    Nothing
; CALLS:       Kernel sys_write
; DESCRIPTION: Sends the predefined control string <ESC>[2J to the
;              console, which clears the full display

%macro ClrScr 0
        push eax            ; Save pertinent registers
        push ebx
        push ecx
        push edx
; Use WriteStr macro to write control string to console:
        WriteStr ClearTerm,CLEARLEN
        pop edx             ; Restore pertinent registers
        pop ecx
        pop ebx
        pop eax
%endmacro



;-------------------------------------------------------------------
; GotoXY:      Position the Linux Console cursor to an X,Y position
; UPDATED:     4/23/2009
; IN:          X in %1, Y in %2
; RETURNS:     Nothing
; MODIFIES:    PosTerm terminal control sequence string
; CALLS:       Kernel sys_write
; DESCRIPTION: Prepares a terminal control string for the X,Y coordinates
;              passed in AL and AH and calls sys_write to position the
;              console cursor to that X,Y position. Writing text to the
;              console after calling GotoXY will begin display of text
;              at that X,Y position.

%macro GotoXY 2                     ; %1 is X value; %2 id Y value
        pushad                      ; Save caller's registers
        xor edx,edx                 ; Zero EDX
        xor ecx,ecx                 ; Ditto ECX
; Poke the Y digits:
        mov dl,%2                            ; Put Y value into offset term EDX
        mov cx,word [Digits+edx*2]  ; Fetch decimal digits to CX
        mov word [PosTerm+2],cx     ; Poke digits into control string
; Poke the X digits:
        mov dl,%1                            ; Put X value into offset term EDX
```

(*continued*)

Listing 10-5: eatmacro.asm (*continued*)

```
        mov cx,word [Digits+edx*2]   ; Fetch decimal digits to CX
        mov word [PosTerm+5],cx      ; Poke digits into control string
; Send control sequence to stdout:
        WriteStr PosTerm,POSLEN
; Wrap up and go home:
        popad                        ; Restore caller's registers
%endmacro


;-----------------------------------------------------------------------
; WriteCtr:     Send a string centered to an 80-char-wide Linux console
; UPDATED:      4/23/2009
; IN:           Y value in %1, String address in %2, string length in %3
; RETURNS:      Nothing
; MODIFIES:     PosTerm terminal control sequence string
; CALLS:        GotoXY, WriteStr
; DESCRIPTION:  Displays a string to the Linux console centered in an
;               80-column display. Calculates the X for the passed-in
;               string length, then calls GotoXY and WriteStr to send
;               the string to the console

%macro WriteCtr 3      ; %1 = row; %2 = String addr; %3 = String length
        push ebx           ; Save caller's EBX
        push edx           ; Save caller's EDX
        mov edx,%3         ; Load string length into EDX
        xor ebx,ebx        ; Zero EBX
        mov bl,SCRWIDTH    ; Load the screen width value to BL
        sub bl,dl          ; Calc diff. of screen width and string length
        shr bl,1           ; Divide difference by two for X value
        GotoXY bl,%1       ; Position the cursor for display
        WriteStr %2,%3     ; Write the string to the console
        pop edx            ; Restore caller's EDX
        pop ebx            ; Restore caller's EBX
%endmacro



global _start          ; Linker needs this to find the entry point!

_start:
        nop                ; This no-op keeps gdb happy...

; First we clear the terminal display...
        ClrScr
; Then we post the ad message centered on the 80-wide console:
        WriteCtr 12,AdMsg,ADLEN
; Position the cursor for the "Press Enter" prompt:
        GotoXY 1,23
; Display the "Press Enter" prompt:
        WriteStr Prompt,PROMPTLEN
```

Listing 10-5: eatmacro.asm (*continued*)

```
; Wait for the user to press Enter:
      WaitEnter
; ...and we're done!
      ExitProg
```

Compare the macros in eatmacro with their procedure equivalents in eat-term. They've shed their RET instructions (and for those macros that invoke other macros, their CALL instructions), but for the most part they consist of almost precisely the same code.

Macros are invoked simply by naming them. Again, don't use the CALL instruction. Just place the macro's name on a line:

```
ClrScr
```

The assembler will handle the rest.

Defining Macros with Parameters

Macros are for the most part a straight text-substitution trick, but text substitution has some interesting and sometimes useful wrinkles. One of these is the ability to pass parameters to a macro when the macro is invoked.

For example, in eatmacro there's an invocation of the macro WriteCtr with three parameters:

```
WriteCtr 12,AdMsg,ADDLEN
```

The literal constant 12 is passed "into" the macro and used to specify the screen row on which the centered text is to be displayed—in this case, line 12 from the top. You could replace the 12 with 3 or 16 or any other number less than the number of lines currently displayed in the Linux console. (If you attempt to position the cursor to a line that doesn't exist in the console, the results are hard to predict. Typically the text shows up on the bottom line of the display.) The other two parameters are passed the address and length of the string to be displayed.

Macro parameters are, again, artifacts of the assembler. They are not pushed on the stack or set into a shared memory area (as with COMMON) or anything like that. The parameters are simply placeholders for the actual values (called *arguments*) that you pass to the macro through its parameters.

Let's take a closer look at the WriteCtr macro to see how this works:

```
%macro WriteCtr 3      ; %1 = row; %2 = String addr; %3 = String length
       push ebx        ; Save caller's EBX
       push edx        ; Save caller's EDX
       mov edx,%3      ; Load string length into EDX
```

```
        xor ebx,ebx        ; Zero EBX
        mov bl,SCRWIDTH    ; Load the screen width value to BL
        sub bl,dl          ; Calc diff. of screen width and string length
        shr bl,1           ; Divide difference by two for X value
        GotoXY bl,%1       ; Position the cursor for display
        WriteStr %2,%3     ; Write the string to the console
        pop edx            ; Restore caller's EDX
        pop ebx            ; Restore caller's EBX
%endmacro
```

So where are the parameters? This is another area where NASM differs radically from Microsoft's MASM. MASM allows you to use symbolic names—such as the word "Row" or "StringLength"—to stand for parameters. NASM relies on a simpler system that declares the number of parameters in the definition of the macro, and then refers to each parameter by number within the macro, rather than by some symbolic name.

In the definition of macro WriteCtr, the number 3 after the name of the macro indicates that the assembler is to look for three parameters. This number must be present—as 0—even when you have a macro with no parameters at all. *Every macro must have a parameter count.* Down in the definition of the macro, the parameters are referenced by number. Therefore, "%1" indicates the first parameter used after the invocation of the macro name "WriteCtr"; "%2" indicates the second parameter, counting from left to right; "%3" indicates the third parameter; and so on.

The actual values passed into the parameters are referred to as *arguments*. Don't confuse the actual values with the parameters. If you understand Pascal, it's *exactly* like the difference between formal parameters and actual parameters. A macro's parameters correspond to Pascal's formal parameters, whereas a macro's arguments correspond to Pascal's actual parameters. The macro's parameters are the labels following the name of the macro in the line in which it is *defined*. The arguments are the values specified on the line where the macro is *invoked*.

Macro parameters are a kind of label, and they may be referenced anywhere *within* the macro—but *only* within the macro. In WriteCtr, the %3 parameter is referenced as an operand to a MOV instruction. The argument passed to the macro in %3 is thus loaded into register EDX.

Macro arguments may be passed as parameters to other macros. This is what happens within WriteCtr when WriteCtr invokes the macro WriteStr. WriteStr takes two parameters, and WriteCtr passes its parameters %2 and %3 to WriteStr as its arguments.

The Mechanics of Invoking Macros

You can pass a literal constant value as an argument to a macro, as the row value is passed to the macro WriteCtr in the eatmacro program. You can also pass a register name as an argument. This is legal and a perfectly reasonable invocation of `WriteCtr`:

```
mov al,4
WriteCtr al,AdMsg,ADLEN
```

Inside the `WriteCtr` macro, NASM substitutes the name of the AL register for the `%1` parameter, so

```
GotoXY bl,%1   ; Position the cursor for display
```

becomes

```
GotoXY bl,al
```

Note well that all the usual rules governing instruction operands apply. Parameter `%1` can only hold an 8-bit argument, because ultimately `%1` is loaded into an 8-bit register inside `GotoXY`. You cannot legally pass register EBP or CX to `WriteCtr` in parameter `%1`, because you cannot directly move a 32-bit or a 16-bit register into an 8-bit register.

Similarly, you can pass a bracketed address as an argument:

```
WriteCtr [RowValue],AdMsg,ADLEN
```

This assumes, of course, that `RowValue` is a named variable defined as an 8-bit data item. If a macro parameter is used in an instruction requiring a 32-bit argument (as are `WriteCtr`'s parameters `%2` and `%3`), then you can also pass labels representing 32-bit addresses or 32-bit numeric values.

When a macro is invoked, its arguments are separated by commas. NASM drops the arguments into the macro's parameters in order, from left to right. If you pass only two arguments to a macro with three parameters, you're likely to get an error message from the assembler, depending on how you've referenced the unfilled parameter. If you pass *more* arguments to a macro than there are parameters to receive the arguments, the extraneous arguments are ignored.

Local Labels Within Macros

The macros I included in eatmacro.asm were designed to be simple and fairly obvious. None of them contains any jump instructions at all, but code in macros can use conditional and unconditional jumps just as code in procedures or program bodies can. There is, however, an important problem with labels used inside macros: labels in assembly language programs must be unique, and yet a macro is essentially duplicated in the source code as many times as it is invoked. This means there will be error messages flagging duplicate labels . . . unless a macro's labels are treated as local.

Local items have no meaning outside the immediate framework within which they are defined. Labels local to a macro are not visible outside the macro definition, meaning that they cannot be referenced except from code within the %MACRO...%ENDMACRO bounds.

All labels defined within a macro are considered local to the macro and are handled specially by the assembler. Here's an example; it's a macro adaptation of a piece of code I presented earlier, for forcing characters in a buffer from lowercase to uppercase:

```
%macro UpCase 2          ; %1 = Address of buffer; %2 = Chars in buffer
        mov edx,%1       ; Place the offset of the buffer into edx
        mov ecx,%2       ; Place the number of bytes in the buffer into ecx
%%IsLC: cmp byte [edx+ecx-1],'a' ; Below 'a'?
        jb %%Bump        ; Not lowercase. Skip
        cmp byte [edx+ecx-1],'z' ; Above 'z'?
        ja %%Bump        ; Not lowercase. Skip
        sub byte [edx+ecx-1],20h ; Force byte in buffer to uppercase
%%Bump: dec ecx          ; Decrement character count
        jnz %%IsLC       ; If there are more chars in the buffer, repeat
%endmacro
```

A label in a macro is made local by beginning it with two percent symbols: %%. When marking a location in the macro, the local label should be followed by a colon. When used as an operand to a jump or call instruction (such as JA, JB, and JNZ in the preceding), the local label is *not* followed by a colon. The important thing is to understand that unless the labels IsLC and Bump were made local to the macro by adding the prefix %% to each, there would be multiple instances of a label in the program (assuming the macro were invoked more than once) and the assembler would generate a duplicate label error on the second and every subsequent invocation.

Because labels must in fact be unique within your program, NASM takes a macro local label such as %%Bump and generates a label from it that will be unique in your program. It does this by using the prefix "..@" plus a four-digit number and the name of the label. Each time your macro is invoked, NASM will change the number, and thus generate unique synonyms for each local label within the macro. The label %%Bump, for example, might become ..@1771.Bump for a given invocation, and the number would be different each time the macro is invoked. This happens behind the scenes and you'll rarely be aware that it's going on unless you read the code dump listing files generated by NASM.

Macro Libraries As Include Files

Just as procedures may be gathered into library modules external to your program, so may macros be gathered into macro libraries. A *macro library* is really nothing but a text file that contains the source code for the macros in the library. Unlike procedures gathered into a module, macro libraries are not separately assembled and must be passed through the assembler each time the program is assembled. This is a problem with macros in general, not only with macros that are gathered into libraries. Programs that manage complexity by dividing code up into macros will assemble more slowly than programs that have been divided up into separately assembled modules. This is less of a problem today than it was 20 years ago, but for very large projects it can affect the speed of the build.

Macro libraries are used by "including" them in your program's source code file. The means to do this is the %INCLUDE directive. The %INCLUDE directive precedes the name of the macro library:

```
%include "mylib.mac"
```

Technically this statement may be anywhere in your source code file, but keep in mind that all macros must be fully defined before they are invoked. For this reason, it's a good idea to use the %INCLUDE directive near the top of your source code file's .text section, before any possible invocation of one of the library macros could occur.

If the macro file you want to include in a program is not in the same directory as your program, you may need to provide a fully qualified pathname as part of the %INCLUDE directive:

```
%include "../macrolibs/mylib.mac"
```

Otherwise, NASM may not be able to locate the macro file and will hand you an error message.

Macros versus Procedures: Pros and Cons

There are advantages to macros over procedures. One of them is speed. It takes time to execute the CALL and RET instructions that control entry to and exit from a procedure. In a macro, neither instruction is used. Only the instructions that perform the actual work of the macro are executed, so the macro's work is performed as quickly as possible.

There is a cost to this speed, and the cost is in extra memory used, especially if the macro is invoked a great many times. Notice in Figure 10-4 that three invocations of the macro WriteStr generate a total of eighteen instructions in memory. If the macro had been set up as a procedure, it would have required the six instructions in the body of the procedure, plus one RET instruction and three CALL instructions to do the same work. This would require a total of eight instructions for the procedure implementation, and 18 for the macro implementation. And if the macro were called five or seven times or more, the difference would grow. *Each time that a macro is called, all of its instructions are duplicated in the program yet another time.*

In short programs, this may not be a problem, and in situations where the code must be as fast as possible—as in graphics drivers—macros have a lot going for them, by eliminating the procedure overhead of calls and returns. It's a simple trade-off to understand: think macros for speed and procedures for compactness.

On the other hand, unless you really *are* writing something absolutely performance-dependent—such as graphics drivers—this trade-off is minor to the point of insignificance. For ordinary software, the difference in size between a procedure-oriented implementation and a macro-oriented implementation might be only two or three thousand bytes, and the speed difference would probably not be detectable. On modern CPUs, the performance of any given piece of software is *very* difficult to predict, and massive storage devices and memory systems make program size far less important than it was a generation ago. If you're trying to decide whether to go procedure or macro in any given instance, other factors than size or speed will predominate.

For example, I've always found macro-intensive software much more difficult to debug. Software tools don't necessarily deal well with macros. The Insight component of the Gdb debugger doesn't show expanded macro text in its source-code window. Insight wasn't designed with pure assembly debugging in mind (Gdb, like most Unix tools, has a powerful C bias) and when you step into a macro, *the source code highlighting simply stops* until execution emerges from the macro. You thus can't step through a macro's code as you can step through procedure or program code. Gdb will still debug as always from the console window, but console debugging is a very painful process compared to the visual perspective available from Insight.

Finally, there's another issue connected with macros that's much harder to explain, but it's the reason I am famously uncomfortable with them: use macros too much, and your code will no longer look like assembly language. Let's look again at the main program portion of the eatmacro.asm program:

```
ClrScr
WriteCtr 12,AdMsg,ADLEN
GotoXY 1,23
WriteStr Prompt,PROMPTLEN
WaitEnter
ExitProg
```

That's the whole main program. The entire thing has been subsumed by macro invocations. Is this assembly language, or is it—good grief!—a dialect of BASIC?

I admit, I replaced the entire main program with macro invocations here to make the point, but it's certainly possible to create so many macros that your assembly programs begin to look like some odd high-level language.

The difficult truth is that macros can clarify what a program is doing, or, used to excess, they can totally obscure how things actually work "under the skin." In my own projects, I use macros solely to reduce the clutter of very repetitive instruction sequences, especially things like setting up registers before making kernel calls. The whole point of assembly programming, after all, is to foster a complete understanding of what's happening down where the software meets the CPU. Anything that impedes that understanding should be used carefully, expertly, and (most of all) *sparingly*—or you might just as well learn C.

11

Strings and Things

Those Amazing String Instructions

At this point in the book we've touched on most of the important facets of assembly language work, including nearly all categories of machine instruction. One category remains, and for my money they're probably the most fascinating of all: the x86 string instructions.

They alone, of all the instructions in the x86 instruction set, have the power to deal with long sequences of bytes, words, or double words in memory at one time. (In assembly language, any contiguous sequence of bytes in memory may be considered a string—not simply sequences of human-readable characters.) More amazingly, some string instructions have the power to deal with these large sequences of bytes in an extraordinarily compact way: by executing a complete instruction loop as a single instruction, entirely within the CPU.

In this chapter, we'll cozy up to assembly language strings, and cover a few more topics related to programming and debugging for Linux.

The Notion of an Assembly Language String

Words fail us sometimes by picking up meanings as readily as a magnet picks up iron filings. The word *string* is a major offender here. It means roughly the same thing in all computer programming, but there are a multitude of small variations on that single theme. If you learned about strings in Pascal (as I did), you'll find that what you know isn't totally applicable when you program in C/C++, Python, Basic, or (especially) assembly.

So here's the Big View: a *string* is any contiguous group of bytes in memory, of any arbitrary size, that your operating system allows. (For Linux, that can be *big*.) The primary defining concept of an assembly language string is that its component bytes are right there in a row, with no interruptions.

That's pretty fundamental. Most higher-level languages build on the string concept in several ways. Pascal implementations that descend from Turbo Pascal treat strings as a separate data type, with a length counter at the start of the string to indicate how many bytes are in the string. In C, a string has no length byte in front of it. Instead, a C string is said to end when a byte with a binary value of 0 is encountered. This will be important in assembly work, much of which relates intimately to C and the standard C library, where C's string-handling machinery lives. In Basic, strings are stored in something called *string space*, which has a lot of built-in code machinery associated with it, to manage string space and handle the "way down deep" manipulation of string data.

When you begin working in assembly, you have to give up all that high-level language stuff. Assembly strings are just contiguous regions of memory. They start at some specified address, continue for some number of bytes, and stop. There is no length counter to indicate how many bytes are in the string, and no standard boundary characters such as binary 0 to indicate where a string starts or ends. You can certainly write assembly language routines that allocate Turbo Pascal-style strings or C-style strings and manipulate them, but to avoid confusion you must think of the data operated on by your routines as Pascal or C strings, rather than assembly language strings.

Turning Your "String Sense" Inside-Out

Assembly strings have no boundary values or length indicators. They can contain any values at all, including binary 0. In fact, you really have to stop thinking of strings in terms of specific regions in memory. You should instead think of strings in terms of the register values that define them.

It's slightly inside out compared to how you think of strings in such languages as Pascal, but it works: you've got a string when you set up a register to point to one. And once you point to a string, the length of that string is defined by the value that you place in register ECX.

This is key, and at the risk of repeating myself, I'll say it again: *Assembly strings are wholly defined by values you place in registers.* There is a set of assumptions about strings and registers baked into the silicon of the CPU. When you execute one of the string instructions (as I will describe shortly), the CPU uses those assumptions to determine which area of memory it reads from or writes to.

Source Strings and Destination Strings

There are two kinds of strings in x86 assembly work. *Source strings* are strings that you read from. *Destination strings* are strings that you write to. The difference between the two is *only* a matter of registers; source strings and destination strings can overlap. In fact, the very same region of memory can be *both* a source string and a destination string, at the same time.

Here are the assumptions that the CPU makes about strings when it executes a string instruction in 32-bit protected mode:

- A source string is pointed to by ESI.

- A destination string is pointed to by EDI.

- The length of both kinds of strings is the value you place in ECX. How this length is acted upon by the CPU depends on the specific instruction and how it's being used.

- Data coming from a source string or going to a destination string must begin the trip from, end the trip at, or pass through register EAX.

The CPU can recognize both a source string and a destination string simultaneously, because ESI and EDI can hold values independently of one another. However, because there is only one ECX register, the length of source and destination strings must be identical when they are used simultaneously, as in copying a source string to a destination string.

One way to remember the difference between source strings and destination strings is by their offset registers. *ESI* means "extended source index," and *EDI* means "extended destination index." "Extended," of course, means that they're 32 bits in size, compared to their 16-bit register portions SI and DI, inherited from the ancient days of 16-bit x86 computing.

A Text Display Virtual Screen

The best way to cement all that string background information in your mind is to see some string instructions at work. In Listing 11-1 I've implemented an interesting mechanism using string instructions: a simple virtual text display for the Linux console.

Back in the days of real-mode programming under DOS on PC-compatible machines, we had unhampered access to the video display refresh buffer on the graphics adapter. If we wrote an ASCII character or string of characters to the region of memory comprising the card's display buffer, wham! The associated text glyphs appeared on the screen instantaneously. In earlier editions of this book I took advantage of that direct-access display machinery, and presented a suite of useful display routines that demonstrated the x86 string instructions.

Under Linux, that's no longer possible. The graphics display buffer is still there, but it's now the property of the Linux kernel, and user-space applications can't write to it or even read from it directly.

Writing text-mode applications in assembly for the Linux console is nowhere near as easy as it was under DOS. In Chapter 10 I explained how (very) simple console terminal control could be achieved by writing escape sequences to the console via INT 80h. However, except for the two or three simplest commands, variations in terminal implementation makes using "naked" escape sequences a little dicey. A given sequence might mean one thing for one terminal and something entirely different for another. Terminal-control libraries like ncurses go to great lengths to detect and adapt to the multitude of terminal types that are out there. Code to do that is not something you can cobble up in an afternoon, and in fact it's too large a topic to treat in detail in an introductory book like this.

However, we can pull a few scurvy tricks, and learn a few things by pulling them. One is to create our own text video refresh buffer in memory as a named variable, and periodically write it out to the Linux console via INT 80h. Our PCs have gotten *very* fast since the DOS era, and text video buffers are not large. A 25 × 80 text display buffer is only 2,000 characters long, and the whole thing can be sent to the console with a single INT 80h sys_write call. The buffer appears instantaneously, at least as far as any human observer can discern.

Placing text in the buffer is a simple matter of calculating the address of a given row and column position in the buffer, and writing ASCII character values into the buffer variable starting at that address. After each modification of the buffer variable, you can update the console display by writing the entire buffer to the console via INT 80h. Jaded experts might call this "brute force" (and it's nowhere near as versatile as ncurses) but it's easy to understand. It doesn't give you control over character color or attributes (underlining, blinking, and so on), but it will give you a good basic understanding of the x86 string instructions.

Look over the code in Listing 11-1. In following sections I'll go through it piece by piece.

Listing 11-1: vidbuff1.asm

```
;   Executable name  : VIDBUFF1
;   Version          : 1.0
;   Created date     : 5/11/2009
;   Last update      : 5/14/2009
;   Author           : Jeff Duntemann
;   Description      : A simple program in assembly for Linux, using NASM 2.05,
;          demonstrating string instruction operation by "faking" full-screen
;          memory-mapped text I/O.
```

Listing 11-1: vidbuff1.asm (*continued*)

```
;
;   Build using these commands:
;     nasm -f elf -g -F stabs vidbuff1.asm
;     ld -o vidbuff1 vidbuff1.o
;

SECTION .data                     ; Section containing initialised data
        EOL     equ 10            ; Linux end-of-line character
        FILLCHR equ 32            ; ASCII space character
        HBARCHR equ 196           ; Use dash char if this won't display
        STRTROW equ 2             ; Row where the graph begins

; The dataset is just a table of byte-length numbers:
        Dataset db 9,71,17,52,55,18,29,36,18,68,77,63,58,44,0

        Message db "Data current as of 5/13/2009"
        MSGLEN  equ $-Message

; This escape sequence will clear the console terminal and place the
; text cursor to the origin (1,1) on virtually all Linux consoles:
        ClrHome db 27,"[2J",27,"[01;01H"
        CLRLEN  equ $-ClrHome     ; Length of term clear string

SECTION .bss                      ; Section containing uninitialized data

        COLS    equ 81            ; Line length + 1 char for EOL
        ROWS    equ 25            ; Number of lines in display
        VidBuff resb COLS*ROWS    ; Buffer size adapts to ROWS & COLS

SECTION .text                     ; Section containing code

global _start                     ; Linker needs this to find the entry point!

; This macro clears the Linux console terminal and sets the cursor position
; to 1,1, using a single predefined escape sequence.
%macro ClearTerminal 0
        pushad                    ; Save all registers
        mov eax,4                 ; Specify sys_write call
        mov ebx,1                 ; Specify File Descriptor 1: Standard Output
        mov ecx,ClrHome           ; Pass offset of the error message
        mov edx,CLRLEN            ; Pass the length of the message
        int 80H                   ; Make kernel call
        popad                     ; Restore all registers
%endmacro


;--------------------------------------------------------------------
; Show:       Display a text buffer to the Linux console
; UPDATED:    5/13/2009
```

(*continued*)

Listing 11-1: vidbuff1.asm (*continued*)

```
; IN:          Nothing
; RETURNS:     Nothing
; MODIFIES:    Nothing
; CALLS:       Linux sys_write
; DESCRIPTION: Sends the buffer VidBuff to the Linux console via sys_write.
;              The number of bytes sent to the console is calculated by
;              multiplying the COLS equate by the ROWS equate.

Show:   pushad                ; Save all registers
        mov eax,4             ; Specify sys_write call
        mov ebx,1             ; Specify File Descriptor 1: Standard Output
        mov ecx,VidBuff       ; Pass offset of the buffer
        mov edx,COLS*ROWS     ; Pass the length of the buffer
        int 80H               ; Make kernel call
        popad                 ; Restore all registers
        ret                   ; And go home!


;------------------------------------------------------------------
; ClrVid:      Clears a text buffer to spaces and replaces all EOLs
; UPDATED:     5/13/2009
; IN:          Nothing
; RETURNS:     Nothing
; MODIFIES:    VidBuff, DF
; CALLS:       Nothing
; DESCRIPTION: Fills the buffer VidBuff with a predefined character
;              (FILLCHR) and then places an EOL character at the end
;              of every line, where a line ends every COLS bytes in
;              VidBuff.

ClrVid: push eax              ; Save caller's registers
        push ecx
        push edi
        cld                   ; Clear DF; we're counting up-memory
        mov al,FILLCHR        ; Put the buffer filler char in AL
        mov edi,VidBuff       ; Point destination index at buffer
        mov ecx,COLS*ROWS     ; Put count of chars stored into ECX
        rep stosb             ; Blast chars at the buffer
; Buffer is cleared; now we need to re-insert the EOL char after each line:
        mov edi,VidBuff       ; Point destination at buffer again
        dec edi               ; Start EOL position count at VidBuff char 0
        mov ecx,ROWS          ; Put number of rows in count register
PtEOL:  add edi,COLS          ; Add column count to EDU
        mov byte [edi],EOL    ; Store EOL char at end of row
        loop PtEOL            ; Loop back if still more lines
        pop edi               ; Restore caller's registers
        pop ecx
        pop eax
```

Listing 11-1: vidbuff1.asm (*continued*)

```
        ret                      ; and go home!


;-----------------------------------------------------------------------
; WrtLn:        Writes a string to a text buffer at a 1-based X,Y position
; UPDATED:      5/13/2009
; IN:           The address of the string is passed in ESI
;               The 1-based X position (row #) is passed in EBX
;               The 1-based Y position (column #) is passed in EAX
;               The length of the string in chars is passed in ECX
; RETURNS:      Nothing
; MODIFIES:     VidBuff, EDI, DF
; CALLS:        Nothing
; DESCRIPTION: Uses REP MOVSB to copy a string from the address in ESI
;               to an X,Y location in the text buffer VidBuff.

WrtLn: push eax           ; Save registers we change
        push ebx
        push ecx
        push edi
        cld                      ; Clear DF for up-memory write
        mov edi,VidBuff ; Load destination index with buffer address
        dec eax          ; Adjust Y value down by 1 for address calculation
        dec ebx          ; Adjust X value down by 1 for address calculation
        mov ah,COLS      ; Move screen width to AH
        mul ah           ; Do 8-bit multiply AL*AH to AX
        add edi,eax      ; Add Y offset into vidbuff to EDI
        add edi,ebx      ; Add X offset into vidbuf to EDI
        rep movsb        ; Blast the string into the buffer
        pop edi          ; Restore registers we changed
        pop ecx
        pop ebx
        pop eax
        ret                      ; and go home!


;-----------------------------------------------------------------------
; WrtHB:        Generates a horizontal line bar at X,Y in text buffer
; UPDATED:      5/13/2009
; IN:           The 1-based X position (row #) is passed in EBX
;               The 1-based Y position (column #) is passed in EAX
;               The length of the bar in chars is passed in ECX
; RETURNS:      Nothing
; MODIFIES:     VidBuff, DF
; CALLS:        Nothing
; DESCRIPTION: Writes a horizontal bar to the video buffer VidBuff,
;               at the 1-based X,Y values passed in EBX,EAX. The bar is
;               "made of" the character in the equate HBARCHR. The
```

(continued)

Listing 11-1: vidbuff1.asm (*continued*)

```
;                default is character 196; if your terminal won't display
;                that (you need the IBM 850 character set) change the
;                value in HBARCHR to ASCII dash or something else supported
;                in your terminal.

WrtHB: push eax          ; Save registers we change
       push ebx
       push ecx
       push edi
       cld               ; Clear DF for up-memory write
       mov edi,VidBuff    ; Put buffer address in destination register
       dec eax           ; Adjust Y value down by 1 for address calculation
       dec ebx           ; Adjust X value down by 1 for address calculation
       mov ah,COLS       ; Move screen width to AH
       mul ah            ; Do 8-bit multiply AL*AH to AX
       add edi,eax       ; Add Y offset into vidbuff to EDI
       add edi,ebx       ; Add X offset into vidbuf to EDI
       mov al,HBARCHR    ; Put the char to use for the bar in AL
       rep stosb         ; Blast the bar char into the buffer
       pop edi           ; Restore registers we changed
       pop ecx
       pop ebx
       pop eax
       ret               ; And go home!


;-------------------------------------------------------------------------
; Ruler:        Generates a "1234567890"-style ruler at X,Y in text buffer
; UPDATED:      5/13/2009
; IN:           The 1-based X position (row #) is passed in EBX
;               The 1-based Y position (column #) is passed in EAX
;               The length of the ruler in chars is passed in ECX
; RETURNS:      Nothing
; MODIFIES:     VidBuff
; CALLS:        Nothing
; DESCRIPTION:  Writes a ruler to the video buffer VidBuff, at the 1-based
;               X,Y position passed in EBX,EAX. The ruler consists of a
;               repeating sequence of the digits 1 through 0. The ruler
;               will wrap to subsequent lines and overwrite whatever EOL
;               characters fall within its length, if it will noy fit
;               entirely on the line where it begins. Note that the Show
;               procedure must be called after Ruler to display the ruler
;               on the console.

Ruler: push eax          ; Save the registers we change
       push ebx
       push ecx
       push edi
```

Listing 11-1: vidbuff1.asm (*continued*)

```
        mov edi,VidBuff  ; Load video address to EDI
        dec eax          ; Adjust Y value down by 1 for address calculation
        dec ebx          ; Adjust X value down by 1 for address calculation
        mov ah,COLS      ; Move screen width to AH
        mul ah           ; Do 8-bit multiply AL*AH to AX
        add edi,eax      ; Add Y offset into vidbuff to EDI
        add edi,ebx      ; Add X offset into vidbuf to EDI
; EDI now contains the memory address in the buffer where the ruler
; is to begin. Now we display the ruler, starting at that position:
        mov al,'1'       ; Start ruler with digit '1'
DoChar: stosb            ; Note that there's no REP prefix!
        add al,'1'       ; Bump the character value in AL up by 1
        aaa              ; Adjust AX to make this a BCD addition
        add al,'0'       ; Make sure we have binary 3 in AL's high nybble
        loop DoChar      ; Go back & do another char until ECX goes to 0
        pop edi          ; Restore the registers we changed
        pop ecx
        pop ebx
        pop eax
        ret              ; And go home!


;-------------------------------------------------------------------------
; MAIN PROGRAM:

_start:
        nop              ; This no-op keeps gdb happy...

; Get the console and text display text buffer ready to go:
        ClearTerminal    ; Send terminal clear string to console
        call ClrVid      ; Init/clear the video buffer

; Next we display the top ruler:
        mov eax,1        ; Load Y position to AL
        mov ebx,1        ; Load X position to BL
        mov ecx,COLS-1   ; Load ruler length to ECX
        call Ruler       ; Write the ruler to the buffer

; Here we loop through the dataset and graph the data:
        mov esi,Dataset  ; Put the address of the dataset in ESI
        mov ebx,1        ; Start all bars at left margin (X=1)
        mov ebp,0        ; Dataset element index starts at 0
.blast: mov eax,ebp      ; Add dataset number to element index
        add eax,STRTROW  ; Bias row value by row # of first bar
        mov cl,byte [esi+ebp]  ; Put dataset value in low byte of ECX
        cmp ecx,0        ; See if we pulled a 0 from the dataset
        je .rule2        ; If we pulled a 0 from the dataset, we're done
        call WrtHB       ; Graph the data as a horizontal bar
        inc ebp          ; Increment the dataset element index
```

(continued)

Listing 11-1: vidbuff1.asm (*continued*)

```
        jmp .blast        ; Go back and do another bar

; Display the bottom ruler:
.rule2: mov eax,ebp       ; Use the dataset counter to set the ruler row
        add eax,STRTROW   ; Bias down by the row # of the first bar
        mov ebx,1         ; Load X position to BL
        mov ecx,COLS-1    ; Load ruler length to ECX
        call Ruler        ; Write the ruler to the buffer

; Thow up an informative message centered on the last line
        mov esi,Message   ; Load the address of the message to ESI
        mov ecx,MSGLEN    ; and its length to ECX
        mov ebx,COLS      ; and the screen width to EBX
        sub ebx,ecx       ; Calc diff of message length and screen width
        shr ebx,1         ; Divide difference by 2 for X value
        mov eax,24        ; Set message row to Line 24
        call WrtLn        ; Display the centered message

; Having written all that to the buffer, send the buffer to the console:
        call Show         ; Refresh the buffer to the console

Exit:   mov eax,1         ; Code for Exit Syscall
        mov ebx,0         ; Return a code of zero
        int 80H           ; Make kernel call
```

REP STOSB, the Software Machine Gun

Our virtual text display buffer is nothing more than a region of raw memory set aside in the .bss section, using the RESB directive. The size of the buffer is defined by two equates, which specify the number of rows and columns that you want. By default I've set it to 25 rows and 80 columns, but 2010-era consoles can display text screens a great deal larger than that. You can change the COLS and ROWS equates to define buffers as large as 255 × 255, though if your terminal window isn't that large, your results will be (to put it charitably) unpredictable. Changing the dimensions of your text display is done by changing one or both of those equates. Whatever other changes must be made to the code are handled automatically. Note that this has to be done at assembly time, as many of the calculations are assembly-time calculations done by NASM when you build the program.

You do not have to match the size of the terminal window precisely to the ROWS and COLS values you choose, as long as the terminal window is *larger* than ROWS × COLS. If you maximize the terminal window (like Konsole) your text display will appear starting in the upper-left corner of the screen.

Machine-Gunning the Virtual Display

When Linux loads your programs into memory, it typically clears uninitialized variables (like VidBuff from Listing 11-1) to binary zeros. This is good, but binary zeros do not display correctly on the Linux console. To look "blank" on the console, the display buffer memory must be cleared to the ASCII space character. This means writing the value 20h into memory from the beginning of the buffer to its end.

Such things should always be done in tight loops. The obvious way is to put the display buffer address into EDI, the number of bytes in your refresh buffer into ECX, the ASCII value to clear the buffer to into AL, and then code up a tight loop this way:

```
Clear:  mov byte [edi],AL      ; Write the value in AL to memory
        inc edi                ; Bump EDI to next byte in the buffer
        dec ecx                ; Decrement ECX by one position
        jnz Clear              ; And loop again until ECX is 0
```

This will work. It's even tolerably fast, especially on newer CPUs; but *all* of the preceding code is equivalent to the following one single instruction:

```
rep stosb
```

Really.

The STOSB instruction is the simplest of the x86 string instructions, and a good place to begin. There are two parts to the instruction as I show it above, a situation we haven't seen before. REP is a new type of critter, called a *prefix*, and it changes how the CPU treats the instruction mnemonic that follows it. We'll get back to REP shortly. Right now, let's look at STOSB itself. The mnemonic means STOre String by Byte. Like all the string instructions, STOSB makes certain assumptions about some CPU registers. It works only on the destination string, so ESI is not involved. However, these assumptions must be respected and dealt with:

- EDI must be loaded with the address of the destination string. (Think: *E*DI, for *d*estination *i*ndex.)
- ECX must be loaded with the number of times the value in AL is to be stored into the string.
- AL must be loaded with the value to be stored into the string.

Executing the STOSB Instruction

Once you set up these three registers, you can safely execute a STOSB instruction. When you do, this is what happens:

1. The byte value in AL is copied to the memory address stored in EDI.

2. EDI is incremented by 1, such that it now points to the next byte in memory following the one just written to.

Note that we're *not* machine-gunning here—not yet, at least. *One* copy of AL is copied to *one* location in memory. The EDI register is adjusted so that it will be ready for the *next* time STOSB is executed.

One very important point to remember is that ECX is *not* decremented by STOSB. ECX is decremented automatically *only* if you put the REP prefix in front of STOSB. Lacking the REP prefix, you have to do the decrementing yourself, either explicitly through DEC or through the LOOP instruction, as I explain a little later in this chapter.

So, you can't make STOSB run automatically without REP. However, you can, if you like, execute other instructions before executing another STOSB. As long as you don't disturb EDI or ECX, you can do whatever you wish. Then when you execute STOSB again, another copy of AL will go out to the location pointed to by EDI, and EDI will be adjusted yet again. (You have to remember to decrement ECX somehow.) Note that you can change the value in AL if you like, but the changed value will be copied into memory. (You may want to do that—there's no law that requires you to fill a string with only one single value. Later, you'll see that it's sometimes very useful to do so.)

However, this is like the difference between a semiautomatic weapon (which fires one round every time you press and release the trigger) and a fully automatic weapon, which fires rounds continually as long as you hold the trigger down. To make STOSB fully automatic, just hang the REP prefix ahead of it. What REP does is beautifully simple: it sets up the tightest of all tight loops completely *inside* the CPU, and fires copies of AL into memory repeatedly (hence its name), incrementing EDI by 1 each time and decrementing ECX by 1, until ECX is decremented down to 0. Then it stops, and when the smoke clears, you'll see that your entire destination string, however large, has been filled with copies of AL.

Man, now *that's* programming!

In the vidbuff1 program presented in Listing 11-1, the code to clear the display buffer is in the clrVid procedure. The pertinent lines are shown here:

```
cld                 ; Clear DF; we're counting up-memory
mov al,FILLCHR      ; Put the buffer filler char in AL
mov edi,VidBuff     ; Point destination index at buffer
mov ecx,COLS*ROWS   ; Put count of chars stored into ECX
rep stosb           ; Blast chars at the buffer
```

The FILLCHR equate is by default set to 32, which is the ASCII space character. You can set this to fill the buffer with some other character, though how useful this may be is unclear. Note also that the number of characters to be written into memory is calculated by NASM at assembly time as COLS times ROWS. This enables you to change the size of your virtual display without changing the code that clears the display buffer.

STOSB and the Direction Flag (DF)

Leading off the short code sequence shown above is an instruction I haven't mentioned before: CLD. It controls something critical in string instruction work, which is the direction in memory that the string operation takes.

Most of the time that you'll be using STOSB, you'll want to run it "uphill" in memory—that is, from a lower memory address to a higher memory address. In clrVid, you put the address of the start of the video refresh buffer into EDI, and then blast characters into memory at successively higher memory addresses. Each time STOSB fires a byte into memory, EDI is incremented to point to the *next higher* byte in memory.

This is the logical way to work it, but it doesn't have to be done that way at all times. STOSB can just as easily begin at a high address and move downward in memory. On each store into memory, EDI can be *decremented* by 1 instead.

Which way that STOSB fires—uphill toward successively higher addresses, or downhill toward successively lower addresses—is governed by one of the flags in the EFlags register. This is the *Direction flag*, DF. DF's sole job in life is to control the direction of action taken by certain instructions that, like STOSB, can move in one of two directions in memory. Most of these (like STOSB and its brothers) are string instructions.

The sense of DF is this: when DF is *set* (that is, when DF has the value 1), STOSB and its fellow string instructions work downhill, from higher to lower addresses. When DF is *cleared* (that is, when it has the value 0), STOSB and its siblings work uphill, from lower to higher addresses. This in turn is simply the direction in which the EDI register is adjusted: When DF is set, EDI is decremented during string instruction execution. When DF is cleared, EDI is incremented.

The Direction flag defaults to 0 (uphill) when the CPU is reset. It is generally changed in one of two ways: with the CLD instruction or with the STD instruction. CLD clears DF to 0, and STD sets DF to 1. (You should keep in mind when debugging that the POPF instruction can also change DF, by popping an entire new set of flags from the stack into the EFlags register.) Because DF's default state is cleared to 0, and all of the string instructions in the vidbuff1 demo program work uphill in memory, it's not technically necessary to include a CLD instruction in the clrVid procedure. However, other parts of a program can change DF, so it's always a good idea to place the appropriate CLD or STD right before a string instruction to ensure that your machine gun fires in the right direction!

People sometimes get confused and think that DF also governs whether ECX is incremented or decremented by the string instructions. Not so! Nothing in a string instruction *ever* increments ECX. ECX holds a count value, not a memory address. You place a count in ECX and it counts down each time that a string instruction fires, period. DF has nothing to say about it.

Defining Lines in the Display Buffer

Clearing VidBuff to space characters isn't quite the end of the story, however. To render correctly on the terminal programs that display the Linux console, display data must be divided into lines. Lines are delimited by the EOL character, ASCII 10. A line begins at the start of the buffer, and ends with the first EOL character. The next line begins immediately after the EOL character and runs until the next EOL character, and so on.

When text is written piecemeal to the console, each line may be a different length. In our virtual display system, however, the entire buffer is written to the console in one INT 80h swoop, as a sequence of lines that are all the same length. This means that when we clear the buffer, we also have to insert EOL characters where we wish each displayed line to end.

This is done in the remainder of the ClrVid procedure. What we have to do is write an EOL character into the buffer every COLS bytes. This is done with a very tight loop. If you look at the second portion of ClrVid, you may notice that the loop in question isn't *quite* ordinary. Hold that thought—I'll come back to the LOOP instruction in just a little bit.

Sending the Buffer to the Linux Console

I need to reiterate: we're talking a *virtual* display here. VidBuff is just a region of memory into which you can write characters and character strings with ordinary assembly language instructions. However, nothing will appear on your monitor until you send the buffer to the Linux console.

This is easy enough. The procedure Show in Listing 11-1 makes a single call to the sys_write kernel service via INT 80h, and sends the entire buffer to the console at once. The EOL characters embedded in the buffer every COLS bytes are treated as EOL characters always are by the console, and force a new line to begin immediately after each EOL. Because all the lines are the same length, sending VidBuff to the console creates a rectangular region of text that will display correctly on any terminal window that is at least COLS by ROWS in size. (Smaller windows will scramble VidBuff's text. Try running vidbuff1 in terminal windows of various sizes and you'll quickly see what I mean.)

What's important is that your programs call Show whenever you want a screen update. This can be done as often as you want, whenever you want. On modern Linux PCs, the update happens so quickly as to appear instantaneous. There's no reason you shouldn't call Show after each write to VidBuff, but that's up to you.

The Semiautomatic Weapon: STOSB without REP

Among all the string instructions, I chose to show you REP STOSB first because it's dramatic in the extreme. But more to the point, it's *simple*—in fact, it's simpler to use REP than not to use REP. REP simplifies string processing from the programmer's perspective, because it brings the instruction loop *inside* the CPU. You can use the STOSB instruction without REP, but it's a little more work. The work involves setting up the instruction loop outside the CPU and making sure it's correct.

Why bother? Simply this: with REP STOSB, you can only store the *same* value into the destination string. Whatever you put into AL before executing REP STOSB is the value that is fired into memory ECX times. STOSB can be used to store *different* values into the destination string by firing it semiautomatically, and changing the value in AL between each squeeze of the trigger.

You lose a little time in handling the loop yourself, outside the CPU, because a certain amount of time is spent in fetching the loop's instruction bytes from memory. Still, if you keep your loop as tight as you can, you don't lose an objectionable amount of speed, especially on modern processors, which make very effective use of cache and don't fetch instructions from memory every time they're executed.

Who Decrements ECX?

Early in my experience with assembly language, I recall being massively confused about where and when the ECX register was decremented when using string instructions. It's a key issue, especially when you *don't* use the REP prefix.

When you use REP STOSB (or REP with any of the string instructions), ECX is decremented automatically, by 1, for each memory access the instruction makes. And once ECX gets itself decremented down to 0, REP STOSB detects that ECX is now 0 and stops firing into memory. Control then passes on to the next instruction in line. But take away REP, and the automatic decrementing of ECX stops. So, also, does the automatic detection of when ECX has been counted down to 0.

Obviously, something has to decrement ECX, as ECX governs how many times the string instruction accesses memory. If STOSB doesn't do it—you guessed it—*you* have to do it somewhere else, with another instruction.

The obvious way to decrement ECX is to use DEC ECX; and the obvious way to determine whether ECX has been decremented to 0 is to follow the DEC ECX instruction with a JNZ (Jump if Not Zero) instruction. JNZ tests the Zero flag, ZF, and jumps back to the STOSB instruction until ZF becomes true. And ZF becomes true when a DEC instruction causes its operand (here, ECX) to become 0.

The LOOP Instructions

With all that in mind, consider the following assembly language instruction loop. Note that I've split it into three parts by inserting two blank lines:

```
DoChar: stosb           ; Note that there's no REP prefix!

        add al,'1'      ; Bump the character value in AL up by 1
        aaa             ; Adjust AX to make this a BCD addition
        add al,'0'      ; Basically, put binary 3 in AL's high nybble

        dec ecx         ; Decrement the count by 1..
        jnz DoChar      ; ..and loop again if ECX > 0
```

Ignore the block of three instructions in the middle for the time being. What those three instructions do is what I suggested could be done a little earlier: change AL in between each store of AL into memory. I'll explain in detail how shortly. Look instead (for now) to see how the loop runs. STOSB fires, AL is modified, and then ECX is decremented. The JNZ instruction tests to see whether the DEC instruction has forced ECX to zero. If so, the Zero flag, ZF, is set, and the loop will terminate. But until ZF is set, the jump is made back to the label DoChar, where STOSB fires yet again.

There is a simpler way, using an instruction I haven't discussed until now: LOOP. The LOOP instruction combines the decrementing of ECX with a test and jump based on ZF. It looks like this:

```
DoChar: stosb           ; Note that there's no REP prefix!
        add al,'1'      ; Bump the character value in AL up by 1
        aaa             ; Adjust AX to make this a BCD addition
        add al,'0'      ; Make sure we have binary 3 in AL's high nybble
        loop DoChar     ; Go back & do another char until ECX goes to 0
```

The LOOP instruction first decrements ECX by 1. It then checks the Zero flag to see if the decrement operation forced ECX to zero. If so, it falls through to the next instruction. If not (that is, if ZF remains 0, indicating that ECX was still greater than 0), then LOOP branches to the label specified as its operand.

The loop keeps looping the LOOP until ECX counts down to 0. At that point, the loop is finished, and execution falls through and continues with the next instruction following LOOP.

Displaying a Ruler on the Screen

As a useful demonstration of when it makes sense to use STOSB without REP (but with LOOP), let me offer you another item for your video toolkit.

The Ruler procedure from Listing 11-1 displays a repeating sequence of ascending digits starting from 1, of any length, at some selectable location on your screen. In other words, you can display a string of digits like this anywhere you'd like:

```
12345678901234567890123456789012345678901234567890123456789012345678901234567890
```

This might allow you to determine where in the horizontal dimension of the console window a line begins or some character falls. The Ruler procedure enables you to specify how long the displayed ruler is, in digits, and where on the screen it will be displayed.

A typical call to Ruler would look something like this:

```
mov eax,1           ; Load Y position to AL
mov ebx,1           ; Load X position to BL
mov ecx,COLS-1      ; Load ruler length to ECX
call Ruler          ; Write the ruler to the buffer
```

This invocation places a ruler at the upper-left corner of the display, beginning at position 1,1. The length of the ruler is passed in ECX. Here, you're specifying a ruler one character shorter than the display is wide. This provides a ruler that spans the full visible width of your virtual text display.

Why one character shorter? Remember that there is an EOL character at the end of every line. This EOL character isn't visible directly, but it's still a character and requires a byte in the buffer to hold it. The COLS equate must always take this into account: if you want an 80-character wide display, COLS must be set to 81. If you want a 96-character wide display, COLS must be set to 97. If you code a call to Ruler as shown above, NASM will do some assembly-time math and always generate a ruler that spans the full (visible) width of the text display.

Over and above the LOOP instruction, there's a fair amount of new assembly technology at work here that could stand explaining. Let's detour from the string instructions for a bit and take a closer look.

MUL Is Not IMUL

I described the MUL instruction and its implicit operands back in Chapter 7. The Ruler procedure uses MUL as well, to calculate an X,Y position in the display buffer where STOSB can begin placing the ruler characters. The algorithm for determining the offset in bytes into the buffer for any given X and Y values looks like this:

```
Offset = ((Y * width in characters of a screen line) + X)
```

Pretty obviously, you have to move Y lines down in the screen buffer, and then move X bytes over from the left margin of the screen to reach your X,Y position. The calculation is done this way inside the Ruler procedure:

```
mov edi,VidBuff       ; Load video address to EDI
dec eax               ; Adjust Y value down by 1 for address calculation
dec ebx               ; Adjust X value down by 1 for address calculation
mov ah,COLS           ; Move screen width to AH
mul ah                ; Do 8-bit multiply AL*AH to AX
add edi,eax           ; Add Y offset into vidbuff to EDI
add edi,ebx           ; Add X offset into vidbuf to EDI
```

The two DEC instructions take care of the fact that X,Y positions in this system are 1-based; that is, the upper-left corner of the screen is position 1,1 rather than 0,0, as they are in some X,Y coordinate systems. Think of it this way: if you want to display a ruler beginning in the very upper-left corner of the screen, you have to write the ruler characters starting at the very beginning of the buffer, at no offset at all. For calculation's sake, then, the X,Y values thus have to be 0-based.

For an 8-bit multiply using MUL, one of the factors is implicit: AL contains the Y value, and the caller passes Ruler the Y value in EAX. We place the screen width in AH, and then multiply AH times AL with MUL. (See Chapter 7's discussion of MUL if it's gotten fuzzy in the interim.) The product replaces the values in both AH and AL, and is accessed as the value in AX. Adding that product and the X value (passed to Ruler in BL) to EDI gives you the precise memory address where the ruler characters must be written.

Now, there's a fairly common bug to warn you about here: MUL is not IMUL—most of the time. MUL and IMUL are sister instructions that both perform multiplication. MUL treats its operand values as unsigned, whereas IMUL treats them as signed. This difference does not matter as long as both factors remain positive in a signed context. In practical terms for an 8-bit multiply, MUL and IMUL work identically on values of 127 or less. At 128 everything changes. Values above 127 are considered negative in an 8-bit signed context. MUL considers 128 to be ... 128. IMUL considers 128 to be -1. Whoops.

You could replace the MUL instruction with IMUL in Ruler, and the proc would work identically until you passed it a screen dimension greater than 127. Then, suddenly, IMUL would calculate a product that is nominally negative . . . but only if you're treating the value as a signed value. A negative number treated as unsigned is a very large positive number, and a memory reference to the address represented by EDI plus that anomalous value will generate a segmentation fault. Try it! No harm done, and it's an interesting lesson. IMUL is for signed values. For memory address calculation, leave it alone and be sure to use MUL instead.

Adding ASCII Digits

Once the correct offset into the buffer for the ruler's beginning is calculated and placed in EDI (and once we set up initial values for ECX and EAX), we're ready to start making rulers.

Immediately before the STOSB instruction, we load the ASCII digit "1" into AL. Note that the instruction MOV AL, '1' does *not* move the binary numeric value 1 into AL! The '1' is an ASCII character (by virtue of being within single quotes) and the character '1' (the "one" digit) has a numeric value of 31h, or 49 decimal.

This becomes a problem immediately after we store the digit '1' into video memory with STOSB. After digit '1' we need to display digit '2'—and to do that we need to change the value stored in AL from '1' to '2'.

Ordinarily, you can't just add '1' to '1' and get '2'; 31h + 31h will give you 62h, which (when seen as an ASCII character) is lowercase letter b, *not* '2'! However, in this case the x86 instruction set comes to the rescue, in the form of a somewhat peculiar instruction called AAA, *Adjust AL after BCD Addition*.

What AAA does is allow us, in fact, to add ASCII character digits together, rather than numeric values. AAA is one of a group of instructions called the BCD instructions, so called because they support arithmetic with Binary Coded Decimal (BCD) values. BCD is just another way of expressing a numeric value, somewhere between a pure binary value like 1 and an ASCII digit like "1." A BCD value is a 4-bit value, occupying the low nybble of a byte. It expresses values between 0 and 9 *only*. (That's what the "decimal" part of "Binary Coded Decimal" indicates.) It's possible to express values greater than 9 (from 10 to 15, actually) in 4 bits, but those additional values are not valid BCD values (see Figure 11-1).

The value 31h is a valid BCD value, because the low nybble contains 1. BCD is a 4-bit numbering system, and the high nybble (which in the case of 31h contains a 3) is ignored. In fact, all of the ASCII digits from '0' through '9' may be considered legal BCD values, because in each case the characters' low 4 bits contain a valid BCD value. The 3 stored in the high four bits of each ASCII digit is ignored.

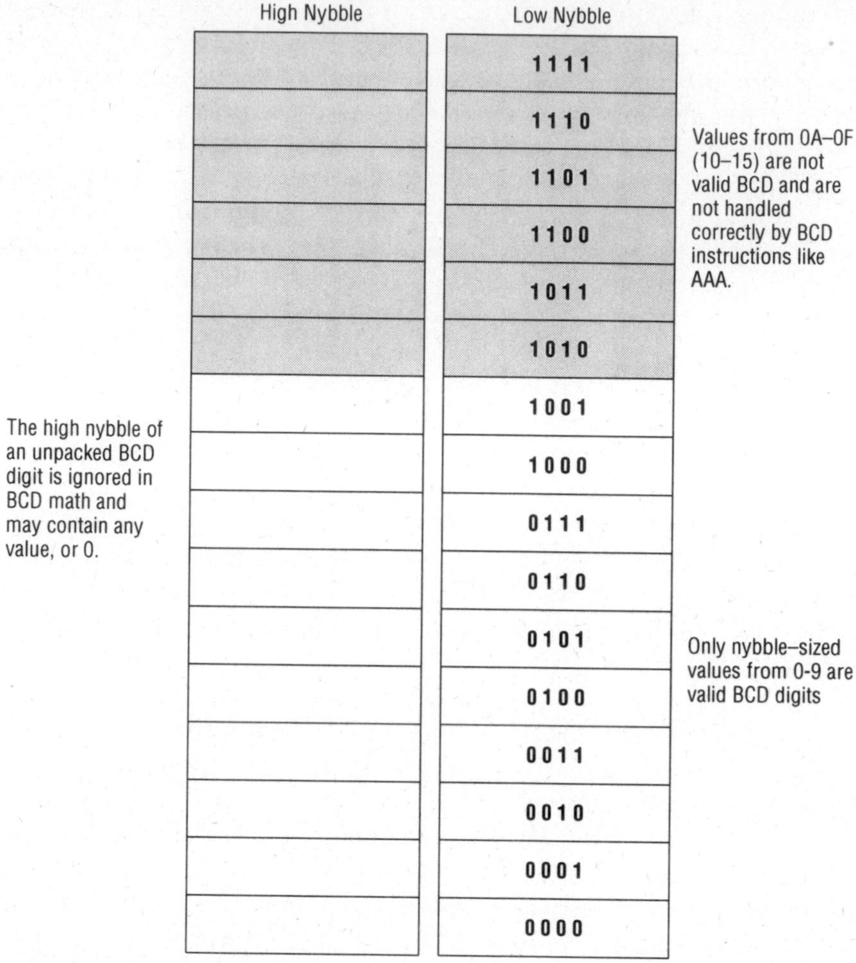

High Nybble   Low Nybble

| 1 1 1 1 |

| 1 1 1 0 |

| 1 1 0 1 | Values from 0A–0F
| 1 1 0 0 | (10–15) are not
| 1 0 1 1 | valid BCD and are
                not handled
| 1 0 1 0 | correctly by BCD
                instructions like
                AAA.

| 1 0 0 1 |

| 1 0 0 0 |

The high nybble of | 0 1 1 1 |
an unpacked BCD
digit is ignored in | 0 1 1 0 |
BCD math and
may contain any | 0 1 0 1 |
value, or 0.
                       | 0 1 0 0 | Only nybble–sized
                                       values from 0-9 are
| 0 0 1 1 | valid BCD digits

| 0 0 1 0 |

| 0 0 0 1 |

| 0 0 0 0 |

Figure 11-1: Unpacked BCD digits

So, if there were a way to perform BCD addition on the x86 CPUs, adding '1' and '1' would indeed give us '2' because '1' and '2' can be manipulated as legal BCD values.

AAA (and several other instructions I don't have room to discuss in this book) gives us that ability to perform BCD math. The actual technique may seem a little odd, but it does work. AAA is in fact a sort of a fudge factor, in that you execute AAA after performing an addition using the normal addition instruction ADD. AAA takes the results of the ADD instruction and forces them to come out right in terms of BCD math.

AAA basically does these two things:

▪ It forces the value in the low 4 bits of AL (which could be any value from 0 to F) to a value between 0 and 9 if they were greater than 9. This is done by adding 6 to AL and then forcing the high nybble of AL to 0. Obviously, if the low nybble of AL contains a valid BCD digit, the digit in the low nybble is left alone.

▪ If the value in AL had to be adjusted, it indicates that there was a carry in the addition, and thus AH is incremented. Also, the Carry flag, CF, is set to 1, as is the Auxiliary Carry flag, AF. Again, if the low nybble of AL contained a valid BCD digit when AAA was executed, then AH is not incremented, and the two Carry flags are cleared (forced to 0), rather than set.

AAA thus facilitates base 10 (decimal) addition on the low nybble of AL. After AL is adjusted by AAA, the low nybble contains a valid BCD digit and the high nybble contains 0. (But note well that this is true *only* if the addition that preceded AAA was executed on two valid BCD operands—and ensuring that those operands are valid is *your* responsibility, not the CPU's!)

This allows us to add ASCII digits such as 1 and 2 using the ADD instruction. Ruler does this immediately after the STOSW instruction:

```
add   al,'1'     ; Bump the character value in AL up by 1
aaa              ; Adjust AX to make this a BCD addition
```

If prior to the addition the contents of AL's low nybble were 9, adding 1 would make the value 0AH, which is not legal BCD. AAA would then adjust AL by adding 6 to AL and clearing the high nybble. Adding 6 to 0A would result in 10, so once the high nybble is cleared, the new value in AL would be 0. Also, AH would have been incremented by 1.

In the Ruler procedure we're not adding multiple decimal columns, but simply rolling over a count in a single column and displaying the number in that column to the screen. Therefore, we just ignore the incremented value in AH and use AL alone.

Adjusting AAA's Adjustments

There is one problem: AAA clears the high nybble to 0. This means that adding '1' and '1' doesn't *quite* equal '2', the displayable digit. Instead, AL becomes binary 2, which in the IBM-850 character set is the dark "smiley face" character. To make the contents of AL a displayable ASCII digit again, we have to add 30h to AL. This is easy to do: just add 0 to AL, which has a numeric value of 30h. So, adding 0 takes 02h back up to 32h, which is the numeric equivalent of the ASCII digit character 2. This is the reason for the ADD AL, '0' instruction that immediately follows AAA. This sounds peculiar, but remember that '0' is the number 30h, not binary 0!

There's a lot more to BCD math than what I've explained here. Much of it involves BCD operations across multiple columns. For example, when you want to perform multiple-column BCD math, you have to take carries into account, which involves careful use of the Auxiliary Carry flag, AF. There are also the AAD, AAM, and AAS instructions for adjusting AL after BCD divides, multiplies, and subtracts, respectively. The same general idea applies: all the BCD adjustment instructions force the standard binary arithmetic instructions to come out right for valid BCD operands.

Ruler's Lessons

The Ruler procedure is a good example of using STOSB *without* the REP prefix. We have to change the value in AL every time we store AL to memory, and thus can't use REP STOSB. Note that nothing is done to EDI or ECX while changing the digit to be displayed, and thus the values stored in those registers are held over for the next execution of STOSB. Ruler is also a good example of how LOOP works with STOSB to adjust ECX downward and return control to the top of the loop. LOOP, in a sense, does outside the CPU what REP does inside the CPU: adjust ECX and close the loop. Try to keep that straight when using any of the string instructions!

16-bit and 32-bit Versions of STOS

Before moving on to other string instructions, it's worth pointing out that there are three different "sizes" of the STOS string instruction: byte, word, and double word. STOSB is the byte-size version demonstrated in Ruler. STOSW stores the 16-bit value in AX into memory, and STOSD stores the 32-bit value in EAX into memory.

STOSW and STOSD work almost the same way as STOSB. The major difference lies in the way EDI is changed after each memory transfer operation. For STOSW, EDI changes by two bytes, either up or down depending on the state of DF. For STOSD, EDI changes by 4 bytes, again either up or down depending on the state of DF.

However, in all cases, with the REP prefix in front of the instruction, ECX is decremented by *one* after each memory transfer operation. It is always decremented, and always by one. ECX counts *operations*. It has nothing to say about memory addresses.

MOVSB: Fast Block Copies

The STOSB instruction is a fascinating item, but for sheer action packed into a single line of assembly code there's nothing that can touch the MOVS instruction. Like STOS, MOVS comes in three "sizes": for handling bytes (MOVSB), 16-bit words

(MOVSW), and 32-bit double words (MOVSD). For working with ASCII characters as we are in this chapter, MOVSB is the one to use.

The gist of the MOVSB instruction is this: a block of memory data at the address stored in ESI is copied to the address stored in EDI. The number of bytes to be moved is placed in the ECX register. ECX counts down after each byte is copied, and the addresses in ESI and EDI are adjusted by one. For MOVSW, the ESI/EDI addresses are adjusted by two after each word is copied, and for MOVSD, they are adjusted by four after each double word is copied. These adjustments are either increments or decrements, depending on the state of DF. In all three cases, ECX is decremented by one each time a data item goes from the source address to the destination address. Remember that ECX is counting memory transfer operations, *not* address bytes.

The DF register affects MOVSB the same way it affects STOSB. By default, DF is cleared, and string operations operate ''uphill'' from low memory toward high memory. If DF is set, then the direction in which string operations work goes the other way, from high memory toward low.

MOVSB can operate either semiautomatically or automatically, just as with STOSB. If the REP prefix is added to MOVSB, then (assuming you have the registers set up correctly) a block of memory will be copied from here to there in just one instruction.

To demonstrate MOVSB, I added a short procedure called WrtLn to Listing 11-1. WrtLn copies a string to a given X,Y location in the display buffer VidBuff. It does a job much like Write in Pascal or print in C. Before calling WrtLn, you place the source address of the string in ESI, the one-based X,Y coordinates in EBX and EAX, and the length of the string, in bytes, in ECX.

The code that does the work in WrtLn is pretty simple:

```
cld                   ; Clear DF for up-memory write
mov edi,VidBuff       ; Load destination index with buffer address
dec eax               ; Adjust Y value down by 1 for address calculation
dec ebx               ; Adjust X value down by 1 for address calculation
mov ah,COLS           ; Move screen width to AH
mul ah                ; Do 8-bit multiply AL*AH to AX
add edi,eax           ; Add Y offset into vidbuff to EDI
add edi,ebx           ; Add X offset into vidbuf to EDI
rep movsb             ; Blast the string into the buffer
```

The code for calculating the offset into VidBuff from the X,Y values using MUL is the same as that in Ruler. In the main program section of vidbuff1, some additional calculation is performed to display a string centered in the visible buffer, rather than at some specific X,Y location:

```
mov esi,Message   ; Load the address of the message to ESI
mov ecx,MSGLEN    ; and its length to ECX
mov ebx,COLS      ; and the screen width to EBX
```

```
sub ebx,ecx        ; Calc diff of message length and screen width
shr ebx,1          ; Divide difference by 2 for X value
mov eax,24         ; Set message row to Line 24
call WrtLn         ; Display the centered message
```

DF and Overlapping Block Moves

The simple demo program vidbuff1 uses MOVSB to copy a message from the .data section of the program into the display buffer. Although WrtLn uses MOVSB to copy the message "uphill" from low memory to high, you could argue that you could just as easily copy it from high memory "downhill" to low, and you would be right. The direction flag, DF, doesn't seem to be more than a matter of preference ... until your source and destination memory blocks overlap.

Nothing mandates that ESI and EDI point to entirely separate areas of memory. The source and destination memory blocks may overlap, and that can often be extremely useful.

Here's an example: consider the challenge of editing text stored in a memory buffer. Suppose you have a string in a buffer and want to insert a character somewhere in the middle of the string. All the characters in the string past the insertion point must be "moved aside" to make room for the new inserted character (assuming there is empty space at the end of the buffer). This is a natural application for REP MOVSB—but setting it up may be trickier than it seems at first glance.

I vividly remember the first time I tried it—which, not coincidentally, was the first time I ever attempted to use MOVSB. What I did is shown schematically in the left portion of Figure 11-2. The goal was to move a string to the right by one position so that I could insert a space character in front of it. (At the time I was using a 16-bit CPU, and the registers were SI, DI, and CX, but the mechanism is precisely the same in 32-bit mode. Only the register names are different today.)

I pointed ESI at the first byte in the string, and EDI to the position I wanted to move the string. I then executed an "uphill" REP MOVSB instruction, and when the smoke cleared I discovered that I had replaced the entire string with its initial character. Yes, it's an obvious mistake ... once you see it actually *happen*.

The right side of the figure shows how such an insert should in fact be done. You must begin at the end of the string and work "downhill" toward the insertion point. The first character move must take the last character of the string into empty buffer space and out of the way of the next character move, and so on. In this way, two areas of memory that overlap by all but one byte can be copied one to the other without losing any data.

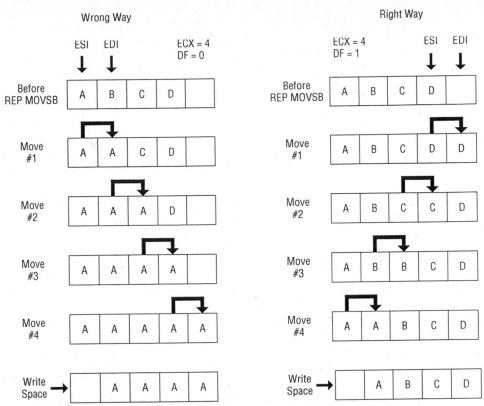

Figure 11-2: Using MOVSB on overlapping memory blocks

It's easy to watch an operation like this happen by setting up a test case in a sandbox program and observing memory with Insight's Memory view. Enter the following sandbox program, build the executable, and then bring it up under Insight:

```
section .data

        EditBuff: db 'abcdefghijklm                '
        ENDPOS     equ 12
        INSRTPOS   equ 5


section .text
        global _start
_start:
        nop
; Put your experiments between the two nops...

        std                        ; down-memory transfer
        mov ebx,EditBuff+INSRTPOS  ; Save address of insert point
```

```
        mov esi,EditBuff+ENDPOS     ; Start at end of text
        mov edi,EditBuff+ENDPOS+1   ; Bump text right by 1
        mov ecx,ENDPOS-INSRTPOS+1   ; # of chars to bump
        rep movsb                   ; Move 'em!
        mov byte [ebx],' '          ; Write a space at insert point

; Put your experiments between the two nops...
        nop
```

Make sure that Insight's Memory view window is open. The string `EditBuff` will be shown at the top of the Memory view. By single-stepping the sandbox code, you can watch the characters "move over" inside the `EditBuff` variable, one by one.

In this example, `ENDPOS` is the zero-based offset of the last character in the string. Note that this is *not* a count, but an offset from the beginning of the buffer. The offset of the final character "m" from the beginning of the buffer is 12 bytes. If you start with the address of `EditBuff` in ESI and add 12 to it, ESI will be pointing at the "m." EDI, in turn, is pointed at the offset of the first buffer position *after* the final character in the string; hence, the `ENDPOS+1` assembly-time calculation.

Deriving the count to be placed into ECX has to take the zero-based nature of the address offsets into account. You have to add 1 to the difference between the string's end position (`ENDPOS`) and the insert position (`INSRTPOS`) to get a correct count of the number of bytes that must be moved.

Note the `STD` instruction that begins the code block. `STD` sets the Direction flag, DF, to 1, which forces string instructions to work "downhill" from high memory toward low memory. DF defaults to 0, so in order for this code to work the `STD` instruction *must* be present!

You can change the insert point in the sandbox example simply by changing the value in `INSRTPOS` and rebuilding the sandbox. For example, to insert the space character at the very beginning of the string, change the value of `INSRTPOS` to 0.

Single-Stepping REP String Instructions with Insight

I should mention here that even though a `REP MOVSB` instruction appears to be a single instruction, it is actually an extremely tight loop implemented as a single instruction. Single-stepping `REP MOVSB` under Insight does *not* execute the whole loop at one blow! Each time you click the Step ASM Instruction button, only one memory transfer operation takes place. If ECX is loaded with a count value of 12, for example, then you have to click Step ASM Instruction 12 times to step your way through the entire instruction.

This is a good thing sometimes, especially if you want to watch memory change while the instruction operates. However, for large count values in

ECX, that's a lot of clicking. If you're confident of the correctness of your string instruction setup, you may want to place a breakpoint on the next instruction after the REP string instruction, and click the Continue button to execute the string instruction at full speed, without pausing after each memory transfer operation. Insight will pause at the breakpoint, and you can continue single-stepping from there.

Storing Data to Discontinuous Strings

Sometimes you have to break the rules. Until now I've been explaining the string instructions under the assumption that the destination string is always one continuous sequence of bytes in memory. This isn't necessarily the case. In addition to changing the value in EAX between executions of STOSB, you can change the *destination address* as well. As a result, you can store data to several different areas of memory within a single very tight loop.

Displaying an ASCII Table

I've created a small demo program, showchar, to show you what I mean. It's not as useful as the Ruler procedure contained in Listing 11-1, but it makes its point and is easy to understand if you've followed me so far. Because the showchar program uses a lot of the same basic machinery as vidbuff1, including the virtual display mechanism and Ruler, I'm not going to show the whole program here. The complete source code file (as with all the code presented in this book) can be downloaded from my assembly language Web page in the listings archive zip file. (The URL is printed in the Introduction to this book.)

The showchar program clears the screen, displays a ruler on line 1, and below that shows a table containing 224 of the 256 ASCII characters, neatly displayed in seven lines of 32 characters each. The table includes the "high" 127 ASCII characters, including foreign-language characters, line-draw characters, and miscellaneous symbols. What it does not display are the very first 32 ASCII characters. Linux treats these as control characters, and even those characters for which glyphs are available are not displayed to the console.

The showchar program introduces a couple of new concepts and instructions, all related to program loops. (String instructions such as STOSB and program loops are intimately related.) Listing 11-2 presents the main body of showchar. All procedures and macros it invokes are present in Listing 11-1. It also uses the following two equates not present in Listing 11-1:

```
CHRTROW equ 2    ; Chart begins 2 lines from top of the display
CHRTLEN equ 32   ; Each chart line shows 32 characters
```

Read the code carefully before continuing with the text.

Listing 11-2: showchar.asm (main program body only)

```
_start:
        nop              ; This no-op keeps gdb happy...

; Get the console and text display text buffer ready to go:
        ClearTerminal  ; Send terminal clear string to console
        call ClrVid    ; Init/clear the video buffer

; Show a 64-character ruler above the table display:
        mov eax,1        ; Start ruler at display position 1,1
        mov ebx,1
        mov ecx,32       ; Make ruler 32 characters wide
        call Ruler       ; Generate the ruler

; Now let's generate the chart itself:
        mov edi,VidBuff      ; Start with buffer address in EDI
        add edi,COLS*CHRTROW  ; Begin table display down CHRTROW lines
        mov ecx,224          ; Show 256 chars minus first 32
        mov al,32            ; Start with char 32; others won't show
.DoLn:  mov bl,CHRTLEN       ; Each line will consist of 32 chars
.DoChr: stosb               ; Note that there's no REP prefix!
        jcxz AllDone         ; When the full set is printed, quit
        inc al               ; Bump the character value in AL up by 1
        dec bl               ; Decrement the line counter by one
        loopnz .DoChr    ; Go back & do another char until BL goes to 0
        add edi,(COLS-CHRTLEN)  ; Move EDI to start of next line
        jmp .DoLn        ; Start display of the next line

; Having written all that to the buffer, send the buffer to the console:
AllDone:
        call Show        ; Refresh the buffer to the console

Exit:   mov eax,1        ; Code for Exit Syscall
        mov ebx,0        ; Return a code of zero
        int 80H          ; Make kernel call
```

Nested Instruction Loops

Once all the registers are set up correctly according to the assumptions made by STOSB, the real work of showchar is performed by two instruction loops, one inside the other. The inner loop displays a line consisting of 32 characters. The outer loop breaks up the display into seven such lines. The inner loop, shown here, is by far the more interesting of the two:

```
.DoChr: stosb            ; Note that there's no REP prefix!
        jcxz AllDone     ; When the full set is printed, quit
        inc al           ; Bump the character value in AL up by 1
```

```
        dec bl              ; Decrement the line counter by one
        loopnz .DoChr       ; Go back & do another char until BL goes to 0
```

The work here (putting a character into the display buffer) is again done by STOSB. Once again, STOSB is working solo, without REP. Without REP to pull the loop inside the CPU, you have to set the loop up yourself.

Keep in mind what happens each time STOSB fires: The character in AL is written to the memory location pointed to by EDI, and EDI is incremented by 1. At the other end of the loop, the LOOPNZ instruction decrements ECX by 1 and closes the loop.

During register setup, we loaded ECX with the number of characters we wanted to display—in this case, 224. Each time STOSB fires, it places another character in the display buffer VidBuff, leaving one less character left to display. ECX acts as the master counter, keeping track of when we finally display the last remaining character. When ECX goes to zero, we've displayed the appropriate subset of the ASCII character set and the job is done.

Jumping When ECX Goes to 0

Hence the instruction JCXZ. This is a special branching instruction created specifically to help with loops like this. In Chapter 10, I explained how it's possible to branch using one of the many variations of the JMP instruction, based on the state of one of the machine flags. Earlier in this chapter, I explained the LOOP instruction, which is a special-purpose sort of a JMP instruction, one combined with an implied DEC ECX instruction. JCXZ is yet another variety of JMP instruction, but one that doesn't watch any of the flags or decrement any registers. Instead, JCXZ watches the ECX register. When it sees that ECX has just gone to zero, it jumps to the specified label. If ECX is still nonzero, then execution falls through to the next instruction in line.

In the case of the inner loop shown previously, JCXZ branches to the "close up shop" code when it sees that ECX has finally gone to 0. This is how the showchar program terminates.

Most of the other JMP instructions have partners that branch when the governing flag is *not* true. That is, JC (Jump on Carry) branches when the Carry flag equals 1. Its partner, JNC (Jump on Not Carry), jumps when the Carry flag is *not* 1. However, JCXZ is a loner. There is *no* JCXNZ instruction, so don't go looking for one in the instruction reference!

Closing the Inner Loop

Assuming that ECX has not yet been decremented down to 0 by the STOSB instruction (a condition watched for by JCXZ), the loop continues. AL is incremented. This is how the next ASCII character in line is selected. The value in AL is sent to the location stored in EDI by STOSB. If you increment the value in AL, then you change the displayed character to the next one in line. For example, if AL contains the value for the character A (65), then incrementing AL changes the A character to a B (66). On the next pass through the loop, STOSW will fire a B at the screen instead of an A.

After the character code in AL is incremented, BL is decremented. Now, BL is not directly related to the string instructions. Nothing in any of the assumptions made by the string instructions involves BL. We're using BL for something else entirely here. BL is acting as a counter that governs the length of the lines of characters shown on the screen. BL was loaded earlier with the value represented by the equate CHRTLEN, which has the value 32. On each pass through the loop, the DEC BL instruction decrements the value of BL by 1. Then the LOOPNZ instruction gets its moment in the sun.

LOOPNZ is a little bit different from our friend LOOP, examined earlier. It's just different enough to get you into trouble if you don't truly understand how it works. Both LOOP and LOOPNZ decrement the ECX register by 1. LOOP watches the state of the ECX register and closes the loop until ECX goes to 0. LOOPNZ watches *both* the state of the ECX register *and* the state of the Zero flag, ZF. (LOOP ignores ZF.) LOOPNZ will only close the loop if ECX < > (not equal to) 0 *and* ZF = 0. In other words, LOOPNZ closes the loop only if ECX still has something left in it *and* the Zero flag, ZF, is not set.

What exactly is LOOPNZ watching for here? Remember that immediately prior to the LOOPNZ instruction, we're decrementing BL by 1 through a DEC BL instruction. The DEC instruction *always* affects ZF. If DEC's operand goes to zero as a result of the DEC instruction, ZF goes to 1 (is set). Otherwise, ZF stays at 0 (remains cleared). So, in effect, LOOPNZ is watching the state of the BL register. Until BL is decremented to 0 (setting ZF), LOOPNZ closes the loop. After BL goes to zero, the inner loop is finished and execution falls through LOOPNZ to the next instruction.

What about ECX? Well, LOOPNZ is in fact watching ECX—but so is JCXZ. JCXZ is actually the switch that governs when the whole loop—both inner and outer portions—has done its work and must stop. So, while LOOPNZ does watch ECX, somebody else is doing that task, and that somebody else will take action on ECX before LOOPNZ can. LOOPNZ's job is thus to decrement ECX, but to watch BL. It governs the inner of the two loops.

Closing the Outer Loop

Does that mean that JCXZ closes the outer loop? No. JCXZ indicates when *both* loops are finished. Closing the outer loop is done a little differently from closing the inner loop. Take another look at the two nested loops:

```
.DoLn:  mov bl,CHRTLEN     ; Each line will consist of 32 chars
.DoChr: stosb              ; Note that there's no REP prefix!
```

```
jcxz AllDone            ; When the full set is printed, quit
inc al                  ; Bump the character value in AL up by 1
dec bl                  ; Decrement the line counter by one
loopnz .DoChr           ; Go back & do another char until BL goes to 0
add edi,COLS-CHRTLEN    ; Move EDI to start of next line
jmp .DoLn               ; Start display of the next line
```

The inner loop is considered complete when we've displayed one full line of the ASCII table to the screen. BL governs the length of a line, and when BL goes to zero (which the LOOPNZ instruction detects), a line is finished. LOOPNZ then falls through to the ADD instruction that modifies EDI.

We modify EDI to jump from the address of the end of a completed line in the display buffer to the start of the next line at the left margin. This means we have to "wrap" by some number of characters from the end of the ASCII table line to the end of the visible screen. The number of bytes this requires is provided by the assembly-time expression COLS-CHRTLEN. This is basically the difference between the length of one ASCII table line and width of the virtual screen (*not* the width of the terminal window to which the virtual screen is displayed!). The result of the expression is the number of bytes that must be moved further into the display buffer to arrive at the start of the next line at the left screen margin.

But after that wrap is accomplished by modifying EDI, the outer loop's work is done, and we close the loop. This time, we do it *unconditionally*, by way of a simple JMP instruction. The target of the JMP instruction is the .DoLn local label. No ifs, no arguments. At the top of the outer loop (represented by the .DoLn label), we load the length of a table line back into the now empty BL register, and then drop back into the inner loop. The inner loop starts firing characters at the buffer again, and will continue to do so until JCXZ detects that CX has gone to 0.

At that point, both the inner and the outer loops are finished, and the full ASCII table has been written into VidBuff. With this accomplished, the buffer can be sent to the Linux console by calling the Show procedure.

Showchar Recap

Let's review what we've just done, as it's admittedly pretty complex. The showchar program contains two nested loops: the inner loop shoots characters at the screen via STOSB. The outer loop shoots *lines* of characters at the screen, by repeating the inner loop some number of times (here, seven).

The inner loop is governed by the value in the BL register, which is initially set up to take the length of a line of characters (here, 32). The outer loop is not explicitly governed by the number of lines to be displayed. That is, you don't load the number 7 into a register and decrement it. Instead, the outer loop continues until the value in ECX goes to 0, indicating that the whole job—displaying all of the 224 characters that we want shown—is done.

The inner and outer loops both modify the registers that STOSB works with. The inner loop modifies AL after each character is fired at the screen. This makes it possible to display a different character each time STOSB fires. The outer loop modifies EDI (the destination index register) each time a *line* of characters is complete. This enables us to break the destination string up into seven separate, noncontiguous lines.

Command-Line Arguments and Examining the Stack

When you launch a program at the Linux console command prompt, you have the option to include any reasonable number of arguments after the pathname of the executable program. In other words, you can execute a program named showargs1 like this:

```
$./showargs1 time for tacos
```

The three arguments follow the program name and are separated by space characters. Note that these are *not* the same as I/O redirection parameters, which require the use of the redirection operators, > or <, and are handled separately by Linux.

When one of your programs begins running, any command-line arguments that were entered when the program was launched are passed to the program by Linux. In this section, I'm going to explain the structure of the Linux stack, which is where command-line arguments are stored. In the next section, you'll see how to access a program's command-line arguments from an assembly language program. In the process, you'll get to see yet another x86 string instruction in action: SCASB.

Virtual Memory in Two Chunks

Back in Chapter 8, I explained the x86 stack conceptually. I glossed over many of the details, especially the way that Linux sets up the stack when a program is executed. It's time to take a closer look.

Understanding the Linux stack requires at least a perfunctory understanding of virtual memory. Linux has always used a virtual memory mechanism to manage the physical memory in your computer. Virtual memory is a handful to explain in detail, but from a height it works this way: Linux can set aside a region of memory anywhere in your computer's physical memory system, and then say, "You should consider the first address of this block of memory 08048000h, and perform all memory addressing accordingly."

This is a fib, but a useful one. Your program can make free use of the block of memory Linux has given it, and assume that it is the only program making use of that memory. Other programs may be given their own blocks of this "virtual" memory, and they may be running at the same time as your program runs. None of these programs running simultaneously is aware of the fact that the others are running, and none can interfere with any of the others.

And this is the really odd part: *Every program given a block of memory may be told that its memory block begins with address 08048000h.* This is true even for programs running simultaneously. Each program thinks that it's running in its own little memory universe, and each one thinks that its memory address begins at the same place.

How is this possible? Away in the background, the Linux kernel accepts every single memory-addressing attempt made by any program's code, and translates that virtual address into a physical memory address somewhere in RAM. This involves a lot of fast work with physical memory tables and even (when necessary) "faking" physical memory in RAM with storage on a hard drive. But the bottom line is that your program gets its own little memory universe, and may assume that whatever memory it has is truly its own. Where precisely that memory exists in the physical memory system is unknown to your program, and unimportant.

When your program begins running, Linux does its virtual-memory magic and sets aside an area of memory for your program's code and its data. For x86-based Linux systems, this block of memory always begins at 08048000h. From there, it runs all the way up to 0BFFFFFFFh (or something in that vicinity; the top address is not always the same, more on which shortly). Now, that's a *lot* of memory: over 3GB. Most PCs are only recently reaching 4GB of installed physical memory. How can Linux hand each running program 3GB of memory if only 2GB (for example) is installed?

Easy: Not every virtual address in that 3GB virtual address space maps to a physical address. In fact, a Linux program's virtual memory space is divided into two blocks, as shown in Figure 11-3. The low block begins at 08048000h and contains your program code, along with the data defined in the .data and .bss sections. It's only as big as it needs to be, given the code and data that you define; and for the simple demo programs shown in this book, it's quite small—perhaps a few hundred bytes.

The high block can be thought of almost in reverse: it begins in high memory and runs down toward low memory. The actual address boundaries of this high block are not always the same. However, the high end of this block (which is sometimes confusingly called the "bottom of the stack") cannot be higher than 0BFFFFFFFh. This high block is your program's stack.

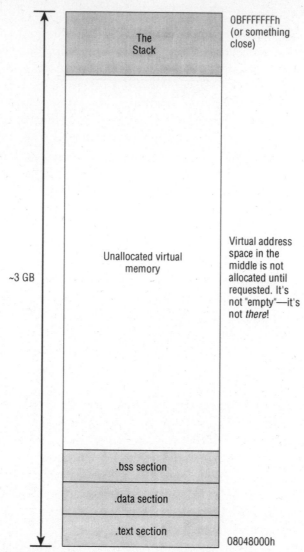

Figure 11-3: A program's virtual memory block at runtime

The apparent immensity of unused space in between the two blocks is an illusion. If your program needs additional memory from that empty middle area, it simply needs to attempt to address that additional memory, and Linux will grant the request—unless the request is for any of several arcane reasons judged excessive or defective. Then Linux may deny the request and terminate the program for misbehavior.

In general, your program code and data will be down somewhere near (but not below) 08048000h. Your stack will be up somewhere near (but not above) 0BFFFFFFFh.

Anatomy of the Linux Stack

The stack is much bigger and more complex than you might think. When Linux loads your program, if places a great deal of information on the stack before letting the program's code begin execution. This includes the fully qualified pathname of the executable that's running, any command-line arguments that were entered by the user when executing the program, and the current state of the Linux environment, which is a collection of textual configuration strings that define how Linux is set up.

This is all laid out according to a plan, which I've summarized in Figure 11-4. First some jargon refreshers: the *top of the stack* is (counterintuitively) at the bottom of the diagram. It's the memory location pointed to by ESP when your program begins running. The *bottom of the stack* is at the top of the diagram. It's the highest address in the virtual address space that Linux gives to your program when it loads your program and runs it. This "top" and "bottom" business is an ancient convention that confuses a lot of people. Memory diagrams generally begin with low memory at the bottom of the page and depict higher memory above it, even though this means that the bottom of the stack is at the top of the diagram. Get used to it; if you're going to understand the literature you have no choice.

Linux builds the stack from high memory toward low memory, beginning at the bottom of the stack and going down-memory from there. When your program code actually begins running, ESP points at the top of the stack. Here's a more detailed description of what you'll find on the stack at startup:

- At ESP is a 32-bit number, giving you the count of the command-line arguments present on the stack. *This value is always at least 1*, even if no arguments were entered. The text typed by the user when executing the program is counted along with any command-line parameters, and this "invocation text" is always present, which is why the count is always at least 1.

- The next 32-bit item up-memory from ESP is the address of the invocation text by which the executable file was run. The text may be fully qualified, which means that the pathname includes the directory path to the file from your /home directory—for example, /home/asmstuff/ asm3ecode/showargs1/showargs1. This is how the invocation text looks when you run your program from Insight. If you use the "dot slash" method of invoking an executable from within the current directory, you'll see the executable name prefixed by "./".

- If any command-line arguments were entered, their 32-bit addresses lie up-memory from ESP, with the address of the first (leftmost) argument followed by the address of the second, and so on. The number of arguments varies, of course, though you'll rarely need more than four or five.

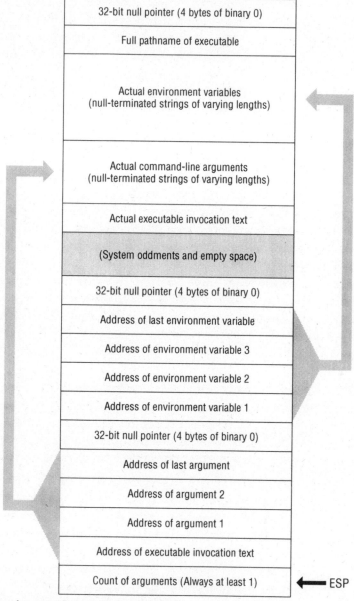

Figure 11-4: Linux stack at program startup

- The list of command-line argument addresses is terminated by a null pointer, which is jargon for 32 bits of binary 0.

- Up-memory from the null pointer begins a longish list of 32-bit addresses. How many depends on your particular Linux system, but it can be close to 200. Each of these addresses points to a null-terminated string (more on those shortly) containing one of the definitions belonging to the Linux environment.

- At the end of the list of addresses of Linux environment variables is another 32-bit null pointer, and that marks the end of the stack's "directory." Beyond this point, you use the addresses found earlier on the stack to access items still further up-memory.

Why Stack Addresses Aren't Predictable

Years ago, the very highest address of the virtual space given to a running program was always 0BFFFFFFFh, and this was always the bottom of the stack. Beginning with the 2.6 version of the Linux kernel, the kernel "randomizes" the boundaries of the stack. Each time your program runs, its stack addresses will be different, often by several million bytes. In addition, there is a variable amount of unused "padding" in memory between the end of the address list and the beginning of the actual string data pointed to by those addresses.

This makes reading a program's memory layout more difficult, but it's for a good cause. If the stack is always reliably located at the same address, buffer overflows can force code onto the stack as data and then malware can execute that code. This execution depends on hard-coding memory addresses into the malware code (because there's no loader to adjust code addresses), but if the stack is (almost) never in precisely the same place twice, this hard-coding of addresses won't work and executing malware code on the stack becomes a *great* deal harder.

This is one of many reasons why Linux is inherently more secure than older versions of Windows, including XP and 2000, where stack addresses can be "guessed" a great deal more easily.

Setting Command-Line Arguments with Insight

In general, Gdb's Insight GUI system isn't bad, and parts of it are indeed excellent. Some of it, however, is pure awfulness. Unfortunately, much of that awfulness lies in the Memory view window, which is the only way to examine the stack using Insight.

When you run Insight with the name of a program to be debugged, the program is not run immediately, but held in memory until you click the Run button. This gives you a chance to set breakpoints before running the program. It also gives you a chance to enter command-line parameters.

To set command-line arguments under Insight, open the Console view, and at the `(gdb)` prompt enter the arguments following the `set args` command:

```
(gdb) set args time for tacos
```

Here you're entering three arguments: `time`, `for`, and `tacos`. After you've entered your arguments at the gdb console, press Enter. To verify the arguments that you entered, you can display them from the Console view with the command `show args`. After all necessary arguments are entered, you can click Run and let the machine pause at your first breakpoint. Once the program begins running, the Memory view goes live and shows real data.

Examining the Stack with Insight's Memory View

There are only two ways to change the address of the memory region on display in the Memory view. One is to click the up or the down arrow buttons in the navigation control. One click will move the view either 16 bytes up-memory or 16 bytes down-memory. Alas, this method is painfully slow; it can take up to three seconds for the display to refresh after a click on one of the arrows. The other method is to type a full 32-bit address (in hex) into the address entry field of the navigation control. Again, alas (and shame on whomever wrote Insight!), the control does *not* accept text pasted from the clipboard.

By default, Insight's memory view will come up set to display from the first byte in your .data section. To view the stack, you must open the Registers view and enter the address shown in ESP into the Memory view navigation control. Then the Memory view will show you the stack starting at the top—that is, at the byte pointed to by ESP.

Figure 11-5 shows the Memory view of the stack for the program showargs1 (see Listing 11-3, below) with three command-line parameters.

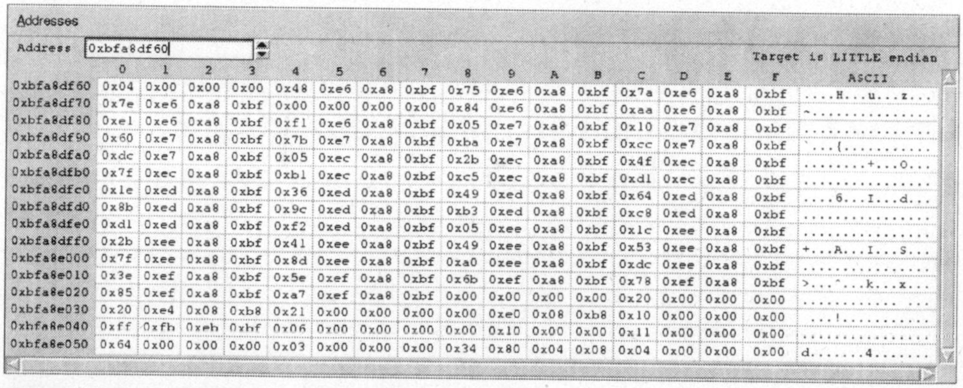
Addresses
Address 0xbfa8df60
Target is LITTLE endian

	0	1	2	3	4	5	6	7	8	9	A	B	C	D	E	F	ASCII
0xbfa8df60	0x04	0x00	0x00	0x00	0x48	0xe6	0xa8	0xbf	0x75	0xe6	0xa8	0xbf	0x7a	0xe6	0xa8	0xbf	....H...u...z...
0xbfa8df70	0x7e	0xe6	0xa8	0xbf	0x00	0x00	0x00	0x00	0x84	0xe6	0xa8	0xbf	0xaa	0xe6	0xa8	0xbf	~...............
0xbfa8df80	0xe1	0xe6	0xa8	0xbf	0xf1	0xe6	0xa8	0xbf	0x05	0xe7	0xa8	0xbf	0x10	0xe7	0xa8	0xbf	....
0xbfa8df90	0x60	0xe7	0xa8	0xbf	0x7b	0xe7	0xa8	0xbf	0xba	0xe7	0xa8	0xbf	0xcc	0xe7	0xa8	0xbf	`...{...........
0xbfa8dfa0	0xdc	0xe7	0xa8	0xbf	0x05	0xec	0xa8	0xbf	0x2b	0xec	0xa8	0xbf	0x4f	0xec	0xa8	0xbf	........+...O...
0xbfa8dfb0	0x7f	0xec	0xa8	0xbf	0xb1	0xec	0xa8	0xbf	0xc5	0xec	0xa8	0xbf	0xd1	0xec	0xa8	0xbf	....
0xbfa8dfc0	0x1e	0xed	0xa8	0xbf	0x36	0xed	0xa8	0xbf	0x49	0xed	0xa8	0xbf	0x64	0xed	0xa8	0xbf	....6...I...d...
0xbfa8dfd0	0x8b	0xed	0xa8	0xbf	0x9c	0xed	0xa8	0xbf	0xb3	0xed	0xa8	0xbf	0xc8	0xed	0xa8	0xbf	....
0xbfa8dfe0	0xd1	0xed	0xa8	0xbf	0xf2	0xed	0xa8	0xbf	0x05	0xee	0xa8	0xbf	0x1c	0xee	0xa8	0xbf	....
0xbfa8dff0	0x2b	0xee	0xa8	0xbf	0x41	0xee	0xa8	0xbf	0x49	0xee	0xa8	0xbf	0x53	0xee	0xa8	0xbf	+...A...I...S...
0xbfa8e000	0x7f	0xee	0xa8	0xbf	0x8d	0xee	0xa8	0xbf	0xa0	0xee	0xa8	0xbf	0xdc	0xee	0xa8	0xbf	....
0xbfa8e010	0x3e	0xef	0xa8	0xbf	0x5e	0xef	0xa8	0xbf	0x6b	0xef	0xa8	0xbf	0x78	0xef	0xa8	0xbf	>...^...k...x...
0xbfa8e020	0x85	0xef	0xa8	0xbf	0xa7	0xef	0xa8	0xbf	0x00	0x00	0x00	0x00	0x20	0x00	0x00	0x00	....
0xbfa8e030	0x20	0xe4	0x08	0xb8	0x21	0x00	0x00	0x00	0x00	0xe0	0x08	0xb8	0x10	0x00	0x00	0x00	....!...........
0xbfa8e040	0xff	0xfb	0xeb	0xbf	0x06	0x00	0x00	0x00	0x00	0x10	0x00	0x00	0x11	0x00	0x00	0x00	....
0xbfa8e050	0x64	0x00	0x00	0x00	0x03	0x00	0x00	0x00	0x34	0x80	0x04	0x08	0x04	0x00	0x00	0x00	d.......4.......

Figure 11-5: The stack in Insight's Memory view

The trick in reading a stack display in the Memory view is to remember that numbers and addresses are 32 bits in size, and that the display is little-endian. That means that the bytes appear in order of reverse significance. In other words, the least significant byte of a 32-bit value comes first, followed by the next more significant byte, and so on. This is why the first four values on the stack are these:

```
0x04 0x00 0x00 0x00
```

This is the 32-bit value 4, which is the count of the three command-line parameters plus the pathname of the executable file.

The same is true of addresses. The least-significant byte of an address comes first, so the four address bytes are presented "backwards" from how you're used to thinking of 32-bit addresses. The first address on the stack is that of the invocation text by which the executable was run. It looks like this:

```
0x48 0xe6 0xa8 0xbf
```

These four bytes represent the 32-bit address 0BFA8E648h.

Relate the stack display in Figure 11-5 to the stack diagram in Figure 11-4. You should have the count value of 4, followed by four 32-bit addresses, followed in turn by four 0-bytes, which is the 32-bit null pointer. (This is a term originating in C programming that is sometimes used in assembly work, even though we don't generally refer to addresses as "pointers.") After the null pointer you will see a long run of additional addresses, followed again by another null pointer.

You can use the Memory view to "follow" an address to the actual data stored up-memory. Type the first address on the stack into the navigation control, and the view will move to that address. In this case, that should be the address of the invocation text of the executable file (see Figure 11-6).

```
Addresses
Address  0xbfa8e648                                                          Target is LITTLE endian
            0    1    2    3    4    5    6    7    8    9    A    B    C    D    E    F   ASCII
0xbfa8e648 0x2f 0x68 0x6f 0x6d 0x65 0x2f 0x6a 0x64 0x75 0x6e 0x74 0x65 0x6d 0x61 0x6e 0x6e  /home/jduntemann
0xbfa8e658 0x2f 0x61 0x73 0x6d 0x77 0x6f 0x72 0x6b 0x2f 0x73 0x68 0x6f 0x77 0x61 0x72 0x67  /asmwork/showarg
0xbfa8e668 0x73 0x31 0x2f 0x73 0x68 0x6f 0x77 0x61 0x72 0x67 0x73 0x31 0x00 0x74 0x69 0x6d  s1/showargs1.tim
0xbfa8e678 0x65 0x00 0x66 0x6f 0x72 0x00 0x74 0x61 0x63 0x6f 0x73 0x00 0x4f 0x52 0x42 0x49  e.for.tacos.ORBI
0xbfa8e688 0x54 0x5f 0x53 0x4f 0x43 0x4b 0x45 0x54 0x44 0x49 0x52 0x3d 0x2f 0x74 0x6d 0x70  T_SOCKETDIR=/tmp
0xbfa8e698 0x2f 0x6f 0x72 0x62 0x69 0x74 0x2d 0x6a 0x64 0x75 0x6e 0x74 0x65 0x6d 0x61 0x6e  /orbit-jdunteman
0xbfa8e6a8 0x6e 0x00 0x47 0x50 0x47 0x5f 0x41 0x47 0x45 0x4e 0x54 0x5f 0x49 0x4e 0x46 0x4f  n.GPG_AGENT_INFO
0xbfa8e6b8 0x3d 0x2f 0x74 0x6d 0x70 0x2f 0x73 0x65 0x61 0x68 0x6f 0x72 0x73 0x65 0x2d 0x46  =/tmp/seahorse-F
0xbfa8e6c8 0x6d 0x5a 0x4b 0x51 0x38 0x2f 0x53 0x2e 0x67 0x70 0x67 0x2d 0x61 0x67 0x65 0x6e  mZKQ8/S.gpg-agen
0xbfa8e6d8 0x74 0x3a 0x34 0x39 0x34 0x38 0x3a 0x31 0x00 0x53 0x48 0x45 0x4c 0x4c 0x3d 0x2f  t.4948.1.SHELL=/
0xbfa8e6e8 0x62 0x69 0x6e 0x2f 0x62 0x61 0x73 0x68 0x00 0x44 0x45 0x53 0x4b 0x54 0x4f 0x50  bin/bash.DESKTOP
0xbfa8e6f8 0x5f 0x53 0x54 0x41 0x52 0x54 0x55 0x50 0x5f 0x49 0x44 0x3d 0x00 0x54 0x45 0x52  _STARTUP_ID=.TER
0xbfa8e708 0x4d 0x3d 0x78 0x74 0x65 0x72 0x6d 0x00 0x58 0x44 0x47 0x5f 0x53 0x45 0x53 0x53  M=xterm.XDG_SESS
0xbfa8e718 0x49 0x4f 0x4e 0x5f 0x43 0x4f 0x4f 0x4b 0x49 0x45 0x3d 0x65 0x35 0x66 0x31 0x33  ION_COOKIE=e5f13
0xbfa8e728 0x66 0x66 0x32 0x35 0x39 0x30 0x64 0x39 0x63 0x37 0x37 0x66 0x37 0x66 0x32 0x37  ff2590d9c77f7f27
0xbfa8e738 0x62 0x62 0x37 0x34 0x39 0x38 0x62 0x35 0x32 0x64 0x66 0x2d 0x31 0x32 0x34 0x32  bb7498b52df-1242
```

Figure 11-6: Command-line arguments in Insight's Memory view

Command-line arguments and environment variables are stored nose-to-tail in memory. Each one is terminated by a single 0 byte (often called a *null*), which is why such strings are called *null-terminated*. Although there's no technical reason for it, command-line arguments and environment variables are stored in the same region of the stack, with the command-line arguments first and the environment variables following.

You can see them in the ASCII column of the Memory view shown in Figure 11-6. Immediately after the tacos parameter, you'll see the first environment variable: ORBIT_SOCKETDIR=tmp/orbit-jduntemann. Just what that means is outside the scope of this book (ORBIT is a CORBA object request broker), but Linux uses the variable to tell whoever needs to know where certain essential ORBIT files are stored on the system.

String Searches with SCASB

Once you understand how the Linux stack is laid out in memory, getting at the command-line arguments is easy. You have what amounts to a table of addresses on the stack, and each address points to an argument. The only tricky part is determining how many bytes belong to each argument, so that you can copy the argument data somewhere else if you need to, or pass it to a Linux kernel call like sys_write. Because each argument ends with a single 0-byte, the challenge is plain: we have to search for the 0.

This can be done in the obvious way, in a loop that reads a byte from an address in memory, and then compares that byte against 0 before incrementing a counter and reading another byte. However, the good news is that the x86 instruction set implements such a loop in a string instruction that doesn't store data (like STOSB) or copy data (like MOVSB) but instead searches memory for a particular data value. This instruction is SCASB (Scan String by Byte), and if you've followed the material already presented on the other string instructions, understanding it should be a piece of cake.

Listing 11-3 demonstrates SCASB by looking at the command-line arguments on the stack and building a table of argument lengths. It then echoes back the arguments (along with the invocation text of the executable file) to stdout via a call to sys_write.

Listing 11-3: showargs1.asm

```
;  Executable name : SHOWARGS1
;  Version         : 1.0
;  Created date    : 4/17/2009
;  Last update     : 5/19/2009
;  Author          : Jeff Duntemann
;  Description     : A simple program in assembly for Linux, using NASM 2.05,
;     demonstrating the way to access command line arguments on the stack.
```

Listing 11-3: showargs1.asm (*continued*)

```
;
;   Build using these commands:
;     nasm -f elf -g -F stabs showargs1.asm
;     ld -o showargs1 showargs1.o
;

SECTION .data                   ; Section containing initialized data

        ErrMsg db "Terminated with error.",10
        ERRLEN equ $-ErrMsg

SECTION .bss                    ; Section containing uninitialized data

; This program handles up to MAXARGS command-line arguments. Change the
; value of MAXARGS if you need to handle more arguments than the default 10.
; In essence we store pointers to the arguments in a 0-based array, with the
; first arg pointer at array element 0, the second at array element 1, etc.
; Ditto the arg lengths. Access the args and their lengths this way:
;         Arg strings:           [ArgPtrs + <index reg>*4]
;         Arg string lengths:    [ArgLens + <index reg>*4]
; Note that when the argument lengths are calculated, an EOL char (10h) is
; stored into each string where the terminating null was originally. This
; makes it easy to print out an argument using sys_write. This is not
; essential, and if you prefer to retain the 0-termination in the arguments,
; you can comment out that line, keeping in mind that the arguments will not
; display correctly without EOL characters at their ends.

        MAXARGS    equ  10      ; Maximum # of args we support
        ArgCount: resd 1        ; # of arguments passed to program
        ArgPtrs:  resd MAXARGS  ; Table of pointers to arguments
        ArgLens:  resd MAXARGS  ; Table of argument lengths

SECTION .text                   ; Section containing code

global _start                   ; Linker needs this to find the entry point!

_start:
        nop                     ; This no-op keeps gdb happy...

; Get the command line argument count off the stack and validate it:
        pop ecx                 ; TOS contains the argument count
        cmp ecx,MAXARGS         ; See if the arg count exceeds MAXARGS
        ja Error                ; If so, exit with an error message
        mov dword [ArgCount],ecx ; Save arg count in memory variable

; Once we know how many args we have, a loop will pop them into ArgPtrs:
        xor edx,edx             ; Zero a loop counter
```

(*continued*)

Listing 11-3: showargs1.asm (*continued*)

```
SaveArgs:
        pop dword [ArgPtrs + edx*4]   ; Pop an arg addr into the memory table
        inc edx                      ; Bump the counter to the next arg addr
        cmp edx,ecx                  ; Is the counter = the argument count?
        jb SaveArgs                  ; If not, loop back and do another

; With the argument pointers stored in ArgPtrs, we calculate their lengths:
        xor eax,eax                  ; Searching for 0, so clear AL to 0
        xor ebx,ebx                  ; Pointer table offset starts at 0
ScanOne:
        mov ecx,0000ffffh            ; Limit search to 65535 bytes max
        mov edi,dword [ArgPtrs+ebx*4] ; Put address of string to search in EDI
        mov edx,edi                  ; Copy starting address into EDX
        cld                          ; Set search direction to up-memory
        repne scasb                  ; Search for null (0 char) in string at edi
        jnz Error                    ; REPNE SCASB ended without finding AL
        mov byte [edi-1],10          ; Store an EOL where the null used to be
        sub edi,edx                  ; Subtract position of 0 from start address
        mov dword [ArgLens+ebx*4],edi   ; Put length of arg into table
        inc ebx                      ; Add 1 to argument counter
        cmp ebx,[ArgCount]           ; See if arg counter exceeds argument count
        jb ScanOne                   ; If not, loop back and do another one

; Display all arguments to stdout:
        xor esi,esi                  ; Start (for table addressing reasons) at 0
Showem:
        mov ecx,[ArgPtrs+esi*4]      ; Pass offset of the message
        mov eax,4                    ; Specify sys_write call
        mov ebx,1                    ; Specify File Descriptor 1: Standard Output
        mov edx,[ArgLens+esi*4]      ; Pass the length of the message
        int 80H                      ; Make kernel call
        inc esi                      ; Increment the argument counter
        cmp esi,[ArgCount]           ; See if we've displayed all the arguments
        jb Showem                    ; If not, loop back and do another
        jmp Exit                     ; We're done! Let's pack it in!

Error: mov eax,4                     ; Specify sys_write call
        mov ebx,1                    ; Specify File Descriptor 2: Standard Error
        mov ecx,ErrMsg               ; Pass offset of the error message
        mov edx,ERRLEN               ; Pass the length of the message
        int 80H                      ; Make kernel call

Exit:  mov eax,1                     ; Code for Exit Syscall
        mov ebx,0                    ; Return a code of zero
        int 80H                      ; Make kernel call
```

The showargs1 program first pops the argument count from the stack into ECX, and if the count doesn't exceed the value in MAXARGS, the count in

ECX is then used to govern a loop that pops the addresses of the arguments themselves into the doubleword table ArgPtrs. This table is used later to access the arguments themselves.

The REPNE SCASB instruction is used to find the 0 byte at the end of each argument. Setting up SCASB is roughly the same as setting up STOSB:

- For up-memory searches (like this one) the CLD instruction is used to ensure that the Direction flag, DF, is cleared.

- The address of the first byte of the string to be searched is placed in EDI. Here, it's the address of a command-line argument on the stack.

- The value to be searched for is placed in AL (here, it's 0).

- A maximum count is placed in ECX. This is done to avoid searching too far in memory in case the byte you're searching for isn't actually there.

With all that in place, REPNE SCASB can be executed. As with STOSB, this creates a tight loop inside the CPU. On each pass through the loop, the byte at [EDI] is compared to the value in AL. If the values are equal, the loop is satisfied and REPNE SCASB ceases executing. If the values are *not* equal, then EDI is incremented by 1, ECX is decremented by 1, and the loop continues with another test of the byte at [EDI].

When REPNE SCASB finds the character in AL and ends, EDI will point to the byte *after* the found character's position in the search string. To access the found character, you must subtract 1 from EDI, as the program does when it replaces the 0 character with an EOL character:

```
mov byte [edi-1],10 ; Store an EOL where the null used to be
```

REPNE vs. REPE

The SCASB instruction is a little different from STOSB and MOVSB in that it is a *conditional* string instruction. STOSB and MOVSB both repeat unconditionally when preceded by the REP prefix. There are no tests going on except testing ECX to see if the loop has gone on for the predefined number of iterations. By contrast, SCASB performs a separate test every time it fires, and every test can go two ways. That's why we don't use the unconditional REP prefix with SCASB, but either the REPNE prefix or the REPE prefix.

When we're looking for a byte in the search string that matches the byte in AL, we use the REPNE prefix, as is done in showargs1. When we're looking for a byte in the search string that does *not* match the byte in AL, we use REPE. You might think that this sounds backwards somehow, and it does. However, the sense of the REPNE prefix is this: *Repeat* SCASB *as long as* [EDI] *does not equal AL*. Similarly, the sense of the REPE prefix is this: *Repeat* SCASB *as long as* [EDI] *equals AL*. The prefix indicates how long the SCASB instruction should continue firing, not when it should stop.

It's important to remember that REPNE SCASB can end for either of two reasons: It finds a match to the byte in AL or it counts ECX down to 0. In nearly all cases, if ECX is zero when REPNE SCASB ends, it means that the byte in AL was not found in the search string. However, there is the fluky possibility that ECX just happened to count down to zero when [EDI] contained a match to AL. Not very likely, but there are some mixes of data where it might occur.

Each time SCASB fires, it makes a comparison, and that comparison either sets or clears the Zero flag, ZF. REPNE will end the instruction when its comparison sets ZF to 1. REPE will end the instruction when its comparison clears ZF to 0. However, to be absolutely sure that you catch the "searched failed" outcome, you *must* test ZF immediately after the SCASB instruction ends.

For REPNE SCASB: Use JNZ.

For REPE SCASB: Use JZ.

Pop the Stack or Address It?

The showargs1 program demonstrates the obvious way to access things on the stack: pop them off the stack into registers or variables. There is another way, and this is a good place to ask an interesting program design question: is it better to pop stack data off the stack into registers or variables, or access data on the stack via memory references, while leaving it in place? Data on the stack, remember, isn't treated specially in any way once it's on the stack. Stack data is in memory, and can be addressed in brackets just like any location in a program's memory space can be addressed, using any legal addressing mode.

On the other hand, once you pop a data item off the stack into a register, it's no longer technically on the stack, because ESP has moved up-memory by the size of the data item. True, the data on the stack is not overwritten by popping it from the stack, but the next time anything is pushed onto the stack, data down-memory from the address in ESP will be overwritten. If that's where a popped data item is, it will be gone, replaced with new stack data.

The only tricky thing about addressing data on the stack is that the top of the stack isn't always in the same place during the run of a program. If your program calls procedures, the value in ESP changes as return addresses are pushed onto the stack and then popped off the stack. Your code can push values onto the stack for temporary storage. It's *very* dicey to rely on an unchanging value of ESP to address the stack except for the very simplest programs.

In most applications, a better method is to create an unchanging copy of the stack pointer by copying ESP into a 32-bit register as soon as the program begins running. A good choice for this is EBP, the 32-bit version of the 16-bit

BP (Base Pointer) register. That's what BP was originally designed to do: save a copy of the original value of the stack pointer, so that subsequent stack operations don't make "nondestructive" addressing of stack data more difficult. If you copy ESP into EBP before your program does anything that alters the value in ESP, you have a "bookmark" into the stack from which you can address anything further up the stack.

I've created a slightly different version of showargs1 to demonstrate how this works. The full program showargs2 is present in the listings archive for this book, but the pertinent code is shown here. Compare it with showargs1 to see how the two programs differ:

```
_start:
        nop                        ; This no-op keeps gdb happy...

        mov ebp,esp                ; Save the initial stack pointer in EBP
; Validate the command line argument count:
        cmp dword [ebp],MAXARGS ; See if the arg count exceeds MAXARGS
        ja Error                   ; If so, exit with an error message

; Here we calculate argument lengths and store lengths in table ArgLens:
        xor eax,eax                ; Searching for 0, so clear AL to 0
        xor ebx,ebx                ; Stack address offset starts at 0
ScanOne:
        mov ecx,0000ffffh          ; Limit search to 65535 bytes max
        mov edi,dword [ebp+4+ebx*4] ; Put address of string to search in EDI
        mov edx,edi                ; Copy starting address into EDX
        cld                        ; Set search direction to up-memory
        repne scasb                ; Search for null (0 char) in string at edi
        jnz Error                  ; REPNE SCASB ended without finding AL
        mov byte [edi-1],10        ; Store an EOL where the null used to be
        sub edi,edx                ; Subtract position of 0 from start address
        mov dword [ArgLens+ebx*4],edi  ; Put length of arg into table
        inc ebx                    ; Add 1 to argument counter
        cmp ebx,[ebp]              ; See if arg counter exceeds argument count
        jb ScanOne                 ; If not, loop back and do another one

; Display all arguments to stdout:
        xor esi,esi                ; Start (for table addressing reasons) at 0
Showem:
        mov ecx,[ebp+4+esi*4]    ; Pass offset of the message
        mov eax,4                 ; Specify sys_write call
        mov ebx,1                 ; Specify File Descriptor 1: Standard Output
        mov edx,[ArgLens+esi*4]  ; Pass the length of the message
        int 80H                    ; Make kernel call
        inc esi                    ; Increment the argument counter
        cmp esi,[ebp]             ; See if we've displayed all the arguments
        jb Showem                  ; If not, loop back and do another
        jmp Exit                   ; We're done! Let's pack it in!
```

Right at the beginning, we create an unchanging copy of the stack pointer by copying ESP into EBP. All other access to the stack is done by way of the address in EBP. The variables `ArgPtrs` and `ArgCount` are gone; the data stored in those two variables in showargs1 is available on the stack, and in showargs2 we leave it on the stack and use it from the stack.

At program startup, the top of the stack contains the argument count, so accessing the argument count is a snap: It's the `dword` quantity at [EBP]. To access items further up the stack (such as the argument addresses), we have to add offsets to EBP. Four bytes up from the argument count is the address of the first argument, so that argument's effective address is [EBP+4]. Every four bytes further up the stack is yet another argument address, until we hit the null pointer. If we use the EBX register as a 0-based counter of arguments, the address of any given argument can be calculated this way:

```
[ebp+4+ebx*4]
```

This is how we used the stack-based argument addresses to find the lengths of arguments and later display them to the console. No popping required, and whatever was on the stack when the program began running remains there, just in case we need it again later on down the line of execution.

For Extra Credit . . .

Practice is always useful, so here's a challenge that you can pursue on your own: rewrite showargs2.asm so that instead of displaying the program's command-line arguments, it displays the full list of Linux environment variables. Most of the challenge will lie in how you address the stack. The addresses of the environment variables are not at some unchanging offset up-memory from EBP. Where they lie depends on how many command-line arguments were entered by the user.

It's actually easier than it sounds. Even one hint would give it away, so put on your thinking cap and see what you come up with. (You can find the answer in the listings archive for this book, but try it yourself first!)

Heading Out to C

Calling External Functions Written in the C Language

There's a lot of value in learning assembly language, most of it stemming from the requirement that you *must* know in detail how everything works, or you won't get very far. This has always been true, from the very dawn of digital electronic computing, but from it follows a fair question: *Do I really have to know all that?*

The fair answer is no. It's possible to write extremely effective programs without having an assembly-level grip on the machine and the operating system. This is what higher-level languages were created to allow: easier, faster programming at a higher level of abstraction. It's unclear how much of today's software would exist at all if it all had to be written entirely in assembly language.

That includes Linux. There are some small portions of Linux written in assembly, but overall the bulk of the operating system is written in C. The Linux universe revolves around the C language, and if you expect to make significant use of assembly language under Linux, you had better be prepared to learn C and use it when necessary.

There is almost immediate payoff: being able to access libraries of procedures written in C. There are thousands of such libraries, and those associated with the Linux operating system are mostly free, and come with C source code. There are pros and cons to using libraries of C functions (as procedures are called in the C culture); but the real reason to learn the skills involved in calling

C functions is that it's part of knowing how everything works, especially under Linux, where the C language has left its fingerprints everywhere you look.

Virtually all the programming examples you'll see for Linux that don't involve interpreted languages such as Perl or Python are in C. Most significant, the C runtime library contains a lot of extremely useful functions but requires that you use the C protocols when making calls to those functions. So if you don't already know the language, buy a book, and get down and bash out some C. You don't need to do a lot of it, but make sure that you understand all the basic C concepts, especially as they apply to function calls. I'll try to fill in the lower-level gaps in this book, but I can't teach the language itself nor all the baggage that comes with it. You may find C a little distasteful (as I did and do) or you may love it, but *you can't escape it*, even if your main interest in Linux lies in assembly language.

What's GNU?

Way back in the late 1970s, a wild-eyed Unix hacker named Richard Stallman wanted his own copy of Unix. He didn't want to pay for it, however, so he did the obvious thing: he began writing his own version. (If it's not obvious to you, well, you don't understand Unix culture.) However, he was unsatisfied with all the programming tools currently available and objected to their high cost as well. So, as a prerequisite to writing his own version of Unix, Stallman set out to write his own compiler, assembler, and debugger. (He had already written his own editor, the legendary EMACS.)

Stallman named his version of Unix *GNU*, a recursive acronym meaning GNU's Not Unix. This was a good chuckle, and one way of getting past AT&T's trademark lawyers, who were fussy in those days about who used the word *Unix* and how. As time went on, the GNU tools took on a life of their own; and as it happened, Stallman never actually finished GNU itself. Other free versions of Unix appeared, and there was some soap opera for a few years regarding who actually owned what parts of which. This so disgusted Stallman that he created the Free Software Foundation as the home base for GNU tools development, and a radical sort of software license called the GNU Public License (GPL), which is sometimes informally called "copyleft." Stallman released the GNU tools under the GPL, which not only required that the software be free (including all source code), but prevented people from making minor mods to the software and claiming the derivative work as their own. Changes and improvements had to be given back to the GNU community.

This seemed to be major nuttiness at the time, but over the years since then it has taken on a peculiar logic and life of its own. The GPL has allowed software released under the GPL to evolve tremendously quickly, because large numbers of people were using it and improving it and giving back the improvements without charge or restriction. Out of this bubbling open-source pot eventually arose Linux, the premier GPL operating system. Linux was built with and is maintained with the GNU tool set. If you're going to program under Linux, regardless of what language you're using, you will eventually use one or more of the GNU tools.

The Swiss Army Compiler

The copy of EMACS that you will find on modern distributions of Linux doesn't have a whole lot of Richard Stallman left in it—it's been rewritten umpteen times by many other people over the past 20-odd years. Where the Stallman legacy persists most strongly is in the GNU compilers. There are a number of them, but the one that you must understand as thoroughly as possible is the GNU C Compiler, gcc. (Lowercase letters are something of an obsession in the Unix world, a fetish not well understood by a lot of people, myself included.)

Why use a C compiler for working in assembly? Mostly this: gcc does much more than simply compile C code. It's a sort of Swiss army knife development tool. In fact, I might better characterize what it does as *building* software, rather than simply *compiling* it. In addition to compiling C code to object code, gcc governs both the assembly step and the link step.

Assembly step? Yes, indeedy. There is a GNU assembler, gas, though it's an odd thing that isn't really intended to be used by human programmers. What gcc does is control gas and the GNU linker ld (which you're already using) like puppets on strings. If you use gcc, especially at the beginner level, you don't have to do much direct messing around with gas and ld.

Let's talk more about this.

Building Code the GNU Way

Assembly language work is a departure from C work, and gcc is first and foremost a C compiler. Therefore, we need to look first at the process of building C code. On the surface, building a C program for Linux using the GNU tools is pretty simple. Behind the scenes, however, it's a seriously hairy business. While it looks like gcc does all the work, what gcc really does is act as master controller for several GNU tools, supervising a code assembly line that you don't need to see unless you specifically want to.

Theoretically, this is all you need to do to generate an executable binary file from C source code:

```
gcc eatc.c -o eatc
```

Here, gcc takes the file eatc.c (which is a C source code file) and crunches it to produce the executable file eatc. (The -o option tells gcc what to name the executable output file.) However, there's more going on here than meets the eye. Take a look at Figure 12-1 as we go through it. In the figure, shaded arrows indicate movement of information. Blank arrows indicate program control.

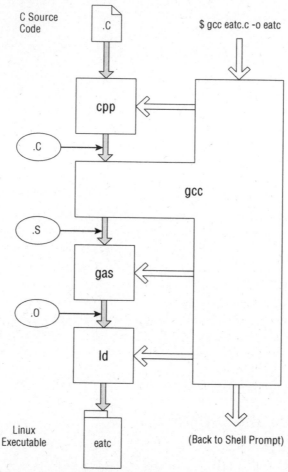

Figure 12-1: How gcc builds Linux executables

The programmer invokes gcc from the shell command line, typically in a terminal window. Gcc takes control of the system and immediately invokes a utility called the C preprocessor, cpp. The preprocessor takes the original C source code file and handles certain items like #includes and #defines. It can be thought of as a sort of macro expansion pass on the C source code file.

When cpp is finished with its work, gcc takes over in earnest. From the preprocessed C source code file, gcc generates an assembly language source code file with an .s file extension. This is literally the assembly code equivalent of the C statements in the original .c file, in human-readable form. If you develop any skill in reading AT&T assembly syntax and mnemonics (more on which a little later) you can learn a *lot* from inspecting the .s files produced by gcc.

When gcc has completed generating the assembly language equivalent of the C source code file, it invokes the GNU assembler, gas, to assemble the .s file into object code. This object code is written out in a file with an .o extension.

The final step involves the linker, ld. The .o file contains binary code, but it's *only* the binary code generated from statements in the original .c file. The .o file does *not* contain the code from the standard C libraries that are so important in C programming. Those libraries have already been compiled and simply need to be linked into your application. The linker, ld, does this work at gcc's direction. The good part is that gcc knows precisely which of the standard C libraries need to be linked to your application to make it work, and it always includes the right libraries in their right versions. So, although gcc doesn't actually do the linking, *it knows what needs to be linked*—and that is valuable knowledge indeed, as your programs grow more and more complex.

At the end of the line, ld spits out the fully linked and executable program file. At that point, the build is done, and gcc returns control to the Linux shell. Note that all of this is typically done with one simple command to gcc!

How to Use gcc in Assembly Work

The process I just described, and illustrated graphically for you in Figure 12-1, is how a C program is built under Linux using the GNU tools. I went into some detail here because we're going to use part—though only part—of this process to make our assembly programming easier. It's true that we don't need to convert C source code to assembly code—and in fact, we don't need gas to convert gas assembly source code to object code. However, we do need gcc's expertise at linking. We're going to tap in to the GNU code-building process at the link stage, so that gcc can coordinate the link step for us.

When you assemble a Linux program using NASM, NASM generates an .o file containing binary object code. Invoking NASM under Linux is typically done this way:

```
nasm -f elf -g -F stabs eatclib.asm
```

This command directs NASM to assemble the file eatclib.asm and generate a file called eatclib.o. The -f elf part tells NASM to generate object code in the ELF format, rather than one of the numerous other object code formats that NASM is capable of producing. The -g -F stabs part enables the generation of debug information in the output file, in the STABS format. The eatclib.o file is not by itself executable. It needs to be linked. Therefore, we call gcc and instruct it to link the program for us:

```
gcc eatclib.o -o eatclib
```

What part of this tells gcc to link and not compile? The only input file called out in the command is an .o file containing object code. This fact alone tells gcc that all that needs to be done is to link the file with the C runtime library to produce the final executable. The `-o eatclib` part tells gcc that the name of the final executable file is to be "eatclib."

Including the `-o` specifier is important. If you don't tell gcc precisely what to name the final executable file, it will punt and name that file "a.out."

Why Not gas?

You might be wondering why, if there's a perfectly good assembler installed automatically with every copy of Linux, I've bothered showing you how to install and use another one. Two reasons:

- The GNU assembler gas uses a peculiar syntax that is utterly unlike that of all the other familiar assemblers used in the x86 world, including NASM. It has a whole set of instruction mnemonics unique to itself. I find them ugly, nonintuitive, and hard to read. This is the AT&T syntax, so named because it was created by AT&T as a portable assembly notation to make Unix easier to port from one underlying CPU to another. It's ugly in part because it was designed to be generic, and it can be recast for any reasonable CPU architecture that might appear.

- More to the point, the notion of a "portable assembly language" is in my view a contradiction in terms. An assembly language should be a direct, complete, one-for-one reflection of the underlying machine architecture. Any attempt to make an assembly language generic moves the language away from the machine and limits the ability of an assembly programmer to direct the CPU as it was designed to be directed. The organization that created and evolves a CPU architecture is in the best position to define a CPU's mnemonics without compromise. That's why I will always use and teach the Intel mnemonics.

If it were just this simple, I wouldn't mention gas at all, as you don't need gas to write Linux assembly language in NASM. However, one of the major ways you'll end up learning many of the standard C library calls is by using them in short C programs and then inspecting the .s assembly output files that gcc generates. Having some ability to read AT&T mnemonics can be useful while you're getting comfortable with C calling conventions. I'll provide an overview of the AT&T syntax a little later in this chapter.

Linking to the Standard C Library

When you write an all-assembly program, like those I've presented in this book so far, you write *all* of it. Apart from an occasional dive into the Linux kernel services, all the code that runs is code that you write yourself. Linking in libraries of external assembly language procedures complicates this picture a little, especially if you weren't the one who wrote the libraries. Linking to functions in the standard C library (which for Linux is called *glibc*) complicates the picture a lot.

In truth, when you create a Linux assembly language program and link to functions in glibc, you're creating a sort of a hybrid. The structure of this hybrid is shown in Figure 12-2.

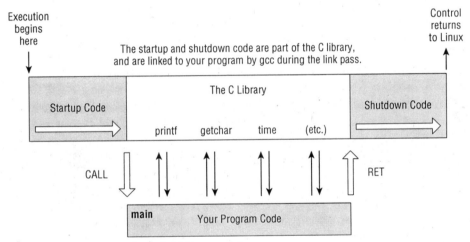

Figure 12-2: Structure of a hybrid C-assembly program

Your program is no longer the simple, start-at-the-top-and-go-down affair that your earlier assembly programs were. Glibc is not just a collection of disjointed functions. It's the standard C runtime library, and as part of its standardness, it dictates a structure to any programs that link to it. This structure includes a block of code that runs before your program begins, and another block of code that runs after your program ends. Your program is called by the startup code as though it were a procedure (with the CALL instruction) and it returns control to the C library code using a RET instruction.

Technically, your program *is* a procedure, and it helps to think of it as one. That's how I've drawn it in Figure 12-2. When Linux begins executing your program, it actually starts not at the top of the code *you* wrote, but at the beginning of the startup code block. When the startup code has done what it must, it executes a CALL instruction that takes execution down into your assembly code. When your assembly language program returns control to its caller via RET, the shutdown code begins executing, and it's the shutdown code that actually returns control to Linux via the necessary INT 80h kernel call.

In between, you can make as many calls into glibc as you like. When you link your program using gcc, the code containing the C library routines that you call is linked into the program. Note well that the startup and shutdown code, as well as all the code for the library calls, are physically present in the executable file that you generate with gcc.

C Calling Conventions

Glibc isn't singling out assembly language programs for special treatment. Pure C programs work the same way, and this is why the main program portion of a C program is called the main *function*. It really is a function, the standard C library code calls it with a CALL instruction, and it returns control to the standard C library code by executing a RET instruction.

The way the main program obtains control is therefore the first example you'll see of a set of rules called the *C calling conventions*. The standard C library is nothing if not consistent, and that is its greatest virtue. All C library functions implemented on x86 processors follow these rules. Bake them into your synapses early, and you'll lose a lot less sleep than I did trying to figure them out.

Here's the view from a height:

- A procedure (which is the more generic term for what C calls a function) must preserve the values of the EBX, ESP, EBP, ESI, and EDI 32-bit registers. That is, although it may use those registers, when it returns control to its caller, the values those registers have must be the same values they had before the function was called. The contents of all other general-purpose registers may be altered at will.

- A procedure's return value is returned in EAX if it is a value 32 bits in size or smaller. Sixty-four-bit integer values are returned in EDX and EAX, with the low 32 bits in EAX and the high 32 bits in EDX. Floating-point return values are returned at the top of the floating-point stack. (I won't be covering floating-point numerics work in this book.) Strings, structures, and other data items larger than 32 bits in size are returned by reference; that is, the procedure returns a 32-bit pointer to them in EAX.

- Parameters passed to procedures are pushed onto the stack in *reverse* order. That is, given the C function MyFunc(foo, bar, bas), bas is pushed onto the stack first, bar second, and foo last. More on this later.

- Procedures themselves do *not* remove parameters from the stack. The caller must do that after the procedure returns, either by popping the procedures off the stack or (much more commonly, since it is usually faster) by adding an offset to the stack pointer ESP. (Again, I'll explain what this means in detail later, when we actually do it.)

- Although not technically a calling convention, this requirement is important: The label naming the point at which your assembly program begins *must* be "`main:`"—not `start:`, nor `Main:`, nor `MAIN:`, nor `Beginning:`. The label at the beginning of your code must be `main:`, and it must be declared global.

Understanding these rules thoroughly will enable you to make calls to the multitude of functions in the standard C library, as well as many other useful libraries, all of which are written in C and follow the conventions as I've described them.

A Framework to Build On

Respecting the C calling conventions in your programs begins with preserving and restoring what I call the sacred registers, as listed above. Every program you write that links to glibc (or to almost any other function library written in C) requires the very same code at its beginning and end, so it's useful to bake the required code into a sort of boilerplate file that you use when you begin any new project intended to be linked with C functions.

I've created such a boilerplate file, called boiler.asm, and it's present in the listings archive for this book. The code for the necessary register saving and restoring is already there. All of the demonstration programs in the rest of this chapter are based on boiler.asm, and you can use it as the foundation for new projects of your own. For a simple example, look ahead to eatclib.asm, in Listing 12-1, which is the boiler.asm file with only five lines of new code added to it.

Saving and Restoring Registers

As I described earlier, one of the odder provisions of the C calling conventions is that a program may not arbitrarily change all general-purpose registers. The registers that cannot be changed by a Linux application linked to C functions are EBX, ESP, EBP, ESI, and EDI. You'll notice that boiler.asm saves these registers onto the stack when the program begins, and then restores them from the stack before giving control back to Linux.

One very important but non-obvious conclusion you must draw from this requirement to save EBX, ESP, EBP, ESI, and EDI is that the other general-purpose registers may be trashed. Yes, trashed—*and not only by you.* When you call procedures written by other people, those procedures may alter the values in EAX, ECX, and EDX. (The stack pointer ESP is a special case and needs special care of a sort not applicable to other registers.) What this means for you is that you *cannot* assume that (for example) a counter value you're tracking in ECX will be left untouched when you call a C library function such as printf().

If you're using ECX to count passes through a loop that calls a library function—or any function that you yourself didn't write—you must save your value of ECX on the stack before you call the library function and restore it after the library function returns. The same applies to EAX and EDX. (EAX is often used to return values from library functions, so it's not a good idea to use it to store counters and addresses and such when you're making library function calls.) If you need to keep their values intact across a call to a library function, you must save them to the stack before the library function is called.

Conversely, the sacred nature of EBX, EBP, ESI, and EDI means that these registers *will* keep their values when you make C library calls. What is binding on you is binding on the C library as well. Library functions that must use these registers save and restore them without any attention from you.

Setting Up a Stack Frame

The stack is extremely important in assembly language work, and this is doubly true in programs that interface with C, because in C (and in truth most other native-code high-level languages, including Pascal) the stack has a central role. The reason for this is simple: Compilers are robots that write assembly language code, and they are not human and clever like you. This means that a compiler has to use what might seem like brute-force methods to create its code, and most of those methods depend heavily on the use of the stack.

Compiler code generation is doctoral thesis stuff and isn't especially relevant to the lessons in this entry-level book. One compiler mechanism that does bear on Linux assembly work is that of the *stack frame*. Compilers depend on stack frames to create local variables in functions, and while stack frames are less useful in pure assembly work, you must understand them if you're going to call functions written by a high-level language compiler.

A stack frame is a location on the stack marked as belonging to a particular function. It is basically the region between the addresses contained in two registers: base pointer EBP and stack pointer ESP. This draws better than it explains; see Figure 12-3.

A stack frame is created by pushing the caller's copy of EBP on the stack to save it, and then copying the caller's stack pointer ESP into register EBP. The first two instructions in any assembly program that honors the C calling conventions must be these:

```
push ebp
mov ebp,esp
```

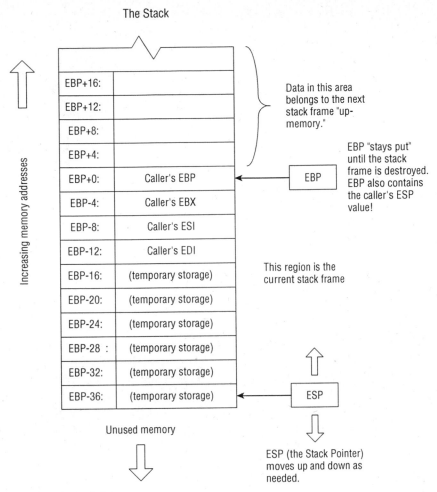

Figure 12-3: A stack frame

After this, you must either leave EBP alone or, if you must use it in a serious pinch, make sure you can restore it before the change violates any C library assumptions. (I *powerfully* recommend leaving it alone!) EBP is considered the anchor of your new stack frame, which is the main reason it shouldn't be changed. There are things stored on the stack above your stack frame (that is, at higher addresses) that often need to be referenced in your code, and EBP is the only safe way to reference them. (These things aren't shown in Figure 12-3, but I'll return to them a little later.)

Less obvious is the fact that EBP is also the hidey-hole in which you stash the caller's stack pointer value, ESP. This is yet another reason not to change EBP once you create your stack frame. Returning control at the end of your program with a random value in ESP is the shortest path to trouble that I could name.

Once EBP is safely anchored as one end of your stack frame, the stack pointer ESP is free to move up and down the stack as required. The first things you need to put on the stack, however, are the caller's values for EBX, ESI, and EDI, as shown in Figure 12-3. They will be popped back off the stack when the stack frame is destroyed at the end of your program, handing back to the caller (which in our case is the startup/shutdown code from the standard C library) the same values that those registers had when the startup code called your program as the function main.

But once EBX, ESI, and EDI are there, you can push and pop whatever you need to for temporary storage. Calling C functions requires a fair amount of pushing and popping, as you'll see shortly.

Destroying a Stack Frame

Before our program ends its execution by returning control to the startup/shutdown code (refer back to Figure 12-2 if this relationship isn't clear), its stack frame must be destroyed. This sounds to many people like something wrong is happening, but not so: the stack frame must be destroyed, or your program will crash. ("Put away" might be better terminology than "destroyed" but programmers prefer colorful language, as you'll learn after you spend any time among them.)

The stack must be clean before we destroy the stack frame and return control. This simply means that any temporary values that we may have pushed onto the stack during the program's run must be gone. All that is left on the stack should be the caller's EBP, EBX, ESI, and EDI values. Basically, if EDI was the last of the caller's values that was saved on the stack, ESP (the stack pointer) had better be pointing to that saved EDI value or there will be trouble.

Once the stack is clean, to destroy the stack frame we must first pop the caller's register values back into their registers, ensuring that the pops are in the correct order. Handing back the caller's EBX value in EDI will still crash your program! With that done, we undo the logic we followed in creating the stack frame: We restore the caller's ESP by moving the value from EBP into ESP, and finally pop the caller's EBP value off the stack:

```
mov esp,ebp
pop ebp
```

That's it! The stack frame is gone, and the stack and sacred registers are now in the same state that they were in when the startup code handed control to our program. It's now safe to execute the RET instruction that sends control to the C library's shutdown code.

Characters Out via puts()

About the simplest useful function in glibc is puts(), which sends characters to standard output. Making a call to puts() from assembly language is so simple it can be done in three lines of code. The program in Listing 12-1 is built on the file boiler.asm, and you can see the boilerplate code for saving and restoring the sacred registers at the beginning and end of the main program.

Calling puts() this way is a good example, in miniature, of the general process we use to call most any C library routine. All C library routines take their parameters on the stack, which means that we have to push either numeric values that fit in 32 bits, or else pointers to strings or other larger data objects located somewhere else. In this case, we push a 32-bit pointer to a text string. Note that we don't pass a length value for the string to puts(), as we did when sending text to the console with the sys_write kernel call. Puts() starts at the beginning of the string, and sends characters to stdout until it encounters a 0 (null) character. However many characters lie between the first byte of the string and the first null is the number of characters that the console receives.

Listing 12-1: eatclib.asm

```
;   Source name     : EATCLIB.ASM
;   Executable name : EATCLIB
;   Version         : 2.0
;   Created date    : 10/1/1999
;   Last update     : 5/26/2009
;   Author          : Jeff Duntemann
;   Description     : Demonstrates calls made into glibc, using NASM 2.05
;                     to send a short text string to stdout with puts().
;
;
;   Build using these commands:
;      nasm -f elf -g -F stabs eatclib.asm
;      gcc eatclib.o -o boiler

[SECTION .data]          ; Section containing initialized data

EatMsg: db "Eat at Joe's!",0

[SECTION .bss]           ; Section containing uninitialized data

[SECTION .text]          ; Section containing code

extern puts              ; Simple "put string" routine from glibc
global main              ; Required so linker can find entry point

main:
        push ebp         ; Set up stack frame for debugger
```

(continued)

Listing 12-1: eatclib.asm (*continued*)

```
        mov ebp,esp
        push ebx        ; Must preserve ebp, ebx, esi, & edi
        push esi
        push edi
;;; Everything before this is boilerplate; use it for all ordinary apps!

        push EatMsg     ; Push address of message on the stack
        call puts       ; Call glibc function for displaying strings
        add esp,4       ; Clean stack by adjusting ESP back 4 bytes

;;; Everything after this is boilerplate; use it for all ordinary apps!
        pop edi         ; Restore saved registers
        pop esi
        pop ebx
        mov esp,ebp     ; Destroy stack frame before returning
        pop ebp
        ret             ; Return control to Linux
```

Formatted Text Output with printf()

The puts() library routine may seem pretty useful, but compared to a few of its more sophisticated siblings, it's kid stuff. With puts() we can only send a simple text string to a file (by default, stdout), without any sort of formatting. Worse, puts() always includes an EOL character at the end of its display, whether we include one in the string data or not. This prevents us from using multiple calls to puts() to output several text strings all on the same line.

About the best you can say for puts() is that it has the virtue of simplicity. For nearly all character output needs, you're way better off using a much more powerful library function called printf(). The printf() function enables us to do a number of truly useful things, all with one function call:

- Output text either with or without a terminating EOL

- Convert numeric data to text in numerous formats, by outputting formatting codes along with the data

- Output text to a file that includes multiple strings stored separately

If you've worked with C for more than half an hour, printf() will be perfectly obvious to you, but for people coming from other languages (such as Pascal, which has no direct equivalent), it may take a little explaining.

The printf() routine will gladly display a simple string like "Eat at Joe's!"—but we can merge other text strings and converted numeric data with that base string as it travels toward standard output, and show it all seamlessly together. This is done by dropping *formatting codes* into the base string, and then passing a data item to printf() for each of those formatting codes, along with the base string. A formatting code begins with a percent sign and includes information relating to the type and size of the data item being merged with the base string, as well as how that information should be presented.

Let's look at a very simple example to start out. Here's a base string containing one formatting code:

```
"The answer is %d, and don't you forget it!"
```

The `%d` formatting code simply tells `printf()` to convert a signed integer value to text, and substitute that text for the formatting code in the base string. Of course, you must now pass an integer value to `printf()`, and I show you how that's done shortly, but when you do, `printf()` will convert the integer to text and merge it with the base string as it sends text to the stream. If the decimal value passed is 42, on the console you'll see this:

```
The answer is 42, and don't you forget it!
```

A formatting code actually has a fair amount of structure, and the `printf()` mechanism as a whole has more wrinkles than I have room here to describe. Any good C reference will explain the whole thing in detail. Table 12-1 lists the most common and useful formatting codes.

Table 12-1: Common printf() Formatting Codes

CODE	BASE	DESCRIPTION
%c	n/a	Displays a character as a character
%d	10	Converts an integer and displays it in decimal
%s	n/a	Displays a string as a string
%x	16	Converts an integer and displays it in hex
%%	n/a	Displays a percent symbol

The most significant enhancement that we can make to the formatting codes is to place an integer value between the `%` symbol and the code letter:

```
%5d
```

This code tells `printf()` to display the value right-justified within a field five characters wide. If you don't include a field width value, `printf()` will simply give the value as much room as its digits require.

Remember that if you need to display a percent symbol, you must include two consecutive percent symbols in the string: The first is a formatting code that tells `printf()` to display the second as itself, and not as the lead-in to a formatting code.

Passing Parameters to printf()

The real challenge in working with printf(), assuming you understand how it works logically, is knowing how to pass it all the parameters that it needs to handle any particular string display. Like the Writeln() function in Pascal, printf() has no set number of parameters. It can take as few parameters as one base string, or as many parameters as you need, including additional strings, character values, and numeric values of various sorts.

All parameters to C library functions are passed on the stack. This is done either directly, by pushing the parameter value itself on the stack, or indirectly, by reference, by pushing the 32-bit address of the parameter onto the stack. For 32-bit or 64-bit data values, we push the values themselves onto the stack. For larger data items such as strings and arrays, we push a pointer to the items onto the stack. (In C jargon, passing the address of something is called *passing a pointer* to that something.)

When multiple parameters are passed to printf(), they all have to be pushed onto the stack, and in a very particular and nonintuitive order: from right to left, as they would appear if you were to call printf() from code written in C. The base string is considered the leftmost parameter and is always pushed onto the stack last. A simple example from C will help here:

```
printf('%d + %d = %d ...for large values of %d.',2,2,5,2);
```

This is a C language statement that calls printf(). The base string is enclosed in quotes and is the first parameter. After the string are several numeric parameters. There must be one numeric value for each of the %d formatting codes embedded in the base string. The order in which these items must go onto the stack starts from the right and reads toward the left: 2,5,2,2, with the base string pushed last. In assembly, it's done this way:

```
push 2
push 5
push 2
push 2
push mathmsg
call printf
add esp,20
```

The identifier mathmsg is the base string, and its address is pushed last of all the parameters. Remember that we don't push the string itself onto the stack. We push the string's *address*, and the C library code will follow the address and fetch the string's data using its own machinery.

The ADD instruction at the end of the sequence represents what you'll hear described as "cleaning up the stack." Each time we push something onto the stack with a PUSH instruction, the stack pointer ESP moves toward low memory by a number of bytes equal to the size of whatever was pushed. In our case here, all parameters are exactly four bytes in size. Five such parameters thus represent 20 bytes of change in ESP for the sake of making the call. After the call is done, ESP must be moved back to where it was before we started pushing parameters onto the stack. By adding 20 to the value in ESP, the stack pointer moves back up-memory by 20 bytes and will then be where it was before we began to set up the `printf()` call.

Not well: If you forget to clean up the stack, or if you clean it up by the wrong number of bytes, your program will almost certainly throw a segmentation fault. Details—dare I call it neatness?—count!

Merging several text strings into the base string is done more or less the same way, using the `%s` code instead of `%d`:

```
push dugongs    ; Rightmost arg is pushed first
push mammals    ; Next arg to the left
push setbase    ; Base string is pushed last
call printf     ; Make the printf() call
add esp,12      ; Stack cleanup: 3 parms x 4 bytes = 12
```

The strings required for the `printf()` call are defined in the .data section of the program:

```
MammalMsg db 'Does the set of %s contain the set of %s?',10,0
Mammals   db 'mammals',0
Dugongs   db 'dugongs',0
```

I haven't shown the entire program here for the sake of brevity—how often do you need to see all the boilerplate?—but by now you should be catching the sense of making calls to `printf()`. Remember three crucial things:

- Parameters are pushed onto the stack from right to left, starting with the function call as it would be written in C. The base string is pushed last. If you're doing anything even a little complex with `printf()`, it helps to write the call out first in C form, and then translate it from there into assembly. It may help even more to first write, compile, and then run a short program in C that tests the `printf()` call, especially if you're doing something ambitious with a lot of strings and formatting codes.

- After the call to `printf()`, we must add to ESP a value equal to the total size of all parameters pushed onto the stack. Don't forget that for strings we're pushing the address of the string, *not* the data contained in the string! For nearly all parameters this will be 4 bytes. For 64-bit integers it will be eight bytes.

- The `printf()` function call trashes everything but the sacred registers. Don't expect to keep values in other registers intact through a call to `printf()`! For example, if we try to keep a counter value in ECX while executing a loop that calls `printf()`, the call to `printf()` will destroy the counter value in ECX. We must save ECX on the stack before each call to a library function, and restore it after the library call returns—or, carefully and with all due diligence, use one of the available sacred registers, such as ESI, EDI, or EBX. (Obviously, do *not* try to use ESP or EBP!)

You should be careful to ensure that all of your string parameters are properly terminated with a binary 0, which is the only way that glibc functions like `puts()` and `printf()` know where the string data ends. And again, if you can't get a `printf()` call to work in assembly, write up a simple one-line C program containing the `printf()` call and see if it works there, and works the way you expect. If it does, you're probably getting the order or the number of the parameters wrong in your assembly program. Never forget that there must be one parameter for each formatting code.

The code listings archive for this book contains answer.asm, a full (if short) example program demonstrating all the `printf()` calls shown in this section.

Data In with fgets() and scanf()

Reading characters from the Linux keyboard using `INT80h` and the `sys_read` kernel call is simple but not very versatile. The standard C library has a better way. In fact, the C library functions for reading data from the keyboard (which is the default data source assigned to standard input) are almost the inverse of those that display data to standard output. This was deliberate, even though there are times when the symmetry gets in the way, as I'll explain a little later.

If you poke around in a C library reference (and you should—there are a multitude of interesting routines there that you can call from assembly programs), you may discover the `gets()` routine. You may have wondered (if I didn't choose to tell you here) why I didn't cover it. The `gets()` routine is simplicity itself: You pass it the name of a string array in which to place characters, and then the user types characters at the keyboard, which are placed in the array. When the user presses Enter, `gets()` appends a null at the end of the entered text and returns. What's not to love?

Well, how big is the array? And how dumb is your user? Here's the catch: There's no way to tell `gets()` when to stop accepting characters. If the user types in more characters than you've allocated room for in an array, `gets()` will gleefully keep accepting characters, and overwrite whatever data is sitting next to your array in memory. If that something is something important, your program will almost certainly malfunction, and may simply crash.

That's why if you try to use `gets()`, gcc will warn you that `gets()` is dangerous. It's ancient, and *much* better machinery has been created in the decades since Unix and the standard C library were first designed. The designated successor to gets() is fgets(), which has some built-in safety equipment—and some complications, too.

The complications stem from the fact that you must pass a file handle to fgets(). In general, standard C library routines whose names begin with *f* act on files. (I'll explain how to work with disk files a little later in this chapter.) You can use fgets() to read text from a disk file—but remember, in Unix terms, your keyboard is already connected to a file, the file called standard input. If we can connect fgets() to standard input, we can read text from the keyboard, which is what the old and hazardous gets() function does automatically.

The bonus in using fgets() is that it enables us to specify a maximum number of characters for the routine to accept from the keyboard. Anything else that the user types will be truncated and discarded. If this maximum value is no larger than the string buffer you define to hold characters entered by the user, there's no chance that using fgets() will crash your program.

Connecting fgets() to standard input is easy. As I explained earlier in this book, Linux predefines three standard file handles, which are linked into your program automatically: stdin (standard input), stdout (standard output), and stderr (standard error). For accepting input from the keyboard through fgets(), you want to use the identifier stdin. It's already there; you simply have to declare it as extern in order to reference it from inside your assembly language programs.

Here's how to use the fgets() function:

1. Make sure you have declared extern fgets and extern stdin along with your other external declarations at the top of the .text section of your program.

2. Declare a buffer variable large enough to hold the string data you want the user to enter. Use the RESB directive in the .bss section of your program.

3. To call fgets(), first push the file handle. Note well that *you must push the handle itself*, not the handle's address! So use the form push dword [stdin].

4. Push the value indicating the maximum number of characters that you want fgets() to accept. Make sure it is no larger than the buffer variable you declare in .bss! The stack must contain the actual value—don't just push the *address* of a variable holding the value. Pushing an immediate value or the contents of a memory variable will work.

5. Push the address of the buffer variable where fgets() is to store the characters entered by the user.

6. Call fgets() itself.

7. As with all library function calls written in C, don't forget to clean up the stack!

This probably sounds worse than it is. In terms of actual code, a call to `fgets()` should look something like the following:

```
push dword [stdin]     ; Push predefined file handle for standard input
push 72                ; Accept no more than 72 characters from keyboard
push InString          ; Push address of buffer for entered characters
call fgets             ; Call fgets()
add esp,12             ; Stack cleanup: 3 parms X 4 bytes = 12
```

Here, the identifier `InString` is a memory variable defined like this:

```
[SECTION .bss]         ; Section containing uninitialized data
InString resb 96       ; Reserve 96 bytes for the string entry buffer
```

Recall that the RESB directive just sets aside space for your variable. That space is not pre-cleared with any particular value, spaces, nulls, or anything. Until the user enters data through `fgets()`, the string storage you allocate using RESB is uninitialized and could contain any garbage values at all. It's generally full of nulls, but Linux makes you no promises about that!

From the user side of the screen, `fgets()` simply accepts characters until the user presses Enter. It doesn't automatically return after the user types the maximum permitted number of characters. (That would prevent the user from backing over input and correcting it.) However, anything the user types beyond the number of permitted characters is discarded.

The charsin.asm file shown later in Listing 12-2 contains the preceding code.

Using scanf() for Entry of Numeric Values

In a peculiar sort of way, the C library function `scanf()` is `printf()` running backwards: Instead of outputting formatted data in a character stream, `scanf()` takes a stream of character data from the keyboard and converts it to numeric data stored in a numeric variable. `scanf()` works very well, and it understands a great many formats that I won't be explaining in this book, especially for the entry of floating-point numbers. (Floating-point values are a special problem in assembly work, and I won't be covering them in this edition.)

For most simple programs you may write while you're getting your bearings in assembly, you'll be entering simple integers, and `scanf()` is very good at that. Using it is simple: Pass `scanf()` the name of a numeric variable in which to store the entered value, and a formatting code indicating what form that value will take on data entry. The `scanf()` function takes the characters typed by the user and converts them to the integer value that the characters represent. For example, `scanf()` will take the two ASCII characters "4" and "2" entered successively and convert them to the base 10 numeric value 42 after the user presses Enter.

What about a prompt string, instructing the user what to type? Well, many newcomers assume that you can combine the prompt with the format code in a single string handed to scanf()—but alas, that won't work. It seems as though it should—after all, you can combine formatting codes with the base string to be displayed using printf(). And in scanf(), you can theoretically use a base string containing formatting codes, but the user would then have to type the prompt as well as the numeric data!

In practical terms, the only string used by scanf() is a string containing the formatting codes. If you want a prompt, you must display the prompt before calling scanf(), using printf(). To keep the prompt and the data entry on the same line, make sure you *don't* have an EOL character at the end of your prompt string.

The scanf() function automatically takes character input from standard input. There's no need to pass it the file handle stdin, as there is with fgets(). There is a separate glibc function, fscanf(), to which you *do* have to pass a file handle, but for integer data entry there's no hazard in using scanf().

Here's how to use the scanf() routine:

1. Make sure that you have declared extern scanf along with your other external declarations at the top of the .text section.

2. Declare a memory variable of the proper type to hold the numeric data read and converted by scanf(). My examples here are for integer data, so you would create such a variable with either the DD directive or the RESD directive. Obviously, if you're going to keep several separate values, you'll need to declare one variable per value entered.

3. To call scanf() for entry of a single value, first push the address of the memory variable that will hold the value. (See the following discussion about entry of multiple values in one call.)

4. Push the address of the format string specifying what format that data will arrive in. For integer values, this is typically the string %d.

5. Call scanf().

6. Clean up the stack.

The code for a typical scanf() call would look like this:

```
push IntVal      ; Push the address of the integer buffer
push Iformat     ; Push the address of the integer format string
call scanf       ; Call scanf to enter numeric data
add esp,8        ; Stack cleanup: 2 parms X 4 bytes = 8
```

It's possible to present scanf() with a string containing multiple formatting codes, so that users can enter multiple numeric values with only one call to scanf(). I've tried this, and it makes for a very peculiar user interface. The feature is better used if you're writing a program to read a text file containing rows of integer values expressed as text, and convert them to actual integer variables in memory. To simply obtain numeric values from the user through the keyboard, it's best to accept only one value per call to scanf().

The charsin.asm program in Listing 12-2 shows how to set up prompts alongside a data entry field for accepting both string data and numeric data from the user through the keyboard. After accepting the data, the program displays what was entered, using printf().

Listing 12-2: charsin.asm

```
;   Source name      : CHARSIN.ASM
;   Executable name  : CHARSIN
;   Version          : 2.0
;   Created date     : 11/21/1999
;   Last update      : 5/28/2009
;   Author           : Jeff Duntemann
;   Description      : A character input demo for Linux, using NASM 2.05,
;                      incorporating calls to both fgets() and scanf().
;
;   Build using these commands:
;     nasm -f elf -g -F stabs charsin.asm
;     gcc charsin.o -o charsin
;

[SECTION .data]                    ; Section containing initialised data

SPrompt  db 'Enter string data, followed by Enter: ',0
IPrompt  db 'Enter an integer value, followed by Enter: ',0
IFormat  db '%d',0
SShow    db 'The string you entered was: %s',10,0
IShow    db 'The integer value you entered was: %5d',10,0

[SECTION .bss]           ; Section containing uninitialized data

IntVal   resd 1          ; Reserve an uninitialized double word
InString resb 128m       ; Reserve 128 bytes for string entry buffer

[SECTION .text]          ; Section containing code

extern stdin             ; Standard file variable for input
extern fgets
extern printf
extern scanf
global main              ; Required so linker can find entry point

main:
```

Listing 12-2: charsin.asm *(continued)*

```
        push ebp            ; Set up stack frame for debugger
        mov ebp,esp
        push ebx            ; Program must preserve ebp, ebx, esi, & edi
        push esi
        push edi
;;; Everything before this is boilerplate; use it for all ordinary apps!

; First, an example of safely limited string input using fgets:
        push Sprompt        ; Push address of the prompt string
        call printf         ; Display it
        add esp,4           ; Stack cleanup for 1 parm

        push dword [stdin]  ; Push file handle for standard input
        push 72             ; Accept no more than 72 chars from keybd
        push InString       ; Push address of buffer for entered chars
        call fgets          ; Call fgets
        add esp,12          ; Stack cleanup: 3 parms X 4 bytes = 12

        push InString       ; Push address of entered string data buffer
        push Sshow          ; Push address of the string display prompt
        call printf         ; Display it
        add esp,8           ; Stack cleanup: 2 parms X 4 bytes = 8

; Next, use scanf() to enter numeric data:
        push Iprompt        ; Push address of the integer input prompt
        call printf         ; Display it
        add esp,4           ; Stack cleanup for 1 parm

        push IntVal         ; Push the address of the integer buffer
        push Iformat        ; Push the address of the integer format string
        call scanf          ; Call scanf to enter numeric data
        add esp,8           ; Stack cleanup: 2 parms X 4 bytes = 8

        push dword [IntVal] ; Push integer value to display
        push Ishow          ; Push base string
        call printf         ; Call printf to convert & display the integer
        add esp,8           ; Stack cleanup: 2 parms X 4 bytes = 8

;;; Everything after this is boilerplate; use it for all ordinary apps!
        pop edi             ; Restore saved registers
        pop esi
        pop ebx
        mov esp,ebp         ; Destroy stack frame before returning
        pop ebp
        ret                 ; Return control to Linux

[SECTION .data]            ; Section containing initialised data
```

(continued)

Listing 12-2: charsin.asm (*continued*)

```
sprompt   db 'Enter string data, followed by Enter: ',0
iprompt   db 'Enter an integer value, followed by Enter: ',0
iformat   db '%d',0
sshow     db 'The string you entered was: %s',10,0
ishow     db 'The integer value you entered was: %5d',10,0

[SECTION .bss]            ; Section containing uninitialized data

intval    resd 1         ; Reserve an uninitialized double word
instring  resb 128       ; Reserve 128 bytes for string entry buffer
```

One shortcoming of the demo program as shown is that it has no validation for entry of numbers. If the user enters ASCII digits expressing a numeric value too large to be contained in a 32-bit integer, or some mixture of characters that doesn't cook down to a numeric value, the value returned to the program by scanf() will be a garbage value with no necessary relation to what the user entered.

Be a Time Lord

The standard C libraries contain a rather substantial group of functions that manipulate dates and times. Although these functions were originally designed to handle date values generated by the real-time clock in ancient AT&T minicomputer hardware that was current in the 1970s, they have by now become a standard interface to any operating system's real-time clock support. People who program in C for Windows use the very same group of functions, and they work more or less the same way irrespective of what operating system you're working with.

By understanding how to call these functions as assembly language procedures, you'll be able to read the current date, express time and date values in numerous formats, apply timestamps to files, and do many other very useful things.

Let's take a look at how it works.

The C Library's Time Machine

Somewhere deep inside the standard C library is a block of code that, when invoked, looks at the real-time clock in the computer, reads the current date and time, and translates that into a standard, 32-bit unsigned integer value. This value is (theoretically) the number of seconds that have passed in the "Unix epoch," which began on January 1, 1970, 00:00:00 universal time. Every second that passes adds one to this value. When you read the current time or date via the C library, what you'll retrieve is the current value of this number.

The number is called `time_t`. The `time_t` value flipped to 10 digits (1 billion seconds since January 1, 1970) on September 9, 2001, at 7:46:40 A.M. UTC. There isn't a Y2K-style hazard in the immediate future, but on 3:14:07 A.M. on January 19, 2038, computers that treat `time_t` as a signed integer will see it roll over to 0, because a 32-bit signed integer can only express quantities up to 2,147,483,647. That's a lot of seconds (and a reasonably long time to prepare) but I'll only be 86, and I expect to be around when it happens.

Not to worry. A properly implemented C library doesn't assume that `time_t` is a 32-bit quantity at all, so when the signed 32-bit `time_t` flips in the year 2038, we'll already be using at least 64-bit values for everything and the whole problem will be put off for another 292 billion years or so. If we haven't fixed it once and for all by then, we'll deserve to go down in the Cosmic Crunch that cosmologists are predicting shortly thereafter.

A `time_t` value is just an arbitrary seconds count and doesn't tell you much on its own, though it can be useful for calculating elapsed times in seconds. Another standard data type implemented by the standard C library is much more useful. A `tm` structure (which is often called a *struct*, and among Pascal people a *record*) is a grouping of nine 32-bit numeric values that express the current time and date in separate useful chunks, as summarized in Table 12-2. Note that although a struct (or record) is nominally a grouping of unlike values, in the current x86 Linux implementation, a `tm` value is more like an array or a data table, because all nine elements are the same size, which is 32 bits, or 4 bytes. I've described it that way in Table 12-2, by including a value that is the offset from the beginning of the structure for each element in the structure. This enables us to use a pointer to the beginning of the structure, and an offset from the beginning to close in on any given element of the structure.

There are C library functions that convert `time_t` values to `tm` values and back. I cover a few of them in this chapter, but they're all pretty straightforward, and once you've thoroughly internalized the C calling conventions, you should be able to work out an assembly calling protocol for any of them.

Note that the `time_t` value is not truly the exact, precise number of seconds since the beginning of the Unix epoch. There are glitches in the way Unix counts seconds, and `time_t` is not adjusted for accumulated astronomical errors in the way that real-world NIST time is. So across short intervals (ideally, less than a year) `time_t` may be considered accurate. Beyond that, assume that it will be off by a few seconds or more, with no easy way to figure out how to compensate for the errors.

Table 12-2: Values Contained in the tm Structure

OFFSET IN BYTES	C LIBRARY NAME	DEFINITION
0	tm_sec	Seconds after the minute, from 0
4	tm_min	Minutes after the hour, from 0
8	tm_hour	Hour of the day, from 0
12	tm_mday	Day of the month, from 1
16	tm_mon	Month of the year, from 0
20	tm_year	Year since 1900, from 0
24	tm_wday	Days since Sunday, from 0
28	tm_yday	Day of the year, from 0
32	tm_isdst	Daylight Savings Time flag

Fetching time_t Values from the System Clock

Any single second of time (at least those seconds after January 1, 1970) can be represented as a 32-bit unsigned integer in a Unix-compatible system. Fetching the value for the current time is done by calling the time() function:

```
push dword 0        ; Push a 32-bit null pointer to stack, since
                    ; we don't need a buffer. Time value is
                    ; returned in eax.
call time           ; Returns calendar time in eax
add esp, byte 4     ; Stack cleanup for 1 parm
mov [oldtime],eax   ; Save time value in memory variable
```

The time() function can potentially return the time_t value in two places: in EAX or in a buffer that you allocate somewhere. To have time() place the value in a buffer, you pass it a pointer to that buffer on the stack. If you don't want to store the time value in a buffer, then you must still hand it a null pointer on the stack. That's why we push a 0 value in the preceding code; 0 is the value of a null pointer.

No other parameters need to be passed to time(). On return, you'll have the current time_t value in EAX. That's all there is to it.

Converting a time_t Value to a Formatted String

By itself, a time_t value doesn't tell you a great deal. The C library contains a function, ctime(), that will return a pointer to a formatted string representation of a given `time_t`. It returns a pointer to a string buried somewhere in the runtime library. This string has the following format:

```
Wed June 3 12:13:21 2009
```

The first field is a three-character code for the day of the week, followed by a three-character code for the month and a two-space field for the day of the month. The time follows, in 24-hour format, and the year brings up the rear. For good measure (though it is sometimes a nuisance), the string as returned by `ctime()` is terminated by a newline.

Here's how you call `ctime()`:

```
push OldTime   ; Push *address* of calendar time value
call ctime     ; Returns pointer to ASCII time string in eax
add esp,4      ; Stack cleanup for 1 parm
```

This looks pretty conventional, but note something here that departs from recent experience with glibc: You pass `ctime()` the *address* of a `time_t` value, not the value itself! You're used to passing 32-bit integer values by pushing the values themselves onto the stack—say, for display by `printf()`. Not so here. A `time_t` value is currently, under Linux, represented as a 4-byte integer, but there is no guarantee that it will always be thus. So, to keep its options open (and to ensure that Unix can be used for thousands or even billions of years to come, egad), the C library requires a pointer to the current time, rather than a time value itself.

You push a pointer to the `time_t` value that you want to represent as a string, and then call `ctime()`. What `ctime()` returns is a pointer to the string, which it keeps somewhere inside the library. You can use that pointer to display the string on the screen via `printf()` or to write it to a text file.

Generating Separate Local Time Values

The C library also provides a function to break out the various components of the date and time into separate values, so that you can use them separately or in various combinations. This function is `localtime()`, and given a `time_t` value, it will break out the date and time into the fields of a `tm` structure, as described in Table 12-2. Here's the code to call it:

```
push OldTime   ; Push address of calendar time value
call localtime ; Returns pointer to static time structure in eax
add esp,4      ; Stack cleanup for 1 parm
```

Here, `OldTime` is a `time_t` value. Given this value, `localtime()` returns in EAX—much in the manner of `ctime()`—a pointer to a `tm` structure within the C library somewhere. By using this pointer as a base address, you can access the fields in the structure. The trick lies in knowing the offset into `tm` for the individual time/date field that you want, and using that offset as a constant displacement from the address base. For example, the code below displays the year field from a `tm` structure to the console using `printf`. Note that the first instruction indexes into `tm` by 20 bytes, which is the offset of the year field from the beginning of the structure:

```
mov edx, dword [eax+20] ; Year value is 20 bytes offset into tm
push edx                ; Push value onto the stack
push yrmsg              ; Push address of the base string
call printf             ; Display string and year value with printf
add esp, byte 8         ; Stack cleanup: 2 parms X 4 bytes = 8
```

By using the displacements shown in Table 12-2, you can access all the other components of the time and the date in the `tm` structure, each stored as a 32-bit integer value.

Making a Copy of glibc's tm Struct with MOVSD

It's sometimes handy to keep a separate copy of a `tm` structure, especially if you're working with several date/time values at once. So, after you use `localtime()` to fill the C library's hidden `tm` structure with date/time values, you can copy that structure to a structure allocated in the .bss or .data section of your program.

Doing such a copy involves the straightforward use of the REP MOVSD (Repeat Move String Double) instruction, introduced in Chapter 11. MOVSD is an almost magical thing: Once you set up pointers to the data area you want to copy, and the place you want to copy it to, you store the size of the area in ECX and let REP MOVSD do the rest. In one operation it will copy an entire buffer from one place in memory to another.

To use REP MOVSD, you place the address of the source data—that is, the data to be copied—into ESI. You move the address of the destination location—where the data is to be placed—in EDI. The number of items to be moved is placed in ECX. You then make sure that the Direction flag, DF, is cleared (for more on this, see Chapter 11) and execute REP MOVSD:

```
mov esi,eax     ; Copy address of static tm from EAX to ESI
mov edi,tmcopy  ; Put the address of the local tm copy in edi
mov ecx,9       ; A tm struct is 9 dwords in size under Linux
cld             ; Clear df to 0 so we move up-memory
rep movsd       ; Copy static tm struct to local copy
```

Here, we're moving the C library's `tm` structure to a buffer allocated in the .bss section of the program. The `tm` structure is nine double words—36 bytes—in size, so we have to reserve that much space and give it a name:

```
TmCopy resd 9  ; Reserve 9 32-bit fields for time struct tm
```

The preceding code assumes that the address of the C library's already filled tm structure is in EAX, and that a tm structure TmCopy has been allocated. Once executed, it will copy all of the tm data from its hidey-hole inside the C runtime library to your freshly allocated buffer.

The REP prefix puts MOVSD in automatic-rifle mode, as explained in Chapter 11. That is, MOVSD will keep moving data from the address in ESI to the address in EDI, counting ECX down by one with each move, until ECX goes to zero. Then it stops.

One frequently made mistake is forgetting that the count in ECX is the count of data items to be moved, *not* the number of bytes to be moved! By virtue of the *D* on the end of its mnemonic, MOVSD moves double words, and the value you place in ECX must be *the number of 4-byte items* to be moved. So, in moving nine double words, MOVSD actually transports 36 bytes from one location to another—but you're counting double words here, not bytes.

The program in Listing 12-3 knits all of these code snippets together into a demo of the major Unix time features. There are many more time functions to be studied in the C library, and with what you now know about C function calls, you should be able to work out calling protocols for any of them.

Listing 12-3: timetest.asm

```
;   Source name      : TIMETEST.ASM
;   Executable name  : TIMETEST
;   Version          : 2.0
;   Created date     : 12/2/1999
;   Last update      : 5/26/2009
;   Author           : Jeff Duntemann
;   Description      : A demo of time-related functions for Linux, using
;                      NASM 2.05
;
;   Build using these commands:
;      nasm -f elf -g -F stabs timetest.asm
;      gcc timetest.o -o timetest
;

[SECTION .data]          ; Section containing initialised data

TimeMsg  db "Hey, what time is it?  It's %s",10,0
YrMsg    db "The year is %d.",10,0
Elapsed  db "A total of %d seconds has elapsed since program began running.",
10,0

[SECTION .bss]           ; Section containing uninitialized data

OldTime  resd 1          ; Reserve 3 integers (doubles) for time values
NewTime  resd 1          ; 32-bit time_t value
```

(continued)

Listing 12-3: timetest.asm (*continued*)

```
TimeDiff resd 1        ; 32-bit time_t value
TimeStr  resb 40       ; Reserve 40 bytes for time string
TmCopy   resd 9        ; Reserve 9 integer fields for time struct tm

[SECTION .text]        ; Section containing code

extern ctime
extern difftime
extern getchar
extern printf
extern localtime
extern strftime
extern time

global main            ; Required so linker can find entry point

main:
        push ebp       ; Set up stack frame for debugger
        mov ebp,esp

        push ebx       ; Program must preserve EBP, EBX, ESI, & EDI
        push esi
        push edi
;;; Everything before this is boilerplate; use it for all ordinary apps!

; Generate a time_t calendar time value with glibc's time() function:
        push 0             ; Push a 32-bit null pointer to stack,
                           ;   since we don't need a buffer.
        call time          ; Returns calendar time in EAX
        add esp,4          ; Clean up stack after call
        mov [OldTime],eax  ; Save time value in memory variable

; Generate a string summary of local time with glibc's ctime() function:
        push OldTime       ; Push address of calendar time value
        call ctime         ; Returns pointer to ASCII time string in EAX
         add esp,4         ; Stack cleanup for 1 parm

        push eax           ; Push pointer to ASCII time string on stack
        push TimeMsg       ; Push pointer to base message text string
        call printf        ; Merge and display the two strings
        add esp,8          ; Stack cleanup: 2 parms X 4 bytes = 8

; Generate local time values into glibc's static tm struct:
        push dword OldTime ; Push address of calendar time value
        call localtime     ; Returns pointer to static time structure in
EAX
        add esp,4          ; Stack cleanup for 1 parm

; Make a local copy of glibc's static tm struct:
```

Listing 12-3: timetest.asm (*continued*)

```
        mov esi,eax            ; Copy address of static tm from eax to ESI
        mov edi,TmCopy         ; Put the address of the local tm copy in EDI
        mov ecx,9              ; A tm struct is 9 dwords in size under Linux
        cld                    ; Clear DF so we move up-memory
        rep movsd              ; Copy static tm struct to local copy

; Display one of the fields in the tm structure:
        mov edx,dword [TmCopy+20] ; Year field is 20 bytes offset into tm
        add edx,1900           ; Year field is # of years since 1900
        push edx               ; Push value onto the stack
        push YrMsg             ; Push address of the base string
        call printf            ; Display string and year value with printf
        add esp,8              ; Stack cleanup: 2 parms X 4 bytes = 8

; Wait a few seconds for user to press Enter so we have a time difference:
        call getchar           ; Wait for user to press Enter

; Calculating seconds passed since program began running:
        push dword 0           ; Push null ptr; we'll take value in EAX
        call time              ; Get current time value; return in EAX
        add esp,4              ; Clean up the stack
        mov [NewTime],eax      ; Save new time value

        sub eax,[OldTime]      ; Calculate time difference value
        mov [TimeDiff],eax     ; Save time difference value

        push dword [TimeDiff]  ; Push difference in seconds onto the stack
        push Elapsed           ; Push addr. of elapsed time message string
        call printf            ; Display elapsed time
        add esp,8              ; Stack cleanup for 1 parm

;;; Everything after this is boilerplate; use it for all ordinary apps!
        pop edi                ; Restore saved registers
        pop esi
        pop ebx
        mov esp,ebp            ; Destroy stack frame before returning
        pop ebp
        ret                    ; Return control to Linux
```

If you ever move to other Unix implementations outside the GNU sphere, keep in mind that the time_t value may already have some other definition than a 32-bit integer. At this time, glibc defines time_t as a 32-bit integer, and you can calculate time differences between two time_t values simply by subtracting them—at least until the year 2038. For other, non-GNU implementations of Unix, it's best to use the difftime() function in the C library to return a difference between two time_t values.

Understanding AT&T Instruction Mnemonics

There is more than one set of instruction mnemonics for the x86 CPUs, and that's been a source of much confusion. An instruction mnemonic is simply a way for human beings to remember what a binary bit pattern such as 1000100111000011 means to the CPU. Instead of writing 16 ones and zeros in a row (or even the slightly more graspable hexadecimal equivalent 89C3h), we say MOV BX,AX.

Keep in mind that mnemonics are just that—memory joggers for humans—and are creatures unknown to the CPU itself. Assemblers translate mnemonics to machine instructions. Although we can agree among ourselves that MOV BX,AX will translate to 1000100111000011, there's nothing magical about the string MOV BX,AX. We could just as well have agreed on "COPY AX TO BX" or "STICK GPREGA INTO GPREGB." We use MOV BX,AX because that's what Intel suggested we do, and since Intel designed and manufactures the CPU chips, it likely knows best how to describe the internals of its own products.

The alternate set of x86 instruction mnemonics, called the *AT&T mnemonics*, arose out of the desire to make Unix as easy to port to different machine architectures as possible. However, the goals of operating system implementers are not the same as those of assembly language programmers; and if your goal is to have a complete and optimally efficient command of the x86 CPUs, you're better off writing code with the Intel set, as I've been teaching throughout this book. Where the AT&T set comes in handy is in understanding the gcc compiler and the standard C library.

AT&T Mnemonic Conventions

When gcc compiles a C source code file to machine code, what it really does is translate the C source code to assembly language source code, using the AT&T mnemonics. Look back to Figure 12-1. The gcc compiler takes as input a .c source code file, and outputs an .s assembly source file, which is then handed to the GNU assembler, gas, for assembly. This is how the GNU tools work on all platforms. In a sense, assembly language is an intermediate language used for the C compiler's benefit. In most cases, programmers never see it and don't have to fool with it.

In most cases. However, if you're going to deal with the standard C library and the multitudes of other function libraries written in C and for C, it makes sense to become at least passingly familiar with the AT&T mnemonics. There are some general rules that, once digested, make it much easier. Here's the list in short form:

- **AT&T mnemonics and register names are invariably lowercase**. This is in keeping with the Unix convention of case sensitivity. I've mixed uppercase and lowercase in the text and examples to get you used to seeing assembly source both ways, but you have to remember that while Intel (and hence NASM) suggest uppercase but will accept lowercase, AT&T *requires* lowercase.

- **Register names are always preceded by the percent symbol, %.** That is, what Intel would write as AX or EBX, AT&T would write as %ax and %ebx. This helps the assembler recognize register names.

- **Every AT&T machine instruction mnemonic that has operands has a single-character suffix indicating how large its operands are.** The suffix letters are *b, w,* and *l,* indicating byte (8 bits), word (16 bits), or long (32 bits). What Intel would write as MOV BX,AX, AT&T would write as movw %ax,%bx. (The changed order of %ax and %bx is *not* an error. See the next rule!)

- **In the AT&T syntax, source and destination operands are placed in the opposite order from Intel syntax.** That is, what Intel would write as MOV BX,AX, AT&T would write as movw %ax,%bx. In other words, in AT&T syntax, the source operand comes first, followed by the destination.

- **In the AT&T syntax, immediate operands are always preceded by the dollar sign ($).** What Intel would write as PUSH 32, AT&T would write as pushl $32. This helps the assembler recognize immediate operands.

- **Not all AT&T instruction mnemonics are generated by gcc.** Equivalents to Intel's JCXZ, JECXZ, LOOP, LOOPZ, LOOPE, LOOPNZ, and LOOPNE have only recently been added to the AT&T mnemonic set, and gcc never generates code that uses them.

- **In the AT&T syntax, displacements in memory references are signed quantities placed outside parentheses containing the base, index, and scale values.** I'll treat this one separately a little later, as you'll see it a lot in .s files and you should be able to understand it.

Examining gas Source Files Created by gcc

The best way to get a feel for the AT&T assembly syntax is to look at an actual AT&T-style .s file produced by gcc. Doing this has two benefits: first, it will help you become familiar with the AT&T mnemonics and formatting conventions. Second, you may find it useful, when struggling to figure out how to call a C library function from assembly, to create a very short C program that simply calls the function of interest, and then examine the .s file that gcc produces when it compiles your C program. The dateis.c program shown below was actually a part of my early research in the 1990s, and I used it to get a sense for how ctime() was called at the assembly level.

You don't automatically get an .s file every time you compile a C program. The .s file is created, but once gas assembles the .s file to a binary object code file (typically an .o file), it deletes the .s file. If you want to examine an .s file created by gcc, you must compile with the −s option. (Note that this is an uppercase *S*. Case matters in the Unix world!) The command looks like this:

```
gcc dateis.c -S
```

Note that the output of this command is *the assembly source file only*. If you specify the −s option, gcc understands that you want to generate assembly source, rather than an executable program file, so it generates only the .s file. To compile a C program to an executable program file, you must compile it again *without* the −s option.

Here's dateis.c, which does nothing more than print out the date and time as returned by the standard C library function `ctime()`:

```
#include <time.h>
#include <stdio.h>

int main()
  {
    time_t timeval;

    (void)time(&timeval);
    printf("The date is: %s", ctime(&timeval));
    exit(0);
  }
```

It's not much of a program, but it does illustrate the use of three C library function calls: `time()`, `ctime()`, and `printf()`. When gcc compiles the preceding program (dateis.c), it produces the file dateis.s, shown in Listing 12-4. I have manually added the equivalent Intel mnemonics as comments to the right of the AT&T mnemonics, so you can see what equals what in the two systems. (Alas, neither gcc nor any other utility I have ever seen will do this for you.)

Listing 12-4: dateis.s

```
    .file       "dateis.c"
    .version    "01.01"
gcc2_compiled.:
.section    .rodata
.LC0:
    .string     "The date is: %s"
.text
    .align 4
```

Listing 12-4: dateis.s (*continued*)

```
.globl main
     .type       main,@function
main:
     pushl %ebp              # push ebp
     movl %esp,%ebp          # mov ebp,esp
     subl $4,%esp            # sub esp,4
     leal -4(%ebp),%eax      # lea eax,ebp-4
     pushl %eax              # push eax
     call time               # call time
     addl $4,%esp            # add esp,4
     leal -4(%ebp),%eax      # lea eax,ebp-4
     pushl %eax              # push eax
     call ctime              # call ctime
     addl $4,%esp            # add esp,4
     movl %eax,%eax          # mov eax,eax
     pushl %eax              # push eax
     pushl $.LC0             # push dword .LC0
     call printf             # call printf
     addl $8,%esp            # add esp,8
     pushl $0                # push dword 0
     call exit               # call exit
     addl $4,%esp            # add esp,4
     .p2align 4,,7
.L1:
     leave                   # leave
     ret                     # ret
.Lfe1:
     .size       main,.Lfe1-main
     .ident      "GCC: (GNU) egcs-2.91.66 19990314/Linux (egcs-1.1.2 release)"
```

One thing to keep in mind when reading this is that dateis.s contains assembly language code produced mechanically by a compiler, *not* by a human programmer! Some things about the code (such as why the label .L1 is present but never referenced) are less than ideal and can only be explained as artifacts of gcc's compilation machinery. In a more complex program there may be some customary use of a label .L1 that doesn't exist in a program this simple.

Some quick things to note here while reading the preceding listing:

- When an instruction does not take operands (call, leave, ret), it does not have an operand-size suffix. Calls and returns look pretty much alike in both Intel and AT&T syntax.

- When referenced, the name of a message string is prefixed by a dollar sign ($), just as numeric literals are. In NASM, a named string variable is considered a variable and not a literal. This is just another AT&T peccadillo to be aware of.

- Note that the comment delimiter in the AT&T scheme is the pound sign (#), rather than the semicolon used in nearly all Intel-style assemblers, including NASM.

AT&T Memory Reference Syntax

As you'll recall from earlier chapters, referencing a memory location (as distinct from referencing its address) is done by enclosing the location of the address in square brackets, like so:

```
mov ax, dword [ebp]
```

Here, we're taking whatever 32-bit quantity is located at the address contained in EBP and loading it into register AX. More complex memory addressing can look like this:

```
mov eax, dword [ebx-4]        ; Base minus displacement
mov al, byte [bx+di+28]       ; Base plus index plus displacement
mov al, byte [bx+di*4]        ; Base plus index times scale
```

All of the preceding examples use the Intel syntax. The AT&T syntax for memory addressing is considerably different. In place of square brackets, AT&T mnemonics use parentheses to enclose the components of a memory address:

```
movb (%ebx),%al               # mov byte al,[ebx] in Intel syntax
```

Here, we're moving the byte quantity at [ebx] to AL. (Don't forget that the order of operands is reversed from what Intel syntax does.) Inside the parentheses you place the base, the index, and the scale, when present. (The base must always be there.) The displacement, when one exists, must be placed in front of and outside the parentheses:

```
movl -4(%ebx),%eax            # mov dword eax,[ebx-4] in Intel syntax
movb 28(%ebx,%edi),%eax       # mov byte eax,[ebx+edi+28] in Intel syntax
```

Note that in AT&T syntax, you don't do the math inside the parentheses. The base, index, and scale are separated by commas, and plus signs and asterisks are not allowed. The schema for interpreting an AT&T memory reference is as follows:

```
±disp(base,index,scale)
```

The ± symbol I use in the preceding schematic example indicates that the displacement is *signed*; that is, it may be either positive or negative, to indicate whether the displacement value is added to or subtracted from the rest of the address. Typically, you only see the sign as explicitly negative; without the minus symbol, it is assumed that the displacement is positive. The displacement and scale values are optional.

What you will see most of the time, however, is a very simple type of memory reference:

```
-16(%ebp)
```

The displacements will vary, of course, but what this almost always means is that an instruction is referencing a data item somewhere on the stack. C code allocates its variables on the stack, in a stack frame, and then references those variables by literal offsets from the value in EBP. EBP acts as a "thumb in the stack," and items on the stack may be referenced in terms of offsets (either positive or negative) from EBP. The preceding reference would tell a machine instruction to work with an item at the address in EBP minus 16 bytes.

Generating Random Numbers

As our next jump on this quick tour of standard C library calls from assembly, let's get seriously random. (Or modestly pseudorandom, at least.) The standard C library has a pair of functions that enable programs to generate pseudorandom numbers. The *pseudo* prefix is significant here. Research indicates that there is no provable way to generate a truly *random*, random number strictly from software. In fact, the whole notion of what *random* really means is a spooky one and keeps a lot of mathematicians off the streets these days. Theoretically, you'd need to obtain triggers from some sort of quantum phenomenon (radioactivity is the one most often mentioned) to achieve true randomness. But lacking a nuclear-powered random-number generator, we'll have to fall back on pseudo-ness and learn to live with it.

A simplified definition of *pseudorandom* would run something like this: a *pseudorandom*-number generator yields a sequence of numbers of no recognizable pattern, but the sequence can be repeated by passing the same *seed value* to the generator. A *seed value* is simply a whole number that acts as an input value to an arcane algorithm that creates the sequence of pseudorandom numbers. Pass the same seed to the generator, and you get the same sequence. However, within the sequence, the distribution of numbers within the generator's range is reasonably scattered and random.

The standard C library contains two functions relating to pseudorandom numbers:

- The srand() function passes a new seed value to the random-number generator. This value must be a 32-bit integer. If no seed value is passed, the value defaults to 1.

- The rand() function returns a 31-bit pseudorandom number. The high bit is always 0 and thus the value is always positive if treated as a 32-bit signed integer.

Once you understand how these functions work, using them is close to trivial.

Seeding the Generator with srand()

Getting the seed value into the generator is actually more involved than making the call that pulls the next pseudorandom number in the current sequence. It's not that the call to srand() is that difficult: you push the seed value onto the stack, and then call srand():

```
push eax     ; Here, the seed value is in eax
call srand    ; Seed the pseudorandom number generator
add esp,4    ; Stack cleanup for 1 parm
```

That's all you have to do! The srand() function does not return a value. But . . . what do you use as a seed value?

Aye, now there's the rub.

If it's important that your programs *not* work with the same exact sequence of pseudorandom numbers every time they run, you clearly don't want to use an ordinary integer hard-coded into the program. You'd ideally want to get a different seed value each time you run the program. The best way to do that (though there are other ways) is to seed calls to srand() with the seconds count since January 1, 1970, as returned by the time() function, explained in the previous section. This value, called time_t, is a signed integer that changes every second, so with every passing second you have a new seed value at your disposal, one that by definition will *never* repeat. (I'm assuming here that the time_t rollover problem mentioned in the previous section will be solved by the year 2038.)

Almost everyone does this, and the only caution is that you must make certain that you don't call srand() to reseed the sequence more often than once per second. In most cases, for programs that are run, do their work, and terminate in a few minutes or hours, you only need to call srand() once, when the program begins executing. If you are writing a program that will remain running for days or weeks or longer without terminating (such as a server), it might be a good idea to reseed your random-number generator once per day.

Here's a short code sequence that calls time() to retrieve the current time_t value, and then hands the time value to srand():

```
push 0       ; Push a 32-bit null pointer to stack
call time     ; Returns time_t value (32-bit integer) in eax
add esp,4    ; Clean up stack
```

```
push eax        ; Push time value in eax onto stack
call srand      ; Time value is the seed value for random gen.
add esp,4       ; Clean up stack
```

The initial push of a null pointer indicates to `time()` that you're not passing in a variable to accept the time value. The null pointer has to be there on the stack to keep the `time()` function happy, however. The value you want to keep is returned in EAX.

Generating Pseudorandom Numbers

Once you've seeded the generator, getting numbers in the pseudorandom sequence is easy: You pull the next number in the sequence with each call to `rand()`. The `rand()` function is as easy to use as anything in the C library: it takes no parameters (so you don't need to push anything onto the stack or clean up the stack afterward) and the pseudorandom number is returned in EAX.

The randtest.asm program in Listing 12-5 demonstrates how `srand()` and `rand()` work. It also demonstrates a couple of interesting assembly tricks, which I'll spend the rest of this section discussing.

Listing 12-5: randtest.asm

```
;   Source name     : RANDTEST.ASM
;   Executable name : RANDTEST
;   Version         : 2.0
;   Created date    : 12/1/1999
;   Last update     : 5/22/2009
;   Author          : Jeff Duntemann
;   Description     : A demo of Unix rand & srand using NASM 2.05
;
;   Build using these commands:
;     nasm -f elf -g -F stabs randtest.asm
;     gcc randtest.o -o randtest
;

[SECTION .data]              ; Section containing initialized data

Pulls      dd 36             ;   How many numbers do we pull?
Display    db 10,'Here is an array of %d %d-bit random numbners:',10,0
ShowArray  db '%10d %10d %10d %10d %10d %10d',10,0
CharTbl db '0123456789ABCDEFGHIJKLMNOPQRSTUVWXYZabcdefghijklmnopqrstuvwxyz-@'

[SECTION .bss]               ; Section containing uninitialized data

BUFSIZE    equ 70            ; # of randomly chosen chars
```

(continued)

Listing 12-5: randtest.asm (*continued*)

```
RandVal   resd 1              ; Reserve an integer variable
Stash     resd 72             ; Reserve an array of 72 integers for randoms
RandChar  resb BUFSIZE+5      ; Buffer for storing randomly chosen chars

[SECTION .text]               ; Section containing code

extern printf
extern puts
extern rand
extern scanf
extern srand
extern time


;-----------------------------------------------------------------------
;  Random number generator procedures  --  Last update 5/22/2009
;
;  This routine provides 5 entry points, and returns 5 different "sizes" of
;  pseudorandom numbers based on the value returned by rand. Note first of
;  all that rand pulls a 31-bit value. The high 16 bits are the most "random"
;  so to return numbers in a smaller range, you fetch a 31-bit value and then
;  right shift it zero-fill all but the number of bits you want. An 8-bit
;  random value will range from 0-255, a 7-bit value from 0-127, and so on.
;  Respects EBP, ESI, EDI, EBX, and ESP. Returns random value in EAX.
;-----------------------------------------------------------------------
pull31: mov ecx,0             ; For 31 bit random, we don't shift
        jmp pull
pull16: mov ecx,15            ; For 16 bit random, shift by 15 bits
        jmp pull
pull8:  mov ecx,23            ; For 8 bit random, shift by 23 bits
        jmp pull
pull7:  mov ecx,24            ; For 7 bit random, shift by 24 bits
        jmp pull
pull6:  mov ecx,25            ; For 6 bit random, shift by 25 bits
        jmp pull
pull4:  mov ecx,27            ; For 4 bit random, shift by 27 bits
pull:   push ecx              ; rand trashes ecx; save shift value on stack
        call rand             ; Call rand for random value; returned in EAX
        pop ecx               ; Pop stashed shift value back into ECX
        shr eax,cl            ; Shift the random value by the chosen factor
                              ;  keeping in mind that part we want is in CL
        ret                   ; Go home with random number in EAX

;-----------------------------------------------------------------------
;  Newline outputter  --  Last update 5/22/2009
;
```

Listing 12-5: randtest.asm (*continued*)

```
;   This routine allows you to output a number of newlines to stdout, given
;   by the value passed in EAX.  Legal values are 1-10. All sacred registers
;   are respected. Passing 0 in EAX will result in no newlines being issued.
;-------------------------------------------------------------------------
newline:
        mov ecx,10      ; We need a skip value, which is 10 minus the
        sub ecx,eax     ;  number of newlines the caller wants.
        add ecx,nl      ; This skip value is added to the address of
        push ecx        ;  the newline buffer nl before calling printf.
        call printf     ; Display the selected number of newlines
        add esp,4       ; Stack cleanup for one parm
        ret             ; Go home
nl db 10,10,10,10,10,10,10,10,10,10,0



;; This subroutine displays numbers six at a time
;; Not intended to be general-purpose...
shownums:
        mov esi, dword [Pulls]  ; Put pull count into ESI
.dorow: mov edi,6               ; Put row element counter into EDI
.pushr: dec edi                 ; Decrement row element counter
        dec esi                 ; Decrement pulls counter
        push dword [Stash+esi*4]; Push number from array onto stack
        cmp edi,0               ; Have we filled the row yet?
        jne .pushr              ; If not, go push another one
        push ShowArray          ; Push address of base display string
        call printf             ; Display the random numbers
        add esp,28              ; Stack cleanup: 7 items X 4 bytes = 28
        cmp esi,0               ; See if pull count has gone to 0
        jnz .dorow              ; If not, we go back and do another row!
        ret                     ; Done, so go home!


;; This subroutine pulls random values and stuffs them into an
;; integer array.  Not intended to be general purpose.  Note that
;; the address of the random number generator entry point must
;; be loaded into edi before this is called, or you'll seg fault!
puller:
        mov esi,dword [Pulls]   ; Put pull count into ESI
.grab:  dec esi                 ; Decrement counter in ESI
        call edi                ; Pull the value; it's returned in eax
        mov [Stash+esi*4],eax   ; Store random value in the array
        cmp esi,0               ; See if we've pulled 4 yet
        jne .grab               ; Do another if ESI <> 0
        ret                     ; Otherwise, go home!


; MAIN PROGRAM:
```

(continued)

Listing 12-5: randtest.asm (*continued*)

```
global main                    ; Required so linker can find entry point

main:
        push ebp          ; Set up stack frame for debugger
        mov ebp,esp
        push ebx          ; Program must preserve EBP, EBX, ESI, & EDI
        push esi
        push edi
;;; Everything before this is boilerplate; use it for all ordinary apps!

; Begin by seeding the random number generator with a time_t value:
Seedit: push 0           ; Push a 32-bit null pointer to stack
        call time        ; Returns time_t value (32-bit integer) in EAX
        add esp,4        ; Stack cleanup for one parm
        push eax         ; Push time_t value in EAX onto stack
        call srand       ; Time_t value is the seed value for random # gen
        add esp,4        ; Stack cleanup for one parm

; All of the following code blocks are identical except for the size of
; the random value being generated:

; Create and display an array of 31-bit random values
        mov edi,pull31   ; Copy address of random # subroutine into EDI
        call puller      ; Pull as many numbers as called for in [pulls]
        push 32          ; Size of numbers being pulled, in bits
        push dword [Pulls] ; Number of random numbers generated
        push Display     ; Address of base display string
        call printf      ; Display the label
        add esp,12       ; Stack cleanup: 3 parms X 4 bytes = 12
        call shownums    ; Display the rows of random numbers

; Create and display an array of 16-bit random values
        mov edi,pull16   ; Copy address of random # subroutine into edi
        call puller      ; Pull as many numbers as called for in [pulls]
        push 16          ; Size of numbers being pulled, in bits
        push dword [Pulls] ; Number of random numbers generated
        push Display     ; Address of base display string
        call printf      ; Display the label
        add esp,12       ; Stack cleanup: 3 parms X 4 bytes = 12
        call shownums    ; Display the rows of random numbers

; Create and display an array of 8-bit random values:
        mov edi,pull8    ; Copy address of random # subroutine into edi
        call puller      ; Pull as many numbers as called for in [pulls]
        push 8           ; Size of numbers being pulled, in bits
        push dword [Pulls] ; Number of random numbers generated
        push Display     ; Address of base display string
        call printf      ; Display the label
```

Listing 12-5: randtest.asm (*continued*)

```
        add esp,12      ; Stack cleanup: 3 parms X 4 bytes = 12
        call shownums   ; Display the rows of random numbers

; Create and display an array of 7-bit random values:
        mov edi,pull7   ; Copy address of random # subroutine into edi
        call puller     ; Pull as many numbers as called for in [pulls]
        push 7          ; Size of numbers being pulled, in bits
        push dword [Pulls] ; Number of random numbers generated
        push Display    ; Address of base display string
        call printf     ; Display the label
        add esp,12      ; Stack cleanup: 3 parms X 4 bytes = 12
        call shownums   ; Display the rows of random numbers

; Create and display an array of 4-bit random values:
        mov edi,pull4   ; Copy addr. of random # subroutine into EDI
        call puller     ; Pull as many #s as called for in [pulls]
        push 4          ; Size of numbers being pulled, in bits
        push dword [Pulls] ; Number of random numbers generate
        push Display    ; Address of base display string
        call printf     ; Display the label
        add esp,12      ; Stack cleanup: 3 parms X 4 bytes = 12
        call shownums   ; Display the rows of random numbers

; Clear a buffer to nulls:
Bufclr: mov ecx, BUFSIZE+5      ; Fill whole buffer plus 5 for safety
.loop:  dec ecx                 ; BUFSIZE is 1-based so decrement first!
        mov byte [RandChar+ecx],0  ; Mov null into the buffer
        cmp ecx,0               ; Are we done yet?
        jnz .loop               ; If not, go back and stuff another null

; Create a string of random alphanumeric characters:
Pulchr: mov ebx, BUFSIZE        ; BUFSIZE tells us how many chars to pull
.loop:  dec ebx                 ; BUFSIZE is 1-based, so decrement first!
        mov edi,pull6           ; For random in the range 0-63
        call puller             ; Go get a random number from 0-63
        mov cl,[CharTbl+eax]    ; Use random # in eax as offset into table
                                ;   and copy character from table into CL
        mov [RandChar+ebx],cl   ; Copy char from CL to character buffer
        cmp ebx,0               ; Are we done having fun yet?
        jne .loop               ; If not, go back and pull another

; Display the string of random characters:
        mov eax,1       ; Output a newline
        call newline    ;  using the newline procedure
        push RandChar   ; Push the address of the char buffer
        call puts       ; Call puts to display it
        add esp,4       ; Stack cleanup for one parm
        mov eax,1       ; Output a newline
```

(continued)

Listing 12-5: randtest.asm (*continued*)

```
        call newline    ;  using the newline subroutine

;;; Everything after this is boilerplate; use it for all ordinary apps!
        pop edi         ; Restore saved registers
        pop esi
        pop ebx
        mov esp,ebp     ; Destroy stack frame before returning
        pop ebp
        ret             ; Return control to Linux
```

Some Bits Are More Random Than Others

Under Linux, the `rand()` function returns a 31-bit unsigned value in a 32-bit integer. (The sign bit of the integer—the highest of all 32 bits—is always cleared to 0.) The Unix documentation for `rand()` and `srand()` indicates that the low-order bits of a value generated by `rand()` are less random than the high-order bits. This means that if you're going to use only some of the bits of the value generated by `rand()`, you should use the highest-order bits you can.

I honestly don't know why this should be so, nor how bad the problem is. I'm not a math guy, and I will take the word of the people who wrote the `rand()` documentation; but it bears on the issue of how to limit the range of the random numbers that you generate.

The issue is pretty obvious: suppose you want to pull a number of random alphanumeric ASCII characters. You don't need numbers that range from 0 to 2 billion. There are only 127 ASCII characters, and in fact only 62 are letters and numbers. (The rest are punctuation marks, white space, control characters, or nonprinting characters such as the smiley faces.) What you want to do is pull random numbers between 0 and 61.

Pulling numbers that range from 0 to 2 billion until you find one less than 62 will take a long time. Clearly, you need a different approach. The one I took treats the 31-bit value returned by `rand()` as a collection of random bits. I extract a subset of those bits just large enough to meet my needs. Six bits can express values from 0 to 63, so I take the highest-order six bits from the original 31-bit value and use those to specify random characters.

It's easy: simply shift the 31-bit value to the right until all bits but the highest-order six bits have been shifted off the right end of the value into oblivion. The same trick works with any (reasonable) number of bits. All you have to do is select by how many bits to shift. I've created a procedure with multiple entry points, where each entry point selects a number of bits to select from the random value:

```
pull31: mov ecx,0  ; For 31 bit random, we don't shift
        jmp pull
pull16: mov ecx,15 ; For 16 bit random, shift by 15 bits
```

```
          jmp pull
pull8:    mov ecx,23  ; For 8 bit random, shift by 23 bits
          jmp pull
pull7:    mov ecx,24  ; For 7 bit random, shift by 24 bits
          jmp pull
pull6:    mov ecx,25  ; For 6 bit random, shift by 25 bits
          jmp pull
pull4:    mov ecx,27  ; For 4 bit random, shift by 27 bits
pull:     push ecx    ; rand() trashes ECX; save shift value on stack
          call rand   ; Call rand() for random value; returned in EAX
          pop ecx     ; Pop stashed shift value back into ECX
          shr eax,cl  ; Shift the random value by the chosen factor
                      ;  keeping in mind that part we want is in CL
          ret         ; Go home with the random number in EAX
```

To pull a 16-bit random number, call pull16. To pull an 8-bit random number, call pull8, and so on. I did discover that the smaller numbers are not as random as the larger numbers, and the numbers returned by pull4 are probably not random enough to be useful. (I left the pull4 code in so you could see for yourself by running randtest.)

The logic here should be easy to follow: you select a shift value, put it in ECX, push ECX onto the stack, call rand(), pop ECX from the stack, and then shift the random number (which rand() returns in EAX) by the value in CL—which, of course, is the lowest eight bits of ECX.

Why does ECX go onto the stack? ECX is not one of the sacred registers in the C calling conventions, and virtually all C library routines use ECX internally and thus trash its value. If you want to keep a value in ECX across a call to a library function, then you have to save your value somewhere before the call, and restore it after the call is complete. The stack is the best place to do that.

I use the pull6 routine to pull random 6-bit numbers to select characters from a character table, thus creating a string of random alphanumeric characters. I pad the table to 64 elements with two additional characters (- and @) so that I don't have to test each pulled number to see if it's less than 62. If you need to limit random values to some range that is not a power of 2, choose the next largest power of 2—but try to design your program so that you don't have to choose random values in a range like 0 to 65. Much has been written in algorithm books about random numbers, so if the concept fascinates you, I direct you there for further study.

Calls to Addresses in Registers

I use a technique in randtest that is sometimes forgotten by assembly new-comers: you can execute a CALL instruction to a procedure address held in a register. You don't always have to use CALL with an immediate label. In other words, the two CALL instructions in the following code snippet are both completely legal and equivalent:

```
mov ebx, pull8 ; Load the address represented by label pull8 into EBX
call pull8     ; Call the address represented by pull8
call ebx       ; Call the address stored in EBX
```

Why do this? You'll find your own reasons over time, but in general it enables you to treat procedure calls as parameters. In randtest, I factored out a lot of code into a procedure called puller, and then called puller several times for different sizes of random number. I passed puller the address of the correct random-number procedure to call by loading the address of that procedure into EDI:

```
; Create and display an array of 8-bit random values:
mov edi,pull8  ; Copy address of random # subroutine into edi
call puller    ; Pull as many numbers as called for in [pulls]
```

Down in the puller procedure, the code calls the requested random-number procedure this way:

```
puller:
      mov esi,dword [pulls]    ; Put pull count into ESI
.grab: dec esi                 ; Decrement counter in ESI
      call edi                 ; Pull the value; it's returned in EAX
      mov [stash+esi*4],eax    ; Store random value in the array
      cmp esi,0                ; See if we've pulled enough yet
      jne .grab                ; Do another if ESI<> 0
      ret                      ; Otherwise, go home!
```

See the CALL EDI instruction? In this situation (where EDI was previously loaded with the address of procedure pull8), what is called is pull8—even though the label "pull8" is nowhere present in procedure puller. The same code in puller can be used to fill a buffer with all the different sizes of random numbers, by calling the procedure address passed to it in EDI.

Calling an address in a register gives you a lot of power to generalize code—just make sure you document what you're up to, as the label that you're calling is not contained in the CALL instruction!

How C Sees Command-Line Arguments

In Chapter 11 I explained how to access command-line arguments from a Linux program as part of a more general discussion of stack frames. One of the odder things about linking and calling functions out of the standard C library in glibc is that the way you access command-line arguments changes, and changes significantly.

The arguments are still on the stack, as is the table of argument addresses. (If you haven't been through that section of Chapter 11 yet, please go to page 427 and study it now or this section won't make much sense.) The problem is that the glibc startup code places other things there as well, and those other things are now in the way.

Fortunately, you have a way past those obstructions, which include important things like the return address that takes execution into the glibc shutdown code and allows your program to make a graceful exit. The way past is your "thumb in the stack," EBP. EBP anchors your access to both your own items (stored down-memory from EBP) and those placed on the stack by glibc, which are up-memory.

Glibc adds a pointer to the stack frame that points to the table of addresses pointing to the arguments themselves. Because we're talking about a pointer to a pointer to a table of pointers to the actual argument strings, the best way to begin is to draw a picture of the lay of the land. Figure 12-4 shows the pointer relationships and stack structures you have to understand to identify and read the command-line arguments.

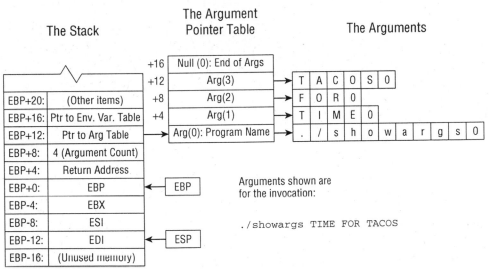

Figure 12-4: Accessing command-line arguments when the C library is present

Immediately above EBP is the return address for your portion of the program. When your code is done, it executes a RET instruction, which uses this return address to take execution back into the C library's shutdown sequence. You don't need to access this return address directly for anything, and you certainly shouldn't change it.

Immediately above the return address, at offset 8 from EBP (as the literature would say, at EBP+8) is an integer count of the number of arguments. Don't be confused: This is a duplicate copy of the argument count that exists just below the table of argument addresses, as described in Chapter 11.

Immediately above the argument count, at EBP+12, is a pointer to the table of argument addresses. Immediately above that, at EBP+16, is a pointer to the table of environment variable pairs. Reading environment variable pairs is done much the same way as reading command-line arguments, so if you understand one, you won't have much trouble with the other.

Even with all that additional indirection, it takes surprisingly little code to display a list of arguments:

```
        mov edi,[ebp+8]   ; Load argument count into EDI
        mov ebx,[ebp+12]  ; Load pointer to argument table into EBX
        xor esi,esi       ; Clear ESI to 0
.showit:
        push dword [ebx+esi*4]  ; Push address of an argument on the stack
        push esi                ; Push argument number
        push ArgMsg             ; Push address of display string
        call printf             ; Display the argument # and argument
        add esp,12              ; Stack cleanup: 3 parms x 4 bytes = 12
        inc esi                 ; Bump argument # to next argument
        dec edi                 ; Decrement argument counter by 1
        jnz .showit             ; If argument count is 0, we're done
```

The argument count and the address of the argument table are at fixed offsets from EBP. The argument count goes into EDI. The address of the argument table goes into EBX. ESI is cleared to 0, and provides an offset into the table of argument addresses. With that accomplished, we go into a loop that pushes the argument pointer, the argument number, and a base string onto the stack and calls `printf()` to display them. After printing each argument, we increment the argument number in ESI and decrement the argument count in EDI. When EDI goes to 0, we've displayed all the arguments, and we're done.

One important note about this program, which I've said before but must emphasize: If you're calling a C library function in a loop, either you must use the sacred registers to hold the counters that govern the loop or you must push them onto the stack before making a library call. The library trashes the nonsacred registers EAX, ECX, and EDX. If you had tried to store the argument count in ECX, the count would have been destroyed the first time you called `printf()`. The sacred nature of EBX, ESI, and EDI makes them ideal for this use.

A full program incorporating the preceding code is present in the listings archive for this book, as showargs3.asm.

Simple File I/O

The final example program I present in this book is nominally about working with disk-based text files. However, it pulls together a lot of assembly tricks and features I've explained earlier and adds a few more. It's the largest and most complex program in this book, and if you can read it and follow the flow of the logic, you've gotten everything from this book that I set out to teach you. It's more like a "real" program than anything else in this book, in that it works with command-line arguments, writes output to a disk file, and does other useful things that any utility you'll set out to build will likely require.

The program textfile.asm in Listing 12-6 creates and fills a text file with text. You can specify the number of lines to be filled in the file, as well as text for the lines. If you don't specify text for the file, the program will generate a line of randomly chosen characters and use that instead. Invoking the program is done like this:

```
$./textfile 150 Time for tacos!
```

This invocation would create a new file (the name of which is fixed in the program as "testeroo.txt") and write the text "Time for tacos!" to the file 150 times before closing the file. If the file testeroo.txt already exists, it will be overwritten from the beginning. If you don't type anything after the line count number, the program will fill the file with random alphanumeric characters. If you don't type an integer as the first argument, textfile will display an error message. If you only type the program name and press Enter, textfile will display several lines explaining what it is and how to use it.

Converting Strings into Numbers with sscanf()

When you type a number on the command line when invoking a program, you can access that number as one of the command-line arguments, through the mechanisms described earlier in this chapter. However, there's a catch: the number is present *as text*, and you can't, for example, just take the textual string "751" and load it into a register or an integer variable. To make use of numeric command-line arguments as *numbers*, you must convert their textual expression into numeric form.

The standard C library has several functions to handle this challenge. Some of them, such as strtod(), are pretty specific and limited, and convert text to only one numeric type. One of them, however, is capable of converting almost any textual expression of a legal numeric value into an appropriate numeric form. This is sscanf(), and it's the one we'll use in Listing 12-6.

The sscanf() function takes three parameters, which you must push on the stack in the following order:

1. First push the address of a numeric variable to contain the numeric value generated by sscanf(). We're generating a 32-bit integer here, so in textfile.asm we pass the address of the memory variable LineCount, which is a 32-bit integer.

2. Now push the address of a formatting code string that tells sscanf() what numeric format you want the input text to be converted to. Here the code string is "%d," which, as you may recall from our printf() discussion, is the code for double words (32-bit integers).

3. Finally, push the address of the text string to be converted to the numeric value that it represents. In textfile.asm, we push the address of arg(1), which is the first command-line argument you type on the command line when you invoke the program.

Once these three addresses are pushed onto the stack, call sscanf(). It returns the converted value in the numeric variable whose address you passed as the first parameter. It also returns a code in EAX to indicate whether the conversion was successful. If the return value in EAX is 0, then an error occurred, and you shouldn't assume that you have anything useful in your numeric variable. If the conversion went through successfully, you'll see the value 1 in EAX.

This is the simplest way to use sscanf(). It can convert whole arrays of numbers at once, but this is a more specialized use that you're unlikely to need when you're just starting out. The string passed to sscanf() as the third parameter may contain multiple formatting codes, and in that case the string whose address you pass as the third parameter should have text describing numeric values for each formatting code present in the format string.

The whole process looks like this:

```
mov ebx,[ebp+12]       ; Put pointer to argument table into ebx
push LineCount         ; Push address of line count integer for sscanf
push IntFormat         ; Push address of integer formatting code
push dword [ebx+4]     ; Push address of arg(1)
call sscanf            ; Call sscanf to convert arg(1) to an integer
add esp,12             ; Stack cleanup: 3 parms x 4 bytes = 12
cmp eax,1              ; Return value of 1 says we got a valid number
je chkdata             ; If we got a valid number, go on; else abort
```

Assuming that the user entered at least one argument on the command line (and the program has already verified this), a pointer to that first argument is located at an offset of 4 from the beginning of the command-line argument pointer table. (The very first element in the table, which we call arg(0), points to the name of the program as the user typed it on the command line.) That's why we push the contents of location [EBX+4] onto the stack; we had already loaded EBX with the address of the argument pointer table. What's located at [EBX+4] is the pointer to arg(1), the first command-line argument. Refer to Figure 12-4 if this is still fuzzy.

Creating and Opening Files

By this time you should be pretty comfortable with the general mechanism for making C library calls from assembly. And whether you realize it or not, you're already pretty comfortable with some of the machinery for manipulating text files. You've already used printf() to display formatted text to the screen by way of standard output. The very same mechanism is used to write formatted text to disk-based text files—you're basically substituting a real disk file for standard output, so understanding text file I/O shouldn't be much of a conceptual leap.

But unlike standard output, which is predefined for you by the C library and always available, you have to create or open a disk-based text file in order to use it. The fopen() function is what does the job.

There are three general ways to open a file: for reading, for writing, and for appending. When you open a file for reading, you can read text from it via such functions as fgets(), but you can't write to the file. When you open a file for writing, whatever may have been in the file before is thrown away, and new material is written starting at the beginning of the file. When you open a file for appending, you may write to the file, but new material is written *after* any existing material, and whatever was originally in the file is retained.

Ordinarily, when you open a file for writing you can't read from it, but there are special modes that allow both reading from and writing to a file. For text files especially (which are what we're speaking of here) that introduces some complications, so for the most part text files are opened for either reading or writing, but not for both at once.

In the Unix file system, if you open a file for either writing or appending and the file does not already exist, the file is created. If you don't know whether a file exists and you need to find out, attempt to open it for *reading* and not for writing, or you'll get a file whether it actually existed earlier or not!

To use fopen(), you must push the following parameters onto the stack before the call:

1. First onto the stack is the address of a code indicating for which mode the file should be opened. The various available modes are listed in Table 12-3. The ones you'll typically use for text files are "r," "w," and "a." These should be defined as short character strings, followed by a null:

```
WriteCode  db 'w',0
OpenCode   db 'r',0
```

2. Next onto the stack is the address of the character string containing the name of the file to be opened.

With those two items on the stack, you make the call to `fopen()`. If the file was successfully opened, `fopen()` will return a file handle in EAX. A file handle is a 32-bit number assigned by Linux to a file during the call to `fopen()`. If the open was unsuccessful, EAX will contain 0. Here's how opening a file for reading looks in code:

```
push opencode   ; Push address of open-for-read code "r"
push ebx        ; Address of the name of the help file is in EBX
call fopen      ; Attempt to open the file for reading
add esp,8       ; Stack cleanup: 2 parms x 4 bytes = 8
cmp eax,0       ; fopen() returns null if attempted open failed
<jump as needed>
```

The process of creating a file and then writing to it is identical, except that you must push the "w" code onto the stack, rather than the "r" code.

Table 12-3: File Access Codes for Use with fopen()

CODE	DESCRIPTION
"r"	Opens an existing text file for reading
"w"	Creates a new text file or opens and truncates an existing file
"a"	Creates a new text file or opens an existing file so that new text is added at the end
"r+"	Opens an existing text file for either writing or reading
"w+"	Creates a new text file or opens and truncates an existing file for both read and write access
"a+"	Creates a new text file or opens an existing file for reading or for writing so that new text may be added at the end

Reading Text from Files with fgets()

When `fopen()` successfully creates or opens a file for you, it returns a file handle in EAX. Keep that file handle safe somewhere—I recommend either copying it to a memory variable allocated for that purpose or putting it in one of the sacred registers. If you store it in EAX, ECX, or EDX and then make a call to almost any C library function, the file handle in the register will be trashed and you'll lose it.

Once a file is opened for reading, you can read text lines from it sequentially with the fgets() function. Each time you call fgets() on an opened text file, it will read one line of the file, which is defined as all the characters up to the next EOL ("newline") character (ASCII 10), which in the Unix world always indicates the end of a text line.

Now, in any given file there's no way of knowing how many characters there will be until the next newline, so it would be dangerous to just turn fgets() loose to bring back characters until it encounters a newline. If you attempt to open the wrong kind of file (a binary code file is one possibility, or a compressed data file), you might bring in thousands of bytes before encountering the binary 10 value that the file system considers a newline. Whatever buffer you had allocated to hold the incoming text would overflow and fgets() would perhaps destroy adjacent data or crash your program.

For that reason, you must also pass a limit value to fgets(). When it begins reading a line, fgets() keeps track of how many characters it has brought in from the file, and when it gets to one short of the limit value, it stops reading characters. It then adds an EOL character to the buffer for the final character and returns.

Set up calls to fgets() this way:

1. Push the file handle returned from fopen() onto the stack.

2. Push the character count limit value. This must be the actual integer value, and not a pointer to the value!

3. Finally, push the address of the character buffer into which fgets() should store the characters that it reads from the file.

With all that done, call fgets(). If fgets() returns a 0 in EAX, then either you've reached the end of the file, or else a file error happened during the read. Either way, there's no more data forthcoming from the file; but without a 0 coming back in EAX, you can assume that valid text is present in the buffer at the address you passed on the stack to fgets().

I used fgets() to create a very simple disk-based help system for textfile.asm. When the user enters no command-line arguments at all, the textfile program reads a short text file from disk and displays it to standard output. If the disk-based help file cannot be opened, textfile displays a short message to that effect. This is a common and courteous thing to do with command-line programs, and I recommend that all utilities you build for everyday use work this way.

The code for the help system is relatively simple and demonstrates both fopen() and fgets():

```
diskhelp:
        push OpenCode    ; Push pointer to open-for-read code "r"
        push ebx         ; Pointer to name of help file is passed in ebx
```

```
            call fopen      ; Attempt to open the file for reading
            add esp,8       ; Clean up the stack
            cmp eax,0       ; fopen returns null if attempted open failed
            jne .disk       ; Read help info from disk file...
            call memhelp    ; ...else from memory if there's help file on disk
            ret
.disk:  mov ebx,eax     ; Save handle of opened file in ebx
.rdln:  push ebx        ; Push file handle on the stack
        push dword HELPLEN  ; Limit line length of text read
        push HelpLine   ; Push address of help text line buffer
        call fgets      ; Read a line of text from the file
        add esp,12      ; Clean up the stack
        cmp eax,0       ; A returned null indicates error or EOF
        jle .done       ; If we get 0 in eax, close up & return
        push HelpLine   ; Push address of help line on the stack
        call printf     ; Call printf to display help line
        add esp,4       ; Clean up the stack
        jmp .rdln
.done:  push ebx        ; Push the handle of the file to be closed
        call fclose     ; Closes the file whose handle is on the stack
        add esp,4       ; Clean up the stack
        ret             ; Go home
```

When the procedure `diskhelp` is called, the caller passes a pointer to the name of the help file to be read in EBX. The code then attempts to open this file. If the attempt to open the help file fails, a very short "fail-safe" help message is displayed from strings stored in the .data section of the program. (This is the call to `memhelp`, which is another short procedure in textfile.asm.) Never leave the user staring at a mute cursor, wondering what's going on!

Once the help file is opened, the code starts looping through a sequence that reads text lines from the opened file with `fgets()`, and then writes those lines to standard output with `printf()`. The maximum length of the lines to be read is defined by the equate HELPLEN. Pushing an equate value on the stack is no different from pushing an immediate value, and that's how the instruction is encoded. But instead of being specified (perhaps differently) at several places all over your source code, the maximum length of your help file lines is defined in only one place and may be changed everywhere it's used by changing that one equate only. Equates are good. Use them whenever you can.

Each time a line is read from the file, the address of the line is pushed onto the stack and displayed with `printf()`. When no more lines are available to be read in the help file, `fgets()` returns a 0 in EAX, and the program branches to the function call that closes the file.

Note the `fclose()` function, which in use is quite simple: You push the file handle of an open file onto the stack, and call `fclose()`. That's all it takes to close the file!

Writing Text to Files with fprintf()

Earlier in this chapter, I explained how to write formatted text to the display by way of standard output, using the printf() function. The standard C library provides a function that writes the very same formatted text to *any* opened text file. The fprintf() function does exactly what printf() does, but it takes one additional parameter on the stack: the file handle of an open text file. The same text stream that printf() would send to standard output is sent by fprintf() to that open file.

I won't bother repeating how to format text for printf() using formatting codes and base strings. It's done the same way, with the exact same codes. Instead, I'll simply summarize how to set up a call to fprintf():

1. Push any values or addresses of values (as appropriate) onto the stack. There's no difference here from the way it's done for a call to printf().

2. Push the address of the base string containing the formatting codes. Again, this is done just as for printf().

3. Finally, and here's where fprintf() differs from printf(), push the file handle of the file to which the text should be written.

Then call fprintf(). Your text will be written to the open file. Note that to use fprintf(), the destination file must have been opened *for either writing or appending*. If you attempt to use fprintf() on a file opened for reading, you will generate an error and fprintf() will return without writing any data at all.

In that event, an error code will be returned in EAX. However, unlike the other functions we've discussed so far, the error code is a negative number, *not* 0! So, although you should compare the returned value against 0, you actually need to jump on a value *less* than 0—rather than 0 itself. Typically, to jump on an fprintf() error condition, you would use JL (Jump if Less), which will jump on a value less than 0.

Here's the fprintf() call from textfile.asm:

```
        push esi        ; ESI is the pointer to the line of text
        push 1          ; Push the first line number
        push WriteBase  ; Push address of the base string
        push ebx        ; Push the file handle of the open file
writeline:
        cmp dword edi,0 ; Has the line count gone to 0?
        je donewrite    ; If so, go down & clean up stack
        call fprintf    ; Write the text line to the file
        dec edi         ; Decrement the count of lines to be written
        add dword [esp+8],1 ; Update the line number on the stack
        jmp writeline   ; Loop back and do it again
donewrite:
        add oop,16      ; Clean up stack after call to fprintf
```

The call to fprintf() is a pretty minor part of this, but there's still something very interesting to note here: The code doesn't clean up the stack immediately after the call to fprintf(). In every other case of a call to a C library function, I have adjusted the stack to remove parameters immediately after the function call. What's different here?

This part of the code from textfile.asm writes a single text line to the output file repeatedly, for a number of times specified in the memory variable LineCount. Remember that the function you're calling doesn't remove parameters from the stack, and almost never modifies them. So instead of wasting time pushing and removing the parameters for every write to the file, I waited until all the calls to fprintf() were finished, and only then (at the label donewrite) cleaned up the stack.

But that leaves the question of changing the line number value for each write. The textfile program writes an initial line number before each line of text written to the file, and that number changes for each line written. But instead of pushing a new line number value for each call to fprintf()(which would require removing and repushing everything else, too), the code reaches right up into the stack and updates the line number value that has been pushed onto the stack, after each call to fprintf():

```
add dword [esp+8],1  ; Update the line number on the stack
```

I counted the number of bytes in each of the parameters passed to fprintf() and worked out where the pushed line number value was on the stack. In this case (and it may change depending on how many values you pass to fprintf()) it was 8 bytes higher on the stack than the position of the stack pointer ESP.

There's nothing dicey about changing parameters that have already been pushed onto the stack, especially if it can save you a whole bunch of pushing and popping. *Just make sure that you know precisely where the things are that you want to change!* Needless to say, attempting to update a counter but changing an address instead can lead to a quick crash. This is assembly language, people. Your cushy chair is gone.

Notes on Gathering Your Procedures into Libraries

Here's a recap of how to go about gathering procedures together into libraries:

- No entry-point definition or register saving has to happen. Just create a new source code file and paste the procedure source code into the file, which must have an .asm file extension.

- Define all of the callable entry points to all procedures in the library, as well as any other identifiers that may be used by other programs and libraries, as global.

- If the procedures call any C library functions, or procedures in other libraries you own or have created, or use variables or other identifiers defined outside the library, declare all such external identifiers as extern.

- When calling library procedures from a program, update the makefile for that program so that the final executable has a dependency on the library.

This last point is the only one that requires additional discussion. The following makefile builds the textfile.asm demo program, which links in a library called linlib.asm. Note that there is an entirely new line specifying how the object file linlib.o is assembled, and indicating that the final binary file textfile depends on both textfile.o and linlib.o.

Because the textfile executable depends on both textfile.o and linlib.o, anytime you make changes to either textfile.asm or linlib.asm, the make utility will completely relink the executable file via gcc. However, unless you change both .asm files, only the .asm file that is changed will be assembled. The magic of make is that it does nothing that doesn't need to be done.

```
textfile: textfile.o linlib.o
        gcc textfile.o linlib.o -o textfile
textfile.o: textfile.asm
        nasm -f elf -g -F stabs textfile.asm
linlib.o: linlib.asm
        nasm -f elf -g -F stabs linlib.asm
```

The complete file, linlib.asm, is present in the listings archive for this book. The procedures it contains have been gathered from other programs shown in this chapter, so it would be repetitive to reprint them all here.

Finally, the textfile.asm program follows, in its entirety. Make sure that you can read all of it—there's nothing here I haven't covered somewhere in this book. And if you want a challenge, here's one for your next project: Adapt textfile to read in a text file, and write it out again with line numbers prepended in front of each line of text. Allow the user to enter on the command line the name of a new file to contain the modified text. Keep the help system and write a new help text file for it.

Pull that off, and you can take a bow: You'll be an assembly language programmer!

Listing 12-6: textfile.asm

```
;   Source name     : TEXTFILE.ASM
;   Executable name : TEXTFILE
;   Version         : 2.0
;   Created date    : 11/21/1999
;   Last update     : 5/29/2009
;   Author          : Jeff Duntemann
```

(continued)

Listing 12-6: textfile.asm (*continued*)

```
;   Description     : A text file I/O demo for Linux, using NASM 2.05
;
;   Build using these commands:
;     nasm -f elf -g -F stabs textfile.asm
;     nasm -f elf -g -F stabs linlib.asm
;     gcc textfile.o linlib.o -o textfile
;
;   Note that this program requires several procedures
;   in an external named LINLIB.ASM.

[SECTION .data]          ; Section containing initialized data

IntFormat   dd '%d',0
WriteBase   db 'Line #%d: %s',10,0
NewFilename db 'testeroo.txt',0
DiskHelpNm  db 'helptextfile.txt',0
WriteCode   db 'w',0
OpenCode    db 'r',0
CharTbl db '0123456789ABCDEFGHIJKLMNOPQRSTUVWXYZabcdefghijklmnopqrstuvwxyz-@'
Err1    db 'ERROR: The first command line argument must be an integer!',10,0
HelpMsg db 'TEXTTEST: Generates a test file.  Arg(1) should be the # of ',10,0
HELPSIZE EQU $-HelpMsg
        db 'lines to write to the file.  All other args are concatenated',10,0
        db 'into a single line and written to the file.  If no text args',10,0
        db 'are entered, random text is written to the file.  This msg ',10,0
        db 'appears only if the file HELPTEXTFILE.TXT cannot be opened. ',10,0
HelpEnd     dd 0


[SECTION .bss]           ; Section containing uninitialized data

LineCount   resd 1           ; Reserve integer to hold line count
HELPLEN     EQU 72           ; Define length of a line of help text data
HelpLine    resb HELPLEN     ; Reserve space for disk-based help text line
BUFSIZE     EQU 64           ; Define length of text line buffer buff
Buff        resb BUFSIZE+5   ; Reserve space for a line of text

[SECTION .text]               ; Section containing code

;; These externals are all from the glibc standard C library:
extern fopen
extern fclose
extern fgets
extern fprintf
extern printf
extern sscanf
```

Listing 12-6: textfile.asm (*continued*)

```nasm
extern time

;; These externals are from the associated library linlib.asm:
extern seedit                 ; Seeds the random number generator
extern pull6                  ; Generates a 6-bit random number from 0-63
extern newline                ; Outputs a specified number of newline chars

global main                   ; Required so linker can find entry point

main:
        push ebp              ; Set up stack frame for debugger
        mov ebp,esp
        push ebx              ; Program must preserve EBP, EBX, ESI, & EDI
        push esi
        push edi
;;; Everything before this is boilerplate; use it for all ordinary apps!

        call seedit           ; Seed the random number generator

;; First test is to see if there are command line arguments at all.
;; If there are none, we show the help info as several lines.  Don't
;; forget that the first arg is always the program name, so there's
;; always at least 1 command-line argument!
        mov eax,[ebp+8]       ; Load argument count from stack into EAX
        cmp eax,1             ; If count is 1, there are no args
        ja chkarg2            ; Continue if arg count is > 1
        mov ebx,DiskHelpNm    ; Put address of help file name in ebx
        call diskhelp         ; If only 1 arg, show help info...
        jmp gohome            ; ...and exit the program

;; Next we check for a numeric command line argument 1:
chkarg2:
        mov ebx,[ebp+12]      ; Put pointer to argument table into ebx
        push LineCount        ; Push address of line count integer for sscanf
        push IntFormat        ; Push address of integer formatting code
        push dword [ebx+4]    ; Push pointer to arg(1)
        call sscanf           ; Call sscanf to convert arg(1) to an integer
        add esp,12            ; Clean up the stack
        cmp eax,1             ; Return value of 1 says we got a number
        je chkdata            ; If we got a number, go on; else abort
        mov eax,Err1          ; Load eax with address of error message #1
        call showerr          ; Show the error message
        jmp gohome            ; Exit the program

;; Here we're looking to see if there are more arguments.  If there
;; are, we concatenate them into a single string no more than BUFSIZE
;; chars in size.  (Yes, I *know* this does what strncat does...)
chkdata:
```

(*continued*)

Listing 12-6: textfile.asm (*continued*)

```
        cmp dword [ebp+8],3   ; Is there a second argument?
        jae getlns            ; If so, we have text to fill a file with
        call randline         ; If not, generate a line of random text
                              ; Note that randline returns ptr to line in esi
        jmp genfile           ; Go on to create the file

;; Here we copy as much command line text as we have, up to BUFSIZE
;; chars, into the line buffer buff. We skip the first two args
;; (which at this point we know exist) but we know we have at least
;; one text arg in arg(2). Going into this section, we know that
;; ebx contains the pointer to the arg table. All other bets are off.
getlns: mov edx,2    ; We know we have at least arg(2), start there
        mov edi,Buff ; Destination pointer is start of char buffer
        xor eax,eax  ; Clear eax to 0 for the character counter
        cld          ; Clear direction flag for up-memory movsb

grab:   mov esi,[ebx+edx*4]  ; Copy pointer to next arg into esi
.copy:  cmp byte [esi],0     ; Have we found the end of the arg?
        je .next             ; If so, bounce to the next arg
        movsb                ; Copy char from [esi] to [edi]; inc edi & esi
        inc eax              ; Increment total character count
        cmp eax,BUFSIZE      ; See if we've filled the buffer to max count
        je addnul            ; If so, go add a null to buff & we're done
        jmp .copy

.next:  mov byte [edi],' '   ; Copy space to buff to separate args
        inc edi              ; Increment destion pointer for space
        inc eax              ; Add one to character count too
        cmp eax,BUFSIZE      ; See if we've now filled buff
        je addnul            ; If so, go down to add a nul and we're done
        inc edx              ; Otherwise, increment the argument count
        cmp edx, dword [ebp+8] ; Compare against argument count
        jae addnul           ; If edx = arg count, we're done
        jmp grab             ; And go back and copy it

addnul: mov byte [edi],0     ; Tack a null on the end of buff
        mov esi,Buff         ; File write code expects ptr to text in esi

;; Now we create a file to fill with the text we have:
genfile:
        push WriteCode       ; Push pointer to file write/create code ('w')
        push NewFilename     ; Push pointer to new file name
        call fopen           ; Create/open file
        add esp,8            ; Clean up the stack
        mov ebx,eax          ; eax contains the file handle; save in ebx

;; File is open. Now let's fill it with text:
        mov edi,[LineCount]  ; The number of lines to be filled is in edi
```

Listing 12-6: textfile.asm (*continued*)

```
        push esi            ; ESI is the pointer to the line of text
        push 1              ; The first line number
        push WriteBase      ; Push address of the base string
        push ebx            ; Push the file handle of the open file

writeline:
        cmp dword edi,0     ; Has the line count gone to 0?
        je donewrite        ; If so, go down & clean up stack
        call fprintf        ; Write the text line to the file
        dec edi             ; Decrement the count of lines to be written
        add dword [esp+8],1 ; Update the line number on the stack
        jmp writeline       ; Loop back and do it again
donewrite:
        add esp,16          ; Clean up stack after call to fprintf

;; We're done writing text; now let's close the file:
closeit:
        push ebx            ; Push the handle of the file to be closed
        call fclose         ; Closes the file whose handle is on the stack
        add esp,4

;;; Everything after this is boilerplate; use it for all ordinary apps!
gohome: pop edi            ; Restore saved registers
        pop esi
        pop ebx
        mov esp,ebp        ; Destroy stack frame before returning
        pop ebp
        ret                ; Return control to to the C shutdown code


;;; SUBROUTINES================================================================


;---------------------------------------------------------------------------


; Disk-based mini-help subroutine  --  Last update 12/5/1999
;
; This routine reads text from a text file, the name of which is passed by
; way of a pointer to the name string in ebx. The routine opens the text file,

; reads the text from it, and displays it to standard output.  If the file
; cannot be opened, a very short memory-based message is displayed instead.
;---------------------------------------------------------------------------


diskhelp:
        push OpenCode   ; Push pointer to open-for-read code "r"
        push ebx        ; Pointer to name of help file is passed in ebx
        call fopen      ; Attempt to open the file for reading
        add esp,8       ; Clean up the stack
```

(continued)

Listing 12-6: textfile.asm (*continued*)

```
            cmp eax,0            ; fopen returns null if attempted open failed
            jne .disk           ; Read help info from disk, else from memory
            call memhelp
            ret
.disk: mov ebx,eax              ; Save handle of opened file in ebx
.rdln: push ebx                 ; Push file handle on the stack
            push dword HELPLEN   ; Limit line length of text read
            push HelpLine        ; Push address of help text line buffer
            call fgets           ; Read a line of text from the file
            add esp,12           ; Clean up the stack
            cmp eax,0            ; A returned null indicates error or EOF
            jle .done            ; If we get 0 in eax, close up & return
            push HelpLine        ; Push address of help line on the stack
            call printf          ; Call printf to display help line
            add esp,4            ; Clean up the stack
            jmp .rdln

.done: push ebx                 ; Push the handle of the file to be closed
            call fclose          ; Closes the file whose handle is on the stack
            add esp,4            ; Clean up the stack
            ret                  ; Go home

memhelp:
            mov eax,1
            call newline
            mov ebx,HelpMsg      ; Load address of help text into eax
.chkln: cmp dword [ebx],0       ; Does help msg pointer point to a null?
            jne .show            ; If not, show the help lines
            mov eax,1            ; Load eax with number of newlines to output
            call newline         ; Output the newlines
            ret                  ; If yes, go home
.show: push ebx                 ; Push address of help line on the stack
            call printf          ; Display the line
            add esp,4            ; Clean up the stack
            add ebx,HELPSIZE     ; Increment address by length of help line
            jmp .chkln           ; Loop back and check to see if we done yet

showerr:
            push eax             ; On entry, eax contains addr of error message
            call printf          ; Show the error message
            add esp,4            ; Clean up the stack
            ret                  ; Go home; no returned values

randline:
            mov ebx,BUFSIZE      ; BUFSIZE tells us how many chars to pull
            mov byte [Buff+BUFSIZE+1],0  ; Put a null at end of buffer first
.loop: dec ebx                  ; BUFSIZE is 1-based, so decrement
            call pull6           ; Go get a random number from 0-63
```

Listing 12-6: textfile.asm (*continued*)

```
        mov cl,[CharTbl+eax]  ; Use random # in eax as offset into table
                             ;   and copy character from table into cl
        mov [Buff+ebx],cl     ; Copy char from cl to character buffer
        cmp ebx,0             ; Are we done having fun yet?
        jne .loop             ; If not, go back and pull another
        mov esi,Buff          ; Copy address of the buffer into esi
        ret                   ;   and go home
```

Conclusion: Not the End, But Only the Beginning

You never really learn assembly language.

You can improve your skills over time, by reading good books on the subject, by reading good code that others have written, and, most of all, by writing lots and lots of code yourself. But at no point will you be able to stand up and say, "I *know* it."

You shouldn't feel bad about this. In fact, I take some encouragement from occasionally hearing that Michael Abrash, author of *Zen of Assembly Language*, *Zen of Code Optimization*, and his giant compendium *Michael Abrash's Graphics Programming Black Book*, has learned something new about assembly language. Michael has been writing high-performance assembly code for almost 30 years, and has become one of the two or three best assembly language programmers in the Western hemisphere.

If Michael is still learning, is there hope for the rest of us?

Wrong question. *Silly* question. If Michael is still learning, it means that *all* of us are students and will always be students. It means that the journey is the goal, and as long as we continue to probe and hack and fiddle and try things that we never tried before, over time we will advance the state of the art and create programs that would have made the pioneers in our field catch their breath in 1977.

The point is not to conquer the subject, but to live with it, and grow with your knowledge of it. Because the journey *is* the goal, with this book I've tried hard to help those people who have been frozen with fear at the thought of starting the journey, staring at the complexity of it all and wondering where the first brick in that Yellow Brick Road might be.

It's *here*, with nothing more than the conviction that you can do it.

You can. The challenge is not limited to assembly language. Consider my own experience: I got out of school in recession year 1974 with a B.A. in English, summa cum laude, with few reliable prospects outside of driving a cab. I finessed my way into a job with Xerox Corporation, repairing copy machines. Books were fun, but paperwork makes money—so I picked up a tool bag and had a fine old time for several years, before maneuvering my way into a computer programming position.

But I'll never forget that first awful moment when I looked over the shoulder of an accomplished technician at a model 660 copier with its panels off, to see what looked like a bottomless pit of little cams and gears and drums and sprocket chains turning and flipping and knocking switch actuators back and forth. Mesmerized by the complexity, I forgot to notice that a sheet of paper had been fed through the machine and turned into a copy of the original document. I was terrified of never learning what all the little cams did and missed the comforting simplicity of the Big Picture—that a copy machine makes copies.

That's square one—discover the Big Picture. Ignore the cams and gears for a bit. You can do it. Find out what's important in holding the Big Picture together (ask someone if it's not obvious) and study that before getting down to the cams and gears. Locate the processes that happen. Divide the Big Picture into subpictures. See how things flow. Only then should you focus on something as small and as lost in the mess as an individual cam or switch.

That's how you conquer complexity, and that's how I've presented assembly language in this book. Some might say I've shorted the instruction set, but covering the instruction set was never the real goal here. The real goal was to conquer your fear of the complexity of the subject, with some metaphors and plenty of pictures and (this really matters!) a light heart.

Did it work? You tell me. I'd really like to know.

Where to Now?

People get annoyed at me sometimes because this book (which has been around in four editions since 1989) does not go more deeply into the subject. I stand firm: This book is about beginnings, and I won't short beginnings in order to add more material at the end. (Books can only be so long!) To go further you will have to set this book aside and continue on your own.

Your general approach should be something like this:

- Study Linux.
- Study assembly language.
- Write code.
- Write more code.

There is no shortage of good books out there on Linux. Here are some that I recommend:

Ubuntu 8.10 Linux Bible by William von Hagen (Wiley, 2009)

If you don't already know Linux well, this is a good book to have on your shelf. It covers almost everything related to *using* Linux, though note that it does not cover programming at all. Even if you're pretty good at Linux, it's always handy to have a well-indexed reference nearby for when you realize that your recall of a particular topic is a little thin.

Beginning Linux Programming, Fourth Edition, by Neil Matthew and Richard Stones (Wrox Press, 2008)

If you've never done any Linux programming of any kind before, this book presents a good overview. It does not address assembly language, but focuses on shell programming, C/C++, and SQL. However, the material related to file programming, terminals, and the Linux environment applies to any sort of programming, and goes much further than I've been able to in this book.

There have never been a lot of books on assembly language, much less good books. Many of the best books on the topic are very old and now mostly obsolete, like Tom Swan's *Mastering Turbo Assembler* (Sams, 1995), which covers mainly DOS, and contains only a little material on Windows.

The Art of Assembly Language by Randall Hyde (No Starch Press, 2003)

In terms of sheer quality, this may be the best book on assembly language ever written. However, it's something of an oddity, in that it describes a "high-level" assembler (HLA), written by Randy himself, that understands a syntax incorporating language elements borrowed from high-level languages like C. I'm of two minds about that. Introducing high-level elements to assembly language can obscure what happens at the very, very bottom of the pond, which is really what you do assembly language for. That said, HLA is what the C language should have been: a low-level language providing access to individual instructions while allowing the sort of high-level data abstraction that makes ambitious programs possible. If you're already an accomplished C programmer, HLA provides a very good path to assembly, but if you're just starting out in assembly, it may be better to write "pure" assembly for awhile until you're sure you understand it all the way down past the last of the turtles.

Professional Assembly Language by Richard Blum (Wrox Press, 2005)

This is a decent intermediate-level book that's a good choice for your "next" text in assembly, and is well worth having for the three chapters on numeric programming alone. (I did not have the space to cover floating-point math at all in this book.) The big downside is that the author mostly uses the gas assembler and the AT&T mnemonics, but as wrongheaded as gas is, you need to understand it and its syntax if you're going to understand much of the literature and Web pages on Linux assembly.

The pickings get pretty slim after that. Other books on assembly exist and I'm sure I've seen most of them, but if I don't mention them here it means I don't recommend them for one reason or another. However, if you spot one that you like and have found it useful, drop me a note and let me know. I pay attention to the field, but I'll be the last person to insist that I never miss anything. Contact me through my assembly language Web page:

```
www.duntemann.com/assembly.htm
```

Stepping off Square One

Okay—with a couple of new books in hand and a good night's sleep behind you, strike out on your own a little. Set yourself a goal, and try to achieve it: something *tough*, such as an assembly language utility that locates all files on a specified directory tree with a given ambiguous filename. That's ambitious for a newcomer and will require some research and study, and (perhaps) a few false starts. But you can do it, and once you do it you'll be a real journeyman assembly language programmer.

Becoming a master takes work, and time. Books can only take you so far. Eventually you will have to be your own teacher and direct your own course of study. These days, mastering assembly means understanding the operating system kernel and its low-level machinery, such as device drivers. You'll need to learn C well to do that, but there's no way around it. More and more, mastering assembly may also involve writing code to run on high-performance graphics coprocessors like those from Nvidia. The gaming industry drives performance computing these days, and although writing high-performance graphics software is a very difficult challenge, the results can be breathtaking.

Whichever route you take, *keep programming*. No matter what sort of code you write, you will learn things while writing it that lead to new challenges. Learning something new always involves the realization that there is a lot more to learn. Study is necessary, but without constant and fairly aggressive practice, study won't help, and static knowledge without reinforcement from real-world experience goes stale in a *big* hurry.

It gets scary at times. The complexity of computing seems to double every couple of years. Still, keep telling yourself: *I can do this*. Believing in the truth of that statement is the essence of stepping away from square one—and the rest of the road, like all roads, is taken one step at a time.

Partial x86 Instruction Set Reference

Instruction	Reference Page	Text Page	CPU
AAA	512	411	
ADC	513	Only in Appendix A	
ADD	515	207	
AND	517	281	
BT	519	306	386+
CALL	521	336, 483	
CLC	523	Only in Appendix A	
CLD	524	411	
CMP	525	411	
DEC	527	215	
DIV	528	411	
INC	529	215	
INT	530	411	

Instruction	Reference Page	Text Page	CPU
IRET	531	260	
J?	532	218, 299, 302	
JCXZ	534	421	
JECXZ	535	Only in Appendix A	386+
JMP	536	298	
LEA	537	315	
LOOP	538	408	
LOOPNZ/LOOPNE	540	422	
LOOPZ/LOOPE	541	Only in Appendix A	
MOV	542	204	
MOVS	544	414	
MOVSX	546	224	386+
MUL	547	225	
NEG	549	223	
NOP	550	Only in Appendix A	
NOT	551	285	
OR	552	283	
POP	554	251	
POPA	555	251, 344	286+
POPAD	555	251, 344	386+
POPF	556	251	
POPFD	557	251	386+
PUSH	558	249	
PUSHA	559	249	286+
PUSHAD	560	249, 344	386+
PUSHF	561	249	
PUSHFD	562	249	386+
RET	563	337	
ROL	564	288	

Instruction	Reference Page	Text Page	CPU
ROR	566	288	
SBB	568	Only in Appendix A	
SHL	570	286	
SHR	572	286	
STC	574	289	
STD	575	405	
STOS	576	402	
SUB	577	302	
XCHG	579	234	
XLAT	580	321	
XOR	581	284	

Notes on the Instruction Set Reference

Instruction Operands

When an instruction takes two operands, the destination operand is the one on the *left*, and the source operand is the one on the *right*. In general, when a result is produced by an instruction, the result replaces the destination operand. For example, in the instruction

```
ADD BX,SI
```

the BX register is added to the SI register, and the sum is then placed in the BX register, overwriting whatever was in BX before the addition.

Flag Results

Each instruction contains a flag summary that looks like the following (the asterisks present will vary from instruction to instruction):

```
O D I T S Z A P C   OF: Overflow flag  TF: Trap flag AF: Aux carry
F F F F F F F F F   DF: Direction flag SF: Sign flag PF: Parity flag
*   ? ? * * * * *   IF: Interrupt flag ZF: Zero flag CF: Carry flag
```

The nine most important flags are all represented here. An asterisk indicates that the instruction on that page affects that flag. A blank space under the flag header means that the instruction does not affect that flag in any way. If a flag is affected in a defined way, it will be affected according to these rules:

OF Set if the result is too large to fit in the destination operand.

IF Set by the STI instruction; cleared by CLI.

TF For debuggers; not used in normal programming and may be ignored.

SF Set when the sign of the result forces the destination operand to become negative.

ZF Set if the result of an operation is zero. If the result is nonzero, then ZF is cleared.

AF Auxiliary carry used for 4-bit BCD math. Set when an operation causes a carry out of a 4-bit BCD quantity.

PF Set if the number of 1-bits in the low byte of the result is even; cleared if the number of 1 bits in the low byte of the result is odd. Used in data communications applications but little else.

CF Set if the result of an add or shift operation carries out a bit beyond the destination operand; otherwise cleared. May be manually set by STC and manually cleared by CLC when CF must be in a known state before an operation begins.

Some instructions force certain flags to become undefined. These are indicated by a question mark under the flag header. "Undefined" means *don't count on it being in any particular state*. Until you know that a flag in a previously undefined state has gone into a defined state by the action of another instruction, do not test or in any other way use the state of the flag.

AAA: Adjust AL after BCD Addition

Flags Affected

```
O D I T S Z A P C   OF: Overflow flag  TF: Trap flag AF: Aux carry
F F F F F F F F F   DF: Direction flag SF: Sign flag PF: Parity flag
?         ? ? * ? * IF: Interrupt flag ZF: Zero flag CF: Carry flag
```

Legal Forms

```
AAA
```

Examples

```
AAA
```

Notes

AAA makes an addition come out right in AL when what you're adding are BCD values rather than ordinary binary values. Note well that AAA does *not* perform the arithmetic itself, but is a postprocessor after ADD or ADC. The AL register is an *implied* operand and may not be explicitly stated—so make sure that the preceding ADD or ADC instruction leaves its results in AL!

A BCD digit is a byte with the high 4 bits set to 0, and the low 4 bits containing a digit from 0 to 9. AAA will yield garbage results if the preceding ADD or ADC acted upon one or both operands with values greater than 09.

After the addition of two legal BCD values, AAA will adjust a non-BCD result (that is, a result greater than 09 in AL) to a value between 0 and 9. This is called a *decimal carry*, as it is the carry of a BCD digit and not simply the carry of a binary bit.

For example, if ADD added 08 and 04 (both legal BCD values) to produce 0C in AL, AAA will take the 0C and adjust it to 02. The decimal carry goes to AH, *not* to the upper 4 bits of AL, which are *always* cleared to 0 by AAA.

If the preceding ADD or ADC resulted in a decimal carry (as in the preceding example), *both* CF and AF are set to 1 and AH is incremented by 1. Otherwise, AH is not incremented and CF and AF are cleared to 0.

This instruction is subtle. See the detailed discussion in the text.

```
r8 = AL AH BL BH CL CH DL DH      r16 = AX BX CX DX BP SP SI DI
sr = CS DS SS ES FS GS            r32 = EAX EBX ECX EDX EBP ESP ESI EDI
m8 = 8-bit memory data            m16 = 16-bit memory data
m32 = 32-bit memory data          i8 = 8-bit immediate data
i16 = 16-bit immediate data       i32 = 32-bit immediate data
d8 = 8-bit signed displacement    d16 = 16-bit signed displacement
d32 = 32-bit unsigned displacement
```

ADC: Arithmetic Addition with Carry

Flags Affected

```
O D I T S Z A P C   OF: Overflow flag   TF: Trap flag AF: Aux carry
F F F F F F F F F   DF: Direction flag  SF: Sign flag PF: Parity flag
*       * * * *     IF: Interrupt flag  ZF: Zero flag CF: Carry flag
```

Legal Forms

```
ADC r8,r8
ADC m8,r8
ADC r8,m8
ADC r16,r16
ADC m16,r16
ADC r16,m16
ADC r32,r32     386+
ADC m32,r32     386+
ADC r32,m32     386+
ADC r8,i8
ADC m8,i8
ADC r16,i16
ADC m16,i16
ADC r32,i32     386+
ADC m32,i32     386+
ADC r16,i8
ADC m16,i8
ADC r32,i8      386+
ADC m32,i8      386+
ADC AL,i8
ADC AX,i16
ADC EAX,i32     386+
```

Examples

```
ADC BX,DI
ADC EAX,5
ADC AX,0FFFFH           ;Uses single-byte opcode
ADC AL,42H              ;Uses single-byte opcode
ADC BP,17H
ADC WORD [BX+SI+Inset],5
ADC WORD ES:[BX],0B800H
```

Notes

ADC adds the source operand and the Carry flag to the destination operand, and after the operation, the result replaces the destination operand. The add operation is an arithmetic add, and the carry allows multiple-precision additions across several registers or memory locations. (To add without taking the Carry flag into account, use the ADD instruction.) All affected flags are set according to the operation. Most important, if the result does not fit into the destination operand, the Carry flag is set to 1.

```
r8 = AL AH BL BH CL CH DL DH      r16 = AX BX CX DX BP SP SI DI
sr = CS DS SS ES FS GS             r32 = EAX EBX ECX EDX EBP ESP ESI EDI
m8 = 8-bit memory data            m16 = 16-bit memory data
m32 = 32-bit memory data          i8 = 8-bit immediate data
i16 = 16-bit immediate data       i32 = 32-bit immediate data
d8 = 8-bit signed displacement    d16 = 16-bit signed displacement
d32 = 32-bit unsigned displacement
```

ADD: Arithmetic Addition

Flags Affected

```
O D I T S Z A P C   OF: Overflow flag  TF: Trap flag AF: Aux carry
F F F F F F F F F   DF: Direction flag SF: Sign flag PF: Parity flag
*       * * * *     IF: Interrupt flag ZF: Zero flag CF: Carry flag
```

Legal Forms

```
ADD r8,r8
ADD m8,r8
ADD r8,m8
ADD r16,r16
ADD m16,r16
ADD r16,m16
ADD r32,r32      386+
ADD m32,r32      386+
ADD r32,m32      386+
ADD r8,i8
ADD m8,i8
ADD r16,i16
ADD m16,i16
ADD r32,i32      386+
ADD m32,i32      386+
ADD r16,i8
ADD m16,i8
ADD r32,i8       386+
ADD m32,i8       386+
ADD AL,i8
ADD AX,i16
ADD EAX,i32      386+
```

Examples

```
ADD BX,DI
ADD AX,0FFFFH    ;Uses single-byte opcode
ADD AL,42H       ;Uses single-byte opcode
ADD EAX,5
ADD BP,17H
AND DWORD [EDI],EAX
ADD WORD [BX+SI+Inset],5
ADD WORD ES:[BX],0B800H
```

Notes

ADD adds the source operand to the destination operand, and after the operation, the result replaces the destination operand. The add operation is an arithmetic add, and does *not* take the Carry flag into account. (To add using the Carry flag, use the ADC Add with Carry instruction.) All affected flags are set according to the operation. Most important, if the result does not fit into the destination operand, the Carry flag is set to 1.

```
r8  = AL AH BL BH CL CH DL DH      r16 = AX BX CX DX BP SP SI DI
sr  = CS DS SS ES FS GS            r32 = EAX EBX ECX EDX EBP ESP ESI EDI
m8  = 8-bit memory data            m16 = 16-bit memory data
m32 = 32-bit memory data           i8  = 8-bit immediate data
i16 = 16-bit immediate data        i32 = 32-bit immediate data
d8  = 8-bit signed displacement    d16 = 16-bit signed displacement
d32 = 32-bit unsigned displacement
```

AND: Logical AND

Flags Affected

```
O D I T S Z A P C   OF: Overflow flag  TF: Trap flag AF: Aux carry
F F F F F F F F F   DF: Direction flag SF: Sign flag PF: Parity flag
*       * * ? * *   IF: Interrupt flag ZF: Zero flag CF: Carry flag
```

Legal Forms

```
AND r8,r8
AND m8,r8
AND r8,m8
AND r16,r16
AND m16,r16
AND r16,m16
AND r32,r32     386+
AND m32,r32     386+
AND r32,m32     386+
AND r8,i8
AND m8,i8
AND r16,i16
AND m16,i16
AND r32,i32     386+
AND m32,i32     386+
AND AL,i8
AND AX,i16
AND EAX,i32     386+
```

Examples

```
AND BX,DI
AND EAX,5
AND AX,0FFFFH         ;Uses single-byte opcode
AND AL,42H            ;Uses single-byte opcode
AND DWORD [EDI],EAX
AND WORD ES:[BX],0B800H
AND WORD [BP+SI],DX
```

Notes

AND performs the AND logical operation on its two operands. Once the operation is complete, the result replaces the destination operand. AND is performed on a bit-by-bit basis, such that bit 0 of the source is ANDed with bit 0 of the destination, bit 1 of the source is ANDed with bit 1 of the destination, and so on. The AND operation yields a 1 if *both* of the operands are 1; and a 0 only if *either* operand is 0. Note that the operation makes the Auxiliary carry flag undefined. CF and OF are cleared to 0, and the other affected flags are set according to the operation's results.

```
r8  = AL AH BL BH CL CH DL DH      r16 = AX BX CX DX BP SP SI DI
sr  = CS DS SS ES FS GS            r32 = EAX EBX ECX EDX EBP ESP ESI EDI
m8  = 8-bit memory data            m16 = 16-bit memory data
m32 = 32-bit memory data           i8  = 8-bit immediate data
i16 = 16-bit immediate data        i32 = 32-bit immediate data
d8  = 8-bit signed displacement    d16 = 16-bit signed displacement
d32 = 32-bit unsigned displacement
```

BT: Bit Test

Flags Affected

```
O D I T S Z A P C   OF: Overflow flag  TF: Trap flag AF: Aux carry
F F F F F F F F F   DF: Direction flag SF: Sign flag PF: Parity flag
              *     IF: Interrupt flag ZF: Zero flag CF: Carry flag
```

Legal Forms

```
BT r16,r16      386+
BT m16,r16      386+
BT r32,r32      386+
BT m32,r32      386+
BT r16,i8       386+
BT m16,i8       386+
BT r32,i8       386+
BT m32,i8       386+
```

Examples

```
BT AX,CX
BT [BX+DI],DX
BT AX,64
BT EAX,EDX
BT ECX,17
```

Notes

BT copies a single specified bit from the left operand to the Carry flag, where it can be tested or fed back into a quantity using one of the shift/rotate instructions. Which bit is copied is specified by the right operand. Neither operand is altered by BT.

When the right operand is an 8-bit immediate value, the value specifies the number of the bit to be copied. In BT AX,5, bit 5 of AX is copied into CF. When the immediate value exceeds the size of the left operand, the value is expressed modulo the size of the left operand. That is, because there are not 66 bits in EAX, BT EAX,66 pulls out as many 32s from the immediate value as can be taken, and what remains is the bit number. (Here, 2.) When the right operand is *not* an immediate value, the right operand not only specifies the bit to be tested but also an offset from the memory reference in the left operand. This is complicated and not covered completely in this book. See a detailed discussion in a full assembly language reference.

```
r8  = AL AH BL BH CL CH DL DH        r16 = AX BX CX DX BP SP SI DI
sr  = CS DS SS ES FS GS              r32 = EAX EBX ECX EDX EBP ESP ESI EDI
m8  = 8-bit memory data              m16 = 16-bit memory data
m32 = 32-bit memory data            i8  = 8-bit immediate data
i16 = 16-bit immediate data          i32 = 32-bit immediate data
d8  = 8-bit signed displacement      d16 = 16-bit signed displacement
d32 = 32-bit unsigned displacement
```

CALL: Call Procedure

Flags Affected

```
O D I T S Z A P C    OF: Overflow flag  TF: Trap flag AF: Aux carry
F F F F F F F F F    DF: Direction flag SF: Sign flag PF: Parity flag
      <none>         IF: Interrupt flag ZF: Zero flag CF: Carry flag
```

Legal Forms

```
CALL <near label>
CALL <far label>
CALL r16
CALL m16
CALL r32        386+
CALL m32        386+
```

Examples

```
CALL InsideMySegment      ;InsideMySegment is a Near label
CALL OutsideMySegment     ;OutsideMySegment is a Far label
CALL BX
CALL EDX
CALL WORD [BX+DI+17]      ;Calls Near address at [BX+DI+17]
CALL DWORD [BX+DI+17]     ;Calls full 32-bit address at [BX+DI+17]
```

Notes

CALL transfers control to a procedure address. Before transferring control, CALL pushes the address of the instruction immediately after itself onto the stack. This allows a RET instruction (see also) to pop the return address into either CS:IP or IP only (depending on whether it is a Near or Far call) and thus return control to the instruction immediately after the CALL instruction.

In addition to the obvious CALL to a defined label, CALL can transfer control to a Near address within a 16-bit general-purpose register, and also to an address located in memory. These are shown in the Legal Forms column as m16 and m32. m32 is simply a full 32-bit address stored at a location in memory that may be addressed through any legal x86 memory-addressing mode. CALL m16 and CALL m32 are useful for creating jump tables of procedure addresses.

There are many more variants of the CALL instruction with provisions for working with the protection mechanisms of operating systems. These are not covered here; for more information you should see an advanced text or a full assembly language reference.

```
r8  = AL AH BL BH CL CH DL DH     r16 = AX BX CX DX BP SP SI DI
sr  = CS DS SS ES FS GS           r32 = EAX EBX ECX EDX EBP ESP ESI EDI
m8  = 8-bit memory data           m16 = 16-bit memory data
m32 = 32-bit memory data          i8  = 8-bit immediate data
i16 = 16-bit immediate data       i32 = 32-bit immediate data
d8  = 8-bit signed displacement   d16 = 16-bit signed displacement
d32 = 32-bit unsigned displacement
```

CLC: Clear Carry Flag (CF)

Flags Affected

```
O D I T S Z A P C   OF: Overflow flag   TF: Trap flag AF: Aux carry
F F F F F F F F F    DF: Direction flag  SF: Sign flag PF: Parity flag
              *      IF: Interrupt flag  ZF: Zero flag CF: Carry flag
```

Legal Forms

```
CLC
```

Examples

```
CLC
```

Notes

CLC simply sets the Carry flag (CF) to the cleared (0) state. Use CLC in situations where the Carry flag *must* be in a known cleared state before work begins, as when you are rotating a series of words or bytes using the rotate instructions RCL and RCR. It can also be used to put CF into a known state before returning from a procedure, to indicate that the procedure had succeeded or failed, as desired.

```
r8 = AL AH BL BH CL CH DL DH        r16 = AX BX CX DX BP SP SI DI
sr = CS DS SS ES FS GS              r32 = EAX EBX ECX EDX EBP ESP ESI EDI
m8 = 8-bit memory data              m16 = 16-bit memory data
m32 = 32-bit memory data            i8 = 8-bit immediate data
i16 = 16-bit immediate data         i32 = 32-bit immediate data
d8 = 8-bit signed displacement      d16 = 16-bit signed displacement
d32 = 32-bit unsigned displacement
```

CLD: Clear Direction Flag (DF)

Flags Affected

```
O D I T S Z A P C   OF: Overflow flag  TF: Trap flag AF: Aux carry
F F F F F F F F F   DF: Direction flag SF: Sign flag PF: Parity flag
    *               IF: Interrupt flag ZF: Zero flag CF: Carry flag
```

Legal Forms

```
CLD
```

Examples

```
CLD
```

Notes

CLD simply sets the Direction flag (DF) to the cleared (0) state. This affects the adjustment performed by repeated string instructions such as STOS, SCAS, and MOVS. Typically, when DF = 0, the destination pointer is increased, and decreased when DF = 1. DF is set to 1 with the STD instruction.

```
r8  = AL AH BL BH CL CH DL DH      r16 = AX BX CX DX BP SP SI DI
sr  = CS DS SS ES FS GS            r32 = EAX EBX ECX EDX EBP ESP ESI EDI
m8  = 8-bit memory data            m16 = 16-bit memory data
m32 = 32-bit memory data           i8  = 8-bit immediate data
i16 = 16-bit immediate data        i32 = 32-bit immediate data
d8  = 8-bit signed displacement    d16 = 16-bit signed displacement
d32 = 32-bit unsigned displacement
```

CMP: Arithmetic Comparison

Flags Affected

```
O D I T S Z A P C   OF: Overflow flag  TF: Trap flag AF: Aux carry
F F F F F F F F F   DF: Direction flag SF: Sign flag PF: Parity flag
*       * * * *     IF: Interrupt flag ZF: Zero flag CF: Carry flag
```

Legal Forms

```
CMP r8,r8
CMP m8,r8
CMP r8,m8
CMP r16,r16
CMP m16,r16
CMP r16,m16
CMP r32,r32     386+
CMP m32,r32     386+
CMP r32,m32     386+
CMP r8,i8
CMP m8,i8
CMP r16,i16
CMP m16,i16
CMP r32,i32     386+
CMP m32,i32     386+
CMP r16,i8
CMP m16,i8
CMP r32,i8      386+
CMP m32,i8      386+
CMP AL,i8
CMP AX,i16
CMP EAX,i32     386+
```

Examples

```
CMP BX,DI
CMP EAX,5
CMP AX,0FFFFH          ;Uses single-byte opcode
CMP AL,42H             ;Uses single-byte opcode
CMP BP,17H
CMP WORD [BX+SI+Inset],5
CMP WORD ES:[BX],0B800H
```

Notes

CMP compares its two operations, and sets the flags to indicate the results of the comparison. *The destination operand is not affected.* The operation itself is identical to subtraction of the source from the destination without borrow (SUB), save that the result does not replace the destination. Typically, CMP is followed by one of the conditional jump instructions—that is, JE to jump if the operands were equal; JNE if they were unequal; and so forth.

```
r8  = AL AH BL BH CL CH DL DH          r16 = AX BX CX DX BP SP SI DI
sr  = CS DS SS ES FS GS                r32 = EAX EBX ECX EDX EBP ESP ESI EDI
m8  = 8-bit memory data                m16 = 16-bit memory data
m32 = 32-bit memory data               i8  = 8-bit immediate data
i16 = 16-bit immediate data            i32 = 32-bit immediate data
d8  = 8-bit signed displacement        d16 = 16-bit signed displacement
d32 = 32-bit unsigned displacement
```

DEC: Decrement Operand

Flags Affected

```
O D I T S Z A P C   OF: Overflow flag  TF: Trap flag AF: Aux carry
F F F F F F F F F   DF: Direction flag SF: Sign flag PF: Parity flag
*       * * * *     IF: Interrupt flag ZF: Zero flag CF: Carry flag
```

Legal Forms

```
DEC m8
DEC m16
DEC m32
DEC r8
DEC r16
DEC r32
```

Examples

```
DEC AL
DEC CX
DEC EBX
DEC BYTE [BP]        ; Decrements the BYTE at [BP]
DEC WORD [BX]        ; Decrements the WORD at [BX]
DEC DWORD [EDX]      ; Decrements the DWORD at [EDX]
```

Notes

Remember that segment registers *cannot* be decremented with DEC. All register-half opcodes are 2 bytes in length, but all 16-bit register opcodes are 1 byte in length. If you can decrement an entire 16-bit register of which only the lower half contains data, use the 16-bit opcode and save a byte.

DEC does *not* affect the Carry flag. (This is a common error.)

As with all instructions that act on memory, memory data forms *must* be used with a data size specifier such as BYTE, WORD, and DWORD. NASM doesn't assume anything!

```
r8 = AL AH BL BH CL CH DL DH      r16 = AX BX CX DX BP SP SI DI
sr = CS DS SS ES FS GS            r32 = EAX EBX ECX EDX EBP ESP ESI EDI
m8 = 8-bit memory data            m16 = 16-bit memory data
m32 = 32-bit memory data          i8 = 8-bit immediate data
i16 = 16-bit immediate data       i32 = 32-bit immediate data
d8 = 8-bit signed displacement    d16 = 16-bit signed displacement
d32 = 32-bit unsigned displacement
```

DIV: Unsigned Integer Division

Flags Affected

```
O D I T S Z A P C    OF: Overflow flag  TF: Trap flag AF: Aux carry
F F F F F F F F F    DF: Direction flag SF: Sign flag PF: Parity flag
?       ? ? ? ?      IF: Interrupt flag ZF: Zero flag CF: Carry flag
```

Legal Forms

```
DIV r8
DIV m8
DIV r16
DIV m16
DIV r32              386+
DIV m32              386+
```

Examples

```
DIV CH               ; AX / CH --> Quotient in AL; remainder in AH
DIV BX               ; DX:AX / BX --> Quotient in AX; remainder in DX
DIV ECX              ; EDX:EAX / ECX --> Quotient in EAX; remainder in EDX
DIV WORD [BX+DI]     ; DX:AX / [BX+DI] --> Quotient in AX; remainder in DX
```

Notes

DIV divides the implicit dividend by the explicit divisor specified in its operand. For dividing by 8-bit quantities, the dividend is assumed to be in AX. For dividing by 16-bit and 32-bit quantities, the dividend is assumed to be in two registers, allowing a much greater range of calculation. The least significant portion of the dividend is placed in the "A" register (AX or EAX) and the most significant portion of the dividend is placed in the "D" register (DX or EDX). Note that even when there is no "high" portion of the dividend, the "D" register is cleared to 0 and cannot be used to hold independent values while a DIV instruction is executed.

Remember that when the operand is a memory value, you *must* place one of the type specifiers BYTE, WORD, or DWORD before the operand.

DIV leaves no information in the flags. Note, however, that OF, SF, ZF, AF, PF, and CF are undefined after DIV.

```
r8 = AL AH BL BH CL CH DL DH      r16 = AX BX CX DX BP SP SI DI
sr = CS DS SS ES FS GS            r32 = EAX EBX ECX EDX EBP ESP ESI EDI
m8 = 8-bit memory data            m16 = 16-bit memory data
m32 = 32-bit memory data          i8 = 8-bit immediate data
i16 = 16-bit immediate data       i32 = 32-bit immediate data
d8 = 8-bit signed displacement    d16 = 16-bit signed displacement
d32 = 32-bit unsigned displacement
```

INC: Increment Operand

Flags Affected

```
O D I T S Z A P C   OF: Overflow flag  TF: Trap flag AF: Aux carry
F F F F F F F F F   DF: Direction flag SF: Sign flag PF: Parity flag
*       * * * *     IF: Interrupt flag ZF: Zero flag CF: Carry flag
```

Legal Forms

```
INC r8
INC m8
INC r16
INC m16
INC r32        386+
INC m32        386+
```

Examples

```
INC AL
INC BX
INC EDX
INC BYTE [BP]   ; Increments the BYTE at [BP]
INC WORD [BX]   ; Increments the WORD at [BX]
INC DWORD [ESI] ; Increments the DWORD at [ESI]
```

Notes

Remember that segment registers *cannot* be incremented with INC. All register-half (r8) opcodes are 2 bytes in length, but all 16-bit register (r16) opcodes are 1 byte in length. If you can increment an entire register of which only the lower half contains data, use the 16-bit opcode and save a byte.

INC does *not* affect the Carry flag. (This is a common error.)

As with all instructions that act on memory, memory data forms *must* be used with a data size specifier such as BYTE, WORD, and DWORD. NASM doesn't assume anything!

```
r8 = AL AH BL BH CL CH DL DH     r16 = AX BX CX DX BP SP SI DI
sr = CS DS SS ES FS GS           r32 = EAX EBX ECX EDX EBP ESP ESI EDI
m8 = 8-bit memory data           m16 = 16-bit memory data
m32 = 32-bit memory data         i8 = 8-bit immediate data
i16 = 16-bit immediate data      i32 = 32-bit immediate data
d8 = 8-bit signed displacement   d16 = 16-bit signed displacement
d32 = 32-bit unsigned displacement
```

INT: Software Interrupt

Flags Affected

```
O D I T S Z A P C    OF: Overflow flag  TF: Trap flag AF: Aux carry
F F F F F F F F F    DF: Direction flag SF: Sign flag PF: Parity flag
      * *            IF: Interrupt flag ZF: Zero flag CF: Carry flag
```

Legal Forms

```
INT3            NASM-specific shorthand for INT 3
INT i8
```

Examples

```
INT3     ; NASM requires this to generate an INT 3 instruction
INT 10H
```

Notes

INT triggers a software interrupt to one of 256 vectors in the first 1,024 bytes of memory. The operand specifies which vector, from 0 to 255. When an interrupt is called, the Flags register is pushed on the stack along with the return address. The IF flag is cleared, which prevents further interrupts (either hardware or software) from being recognized until IF is set again. TF is also cleared.

A special form of the instruction allows calling Interrupt 3 with a single-byte instruction. Debuggers use Interrupt 3 to set breakpoints in code by replacing an instruction with the single-byte opcode for calling Interrupt 3. NASM does not recognize this, and if you want to use INT 3 for some reason (and that instruction form isn't of much use unless you're writing a debugger), you must use a special mnemonic form, INT3, rather than INT 3. This is advanced stuff; be careful.

Virtually all your applications of INT will use the other form, which takes an 8-bit immediate numeric value.

Always return from a software interrupt service routine with the IRET instruction. IRET restores the flags that were pushed onto the stack by INT, and in doing so clears IF, allowing further interrupts.

```
r8 = AL AH BL BH CL CH DL DH       r16 = AX BX CX DX BP SP SI DI
sr = CS DS SS ES FS GS             r32 = EAX EBX ECX EDX EBP ESP ESI EDI
m8 = 8-bit memory data             m16 = 16-bit memory data
m32 = 32-bit memory data           i8 = 8-bit immediate data
i16 = 16-bit immediate data        i32 = 32-bit immediate data
d8 = 8-bit signed displacement     d16 = 16-bit signed displacement
d32 = 32-bit unsigned displacement
```

IRET: Return from Interrupt

Flags Affected

```
O D I T S Z A P C    OF: Overflow flag  TF: Trap flag AF: Aux carry
F F F F F F F F F    DF: Direction flag SF: Sign flag PF: Parity flag
* * * * * * * * *    IF: Interrupt flag ZF: Zero flag CF: Carry flag
```

Legal Forms

```
IRET
```

Examples

```
IRET
```

Notes

IRET *must* be used to exit from interrupt service routines called through INT or through interrupt hardware such as serial ports and the like. IRET pops the return address from the top of the stack into CS and IP, and then pops the next word from the stack into the Flags register. *All flags are affected.*

If the interrupt was triggered by hardware, additional steps may be necessary to prepare the hardware for another interrupt before IRET is executed. Consult your hardware documentation.

When using NASM, the actual opcode generated for IRET depends on the BITS setting, and governs whether a 16-bit return or 32-bit return is generated.

In protected mode, user-space applications cannot contain interrupt service routines and thus cannot use IRET.

```
r8 = AL AH BL BH CL CH DL DH     r16 = AX BX CX DX BP SP SI DI
sr = CS DS SS ES FS GS           r32 = EAX EBX ECX EDX EBP ESP ESI EDI
m8 = 8-bit memory data           m16 = 16-bit memory data
m32 = 32-bit memory data         i8 = 8-bit immediate data
i16 = 16-bit immediate data      i32 = 32-bit immediate data
d8 = 8-bit signed displacement   d16 = 16-bit signed displacement
d32 = 32-bit unsigned displacement
```

J?: Jump on Condition

Flags Affected

```
O D I T S Z A P C   OF: Overflow flag  TF: Trap flag AF: Aux carry
F F F F F F F F F    DF: Direction flag SF: Sign flag PF: Parity flag
    <none>           IF: Interrupt flag ZF: Zero flag CF: Carry flag
```

Legal Forms	Descriptions	Jump If Flags Are
JA/JNBE d	(Jump If Above/Jump If Not Below or Equal)	CF=0 AND ZF=0
JAE/JNB d	(Jump If Above or Equal/Jump If Not Below)	CF=0
JB/JNAE d	(Jump If Below/Jump If Not Above or Equal)	CF=1
JBE/JNA d	(Jump If Below or Equal/Jump If Not Above)	CF=1 OR ZF=1
JE/JZ d	(Jump If Equal/Jump If Zero)	ZF=1
JNE/JNZ d	(Jump If Not Equal/Jump If Not Zero)	ZF=0
JG/JNLE d	(Jump If Greater/Jump If Not Less or Equal)	ZF=0 OR SF=OF
JGE/JNL d	(Jump If Greater or Equal/Jump If Not Less)	SF=OF
JL/JNGE d	(Jump If Less/Jump If Not Greater or Equal)	SFOF
JLE/JNG d	(Jump If Less or Equal/Jump If Not Greater)	ZF=1 OR SFOF
JC d	(Jump If Carry flag set)	CF=1
JNC d	(Jump If Carry flag Not set)	CF=0
JO d	(Jump If Overflow flag set)	OF=1
JNO d	(Jump If Overflow flag Not set)	OF=0
JP/JPE d	(Jump If PF set/Jump if Parity Even)	PF=1
JNP/JPO d	(Jump If PF Not set/Jump if Parity Odd)	PF=0
JS d	(Jump If Sign flag set)	SF=1
JNS d	(Jump If Sign flag Not set)	SF=0

d without NEAR = 8-bit signed displacement; use NEAR before d to specify segment-wide displacement.

Examples

```
JB HalfSplit      ;Jumps if CF=1
JLE TooLow        ;Jumps if either ZF=1 or SFOF
JG NEAR WayOut    ;Jumps if greater to 16-bit displacement
                  ; in real mode or 32-bit displacement in
                  ; 32-bit protected mode.
```

Notes

By default all these instructions make a short jump (127 bytes forward or 128 bytes back) if some condition is true, or fall through if the condition is not true. The conditions all involve flags, and the flag conditions in question are given to the right of the mnemonic and its description, under "Legal Forms."

The mnemonics incorporating "above" or "below" are for use after unsigned comparisons, whereas the mnemonics incorporating "less" or "greater" are for use after signed comparisons. "Equal" and "Zero" may be used after either unsigned or signed comparisons.

NASM allows use of the segment-wide form by inserting the NEAR keyword after the instruction mnemonic. In real mode this allows the use of a 16-bit signed displacement, and in 32-bit protected mode this allows the use of a 32-bit signed displacement. Use of NEAR is supported only with 386 and later CPUs.

```
r8  = AL AH BL BH CL CH DL DH        r16 = AX BX CX DX BP SP SI DI
sr  = CS DS SS ES FS GS              r32 = EAX EBX ECX EDX EBP ESP ESI EDI
m8  = 8-bit memory data              m16 = 16-bit memory data
m32 = 32-bit memory data             i8  = 8-bit immediate data
i16 = 16-bit immediate data          i32 = 32-bit immediate data
d8  = 8-bit signed displacement      d16 = 16-bit signed displacement
d32 = 32-bit unsigned displacement
```

JCXZ: Jump If CX = 0

Flags Affected

```
O D I T S Z A P C   OF: Overflow flag  TF: Trap flag AF: Aux carry
F F F F F F F F F   DF: Direction flag SF: Sign flag PF: Parity flag
       <none>       IF: Interrupt flag ZF: Zero flag CF: Carry flag
```

Legal Forms

```
JCXZ <short displacement>
```

Examples

```
JCXZ AllDone  ;Label AllDone must be within 127 bytes!
```

Notes

Many instructions use CX as a count register, and JCXZ allows you to test and jump to see if CX has become 0. The jump may only be a short jump (that is, no more than 127 bytes forward or 128 bytes back) and will be taken if CX = 0 at the time the instruction is executed. If CX is any value other than 0, execution falls through to the next instruction. *See also* the *Jump on Condition* instructions.

JCXZ is most often used to bypass the CX = 0 condition when using the LOOP instruction. Because LOOP decrements CX before testing for CX = 0, if you enter a loop governed by LOOP with CX = 0, you will end up iterating the loop 65,536 times, hence JCXZ.

```
r8 = AL AH BL BH CL CH DL DH      r16 = AX BX CX DX BP SP SI DI
sr = CS DS SS ES FS GS            r32 = EAX EBX ECX EDX EBP ESP ESI EDI
m8 = 8-bit memory data            m16 = 16-bit memory data
m32 = 32-bit memory data          i8 = 8-bit immediate data
i16 = 16-bit immediate data       i32 = 32-bit immediate data
d8 = 8-bit signed displacement    d16 = 16-bit signed displacement
d32 = 32-bit unsigned displacement
```

JECXZ: Jump If ECX = 0

Flags Affected

```
O D I T S Z A P C   OF: Overflow flag  TF: Trap flag AF: Aux carry
F F F F F F F F F   DF: Direction flag SF: Sign flag PF: Parity flag
    <none>          IF: Interrupt flag ZF: Zero flag CF: Carry flag
```

Legal Forms

```
JECXZ <short displacement>    386+
```

Examples

```
JECXZ AllDone       ;Label AllDone must be within 127 bytes!
```

Notes

This instruction operates identically to JCXZ except that the register tested is ECX, and not CX.

JECXZ is most often used to bypass the ECX = 0 condition when using the LOOP instruction. Because LOOP decrements ECX before testing for ECX = 0, if you enter a loop governed by LOOP with ECX = 0, you will end up iterating the loop 2,147,483,648 times, hence JECXZ.

```
r8 = AL AH BL BH CL CH DL DH      r16 = AX BX CX DX BP SP SI DI
sr = CS DS SS ES FS GS            r32 = EAX EBX ECX EDX EBP ESP ESI EDI
m8 = 8-bit memory data            m16 = 16-bit memory data
m32 = 32-bit memory data          i8 = 8-bit immediate data
i16 = 16-bit immediate data       i32 = 32-bit immediate data
d8 = 8-bit signed displacement    d16 = 16-bit signed displacement
d32 = 32-bit unsigned displacement
```

JMP: Unconditional Jump

Flags Affected

```
O D I T S Z A P C   OF: Overflow flag  TF: Trap flag AF: Aux carry
F F F F F F F F F   DF: Direction flag SF: Sign flag PF: Parity flag
    <none>          IF: Interrupt flag ZF: Zero flag CF: Carry flag
```

Legal Forms

```
JMP <short displacement>
JMP <near label>
JMP <far label>
JMP r16
JMP r32                386+
JMP m16
JMP m32
```

Examples

```
JMP RightCloseBy        ;Plus or minus 128 bytes
JMP InsideMySegment     ;To 16-bit offset from CS
JMP OutsideMySegment    ;To immediate 32-bit address
JMP DX                  ;To 16-bit offset stored in DX register
JMP EAX                 ;To 32-bit offset stored in EAX register
JMP WORD [BX+DI+17]     ;To Near address stored at [BX+DI+17]
JMP DWORD [EBX+EDI+17]  ;To full 32-bit address stored at [EBX+EDI+17]
```

Notes

JMP transfers control unconditionally to the destination given as the single operand. In addition to defined labels, JMP can transfer control to a 16-bit signed offset from IP (or 32-bit signed offset from EIP) stored in a general-purpose register, or to an address (either Near or Far) stored in memory and accessed through any legal addressing mode. These m16 and m32 forms are useful for creating jump tables in memory, where a jump table is an array of addresses. For example, JMP [BX+DI+17] would transfer control to the 16-bit offset into the code segment found at the based-indexed-displacement address [BX+DI+17].

No flags are affected, and, unlike CALL, no return address is pushed onto the stack.

```
r8 = AL AH BL BH CL CH DL DH      r16 = AX BX CX DX BP SP SI DI
sr = CS DS SS ES FS GS            r32 = EAX EBX ECX EDX EBP ESP ESI EDI
m8 = 8-bit memory data            m16 = 16-bit memory data
m32 = 32-bit memory data          i8 = 8-bit immediate data
i16 = 16-bit immediate data       i32 = 32-bit immediate data
d8 = 8-bit signed displacement        16 = 16-bit signed displacement
d32 = 32-bit unsigned displacement
```

LEA: Load Effective Address

Flags Affected

```
O D I T S Z A P C    OF: Overflow flag   TF: Trap flag AF: Aux carry
F F F F F F F F F    DF: Direction flag SF: Sign flag PF: Parity flag
    <none>           IF: Interrupt flag ZF: Zero flag CF: Carry flag
```

Legal Forms

```
LEA r16,m<any size>
LEA r32,m<any size>
```

Examples

```
LEA EBX,[EAX+EDX*4+128]    ;Loads calculated address into EBX
LEA BP,MyWordVar           ;Loads offset of MyWordVar to BP
```

Notes

LEA derives the offset of the source operand from the start of its segment and loads that offset into the destination operand. The destination operand must be a register and *cannot* be memory. The source operand must be a memory operand, but it can be any size. The address stored in the destination operand is the address of the first byte of the source in memory, and the size of the source in memory is unimportant.

This is a good, clean way to place the address of a variable into a register prior to a procedure or interrupt call.

LEA can also be used to perform register math, since the address specified in the second operand is *calculated* but not *accessed*. The address can thus be an address for which your program does not have permission to access. Any math that can be expressed as a valid address calculation may be done with LEA.

This is one of the few places where NASM does not require a size specifier before an operand that gives a memory address—again, because LEA calculates the address but moves no data to or from that address.

```
r8 = AL AH BL BH CL CH DL DH    r16 = AX BX CX DX BP SP SI DI
sr = CS DS SS ES FS GS          r32 = EAX EBX ECX EDX EBP ESP ESI EDI
m8 = 8-bit memory data          m16 = 16-bit memory data
m32 = 32-bit memory data        i8 = 8-bit immediate data
i16 = 16-bit immediate data     i32 = 32-bit immediate data
d8 = 8-bit signed displacement  d16 = 16-bit signed displacement
d32 = 32-bit unsigned displacement
```

LOOP: Loop until CX/ECX = 0

Flags Affected

```
O D I T S Z A P C     OF: Overflow flag  TF: Trap flag AF: Aux carry
F F F F F F F F F     DF: Direction flag SF: Sign flag PF: Parity flag
      <none>          IF: Interrupt flag ZF: Zero flag CF: Carry flag
```

Legal Forms

```
LOOP d8
```

Examples

```
LOOP PokeValue
```

Notes

LOOP is a combination decrement counter, test, and jump instruction. It uses the CX register in 16-bit modes, and ECX in 32-bit modes. The operation of LOOP is logistically identical in both modes, and I use 32-bit coding as an example here.

LOOP simplifies code by acting as a DEC ECX instruction, a CMP ECX,0 instruction, and JZ instruction, all at once. A repeat count must be initially loaded into ECX. When the LOOP instruction is executed, it first decrements ECX. Then it tests whether ECX = 0. If ECX is *not* 0, LOOP transfers control to the displacement specified as its operand:

```
        MOV ECX,17
DoIt:   CALL CrunchIt
        CALL StuffIt
        LOOP DoIt
```

Here, the two procedure CALLs will be made 17 times. The first 16 times through, ECX will still be nonzero and LOOP will transfer control to DoIt. On the 17th pass, however, LOOP will decrement ECX to 0, and then fall through to the next instruction in sequence when it tests CX.

LOOP does *not* alter any flags, even when ECX is decremented to 0. *Warning:* Watch your initial conditions! If you're in 16-bit mode and CX is initially 0, LOOP will decrement it to 65,535 (0FFFFH) and then perform the loop 65,535 times. Worse, if you're working in 32-bit protected mode and enter a loop with

ECX = 0, the loop will be performed over 2 *billion* times, which might be long enough to look like a system lockup.

```
r8 = AL AH BL BH CL CH DL DH      r16 = AX BX CX DX BP SP SI DI
sr = CS DS SS ES FS GS            r32 = EAX EBX ECX EDX EBP ESP ESI EDI
m8 = 8-bit memory data            m16 = 16-bit memory data
m32 = 32-bit memory data          i8 = 8-bit immediate data
i16 = 16-bit immediate data       i32 = 32-bit immediate data
d8 = 8-bit signed displacement    d16 = 16-bit signed displacement
d32 = 32-bit unsigned displacement
```

LOOPNZ/LOOPNE: Loop While CX/ECX > 0 and ZF = 0

Flags Affected

```
O D I T S Z A P C   OF: Overflow flag  TF: Trap flag AF: Aux carry
F F F F F F F F F   DF: Direction flag SF: Sign flag PF: Parity flag
    <none>          IF: Interrupt flag ZF: Zero flag CF: Carry flag
```

Legal Forms

```
LOOPNZ d8
LOOPNE d8
```

Examples

```
LOOPNZ StartProcess
LOOPNE GoSomewhere
```

Notes

LOOPNZ and LOOPNE are synonyms and generate identical opcodes. Like LOOP, they use either CX or ECX depending on the CPU's BITS setting; hence the current "bit-ness" of the CPU. LOOPNZ/LOOPNE decrements ECX and jumps to the location specified in the target operand if ECX is not 0 and the Zero flag, ZF, is 0. Otherwise, execution falls through to the next instruction.

This means that the loop is pretty much controlled by ZF. If ZF remains 0, then the loop is looped until ECX is decremented to 0; but as soon as ZF is set to 1, the loop terminates. Think of it as "Loop While Not Zero Flag."

Keep in mind that LOOPNZ does not *itself* affect ZF. Some instruction within the loop (typically one of the string instructions) must do something to affect ZF to terminate the loop before CX/ECX counts down to 0.

```
r8 = AL AH BL BH CL CH DL DH      r16 = AX BX CX DX BP SP SI DI
sr = CS DS SS ES FS GS            r32 = EAX EBX ECX EDX EBP ESP ESI EDI
m8 = 8-bit memory data            m16 = 16-bit memory data
m32 = 32-bit memory data          i8 = 8-bit immediate data
i16 = 16-bit immediate data       i32 = 32-bit immediate data
d8 = 8-bit signed displacement    d16 = 16-bit signed displacement
d32 = 32-bit unsigned displacement
```

LOOPZ/LOOPE: Loop While CX/ECX > 0 and ZF = 1

Flags Affected

```
O D I T S Z A P C   OF: Overflow flag  TF: Trap flag AF: Aux carry
F F F F F F F F F   DF: Direction flag SF: Sign flag PF: Parity flag
    <none>          IF: Interrupt flag ZF: Zero flag CF: Carry flag
```

Legal Forms

```
LOOPZ d8
LOOPE d8
```

Examples

```
LOOPZ SenseOneShots
LOOPE CRCGenerate
```

Notes

LOOPZ and LOOPE are synonyms and generate identical opcodes. Like LOOP, they use either CX or ECX depending on the BITS setting; hence the current "bit-ness" of the CPU. LOOPZ/LOOPE decrements ECX and jumps to the location specified in the target operand if ECX is not 0 and the Zero flag ZF is 1. Otherwise, execution falls through to the next instruction.

This means that the loop is pretty much controlled by ZF. If ZF remains 1, the loop is looped until CX is decremented to 0; but as soon as ZF is cleared to 0, the loop terminates. Think of it as "Loop While Zero Flag."

Keep in mind that LOOPZ does not *itself* affect ZF. Some instruction within the loop (typically one of the string instructions) must do something to affect ZF to terminate the loop before CX/ECX counts down to 0.

```
r8 = AL AH BL BH CL CH DL DH      r16 = AX BX CX DX BP SP SI DI
sr = CS DS SS ES FS GS            r32 = EAX EBX ECX EDX EBP ESP ESI EDI
m8 = 8-bit memory data            m16 = 16-bit memory data
m32 = 32-bit memory data          i8 = 8-bit immediate data
i16 = 16-bit immediate data       i32 = 32-bit immediate data
d8 = 8-bit signed displacement    d16 = 16-bit signed displacement
d32 = 32-bit unsigned displacement
```

MOV: Move (Copy) Right Operand into Left Operand

Flags Affected

```
O D I T S Z A P C    OF: Overflow flag  TF: Trap flag AF: Aux carry
F F F F F F F F F    DF: Direction flag SF: Sign flag PF: Parity flag
    <none>           IF: Interrupt flag ZF: Zero flag CF: Carry flag
```

Legal Forms

```
MOV r8,r8
MOV m8,r8
MOV r8,m8
MOV r8,i8
MOV m8,i8
MOV r16,r16
MOV m16,r16
MOV r16,m16
MOV m16,i16
MOV r16,i16
MOV r32,r32     386+
MOV m32,r32     386+
MOV r32,m32     386+
MOV r32,i32     386+
MOV m32,i32     386+
MOV sr,r16
MOV sr,m16
MOV r16,sr
MOV m16,sr
```

Examples

```
MOV AL,BH
MOV EBX,EDI
MOV BP,ES
MOV ES,AX
MOV AX,0B800H
MOV ES:[BX],0FFFFH
MOV CX,[SI+Inset]
```

Notes

This is perhaps the most frequently used instruction. The source (right) operand is copied into the left (destination) operand. The source operand is not changed.

The flags are not affected.

```
r8 = AL AII BL BH CL CH DL DH        r16 = AX BX CX DX BP SP SI DI
sr = CS DS SS ES FS GS               r32 = EAX EBX ECX EDX EBP ESP ESI EDI
m8 = 8-bit memory data               m16 = 16-bit memory data
m32 = 32-bit memory data             i8 = 8-bit immediate data
i16 = 16-bit immediate data          i32 = 32-bit immediate data
d8 = 8-bit signed displacement       d16 = 16-bit signed displacement
d32 = 32-bit unsigned displacement
```

MOVS: Move String

Flags Affected

```
O D I T S Z A P C   OF: Overflow flag  TF: Trap flag AF: Aux carry
F F F F F F F F F   DF: Direction flag SF: Sign flag PF: Parity flag
     <none>          IF: Interrupt flag ZF: Zero flag CF: Carry flag
```

Legal Forms

```
MOVSB
MOVSW
MOVSD              386+
```

Examples

```
MOVSB      ;Copies byte at [ESI] to [EDI]
MOVSW      ;Copies word at [ESI] to [EDI]
MOVSD      ;Copies double word at [ESI] to [EDI]
REP MOVSB  ;Copies memory region starting at [ESI] to region
           ; starting at [EDI], for CX/ECX repeats, one byte
           ; at a time
```

Notes

MOVS copies memory in 8-bit (MOVSB), 16-bit (MOVSW), or 32-bit (MOVSD) chunks, from the address stored in EDI to the address stored in ESI.

For 16-bit modes, ES must be the segment of the destination and cannot be overridden. In 32-bit protected mode, all segments are congruent; thus, ES does not need to be specified explicitly. Similarly, ES:DI or EDI must always be the destination offset.

By placing an operation repeat count (not a count of data units!) in CX/ECX and preceding the mnemonic with the REP prefix, MOVS can do an automatic "machine-gun" copy of data from a memory region starting at [ESI] to a memory region starting at [EDI].

After each copy operation, SI/ESI and DI/EDI are adjusted (see next paragraph) by either by 1 (for 8-bit operations), 2 (for 16-bit operations), or 4 (for 32-bit operations), and CX/ECX is decremented by 1. Don't forget that CX/ECX counts *operations* (the number of times a data item is copied from source to destination), *not* bytes!

Adjusting means incrementing if the Direction flag is cleared (by CLD), or decrementing if the Direction flag has been set (by STD).

```
r8  = AL AH BL BH CL CH DL DH          r16 = AX BX CX DX BP SP SI  DI
sr  = CS DS SS ES FS GS                r32 = EAX EBX ECX EDX EBP ESP ESI EDI
m8  = 8-bit memory data                m16 = 16-bit memory data
m32 = 32-bit memory data               i8  = 8-bit immediate data
i16 = 16-bit immediate data            i32 = 32-bit immediate data
d8  = 8-bit signed displacement        d16 = 16-bit signed displacement
d32 = 32-bit unsigned displacement
```

MOVSX: Move (Copy) with Sign Extension

Flags Affected

```
O D I T S Z A P C    OF: Overflow flag  TF: Trap flag AF: Aux carry
F F F F F F F F F    DF: Direction flag SF: Sign flag PF: Parity flag
     <none>          IF: Interrupt flag ZF: Zero flag CF: Carry flag
```

Legal Forms

```
MOVSX r16,r8          386+
MOVSX r16,m8          386+
MOVSX r32,r8          386+
MOVSX r32,m8          386+
MOVSX r32,r16         386+
MOVSX r32,m16         386+
```

Examples

```
MOVSX AX,AL
MOVSX CX,BYTE [EDI]          ; Acts on the byte at EDI
MOVSX ECX,DL
MOVSX ESI,DWORD [EBX+EDI]    ; Acts on the doubleword at EBX+EDI
```

Notes

MOVSX operates like MOV, but copies values from source to destination operands with sign extension. That is, it carries the sign bit of the smaller source operand to the sign bit of the larger destination operand. This way, for example, a 16-bit signed value in AX will still be a signed value when copied into 32-bit register EDX. Without sign extension, the sign bit of AX would simply become another bit in the binary value copied into EDX, and the value in EDX would bear no resemblance to the supposedly identical value in AX.

The destination operand must be a register. MOVSX can copy data *from* a memory location, but not *to* a memory location. Also note that the destination operand must be a wider value than the source operand; that is, MOVSX will copy from an 8-bit or 16-bit value to a 32-bit value, but not a 16-bit to a 16-bit, nor 32-bit to 32-bit.

MOVSX is only present in 386 and later CPUs. It does not affect any flags.

```
r8 = AL AH BL BH CL CH DL DH      r16 = AX BX CX DX BP SP SI DI
sr = CS DS SS ES FS GS            r32 = EAX EBX ECX EDX EBP ESP ESI EDI
m8 = 8-bit memory data            m16 = 16-bit memory data
m32 = 32-bit memory data          i8 = 8-bit immediate data
i16 = 16-bit immediate data       i32 = 32-bit immediate data
d8 = 8-bit signed displacement    d16 = 16-bit signed displacement
d32 = 32-bit unsigned displacement
```

MUL: Unsigned Integer Multiplication

Flags Affected

```
O D I T S Z A P C   OF: Overflow flag  TF: Trap flag AF: Aux carry
F F F F F F F F F   DF: Direction flag SF: Sign flag PF: Parity flag
*       ? ? ? ? *   IF: Interrupt flag ZF: Zero flag CF: Carry flag
```

Legal Forms

```
MUL r8
MUL m8
MUL r16
MUL m16
MUL r32            386+
MUL m32            386+
```

Examples

```
MUL CH              ; AL * CH --> AX
MUL BX              ; AX * BX --> DX:AX
MUL ECX             ; EAX * ECX --> EDX:EAX
MUL WORD [BX+DI]    ; AX * [BX+DI] --> DX:AX
```

Notes

MUL multiplies its operand by AL, AX, or EAX, and the result is placed in AX, in DX:AX, or in EDX:EAX. If MUL is given an 8-bit operand (either an 8-bit register or an 8-bit memory operand), the results will be placed in AX. This means that AH will be affected, even if the results will fit entirely in AL.

Similarly, if MUL is given a 16-bit operand, the results will be placed in DX:AX, *even if the entire result will fit in AX!* It's easy to forget that MUL affects DX on 16-bit multiplies, and EDX in 32-bit multiplies. Keep that in mind!

Note: It's easy to assume that IMUL is identical to MUL save for IMUL's ability to operate on signed values. Not so: IMUL has more legal instruction forms and considerably more complexity than MUL.

The Carry and Overflow flags are cleared to 0 if the result value is 0; otherwise, both are set to 1. Remember that SF, ZF, AF, and PF are undefined after MUL.

```
r8 = AL AH BL BH CL CH DL DH        r16 = AX BX CX DX BP SP SI DI
sr = CS DS SS ES FS GS              r32 = EAX EBX ECX EDX EBP ESP ESI EDI
m8 = 8-bit memory data              m16 = 16-bit memory data
m32 = 32-bit memory data            i8 = 8-bit immediate data
i16 = 16-bit immediate data         i32 = 32-bit immediate data
d8 = 8-bit signed displacement      d16 = 16-bit signed displacement
d32 = 32-bit unsigned displacement
```

NEG: Negate (Two's Complement; i.e., Multiply by -1)

Flags Affected

```
O D I T S Z A P C   OF: Overflow flag  TF: Trap flag AF: Aux carry
F F F F F F F F F    DF: Direction flag SF: Sign flag PF: Parity flag
*       * * * *      IF: Interrupt flag ZF: Zero flag CF: Carry flag
```

Legal Forms

```
NEG r8
NEG m8
NEG r16
NEG m16
NEG r32         386+
NEG m32         386+
```

Examples

```
NEG AL
NEG DX
NEG ECX
NEG BYTE [BX]    ; Negates BYTE quantity at [BX]
NEG WORD [DI]    ; Negates WORD quantity at [BX]
NEG DWORD [EAX]  ; Negates DWORD quantity at [EAX]
```

Notes

This is the assembly language equivalent of multiplying a value by -1. Keep in mind that negation is *not* the same as simply inverting each bit in the operand. (Another instruction, NOT, does that.) The process is also known as generating the *two's complement* of a value. The two's complement of a value added to that value yields zero. $-1 = \$FF$; $-2 = \$FE$; $-3 = \$FD$; and so forth.

If the operand is 0, CF is cleared and ZF is set; otherwise, CF is set and ZF is cleared. If the operand contains the maximum negative value for the operand size, the operand does not change, but OF and CF are set. SF is set if the result is negative, or else SF is cleared. PF is set if the low-order 8 bits of the result contain an even number of set (1) bits; otherwise, PF is cleared.

Note: You *must* use a size specifier (BYTE, WORD, DWORD) with memory data!

```
r8 = AL AH BL BH CL CH DL DH      r16 = AX BX CX DX BP SP SI DI
sr = CS DS SS ES FS GS            r32 = EAX EBX ECX EDX EBP ESP ESI EDI
m8 = 8-bit memory data            m16 = 16-bit memory data
m32 = 32-bit memory data          i8 = 8-bit immediate data
i16 = 16-bit immediate data       i32 = 32-bit immediate data
d8 = 8-bit signed displacement    d16 = 16-bit signed displacement
d32 = 32-bit unsigned displacement
```

NOP: No Operation

Flags Affected

```
O D I T S Z A P C   OF: Overflow flag  TF: Trap flag AF: Aux carry
F F F F F F F F F   DF: Direction flag SF: Sign flag PF: Parity flag
    <none>          IF: Interrupt flag ZF: Zero flag CF: Carry flag
```

Legal Forms

```
NOP
```

Examples

```
NOP
```

Notes

This, the easiest-to-understand of all 86-family machine instructions, simply does nothing. Its job is to take up space in sequences of instructions. When fetched by the CPU, NOP is executed as XCHG AX,AX. Therefore, some work is actually done, but it's not *useful* work, and no data is altered anywhere. The flags are not affected. NOP is used for "NOPping out" machine instructions during debugging, leaving space for future procedure or interrupt calls, or padding timing loops—though padding timing loops is no longer quantifiable, given the ability of modern x86 CPUs to perform various context-sensitive optimizations on executing code. *Precise assembly-time prediction of instruction execution time is no longer possible!*

```
r8 = AL AH BL BH CL CH DL DH     r16 = AX BX CX DX BP SP SI DI
sr = CS DS SS ES FS GS           r32 = EAX EBX ECX EDX EBP ESP ESI EDI
m8 = 8-bit memory data           m16 = 16-bit memory data
m32 = 32-bit memory data         i8 = 8-bit immediate data
i16 = 16-bit immediate data      i32 = 32-bit immediate data
d8 = 8-bit signed displacement   d16 = 16-bit signed displacement
d32 = 32-bit unsigned displacement
```

NOT: Logical NOT (One's Complement)

Flags Affected

```
O D I T S Z A P C   OF: Overflow flag  TF: Trap flag AF: Aux carry
F F F F F F F F F   DF: Direction flag SF: Sign flag PF: Parity flag
    <none>          IF: Interrupt flag ZF: Zero flag CF: Carry flag
```

Legal Forms

```
NOT r8
NOT m8
NOT r16
NOT m16
NOT r32      386+
NOT m32      386+
```

Examples

```
NOT CL
NOT DX
NOT EBX
NOT WORD [SI+5]
```

Notes

NOT inverts each individual bit within the operand separately. That is, every bit that was 1 becomes 0, and every bit that was 0 becomes 1. This is the "logical NOT" or "one's complement" operation. *See* the *NEG* instruction for the negation, or two's complement, operation.

After execution of NOT, the value FFH would become 0; the value AAH would become 55H. Note that the Zero flag is *not* affected, even when NOT forces its operand to 0.

Note: You *must* use a size specifier (BYTE, WORD, DWORD) with memory data.

```
r8 = AL AH BL BH CL CH DL DH     r16 = AX BX CX DX BP SP SI DI
sr = CS DS SS ES FS GS           r32 = EAX EBX ECX EDX EBP ESP ESI EDI
m8 = 8-bit memory data           m16 = 16-bit memory data
m32 = 32-bit memory data         i8 = 8-bit immediate data
i16 = 16-bit immediate data      i32 = 32-bit immediate data
d8 = 8-bit signed displacement    d16 = 16-bit signed displacement
d32 = 32-bit unsigned displacement
```

OR: Logical OR

Flags Affected

```
O D I T S Z A P C   OF: Overflow flag  TF: Trap flag AF: Aux carry
F F F F F F F F F    DF: Direction flag SF: Sign flag PF: Parity flag
*       * * ? * *    IF: Interrupt flag ZF: Zero flag CF: Carry flag
```

Legal Forms

```
OR r8,r8
OR m8,r8
OR r8,m8
OR r16,r16
OR m16,r16
OR r16,m16
OR r32,r32     386+
OR m32,r32     386+
OR r32,m32     386+
OR r8,i8
OR m8,i8
OR r16,i16
OR m16,i16
OR r32,i32     386+
OR m32,i32     386+
OR AL,i8
OR AX,i16
OR EAX,i32     386+
```

Examples

```
OR EBX,EDI
OR AX,0FFFFH          ;Uses single-byte opcode
OR AL,42H             ;Uses single-byte opcode
OR WORD [EBX],0B8C0H
OR WORD [BP+SI],DX
```

Notes

OR performs the OR logical operation between its two operands. Once the operation is complete, the result replaces the destination operand. OR is performed on a bit-by-bit basis, such that bit 0 of the source is ORed with bit 0 of the destination, bit 1 of the source is ORed with bit 1 of the destination, and so on. The OR operation yields a 1 if one of the operands is 1; and a 0 only if both operands are 0. Note that the operation makes the Auxiliary carry flag undefined. CF and OF are cleared to 0, and the other affected flags are set according to the operation's results.

Note: You *must* use a size specifier (BYTE, WORD, DWORD) with memory data.

```
r8  = AL AH BL BH CL CH DL DH        r16 = AX BX CX DX BP SP SI DI
sr  = CS DS SS ES FS GS              r32 = EAX EBX ECX EDX EBP ESP ESI EDI
m8  = 8-bit memory data              m16 = 16-bit memory data
m32 = 32-bit memory data             i8  = 8-bit immediate data
i16 = 16-bit immediate data          i32 = 32-bit immediate data
d8  = 8-bit signed displacement      d16 = 16-bit signed displacement
d32 = 32-bit unsigned displacement
```

POP: Pop Top of Stack into Operand

Flags Affected

```
 O D I T S Z A P C   OF: Overflow flag  TF: Trap flag AF: Aux carry
 F F F F F F F F F    DF: Direction flag SF: Sign flag PF: Parity flag
     <none>           IF: Interrupt flag ZF: Zero flag CF: Carry flag
```

Legal Forms

```
POP r16
POP m16
POP r32
POP m32
POP sr
```

Examples

```
POP WORD [BX]
POP EAX
POP DX
POP DWORD [EAX+ECX]
POP ES
```

Notes

It is impossible to pop an 8-bit item from the stack. Also remember that the *top of the stack* is defined (in 16-bit modes) as the word at address SS:SP, and there's no way to override that using prefixes. In 32-bit modes, the top of the stack is the DWORD at [ESP]. There is a separate pair of instructions, PUSHF and POPF, for pushing and popping the Flags register.

All register forms have single-byte opcodes. NASM recognizes them and generates them automatically, even though there are larger forms in the CPU instruction decoding logic.

```
r8 = AL AH BL BH CL CH DL DH    r16 = AX BX CX DX BP SP SI DI
sr = CS DS SS ES FS GS          r32 = EAX EBX ECX EDX EBP ESP ESI EDI
m8 = 8-bit memory data          m16 = 16-bit memory data
m32 = 32-bit memory data        i8 = 8-bit immediate data
i16 = 16-bit immediate data     i32 = 32-bit immediate data
d8 = 8-bit signed displacement  d16 = 16-bit signed displacement
d32 = 32-bit unsigned displacement
```

POPA/POPAD: Pop All GP Registers

Flags Affected

```
O D I T S Z A P C   OF: Overflow flag  TF: Trap flag AF: Aux carry
F F F F F F F F F   DF: Direction flag SF: Sign flag PF: Parity flag
      <none>        IF: Interrupt flag ZF: Zero flag CF: Carry flag
```

Legal Forms

```
POPA        286+
POPAD       386+
```

Examples

```
POPA       ; Pops all 8 16-bit regs from stack. SP value is discarded
POPAD      ; Pops all 8 32-bit regs from stack. ESP value is discarded.
```

Notes

POPA pushes all 16-bit general-purpose registers onto the stack. This instruction is present on the 286 and later CPUs and is not available in the 8086/8088. The eight 16-bit general-purpose registers are popped in this order:

DI, SI, BP, SP, BX, DX, CX, AX

There's one wrinkle here: the SP value popped off the stack by POPA is *not* popped back into SP! (That would be insane, since we're using SP to manage the stack as we pop values off of it.) The value in SP's position on the stack is simply discarded when instruction execution reaches it.

POPAD is the 32-bit equivalent of POPA. It pops all eight 32-bit register values from the stack into the registers, with the exception of ESP, in this order:

EDI, ESI, EBP, ESP, EBX, EDX, ECX, EAX

The value pushed onto the stack for ESP is discarded by POPAD and does not replace the current value of ESP.

POPA and POPAD are usually used in conjunction with PUSHA and PUSHAD, but nothing guarantees this. If you pop garbage values off the stack into the general-purpose registers, well, interesting things (in the sense of the old Chinese curse) can and probably will happen.

```
r8 = AL AH BL BH CL CH DL DH      r16 - AX BX CX DX BP SP SI DI
sr = CS DS SS ES FS GS            r32 = EAX EBX ECX EDX EBP ESP ESI EDI
m8 = 8-bit memory data            m16 = 16-bit memory data
m32 = 32-bit memory data          i8 = 8-bit immediate data
i16 = 16-bit immediate data       i32 = 32-bit immediate data
d8 = 8-bit signed displacement    d16 - 16-bit signed displacement
d32 = 32-bit unsigned displacement
```

POPF: Pop Top of Stack into 16-Bit Flags

Flags Affected

```
O D I T S Z A P C   OF: Overflow flag  TF: Trap flag AF: Aux carry
F F F F F F F F F   DF: Direction flag SF: Sign flag PF: Parity flag
* * * * * * * * *   IF: Interrupt flag ZF: Zero flag CF: Carry flag
```

Legal Forms

```
POPF
```

Examples

```
POPF
```

Notes

POPF pops the 16-bit word at the top of the stack into the Flags register. *The top of the stack* is defined as the word at SS:SP, and there is no way to override that with prefixes.

SP is incremented by 2 *after* the word comes off the stack. Remember that SP always points to either an empty stack or real data. There is a separate pair of instructions, PUSH and POP, for pushing and popping other register data and memory data.

PUSHF and POPF are most often used in writing 16-bit interrupt service routines, where you must be able to save and restore the environment—that is, all machine registers—to avoid disrupting machine operations while servicing the interrupt.

There is a separate pair of instructions, PUSHFD and POPFD, for pushing and popping the 32-bit EFlags register.

```
r8 = AL AH BL BH CL CH DL DH        r16 = AX BX CX DX BP SP SI DI
sr = CS DS SS ES FS GS              r32 = EAX EBX ECX EDX EBP ESP ESI EDI
m8 = 8-bit memory data              m16 = 16-bit memory data
m32 = 32-bit memory data            i8 = 8-bit immediate data
i16 = 16-bit immediate data         i32 = 32-bit immediate data
d8 = 8-bit signed displacement      d16 = 16-bit signed displacement
d32 = 32-bit unsigned displacement
```

POPFD: Pop Top of Stack into EFlags

Flags Affected

```
O D I T S Z A P C   OF: Overflow flag  TF: Trap flag AF: Aux carry
F F F F F F F F F   DF: Direction flag SF: Sign flag PF: Parity flag
* * * * * * * * *   IF: Interrupt flag ZF: Zero flag CF: Carry flag
```

Legal Forms

```
POPFD
```

Examples

```
POPFD        386+
```

Notes

POPFD pops the double word (4 bytes) at the top of the stack into the EFlags register. In 32-bit protected mode, the *top of the stack* is defined as the DWORD at [ESP].

ESP is incremented by 4 *after* the word comes off the stack. Remember that ESP always points to either an empty stack or real data. There is a separate pair of instructions, PUSH and POP, for pushing and popping other register data and memory data, in both 16-bit and 32-bit sizes. There is also a separate pair of instructions, PUSHF and POPF, for pushing and popping the 16-bit Flags register.

```
r8 = AL AH BL BH CL CH DL DH        r16 = AX BX CX DX BP SP SI DI
sr = CS DS SS ES FS GS              r32 = EAX EBX ECX EDX EBP ESP ESI EDI
m8 = 8-bit memory data             m16 = 16-bit memory data
m32 = 32-bit memory data           i8 = 8-bit immediate data
i16 = 16-bit immediate data        i32 = 32-bit immediate data
d8 = 8-bit signed displacement     d16 = 16-bit signed displacement
d32 = 32-bit unsigned displacement
```

PUSH: Push Operand onto Top of Stack

Flags Affected

```
O D I T S Z A P C   OF: Overflow flag  TF: Trap flag AF: Aux carry
F F F F F F F F F   DF: Direction flag SF: Sign flag PF: Parity flag
    <none>          IF: Interrupt flag ZF: Zero flag CF: Carry flag
```

Legal Forms

```
PUSH r16
PUSH m16
PUSH r32      386+
PUSH m32      386+
PUSH sr
PUSH i8       286+
PUSH i16      286+
PUSH i32      386+
```

Examples

```
PUSH WORD [EBX]
PUSH EAX
PUSH DI
PUSH DWORD 5
PUSH WORD 1000H
```

Notes

It is impossible to push an 8-bit item onto the stack. Also remember that the *top of the stack* is defined (in 16-bit modes) as the word at address SS:SP, and there's no way to override that using prefixes. In 32-bit modes, the top of the stack is the DWORD at [ESP]. There is a separate pair of instructions, PUSHF and POPF, for pushing and popping the Flags register.

There are special forms of PUSH for pushing the segment registers, but these are not listed here because they cannot be used in ordinary Linux user-space programming.

Also remember that SP/ESP is decremented *before* the push takes place; SP points to either an empty stack or real data.

```
r8 = AL AH BL BH CL CH DL DH      r16 = AX BX CX DX BP SP SI DI
sr = CS DS SS ES FS GS            r32 = EAX EBX ECX EDX EBP ESP ESI EDI
m8 = 8-bit memory data            m16 = 16-bit memory data
m32 = 32-bit memory data          i8 = 8-bit immediate data
i16 = 16-bit immediate data       i32 = 32-bit immediate data
d8 = 8-bit signed displacement    d16 = 16-bit signed displacement
d32 = 32-bit unsigned displacement
```

PUSHA: Push All 16-Bit GP Registers

Flags Affected

```
O D I T S Z A P C   OF: Overflow flag  TF: Trap flag AF: Aux carry
F F F F F F F F F   DF: Direction flag SF: Sign flag PF: Parity flag
    <none>          IF: Interrupt flag ZF: Zero flag CF: Carry flag
```

Legal Forms

```
PUSHA            286+
```

Examples

```
PUSHA
```

Notes

PUSHA pushes all 16-bit general-purpose registers onto the stack. This instruction is present on the 286 and later CPUs and is not available in the 8086/8088.

The registers are pushed in this order:

AX, CX, DX, BX, SP, BP, SI, DI

However, note that the value of SP pushed is the value SP had *before* the first register was pushed onto the stack. In the course of executing PUSHA, the stack pointer is decremented by 16 bytes (8 registers × 2 bytes each).

The pushed value of SP is not considered useful and is discarded by POPA.

```
r8 = AL AH BL BH CL CH DL DH        r16 = AX BX CX DX BP SP SI DI
sr = CS DS SS ES FS GS              r32 = EAX EBX ECX EDX EBP ESP ESI EDI
m8 = 8-bit memory data             m16 = 16-bit memory data
m32 = 32-bit memory data           i8 = 8-bit immediate data
i16 = 16-bit immediate data        i32 = 32-bit immediate data
d8 = 8-bit signed displacement     d16 = 16-bit signed displacement
d32 = 32-bit unsigned displacement
```

PUSHAD: Push All 32-Bit GP Registers

Flags Affected

```
O D I T S Z A P C   OF: Overflow flag  TF: Trap flag AF: Aux carry
F F F F F F F F F   DF: Direction flag SF: Sign flag PF: Parity flag
   <none>           IF: Interrupt flag ZF: Zero flag CF: Carry flag
```

Legal Forms

```
PUSHAD          386+
```

Examples

```
PUSHAD
```

Notes

PUSHA pushes all 32-bit general-purpose registers onto the stack. This instruction is present on the 386 and later CPUs and is not available in the 8086, 8088, or 286.

The registers are pushed in this order:

EAX, ECX, EDX, EBX, ESP, EBP, ESI, EDI

However, note that the value of ESP pushed is the value SP had *before* the first register was pushed onto the stack. In the course of executing PUSHAD, the stack pointer is decremented by 32 bytes (8 registers × 4 bytes each).

The pushed value of ESP is not considered useful and is discarded by POPAD.

```
r8  = AL AH BL BH CL CH DL DH      r16 = AX BX CX DX BP SP SI DI
sr  = CS DS SS ES FS GS            r32 = EAX EBX ECX EDX EBP ESP ESI EDI
m8  = 8-bit memory data            m16 = 16-bit memory data
m32 = 32-bit memory data           i8  = 8-bit immediate data
i16 = 16-bit immediate data        i32 = 32-bit immediate data
d8  = 8-bit signed displacement    d16 = 16-bit signed displacement
d32 = 32-bit unsigned displacement
```

PUSHF: Push 16-Bit Flags onto Stack

Flags Affected

```
O D I T S Z A P C   OF: Overflow flag  TF: Trap flag AF: Aux carry
F F F F F F F F F   DF: Direction flag SF: Sign flag PF: Parity flag
      <none>         IF: Interrupt flag ZF: Zero flag CF: Carry flag
```

Legal Forms

```
PUSHF
```

Examples

```
PUSHF
```

Notes

PUSHF simply pushes the current contents of the 16-bit Flags register (*not* the 32-bit EFlags!) onto the top of the stack. *The top of the stack* is defined as the word at SS:SP in 16-bit modes, and there is no way to override that with prefixes.

SP is decremented *before* the word goes onto the stack. Remember that SP always points to either an empty stack or real data. There is a separate pair of instructions, PUSH and POP, for pushing and popping other register data and memory data.

The Flags register is not affected when you *push* the flags, but only when you pop them back with POPF.

PUSHF and POPF are most often used in writing interrupt service routines, where you must be able to save and restore the environment—that is, all machine registers—to avoid disrupting machine operations while servicing the interrupt.

```
r8 = AL AH BL BH CL CH DL DH     r16 = AX BX CX DX BP SP SI DI
sr = CS DS SS ES FS GS           r32 = EAX EBX ECX EDX EBP ESP ESI EDI
m8 = 8-bit memory data           m16 = 16-bit memory data
m32 = 32-bit memory data         i8 = 8-bit immediate data
i16 = 16-bit immediate data      i32 = 32-bit immediate data
d8 = 8-bit signed displacement   d16 = 16-bit signed displacement
d32 = 32-bit unsigned displacement
```

PUSHFD: Push 32-Bit EFlags onto Stack

Flags Affected

```
O D I T S Z A P C   OF: Overflow flag  TF: Trap flag AF: Aux carry
F F F F F F F F F    DF: Direction flag SF: Sign flag PF: Parity flag
    <none>           IF: Interrupt flag ZF: Zero flag CF: Carry flag
```

Legal Forms

```
PUSHFD        386+
```

Examples

```
PUSHFD
```

Notes

PUSHFD simply pushes the current contents of the 32-bit EFlags register onto the top of the stack. The *top of the stack* in 32-bit modes is defined as the word at [ESP]. ESP is decremented *before* the EFlags double word goes onto the stack. Remember that ESP always points to either an empty stack or real data. There is a separate pair of instructions, PUSH and POP, for pushing and popping other register data and memory data, and (in the 286 and later processors) immediate data.

The EFlags register is not affected when you *push* the flags, but only when you pop them back with POPFD.

```
r8 = AL AH BL BH CL CH DL DH     r16 = AX BX CX DX BP SP SI DI
sr = CS DS SS ES FS GS           r32 = EAX EBX ECX EDX EBP ESP ESI EDI
m8 = 8-bit memory data           m16 = 16-bit memory data
m32 = 32-bit memory data         i8 = 8-bit immediate data
i16 = 16-bit immediate data      i32 = 32-bit immediate data
d8 = 8-bit signed displacement   d16 = 16-bit signed displacement
d32 = 32-bit unsigned displacement
```

RET: Return from Procedure

Flags Affected

```
O D I T S Z A P C    OF: Overflow flag  TF: Trap flag AF: Aux carry
F F F F F F F F F     DF: Direction flag SF: Sign flag PF: Parity flag
    <none>            IF: Interrupt flag ZF: Zero flag CF: Carry flag
```

Legal Forms

```
RET
RETN
RETF
RET i8
RETN i8
RET i16
RETF i16
```

Examples

```
RET
RET 12H
RETN
RETF 117H
```

Notes

There are two kinds of returns: Near and Far, where Near is within the current code segment and Far is to some other code segment. (This is not an issue in 32-bit protected mode, for which there is only one code segment.) Ordinarily, the RET form is used, and the assembler resolves it to a Near or Far return opcode to match the procedure definition's use of the NEAR or FAR specifier. Specifying RETF or RETN may be done when necessary.

RET may take an operand indicating how many bytes of stack space are to be released on returning from the procedure. This figure is subtracted from the stack pointer to erase data items that had been pushed onto the stack for the procedure's use immediately prior to the procedure call.

```
r8 = AL AH BL BH CL CH DL DH      r16 = AX BX CX DX BP SP SI DI
sr = CS DS SS ES FS GS            r32 = EAX EBX ECX EDX EBP ESP ESI EDI
m8 = 8-bit memory data            m16 = 16-bit memory data
m32 = 32-bit memory data          i8 = 8-bit immediate data
i16 = 16-bit immediate data       i32 = 32-bit immediate data
d8 = 8-bit signed displacement    d16 = 16-bit signed displacement
d32 = 32-bit unsigned displacement
```

ROL: Rotate Left

Flags Affected

```
O D I T S Z A P C   OF: Overflow flag  TF: Trap flag   AF: Aux carry
F F F F F F F F F   DF: Direction flag SF: Sign flag   PF: Parity flag
*               *   IF: Interrupt flag ZF: Zero flag   CF: Carry flag
```

Legal Forms

```
ROL r8,1
ROL m8,1
ROL r16,1
ROL m16,1
ROL r32,1       386+
ROL m32,1       386+
ROL r8,CL
ROL m8,CL
ROL r16,CL
ROL m16,CL
ROL r32,CL      386+
ROL m32,CL      386+
ROL r8,i8       286+
ROL m8,i8       286+
ROL r16,i8      286+
ROL m16,i8      286+
ROL r32,i8      386+
ROL m32,i8      386+
```

Examples

```
ROL AL,1
ROL WORD [BX+SI],CL
ROL BP,1
ROL DWORD [EBX+ESI],9
ROL BP,CL
```

Notes

ROL rotates the bits within the destination operand to the left, where left is toward the most significant bit (MSB). A rotate is a shift (*see* SHL and SHR) that wraps around: the leftmost bit of the operand is shifted into the rightmost bit, and all intermediate bits are shifted one bit to the left. Except for the direction the shift operation takes, ROL is identical to ROR.

The number of bit positions shifted may be specified either as an 8-bit immediate value or by the value in CL—*not* CX or ECX. (The 8086 and 8088 are limited to the immediate value 1.) Note that while CL may accept a value up to 255, it is meaningless to shift by any value larger than 16, *even though the shifts are actually performed on the 8086 and 8088*. (The 286 and later limit the number of shift operations performed to the native word size except when running in Virtual 86 mode.)

The leftmost bit is copied into the Carry flag on each shift operation. OF is modified *only* by the shift-by-one forms of ROL; after shift-by-CL forms, *OF becomes undefined*.

```
r8  = AL AH BL BH CL CH DL DH      r16 = AX BX CX DX BP SP SI DI
sr  = CS DS SS ES FS GS            r32 = EAX EBX ECX EDX EBP ESP ESI EDI
m8  = 8-bit memory data            m16 = 16-bit memory data
m32 = 32-bit memory data           i8  = 8-bit immediate data
i16 = 16-bit immediate data        i32 = 32-bit immediate data
d8  = 8-bit signed displacement    d16 = 16-bit signed displacement
d32 = 32-bit unsigned displacement
```

ROR: Rotate Right

Flags Affected

```
O D I T S Z A P C   OF: Overflow flag  TF: Trap flag  AF: Aux carry
F F F F F F F F F   DF: Direction flag SF: Sign flag  PF: Parity flag
*               *   IF: Interrupt flag ZF: Zero flag  CF: Carry flag
```

Legal Forms

```
ROR r8,1
ROR m8,1
ROR r16,1
ROR m16,1
ROR r32,1      386+
ROR m32,1      386+
ROR r8,CL
ROR m8,CL
ROR r16,CL
ROR m16,CL
ROR r32,CL     386+
ROR m32,CL     386+
ROR r8,i8      286+
ROR m8,i8      286+
ROR r16,i8     286+
ROR m16,i8     286+
ROR r32,i8     386+
ROR m32,i8     386+
```

Examples

```
ROR AL,1
ROR WORD [BX+SI],CL
ROR BP,1
ROR DWORD [EBX+ESI],9
ROR BP,CL
```

Notes

ROR rotates the bits within the destination operand to the right, where right is toward the least significant bit (LSB). A rotate is a shift (*see* SHL and SHR) that wraps around: the rightmost bit of the operand is shifted into the leftmost bit, and all intermediate bits are shifted one bit to the right. Except for the direction the shift operation takes, ROR is identical to ROL.

The number of bit positions shifted may be specified either as an 8-bit immediate value or by the value in CL—*not* CX or ECX. (The 8086 and 8088 are limited to the immediate value 1.) Note that while CL may accept a value up to 255, it is meaningless to shift by any value larger than 16—or 32 in 32-bit mode—*even though the shifts are actually performed on the 8086 and 8088.* (The 286 and later limit the number of shift operations performed to the native word size except when running in Virtual 86 mode.)

The rightmost bit is copied into the Carry flag on each shift operation. OF is modified *only* by the shift-by-one forms of ROR; after shift-by-CL forms, *OF becomes undefined.*

```
r8  = AL AH BL BH CL CH DL DH        r16 = AX BX CX DX BP SP SI DI
sr  = CS DS SS ES FS GS              r32 = EAX EBX ECX EDX EBP ESP ESI EDI
m8  = 8-bit memory data              m16 = 16-bit memory data
m32 = 32-bit memory data             i8  = 8-bit immediate data
i16 = 16-bit immediate data          i32 = 32-bit immediate data
d8  = 8-bit signed displacement      d16 = 16-bit signed displacement
d32 = 32-bit unsigned displacement
```

SBB: Arithmetic Subtraction with Borrow

Flags Affected

```
O D I T S Z A P C    OF: Overflow flag  TF: Trap flag AF: Aux carry
F F F F F F F F F    DF: Direction flag SF: Sign flag PF: Parity flag
*       * * * *      IF: Interrupt flag ZF: Zero flag CF: Carry flag
```

Legal Forms

```
SBB r8,r8
SBB m8,r8
SBB r8,m8
SBB r16,r16
SBB m16,r16
SBB r16,m16
SBB r32,r32     386+
SBB m32,r32     386+
SBB r32,m32     386+
SBB r8,i8
SBB m8,i8
SBB r16,i16
SBB m16,i16
SBB r32,i32     386+
SBB m32,i32     386+
SBB r16,i8
SBB m16,i8
SBB r32,i8      386+
SBB m32,i8      386+
SBB AL,i8
SBB AX,i16
SBB EAX,i32     386+
```

Examples

```
SBB BX,DI
SBB AX,0FFFFH       ;Uses single-byte opcode
SBB AL,42H          ;Uses single-byte opcode
SBB BP,17H
SBB WORD [BX+SI+Inset],5
SBB WORD [ES:BX],0B800H
```

Notes

SBB performs a subtraction with borrow, where the source is subtracted from the destination, and then the Carry flag is subtracted from the result. The result then replaces the destination. If the result is negative, the Carry flag is set. To subtract without taking the Carry flag into account (i.e., without borrowing), use the SUB instruction.

```
r8 = AL AH BL BH CL CH DL DH      r16 = AX BX CX DX BP SP SI DI
sr = CS DS SS ES FS GS            r32 = EAX EBX ECX EDX EBP ESP ESI EDI
m8 = 8-bit memory data            m16 = 16-bit memory data
m32 = 32-bit memory data          i8 = 8-bit immediate data
i16 = 16-bit immediate data       i32 = 32-bit immediate data
d8 = 8-bit signed displacement    d16 = 16-bit signed displacement
d32 = 32-bit unsigned displacement
```

SHL: Shift Left

Flags Affected

```
O D I T S Z A P C   OF: Overflow flag  TF: Trap flag AF: Aux carry
F F F F F F F F F   DF: Direction flag SF: Sign flag PF: Parity flag
*       * * ? * *   IF: Interrupt flag ZF: Zero flag CF: Carry flag
```

Legal Forms

```
SHL  r8,1
SHL  m8,1
SHL  r16,1
SHL  m16,1
SHL  r32,1      386+
SHL  m32,1      386+
SHL  r8,CL
SHL  m8,CL
SHL  r16,CL
SHL  m16,CL
SHL  r32,CL     386+
SHL  m32,CL     386+
SHL  r8,i8      286+
SHL  m8,i8      286+
SHL  r16,i8     286+
SHL  m16,i8     286+
SHL  r32,i8     386+
SHL  m32,i8     386+
```

Examples

```
SHL  AL,1
SHL  WORD [BX+SI],CL
SHL  BP,1
SHL  EAX,9
SHL  BP,CL
```

Notes

SHL shifts the bits within the destination operand to the left, where left is toward the most significant bit (MSB). The number of bit positions shifted may be specified either as an 8-bit immediate value or by the value in CL—*not* CX or ECX. (The 8086 and 8088 are limited to the immediate value 1.) Note that while CL may accept a value up to 255, it is meaningless to shift by any value larger than 16—or 32 in 32-bit mode—*even though the shifts are actually performed on the 8086 and 8088.* (The 286 and later limit the number of shift operations performed to the native word size except when running in Virtual 86 mode.) The leftmost bit of the operand is shifted into the Carry flag; the rightmost bit is cleared to 0. The Auxiliary carry flag, AF, becomes undefined after this instruction. OF is modified *only* by the shift-by-one forms of SHL; after any of the shift-by-CL forms, *OF becomes undefined.*

SHL is a synonym for SAL (Shift Arithmetic Left). Except for the direction of the shift operation, SHL is identical to SHR.

```
r8 = AL AH BL BH CL CH DL DH       r16 = AX BX CX DX BP SP SI DI
sr = CS DS SS ES FS GS             r32 = EAX EBX ECX EDX EBP ESP ESI EDI
m8 = 8-bit memory data             m16 = 16-bit memory data
m32 = 32-bit memory data           i8 = 8-bit immediate data
i16 = 16-bit immediate data        i32 = 32-bit immediate data
d8 = 8-bit signed displacement     d16 = 16-bit signed displacement
d32 = 32-bit unsigned displacement
```

SHR: Shift Right

Flags Affected

```
O  D  I  T  S  Z  A  P  C     OF: Overflow flag   TF: Trap flag  AF: Aux carry
F  F  F  F  F  F  F  F  F      DF: Direction flag  SF: Sign flag  PF: Parity flag
*        *  *  ?  *  *         IF: Interrupt flag  ZF: Zero flag  CF: Carry flag
```

Legal Forms

```
SHR r8,1
SHR m8,1
SHR r16,1
SHR m16,1
SHR r32,1      386+
SHR m32,1      386+
SHR r8,CL
SHR m8,CL
SHR r16,CL
SHR m16,CL
SHR r32,CL     386+
SHR m32,CL     386+
SHR r8,i8      286+
SHR m8,i8      286+
SHR r16,i8     286+
SHR m16,i8     286+
SHR r32,i8     386+
SHR m32,i8     386+
```

Examples

```
SHR AL,1
SHR WORD [BX+SI],CL
SHR BP,1
SHR EAX,9
SHR BP,CL
```

Notes

SHR shifts the bits within the destination operand to the right, where right is toward the least-significant bit (LSB). The number of bit positions shifted may be specified either as an 8-bit immediate value or by the value in CL—*not* CX or ECX. (The 8086 and 8088 are limited to the immediate value 1.) Note that while CL may accept a value up to 255, it is meaningless to shift by any value larger than 16—or 32 in 32-bit mode—*even though the shifts are actually performed on the 8086 and 8088*. (The 286 and later limit the number of shift operations performed to the native word size except when running in Virtual 86 mode.) The rightmost bit of the operand is shifted into the Carry flag; the leftmost bit is cleared to 0. The Auxiliary carry flag, AF, becomes undefined after this instruction. OF is modified *only* by the shift-by-one forms of SHL; after any of the shift-by-CL forms, *OF becomes undefined*.

SHR is a synonym for SAR (Shift Arithmetic Right). Except for the direction of the shift operation, SHR is identical to SHL.

```
r8  = AL AH BL BH CL CH DL DH      r16 = AX BX CX DX BP SP SI DI
sr  = CS DS SS ES FS GS            r32 = EAX EBX ECX EDX EBP ESP ESI EDI
m8  = 8-bit memory data            m16 = 16-bit memory data
m32 = 32-bit memory data           i8  = 8-bit immediate data
i16 = 16-bit immediate data        i32 = 32-bit immediate data
d8  = 8-bit signed displacement    d16 = 16-bit signed displacement
d32 = 32-bit unsigned displacement
```

STC: Set Carry Flag (CF)

Flags Affected

```
O D I T S Z A P C   OF: Overflow flag  TF: Trap flag AF: Aux carry
F F F F F F F F F   DF: Direction flag SF: Sign flag PF: Parity flag
              *      IF: Interrupt flag ZF: Zero flag CF: Carry flag
```

Legal Forms

```
STC
```

Examples

```
STC
```

Notes

STC changes the Carry flag, CF, to a known set state (1). Use it prior to some task that needs a bit in the Carry flag. It can also be used to put CF into a known state before returning from a procedure, to indicate that the procedure succeeded or failed, as desired.

```
r8 = AL AH BL BH CL CH DL DH      r16 = AX BX CX DX BP SP SI DI
sr = CS DS SS ES FS GS            r32 = EAX EBX ECX EDX EBP ESP ESI EDI
m8 = 8-bit memory data            m16 = 16-bit memory data
m32 = 32-bit memory data          i8 = 8-bit immediate data
i16 = 16-bit immediate data       i32 = 32-bit immediate data
d8 = 8-bit signed displacement    d16 = 16-bit signed displacement
d32 = 32-bit unsigned displacement
```

STD: Set Direction Flag (DF)

Flags Affected

```
O D I T S Z A P C    OF: Overflow flag  TF: Trap flag AF: Aux carry
F F F F F F F F F    DF: Direction flag SF: Sign flag PF: Parity flag
        *            IF: Interrupt flag ZF: Zero flag CF: Carry flag
```

Legal Forms

```
STD
```

Examples

```
STD
```

Notes

STD simply changes the Direction flag, DF, to the set (1) state. This affects the adjustment performed by repeated string instructions such as STOS, SCAS, and MOVS. Typically, when DF = 0, the destination pointer is increased, and decreased when DF = 1. DF is cleared to 0 with the CLD instruction.

```
r8 = AL AH BL BH CL CH DL DH        r16 = AX BX CX DX BP SP SI DI
sr = CS DS SS ES FS GS              r32 = EAX EBX ECX EDX EBP ESP ESI EDI
m8 = 8-bit memory data              m16 = 16-bit memory data
m32 = 32-bit memory data            i8 = 8-bit immediate data
i16 = 16-bit immediate data         i32 = 32-bit immediate data
d8 = 8-bit signed displacement      d16 = 16-bit signed displacement
d32 = 32-bit unsigned displacement
```

STOS: Store String

Flags Affected

```
O D I T S Z A P C    OF: Overflow flag  TF: Trap flag AF: Aux carry
F F F F F F F F F    DF: Direction flag SF: Sign flag PF: Parity flag
    <none>           IF: Interrupt flag ZF: Zero flag CF: Carry flag
```

Legal Forms

```
STOSB
STOSW
STOSD        386+
```

Examples

```
STOSB           ;Stores AL to [EDI]
STOSW           ;Stores AX to [EDI]
STOSD           ;Stores EAX to [EDI]
REP STOSW       ;Stores EAX to [EDI] and up, for ECX repeats
```

Notes

STOS stores AL (for 8-bit store operations), AX (for 16-bit operations), or EAX (for 32-bit operations) to the location at [EDI]. For 16-bit modes, ES must contain the segment address of the destination and cannot be overridden. For 32-bit protected mode, all segments are congruent, so ES does not need to be specified explicitly. Similarly, DI or EDI must always be the destination offset.

By placing an operation repeat count (not a byte count!) in CX/ECX and preceding the mnemonic with the REP prefix, STOS can do an automatic "machine-gun" store of AL/AX/EAX into successive memory locations beginning at the initial [EDI]. After each store, DI/EDI is adjusted (see next paragraph) by either by 1 (for 8-bit store operations), 2 (for 16-bit store operations), or 4 (for 32-bit store operations), and CX/ECX is decremented by 1. Don't forget that CX/ECX counts *operations* (the number of times a data item is stored to memory), not bytes!

Adjusting means incrementing if the Direction flag is cleared (by CLD), or decrementing if the Direction flag has been set (STD).

```
r8 = AL AH BL BH CL CH DL DH      r16 = AX BX CX DX BP SP SI DI
sr = CS DS SS ES FS GS            r32 = EAX EBX ECX EDX EBP ESP ESI EDI
m8 = 8-bit memory data            m16 = 16-bit memory data
m32 = 32-bit memory data
i16 = 16-bit immediate data       i8 = 8-bit immediate data
                                  i32 = 32-bit immediate data
d8 = 8-bit signed displacement    d16 = 16-bit signed displacement
d32 = 32-bit unsigned displacement
```

SUB: Arithmetic Subtraction

Flags Affected

```
O D I T S Z A P C   OF: Overflow flag  TF: Trap flag AF: Aux carry
F F F F F F F F F   DF: Direction flag SF: Sign flag PF: Parity flag
*       * * * *     IF: Interrupt flag ZF: Zero flag CF: Carry flag
```

Legal Forms

```
SUB r8,r8
SUB m8,r8
SUB r8,m8
SUB r16,r16
SUB m16,r16
SUB r16,m16
SUB r32,r32      386+
SUB m32,r32      386+
SUB r32,m32      386+
SUB r8,i8
SUB m8,i8
SUB r16,i16
SUB m16,i16
SUB r32,i32      386+
SUB m32,i32      386+
SUB r16,i8
SUB m16,i8
SUB r32,i8       386+
SUB m32,i8       386+
SUB AL,i8
SUB AX,i16
SUB EAX,i32      386+
```

Examples

```
SUB BX,DI
SUB AX,0FFFFH   ;Uses single-byte opcode
SUB AL,42H      ;Uses single-byte opcode
SUB BP,17H
SUB ECX,DWORD [ESI+5]
SUB EAX,17
SUB WORD [BX+SI+Inset],5
SUB WORD [ES:BX],0B800H
```

Notes

SUB performs a subtraction without borrow, where the source operand is subtracted from the destination operand, and the result replaces the destination operand. If the result is negative, the Carry flag, CF, is set. Multiple-precision subtraction can be performed by following SUB with SBB (Subtract with Borrow), which takes the Carry flag into account as an arithmetic borrow.

```
r8  = AL AH BL BH CL CH DL DH        r16 = AX BX CX DX BP SP SI DI
sr  = CS DS SS ES FS GS              r32 = EAX EBX ECX EDX EBP ESP ESI EDI
m8  = 8-bit memory data              m16 = 16-bit memory data
m32 = 32-bit memory data             i8  = 8-bit immediate data
i16 = 16-bit immediate data          i32 = 32-bit immediate data
d8  = 8-bit signed displacement      d16 = 16-bit signed displacement
d32 = 32-bit unsigned displacement
```

XCHG: Exchange Operands

Flags Affected

```
O D I T S Z A P C   OF: Overflow flag  TF: Trap flag AF: Aux carry
F F F F F F F F F   DF: Direction flag SF: Sign flag PF: Parity flag
    <none>          IF: Interrupt flag ZF: Zero flag CF: Carry flag
```

Legal Forms

```
XCHG r8,r8
XCHG r8,m8
XCHG r16,r16
XCHG r16,m16
XCHG r32,r32    386+
XCHG r32,m32    386+
```

Examples

```
XCHG AL,DH
XCHG BH,BYTE [SI]
XCHG SP,BP
XCHG DX,WORD [DI]
XCHG ESI,EDI
XCHG ECX,DWORD [EBP+38]
XCHG AX,BX   ; Uses single-byte opcode
```

Notes

XCHG exchanges the contents of its two operands. This is why there is no form of XCHG for identical operands; that is, XCHG AX,AX is not a legal form because exchanging a register with itself makes no logical sense. (However, the CPU performs the internal equivalent of XCHG AX,AX as the no-operation, or NOP, instruction.)

Exchanging an operand with AX may be accomplished with a single-byte opcode, saving fetch time and code space. All good assemblers recognize these cases and optimize for them, but if you are hand-assembling inline assembly statements for some high-level language, keep the single-byte special cases in mind.

```
r8 = AL AH BL BH CL CH DL DH       r16 = AX BX CX DX BP SP SI DI
sr = CS DS SS ES FS GS             r32 = EAX EBX ECX EDX EBP ESP ESI EDI
m8 = 8-bit memory data             m16 = 16-bit memory data
m32 = 32-bit memory data           i8 = 8-bit immediate data
i16 = 16-bit immediate data        i32 = 32-bit immediate data
d8 = 8-bit signed displacement     d16 = 16-bit signed displacement
d32 = 32-bit unsigned displacement
```

XLAT: Translate Byte via Table

Flags Affected

```
O D I T S Z A P C    OF: Overflow flag  TF: Trap flag AF: Aux carry
F F F F F F F F F    DF: Direction flag SF: Sign flag PF: Parity flag
      <none>          IF: Interrupt flag ZF: Zero flag CF: Carry flag
```

Legal Forms

```
XLAT
XLATB (synonym)
```

Examples

```
XLAT
```

Notes

XLAT performs a table translation of the 8-bit value in AL. All operands are implicit. The value in AL is treated as the index into a table in memory, located at the address contained in EBX. When XLAT is executed, the value at [EBX+AL] replaces the value previously in AL.

The table located at the 32-bit address in EBX does not have to be 256 bytes in length, but a value in AL larger than the length of the table will result in an undefined value being placed in AL, with the additional possibility of a segmentation fault if the table is at the edge of the program's memory space.

```
r8 = AL AH BL BH CL CH DL DH      r16 = AX BX CX DX BP SP SI DI
sr = CS DS SS ES FS GS            r32 = EAX EBX ECX EDX EBP ESP ESI EDI
m8 = 8-bit memory data            m16 = 16-bit memory data
m32 = 32-bit memory data          i8 = 8-bit immediate data
i16 = 16-bit immediate data       i32 = 32-bit immediate data
d8 = 8-bit signed displacement    d16 = 16-bit signed displacement
d32 = 32-bit unsigned displacement
```

XOR: Exclusive Or

Flags Affected

```
O D I T S Z A P C   OF: Overflow flag  TF: Trap flag AF: Aux carry
F F F F F F F F F   DF: Direction flag SF: Sign flag PF: Parity flag
*       * * ? * *   IF: Interrupt flag ZF: Zero flag CF: Carry flag
```

Legal Forms

```
XOR r8,r8
XOR m8,r8
XOR r8,m8
XOR r16,r16
XOR m16,r16
XOR r16,m16
XOR r32,r32     386+
XOR m32,r32     386+
XOR r32,m32     386+
XOR r8,i8
XOR m8,i8
XOR r16,i16
XOR m16,i16
XOR r32,i32     386+
XOR m32,i32     386+
XOR AL,i8
XOR AX,i16
XOR EAX,i32     386+
```

Examples

```
XOR BX,DI
XOR AX,0FFFFH   ;Uses single-byte opcode
XOR AL,42H      ;Uses single-byte opcode
XOR EBX,DWORD [EDI]
XOR WORD [ES:BX],0B800H
XOR WORD [BP+SI],DX
```

Notes

XOR performs the exclusive OR logical operation between its two operands. Once the operation is complete, the result replaces the destination operand. XOR is performed on a bit-by-bit basis, such that bit 0 of the source is XORed with bit 0 of the destination, bit 1 of the source is XORed with bit 1 of the destination, and so on. The XOR operation yields a 1 if the operands are different, and a 0 if the operands are the same. Note that XOR makes the Auxiliary carry flag, AF, undefined. CF and OF are cleared to 0, and the other affected flags are set according to the operation's results.

```
r8  = AL AH BL BH CL CH DL DH      r16 = AX BX CX DX BP SP SI DI
sr  = CS DS SS ES FS GS            r32 = EAX EBX ECX EDX EBP ESP ESI EDI
m8  = 8-bit memory data            m16 = 16-bit memory data
m32 = 32-bit memory data           i8  = 8-bit immediate data
i16 = 16-bit immediate data        i32 = 32-bit immediate data
d8  = 8-bit signed displacement    d16 = 16-bit signed displacement
d32 = 32-bit unsigned displacement
```

Character Set Charts

This appendix contains summaries of two character sets commonly used on PC-compatible machines. The first is for the IBM-850 character set, which is commonly available on Linux terminal utilities like Konsole and GNOME Terminal. The second is the older "Code Page 437" set, which is basically the character set coded into the BIOS ROM of IBM-compatible PCs.

There is one glyph block for each character in each set. Each glyph block includes the following information:

- The three-digit decimal form of the character number, from 000–255. These are in the upper-right corner of each block.

- The hexadecimal form of the character number, from 00–FF. These are in the lower-left corner of each block.

- The character glyph is in the center of the block.

- For control characters from 0–31, the name of the control character (for example, NAK, DLE, CR, etc.) is printed vertically in the lower-right corner of the block.

Note that the IBM-850 character set is not loaded by default in common Linux terminal utilities, and must be specifically selected from the options or settings menu before the character set will be displayed in the terminal window. For more on this, see the section "Linux and Terminals" in Chapter 6.

ASCII & PC Extended Characters - Code Page 437

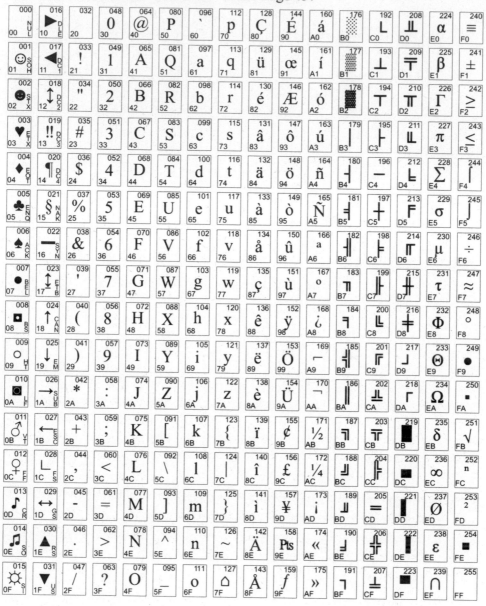

ASCII & PC Extended Characters - IBM-850

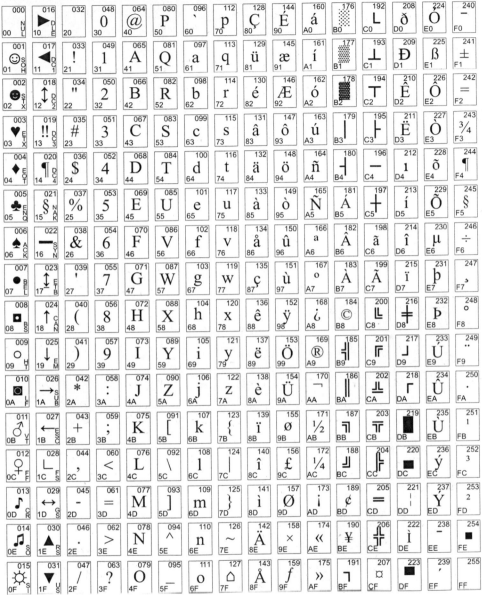

Index

Symbols and Numbers

: (colon), in label syntax, 241–242

\# (pound sign), comment delimiter in AT&T mnemonics, 474

$ (dollar sign)
deriving string location with, 246
for immediate operand in AT&T mnemonic, 471

% (percent symbol), AT&T mnemonic conventions for register names, 471

; (semicolons), as comment delimiters, 124

? (question mark), for undefined flags, 510

[ ] (brackets), for effective address of data item in memory, 210

' (single quote) or " (double quotes), in string variable syntax, 243

1-bits, looking for with TEST, 304–306

8-bit binary values, 292

8-bit computers, 57, 63

8-bit registers, 93

16-bit computers, 57

16-bit CPUs
changes in CPU architecture, 67
general-purpose registers and, 92–93
registers and, 88

16-bit registers
20-bit addresses from, 88–90
burden of, 317–318
overview of, 90–91

20-bit addresses, from 16-bit register, 88–90

32-bit computers
changes in CPU architecture, 67–68
overview of, 57

32-bit CPUs
general-purpose registers and, 92
registers and, 88

32-bit registers, 90–91

64-bit computers
changes in CPU architecture, 67–68
overview of, 57

64-bit "Long Mode"
overview of, 106–107
possibilities vs. realities, 107–108

64K, real flat mode and, 97

8080 CPUs, 79–80

8086 CPUs
memory model for, 80–82
Programmer's Reference Pocket Guide for, 231

A

A Programming Language (APL), 109, 327

AAA (Adjust AL after BCD Addition)
adding ASCII digits to screen ruler, 411–413
adjusting AAA's adjustments, 413–414
reference, 512

Abrash, Michael, 54

ADC (Arithmetic Addition with Carry), 513–514

ADD (Arithmetic Addition)
accessing register data, 207–209
adding source and destination operands, 207
multiplying by shifting and adding, 297–298
operands of, 220
reference, 515–516
speed of, 229

adders, CPU gates and, 65
addition, in hex
  multicolumn addition, 35
  single-column additions, 32–34
address pins
  on CPUs, 58
  on memory chips, 52
addresses. *See also* memory addresses
  in Assembly Language Game, 11–12
  memory addresses vs. I/O addresses, 60
  memory cells and, 52
  why stack addresses are not predictable, 429
addressing data
  confusing data and its address, 210
  effective addresses, 210
  immediate addresses, 205–207
  register addresses, 205–207
AF (auxiliary flag)
  DEC EBX instruction clearing, 217
  in EFlags register, 214
  flag rules, 510
  INC EAX instruction and, 218
AIX, 178
AMD
  dual-core CPUs, 73–74
  Intel-compatible chips, 66
  redesigning chip microarchitecture, 69
AND (Logical AND)
  anatomy of, 283
  applied to x86 instruction set, 281–282
  masking bits with, 282
  masking nybbles with, 292–293
  reference, 517–518
  TEST instruction performing, 304–306
  truth table for, 281
APL (A Programming Language), 109, 327
architecture, CPUs, 67–68
arguments, macro parameters as, 385–386
arithmetic
  addition. *See* ADD (Arithmetic Addition)
  applied mathematics and, 15–16
  CMP (Arithmetic comparison), 301–302, 524–525
  division. *See* DIV (Arithmetic division)
  machine instructions performing, 62
  multiplication. *See* multiplication
  signed values and, 221
  subtraction. *See* subtraction
arithmetic, in hex
  multicolumn addition, 35
  multicolumn subtraction, 32
  overview of, 32

single-column additions, 32–34
single-column subtraction, 35–37
ASCII
  adding ASCII digits to ruler, 411–413
  binary values converted into ASCII
    equivalents, 376–377
  character encoding in, 177–178
  character strings and, 243–244
  displaying ASCII table, 419–420
  displaying binary values as ASCII digits, 292
  translation tables, 348
.ASM files
  linking object code file to, 135–136
  as source code files, 131
assemblers
  errors, 132–133
  function of, 121
  gas (GNU assembler). *See* gas (GNU assembler)
  generating object code files from source code files, 125
  NASM. *See* NASM
  for source code files, 125–126, 131–132
  as translator program, 122
  warning messages, 134–135
assembly language
  defined, 122–123
  development process, 128–129
  translating into object code, 121
Assembly Language Game
  addresses in, 11–12
  code and data in, 10–11
  overview of, 9–10
assembly language, program dissection
  accessing Linux kernel services from stack, 254
  .bss section, 240–241
  .data section, 240
  deriving string length with EQU and $, 244–246
  designing non-trivial program, 264
  initial comment blocks, 239–240
  INT 80h access and portability myths, 262–263
  interrupts, 254–259
  labels, 241–242
  LIFO (last in, first out) stack order, 246–248
  "off by one" error, 273–277
  POP instructions, 251–253
  problem definition phase of design, 264–265
  program bones, 237–239

PUSH instructions, 249–251
returning to Linux kernel services from
    stack, 259–261
scanning buffered I/O file, 271–273
short-term storage, 253–254
software vs. hardware interrupts, 261–262
stack mechanism and, 246
stacking upside down, 248–249
starting program with pseudo-code,
    265–266
string variables, 242–244
successive refinement of, 266–271
.text section, 241
tips for, 277–278
variables for initialized data, 242
assembly language, programming models
overview of, 96–97
    protected mode flat model, 101–104
    real mode flat model, 97–99
    real mode segmented model, 99–101
assembly language, programming process
assembler errors, 132–133
    assembling program with NASM, 143–145
    assembling source code file, 131–132
    big endian and little endian and, 117–121
    binary files vs. text files, 111–112
    comments, 123–124
    converting text to code, 121
    debugging, 138–139
    defining assembly language, 122–123
    development process, 128–130
    editing program, 142–143
    editing source code file, 131
    editors for inspecting files, 112–116
    errors vs. bugs, 137–138
    example, 139–140
    files, 110–111
    fixing errors, 134
    installing software for, 140–142
    interpreting raw data, 116–117
    linker errors, 136
    linking object code file, 135–136
    linking program with ld utility, 145–146
    object code and linkers, 125–128
    overview of, 109–110
    relocatability, 128
    running program in debugger,
        147–153
    testing .EXE file, 136–137, 146–147
    warning messages, 134–135
    working directories and, 129–131
    "write-only" code, 124–125
assembly-time calculations, 244–246

AT&T mnemonic conventions
    AT&T memory reference syntax, 474–475
    examining AT&T gas source file produced
        by gcc, 471–474
    overview of, 470–471

B
Babbage, Charles, 48
backward compatibility
    CPU architecture and, 67
    virtual 86 mode for, 83
base, of number systems
    base 2. See binary numbers (base 2)
    base 8. See octal numbers (base 8)
    base 10. See decimal numbers (base 10)
    conversion between number systems, 24
    counting in base 4, 16
    dissecting base 4 numbers, 18–20
    essence of, 20
    units column, 23
Base + Displacement, protected mode
    addressing, 310
Base + Index, protected mode addressing,
    310–311
base pointer. See EBP (base pointer)
BASIC
    learning programming languages, 110
    simple programming in, 12
    strings, 394
Basic Input/Output System (BIOS)
    direct calls not allowed by protected mode,
        106
    overview of, 71
BCD (Binary Coded Values), 411–414
Berkeley Software Distribution (BSD), 156
binary 0, indicating lack of voltage on
    transistor switch, 50
Big Bux board game, 6–9
big endian, 117–121
binary 1, indicating presence of voltage on
    transistor switch, 50
binary codes, machine instructions as, 64
binary editors, for inspecting/working with
    files, 112
binary files. See also object code files
    converting text to, 121
    text files compared with, 111–112
binary numbers (base 2)
    base 10 compared with, 16
    bit shifting and, 287
    columns, 39–40
    converting decimal to, 41–42

binary numbers (base 2) *(continued)*
    converting to decimal, 40–41
    hex as shortcut for, 43–44
    overview of, 38
    reason for using, 42–43
    signed and unsigned values, 221
BIOS (Basic Input/Output System)
    direct calls not allowed by protected mode, 106
    overview of, 71
bit mapping, 279–280
bit masks, 282
bits
    chip capacity and, 50–51
    converting hex numbers to hex digits, 289–292
    defined, 50
    AND instruction, 281–282
    looking for 1-bits with TEST, 304–306
    looking for O-bits with BT (Bit Test), 306–307
    masking, 282
    measuring memory in, 54
    multiplying by shifting and adding, 295–298
    NOT instruction, 285–286
    numbering, 280
    OR instruction, 283
    overview of, 279–280
    rotating, 288–289
    shifting, 286–287
    sign bit, 221
    XOR instruction, 284–285
bitwise logical instructions
    AND instruction, 281–282
    NOT instruction, 285–286
    OR instruction, 283
    overview of, 280–281
    segment registers not responding to, 285–286
    XOR instruction, 284–285
Bless Hex Editor
    big endian vs. little endian, 117–121
    inspecting files with, 112–116
    interpreting raw data with, 116–117
blue cards, for jogging memory, 231
board games
    assembly-language programming as, 9–10
    Big Bux, 6–9
    as metaphor for assembly-language programming, 5–6
boiler.asm, 447
bookmarks, Kate, 169–170

Boolean logic
    AND instruction, 281–282
    NOT instruction, 285–286
    OR instruction, 283
    overview of, 280–281
    segment registers not responding to, 285–286
    using AND instruction for masking out bits, 282
    XOR instruction, 284–285
borrows
    multiple column subtraction in hex, 37–38
    single column subtraction in hex, 35–37
BOS (bottom of stack), Linux stack, 427
boundary values, strings not having, 394
box analogy, for computers (Nelson), 74–75
breakpoints, Insight Debugger, 198
BSD (Berkeley Software Distribution), 156
.bss section
    in assembly language program, 240–241
    data in, 348
    stack and, 248
BT (Bit Test)
    looking for O-bits with, 306–307
    reference, 519–520
buffered I/O file, 271–273
buffers
    accessing from procedures, 343
    data buffers defined in .bss section, 240–241
    defining lines in display buffer, 406
    sending virtual display buffer to Linux console, 406–407
    text video buffers, 396
bugs
    accidental recursion, 341
    vs. errors, 137–138
    flag etiquette, 341–342
    locating and identifying, 138–139
BYTE , size specifiers, 211
bytes
    counting from zero, 82–83
    CPU reading to/writing from memory, 58–59
    illustration of 1 megabyte memory system, 56
    machine instructions and, 62
    measuring memory in, 54–55
    offset address and, 89
    RAM chips and, 55
    splitting into two nybbles, 292–293
    unique numeric addresses, 57

C

C calling conventions, 446–447

C language

AT&T mnemonic conventions, 470–475

boiler.asm as framework to build on, 447

building C code with GNU, 441–443

C calling conventions, 446–447

CALL instruction to address in registers as randtest technique, 483–484

command-line arguments, 484–486

converting time_t values to formatted strings, 464–465

copying tm structure with MOVSD, 466–469

creating and opening files, 489–490

destroying a stack frame, 450

examining AT&T gas source file, 471–474

fetching time_t values from system clock, 464

fgets() and scanf() functions for data input, 456–458

fgets() function for reading text from files, 490–493

file I/O, 487

GNU and. See GNU

learning, 110

linking to C library, 445–446

Linux and, 439–440

localtime(), 465–466

passing parameters to printf(), 454–456

printf() function for formatting text, 452–453

procedures gathered into libraries, 494–501

puts() function for outputting characters, 451

rand() function for generating pseudorandom numbers, 477–482

random number generation, 475–476

saving/restoring registers, 447–448

scanf() function for entering numeric values, 458–462

setting up a stack frame, 448–450

srand() function for getting seed value for random numbers, 476–477

sscanf() function for converting strings into numbers, 487–489

strings, 394

time and date functions, 462–464

why some bits are more random than others, 482–483

C library

boiler.asm as framework to build on, 447

C calling conventions, 446–447

destroying a stack frame, 450

gathering procedures into, 494–501

overview of, 445–446

puts() function for outputting characters, 451

saving/restoring registers, 447–448

setting up a stack frame, 448–450

C preprocessor (cpp), 442

C++ compilers, 122

cache, transistor switches for, 64

calculators, hex, 28

CALL

calling procedures, 336–337

linking to C library, 445

local data and, 346

reference, 521–522

register address as randtest technique, 483–484

call gate, kernel, 255

calling procedures

calls within calls, 338–340

LoadBuff example, 336–337

stack frame and, 346

carriage returns, 115

case sensitivity

AT&T mnemonic conventions, 471

labels, 241

central processing units. See CPUs (central processing units)

CF (carry flag)

bumping into when shifting bits, 287

CLC (Clear Carry Flag), 522

in EFlags register, 215

flag rules, 510

MUL instruction and, 227–228

setting know value into, 289

STC (Set Carry Flag), 572

uses of, 301

chains of dependencies, Make utility, 189–191

character encoding, in Konsole, 177–178

character sets

APL, 327

Code Page 437, 582

IBM-850, 583

overview of, 581

character strings

as immediate data, 207

overview of, 243

character translation, 348

characters

conversion, 318

puts() for outputting in C, 451

translating with MOV or XLAT, 320–325

characters *(continued)*
  translation tables, 318–320
  translation tables instead of calculations, 325
Chinese boxes method, 329
CLC (Clear Carry Flag), 523
CLD (Clear Direction Flag), 524
clocking rates, CPUs and, 68
CMP (Arithmetic comparison)
  for comparing values, 301–302
  reference, 525–526
code
  converting text to, 121
  costs of dead code, 367
  game steps as, 11
  procedures as boxes for, 329–336
Code Page 437 character set, 582
code reuse
  linkers and, 127
  procedures and, 367–368
code segment registers. *See* CS (code segment) registers
columns
  in binary system, 39–40
  in hexadecimal system, 26
  in number systems generally, 23–24
  in octal system, 23–24
command-line arguments
  C language, 484–486
  examining stack with, 424
  setting with Insight, 429–430
comment blocks, 123
comments
  adding comment headers to procedures, 370–371
  critical nature of, 124
  initial comment block in programs, 239–240
  overview of, 123
  "write-only" code and, 124–125
COMPARE instructions, comparing data with, 11
compatibility
  CPU architecture and, 67
  virtual 86 mode for backward compatibility, 83
compilers
  vs. assemblers, 122
  conditional compilation, 263
  function of, 121
  gcc. *See* gcc (GNU C compiler)
complexity, managing
  breaking actions down into smaller actions, 328–329

macros. *See* macros
  overview of, 327–328
  procedures. *See* procedures
Computer Lib/Dream Machines (Nelson), 74–75
computer programs. *See also* assembly language, programming process
  as laundry list, 1–2
  as series of program instructions, 9
  as table of binary machine instructions, 63–64
computers
  8-bit, 16-bit, 32-bit, and 64-bit, 57, 63, 67–68
  RAX computer in high school class, 45–46
  thinking like humans, 4
conditional compilation, 263
conditional jumps
  JNZ (Jump If Not Zero), 218
  out of range, 354
  overview of, 299–300
conditional string instructions, SCASB as, 435
console, Linux
  control cautions, 377–378
  cursor control, 371–377
  sending virtual display buffer to, 406–407
console applications
  Linux, 176–177
  Windows OSs, 102
Console view, Insight
  setting command-line arguments, 429–430
  viewing EFlag values with, 216–217
  viewing state of flags with, 228
constant data, placing in procedure definitions, 348–350
COSMAC ELF, 46–47
count register, 286
<count> operand, for shifting bits, 286–287
CP/M operating system, 70, 79–82
cpp (C preprocessor), 442
CPUs (central processing units)
  8080, 79–80
  8086, 80–82
  architectures, 67–68
  changing the course of fetch and execute, 65–66
  data bus and, 59–60
  fetch and execute process, 63–64
  improvements to, 68
  machine instructions and, 62
  multiple CPU systems, 73–74
  multitasking and, 72

number of transistors switches on, 64–65

overview of, 57–58

program controlling, 61

recognizing source strings and destination strings, 395

register data shored on internal registers, 207–209

registers, 60–61

talking to memory system, 58–59

what it does vs. how it does it, 66–67

CS (code segment) registers

8086/8088 CPUs, 82

machine instructions stored in, 95

overview of, 91

ctime(), in C, 464–465

Ctrl+F (search), 171

Ctrl+R (replace), 172

current code segment, 95

cursor control

cautions regarding, 377–378

in Linux console, 371–377

cursor movement, Kate editing controls, 169

D

data

addresses for, 11

definitions of data items in .data section of program, 240

local, 346–347

numeric in Assembly Language Game, 11

placing constant data in procedure definitions, 348–350

procedures and, 342–343

storage in board games, 5, 10–11

storing data to discontinuous strings, 419–424

data, as operands

confusing data and its address, 210

immediate data, 205–207

memory data, 209–210

register data, 207–209

data bus, CPU/device communication over, 59–60

data definition directives, 242

Data Display Debugger (DDD), 194

data input, in C

fgets() and scanf() functions for, 456–458

scanf() function for entering numeric values, 458–462

data items, accessing from procedures, 343

data output, in C

printf() function for formatting text output, 452–453

puts() function for outputting characters, 451

data pins, on memory chips, 52

.data section

in assembly language program, 240

stack and, 248

data segment (DS) register, 91

DB (Define Byte) directive, 242

DD (Define Double) directive, 242, 244

DDD (Data Display Debugger), 194

dead code, costs of, 367

DEBUG, 139

debuggers

debugging source code, 128

Gdb. See Gdb debugger

Insight Debugger. See Insight Debugger

installing, 140

KDbg. See KDbg

locating and identifying bugs, 138–139

running program in, 147–153

DEC (Decrement operand)

altering data with, 11

conditional jumps and, 299

decrementing operand by one, 215–216

ECX register and, 408–409

as means of getting negative numbers, 221–222

reference, 527

DEC (Digital Equipment Corporation), 20

decimal numbers (base 10)

conversion to, 24

converting binary to, 40–41

converting hex to, 28–29, 31

converting to binary, 41–42

converting to hex, 29–32

hex calculators, 28

hex equivalents, 25–27

human numbering system based on 10 fingers (digits) of hand, 16

octal equivalents, 22

Registers view displaying register value as, 223–224

Delphi

file processing in, 121

learning, 110

visual programming in, 12

dependencies
    chains of, 189–191
    Make utility and, 187–188
destination addresses, storing data to
    discontinuous strings, 419
destination operand
    immediate data and, 206
    machine instructions and, 205
    sum of source and destination operands, 207
destination strings
    putting display buffer address into EDI, 403
    types of strings in x86, 395
detours, 8, 11
development process
    assembler errors, 132–133
    assembler warning messages, 134–135
    assembling source code file, 131–132
    debuggers and, 138–139
    editing source code file, 131
    errors vs. bugs, 137–138
    linker errors, 136
    linking object code file, 135–136
    overview of, 128–130
    testing .EXE file, 136–137
    working directories and, 129–131
DF (direction flag)
    CLD (Clear Direction Flag), 523
    in EFlags register, 214
    overlapping blocks moves and, 416–418
    STD (Set direction flag), 573
    STOSB instruction and, 405–406
    uses of, 301
Difference Engine (Babbage), 48
Digital Equipment Corporation (DEC), 20
Digits tables, using lookup tables, 293–295
DIMMs (Dual Inline Memory Modules), 56
directories
    creating and using project directories in
        Kate, 173–175
    working directories in development
        process, 129–131
discontinuous strings, storing data to,
    419–424
disks, Kate file management and, 166–167
displacements, protected mode, 309–310
displays. See screens; virtual text display
DIV (Arithmetic division)
    as implicit operand, 226
    SHR (Shift Right) compared with, 209
    slowness of, 229–230
    unsigned division with, 228–229
    reference, 528

DLLs (dynamic link libraries), 78
DOS
    calling procedures within procedures, 340
    overview of, 71
    real mode segmented model and, 78, 99
    Unix and, 156
double word
    DD directive, 242, 244
    measuring memory in, 54
DS (data segment) register, 91
Dual Inline Memory Modules (DIMMs), 56
dual-core CPUs, 73–74
DumpChar procedures, 347–348
DumpLin, hex dump line variable, 347–348
Dunn, Jim, 329
DW (Define Word) directive, 242, 244
DWORD, size specifiers, 211
dynamic link libraries (DLLs), 78

E
EAX register, viewing in Register view,
    206–207
EBP (base pointer)
    accessing command-line arguments, 485
    copying ESP into, 436–438
    destroying stack frame in C, 450
    setting up stack frame in C, 448–450
Eclipse IDE, for Linux, 157
ECX register
    decrementing when using string
        instructions, 407–408
    decrementing with loop instructions,
        408–409
    jumping when ECX goes to O, 421
EDI (extended destination index)
    for destination strings, 395
    DF (direction flag) for
        incrementing/decrementing, 405
    putting display buffer address into, 403
editing
    example program, 142–143
    source code files, 131
editing controls, in Kate, 168–172
editors
    gedit, 131, 140, 142–143
    hex editors, 112
    for inspecting files, 112–116
    Kate. See Kate text editor
effective address
    calculations, 308–309
    of data item in memory, 210
    LEA instruction, 315–316, 537

EFlags register
  bumping into Carry flag when shifting bits, 287
  descriptions of flags in, 212, 214–215
  illustration of, 213
  overview of, 212
  reference documentation for, 232
  watching with Register view, 216–218
EIP. *See* IP (instruction pointer)
electricity, relay switches and, 48
EMACS editor, 440
end of line markers. *See* EOL (end of line) markers
EOL (end of line) markers
  comment delimiters, 124
  defining lines in display buffer, 406
  table of EOL characters, 349
EQU (equate) directive
  changing text display buffer, 402
  deriving string length with, 244–246
equal operator
  arithmetic tests after CMP instruction, 305
  jumps based on, 302
errors
  adding error handling to program, 270–273
  assemblers, 132–133
  vs. bugs, 137–138
  dividing by zero and, 229
  jump out of range, 354
  linkers, 136
  "off by one" error, 273–277
ES (extra segment) register, 91
ESC character, 375
escape sequences
  Konsole, 377–378
  Linux console controlled by, 375–376
  terminal control with, 183–184
ESP (stack pointer)
  anatomy of Linux stack, 427
  destroying stack frame in C, 450
  overview of, 247–248
  popping the stack vs. addressing, 436–438
  setting up stack frame in C, 448–450
  for source strings, 395
.EXE (executable) files
  linking libraries into programs, 366–367
  linking object code files to, 125–128
  testing, 136–137, 146–147
expanding macros, 379
expansion slots, 60
exporting file, as HTML, 167
extended destination index. *See* EDI (extended destination index)

EXTERN. *See* external procedures
external procedures
  declaring, 356–357
  mechanics of, 357–361
external references, object modules, 127
extra segment (ES) register, 91

F
far jumps, 354
fast block copies
  MOVSB instructions for, 414–416
  overlapping blocks moves, 416–418
fetch and execute process, CPUs and, 63–64
fgets(), C language
  for data input, 457–458
  for reading text from files, 490–493
field-effect transistors, 49
file I/O, in C
  creating and opening files, 489–490
  fgets() for reading text from files, 490–493
  overview of, 487
  sscanf() for converting strings into numbers, 487–489
file management, Kate, 164–167
  overview of, 164–165
  working with, 165–167
files
  binary vs. text, 111–112
  bookmarking, 169
  converting text to code, 121
  editors for inspecting files, 112–116
  Kate templates for, 161
  Make utility for checking updates, 189
  processing in programming, 110–111
  Unix, 178–180
Filesystem Browser, in Kate, 164–165
filters
  hexdump1.asm program as, 289–292
  text filters, 182–183, 278
firmware, 71
fixing errors, 134
flags
  changing program execution, 218–220
  CMP instructions for comparing values, 301–302
  conditional jumps and, 299–300
  CPU registers, 66
  descriptions of flags in EFlags register, 212, 214–215
  EFlags register. *See* EFlags register
  etiquette bug, 341–342

flags *(continued)*
  etiquette for instructions, 215–216
  illustration of EFlags register, 213
  instruction flag summaries, 509–510
  overview of, 212
  reference documentation for, 232
  register, 96
  uses of, 301
  watching with Register view, 216–218
folders, Kate file management, 166
`fopen()`, creating/opening files in C,
    489–490
formatting text, in C language, 452–453
FS register, 91

G
gas (GNU assembler)
  assembling C and, 441, 443
  examining AT&T gas source file produced
      by gcc, 471–474
  reasons for not using, 444–445
gates, CPU switches, 64–65
gcc (GNU C compiler)
  applied to assembly work, 443–444
  AT&T mnemonic conventions and,
      470–471
  building code in C, 441–443
  examining AT&T gas source file produced
      by, 471–474
  overview of, 441
Gdb debugger
  limitations of, 194
  local labels and, 352
  overview of, 139–140
  running program in, 147–153
  viewing Eflag values with, 216–217
gedit
  editing program in, 142–143
  as Linux text editor, 131
  preinstalled in Ubuntu Linux, 140
general-purpose registers
  C calling conventions and, 447
  CPUs and, 91–93
  procedures using, 344
`gets()`, in C, 456–457
gigabits (G), of memory, 51
gigabytes (GB), of memory, 56
glibc
  accessing command-line arguments, 485
  C calling conventions, 446–447
  copying `tm` structure with `MOVSD`,
      466–469

`ctime()`, 464–465
`fgets()`, 457–458, 490–493
`fopen()`, 489–490
`fprintf()`, 493–494
`gets()`, 456–457
linking to, 446
`localtime()`, 465–466
overview of, 445
`printf()`, 452–456
`puts()`, 451
`rand()`, 477–482
`scanf()`, 458–462
`srand()`, 476–477
`sscanf()`, 487–489
`time_t` values, 463–464
global data, 342
global labels
  defined, 351–352
  style syntax for, 353
global procedures
  declaring, 356–357
  mechanics of, 361–365
Gnome Application Installer, 140
GNOME Terminal, 176
GNU
  assembler. *See* gas (GNU assembler)
  gcc (GNU C compiler), 441
  gcc applied to assembly work, 443–444
  overview of, 440–441
  process of building C code, 441–443
  reasons for not using gas assembler,
      444–445
GNU Public License (GPL), 440–441
GPL (GNU Public License), 440–441
greater than operator, 302, 303
greater than or equal to operator, 302
GS register, 91
GUI apps, Linux, 185–186

H
hardware interrupts, 261–262
headers, adding comment headers to
    procedures, 370–371
heap, allocating variables on fly, 248
hex calculators, 28
hexadecimal editors, 112
hexadecimal numbers (base 16)
  arithmetic in, 32
  converting decimal to, 29–32
  converting hex numbers to hex digits with
      hexdump1 program, 289–292
  converting to decimal, 28–29, 31

counting in, 25–26
decimal compared with, 16
hex as shortcut for binary, 43–44
hex calculators, 28
multicolumn addition, 35
multicolumn subtraction, 37–38
overview of, 24–25
Registers view displaying register value as, 223–224
single-column additions, 32–34
single-column subtraction, 35–37
hexdump1.asm program, 289–292
hexdump2.asm program, 329
HexStr, 295–298
HTML, exporting file as, 167

I

IA-32, CPU architecture, 68
IBM-850
character encoding scheme, 178–179
character set, 583
IDEs (interactive development environments)
Eclipse and KDevelop, 157
Kate. See Kate text editor
provided by Turbo Pascal, 156
IF (interrupt flag)
DEC and INC instructions not effecting, 218
in EFlags register, 214
flag rules, 510
IF statements, in conditional compilation, 263
immediate addressing, 205–207
immediate data
accessing, 205–207
as operand, 205
implicit operands
DIV, 229
MUL, 227
overview of, 225–226
IMUL (signed integer multiplication)
MUL instruction compared with, 410–411
reference, 527–528
INC (Increment operand)
altering data with, 11
incrementing operand by one, 215–216
reference, 529
include files
macro libraries as, 388–389
macros compared to, 379

Index x Scale + Displacement, protected mode addressing, 312–313
initial comment block, in assembly language program, 239–240
initialized data, variables for, 242
in-line assembly, compilers and, 122
inner loop, closing, 421–422
Insight Debugger
Console view, 216–217
Kill command, 204
Memory view, 199–200, 430–432
overview of, 194–195
Registers view, 198–199
running, 195
setting command-line arguments with, 429–430
single-stepping REP string instructions with Insight, 418–419
source code window, 197
viewing EAX register in Register view, 206–207
watching flags with Register view, 216–218
windows of, 195–197
instruction pointer. See IP (instruction pointer)
instructions
comments and, 123–124
mnemonics and operands as, 123
INT (software interrupt)
reference, 530
returning from Linux kernel services from stack, 259–261
software vs. hardware interrupts, 261–262
using Linux kernel services via INT 80h, 254–259
INT 80h
access and portability myths, 262–263
accessing kernel services from stack, 254–259
exiting program via, 260–261
Intel
dual-core CPUs, 73–74
memory system, 54–55
redesigning chip microarchitecture, 69
role in developing CPU, 58
x86 chips, 66
interactive development environments. See IDEs (interactive development environments)
interrupt vector table, 255–256
interrupt vectors
defined, 255
riding into Linux, 258

interrupts
  IRET (return from interrupt), 260, 531
  returning from Linux kernel services from stack, 259–261
  software. See INT (software interrupt)
  software vs. hardware, 261–262
  using Linux kernel services via INT 80h, 254–259
invoking macros, 386–387
I/O (input/output), in C
  data input. See data input, in C
  data output. See data output, in C
  file I/O. See file I/O, in C
I/O (input/output), scanning buffered I/O file, 271–273
I/O addresses, of peripheral devices, 60
I/O redirection
  filters and, 183
  overview of, 180–182
  printing standard input data in hex format, 335
IP (instruction pointer)
  changing the course of fetch and execute, 66
  CPU register for, 63
  overview of, 95–96
IRET (return from interrupt), 260, 531

J

J? (Jump on condition), 532–533
JA (Jump if Above), 303
JCXZ (Jump if CX=0), 421, 534
JECXZ (Jump if ECX=0), 535
JG (Jump if Greater), 303
JLE (Jump if Less than or Equal), 302
JMP (Unconditional jump), 222
  format for unconditional jumps, 300–301
  local labels and, 353
  reference, 536
  unconditional jumps, 298
JNG (Jump if Not Greater than), 302
JNZ (Jump If Not Zero), 218–219, 300–301
jump instructions
  categories of, 302–303
  conditional, 218–219, 299–300
  greater than vs. above, 303
  jump or don't jump, 66
  jumping on absence of a condition, 300–301
  local labels and, 353
  mnemonics and synonyms for, 304
  short, near, and far jumps, 354–355
  unconditional, 298
JZ (Jump if Zero), 299–300

K

Kate text editor
  adding items to toolbar, 167–168
  configuring, 160–162
  creating and using project directories, 173–175
  creating sandbox session in, 203
  editing controls, 168–172
  editing example program, 142
  file management, 164–167
  installing, 157–158
  invoking Make from, 191–193
  launching, 158–160
  overview of, 157
  sessions, 162–163
  terminal window in, 173
  using while programming, 172–175
  window focus when working with, 175
KDbg
  Insight Debugger compared with, 198
  installing, 141–142
  limitations of, 194
  running program in debugger, 147–153
KDevelop, 157
kernel
  accessing kernel services from stack, 254
  call gate, 255
  Linux, 73
  returning to kernel services stack from, 259–261
kernel space, Linux, 73
Kill command, Insight Debugger, 204
kilobits (K), of memory, 51
Konsole
  adding key binding to, 192–193
  character encoding in, 177–179
  escape sequences, 184, 377–378
  overview of, 143
KWrite editor, 159

L

labels
  descriptive names of programs, 218–219
  duplicating use of, 350
  forcing local label access, 353
  global, 351
  local, 350–353
  overview of, 241–242
  representing addresses, 246
  in .text section of program, 241

laundry list
  computer program as, 1–2
  tests in, 2–3
ld linker
  building code in C and, 443
  linking program with, 145–146
LEA (Load Effective Address), 315–316, 537
lease significant byte (LSB), of BX register,
      208
least significant bit, bit numbering, 280
legend, 6–7
length indicators, strings not having in
      assembly language, 394
less than operator, 302
less than or equal to operator, 302
libraries
  building external procedure library, 355
  C language, 439–440
  dangers of too many procedures and too
      many libraries, 366–367
  global data and, 342
  linking into programs, 365–367
  Linux C library. *See* glibc
  macro libraries as include files, 388–389
line feeds, 115
lines, defining in display buffer, 406
linkers. *See also* ld linker
  building code in C and, 443
  debugging information and, 128
  errors, 136
  function of, 127
  linking libraries into programs, 366–367
  linking program, 145–146
  object code to executable, 125–127,
      135–136
  preinstalled, 140
  relocatability and, 128
Linux
  big endian vs. little endian, 120
  development of, 156
  GNU. *See* GNU
  GUI apps for, 185
  memory model for 32-bit Linux, 78
  OSs (operating systems), 73
Linux console
  control cautions, 377–378
  cursor control, 371–377
  sending virtual display buffer to, 406–407
  text console, 102
  tools, 176–177
Linux kernel services
  accessing from stack, 254
  returning to stack from, 259–261

Linux tools
  adding items to Kate toolbar, 167–168
  chains of dependencies, 189–191
  character encoding in Konsole, 177–178
  configuring Kate, 160–162
  console applications, 176–177
  dependencies, 187–188
  file updates and, 189
  GUI apps, 185–186
  Insight Debugger, 194–195
  installing Kate, 157–158
  invoking Make from Kate, 191–193
  I/O redirection, 180–182
  Kate editing controls, 168–172
  Kate file management, 164–167
  Kate sessions, 162–163
  Kate text editor, 157
  launching Kate, 158–160
  Make utility, 186–187
  overview of, 156–157
  running Insight Debugger, 195, 197–200
  standard Unix files, 178–180
  terminal control with escape sequences,
      183–184
  terminals, 176
  text filters, 182–183
  touch command for forcing builds,
      193–194
  using Kate while programming, 172–175
  windows of Insight Debugger, 195–197
LinuxAsmTools, 378
little endian, 117–121, 206
local data
  overview of, 342
  procedures and, 346–347
local labels
  forcing local label access, 353
  jump lengths and, 350–353
  label reuse and, 350
  within macros, 387–388
  style syntax for, 353
localtime(), in, 465–466
logic
  computers and humans, 4
  machine instructions performing logical
      operations, 62
logical AND. *See* AND (Logical AND)
logical Exclusive OR (XOR), 284–285,
      579–580
logical NOT, 285–286, 549
logical OR, 283, 550–551
lookup tables, 293–295
LOOP (Loop until CX/ECX=0)

LOOP (Loop until CX/ECX=0) *(continued)*
  decrementing EXC register, 408–409
  displaying ruler on screen, 409
  reference, 538–539
LOOPNZ/LOOPNE (Loop while CX/ECX>0
  and ZF=0), 540
LOOPNZ/LOOPNE (Loop while CX/ECX>0
  and ZF=1), 541
loops
  closing inner loop, 421–422
  closing outer loop, 422–423
  decrementing EXC register, 408–409
  nested instruction loops, 420–421
  repeating instructions with, 219–220
  scanning a buffer and, 272
LSB (lease significant byte), of BX register,
  208

M

Mac OS/X, 156
machine instructions
  changing the course of fetch and execute,
    65–66
  computer programs as table of binary
    machine instructions, 63–64
  CPU controlled by, 62
  mnemonics for, 123
  overview of, 201
  program translators, 121
  as steps, 66
  storing in CS (code segment) registers,
    95
machine instructions (x86)
  confusing data and its address, 210
  DIV, 228–229
  EFlags register, 212–215
  flags changing program execution,
    218–220
  flags reference, 232
  immediate data and immediate addressing,
    205–207
  implicit operands, 225–226
  INC and DEC, 215–216
  list of, 507–509
  memory data, 209–210
  minimal NASM program for use with
    sandbox, 202–204
  MOVSX , 224–225
  MUL, 226–228
  NEG , 233–236
  negative numbers and, 221–224
  real mode and, 211–212
  reference, 230–232
  register data and register addressing,
    207–209
  sandbox for experimenting with, 201–202
  signed and unsigned values, 221
  size of memory data, 211
  slowness of MUL and DIV, 229–230
  source and destination operands, 205
  watching flags with Insight's Register view,
    216–218
macros
  defining with parameters, 385–386
  invoking, 386–387
  local labels within, 387–388
  macro libraries as include files, 388–389
  mechanics of defining, 379–385
  overview of, 378–379
  procedures compared to, 379–385,
    389–391
maintainability, of procedures, 367–368
Make utility
  chains of dependencies, 189–191
  dependencies, 187–188
  file updates, 189
  invoking from Kate, 191–193
  overview of, 186–187
  touch command for forcing builds,
    193–194
makefiles
  defined, 187
  dependencies, 187–188
  hexdump2.asm program and, 335
  for sandbox, 203
masking
  bits, 282
  nybbles, 292–293
MASM, 386
mass storage, as serial-access device,
  52
mathematics, emphasis on applied
  mathematics in schools, 15–16
megabits (M), of memory, 51
megabytes (MB), of memory, 56, 82–83
memory
  defined, 48
  principle of staying out of memory
    (Abrash), 54
  switches as on/off memory device,
    47–48
  terms for, 85
  units of measurement, 54–55
memory access time, memory chips,
  53–54

memory addresses
  20-bit addresses, 88–90
  8080 CPU and, 79–80
  AT&T memory reference syntax,
    474–475
  I/O addresses compared to, 60
  as key to assembly language, 12–13
  in megabytes, 82–83
  memory models and, 77–79
  protected mode rules for, 307–308
  protected mode schemes for, 309
  real mode and, 211–212
  segment address compared with, 87
memory cells
  addresses, 52
  silicon chip capacity and, 51
  transistor switches and, 49–50
memory chips
  access time, 53–54
  addresses, 52
  bit capacity of, 51
  bits per address, 55
  CPU (central processing unit). See CPUs
    (central processing units)
  DIMMs (Dual Inline Memory Modules), 56
  function in computers, 46–47
  Intel memory system, 54–55
  peripherals and, 59–60
  redesigning chip microarchitecture, 69
  summary of, 57
memory data
  as operand, 205
  overview of, 209–210
  size of, 211
memory models
  64-bit "Long Mode", 106–108
  8080 CPU and, 79–80
  8086 CPU and, 80–82
  blinders, 83–85
  nature of megabytes in real mode memory,
    82–83
  overview of, 77–79
  protected mode flat model, 101–104
  real mode flat model, 97–99
  real mode segmented model, 99–101
  virtual 86 mode for backward
    compatibility, 83
memory system
  access methods, 57
  CPU communication with, 58–59
  illustration of 1 megabyte memory system,
    56
  Intel, 54–55

Memory view, Insight Debugger, 199–200,
  430–432
memory-mapped video, not allowed by
  protected mode, 104–105
microarchitecture, CPUs, 68
mnemonics
  AT&T. See AT&T mnemonic conventions
  for jump instructions, 304
  machine instructions and, 123
modules
  .asm files as, 355
  external, 357–359
  object modules. See object code files
most significant byte (MSB), of BX register,
  208
motherboard, peripherals on, 60
MOV (Move/copy right operand into left
  operand)
  for moving data, 204
  reference, 542–543
  source and destination operands, 205
  speed of, 229
  translating characters with MOV or XLAT,
    320–325
MOVE instructions, moving data into storage,
  11
MOVS (Move string)
  reference, 544–545
  sizes of, 414–415
MOVSB
  DF and overlapping block moves, 416–418
  for fast block copies, 414–416
  REP MOVSB , 418–419
  types of MOVS instructions, 414
  WrtLn procedure demonstrating, 415–416
MOVSD, 415, 466–469
MOVSW, 415
MOVSX, 224–225, 547
MSB (most significant byte), of BX register,
  208
MS-DOS, 99. See also DOS
MUL (Unsigned integer multiplication)
  CF (carry flag) and, 227–228
  as implicit operand, 226
  IMUL compared with, 410–411
  overview of, 226–227
  reference, 547–548
  slowness of MUL and DIV, 229–230
multibyte values, big endian and little
  endian, 117–121
multicolumn arithmetic, in hex
  addition, 35
  subtraction, 37–38

multiplication
  IMUL (signed integer multiplication),
    410–411, 527–528
  MUL, see MUL (Unsigned integer
    multiplication)
  by shifting and adding, 295–298
multitasking
  Linux and, 73
  Windows 95 (preemptive), 71–72

N

nanoseconds, of memory access time, 53–54
NASM
  assembling programs, 143–145, 443
  assembling source code files, 131–132
  defining data within a procedure, 349
  defining macros with parameters, 386
  error messages, 133
  as a filter, 182–183
  forcing local label access, 353
  installing, 140–141
  Kate editor mode and, 160
  labels, 219
  minimal program for use with sandbox,
    202–204
  one step assembly and, 125
  opcodes for short jumps, 354–355
  size specifier with, 220
ncurses, Unix C library for managing
  console, 378
near jumps, 354
NEG (Negate)
  calculating two's complement, 223
  reference, 233–236, 549
negative numbers, 221–224
  signed values, 221
  two's complement for expressing, 222–223
Nelson, Ted, 74
nested instruction loops, 420–421
nested procedures, recursion and, 340
network port, as peripheral device, 58–59
New Math, 15
Newlines procedure, 349–350
non-trivial programs, designing, 264
NOP (No operation), 550
NOT (Logical Not), 285–286, 551
not equal operator, 302
not greater than operator, 302
not greater than or equal to operator, 302
not less than operator, 302
notes, saving programming notes, 277
null-terminated strings, 432

numbering bits, 280
numbers
  in assembly-language programming, 9
  base 2. *See* binary numbers (base 2)
  base 4, 16, 18–20
  base 8. *See* octal numbers (base 8)
  base 10. *See* decimal numbers (base 10)
  base 16. *See* hexadecimal numbers (base 16)
  essence of a number base, 20
  sscanf() for converting strings into
    numbers, 487–489
numeric values
  scanf() for entering in C, 458–462
  singed and unsigned, 221
nybbles
  bytes and, 54
  shifting high nybble into low nybble, 293
  splitting two bytes into, 292–293

O

O-bits, looking for with BT (Bit Test),
  306–307
object code files
  as intermediate step between source code
    and executable code, 125
  linkers and, 135–136
  linking to executable, 128–129
  program translators and, 121
object modules. *See* object code files
octal numbers (base 8)
  counting in, 21–22
  DEC (Digital Equipment Corporation) and,
    20–21
OF (overflow flag)
  DEC EBX instruction clearing, 217
  in EFlags register, 212
  flag rules, 510
  uses of, 301
"off by one" error, 273–277
offset addresses
  general-purpose registers for, 91
  segments and, 89–90
one's complement, see NOT (Logical Not)
operands
  <count>, 286–287
  ADD. *See* ADD (Arithmetic Addition)
  assembly language, 123
  AT&T mnemonic conventions for, 471
  data as. *See* data, as operands
  DEC. *See* DEC (Decrement operand)
  DIV, 229
  implicit and explicit, 225–226

INC. *See* INC (Increment operand)
incrementing/decrementing, 215–216
machine instructions and, 204
MOV. *See* MOV (move/copy right operand into left operand)
MUL, 227
POP. *See* POP (Pop top of stack into operand)
PUSH . *See* PUSH (Push operand onto top of stack)
source and destination operands, 205–207
symbols for, 234–235
syntax for instruction operands, 509
XCHG , 209, 577
OR (Logical OR), 283, 552–553
OSs (operating systems)
multiple CPU systems, 73–74
multitasking and, 71–72
as overall manager, 70
ROM (read-only memory) and, 71
UNIX/Linux, 73
outer loop, closing, 422–423
overflow flag. *See* OF (overflow flag)
Owens, Jeff, 378

P
package managers, 140
paragraph boundaries, 85–86
paragraphs, as measure of memory, 85
parameters, defining macros, 385–386
parameters, in C
passing to printf(), 454–456
passing to procedures, 446
parity flag. *See* PF (parity flag)
Pascal
compilers, 122
learning, 110
simple programming in, 12
strings, 394
treating numbers symbolically, 9
passing a pointer, C jargon, 454
PC DOS operating system, 71. *See also* DOS
peripherals
CPU and, 58
data bus and, 59–60
registers and, 61
Perl, 110
PF (parity flag)
DEC EBX instruction clearing, 217
in EFlags register, 214–215
flag rules, 510
INC EAX instruction and, 218

Plugin Manager, Kate, 161
POP (Pop top of stack into operand)
overview of, 251–253
reference, 554
saving caller's register values and, 344
pop instructions
vs. addressing stack, 436–438
retrieving from stack, 247–248
POPA/POPAD (Pop all GP registers), 251–253, 344–345, 555
POPF (Pop top of stack into 16-bit flags), 251–253, 556
POPFD (Pop top of stack into EFlags), 251–253, 557
porting, from CPU 8080 to 8086, 80–82
ports, protected mode and, 105–106
power consumption, CPUs and, 68
preemptive multitasking, in Windows 95, 71–72
prefixes
REP, 403
REPNE vs. REPE, 435–436
printf(), C language
for formatting text, 452–453
passing parameters to, 454–456
for writing text to files, 493–494
printing, Kate file management and, 167
problem definition, designing non-trivial program, 264–265
PROCEDURE, as detour in Assembly Language Game, 11
procedures, see also RET (Return from procedure). *See also* CALL
addresses for, 11
art of crafting, 367
as boxes for code, 329–336
calling, 336–337
calls within calls, 338–340
cursor control in Linux console, 371–375
dangers of accidental recursion, 340–341
dangers of too many procedures and too many libraries, 366–367
data and, 342–343
deciding what should be a procedure, 368–369
DumpLin and DumpChar, 347–348
external library for, 355
flag etiquette bug and, 341–342
forcing local label access, 353
global and external declarations, 356–357
linking libraries into programs, 365–367
local data and, 346–347
local labels and jump lengths, 350–353

procedures, see also RET (Return from procedure). *See also* CALL *(continued)*
  macros compared to, 379–385, 389–391
  maintainability and reuse, 367–368
  mechanics of external, 357–361
  mechanics of global, 361–365
  placing constant data in procedure definitions, 348–350
  returning, 337–338
  saving caller's register values, 343–346
  short, near, and far jumps, 354–355
  size requirements and, 369
  structure of, 337–338
procedures, in C
  C calling conventions, 446–447
  gathering into C libraries, 494–501
processors. *See* CPUs (central processing units)
program counters, addresses and, 11–12
Program Instructions, 9
program segment prefix (PSP), 79, 98
program translators, 121
Programmer's Reference Pocket Guide, 231
programming languages, 109–110
programs/programming. *See* assembly language, programming process; computer programs
project directories, creating and using in Kate, 173–175
protected mode
  Base + Displacement addressing, 310
  Base + Index addressing, 310–311
  displacements, 309–310
  effective address calculations, 308–309
  illustration of protected-mode OS, 74
  Index x Scale + Displacement addressing, 312–313
  other addressing schemes, 313–315
  rules for memory addressing, 307–308
  Windows OSs and, 71–72
protected mode flat model, 78, 101–104
protected mode, what not allowed
  direct calls into BIOS, 106
  direct-access to port hardware, 105–106
  memory-mapped video, 104–105
  overview of, 104
pseudo-code
  hexdump2.asm program as, 335–336
  "off by one" error, 273–277
  starting program with, 265–266
  successive refinement of, 266–271

pseudorandom numbers, in C
  CALL instruction to address in registers as randtest technique, 483–484
  explanation of why some bits are more random than others, 482–483
  overview of, 475–476
  rand() function for generating, 477–482
  srand() function for getting seed value, 476–477
PSP (program segment prefix), 79, 98
PUSH (Push operand onto top of stack)
  local data and, 346
  overview of, 249–250
  reference, 558
  saving caller's register values with, 344
push instructions
  adding to stack, 247–248
  overview of, 249–251
PUSHA (Push all 16-bit GP registers), 249–250, 559
PUSHAD (Push all 32-bit GP registers)
  overview of, 249–250
  reference, 560
  saving caller's register values with, 344–345
PUSHF (Push 16-bit flags onto stack), 249–250, 561
PUSHFD (Push 32-bit EFlags onto stack), 249–250, 562
puts(), C language, 451
Python, 9

Q

quad word, for measuring memory, 54

R

RAM (random-access memory)
  chip capacity, 51
  illustration of RAM chip, 53
  memory system on, 55
  translating virtual address into physical memory, 425
rand(), C language, 477–482
random access, 52–53
random numbers. *See* pseudorandom numbers, in C
random-access memory. *See* RAM (random-access memory)
randtest.asm, 477–482
raw data, interpreting, 116–117
RAX computer, 45–46

RCL (Rotate Carry Left), 288–289
RCR (Rotate Carry Right), 288–289
read-only memory (ROM), 71
real mode
  memory, 82
  memory addresses and, 211–212
real mode flat model
  overview of, 78
  programming model for x86 CPU, 97–99
real mode segmented model
  megabytes of addressable memory, 82–83
  overview of, 78, 99–101
  paragraph boundaries and, 86
  seeing megabytes of memory through
      blinders, 83–85
  segments in, 85
recursion, 340, 341
reference documentation
  for beginners, 231–232
  for flags, 232
  overview of, 230–231
register addressing
  accessing register data, 207–209
  overview of, 205–207
register data
  as operand, 205
  overview of, 207–209
register halves, 8-bit registers, 93–95
registers
  16-bit and 32-bit, 90–91
  20-bit addresses from 16-bit registers, 88–90
  burden of 16-bit registers, 317–318
  CPUs and, 60–61
  defined, 88
  flags register, 96
  general-purpose registers, 91–93
  instruction pointer and, 63, 95–96
  memory addresses and, 211–212
  peripherals, 61
  procedures and, 343
  register halves and, 93–95
  saving caller's register values, 343–346
  saving/restoring when linking to C
      libraries, 447–448
  string defined by register values, 395
Registers view, Insight Debugger
  displaying register's value in three formats,
      223–224
  overview of, 198–199
  viewing EAX register with, 206
  viewing flags with, 216–218
relay switches, 48
relocatability, linkers and, 128

REP prefix
  copying tm structure with MOVSD, 466–469
  ECX decrement and, 408–409
  MOVSB with, 418–419
  single-stepping with Insight Debugger,
      418–419
  STOSB with, 403–404
  STOSB without, 407
REPE prefix, 435–436
REPNE prefix, 435–436
repositories, package managers, 140
  RESB directive, 402
  RET (Return from procedure), 563
  LoadBuff example, 337–338
  recursion and, 340–341
  reference, 561
  returning control to caller, 446
reuse. See code reuse
ROL (Rotate Left), 288–289, 564–565
ROM (read-only memory), 71
ROR (Rotate Right), 288–289, 566–567
rotating bits, 288–289
Ruler procedure
  adding ASCII digits, 411–413
  displaying, 409
  lesson learned, 414
  MUL instruction compared with IMUL,
      410–411
runtime errors, 137–138

S
sandbox
  minimal NASM program for using with,
      202–204
  for working with x86 machine instructions,
      201–202
SBB (Arithmetic subtraction with borrow),
    568–569
scanf(), C language, 458–462
SCASB (Scan String by Byte), 432–435
screens. See also virtual text display
  displaying ruler on, 409
  MUL instruction compared with IMUL,
      410–411
searches
  search and replace, 172
  text, 171–172
seed values
  for random numbers, 475
  srand() function for getting seed value of
      random numbers, 476–477
segment addresses, 86–87

segment registers
  not responding to bitwise logical
    instructions, 285–286
  porting from CPU 8080 to 8086, 80–82
  protected flat mode model and, 102
  real flat mode and, 97
segments
  as horizons not places, 88
  making 20-bit addresses out of 16-bit
    registers, 88–90
  nature of, 85–87
  offset addresses and, 89–90
selecting text, in Kate, 170–171
semicolons (;), as comment delimiters,
  124
serial-access devices, 52
services dispatcher, Linux, 256
Session Chooser dialog, Kate, 159
sessions, Kate
  file management and, 165–167
  overview of, 162–163
SF (sign flag)
  DEC EBX instruction clearing, 217
  in EFlags register, 214
  flag rules, 510
  uses of, 301
shifting bits
  <count> operand for, 286–287
  how it works, 287
  multiplying by shifting and adding,
    295–298
  SHR and SHL instructions, 286
SHL (Shift Left)
  multiplying by shifting and adding,
    296–298
  reference, 570–571
  shifting bits, 286
short jumps, conditional jumps,
  354–355
short-term storage, stack for, 253–254
showchar program
  closing inner loop, 421–422
  closing outer loop, 422–423
  displaying ASCII table, 419–420
  nested instruction loops, 420–421
  recapping, 423–424
SHR (Shift Right)
  compared with DIV, 209
  masking unwanted nybbles, 293
  reference, 572–573
  shifting bits, 286
sign bit, 221
sign flag. See SF (sign flag)

signed values
  jump instructions and, 302–304
  MOVSX for moving, 224–225
  overview of, 221
  ranges of, 223
silicon chips. See also memory chips
  bit capacity of, 51
  CPU (central processing unit), 58
size specifiers
  for memory data, 211
  using with NASM, 220
SMP (symmetric multiprocessing), 73
software, package managers for installing,
  140
software interrupts
  vs. hardware interrupts, 261–262
  nature of, 254–255
source code files
  .ASM file extension for, 131
  assembling, 125–126, 131–132
  debugging information in, 128
  editing, 131
  examining AT&T gas source file produced
    by gcc, 471–474
  Kate editing controls for, 168–172
source code highlighting, macros and, 390
source code window, Insight Debugger, 195,
  197
source operand
  immediate data and, 206
  machine instructions and, 205
  sum of source and destination operands,
    207
source strings, types of strings in x86, 395
SpeedCrunch calculators, 28
srand(), C language, 476–477
SS (stack segment) register, 91
sscanf(), C language, 487–489
stack
  anatomy of Linux stack, 427–429
  calling procedures within procedures and,
    340
  examining with command-line arguments,
    424
  examining with Insight's memory view,
    430–432
  LIFO (last in, first out), 246–248
  overview of, 246
  POP instructions, 251–253
  popping vs. addressing, 436–438
  PUSH instructions, 249–251
  real flat mode model and, 98–99
  saving caller's register values and, 344–345

for short-term storage, 253
upside down structure of, 248–249
why stack addresses are not predictable, 429
stack frame
    calling procedures and, 346
    destroying, 450
    setting up, 448–450
stack pointer. *See* ESP (stack pointer)
stack segment (SS) register, 91
Stallman, Richard, 440–441
standard error (stderr), Unix files, 179
standard input (stdin), Unix files, 179
standard output (stdout), Unix files, 179
STC (Set carry flag), 574
STD (Set direction flag), 575
steps
    in Assembly Language Game, 10
    in board games, 5
    in laundry list, 2–3
    machine instructions as, 66
    summary, 12
storage
    in board games, 5
    CPU registers for, 60–61
    cubbyholes in Assembly Language Game, 11
    short-term storage in stack, 253–254
STOS (Store String)
    16-bit and 32-bit versions of, 414
    reference, 576
STOSB (Store String by Byte)
    for clearing display buffer memory, 403
    DF (direction flag) and, 405–406
    ECX decrement and, 408–409
    executing , 404–405
    nested instruction loops, 420–421
    REP and, 407
    Ruler procedure using STOSB without REP, 409–414
    setting up registers for showchar program, 420
string variables
    deriving string length with EQU and $, 244–246
    overview of, 242–244
strings
    converting time_t values to formatted strings, 464–465
    ECX decrement and, 408–409
    HexStr, 295–298
    moving. *See* MOVS (Move string)
    not having boundary values or length indicators, 394

overview of, 393–394
searching with SCASB, 432–435
single-stepping REP string instructions with Insight, 418–419
source strings and destination strings, 395
sscanf() for converting into numbers, 487–489
storing by byte. *See* STOSB (Store String by Byte)
storing data to discontinuous strings, 419–424
virtual text display example. *See* virtual text display
subtraction
    SBB (Arithmetic subtraction with borrow), 568–569
    SUB (Arithmetic subtraction), 577–578
subtraction, in hex
    borrows and, 35–37
    overview of, 32
successive refinement
    designing non-trivial program, 266–271
    of programs, 277
switches
    as on/off memory device, 47–48
    transistor, 48–49
symbol tables, linkers building, 127
symmetric multiprocessing (SMP), 73
Synaptic Package Manager, 140, 141
system clock
    CPU and, 63
    fetching time_t values from, 464

T

tables
    accessing from procedures, 343
    displaying ASCII table, 419–420
    using lookup tables, 293–295
    writing values to, 295
terminal emulation, Unix/Linux, 176
terminal utilities, Konsole, 143
terminal window
    in Kate, 173
    text display and, 402
terminals
    character encoding in Konsole, 177–179
    console applications, 176–177
    control cautions for Linux terminals, 377–378
    escape sequences controlling, 183–184
    not launching Kate via terminal command, 159

terminals *(continued)*
  synchronization of, 161
  Unix/Linux, 176
TEST instruction, looking for 1-bits with, 304–306
tests
  in Assembly Language Game, 10
  in board games, 5
  as choice between two alternatives, 3–4
  conditional jumps and, 299–300
  .EXE file, 136–137, 146–147
  jump or don't jump, 66
  in laundry list, 2–3
  looking for 1-bits with TEST, 304–306
  looking for O-bits with BT (Bit Test), 306–307
text
  fgets() for reading text from files, 490–493
  formatting in C, 452–453
  printf() function for writing text to files, 493–494
  searching by, 171–172
  selecting in Kate, 170–171
text display, virtual. *See* virtual text display
text editors
  editing program in, 142–143
  editing source code file, 131
  fixing errors, 134
  Kate. *See* Kate text editor
text files
  accounting for differences in display order, 117–118
  vs. binary files, 111–112
  converting to code, 121
  inspecting with Bless Hex Editor, 113–116
  interpreting raw data, 116–117
  makefiles, 187
text filters, 182–183, 278
text output, in C
  passing parameters to printf(), 454–456
  printf() function for formatting text, 452–453
.text section
  in assembly language program, 241
  code in, 348
  stack and, 248
text substitution, macros as, 385
text video buffers, creating, 396
textfile.asm, 495–501
TF (trap flag)
  in EFlags register, 214
  flag rules, 510

TI Programmer (hex calculator), 28
time and date functions, in C
  converting time_t values to formatted strings, 464–465
  copying tm structure with MOVSD, 466–469
  fetching time_t values from system clock, 464
  localtime(), 465–466
  overview of, 462–464
time_t values, C language
  converting to formatted strings, 464–465
  fetching from system clock, 464
timestamp, Make utility and, 189
tm structure, C language
  copying with MOVSD, 466–469
  overview of, 463
  values in, 464
toolbars, adding items to Kate toolbar, 167–168
top of stack (TOS)
  anatomy of Linux stack, 427
  procedures and, 346
Torvalds, Linus, 73, 156
TOS (top of stack)
  anatomy of Linux stack, 427
  procedures and, 346
touch command, for forcing builds, 193–194
transient programs, CP/M-80 and, 79
transistor switches
  CPUs and, 64–65
  memory cells and, 49–50
  overview of, 48–49
translation tables
  character translation, 318–320, 348
  instead of calculations, 325
translators
  assembly language as, 122
  converting text files to binary files, 121
trap flag (TF)
  in EFlags register, 214
  flag rules, 510
truth table, for AND operators, 281
Turbo Assembler Quick Reference Guide, 231
Turbo Pascal, 156, 394
two's complement, 222–223

U

Ubuntu Linux calculator, 28
unconditional jumps
  jumping on absence of a condition, 300–301
  overview of, 298
Unicode standard, for text files, 111

units column, in number bases, 23
Unix
    DOS and, 156
    ncurses C library for managing console, 378
    OSs (operating systems), 73
    standard Unix files, 178–180
unsigned values
    jump instructions and, 302–304
    overview of, 221
    Registers view displaying register value as, 223–224
    unsigned division, 228–229
USB port, as peripheral device, 58–59
user space, Linux, 73

V
variables
    allocating on fly, 248
    deriving string length with EQU and $, 244–246
    for initialized data, 242
    string variables, 242–244
    vidbuff1.asm, 396–402
video, memory-mapped video not allowed by protected mode, 104–105
video display, as peripheral device, 58–59
virtual 86 mode, for backward compatibility, 83
virtual addresses, translating into physical memory, 425
virtual memory, 102, 424–426
virtual text display
    changing dimensions of, 402
    creating, 395–402
    defining lines in display buffer, 406
    executing STOSB instruction, 404–405
    sending virtual display buffer to Linux console, 406–407
    STOSB instruction and DF (direction flag), 405–406
    STOSB instruction for clearing display buffer memory, 403
Visual Basic
    file processing in, 121
    learning, 110
    visual programming in, 12

W
warning messages, in programming process, 134–135
whitespace, text files and, 111
Windows calculator, 28
Windows NT, Unix as inspiration for, 73
Windows OSs
    console applications, 102
    Linux GUI apps for, 185
    protected flat mode and, 78
    protected mode and, 71–72
WORD, size specifiers, 211
word processors, 111
words
    DW directive, 242, 244
    measuring memory in, 54
"write-only" code, 124–125

X
x86 CPUs
    backward compatibility with 8086 and 8088, 83
    instruction mnemonics. See AT&T mnemonic conventions
    instruction pointer and, 95–96
    Intel role in developing, 66
    reference guide for, 231–232
    speed optimization, 230
x86 instruction set. See machine instructions
XCHG (Exchange operands), 209, 579
XLAT (Translate byte via table), 320–325, 580
XOR (Exclusive OR), 284–285, 581–582

Z
zero, dividing by produces error, 229
ZF (zero flag)
    conditional jumps and, 299
    DEC EBX instruction clearing, 217
    in EFlags register, 214
    flag rules, 510
    INC EAX instruction and, 217
    JNZ (Jump If Not Zero) and, 218–219
    uses of, 301

CPSIA information can be obtained at www.ICGtesting.com
Printed in the USA
BVOW02n0428030215

385766BV00002B/3/P